MAKÚK

JOHN SUTTON LUTZ

MAKÚK

A New History of Aboriginal-White Relations

UBCPress · Vancouver · Toronto

15 14 13 12 11 10 09 08   5 4 3 2 1

Printed in Canada on acid-free paper

LIBRARY AND ARCHIVES CANADA CATALOGUING IN PUBLICATION

Lutz, John S. (John Sutton), 1959-
     Makúk: a new history of Aboriginal-white relations / John Sutton Lutz.

Includes bibliographical references and index.
ISBN 978-0-7748-1139-2 (bound) ; ISBN 978-0-7748-1140-8 (pbk.)

     1. Whites – British Columbia – Relations with Indians – History. 2. Indians of North America – British Columbia – Economic conditions. 3. Indians of North America – Employment – British Columbia – History. 4. Indians of North America – Commerce – British Columbia – History. 5. Indians of North America – Canada – Government relations. 6. British Columbia – Ethnic relations. I. Title.

E78.C2L88 2008   971.1004'97   C2008-900642-9

Canada

UBC Press gratefully acknowledges the financial support for our publishing program of the Government of Canada through the Book Publishing Industry Development Program (BPIDP), and of the Canada Council for the Arts, and the British Columbia Arts Council.

This book has been published with the help of a grant from the Canadian Federation for the Humanities and Social Sciences, through the Aid to Scholarly Publications Programme, using funds provided by the Social Sciences and Humanities Research Council of Canada, and with the support of the Faculty of Humanities, University of Victoria.

UBC Press
The University of British Columbia
2029 West Mall
Vancouver, BC V6T 1Z2
604-822-5959 / Fax: 604-822-6083
www.ubcpress.ca

Contents

Maps, Figures, and Tables

Preface: *Makúk*

Makúk may well have been the first word exchanged by Aboriginal and European peoples on North America's Northwest Coast. James Cook, the first European visitor to land on what is now British Columbia, heard it even before he dropped anchor. The Mowachaht, whom the British explorer met at what is now known as Yuquot on Nootka Island, used the word *makúk* to attempt to convey several messages.

First and foremost, *makúk* meant "let's trade." The Mowachaht were keen to exchange their furs and other items for the metal goods Cook carried with him. Second, the word implied that the Mowachaht would not be intimidated by the well-armed white men into giving even so much as their grass away. Finally, in using the word *makúk* the Mowachaht were offering Cook and his crew their first lesson in a language of intercultural communication.

Yuquot, which Cook and later Europeans called Nootka, or Friendly Cove, thanks to the welcome they received there, became the centre for European trade on the Northwest Coast of North America from 1778 to the late 1790s. Every trading vessel stopped there, and the Spanish established a settlement there. Beginning with *makúk*, the Mowachaht, along with their Nuu-chah-nulth relatives along the west coast of Vancouver Island and Cape Flattery to the south, taught the Europeans a basic trading vocabulary. When trade shifted to the territory of the Chinook people at the mouth of the Columbia River after 1800, the traders took this simple jargon with them.

Yuquot and the Chinook villages at the mouth of the Columbia were already established trade centres when Europeans arrived. The Chinook added the "Nootka Jargon" to their own trading jargon, which they then taught to other foreign traders.[1] This Chinook "jargon," or *wawa* (to distinguish it from the language spoken by the Chinook people), then spread to other aboriginal groups via the fur traders. English and French words for introduced items were added to the language (e.g., *polallie*, from the voyageur French "pouderie," for powder; *lahache*, for axe; and *lum*, for rum.) The jargon spread northward and eastward so that, by the late 1880s,

The Moment we landed I sent some [men] to cut grass not thinking that the Natives could or would have the least objection, but it proved otherways for the Moment our people began to cut they stopped them and told them they must *Makook* for it, that is first buy it.

Captain James Cook, Friendly Cove, 1778

Captain James Cook

Maquinna, Chief of the Mowachaht

◄ Cook's crew exchanging items with the Mowachaht, 1778 (see p. xii)

I've Begun a Vocabulary

I have begun making a vocabulary of the Chenooke gibberish, by which we communicate with the Indians – it is a vile compound of English, French, American & the Chenooke dialect.

William Fraser Tolmie, *The Journals of William Fraser Tolmie,* June 25, 1833

Chinook Dictionary

Now, if the learner will just turn to ... "Makook" – "Buy" which also signifies "Sell, etc" this tending to puzzle the person who understands it only in one sense when hears it used by an Indian [meaning?] quite opposite.

Harry Guillod, *Chinook Dictionary* [1862-88]

Harry Guillod, ca. 1880

the anthropologist Franz Boas was among many to remark that it would be impossible to get around British Columbia without it.[2]

This "rough-edged tongue with the whiff of commerce about it," as poet Gary Geddes described it, was born of exchange, at the crossroads of cultures, where novel experiences arise and new language is needed. Sites of exchange and translation of languages also become sites of transformation: just the places where the "Trickster" gets involved. In the European tradition, the ancient Greeks attributed the invention of language to Hermes – the Trickster in their pantheon of gods. Plato thought that spoken language was itself a byproduct of bargaining between peoples. On North America's Northwest Coast, a story from the Nuxalk people tells us the Creator thought one language would be enough for all peoples, but Raven (the Trickster), made many languages in order to have more sport in the spaces of misunderstanding.[3] Certainly, the Trickster was at work in Chinook jargon.

The Nuu-chah-nulth word *makúk* (*makook, mahkook, ma-kuk, maá-kuk*) was central to this trading jargon. It means "to exchange" – in all possible ways. The expression *náika tík-a makúk kiúu-ten* translates not only as "I want to buy that horse" but also as "I want to sell that horse" and "I want to trade that horse." In response, a potential trading partner might reply: *Kloshe,* which generally means "good" but has forty-five other meanings, including "graceful" and "useful." The buyer-seller might then say, *Maika skookum,* but since *skookum* means both "strong" and "demon," he or she could be saying "he (the horse) is strong" or "he is a demon." Words and phrases that sound alike also caused confusion. *Naika weght chako maika,* sounds very much like *Naika wake chako maika,* but the former means "I will come to you tomorrow" and the latter "I will not come to you."

To make the language simple, but also more confusing, there are no articles, no gendered pronouns, and no tenses. In its role as a medium of communication between different peoples with different ways of putting language together – and with vastly different concepts of time, space, and gender – all such markers were left out. The main preposition in the language, *kopa,* can mean completely opposite things: "to" and "from" as well as "in," "on," "under," "about," and "around." The main conjunction *pi* means "and" as well as "but." Add to this the many regional variations in vocabulary, pronunciation, usage, and spelling, and it is not surprising that the fifty-plus Chinook jargon dictionaries in circulation prior to 1935 sometimes offered contradictory definitions. Charles Buchanan, who taught the language in the late nineteenth century, put it this way: "The Chinook word is elastic and expressed a broad and general idea rather than one altogether specific."[4] It was a language of approximate meaning.

After Cook's landing in 1778, the jargon existed in a negotiated cultural space, neither fully Aboriginal nor fully European. If any one cultural group tried to push the language towards greater specificity, the referents were not available to the others, thus defeating the jargon's purpose. The various groups settled on a language amorphous enough that each could interpret it in a way that made sense within its own cultural framework. It was a language of deliberate ambiguity.

The vagueness that allowed the jargon to connect vastly different worlds led, of course, to misunderstandings. And these had their uses. If the Nlaka'pamux of the Fraser River wanted to interpret the Chinook words used by the Anglican Bishop of Columbia to refer to the Christian God – *Saghalie Tayee Papa* (literally, "the above chief father") – as the Sun and Creator, both sides could feel they had some common ground. Other "misunderstandings" were, of course, counterproductive, or caused offence, such as when a Methodist clergyman, wishing to address a gathering of Aboriginal People as "Children of the Forest," could, through his Chinook lexicon, get no closer than "Little men among big stick."[5]

In a few locations the jargon developed into a full Creole (it became the first language of children growing up in intercultural situations), but it remained largely a pidgin, a second language, used for intercultural communication and miscommunication.[6] From a trading language it became the language of work, used in the mills, canneries, and hop fields where Aboriginal People interacted with European immigrants, other Northwest Coast aboriginal groups with whom they shared no common language, Asians, and Hawaiians.[7] A language of material exchange, it was pressed into service as a language of cultural exchange: missionaries used Chinook to explain the gospel, teachers taught with it, anthropologists studied Aboriginal Peoples with it, treaties were negotiated through it, and court cases were tried in it.[8] It was even used as a medium of artistic expression: homesick Aboriginal People composed songs in it, and romantic non-aboriginal writers composed poetry in it.[9] Harry Assu, a Kwakwaka'wakw hereditary chief from Cape Mudge, recalled that, in the early twentieth century, Chinook "was all that was spoken in dealings between Indian and non-Indian people." As late as the 1930s, the jargon was still the main means of aboriginal/non-aboriginal interaction in the less populated parts of British Columbia, such as the Chilcotin.[10]

Chinook jargon is, itself, an example of *makúk* – exchange – between two cultures. James Cook's uncertainty about the term in 1778 was the opening act of a long and ongoing dialogue. From 1778 to the early twentieth century, virtually every exchange between Northwest Coast Aboriginal People and immigrants – be it to do with religion, the law, work,

Indian Point of View

Chinook ... is not as complicated as it looks ... You have merely to remember the Indian point of view to get the expression of almost any idea.

W.S. Phillips, *The Chinook Book,* 1913

White Man's Talk

They [Indians] have a great aversion to learning the English language, contenting themselves with the jargon which they look upon as a sort of whiteman's talk.

James Swan, *The Northwest Coast,* 1857

James Swan with his Haida collaborator Johnny Kit Elswa in Victoria, 1883

James Cook's
crew exchanges
items with the
Mowachaht at
Friendly Cove,
1778

The Lingua Franca

Hundreds of Indians of the Comox and
Cowichan tribes work on steamers, in
saw mills and factories; their language is
Chinook, originally pure language of the
Chinook Indian, today so mixed with
Spanish, French, and English words that
Europeans can learn it easily. In British
Columbia Chinook is what the *lingua
franca* is in the Levant. To the traveller in
regions as far north as the Aleutian, it
may be more useful than all modern
languages combined.

Ernest von Hesse-Wartegg, "A Visit to the
Anglo Saxon Antipodes from Canada and
Newfoundland, 1889," ca. 1887

barter, sex, or love – was consummated in a language whose very construction guaranteed misunderstandings.[11] These misunderstandings became the basis for subsequent conventions and relationships. When English, which was taught to Aboriginal Peoples in schools, eclipsed Chinook as the language of intercultural exchange, the ambiguities and misunderstandings were already well entrenched in aboriginal/non-aboriginal relations. This book is all about makúk and how those misunderstandings still shape relations today.

MAKÚK

ONE

Introduction: Molasses Stick Legs

What is today Vancouver's financial district was clothed in giant red cedars when Englishman John Morton and two friends hammered the last spike into their shanty. Soon after, three Aboriginal People arrived on the scene:

> The Indian and two klootchmen approached the cabin and started to talk Chinook. They [the three Englishmen] did not understand the Indians and could not make the Indians understand them ...
>
> This may not be correct but it is as near as I can recall it. The Indians were trying to impart some information but could make no headway, so at last, how they managed it I don't know, but the Indians got them to leave the form on which they were sitting ...
>
> Then the two Indian girls started bouncing about, jumping in the air backwards and forwards over the form like two wild things, and they could jump like deer. This went on for fifteen minutes with the White Men very much puzzled, not understanding what it all meant.
>
> Eventually the girls tired themselves out and had to give up the performance. Neither succeeded in making themselves understood, and, bye and bye the Indians walked off in disgust.[1]

John Morton

In this first encounter, in the summer of 1862, the misunderstandings were obvious. At first the Aboriginal People tried to speak with Morton in the lingua franca of the territory, Chinook jargon. When words failed, the aboriginal visitors turned to gestures, then action. Still no comprehension. John Morton and his friends were left wondering: "what did it all mean?"

Discussion between Aboriginal and non-Aboriginal People seems so much easier today. All across the world, settler populations are involved in historic and ongoing conversations with Indigenous Peoples. This dialogue takes many forms: treaty talks; Royal Commissions; armed stand-offs; parliamentary hearings; Congressional hearings; court challenges; local, provincial, state and national negotiations; and casual conversation in our homes and workplaces.

◄ Detail of Stan Greene exchange painting (see p. 6)

We no longer have the vast cultural gaps that Morton and his Musqueam visitors had to overcome. Aboriginal and non-Aboriginal People generally dress the same way, live in similar houses, shop in the same malls, and watch the same TV shows. In conversation with each other, we now use the same language. Or do we? As we come to grips with major issues of the day – racism, aboriginal title, self-government, treaties, reserve poverty, the legacy of residential schools – are we really engaged in the same conversation with the same points of reference? The gap in communication is more subtle than it was in 1862 and, consequently, more difficult to see. In looking back to the earliest encounters between Europeans and indigenous people, a history of misunderstanding comes into focus.

That 1862 meeting between the newcomer Morton and the long-time owners of the land had the potential for tension and violence. What was it that the aboriginal visitors were so anxious to convey? Was it a welcome? A warning? Apparently neither. It was a job interview. Morton was later told that the male was simply trying to *makúk mamook* – to hire out the young women who were "young and supple, and who proved it by [their] agility."[2]

This book is about *makúk* – exchanges – between Aboriginal People and immigrants, and the misunderstandings that have arisen from them. It is a historical study of a particular kind of exchange – *mamook*, meaning "work for pay" in Chinook jargon – and its connections with race, family, and economy. *Makúk* focuses on British Columbia, Canada, to look at an international process – the displacement of Aboriginal Peoples from control of resources, the resettlement of land by people of European descent, and the partial incorporation of Aboriginal Peoples into the new Euro-Canadian economy and into the modern welfare state. The rationale behind the displacement of Aboriginal Peoples was one that Europeans invoked across the globe, although the techniques of dispossession have surely differed from place to place.

This book also focuses on the work-for-pay exchange between Aboriginal People and immigrants of European stock, the two most prominent cultural groups in colonial British Columbia, and follows the patterns of this exchange from its origins through to the present. In following these patterns over the long term, a surprising fact emerges: the high rates of unemployment and welfare dependency among contemporary aboriginal communities are recent historical phenomena, with observable roots and causes. In 1996, the annual income of registered Indians in Canada was half of that of non-Indians. If we compare Aboriginal People to others who live in comparable communities, economists can show that about 42 percent of this difference is the result of geographical and locational factors.

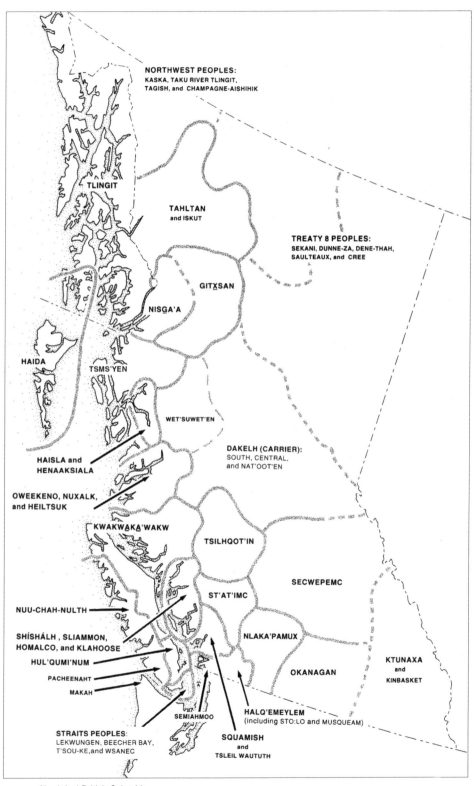

NORTHWEST PEOPLES:
KASKA, TAKU RIVER TLINGIT,
TAGISH, and CHAMPAGNE-AISHIHIK

TLINGIT

TAHLTAN
and ISKUT

TREATY 8 PEOPLES:
SEKANI, DUNNE-ZA, DENE-THAH,
SAULTEAUX, and CREE

GITXSAN

NISG̲A'A

HAIDA

TSMS'YEN

WET'SUWET'EN

DAKELH (CARRIER):
SOUTH, CENTRAL,
and NAT'OOT'EN

HAISLA and
HENAAKSIALA

OWEEKENO, NUXALK,
and HEILTSUK

KWAKW̲AK̲A'WAKW

TSILHQOT'IN

SECWEPEMC

ST'AT'IMC

NUU-CHAH-NULTH

SHÍSHÁLH , SLIAMMON,
HOMALCO, and KLAHOOSE

NLAKA'PAMUX

HUL'QUMI'NUM

PACHEENAHT

KTUNAXA
and
KINBASKET

OKANAGAN

MAKAH

SEMIAHMOO

HALQ'EMEYLEM
(including STO:LO and MUSQUEAM)

STRAITS PEOPLES:
LEKWUNGEN, BEECHER BAY,
T'SOU-KE,and WSANEC

SQUAMISH
and
TSLEIL WAUTUTH

MAP I.I Aboriginal British Columbia

Exchange of fish for
blankets, the main
commodities exchanged
at Fort Langley until the
gold rush, as drawn by
Stó:lō artist Stan Greene

Another 5 percent of this gap can be explained by the younger age structure and lower educational levels of Aboriginal People.[3] The explanation of the other half of this difference lies in our history.

As a theme, *makúk* (exchange) is at the heart of many of the diverse interactions between indigenous peoples worldwide and Europeans. Even before Aboriginal people and Europeans learned to converse, they established a connection based on the trading of goods, a relationship that formed the foundation for more complex exchanges: conversation, wage labour, treaties, and marriage, to name a few. Viral, genetic, and biological exchanges accompanied these new interactions.[4] Of all these forms of exchange, I focus on wages and welfare because aboriginal work for pay, or the lack of it, is central to an understanding of Euro-Canadian expansion into British Columbia and is the core of the discussion about what others have called the "Indian problem" – the place of Aboriginal People in Canadian society today.

Ideas about what constitutes "real" work are at the heart of Canadian history and colonial histories worldwide. To eighteenth- and nineteenth-century Europeans, labour was the source of all value and provided the right to ownership. Europeans invoked the philosophy of John Locke: "Whatsoever, then, he removes out of a state that nature hath provided and left it in, he hath mixed his labour with ... [he] thereby makes it his property." The argument was that the fishing, hunting, gathering, building, and even farming that Aboriginal Peoples did was not labour – at least not in a way that met the definition of classical economics. Such efforts did not sufficiently remove items from their "state of nature."[5] European fishing, trapping, farming, and manufacturing, on the other hand, *were* considered to mix labour with nature and so were invoked as justification for making the land, waters, and resources European "property."

Historical geographer Cole Harris reminds us that culture and space are not separate categories. Land only becomes divisible and ownable when labour is applied to survey and fence it.[6]

Labour is also at the core of how Europeans and, later, North Americans, valued themselves. Before the Reformation, work was tied to need, profit was unclean, and merchants were outcasts – un-Christian because of their selfishness. Beginning with the Protestants in sixteenth-century Europe (earlier among the Jews) and later spreading to Catholic countries and all of Europe's outposts, peoples' worth has been valued according to their conformity with what Max Weber called the "Protestant work ethic." By the new standards, a person's value as a human being was related to his or her willingness to work long hours, to sacrifice leisure, and to pursue wealth beyond her/his basic material needs. From pariahs, merchants became the pillars of the church and the leaders of the community. Since then, Western culture has generally reserved the highest status to those most successful at hoarding wealth.

Aboriginal cultures, which, culturally and economically, valued "leisure time" did not measure up to this "work ethic." In the words of the eighteenth-century legal theorist E. de Vattel, "There are those who, to avoid labour, choose to live by hunting" and, because of that choice, have no reason to complain when their land is usurped by farmers – productive and worthy members of society.[7] The myth of the "lazy Indian," derived from peculiar views about labour that were prevalent in European culture of the time, was invoked to transfer lands from Aboriginal Peoples to colonial states and then to colonists.

There is a widespread misconception that, after the arrival of Europeans in British Columbia, Aboriginal Peoples remained outside the capitalist economy in what Cardell Jacobsen has called, within an American context, an "economy of uselessness." Canadian authors such as Noel Dyck have likewise argued that "this situation is quite different from that of colonial regimes ... where the exploitation of native labour was from the outset a fundamental feature of the economy." Dyck makes the same point as does Robin Fisher in his pioneering work on aboriginal/non-aboriginal relations in British Columbia. Fisher argued that, with the 1858 gold rush, the colonies that comprise modern British Columbia changed from "colonies

No Reason to Complain

Those who still persue this idle mode of life [fishing and hunting] usurp more extensive territories than, with a reasonable share of labour, they would have occassion for, and have, therefore, no reason to complain if other nations, more industrious and too closely confined come and take possession of a part of those lands.

Emmerich de Vattel, *The Law of Nations*, 1861

In a *Victoria Times* cartoon, lazy Indians are depicted as impeding progress (May 16, 1910)

of exploitation, which made use of indigenous manpower, to colonies of settlement, where the Indians became at best, irrelevant."[8]

One of the goals of this book is to reverse this idea. The European economy of the eighteenth and nineteenth centuries depended on aboriginal labour. A closer look shows that Aboriginal Peoples never became irrelevant, not even in the twentieth century, not even to the Euro-Canadian immigrants who tried to make them invisible. In fact, the attempt to "vanish the Indians," ironically, brought them into national visibility. The efforts to marginalize them made them, paradoxically, a central preoccupation of the Canadian state. Aboriginal People were drawn into peaceful exchange and paid-work relationships, and this is important, not least because this made them unwitting participants in the very process that was transforming and displacing their own economies. Ignoring aboriginal participation in the workforce misses the role that wage labour played in the larger project of the "peaceable subordination" of Canadian Aboriginal Peoples and the establishment of modern Canada.

By "peaceable subordination" I am referring to strategies used by certain European colonists and colonial states to dominate occupied lands while publicly deploring the violence of conquest. The dispossession of Aboriginal Peoples was cloaked in this language of incorporation, through which they were supposed to be brought into a state of civilization by the extension of Christianity, education, private property, capitalist social relations, British justice, and, ultimately, the social welfare state. In Canada, compared to many other settler colonies, the dislocation of Aboriginal Peoples was a largely peaceable process that declared, with Psalm 72, "precious shall be their blood in his sight." But if violence was not often visible, it was not too far below the horizon. The same Psalm 72, from which the name "Dominion" for the Dominion of Canada was taken, also says that those who do not bow down before Him shall "lick the dust."[9]

It has been too easy to link the historical characterization of the "irrelevant Indian" with current reports of high unemployment and high rates of welfare dependency. It is easy to assume (as surveys show many Canadians do) that, ever since the fur trade, "lazy Indians" have been sidelined on their reserves collecting government handouts. This assumption, based on a particular interpretation of the past, plays a prominent role in current policy debate. It is visible in public and editorial responses to the ongoing treaty process in British Columbia. As Elizabeth Furniss shows, it plays itself out in the politics and personal relations of rural British Columbia. It has also manifested itself in the learned opinions of the court. In a landmark 1990 court case, BC Chief Justice Allan McEachern incorporated a variant of this view into his decision to deny aboriginal title.[10]

The history of aboriginal work-for-pay connects the extension of European colonialism with the social history of Aboriginal Peoples. Work-for-pay is connected to all other aspects of social life because it always exists in a relationship with other kinds of work – harvesting wild foods, maintaining a household, raising children. How families take shape, how children are raised, how men and women relate to one another are all linked to what work is done and how it is shared. The amount a household participated in a subsistence economy also dramatically affected how it functioned in the labour market since a viable "bush economy" (or what I call moditional economy) meant that wage work was optional.[11]

From today's vantage point, work-for-pay seems to be a straightforward form of exchange, but labour historians have revealed that our current wage-labour system is not a "natural" form of social relations. In Europe an intensive period of indoctrination and coercion was necessary before workers accepted wage labour and its accompanying work ethic, and a similar process occurred during the industrialization of North America.[12] In fact, work for pay is a complicated exchange involving, for the worker: class-relations, subordination, work discipline, and a specialized division of labour. A close study of the relationship between Aboriginal Peoples and the European capitalist economy offers insights about the relationship between Canadians generally, work, and the welfare state.[13]

Even the simplest form of exchange – barter – cannot be taken for granted when it involves crossing cultural boundaries. Consider this *makúk*, which took place on Burrard Inlet (seventy years before Morton's failed attempt at communication) when Captain George Vancouver and his crew became the first Europeans to enter the inlet and meet the Musqueam people. Vancouver recorded the following in his log:

> Here we were met by about fifty Indians in canoes, who conducted themselves with great decorum and civility, presenting us with several fish cooked and undressed of a sort ... resembling smelt. These good people, finding we were inclined to make some return for their hospitality showed much understanding in preferring iron to copper ... The major part of the canoes twice paddled forward, assembled before us, and each time a conference was held ... The subject matter, which remained a profound secret to us, did not appear to be of an unfriendly nature, as they soon returned, and, if possible, expressed additional cordiality and respect ... they possessed no European commodities or trinkets, excepting some rude ornaments apparently made from sheet copper; this circumstance and the general tenor of their behaviour gave us reason to conclude that we were the first white people from a civilized country that they had yet seen.[14]

Indians Choose Not to Work on Sunday

[Christian] teaching has civilised and evangelized these men, and prepared them to become docile and industrious, whereas before they were fierce and indolent.

Rev. W.H. Collison, *In the Wake of the War Canoe*, 1915

Rev. Collison with parishioners Kincolith Chief Paul Klaydach (Claytha) and Councillor James Robinson at Royal Commission Hearings in Kincolith, October 1915

Conquered by Relentless Energy

[Aboriginal People] were not as industrious in the new economic climate as was thought to be necessary by the newcomers in the Colony ... They became a conquered people, not by force of arms ... but by an invading culture and a relentless energy with which they would not, or could not compete.

Chief Justice Allan McEachern, *Reasons for Judgement*, 1991

Captain George
Vancouver

Now, compare this to an aboriginal account told by August Jack Khahtsahlano of the encounter with Vancouver in the same region. Like Vancouver's account, it focuses on the exchange of goods:

> Old people say Indians see first ship they think it an island with three dead trees, might be a schooner, might be a sloop; two masts and bowsprit, sails tied up. Indian braves in about twenty canoes come down Squamish River, go see. Get nearer, see men on island, men have black clothes with high hat coming to point at top ... Whitemans give Indians ship bisquit Indian not know what bisquit for. Before whitemans come Indians have little balls, not very big; roll them along ground, shot at them with bow and arrow for practice, teach young Indian so as not to miss deer. Indian not know ship's bisquit good to eat, so roll them along ground like little practice balls shoot at them, break them up. Then whitemans on schooner give molasses same time bisquit. Indian not know what it of, so Indian rub on leg for medicine. You know Indian sit on legs for long time in canoe; legs get stiff. Rub molasses on legs make stiffness not so bad. Molasses stick legs bottom of canoe.[15]

There are a few parallels in the two accounts.[16] What is more striking, however, are the conflicting realities represented in the accounts – realities rooted in radically different cultural premises. The Musqueam were engaged in a ritual greeting, making speeches and presenting gifts. The explorers were surveying and glad to have the chance to acquire a few fish, unaware that the cordial conferences to which they were being treated were formal welcome speeches.[17] The explorers perceived that iron was the most significant exchange item for the Aboriginal People, but the local people remembered the biscuits and molasses. These ship staples offer the best example of different realities. What had been food to the Europeans became targets and ointment to the locals. It is tempting to dismiss the aboriginal story as an attempt to tell a joke at their own expense, but that would miss an important point: *what was given may not be what was received.*

These contrasting interpretations are key to the argument that underlies this book. Exchange is a process that involves the translation of meaning as well as goods. When goods changed hands, "what they were good for" was also transformed. The "molasses stick legs" story is one example among many of how objects in circulation from one culture to another are often transformed by the act of exchange itself. This type of story recurs frequently in indigenous accounts of first contact in British Columbia and elsewhere. In Nuu-chah-nulth oral histories biscuits and molasses were understood to be bones and blood; by one account the Skidegate Haida took soap offered by the traders to be food; in stories from Massett the first

August Jack Khahtsahlano

TWO

Pomo Wawa: The Other Jargon

The development of a separate scholarly language is necessary in any specialized field. There are medical terms that are only current among doctors and nurses, scientific terms not understood outside the laboratory, and legal terms unfamiliar outside a courtroom. As one delves past the surface of any subject, one needs terms that are more precise than those available for general discussions. In practice, disciplinary jargon sets up barriers to communication between specialists and a wider audience, between disciplines, and even within disciplines. Moreover, scholars mistakenly, and often unintentionally, invoke the "Peerless Principle": the fewer of their peers who can understand them the smarter they must be.

Chinook jargon, or wawa, evolved to provide a space for communication between peoples of different cultures. In the last few decades, the postmodern (pomo) vocabulary has served as a kind of lingua franca allowing scholars to communicate across disciplines. As with the other wawa, crossing boundaries of disciplinary cultures has led to a negotiated language filled with ambiguity. Scholars pick up terms used by others and redefine them. Michel Foucault, one of the fathers of pomo wawa, explained this process: "The only valid tribute to [another scholar's concept]," he said, is "to use it, to deform it, to make it groan and protest."[1] Take the simple notion of something "in between." After the pomo scholars go to work, we have a range of synonyms: ambiguous, indeterminate, interstitial, hybridity, hybridization, hyphenated, liminal, marginal, polyvalent, porous, to name only the common ones.

Much of the pomo wawa has been expressly political, the goal being to show how colonial processes have marginalized indigenous peoples around the world. Ironically, as Linda Tuhwai Smith, a Maori writer, points out in her work *Decolonizing Methodologies*, sympathetic postcolonial writing leaves indigenous peoples out – partly because the language of critique is inaccessible and partly because they cannot recognize themselves in it: "There can be no post-modern for us until we have settled some business of the modern."[2]

This book is part of a dialogue conducted in pomo wawa as well as a conversation aimed at settling the business of the modern as it applies to

More Unsettling ...

The two disciplines [history and anthropology] do not always speak the same language; more unsettling, they sometimes use the same words to mean vastly different things.

Nancy Farriss, from the Foreword of *The Social Life of Things*, 1986

◀ Aboriginal spinners, Metlakatla, ca. 1881 (see p. 19)

Aboriginal and non-Aboriginal Canadians.[3] In this section I acknowledge and engage my sources of scholarly inspiration, explain my analytical levers, introduce my methodology, suggest the range of sources, and explore my role as an observer and speaker in this extended dialogue.

Methods

I use a simple, overarching methodology: dialogue. I sought examples of the thoughts and voices of Aboriginal and non-Aboriginal Peoples in historical records as well as among contemporary Aboriginal People who would engage with me "in an exchange about exchange." Research is always an interactive discussion with people and texts. I highlight my dialogue with other writers, interviewees, journalists, colleagues, and friends and keep the historic dialogue in the foreground by quoting exchanges in Chinook Wawa. Most important, I understand that I am engaged in a conversation (both imagined as I write and forthcoming after publication) with readers. The method is "ethnohistorical" in its fullest sense. I put both parties to a historic encounter under the same lens, treating the interpretations of the observer and the observed as equally factual and equally mytho-historical.[4] (We are all somebody else's "ethno," after all.) This "expanded ethnohistory" uses the traditional qualitative methods of the ethnohistorian, including interviewing and archival research, and quantitative methods including statistics.

Some of these methods, like interviewing and statistical research, are sometimes thought of as antithetical to one another (as are other pairings brought together here, e.g., macro- vs microhistory, postmodern vs empirical research, economic or cultural history). Yet, when we link the discourse analysis in Chapter 2 with the micro experiences discussed in Chapters 4 and 5 to the macro-examinations offered in Chapters 6, 7, and 8, each functions to explain and situate the other. The binaries of the "unmoving history" of the structuralists and the discontinuity of the ethnographer, the "unitary explanation" offered by the modernist and the "complex, multi-layered variability" cited by the postmodernist, fold in on one another. One describes structure, the other agency. Neither exists without the other.

Sources: Rematerializing the Disappeared

Traditionally, historians have sought our informants in various archival sources: diaries, letters, newspapers, and government documents.[5] This has meant that, when we have been discussing aboriginal/non-aboriginal relations, we have been doing it almost exclusively with Europeans, almost all of them male. What different conclusions might be reached if we chose new conversational partners and re-evaluated the old ones?

Where Does It Fit?

While microhistory has the advantages of illuminating previously unknown behaviors and beliefs ... the problem of context legitimately worries those who want to know ... is it typical, or is it unusual? Does it "fit" within the bigger picture of history and, if so, how?

Ruth Sandwell, *Contesting Rural Space*, 2005

Ruth Sandwell

To move the discussion of aboriginal history past the limits of "white" observations, I try to find aboriginal conversational partners. For the memorial past I have interviewed elders and elected officials from the communities I have studied. As Julie Cruikshank's and Wendy Wickwire's ongoing work illustrates, there is a large amount of aboriginal history (stretching back to the contact era) still extant in the stories of people who live in the province.[6] Oral history is as much a relationship as it is a method, and the scope of a single oral history project is necessarily limited to a few communities. To extend the breadth of the book, I have been very thankful for access to oral history programs conducted by others.[7]

For the past that the living no longer remember, I use other strategies to find aboriginal voices. First, a number of autobiographies, biographies, and ethnographies of Aboriginal Peoples have appeared in print over the last fifty years.[8] While the extent of the written and oral testimony does not approach the volume of accounts left by non-aboriginals, it is richer than we might expect. In addition to these formal autobiographies, there are several first-hand accounts, buried deep in government, missionary, and/or ethnological reports while others remain in manuscript form or as cassette recordings tucked in archives scattered from British Columbia to London.[9] One of the most remarkable of these is the daily diary of Arthur Wellington Clah (T'amks), which he kept from 1860 to 1910, which survives at the Wellcome Institute in London. Still other accounts from Aboriginal People are now available, thanks in part to the Freedom of Information Act, in the files of government officials in the form of letters and petitions to the Department of Indian Affairs.[10]

Of course, conversations with recorded informants have their own limitations. David Murray's *Forked Tongues: Speech, Writing and Representation in North American Indian Texts* points out the importance of critically evaluating aboriginal accounts recorded by others. Of the stories that were told, which were published and why? What happened to the stories in the process of translation, editing, and publishing?[11] An example of the pitfalls of using these sources uncritically may be found in the much-reproduced speeches attributed to Dumawamish Chief Seattle, which, upon closer examination, have been revealed to be the largely fictitious renderings of a local newspaper editor.[12] These cautions are particularly relevant here, because, for various reasons discussed below, even this material under-emphasizes aboriginal involvement in paid labour.

The impact of mediation by non-aboriginal "interpreters" is particularly significant when reading the ethnographic literature. Franz Boas, often described as the "father of North American anthropology," studied the Aboriginal Peoples of British Columbia (through the medium of Chinook

Ts'msyen diarist Arthur Wellington Clah (T'amks)

jargon), as did other internationally known anthropologists.[13] What is peculiar about most of this classic anthropological-ethnographic literature (which forms the overwhelming bulk of "scholarly knowledge" about Aboriginal Peoples) is that it was not interested in what Aboriginal People were actually doing when the information was being gathered. Its focus was on what Aboriginal People did, made, and sometimes thought before they had met Europeans. Because the stories and artefacts sought made as little reference as possible to non-aboriginal worlds, these ethnographers have perpetuated the myth that Aboriginal Peoples lived a life that was "suspended in time," existing outside a larger colonial society. Ironically, anthropologists ignored contemporary labour as they fetishized the embodied labour found in historical artefacts. In their own way, anthropologists too have "vanished" Indians and contributed to the stereotypes that exist around Aboriginal People and work.[14]

A relatively recent contribution is histories written by aboriginal authors or commissioned by aboriginal groups.[15] On the whole, these works pay attention to the local oral record and so introduce otherwise overlooked voices into the historical conversation. Despite this recent chorus of aboriginal voices, some parts of the past are still not much noticed because the autobiographies, biographies, and band histories have largely adopted a variant of the ethnographic voice. Most are self-conscious attempts to stress the uniqueness of aboriginal culture and to respond to reader interest. They stress "Indianness" at the expense of a more prosaic participation in the "whiteman's world," and they stress continuity over change. Unpaid, subsistence, and craft work is highlighted, while paid work, when it appears at all, is usually incidental to other stories. Mary Pratt refers to these types of accounts as "auto-ethnography": Aboriginal People tell their own stories but in an idiom that has been heavily influenced by non-aboriginal ethnographies.[16]

If paid work does not fit with the goals of ethnographies, auto-ethnographies, or aboriginal biographies, we can supplement these accounts by re-evaluating the more commonly used sources generated by Euro-Canadians with an eye to understanding their inherent bias. Until 1871 these records are very spotty. In the Hudson's Bay Company fort journals there are regular, though often elliptic, references to employing Aboriginal People in such activities as gardening and construction. Early settlers' accounts tend to make indigenous inhabitants invisible, and when they are mentioned as being employed, their work habits are usually demeaned. Local newspaper reports were apt to mention aboriginal workers but only as a plague that kept down the wages of white workers.[17] On the other hand, missionary accounts, particularly those from the Christian model

Aboriginal spinners at the model Christian village of Metlakatla, ca. 1881

village at Metlakatla, do highlight aboriginal labour. These emphasize, even exaggerate, the success of the missionaries in "civilizing" their charges. Part of this civilizing had to do with showing that Aboriginal People could work "practically as white men."[18]

After British Columbia's confederation with Canada in 1871, the observation of, and record keeping about, Aboriginal People intensified with new structures of state monitoring. The following year federal Indian Agents were appointed in BC, and by 1882 they were located in agencies around the south of the province with the specific mandate to report on the "progress" of Indians. Agents made annual reports on the main activities of the Indians in their agencies, and these constitute some of the most detailed renderings of aboriginal work that have survived. Heavily laden with moralizing judgments, the early reports of the agents were candid assessments of which Indians were "good" (i.e., working and self-supporting), "some good," or "no good" (i.e., prone to potlatching but little interested in paid work). After the turn of the twentieth century, agents were told to refrain from putting their personal judgments in their reports and to emphasize the "progress" that Indians were making.[19]

There were several checks on the extent to which an agent could make himself look good by exaggerating the self-supporting nature of Indians and their incorporation into the workforce. One was the annual income and production statistics that had to be furnished. Agents could not consistently record increases in these figures at the same time as they expanded relief expenditures. Agents who did not respond to Indian requests for relief often found themselves under fire from both Aboriginal People and missionaries.[20] The most telling check on government agents is the letters written by Aboriginal People, sometimes through a translator, to government officials and filed with the latter's records. These letters, often

Wet'suwet'en fishing at Moricetown

protests about unfair behaviour or requests for help, constitute some of the best surviving evidence of Aboriginal People's daily struggles to earn a living and maintain control over their lives.

At the same time other government agencies were collecting information on Aboriginal People, with goals that were different, even contradictory, to those of the Department of Indian Affairs. The federal Department of Fisheries established a network of fishery overseers to limit aboriginal fishing rights on every stream in the province. These overseers recorded the numbers of Aboriginal People fishing and the size of their catches. The provincial Wildlife Branch likewise established agents to license traplines, guides, and hunters in order to limit aboriginal wildlife harvesting. These and other reports of the federal and provincial departments of mines, railways, agriculture, and lands offer a check on the more enthusiastic Indian Agent reports.

Capitalists who depended on aboriginal labour and resources were also attuned to the activities of aboriginal workers. Detailed business records survive from the nineteenth-century fur trade and from fishing and fish-processing industries in the twentieth century. These records are particularly valuable because BC employers relied on a workforce segregated by race, with the result that records were kept according to racial divisions.

Since the late nineteenth century, Aboriginal Peoples have been at the centre of an increasing number of separate, but linked, information-gathering enterprises on the part of government, churches, ethnologists, and business. Since then, no segment of the Canadian population, outside of hospitals, mental institutions, and prisons, has been monitored and reported upon to the same degree as have Aboriginal People.[21] We have a surprisingly large base of information about aboriginal history, if we know how to read it. All the sources are partial, in both senses of the word, and because of our largely uncritical reliance on them, we have been misled for a long time.

Levers and Fulcrums

It is a simple physical principle that, by using the appropriate lever, one small person can lift an enormous weight. I have picked up the tools of others and used or adapted them, like levers, to heft some of the issues that weigh on me. I hope that concepts such as "dialogism," "transformational exchange," "peaceable subordination," "enframement," and "moditional economy" give my observations, interviews, and research some analytical reach. Always, the fulcrum is dialogue.

In his work on literary texts and literary dialogue Russian semiotician Mikhail Bakhtin offers numerous insights to historians, but it is his concept of "dialogism" that is one of the main levers used in this book. Dialogism focuses on the interactive aspect of speech, a quality that can be extended to include exchange more generally: nothing is said that does not take the listener into account. In Bakhtin's words: "The speaker seeks to orient his discourse ... in relation to the horizon of the other, the one who does the understanding, and he enters into a dialogical relation with some aspects of the second horizon" even to the point where he/she reorients his/her own conceptual horizon.[22] Every utterance is situated within a history of dialogue from which it cannot be separated, a phenomenon known as "intertextuality."[23]

Anthropologists have extended the dialogic encounter from Bakhtin's literary analyses to intercultural interactions and exchanges of goods. John and Jean Comaroff focused on cross-cultural dialogue during the process of African missionization. Michael Harkin has applied the dialogic concept to the relationships between the Heiltsuk people on British Columbia's central coast and Euro-Canadians. He points out that dialogue is a process of negotiation of meanings, presentation, and representation of self and other: "Its currency included speech acts, symbolic actions, material exchange, violence, marriage, imitation, legislation, and witchcraft. Each *utterance* transformed the dialogue, and to a greater or lesser degree, the lifeworlds of the interlocutors."[24]

I use the concept of dialogism to decentre the prevailing historiography, which is based primarily on European voices, and to include and

Dialogism

No utterance in general can be attributed to the speaker exclusively; it is *the product of the interaction of the interlocutors*, and broadly speaking, the product of the whole complex *social situation* in which it has occurred.

Mikhail Bakhtin, *Problems of Literacy and Ethics, 1975*

Across the Edges of Civilizations

...the circulation of objects, especially across the edges of societies, civilizations, and trading regimes, is not merely a physical process but is also a movement and displacement of competing conceptions of things.

Nicholas Thomas, *Entangled Objects, 1991*

Nicholas Thomas

compare aboriginal views of the colonial process. This comparison of voices reveals the continuing existence of different meanings in similar utterances: "the two sides use some of the same language and describe some of the same events but often disagree on the meaning." According to Bakhtin, "a word, discourse, language undergoes dialogization when it becomes relativized, deprivileged, aware of competing definitions for the same things."[25]

In the process of understanding the interaction between Europeans and Aboriginal Peoples, it is important to set aside one of the connotations of dialogue that carries over from everyday usage. In ordinary usage, the term "dialogue" may imply an equality or equivalency between the two parties. In this work, where dialogue refers to the full range of communication (including violence) no such power equality between the parties is implied. To say that Aboriginal Peoples engaged in a dialogue with Europeans does not suggest that both parties had the same power to shape that dialogue. Indeed, the power imbalances in that dialogue, expressed through wage work and welfare as well as in many other ways, were precisely what accounts for the dispossession/subordination of Aboriginal Peoples.

Transformational Exchange

Since the 1770s on the Northwest Coast, Aboriginal Peoples have been engaged in a dialogue with Europe and, more recently, with liberalism, capitalism, and modernity. This dialogue has been conducted through sign language, through Chinook jargon, trade, wage work, religion, violence, and a myriad of other ways. It is the transformation and jostling of meaning at the point of these exchanges that is my concern. I start with Nicholas Thomas' observation that "the circulation of objects, especially across the edges of societies, civilizations, and trading regimes, is not merely a physical process but is also a movement and displacement of competing conceptions of things." I refer to this as "transformational exchange" and describe its features more fully on pages 10-11.

But if objects are transformed by the act of exchange, then what happens when people move across cultural divides and move in and out of modernity and the capitalist economy? They, too, are transformed.[26]

The aboriginal dialogue with capitalism was complex. The capitalist workplace was not just a *place*, it was the embodiment of a social system based on private property, individualism, rationalism, subordination, and discipline. When Aboriginal People engaged in work-for-pay they joined a dynamic process in which livelihoods were and are constantly being transformed and reorganized according to how the changing needs of capital interacted with culture.

The European economy simultaneously imposed on and was welcomed and used by Aboriginal Peoples. In her study of the Puget Sound region, historian Alexandra Harmon noted that the "strategic congruities" between the values of Aboriginal Peoples and Europeans enabled them to benefit from each other's abilities and desires while pursuing separate agendas. As Homi Bhabha argues, "The borderline engagement of cultural difference may as often be consensual as conflictual."[27]

Moditional Economy

The incorporation of Aboriginal Peoples into the capitalist economy did not involve the destruction of their non-capitalist economies; rather, the expansion of capitalism depended, as it often does in the colonial world, on the co-existence of the two economies. So-called "modernization" rarely operated through substituting the traditional economy with the capitalist; rather, the one was usually added to the other. According to that keen-eyed critic of capitalism, Karl Marx, capitalism encounters traditional relations "as a barrier and hence gets ideally beyond it, [but] it does not by any means follow that it has *really* overcome it. Capitalism overwhelms some traditional barriers but others are just as constantly posited," so certain elements of traditional society are reinforced as others are transformed or destroyed.[28] One striking example of the new economy reinforcing the old is the slave-raiding and head-taking that formed part of the long migration of northern Aboriginal Peoples towards work for wages in the sawmills of Puget Sound in the 1850s.[29]

These economies, which combined the traditional modes of reproduction and production (for subsistence, prestige goods, and exchange – trade was always a part of the pre-European economy) with new modes of production for exchange in a capitalist market, have often been dismissed as transitional and on the road to a modern, fully capitalist economy. In fact, they are as resilient and as long-lived as capitalism. Historically, people have engaged in multiple modes of production at different times of the day and year: they hunted, fished, gathered, farmed, raised their children, and exchanged their labour in different combinations, and as opportunities presented themselves. I refer to this mixed-mode production system as the "moditional economy."

It turns out that, while Aboriginal Peoples had their distinctive modes, the moditional economy was shared by rural Canadians everywhere. As Ruth Sandwell has shown for Salt Spring Island in southwestern British Columbia, as Gérard Bouchard and José Igartua have shown for the Sagueney region of Quebec, and as Daniel Samson has shown for the Atlantic provinces, the mixture of wage work, small-scale commodity

Capitalist Discipline

The capitalist economy gave rise to a specific modality of disciplinary power, whose general formulas ... could be operated in the most diverse political regimes, apparatuses or institutions.

Michel Foucault, *Discipline and Punish*, 1977

Michel Foucault

Civilization Is Due ... to Working

Most of the civilization observed among the Nanaimo Indians is due to their males working among the white men, in and about the mines, and on board steamers, and to their females washing and performing other domestic work for white families, rather than to the missionary efforts of any religious body.

Letter from Mr. E.W. Gordon to Mr. Dewdney, 1891

production (such as farming or fishing), subsistence fishing, hunting, and gathering was typical of rural Canadian life. Families did not see themselves as belonging to one economy or another; they dipped into them all as opportunities and needs presented themselves. As one of Ruth Sandwell's interviewees told her, "I don't think you understand. The farming never did pay. We always had to do something else to keep the farm going."[30]

Beginning in the 1920s, with the introduction of mothers' pensions, followed by relief (welfare), old-age pensions, family allowance, and unemployment insurance, the state added a new mode of "transfer payments" to the moditional economy. Today fewer and fewer Canadians take part in the subsistence economy, and more and more live in urban centres as wage labourers. But the moditional economy has not been superseded, only the relative proportion of the contribution of two modes has shifted. Subsistence foods might be limited to a jar of jam a neighbour had picked fruit for and preserved, and wages may dominate, but all of us get some input from the state, and many, through pension plans, have small-scale capitalist investments.

In his extensive studies of the Saguenay region of Quebec, Gérard Bouchard developed a concept related to that of moditional economy – "co-integration." Co-integrated economies link metropolitan with rural areas so as to facilitate "traditional" and non-liberal cultural practices at the margin and economic liberalism at the core. The local economies are "primarily driven by the dynamics of reproduction" and are characterized by multifaceted economic activity, including seasonal wage labour and the combination of labour inputs from the different members of the family.[31] What these economies are and how they change in particular circumstances must be determined empirically.

Peaceable Subordination

Embedded in the concept of the moditional economy is the key notion that each part of the "mode" of the economy depends to some degree on the other. For Aboriginal Peoples in Canada, the maintenance of their distinct subsistence and prestige economies depended on capitalist wage work, just as the expansion of capitalism into British Columbia depended on aboriginal labour. However, in selling their labour, even to enable them to more fully engage in their own gifting economy, Aboriginal Peoples entered a process that was ultimately to displace them.

The simultaneous existence of conflict and consent, collaboration and coercion, is deeply embedded in the work-for-pay exchange and the peaceable subordination of Aboriginal Peoples in Canada. By "peaceable subordination" I mean the techniques of power that the British used to secure colonies, all the while decrying the violence used by other colonial powers (including themselves, when necessary). Here, the dispossession of Aboriginal Peoples was cloaked in terms of incorporation, of bringing them into "a new order of things" with the benefits of Christianity, civilization, and the rule of British law.[32]

The term "peaceable subordination" contains within it the paradoxes of the British colonial projects highlighted by Ranajit Guha. First, the British were financing a home society that was based on the principles of liberalism with a foreign empire that denied to the colonized the entitlements of the liberal state. Peaceable colonization was closer to liberalism than was outright conquest, but subordination was, nonetheless, the goal. Britain established its domination based on the promise of the distant but eventual extension of liberal-democratic institutions to the colonized.[33]

The preserve-and-destroy dialectics of capitalism contribute to peaceable subordination. This is because, within the traditional society, there are always opportunities for some to preserve or enhance their power thanks to capitalist relations even as others are displaced by them. The colonizer can usually find some element of the colonized population, often within the elite, who will benefit from, and cooperate in, the new social order. That the privileges gained by cooperation may be short-lived does not matter. Decisions are based on what is known at the time and, given that knowledge, on what one can reasonably predict.

Peaceable subordination occurs through a process that I refer to as "enframement." When Aboriginal Peoples entered the capitalist work place, they entered a foreign cultural framework. And the longer they spent within this foreign cultural framework, the more their original framework had to adjust. Over the long run, engagement in wage work and in missionization, as Harkin shows, or in bureaucratic structures, as Paul Nadasdy's *Hunters and Bureaucrats* shows, alters the terms of engagement and, ultimately, the original cultural frame.

A second kind of enframement was also at work. Through bureaucratic and legal manoeuvres, the state established a set of legal frameworks that did not, at first, impinge upon indigenous peoples because there were no means to enforce them. These included the 1849 declaration that British Law applied to British Columbia; the Indian Act, 1876, which was enacted when there only two Indian Agents for the forty to sixty thousand Aboriginal People in BC; the Fisheries Act (extended to BC in 1877); and so on. Over time, these frames built on each other, leaving Aboriginal Peoples an ever-decreasing space within which to operate. Cole Harris's *Making Native Space* and Douglas Harris's *Fish, Law and Colonialism* are both excellent illustrations of enframement and peaceable subordination in BC.[34]

JACK CANUCK "POINTS WITH PRIDE."
UNCLE SAM—Yes, Jack, I'm a pretty considerable big nation, but I see I kin sit at your feet and learn a few things!

In this 1898 *Toronto Globe* cartoon, Johnny Canuck contrasts Canada's "peaceable subordination" with American mob rule familiar to Uncle Sam.

A Peaceful Takeover

I think the agenda was to take over the country as peacefully as possible without big wars; that was the agenda and try to make treaties and put us on reserves and be nice little Indians.

The Honourable Leonard (Len) Marchand, Okanagan, in the film *A Forgotten Legacy: Spirit of Reclamation* (2002)

Despite the ever-shrinking space within these frames, subjugation was never complete. Aboriginal culture was transformed but not destroyed. Guha calls this type of situation – in which Aboriginal Peoples are under Canadian domination and have incorporated some of the Euro-Canadian worldview, yet still maintain distinct spiritual, economic, and cultural ideas – "domination without hegemony."[35] The rest of this book explores how Aboriginal Peoples came to be dominated through dialogic relations with colonists, the state, and the capitalist economy.

Who Speaks?

We must now look at one of the lessons that postmodernism teaches about the role of the author/speaker. First, there is no such thing as disinterested scholarship. The topics upon which we choose to write, our interpretations of them, the arguments we derive from them, and what counts as fact depend upon who we are and what our interests are. To a greater or lesser degree, my identity as a white, male, Canadian, Buddhist, academic, father, and spouse is imprinted upon what I write. A simple-minded postmodernism would propose that I ought not to write about any one other than my own kind, time, and place.

A more sophisticated postmodernism reminds us that identity is fluid and is full of contradictions. Canadian poet Roy Miki suggests that identity is not "a residence but a performance of multiple and often contradictory positions." There is no single voice among white Canadians, among colonizing populations, or among indigenous peoples. There are collaborators among the colonized, quislings among the colonists. Michael Taussig and Nicholas Thomas show that colonialism is a fragmented culture within which neither the voices of the West nor the voices of the Natives are monolithic, stable, or regionally localized. Moreover, as Renato Rosaldo and Kirin Narayan point out, there are no pure natives, no pure colonizers, only hybrids (culturally if not biologically). Narayan suggests that anthropologists (and academics more generally) "are all incipiently bi- (or multi-) cultural in that [we] belong to worlds both personal and professional."[36] We have all been decentred by our dialogue with one another.

The Exotopic Trick

If the goal of scholarship is to get inside another person or culture and so be able to speak for them, our multifaceted positioning would doom the enterprise from the start (even before we encountered the problem of temporality). But that is not my goal. "I am not ... seeking either to become natives or mimic them. Only romantics or spies would seem to find

The Researcher

Someone, an authoritative, explorative, elegant, learned voice, speaks and analyzes, amasses evidence, theorizes, speculates about everything – except itself. Who speaks? For what and to whom?

Edward W. Said, "Representing the Colonized: Anthropology's Interlocutors," 1989

Edward W. Said

a point in that," opined the eminent anthropologist Clifford Geertz: "We are seeking, in the widened sense of the term in which it encompasses very much more than talk, to converse with them, a matter a great deal more difficult ... than is commonly recognized."[37]

The key, and usually unremarked, problem is not that we are distanced from the language/cultural horizons of our interlocutors. The problem is that we are insufficiently distanced from our own worldview. The biggest obstacle is not so much knowing the other (that is what dialogue is for) as it is knowing oneself.

To be sure, as Bakhtin says, "to enter in some measure into an alien culture and look at the world through its eyes, is a necessary moment in the process of understanding." But there is "an enduring image that is partial and therefore false, according to which to better understand a foreign culture one should live in it and, forgetting one's own, look at the world through the eyes of this culture."[38] Even if "going native" were possible, it would be misguided because the ultimate scholarly goal is not only empathy but understanding. Understanding requires a platform that exists outside (or at least partially outside) a culture and that enables one to view it as a social rather than as a natural construct. That enables us to compare it with other cultures. If we do not have a critical distance from our own language and culture, our own historical and mythic consciousness, we cannot begin to understand how we are determined by it: difference itself becomes negative and other cultures inferior. Only the insider-outsider, or the outsider-insider, has the possibility of turning the ethnographic lens on both sides of a dialogue.

So there is a double challenge: how to become enough of an insider to have a partial understanding of the other side of the dialogue and enough of an outsider to have a partial understanding of one's own side of the dialogue. This place, which Bakhtin refers to as "exotopy," "does not renounce its self, its place in time [or] its culture" in relation to that which we are trying to understand. In other words, a self-aware positioning in one culture (be it ethnic or academic) is necessary if one is to engage in effective conversation with another.

Conversations with the dead are, of course, fraught with many difficulties. First, there is the problem of finding authentic aboriginal voices in the record of the past. A vast literature asks, in the words of Gayatri Spivak, whether or not the subaltern (native) can speak.[39] Second, there is the untranslatability of aboriginal experience when the dialogue is presented in the idiom of only one party. Finally, in holding conversations with the dead, we no longer have access to the original witnesses – those

Going Native

Everyone who would represent the past must "go native" in some way or be condemned always only to represent the present. Even the "native" must "go native" in finding a past ... Few of us can deny the hegemonic mode in our translations of other linguistic forms into our own. "Going native," for all the scandal it seems to cause, is actually a very difficult thing to do.

Greg Dening, *Performances,* 1996

Greg Dening

who might have been able to refute or to explain. These are the key problems of historical investigation, but they are not unique to the engagement between colonial and indigenous cultures. They belong to a larger category: the problem of temporality. We can *only* engage the past from the position of the present and with our current sensibilities and idioms. Spivak and Rey Chow see these issues as constituting a wall that prevents any investigation. Historians use the space between present and past as the place to start – not end – our investigations.[40] Spivak, Chow, and some other postcolonialist writers have forced us to confront how we impose our own projections onto the research material, but they underestimate the historical enterprise. For the past within living memory, interviewing, of course, allows "the native" to speak. For the past that extends beyond living memory, we turn to the archives. Not only are aboriginal voices implicitly contained in the hybridity of the colonial texts, as Homi Bhabha and Benita Parry argue, but detailed archival work also turns up numerous locations where aboriginal voices (sometimes in their own languages) have been directly recorded in interviews, in Royal Commissions, in songs, and in letters as accurately as have the voices of the immigrants.[41] Not only

A
DICTIONARY
of the
CHINOOK
JARGON

Compiled
by

B. J. SPALDING,
Pender Island,
BRITISH COLUMBIA

Spalding's 1947 dictionary was one of more than fifty Chinook jargon dictionaries circulating in British Columbia and the American Pacific Northwest between 1858 and 1950.

"can the subaltern speak," but s/he speaks within a vast archive in multiple and often contradictory voices.

If discourse is understood as involving all the means that Aboriginal People and colonialists used to communicate, then all aboriginal resistance to, as well as participation in, colonialism is a part of that dialogue.

Jean François Lyotard's notion of *différend*, the untranslatability of experience across time and culture, reminds us of the difficulty of understanding cultural categories that exist outside our own experience.[42] Hence the importance of Chinook jargon. Chinook was the language of intercultural dialogue in British Columbia and the Pacific Northwest from the end of the eighteenth century to the early decades of the twentieth century. Aboriginal People referred to it as the "white man's language" and whites referred to it as "speaking Indian." It was a language of cultural interaction, of improvisation, and it was built cooperatively. Through it the indigene speaks and the colonist speaks back. Its form and ambiguity capture not only "the untranslatability of the native's experience and the history of that untranslatablity" but also the untranslatability of the white experience.[43] It is the quintessential language of hybridity, and it exposes a space of communication and mis-communication.

Mikhail Bakhtin would describe Chinook jargon as an intentional semantic hybrid in which "there are always two consciousnesses, two language-intentions [and] two voices." As he points out, "Intentional semantic hybrids are inevitably internally dialogic. Two points of view are not mixed, but set against each other dialogically."[44] Finally, "One language can, after all, see itself only in the light of another language."[45] Hence the need for a dialogue between the *wawas*: pomo and Chinook.

THREE

Making the Lazy Indian

What is an Indian? Between the lines, Burton Kewayosh, an Ojibwa, and Homer Barnett, an anthropologist (both quoted on the right), proposed similar definitions. Being an "Indian" means hunting and fishing and, perhaps, small-scale farming. If one engaged in large-scale farming and had a good house and a boat, then he "practically" ceased being an Indian. For all "practical" purposes, these activities turned an Indian into a white. Real Indians did not "work."[1]

In this chapter, I look at why we know so little about the history of Aboriginal Peoples after the time of European settlement and, particularly, why we do not know about the history of aboriginal work. The answer to these questions lies in the two quotes to the right. It lies in the definition of "Indian" as "outside the workforce." Many have gone further, adding a pejorative twist to this: "Indians" have been defined as lazy. Once this definition was established, the idea of aboriginal work seemed like an oxymoron, and so a history of it was not pursued. This chapter looks at how Aboriginal Peoples came to be defined as "lazy" in the first place, and then it looks at how the process of "laz-i-fying" Indians came to be forgotten.

Making Indians

When Captain George Vancouver explored Burrard Inlet in 1792 and called the indigenous people he met "Indians," he placed them in a category already familiar to Europeans.[2] With this naming, the indigenous peoples of the Northwest Coast were classified with all the Aboriginal Peoples of North America, South America, and Central America, not to mention, thanks to the famous, if disoriented, navigator Christopher Columbus, the inhabitants of India. Physical (phenotypical) differences had something to do with this racial classification. The people Vancouver encountered on the Northwest Coast did have certain physical features that were different from those of him and his crew.

Yet, the phenotypical features of the people did not cry out for those people to be defined as Indians. Indigenous peoples of the Americas had a vast range of skin colours and facial features. The earliest European explorers

Up until the time when I was a boy we were still Indians. We lived by hunting and fishing and small farming.

Burton Kewayosh, from the 1961 CBC radio program, *The Way of the Indian*

Tommy Paul ... was the most prosperous man on the West Saanich Reserve owning a good house, a gas boat, cultivated fields and some livestock ... Practically he was a white man.

Homer Barnett, *The Coast Salish of British Columbia*, 1955

Tommy Paul, early 1930s

◀ Detail of *Amerigo Vespucci Discovers America* (see p. 32)

A late sixteenth-century engraving from Jan Van der Straet's *Amerigo Vespucci Discovers America*. The name "Indian" had less to do with "racial" features of Aboriginal People and more to do with the relationship Europeans wanted to have with them.

to the northwest coast of North America, Juan Perez and James Cook, thought that the "whiteness of [their] skin appeared almost equal to that of Europeans."[3] If physical characteristics had been the main criterion for racial categorization, then some of these Northwest Coast peoples could have easily fit into Asian or European categories. But racial definition does not depend on physical differences.[4] The category "Indian" had less to do with phenotypical features than it did with the relationship Europeans wished to have with Aboriginal Peoples. "Indian" was a useful category for occupants of newly encountered lands.

For Columbus the word "Indian" meant "inhabitant of India" and did not have the racial implications it had for Cook or Vancouver three hundred years later. In Columbus' time the word "race" did not exist in common parlance. As a concept it emerged in the sixteenth century, growing out of a folk category associated with inherited traits observed in animal breeding. By the eighteenth century, the word had spread into all European languages and had been expanded to include inheritable traits in humans. By the time of Vancouver's voyage, scientists had adopted these folk categories and divided human beings into "scientific" categories or races.[5]

The most influential among these scientists was Carl Linnaeus, who worked out a system through which he could classify all living things according to certain visible criteria. When it came to classifying humankind, he brought his knowledge of heredity together with descriptions of seafarers returning from distant regions of the world. In his historic *System*

Naturae of 1758, Linnaeus proposed that homo sapiens fell into six varieties, including monsters (i.e., dwarfs and giants), wild men, Africans, Americans (Indians), Asiatics, and Europeans.[6]

Linnaeus, like other classifiers of his time, associated phenotypical features with social characteristics. He described the American Indian as copper-coloured, with straight, black hair and thick, wide nostrils, along with a scanty beard. This racial type was also socially obstinate, content, and free. Asiatics were melancholy, rigid, severe, haughty, and covetous. Africans were phlegmatic, relaxed, crafty, indolent, and negligent. By contrast, Europeans were sanguine, gentle, acute, and inventive. Systems of governance were also linked to racial type. Asiatics were governed by opinions, Africans by caprice, and Americans (Indians) by custom. Europeans alone were defined as "governed by laws."[7]

Linnaeus had defined the American Indians as "obstinate and carefree" and the African race as "indolent," but the negative typing of non-Europeans blurred when one was in the field. In fact, wherever Europeans met indigenous populations, their conclusions were strikingly similar to those of Linnaeus. The Hottentots of South Africa were rebuked for their "idleness and sloth," the indigenous peoples of the Philippines for laziness and filth.[8] Nothing, it was said, could rouse the native South Americans from "indolent habits and indifference."[9] The most authoritative observers reported that "indolence pervades all classes of the Egyptians."[10] The Fijians' "mental apathy, laziness and improvidence" was said to "arise from their climate, their diet and their communal institutions."[11] Likewise, the early visitors to the Northwest Coast were unanimous in their condemnation of Indians as indolent or lazy.[12] Robert Brown, who studied the Aboriginal Peoples of British Columbia in the 1860s, summarized the general attitude in his encyclopaedic 1871 *Races of Mankind*: "the Central Africans, *like all barbarous or savage people,* are a lazy race."[13] Lazy, it seems, was part of the imperial definition of the "other," and Aboriginal Peoples were certainly other.

The idea of aboriginal laziness was contrasted to "industriousness" and "hard work," which was supposed to characterize European nations. Yet, this contrast breaks down at every level. First, European aristocrats often complained about the laziness of European peasants and workers, so clearly this did not distinguish Aboriginal People from Europeans. Even in BC progressive citizens were constantly complaining about the lack of industry and laziness of the small white farmer. What "lazy" really meant to these upper-class commentators was not willing to work like indentured serfs paying due deference to the "lords" who needed serving. As industry replaced agriculture in Europe, the more regulated and intensified work of factory labourers replaced indentured farm labour as the standard for work. Laziness came to mean unwilling to work for fourteen hours a day at routine factory labour under quasi-military discipline for subsistence pay.[14] Second, the very aristocrats who were not satisfied at the level of industry displayed by their indentured serfs defined themselves by the fact that they did absolutely no work. In Europe, idleness was a marker of upper-class status.

What constitutes appropriate labour evolved historically as an interpretive endeavour to understand human social organization. However, it also became a tool that could be deployed against non-Western peoples.[15] Indigenous people had to be defined as lazy and unproductive because then and only then could Europeans invoke the religious or philosophic justification for occupying their territories and displacing them. Europeans resorted to their "labour theory of value," crystallized by John Locke and Emmerich de Vattel in the mid-eighteenth century, which accorded ownership of land to those who removed it "from a state of nature" and improved it. European colonists had to overlook the different agriculture, mariculture, and silviculture practices of indigenous peoples to characterize the non-European world as "in a state of nature."[16] They also had to characterize the productive activities of indigenous civilizations as "not labour" in order to declare America "unowned" and available for the taking. So, aboriginal labour was framed as existing outside the economy.

Laziness and Leisure

When fur traders followed explorers, they inherited the definition of the Indian as lazy and extended it into a dominant stereotype, despite the abundant evidence of Aboriginal People being productively occupied. In his 1825 tour of inspection, George Simpson, governor of the Hudson's Bay Company, declared the Indians of the Columbia River Valley to be "indolent and lazy to the extreme." John McLeod thought the northern Okanagan people "an indolent and improvident Set," and in 1839 Dugald McTavish described the Chinook as most miserable "owing to their laziness."[17]

Not that the fur traders observed Aboriginal People doing nothing. In salmon season or bulb and berry season Aboriginal People worked from dawn to dusk. Fur trader Gabriel Franchère offered a contrary view of the Columbia River people: "They possess, to an eminent degree, the qualities *opposed* to indolence, improvidence, and stupidity; the chiefs, above all, are distinguished for their good sense and intelligence. Generally speaking they have a ready intellect and a tenacious memory."[18] As Mary Black-Rogers points out, "indolence" to the fur traders did not mean someone who did little, rather it was "an attribute of those who show[ed] independence of the fur trade." Indians were *indolent*, according to the fur traders, because they had little need for European goods (and so chose not to hunt furs extensively) and because they enjoyed long periods of leisure between food gathering seasons.[19] This use of the term "indolent," meaning a lack of interest in participating in a European form of labour subordination and refusing to exchange subsistence activities for accumulation, coincided with Linnaeus's racial categorization of Indians as "content and free."[20]

Even leisure, which Aboriginal People seemed to enjoy in abundance, was an important part of the economy. Leisure time spent in storytelling, lounging, gambling, and travelling to pay social visits was not the wasted time it seemed to the Europeans. In an economy in which trade was interpersonal, food was shared communally, spiritual and practical knowledge was transmitted through stories, and community economic activities required consensus, so-called leisure time was, in fact, essential economic time. In a culture in which the spiritual and economic were not separable, time spent on spirit quests, salmon ceremonies, prayer, and appeasing unhappy spirits was vital to the economy.[21]

While the officers of the fur trade, the literate observers who kept tabs on Aboriginal People, spent most of their days between the semi-annual coming and going of brigades in idleness, elders in the aboriginal communities warned against wasting time.[22] Aboriginal cultures in British Columbia existed in an economy of reciprocity: everyone was expected to contribute in accordance with their abilities and place in society. In such cultures the lazy were a liability for a large extended family and were disparaged and even shunned. Homer Barnett, in his ethnography of the Coast Salish, noted that "children were impressed with the importance of industry and ambition from an early age. Laziness was the worst of all faults." The Saanich called lazy people *swiwalas* as opposed to *qeʾmat*, or poor men (i.e., commoners without canoes or other property). The Comox just called them bad people.[23] Edna Bobb explained that the worst people among the Stó:lō were *suːmet*, or lazy people. To the Athapascan-speaking Ulkatcho Carrier people "the ideal person was one who was not lazy, who hunted all the time and was enterprising in trade. Even children ... were openly criticized for 'playing too much.'" Someone who was lazy and had to ask food from others was called a "dried fish slave" among the Tlingit of the Alaskan panhandle.[24]

By contrast, the accumulation of wealth goods was highly valued among the Northwest Coast peoples. In the Coast Salish languages the word for "to become rich" and "to become a leader" was the same. *Siʔém?* meant leader, rich, and important. But one did not get rich just by one's own initiative. One needed the assistance of spirit helpers. Successful labouring and its resultant wealth was an affirmation that the spiritual beings who

Civilization Equals Labour

The naturally indolent character of too many men of Indian blood disposes them to accept offers to farm on shares, which fostering their disinclination for constant labor admits of their subsisting, although miserably, while leading a life of idleness. This engenders habits opposed to temperate and virtuous living ... No true civilization can prevail apart from labor.

William Spragge, Deputy Superintendent of Indian Affairs, 1865

Among the Salish

One kind of person only, of any class, was despised, and individuals in this category might crop up in any family. They were the "lazy men," the worthless ones who were without ambition or self respect.

Homer Barnett, *Coast Salish of British Columbia*, 1955

ensured good hunting, fishing, or harvesting were being honoured and were satisfied. One's physical labour and spiritual power were intertwined.[25]

The European observations about work and laziness remind us that defining race is about making boundaries, drawing lines, erecting fences, and then declaring what is on the other side of the fence to be "beyond the pale." Racial boundaries, like fences, need to be maintained, and so ideas of race and racial characteristics are constantly being updated, reinforced, and redefined. Named in the eighteenth century by Vancouver and renamed and remade many times since, the category "Indian" as applied in what is now British Columbia was not so much a matter of mistaken identity on the part of Christopher Columbus as it was a created identity – one that has been recreated by successive waves of newcomers.[26]

It is no coincidence that the term "race" and the ideology of racial hierarchies, which puts "whites" at the top of the list, developed during the era of European colonial expansion. The same year that Linnaeus published his *System Naturae*, 1758, Emmerich de Vattel published his *Law of Nations*, in which he argued that those who choose to avoid labour, choosing instead to hunt and fish, have "no reason to complain if other nations, more industrious and too closely confined, come to take possession of a part of those lands." A century later such thinking was used to justify the insatiable appetite of the new colonists to British Columbia: those whom the Stó:lō called *Xwelitem* – "the hungry people." The settlers agreed that "the indolent, contented savage, must give place to the busteling [sic] sons of civilization & Toil."[27] So long as "Indians" were defined as "lazy" or "vanishing" (preferably both), their displacement by the virile, enterprising white race was seen as legitimate.

Vanishing Indians

Understanding "Indian" as a category created by Europeans, with attached meanings like indolence and inferiority, makes sense of historical evidence that is otherwise quite contradictory. How also might you reconcile evidence like that in Charles Forbes' 1862 guide to Vancouver Island, which states that "[Indian] labour cannot be depended on, and with one or two slight exceptions at present forms no point of consideration in the labour market" with that of a principal Vancouver Island newspaper, the *Victoria Gazette*, which complained in May 1860 that, "among the numerous drawbacks from which our Colony suffers, is that of the superabundance of Indian labor, to the extent of almost entirely excluding the white working man"?[28]

What are we to make of the fact that in 1867, in his guide to the colony, A.A. Harvey describes Aboriginal People as "valueless in the labour market," while in 1875 Attorney General George Walkem wrote: "In the present

Rightly Appropriated

According to the strict rule of international law, territory occupied by a barbarous or wholly uncivilized people may be rightly appropriated by a civilized or Christian nation.

British Columbian, June 1, 1869

infancy of British Columbia, the Indians of this class have proved invaluable in the settled portions of this province"? What do we make of Chief Justice Begbie's 1885 assessment of BC Indians as "a race of laborious independent workers"?[29]

Sometimes one commentator made contradictory statements about the same aboriginal groups during the same time period. For example, in his 1849 report, surveyor W.C. Grant wrote of the Aboriginal People on southern Vancouver Island: "Those who are able to work are all anxious to be employed. They are very quick at receiving instruction and many of them ... were tolerably good hands with the axe and the spade." A short time later, on 8 August 1851, Grant commented in a letter to William Brodie that the natives on southern Vancouver Island are "as useless as they are harmless." Two years later he apparently reversed himself, writing that the same people, "with the proper superintendence are capable of being made very useful. They all live by fishing but take kindly to any kind of rough agricultural employment."[30]

Sketch of Chief Kakalatza of the Somenos, a group that explorer Robert Brown described as "a very lazy set"

We might dismiss this as one man's schizophrenia if it were not for the fact that it is a relatively common pattern. Robert Brown, the ethnographer mentioned above, described the Somenos, a subgroup of the Cowichan, as "a very lazy set ... only caring to work if they get high wages," while a few pages later he states: "to judge them as you see them loafing about the white settlements is like judging a man by the coat on his back." In 1861 the *Victoria Colonist* described the Indians' "habits of indolence, roaming propensities, and natural repugnance for manual labour," but in 1860 it had noted "that most of the laboring work done about town is performed by Indians." In 1860 and 1862 its editorials complained that white men could not get work because Aboriginal People were doing it all.[31]

If European observers knew that "Indians" were lazy by definition, yet saw them working everywhere in the colony "with a surprising degree of industry," the result was bound to be a certain amount of contradictory commentary.[32] This is particularly true when aboriginal "industry" took forms that were not in keeping with European notions of time, discipline, and subordination. Aboriginal People's way of entering the paid workforce – generally for short periods – and their reasons for quitting (often to engage in cultural or subsistence work) frustrated Europeans and became further proof of Indian laziness. This underlies the sentiments of Indian Agent W.H. Lomas, who noted: "In the towns of Victoria and Nanaimo individual instances occur where young Indians have learned trades, and are on many subjects as shrewd as the average white man but unfortunately, their intelligence is only superficial, and the true Indian often appears through a coating of veneer."[33]

It's Anglo-Saxon Bone That We Want

The [type] of "bone, muscle and intellect" that is required here differs materially from the Indian or African. It is Caucasian – Anglo-Saxon bone ... that we want.

British Colonist, February 19, 1861

Aboriginal People were often contrasted with Chinese immigrants, who were usually described as more industrious. Investigation of these characterizations suggests an explanation for the comparison. The Chinese in 1880s British Columbia were a true "landless proletariat": they either worked or they starved. But for Aboriginal People, paid work was still a supplement to a rich subsistence base. Much of the Lekwungen's "earnings" were "saved" for potlatch goods. If wages fell to a near subsistence level, it was not worthwhile for Aboriginal People to work. But the Chinese immigrants had no choice.

Beyond price, there were other reasons for the popularity of Chinese labour. Chinese domestic servants were willing to "live in" and be on-call all the time, whereas aboriginal domestics preferred to live in their own homes. Moreover, as one observer testified to a Royal Commission on Chinese immigration, it was more prestigious to have an oriental houseboy than an aboriginal one. The "exotic" status of the Chinese may also account for the partial displacement of aboriginal women by Chinese women in Victoria's red light district.[34]

Drawing showing former *British Colonist* editor Amor de Cosmos' support for a petition to prevent Chinese railway labour (*Canadian Illustrated News,* April 21, 1879)

Employers often gave a third reason for employing the Chinese: their supposed reliability relative to Aboriginal People. Some employers, such as cannery owner Charles Todd, characterized Aboriginal People as "short-sighted and unreasonable. Even after their advances they come down late, giving excuses that their hay took time, or something like that."[35] Later, the trade magazine *Lumberman and Contractor* repeatedly claimed that the forest industry needed oriental labour because "Indians" were too ready to quit to go to a potlatch. By contrast, "Chinamen," the magazine said, would find a replacement if they themselves could not come to work.[36] From an employer's point of view, Chinese labourers probably *were* more reliable and easier to discipline than were Aboriginal People because they were more dependent on wage labour. Aboriginal People were more independent and were engaged in an alternative economic system, which affected their availability for paid work.

Yet, in evaluating this evidence offered by contemporary observers, we have to appreciate that the Chinese were "racialized" as much as were Indians. The positive assessments of Chinese came in the context of employers arguing that they were necessary as cheap labour. Arguing that Aboriginal People were unreliable and that they could not do the job was also a tactic to ensure the Chinese would be admitted and that the overall labour force would be large enough to keep wages down. Commentators who had no interest in employing Chinese often branded them as "lazy" and "thieving," using the same derogatory terms directed at Aboriginal People. Other commentators used the reputed industriousness and thriftiness of the Chinese as reason to exclude them, since whites could not compete. The real problem with Chinese and aboriginal labour was that it was not White labour.[37]

We know so little about the history of aboriginal labour because Indians were defined "as [of] no account in the labour force" and so are overlooked in discussions of the labour that occurred in the colony/province. A classic example of this oversight concerns the historical accounts of the origins of industrial sawmilling in British Columbia. Most of these are based on the written recollections of observers like R.C. Mayne, whose 1862 travel account reported that the first industrial sawmill in the west coast colonies had "been erected in a most solid fashion by English labourers ... Seventy white men [were] employed at and about the premises." This is the accepted account of employment at the first "factory" in the colonies – the largest industrial sawmill on the west coast of North America. Given the low number of "white men" in the colony, Mayne's figure for employment seems more credible than that of Reverend Matthew MacFie, who, in his *Vancouver Island and British Columbia*, mentioned two to three hundred hands employed at the same Alberni mill. It is Mayne's figures that are

As for the Mills

As for the mills, they are principally worked by Indians, half-breeds, Chinese and Japs who are paid 75 Cents to 1.00/day .... Indians who work in logging camps, sawmills, or on board boats, etc, being strong and active, obtain about the same wage as white men.

R.E. Gosnell, *Year Book of British Columbia and Manual of Provincial Information for 1897*

used in the histories of the forest industries in British Columbia.[38] Yet Mayne's and MacFie's figures are reconciled by artist Frederick Whymper, who, in an obscure book about his travels in Alaska, noted that when he visited Alberni "two hundred workmen representing a dozen nationalities, and, including among the number, Kanakas from the Sandwich Islands, and Indians and half-breeds of many tribes – were busily engaged in the mill and neighbourhood."[39]

Whymper's exceptional recollection suggests that many historical accounts, like Mayne's, count only "white" men when they mention the number of "men" employed. The history of aboriginal workers is not known because they were not counted. This observation is important enough – in that it reinserts Aboriginal People into the capitalist labour force – but its importance goes beyond that. It ought to recast the entire way we think about historic aboriginal/non-aboriginal relations. Historian Martin Robin, using the standard accounts, thought that "it was not merely shrinking numbers of the 'vanishing Red Men' which accounted for the low participation of Indians in the new industrial system. By inclination and habit, the Indian did not fit the new industrial mode."[40] But, if Whymper is to be believed, Aboriginal People were part of the new industrial system from the moment it arrived on the British Columbia coast. It was Mayne who, by writing only about *white* labour, "vanished" the aboriginal and Hawaiian (Kanaka) workers, who accounted for over half the workforce.

Of course, Aboriginal Peoples are not the only ones given little, or partial, attention in these historical sources. Other non-white ethnic groups, women, and workers in general are also difficult to find. As a result, historians interested in these "peoples without histories" have turned to what are called "routinely generated" sources, such as censuses, parish records, tax rolls, directories, court records, and voters' lists. These records were systematically collected for routine purposes and often include groups not much mentioned by elite observers.

However, even here, Aboriginal Peoples have been vanished more effectively than most. Legally and racially defined as "other," Aboriginal Peoples are absent from many sources commonly used by social historians. The predecessor to the federal census, the "Blue Books" (the annual statistical registers of the colonies) annually enumerated the "White Race," the "Coloured Race" (i.e., Blacks and Hawaiians), and the "Chinese Race" but not Aboriginal Peoples. The federal census of 1871 used the Blue Book figures and set the population of British Columbia at 10,586, mentioning in a footnote that "no account is taken of the Aboriginal People, details of which are wanting."[41] In fact, the invisible Aboriginal Peoples outnumbered non-Aboriginal Peoples by more than two to one in the new province.

The first federal census of British Columbia, conducted in 1881, made little effort to gather more than the numbers of Aboriginal Peoples and, even then, underestimated the population.[42] Most enumerators just wrote "Indian" in the space provided for names and either made no entry under occupation or took little care with this category, making whole nations "fishermen" and others "hunters." The next census, in 1891, though more carefully collected, did not ask about ethnic origin, so it is impossible to generalize from it about aboriginal work. The 1901 decennial census put Aboriginal People on a special schedule, so they were not asked the questions about employment that appear on the regular schedules. As late as 1951, census takers categorized Indians living on reserves as "neither employed nor unemployed," and so they do not appear in census employment tables.

Aboriginal Peoples and the federal government sometimes shared the same ideas about work. In 1915 Chief John of the Ulkatcho band in British Columbia did not count Kapoose and Kahoose as band members because "they were Ulkatcho Indians but lived after the manner of the white people."[43] Where routinely generated sources did touch on the lives of Aboriginal People, they established a set of categories that reflected the values of the information collectors rather than those of the Aboriginal People. Enumerators had no choice but to record aboriginal households in categories that were suited to Euro-American society, even though Aboriginal People organized themselves according to very different family structures.[44]

If we cannot find out much about aboriginal work from the census – the standard source for social historians – what about other routinely generated sources? Prohibited from voting, Aboriginal People do not appear on provincial voters' lists until after 1949, and they do not appear on federal lists until 1960. Exempt from taxation, they do not appear on tax rolls. Like other marginal groups, they were barely touched by directory compilers until well into the twentieth century. Aboriginal People were intermittently evangelized, but church records are spotty and, like many other sources, inconsistent in their use of variant spellings of both aboriginal and adopted European names.

Like the archival sources for sawmilling, the annual statistical reports of the British Columbia Department of Mines have used their own sleights of hand to make Aboriginal People vanish. The annual statistics divided the number of gold miners into only two categories: white and Chinese. As a result, histories of mining have centred around these two cultural groups, despite the fact that other sources reveal that there were hundreds and perhaps thousands of aboriginal gold miners.[45]

Count Them, Then Get Their Land

We had considerable trouble with the Indians making them understand what we were doing ... Chief supposed our mission was to find out how many of them there were and then the government would do away with them to get their land.

Fred Greer, enumerator, Department of Agriculture, June 29, 1892

Employing the Indians

A large quantity of coal may at any time be got there [near Beaver Cove] by employing the Indians, who are numerous and ... by no means averse to such employment ... On one occasion when we employed them for that purpose, they brought in upwards of ninety tons in a few days, which they dug with hatchets and other inconvenient implements and there is no doubt that with the proper excavating tools they would have done the work much more expeditiously.

James Douglas and Peter S. Ogden to J.A. Duntze, September 7, 1846

James Douglas, Chief Factor of Fort Victoria and later governor of Vancouver Island and British Columbia

This vanishing act was even more profound when it came to coal mining. Alongside categories for white and Chinese coal miners, annual reports do have a category for Indians, but it disappears in the mid-1880s despite a continuing aboriginal presence. Moreover, the reports caution us that the figures do not include miners' helpers. Other sources reveal that miners' helpers were disproportionately made up of Chinese and Aboriginal People.[46]

This is partly why the only history of coal mining on the coast declares that the opening of the first mine at Fort Rupert marked a new stage in BC history. The author, Eric Newsome, wrote: "With the digging of coal the Indians had become irrelevant." A re-examination of the primary documents reveals a different story. *All* of the coal mined at Fort Rupert, over 3,600 tons in three years, was mined by Aboriginal People. Though there were imported Scottish miners at Fort Rupert who unsuccessfully explored for new seams, they did "not raise one square inch of coal." In 1858, when the centre of mining had moved to Nanaimo, the *Victoria Gazette* reported: "There are some thirty or forty miners, mostly Indians, constantly employed in getting out the coal, and the lead has now been worked a quarter of a mile." Moreover, other evidence tells us that Aboriginal People continued working in the mines well into the twentieth century.[47] All these examples tell us that the historical record is suspect and that documenting aboriginal labour is more than a matter of recounting, it is a matter of recasting the entire history of the region.

Forgetting and Remembering

The work of historians involves creating an account of the past based on evidence that exists in the present. For the reasons laid out above, much of the surviving historical evidence completely misses the record of aboriginal work. Historians like Eric Newsome, Martin Robin, Robin Fisher, and others have, with few exceptions, taken the absences in the record at face value and have unwittingly turned these omissions, and along with them the "lazy Indian" stereotype, into historical fact. First white settlers and then historians erased Indians, either by leaving them out of their accounts or by placing them on the margins, where they were barely visible. The "red men" have not vanished from the historical landscape: they have *been* vanished.

When historians write about BC Aboriginal Peoples, they generally use one of three broad storylines, or metanarratives and each has contributed in its own way to disappearing the history of aboriginal workers. One of the earliest and most enduring of these presented "Indians" as unassimilable and, thus, as obstacles to economic development, or "progress." This perspective, although found in early twentieth-century Canadian texts, is best exemplified in the work of an American, Frederick Jackson Turner. His "The Significance of the Frontier in American History" argues that the destruction of indigenous peoples is part of the trial by fire from which a new nation and a new people would be born.[48] There is a "progressive" variant of this argument: Aboriginal Peoples should exchange their "primitive existence" for "civilization" under the guiding hand of the missionary, teacher, or government agent. Although now out of fashion in the scholarly world, these ideas still have wide currency, and, as recently as 1991, formed the basis for a major legal decision that rejected aboriginal land claims.[49]

A second metanarrative is sometimes summed up in the phrase "fatal impact." Trade and contact between an avaricious European world and an (often romanticized) aboriginal culture resulted in the destruction of the latter. This is usually accounted for by superior European technology, aboriginal passivity, and the inherently static nature of "primitive society." This is often a thinly veiled critique of a capitalist society that has flattened indigenous cultures that have stood in its path. Often this metanarrative devalues contemporary aboriginal society as being only the "debris" of an idyllic aboriginal past. Both versions portray Aboriginal Peoples as victims of superior force and deny them a role in the making of their own history.[50]

The third metanarrative is more subtle. Best known in British Columbia from Robin Fisher's work, it considers the period following first contact as one of cultural effervescence. This is sometimes called the "enrichment thesis" because Aboriginal Peoples, who, it is argued, had a great deal of control over the fur trade, were able to choose the aspects of the immigrant culture they wished to adopt and, thereby, enrich their own culture. This narrative restores agency to Aboriginal Peoples but only temporarily. The fatal impact of European settlement, it seems, was not averted, only delayed:

> The fur trade had stimulated Indian culture by adding to Indian wealth and therefore to the scope of Indian creativity. Settlement on the other hand, often had the effect of subtracting from Indian wealth and this tended to stultify Indians ... The Indians had been able to mould the fur trade to their benefit, but settlement was not malleable; it was unyielding and aggressive. It imposed its demands on Indians without compromise.[51]

Settlement, not contact, marked the demise of aboriginal culture and history.

Historical Genocide

It frequently happens that the historian, though he professes more humanity than the trapper, mountain man or golddigger ... really exhibits and practices a similar inhumanity ... wielding a pen instead of a rifle.

Henry David Thoreau, journal entry, February 3, 1859

All three metanarratives have certain features in common. First, they see aboriginal-white relations as marked by a distinct turning point, either at contact or at the beginning of settlement. Second, they describe the process of colonialism and the expansion of a capitalist economy as relatively uniform across space and among Aboriginal Peoples. Third, they all exclude Aboriginal Peoples from history after this turning point. Finally, they have based their theorizing exclusively on white observations.

There have been several attempts to challenge these metanarratives by focusing on the involvement of Aboriginal People in the workforce. Sarah Carter's work, *Lost Harvests*, found that Aboriginal Peoples on the Canadian Prairies actively turned to farming when their buffalo-based economy declined. Carter's evidence suggests that aboriginal farmers were doing well relative to their non-aboriginal neighbours until the latter complained about unfair competition from "state-supported Indians." Responding to this pressure, the federal government prevented Aboriginal People from becoming commercial farmers and encouraged them to take up subsistence farming – a policy that led to long-term poverty. Carter concluded that government policy rather than aboriginal culture was the major factor in accounting for the economic marginalization of Aboriginal Peoples. This finding is echoed in Leo Waisberg and Tim Holzkamm's study of the Ojibwa in northwest Ontario and Ellice Gonzalez' study of the Mi'kmaq.[52] I take up the argument that Indians were "made unemployed" by government policy in Chapters 7 and 8.

Kenneth Coates's look at aboriginal/non-aboriginal relations in the Yukon Territory, *Best Left as Indians*, highlights cultural differences between Aboriginal Peoples and immigrants. He concludes that what is often thought to be "a marginal place" in the "white" economy was, in some respects, preferred by Aboriginal Yukoners. "The Natives' lack of interest in the aggressive, acquisitive materialism of the industrial world ensured that few accepted the discipline and control of the non-Native work place." Like elsewhere, "laziness" was a feature of not being a full-time wage worker. Participating in a subsistence economy and occasionally making seasonal incursions into wage labour permitted Aboriginal Yukoners to maintain important elements of their culture. At the same time, Coates shows how aboriginal choices were severely circumscribed. Their "tangential and peripheral" role may have been a positive choice on their part; however, given the "racial economic barriers barring them from work in the white man's world," there was not much to choose from, particularly in the 1950s and 1960s.[53]

Frank Tough's economic history of northern Manitoba between 1870 and 1930 argues that Aboriginal Peoples had little choice but to accept the dependent role left them by the incursions of capitalism and state welfare policy. He calls for more attention to the structure of markets and modes of production as well as to the extraction of surplus value on the part of interests external to the region.[54]

In British Columbia, the main challenge to the thesis that Aboriginal Peoples were marginalized with the coming of industrial capitalism is Rolf Knight's *Indians at Work: An Informal History of Indian Labour in British Columbia, 1858-1930*. What is most refreshing about Knight's work is that it breaks free of the sources that had circumscribed scholarship in this field and found that oral accounts by Aboriginal People were full of references to work.[55] Knight's sources suggested that aboriginal labourers may have entered the industrial economy in large numbers and that wage labour might have been an important source of income for Aboriginal People as late as the Great Depression. Characterizing his own work as an "informal study," he admits to its preliminary nature: "It will be evident that much of the data for a complete labour history of Indian people in British Columbia is missing here. The present account raises more questions than it answers."[56] Knight did succeed in his goal of opening new avenues of inquiry that have since been followed by scholars of BC and adjacent territories. Few, however, have followed his lead in examining anything other than archival sources.

By rejecting the assumption, sometimes stated and sometimes implied, that "ongoing traditional values and attitudes somehow limit Indian job capacities," Knight stressed aboriginal similarities with other labourers and opened a debate that has been joined by Alicja Muszynski, Evelyn Pinkerton, and Dianne Newell. While Knight took pains to emphasize the similarity of aboriginal and non-aboriginal workers,[57] Muszynski's and Pinkerton's studies of aboriginal fishers and fish processing labourers stressed the differences. In Pinkerton's words, "Work rhythms and work discipline in a pre-industrial society organized by kin obligations and authority of the chief differ, of course, from rhythms of industrial production ... Moreover, the safety net offered by Indian communities and by the Indian's ability to rely on traditional subsistence did not create the most favourable conditions for the development of a highly disciplined capitalist workforce."[58]

According to Muszynski and Pinkerton, Aboriginal People were first incorporated into the industrial labour force, at least in the fish processing industry, because their subsistence economy meant that they could be paid less than immigrants. The cheap price of aboriginal labour was essential to early enterprises, but, ultimately, the subsistence economy allowed Aboriginal People the independence to reject capitalist work discipline. Since Aboriginal People could not be exploited as much as other labourers,

Indian Loggers Were ... Loggers

Whatever ... distinct cultural traditions they maintained, Indian loggers were loggers, Indian longshoremen were longshoremen, Indian cannery workers were cannery workers.

Rolf Knight, *Indians at Work*, 1978

White sawyer captured in Haida argillite carving

employers replaced them with more tractable Chinese and Japanese immigrants. Their argument raises interesting questions, but its conclusion does not entirely square with the evidence that aboriginal women remained vital to the fish processing industry until the 1950s, when most of the plants closed. This evidence is limited to a sampling of published reports. Dianne Newell delves into the unpublished correspondence of the canners as well as documents of the Department of Fisheries and the Department of Indian Affairs. She argues that Aboriginal People actively joined the capitalist economy through their work in the fishing industry and that the state bears the primary responsibility for their displacement – an argument supported by Douglas Harris.[59]

Richard Mackie provides the best evidence that the division between a fur trade economy and a wage economy was imposed by historians. He documents the participation of Aboriginal People in a wide range of paid labour for the Hudson's Bay Company, including construction, fishing and fish preserving, logging, sawmilling, mining, ice harvesting, cranberry harvesting, and so on. They were also employed as ploughmen, messengers, sailors, shepherds, and shearers – all this alongside their work in the fur trade.[60]

These studies of different places, times, and circumstances point to a history of aboriginal work-for-pay, but they come to a variety of conclusions. Might the different conclusions in these regional studies be a feature of different indigenous social structures? To answer this question we must extend our idea of history back before the arrival of Europeans, remembering that different Aboriginal Peoples will likely have different histories of work.

With the exception of Knight's work, the histories mentioned rely primarily on non-aboriginal statements about Aboriginal Peoples' reasons for going to work, for how they conducted themselves at work, and for quitting work. What histories would have been written had we asked Aboriginal People?

If we listen to aboriginal voices, some of the apparent contradictions dissolve. Aboriginal People did not choose to be loggers or Indians, modern or traditional, spiritual or materialistic; rather, they experienced these aspects of their lives within an integrated whole. Aboriginal People made choices after considering the full range of subsistence resources, wage work, and state payments available to them. Aboriginal voices, which are interspersed throughout this book, suggest to me that Aboriginal Peoples constructed their own, distinctive "moditional" economy. They alternated work and leisure but were no "lazier" than were immigrants.

Europeans had to call "Indians" lazy in order to legitimate the occupation of their land. The colonizers seized on the different way that indigenous people worked – periods of hard work followed by periods of leisure – and the fact that many quit when they had accumulated what they needed from wage work as proof of their preconceptions. When it came to counting aboriginal work, the awkward fit between the preconceptions and the abundant evidence of aboriginal workers must have contributed to the gaping absence of Aboriginal People from the census and other key records. This constructed gap in the historical record allows the "lazy" stereotype to persist and be resurrected as a comfortable explanation for aboriginal poverty today and as an argument against modern treaties or any form of "redress" for the earlier displacement.

Integrating aboriginal voices with non-aboriginal voices turns history into dialogue.[61] In acknowledging competing narratives, definitions, and worldviews, history becomes a transformative process that can help rematerialize Aboriginal Peoples who have been disappeared from our history. In the process, the historical conversation becomes more complete, comprehensible, and lively.

FOUR

The Lekwungen

When the people of Victoria, British Columbia, awoke on the morning of October 16, many slid into their slippers and padded through their comfortable homes to retrieve the morning paper, the *Colonist,* from their doorsteps. The name of the paper did not strike them as out of place – the *Colonist* had been the main newspaper in the city since 1858.[1]

On this chilly October morning, the headlines warned that "Indians Face Starvation as Winter Approaches." The paper went on to describe the poverty of the nearby Indian reserve and warned of actual starvation if drastic action were not taken. John Albany, chief of the Lekwungen people, confirmed the desperate predictions: "It is going to be a tough winter. It is going to be worse than ever." The year was 1960.

The Lekwungen had not always been poor. Compare the October 1960 article to the report of October 25, 1881, also about the Lekwungen: "The great bulk of these Indians are really well off this winter; having had good crops of potatoes, the salmon run promising well and so many of them having earned good wages during the summer." In the summer of 1881 the aboriginal villages around Victoria had been "almost entirely deserted, men, women, and children having found paying employment at the salmon canneries on the Fraser River." In addition to fishing and canning, a contemporary observer noted that the Lekwungen "men on the wharves and otherwise, and the females as washerwomen, seamstresses, laundresses, earn much and spend it all in the City."[2]

It is actually possible to compare the wealth and poverty of the Lekwungen between these two reports. In 1881, the Indian Agent estimated that the Indians of southern Vancouver Island "brought back over $15,000 in wages from the fisheries," plus income from the other sources mentioned above. A 1969 survey of the registered Indians in the same area found their total earned income to be $31,385. When we divide these figures by the aboriginal population, the per capita income of southern Vancouver Island Indians, from *fishing alone,* was $92.46 in 1881 (in 1969 dollars), while, in 1969, the per capita earned income from *all sources* was only $56.93. Even allowing for wide margins of error, both the qualitative and

◄ Weaver in a Paul Kane painting (see p. 63)

quantitative evidence suggest that the Lekwungen and other Aboriginal Peoples of the Saanich Peninsula were worse off financially in the 1960s than they were in the 1880s.[3]

This chapter asks how a "century of progress" for Canada could have been a "century of impoverishment" for Aboriginal Peoples, and it does so by focusing on one community's experience. It is a microhistory that looks, in particular, at the Lekwungen people as well as at their Coast Salish neighbours on southern Vancouver Island.

The Lekwungen are now legally known as the Songhees and Esquimalt bands, and their ancestral home is now occupied by the urban core of Victoria. Prior to 1876, "Songhees" was a term Europeans used to refer to a group of families speaking the Lkungen dialect of Straits Salish. The Indian Act of that year split the Songhees into three bands – the Esquimalt, Discovery Island, and the Songhees – by tying each group to a reserve and defining an Indian band as a group of Indians for whom land had been allocated. Subsequently, the Discovery Island band merged with the Songhees band. Culturally, the Lekwungen share much with other Coast Salish peoples, both those of Vancouver Island and those of the adjoining mainland (see Map 4.1).

The Lekwungen have been singled out for study because, of all the Aboriginal Peoples in British Columbia and western Canada, they were the best positioned to succeed within the European, capitalist economy. Their territory was settled by immigrants early in the period of Western European-Aboriginal contact, and, since then, the Lekwungen have been continuously involved with the immigrant economy. Rapid white settlement had a negative impact upon their subsistence economy, but it meant that, from the 1860s onward, the Lekwungen had a wide range of possible vocations in this urban area.

It is not entirely a coincidence that the Lekwungen found an urban centre growing up on their land and around their reserve. The Lekwungen played an important role in the series of events that led to Victoria being chosen as the capital of the colony-cum-province and subsequently becoming the province's largest urban centre in the nineteenth century (since then, the second largest). The Lekwungen welcomed the fur traders into their territory, and it was this welcome, and the landscape that they had turned into a parkland, that helped persuade the Hudson's Bay Company to select Lekwungen land as their headquarters and colonial capital.

Finally, the Lekwungen are important because a uniquely favourable financial situation resulted from the exchange of their original reserve for another in the suburbs of Victoria. As part of the 1911 relocation agreement, every family received $10,000 in cash (approximately $265,000 in

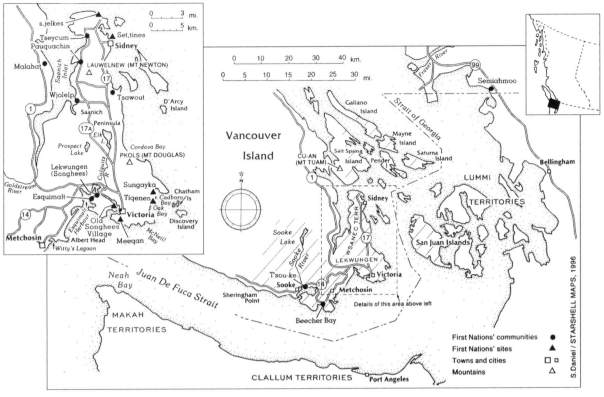

MAP 4.1   Straits territories

2008 dollars). Not only were they advantageously located when it came to the proximity to wage-work opportunities, but for the years immediately after 1911, at least, they were well provided with investment capital. If any aboriginal group in Canada was well positioned to take advantage of, and succeed in, the capitalist economy, it was the Lekwungen. Yet, somehow, this did not happen. This chapter takes a detailed look at one particular aspect of *mákuk*, the role of the immigrant economy in the life of the Lekwungen.

Of Reef Nets, Camas Patches, and Potlatches

The Lekwungen likely had their first close look at Europeans when the Spaniard Manuel Quimper was rowed ashore at what is now called Royal Roads, just west of Victoria, on June 30, 1790, "Having disembarked with most of the seamen and soldiers and carr[ying] ashore a Cross which they adored on their knees." The troops sang a litany as they carried the cross in procession. At the end of the procession they planted the cross, and in a mound of stones at its foot they planted a bottle sealed with pitch and containing the "*Acta de Possesion*."[4] Having claimed the land and its peoples

In reef-netting, however, the gear was assembled and operated by a group working under the direction of the owner of the location or his deputy. The owner gave the crew part of the catch in exchange for their help; he hired them. This type of cooperation might be called capitalistic.

Wayne Suttles, *Economic Life of the Coast Salish of Haro and Rosario Straits*, 1974

Spanish ships *Sutil* and *Mexicana*, commanded by Galiano and Valdés, in Lekwungen waters (near present-day Victoria), 1792

for Spain, Quimper and his crew coasted along southern Vancouver Island, passing through the entire territory of the Lkungen-speaking people. Their permanent and seasonal villages were spread along the southern coast of Vancouver Island from Esquimalt Lagoon to Cordova Bay and through the islands as far east as San Juan Island (see Map 4.2 Territory of the Lekwungen).[5]

As Quimper's ship passed the islands of Haro Strait the Lekwungen paddled out from their summer camps and gave him information about the coast and their neighbours, although how they communicated with each other is not recorded. Quimper then crossed to the south side of the straits before returning to Vancouver Island and what he called Córdoba (Esquimalt) Harbour, now part of Greater Victoria. Here he met three canoes that had come from across the straits to harvest what Quimper called "seeds" but what, more probably, were camas bulbs.[6]

Quimper identified Esquimalt as a good anchorage, and it became a stop-over for subsequent Spanish explorers. In 1791, two Spanish ships under Francisco de Eliza y Reventa revisited the harbour. One of them, the *San Carlos*, anchored in the harbour for several weeks while the other explored the islands and straits east and north of Esquimalt. Like the first encounter, it was peaceful, until, according to the Spaniards, "the Schooner *Saturnina* was obliged to open fire in order to protect the launch of the packet-boat *San Carlos* against the canoes of the natives: the launch had approached them and they made determined efforts to take her."[7]

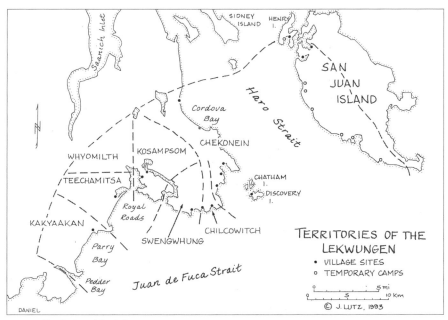

MAP 4.2 Territories of the Lekwungen

This event may coincide with a story that has been preserved among the Lekwungen and that suggests that at least one of them, *s^ntl'o?áy?l*, known in English as Jimmy Chickens, was forced into service on a Spanish ship, where he worked for three years before escaping back to his native village. The Spanish records do not mention seizing any Aboriginal People (though some children, believed to be slaves, were "bought" at other locations).[8]

By contrast, the expedition of the following year had no such eruptions of violence. The two ships commanded by Spaniards Galiano and Valdés were escorted into Cordoba, or Esquimalt. Tetacus (Tatoosh) a leading man of the Makah people, who were on friendly terms with the Lekwungen, hitched a ride with them.[9]

Near Esquimalt, several canoes came alongside with four or five Aboriginal People in each, offering what the Spanish journal calls "sheepskins" in exchange for copper. The two parties could not come to terms and no bargain was made; instead, the Aboriginal People offered what the Spanish took to be "fruit, like figs in shape, black, and of a floury character, with a salt taste" in return for some strings of glass beads.

This account brings to mind the "molasses sticks legs" story told by the Squamish about Vancouver's visit, only this time it was the Spanish who did not comprehend what was offered to them: they thought that the fleece of a special woolly dog bred by the Lekwungen was sheepskin, and they mistook camas bulbs for salty "figs."[10]

Makah Chief Tetacus (Tatoosh)

Further into Haro Straits other canoes came alongside offering "mulberries."[11] These exchanges succeeded in spite of the profound differences between the Spanish and the Lekwungen worldviews. The gap was neatly summarized in a "conversation" between Tetacus and the Spaniards, Valdés and Galiano, and recorded in the latter's journal: "[Tetacus] assured us that he had seen [an eagle] swoop down suddenly from a height to the sea near his house, fasten on a whale and bear it away. Valdés retorted that he must have been sleeping when he believed he had seen such an extraordinary thing, and he assured us that he was as wide awake as now."[12]

The Lekwungen world was inhabited, not just by humans, plants, and animals, but also by *skwinonet*, spirits or spirit helpers associated with living things and "natural" phenomena. *Skwinonet,* both benevolent and otherwise, could move from the visible world to parallel, invisible worlds or worlds located under the sea, underground, or in the sky. In an earlier time these worlds were easier for the Lekwungen to visit. But by the time the Europeans arrived, only in special circumstances – such as during vision quests, dream-states, or near-death experiences – could humans visit these other realms and return with special knowledge, powers, and/or a guardian spirit.[13]

Still, the Lekwungen landscape was imbued with links to and reminders of spirit power. Various features of the landscape, such as the rock *Camosun*, along the remarkable finger of water Victorians now call the "Gorge," were reminders of the time when the transformer, *Xehals*, walked the land, turning people into fish, trees, and at this place, stone, and making sure there was food for everyone to eat. Just opposite the future site of Fort Victoria was *Pallatsis*, the place of cradles, a potent place where infant's cradles and the dancing gear of teenagers would be left so that the *skwinonet* (power) of the place would protect the children. On San Juan Island, the place where one of the first Lekwungen fell to earth from the sky was known. Lekwungen geography was and is inseparable from their spiritual power and their stories.[14]

One of the best accounts of the Salish connection with the spirit world is found in the narrative of John Fornsby, a Salish man from the Skagit nation, which is closely related to the Lekwungen. Fornsby told how certain people acquired powers, sometimes hunting or fishing power, sometimes canoe-building, healing, gambling, or protecting power. These powers were usually associated with animals, trees, or natural forces, although, in more recent times, certain people acquired the spirit power of locomotives and steamships. Youths, both male and female, often acquired their first spirit helpers on special quests. *Skwinonet* also made itself known in dreams. Fornsby's power came from the river in which he swam and from the lizard and snake. He often called forth his power by singing.[15]

In Order to Receive in Exchange

We gave them each a metal button, and made more gifts of the same kind in order to receive something in exchange, not being lavish in their offerings but bartering, seeing that for each thing which they presented we gave them a string of beads or a piece of sea bisquit. They also gave us [shells] ... and there was also taken from them a dogskin cloak decorated with feathers and a tanned skin.

Dionisio Alcalá Galiano, *Relación del viage,* 1792

While to the Salish the land and seascape and all living things had a spiritual dimension, to the newcomers they did not: all of them could be measured precisely in three physical dimensions and recorded, drawn, or mapped in two. Even humans could be rendered in a two-dimensional form, and the newcomers seemed to have an insatiable desire to capture the people of the Northwest Coast in this fashion. The only spiritual presence on the newcomer's horizon was their one God, who had deputized the Europeans to take dominion over all living things – including Aboriginal Peoples.

As vast as the gulf was between the two peoples, there were bridges too. Both organized their societies along class lines, both had hierarchical systems of authority, and both had parallel ideas about the sexual division of labour. Both groups had surpluses and both had systems of property ownership that benefited individuals who accumulated wealth. From the first meeting between the Lekwungen and the Spanish there was also a mutual recognition of the benefit of exchange.

The Europeans brought with them a "fee-simple" concept of property relations, commonly called "private property," where ownership could be bought and sold, and where the current owner was solely responsible for the management and disposal of the property and had exclusive control over the wealth derived from it. The European social system stressed the importance of accumulating, investing, and hoarding wealth as a route to increasing status and comfort.

The Lekwungen, in common with the other Northwest Coast Aboriginal Peoples, had a more intricate system of property relations. It encompassed material goods as well as "spiritual property" and involved several different and overlapping concentric rings of "ownership." Valuable resource-gathering sites, such as reef net locations, seal rocks, and camas beds, were "owned" by extended families rather than by individuals. The family heads stewarded and managed the use of resources. This was both a right, with benefits attached, and a responsibility. Ownership was inherited or passed on by marriage, not bought, and it was renewed by distributing resource surpluses at ceremonial feasts. Failure on the part of the family head to manage the resource productively implied a loss of spiritual power and meant a loss of prestige, as did failure to share. Bad harvests, if protracted, could mean loss of position. Like the European system, the Lekwungen system stressed the accumulation of wealth through exchange; however, in the Lekwungen world, status (and ownership rights) was only sustainable through a ceremonial redistribution of that wealth.[16]

Another level of ownership applied to the remaining territory, to which no single family had particular claims. The Lekwungen owned this land in

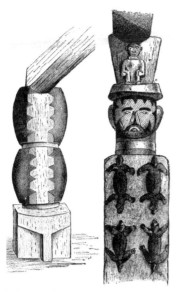

Lekwungen house posts, sketched by
Franz Boas, 1885

common. Less productive clam beds and berry patches were usually in this
category, as were hunting territories. All Lekwungen could hunt, gather
on, and otherwise use this land, as could members of other groups if granted
permission.

A third level of ownership applied to such tangible and spiritual items
as nets, weirs, and other portable goods used at resource sites as well as
houses, canoes, and regalia. These were family property, sometimes under
the stewardship of the members of the family that assisted in their manufacture, sometimes under the head of the family. Ownership of these items
did not have to be renewed and could be bought, traded, or wagered.

Families also owned spiritual and knowledge-related "goods," including the family history. These were passed from grandparent to grandchild
and included the family genealogy, with its associations to the spirit world
and illustrious ancestors; a stock of names derived from these stories; and
the songs and dances that recounted them. This type of property was not
normally bought or sold but could be given, particularly as part of a wedding or naming gift.[17]

Finally, individual Lekwungen owned what might be called "private
property." This included utensils of everyday use, wealth goods held in
preparation for distribution, and spiritual knowledge derived from personal visions. Slaves were the private property of those who could afford
them. "Wealth included those articles which could be used as potlatch
goods, articles which were acceptable in the payment of debts ... articles
which were consumption goods, but more or less luxury items."[18] This
category of property most closely approximated the European notion of
private property. The goods in this category could be traded, given as gifts,
or gambled at the discretion of the owners. Husbands and wives held their
property separately. Tools and ornaments might be interred with individuals when they died, while more substantial property was usually transferred
from fathers to sons and from mothers to daughters.[19]

Although food was gathered by individuals, often from sites owned by
families, it was subject to special regulations that acknowledged its connection to the spiritual world. Food was often described as *xe'xe*, or "sacred."[20]
The first salmon caught in a season was treated as an honoured guest, as
were the first bear and deer. The reverence for food also extended to the
inanimate: prayers were said before berry picking, and the first berries were
eaten after a ritual of thanks. The artist Paul Kane, visiting the Lekwungen
in 1846, described a dance performed "both before and after any important
action of the tribe, such as fishing, gathering camas, or going on a war
party." Within the network of extended friends and family, food could not
be sold or traded. It was shared with those who visited or with those who

appeared to need it. Families could accumulate food for a feast, but it could not be hoarded in times of want. Food could, however, be traded with strangers and directly converted into wealth; however, contact with true strangers, unconnected by kin, was limited.[21]

Wayne Suttles described the goods in the Straits Salish economy as circulating in two distinct but linked economies. Food circulated within a "subsistence economy," where individual gatherers and heads of families had some, but not full, control over its distribution. Other goods, including slaves owned by individuals and families, circulated in a "wealth economy." The two economies functioned separately but were interconnected at various points. Food, which was relatively abundant, was directly convertible into wealth only in certain circumstances. It could also be converted indirectly: for example, surplus food could be given as "gifts" to one's in-laws, for which they might return wealth goods, or it could function to free up labour to be used in the production of wealth goods. Food could also be traded for other food or goods with "strangers" (i.e., those outside the network of reciprocal kin obligations).[22]

Before the introduction of exotic European goods, wealth goods such as slaves, canoes, elk-skin armour, weapons, regalia, and ornamental items (e.g., cowrie and dentalia shells) were exchanged between villages on the Northwest Coast. But for most, including the Lekwungen, the most important wealth goods were "blankets." These blankets, woven from dog wool and the wool of mountain goats, had a prestige value that far exceeded their utility. Because of their value, portability, and divisibility, blankets also functioned as a relatively standardized medium of exchange.[23]

The Lekwungen had much need for wealth. Gambling was a popular pastime, and large sums were wagered. "They are so passionately fond of this [gambling game lehallum] that they frequently pass two or three consecutive days and nights at it without ceasing," reported Paul Kane, who was at Fort Victoria when the Cowichan came to gamble with the Lekwungen. Success at gambling was seen as a demonstration of a special kind of spiritual power, and gambling was often accompanied by songs to summon these spirits. An indication of the stakes that might be involved comes from John Fornsby, who recounted a session in which his uncle wagered a canoe worth $100 against a slave of his Snohomish competitor. "My uncle pretty near won the slave," but in the end, "he lost his canoe."[24]

Goods, and later money, were also needed to purchase services from those with special powers. Fornsby paid the elder who gave him his adult name, *t'sa'lwulq*; when Fornsby came to Victoria to heal the Lekwungen Michael Cooper, he was paid for his services in goods. Boas heard from

It Costs Money to Learn a Spell

It costs money to learn a [spell] and it takes time. The young man comes and sits beside the old man who knows it. He pays each time and it may take a year to learn it ... You might have to pay a hundred dollars, whether you've learned it or not.

Patrick George, Lummi Salish, ca. 1949

Everyone Calls Them Potlatches

Potlatch is a Chinook jargon word. Everybody spoke this trade language when I was young. We call these big potlatches p̓əsa in our language, but now it's called potlatch by Indians and everybody else up and down the coast ... Important families call the people to a potlatch. Then we tell our family history and show our dances and give away names that go with the dances. We give away money and goods to everybody who's invited, and that's what the word potlatch means: "giving away."

Harry Assu, Kwakwa̱ka̱ʼwakw, *Assu of Cape Mudge*, 1989

Lekwungen Chief Sqwameyuks' potlatch, April 1874

his Lekwungen informants that rich people often kept a shaman on a sort of "retainer" to protect their welfare.[25] Patrick George, a Lummi Salish, recalled that, even after the Europeans arrived, his people purchased certain "magic spells" to assist them in hunting, fishing, or finding a suitor.[26]

Gifts were also needed to pay those people who prepared the cradle for newborn children, performed different functions at potlatches, prepared the dead for burial, and so on. According to the accounts collected by Paul Kane in 1846 and Franz Boas in 1889, gifts were also given at winter spirit dances, where they marked the "coming out" of people who had acquired powers through a spirit quest and where they were used to back claims to the right to use prestigious ancestral names or to perform particular ritual dances and songs. Heavy payments were required to induct people into the secret societies and to pay compensation to those who might be offended.[27]

The Lekwungen needed wealth for a whole host of reasons, but the most important was the potlatch. "Potlatch" is shorthand for a variety of ceremonies conducted among Northwest Coast Aboriginal Peoples and involving the distribution of gifts. The social function of the potlatch was to demonstrate and validate status as well as the "ownership" of resources. The occasions that prompted potlatches varied among different Northwest Coast groups. For the Lekwungen and other Straits Salish, potlatches were held to mark significant events, including marriage and the inheritance of rights. Potlatches might also be held to wipe away shame caused by oneself or one's family or to pay debts incurred at earlier potlatches or ceremonial events. Among the Lekwungen, potlatches were usually hosted by a number of families, each with its own event to memorialize, and often centred on marriages.[28]

Marriages were generally arranged between two families of similar social standing who lived in different communities, and they were cemented

by an exchange of property, followed by a chain of reciprocal food and wealth exchanges. Several Lekwungen stories emphasize the romantic attraction between young people, which suggests that such attraction was considered to be ideal before a marriage was "arranged."[29] Among commoners, marriage ceremonies were quite simple, but higher-status members of Straits Salish society staged elaborate wedding feasts. These were highly ritualized, diplomatic events that often served to establish or renew peaceful relations between two communities.

The value of women in Coast Salish society was reflected in this marriage ritual performed by those of high status. After a marriage was arranged by intermediaries, it was customary for the groom to arrive at the bride's house with his father and other male relatives and make a ritual request to allow the marriage. The door was always barred to them, and only after repeated entreaties by the groom's relatives would the party be admitted. Having gained admittance, attempts would be made to arrange the marriage but to no avail. The groom's party would retire, leaving the groom sitting on the floor inside the bride's family home, where he might remain for several days, ignored and unfed by his future in-laws. Every day the groom's party would return for more speech-making regarding the desirability of the union, the generosity of the boy's relatives, the virtues of the boy and the girl. Finally, the bride's family would relent and accept a gift from the groom's family, initiating a series of reciprocal gift exchanges.[30]

The practice of polygyny (having multiple wives) among high-status men was, in part, a recognition of the importance of women as producers of goods and reproducers of labour. Polygyny had other practical and social purposes. Marriages were often diplomatic unions, establishing a basis for friendly relationships between households, particularly those in different villages. Principally, as Suttles explains, this connection provided each set of in-laws with some access to the resources controlled by the other, some measure of "safe passage" through the other's territories, and often some spiritual or ceremonial privileges.[31] It also established a gift-exchange cycle, whereby one's in-laws would bring the rare and valuable commodities of their territory as gifts. Recipients were bound, however, to return the equivalent on a return visit. Finally, for the men, increased status was associated with many wives and with inter-village links, which widened one's potlatch community and increased the number of high-ranking guests who might attend.[32]

One such event, described by John Fornsby and tentatively dated in the late 1850s, involved the marriage of Lekwungen "chief" Waxo'l' to the Swinomish daughter of Chief Joseph. The relatives of the bride sent invitations to the Lummi, the Lower Skagit, and the Upper Skagit to witness the marriage.[33] The guests arrived on the appointed day, singing their spirit-power songs. A *xadsa'tl* competition was held, involving two teams, one from the Lummi and the other from the Skagit nation, each trying to pull members of the opposing team over a horizontal pole. Later, the guests were feasted, and the next day, gift giving began. The hosts had their blankets and other presents piled high on the roof of a house. They called the name of each of the special guests, and, as the guest came forward, the appropriate number of blankets were passed down. Then a raft was made between two canoes and piled high with gifts (in this case, blankets, caps, shirts, and guns, but in other cases, slaves as well). This was a "free-for-all." When the raft was pushed about twenty feet offshore, the new couple began to throw the goods to the assembled people. The recipients held long poles and jostled each other as they attempted to "catch" the goods as they were thrown towards shore:

> They threw caps first. That was the first cap that came in. [The Swinomish] had never seen caps before. My father got one. The people got sticks to catch things. They threw them up so high that people could get them with their sticks. One man cut shirts up and gave each person a piece. The Indians here had never seen shirts before. They threw blankets. If four fellows caught the same blanket on their sticks, they tore the blanket into four pieces. Finally they got guns and threw them up too ... The Skagits got their first guns and first blankets at that time. These were little blankets with marks on the end.[34]

In return for the gifts from the Lekwungen "chief" and his wife, the Swinomish in-laws later brought food gifts to Victoria.[35]

The guests at a potlatch were, in a sense, paid to witness the ceremony and, thereby, acknowledge the legitimacy of the wedding, the inheritance, the name claimed, the shame erased, the debt paid, and so on. But the relationship was more complex than this since, in accepting gifts, the high-status recipient was also accepting his/her own obligation to return gifts at a future potlatch of her/his own.[36] Anthropologist Homer Barnett described the relationship this way:

> Donor A at his potlatch might give twenty blankets to B. When B in turn gave a potlatch, he invited A and gave him any number that he wished, let us say fifty. This gift was called by a term signifying "thanks for coming to my potlatch." At the same time, but separately, so that the distinction was clear, B added twenty blankets which were in reality a repayment of A's twenty blankets ... When A again gave a potlatch and called B's name, he would give

any number he pleased, say twenty-five, and then add fifty more as a return of the fifty given him by B.[37]

The Lekwungen language reveals an emphasis on accumulation and distribution: the word for "leader," *siem*, also means "rich." The most prestigious thing a Lekwungen could do was to give away more wealth than any of his predecessors, leaving himself socially enriched although poor in goods. In the meantime, however, his rights to the resource sites that generated the wealth had been affirmed. It might help to think of this as the giving away of "interest" or "dividends" rather than the wealth (resource site) itself, which remained in the family's hands and, over time, renewed its wealth. Since he knew his peers were accumulating property in an attempt to potlatch still greater amounts, the *siem* and his family had a powerful incentive to begin accumulating immediately for their next potlatch.

The incentives to accumulate were as strong or stronger among the Lekwungen than they were in the alien European society that was establishing links with them in the late eighteenth and early nineteenth centuries. In the nineteenth century, in both Lekwungen and British society, one's social class was determined at birth. Among the Lekwungen one could improve one's rank within a class via opulent potlatches. The worst fault one could have was to be *séxws^xw*, or lazy.[38]

The social relationships surrounding family-owned salmon reef net sites and camas beds require special investigation because they loomed large in Lekwungen life and conditioned relationships with the European immigrants. Embedded in the production systems linked to these two resources was a distinct gendered division of labour. In contrast to the more northern Northwest Coast societies (e.g., the Ts'msyen, Haida, and Tlingit), where descent was reckoned matrilineally, the Lekwungen and other Coast Salish peoples, like Europeans, recognized descent bilaterally, from both paternal and maternal lines, with emphasis on the paternal. The Lekwungen's *siem* – heads of households – which Europeans identified as "chiefs," were all male. This position, along with its prerogatives and obligations, generally passed from a *siem*, on his death, to his eldest son; if there were no sons, then it passed to a brother and his sons. Because he controlled access to major resource sites, a *siem* controlled the wealth of the household and managed the major items of property as well as ceremonial privileges.[39]

Although not so highly stratified as northern Northwest Coast societies, the Lekwungen were divided into three classes: "Good People" or nobles, from which the *siem* would be drawn, commoners, and slaves.[40] In 1839, slaves, plus the offspring of masters and slaves, apparently outnumbered commoners and nobles combined.[41]

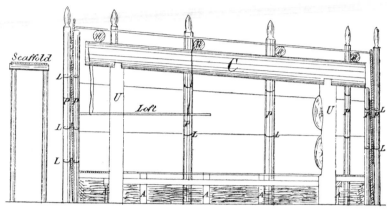

Lekwungen house profile, sketched by Franz Boas, 1885

Villages consisted of a number of extended families, each occupying a large winter house. In 1847, Paul Kane, who had travelled much of the Canadian west, described their "lodges" as "the largest buildings of any description that I have met with among the Indians. They are divided in the interior into compartments, [using rush mats] so as to accommodate eight to ten families." One Lekwungen house (at the abandoned village on Garrison Island) was later measured and found to be four hundred feet by forty feet. Their size is also suggested by Father Bolduc's account of his 1843 visit to the Lekwungen village of *Sungayka* (Cadboro Bay), when he was able to crowd all present (over five hundred people) into one house.[42]

Households usually consisted of a male *siem*, his brothers, sons, and all their wives and children. It was also common to include unmarried sisters, widows, orphans, and perhaps nephews in the household, as well as slaves. Although, theoretically, blood relationship was as strong on the maternal side as on the paternal, a wife usually lived with her husband's family.

Except for the fact that the *siem* might have more than one wife, the newcomers could easily see him as an aboriginal equivalent to an aristocratic patriarch – indeed they sometimes referred to important *siem* (such as Chee-al-thluk of the Lekwungen) as "kings" and to their wives as "queens."[43] Nonetheless, the *siem*'s power lay strictly in his prestige and his ability to persuade and reward. Collective actions, such as moving to a seasonal camp, holding a feast, or waging war, depended on the *siem* using his prestige and persuasive powers.[44]

There was a gendered division of labour based on zones of exclusion and derived from the belief that women were "spiritually potent" while menstruating, following childbirth, and during menopause. In this state their inherent spirit power weakened or destroyed the spiritual power of male hunters or fishers and rendered their tools useless. As a result, men

If the King Wants a Salmon

If King Freezie [Chee-al-thuk] he wanted a salmon he had to catch it like any other of his subjects and as for clams it was the duty of the Queen to dig them up.

J.R. Anderson, "Notes and Comments on Early Days," 1912

Lekwungen weaver and loom with "woolly dog" in an 1847 painting by Paul Kane

were responsible for hunting and fishing as well as building. Women, children, and the elderly harvested domestic and wild crops and shellfish. Women were in charge of food preservation and preparation as well as the production of textiles and most woven products.[45] Men were not prohibited from doing "women's work" and, for short periods, where time was of the essence, some tasks, like harvesting camas or shellfish, might involve whole households.[46]

Men and women worked in separate but interdependent productive activities. Men fished and hunted; women made the baskets and other vessels in which the food would be stored and preserved the catch so that it would be available throughout the year and for feasts. Men made the nets for catching fish, deer, or ducks from twine made by women. Men produced most of the protein in the Lekwungen diet, while women produced the carbohydrates, starches, and other vegetables and fruits essential to their diet.

Subsistence production was relatively balanced by gender, but when it came to the production of prestige goods, women's contribution probably dominated. Men played a role – through the acquisition of slaves in warfare and in manufacturing canoes as well as other hunting implements that might be given at a potlatch – but the most important wealth items were blankets, and these were woven by women.

The Coast Salish, including the Lekwungen and their immediate Nuu-chah-nulth neighbours, were unique in North America in that they husbanded and sheared a dog specially bred for its wool. Wool-bearing dogs were the property of women, who kept them segregated, often on small islands, in order to prevent cross-breeding with other dogs. Myron Eells, speaking of the Lekwungen's southern neighbours, recorded that "a woman's

The head man knows how
to put it together. There's a
hole left in the middle [of
the net] which each piece
touched. It's big enough for
a big salmon to go through
but it won't; if it goes
through it dies. That's the
way it's made.

Louie Pilkey, Wsanec, ca. 1949

Reef net with crew

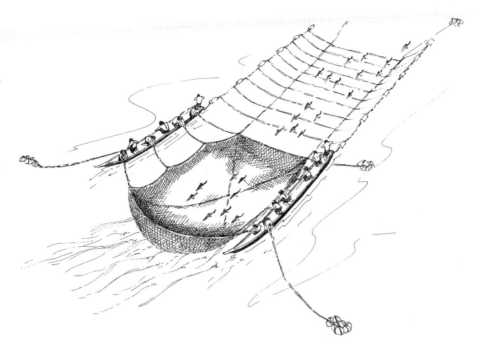

wealth was often estimated by the number of such dogs she owned." Women
sheared these special dogs, spun their wool, and wove the blankets on large
looms. Women and children gathered and prepared the cedar bark for the
warp. The wool for the weft was partly mountain goat wool traded from
the Squamish and Nooksack on the mainland, but the main source was the
dogs, the Lekwungen's only domesticated animal. These were the most
valuable items the Lekwungen offered in exchange to the first Europeans
they encountered.[47]

In addition to the blankets, women also made baskets and mats as
trade and gift items, harvested and stored camas (and later potatoes) that
were exchanged for the food products of other nations, and tanned the
hides that were occasionally used as items of exchange.[48]

Although tasks were specifically gendered, gender was not necessarily
determined by biological sex. Boas noted among the Lekwungen that "sometimes men assume women's dress and occupations and *vice versa*. Such individuals are called *st'o̱mEtcE*."[49]

The Lekwungen and other Straits Salish depended heavily on fish for
subsistence: archaeologists estimate that over 90 percent of the protein of
their Fraser River neighbours came from fish or higher marine animals.[50]
However, unlike their neighbours, the Straits people had no major salmon
rivers. To intercept the fish on their way to the Fraser and other spawning
rivers, the Straits Salish perfected a complicated technique of reef netting.
At specific reefs located along the coastal migration route of the sockeye

salmon, where the water was shallow and the route for the fish constricted, an elaborate net was suspended between two canoes. When a school of salmon swam into the net, the floor was raised and the salmon lifted into the canoes.

Like most elements of Lekwungen life, the harvesting of food linked the spiritual and the material. Each year men wove elaborate nets with cord made by women, and it was known that the salmon people themselves had taught the people how to make the net. A specialist in ritual would advise and assist in making the net, and a hole, called a vulva, would be left in it. The Salish believed that only the salmon who wished to sacrifice themselves would stay in the net and that the others would swim through. Each species of salmon had an honorific name, most identifying them as family, like the Coho, which was known as "the parent of your daughter or son-in-law." Even the fishing camps were ritually constructed to mirror the fishing process: the crews of the two different canoes lived in separate structures with the fish-drying racks between them. New fishing captains had to be specially invested and wore a distinctive hat as a mark of their position. Songs were sung to lure the fish into the net and to thank them as they were being gathered. A ceremony was held to honour and thank the first sockeye salmon to be netted at each reef location.[51]

According to Wsanec elder Earl Claxton, it was not so much that the Wsanec and Lekwungen owned the reef-net sites as that families belonged to the fishing sites and their names were derived from them. The Lekwungen families belonged to a dozen or more reef-net sites, most of them located along the west shore of San Juan Island (see Map 4.2) and each of which was managed by a *siem*.[52] The *siem* might fish as captain of the reef net

Reef Net Songs

When they are out at the reef net and the captain first sees the fish he starts to sing:

tA'tcel ce'yls
(He is) coming (my) oldest brother

tA'tcel ce'yls
(He is) coming (my) oldest brother

hA'nel ce'yls
Thank you oldest brother.

Julius Charles, Lummi and Semiahmoo (born ca. 1865), recorded 1942

Julius Charles

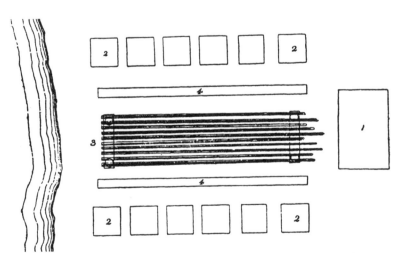

Boas sketch of a reef-net camp site, showing *siem's* house (1), huts for the crews of two boats (2), drying racks (3), and roasting trenches (4).

crew or, according to Boas, among the Lekwungen it was more common to "hire" a good fisher, who would receive two day's catch and a few blankets as payment.[53] The crew of six to fourteen men was "hired" by the *siem* from kin and non-kin within or without the Lekwungen. The crew would start preparations in May – making the net, establishing the fishing camp, and placing anchors – so as to be ready for the start of the sockeye salmon run in mid-July. The *siem*'s family would feed the crew through the fishing season and pay them with a share of the catch. According to most elders, crew members would each take their share of the catch first and then continue fishing for the owner, though Lekwungen Ned Williams reported that, in his more recent experience, the crew would change every day, each taking a share and the owner getting the surplus.[54]

If it was a poor salmon season, the owner of the reef net site might be impoverished as he would have to feed the crew regardless of the catch. In good years the surplus might, however, be enormous. In 1892, when the fish runs had already started to come under pressure from commercial cannery-fishing, one observer noted:

> When fish are running in good numbers ten to fifteen Indians form a crew for a reef net, and a haul can be made every minute or two if necessary. Some of the Indians are very expert at this kind of fishing and have taken as many as 2,000 salmon in a day. In such cases the clutchmen [klootchmen] come out with canoes and boat the fish ashore so that the operations of those engaged in fishing will not be interrupted.

The catch on these very good days would be sufficient to feed a family of eighteen for a year.[55]

Reef-net sites were not the only resource sites owned by families: ownership extended to rich terrestrial locations as well. Although usually remembered as the "salmon people," the Straits Salish and other Coast Salish groups could just as accurately be called the "camas people." They had altered their environment to ensure regular and reliable crops of camas (*Camassia quamash* and *C. leichtlinii*), a flowering plant whose bulb provided the bulk of the starch in their diet. Prime camas patches were owned by the extended families.

The Lekwungen established their villages along the southeast coast of Vancouver Island in a microclimate that was the driest, sunniest property of the entire Northwest Coast. The Lekwungen territory experienced moist cool winters and warm, dry summers, which favoured plants with bulbs. Many varieties of these were harvested and used by the Lekwungen, but camas was "the queen root of this clime."[56] Sometimes called an "onion" by

Flower and bulb of the camas plant, staple of the Lekwungen

Europeans, the bulb of the camas has a sweet taste when steamed. Early white visitors to the straits area commented on the aboriginal use of camas and usually commented favourably on the flavour of this plant.[57]

Although naturally occurring, the camas was husbanded and cultivated by aboriginal women in April and May, when it was in flower and easily visible. The women separated out the *death camas* (*Zydaedenus venosus*), with its white flowers, from the edible camas, with its blue flowers. This "weeding" and harvesting also served to loosen and aerate the soil, and, at least among some groups of the Coast Salish, the seed would be broken from the stems and planted in the loose soil.[58] The women would return to dig up the plants once the flowers withered. In order to maintain the open meadows necessary for the propagation of the camas, Lekwungen owners regularly burned the prairies at the end of the season: "Their object is to clear away the thick fern and underwood in order that the roots and fruits on which they in a measure subsist may grow more freely and be more easily dug up."[59]

The best record of family ownership that we have for the camas beds dates from shortly after the establishment of the Colony of Vancouver Island.[60] In order to acquire formal title to the lands that he had occupied and to open up settlement for the newly established colony, Governor James Douglas, at the behest of the British Colonial Office, signed individual treaties in 1850 with six family groupings, which, together, comprised the Lekwungen: the Teechamitsa, the Kosampson, the Swengwhung, the Chilcowitch, the Whyomilth, and the Chekonein. Unlike his treaties with the Wsanec, where Douglas found it "impossible to discover among the numerous claimants the real owners," the Lekwungen people were quite clear about which groups had rights to which pieces of land (see Map 4.2). The treaties recognized the prior ownership of each of these groups to a specific territory, including those that contained the camas patches.[61]

Ironically, it was the open camas prairies, maintained by the Lekwungen's regular burning, that attracted European settlement to their territory. When he first visited in 1842, just fifty years after the Spanish had "adored the cross" on these shores, Douglas called the site a "perfect Eden."[62] To Douglas, the existence of such a place, more resembling "the close sward of a well managed lea, than the produce of an uncultivated waste," was scarcely believable. But believe it he did, and because of this vast prairie, in his words "nearly 6 miles square containing a great extent of valuable tillage and pasture land equally well adapted for the plough or for feeding stock," he chose the site to build the future headquarters of the Hudson's Bay Company and, later, the colonial and provincial capital of British Columbia.[63]

The Lekwungen regularly burned off forest cover to create camas meadows.

In retrospect, it is clear that Douglas's Eden was *Meeqan*, as the local people knew it, one of the Northwest Coast's prime camas fields. Douglas *had* indeed stumbled upon "a well managed lea" – but the style of agriculture, silviculture, and ownership was not one that he understood.

In the Trail of the Comet, 1843-85

A brilliant comet, probably the brightest ever seen and certainly the most spectacular cosmic event of the century, stretched itself across half of the Lekwungen night sky in March and April, 1843. It was so bright it remained visible even during the day. It appeared first on March 15, the very day the *Beaver*, first steamship on the Northwest Coast, dropped its anchor in Lekwungen territory, firing its cannons to call attention to itself.[64]

It is impossible to know now what impression the coincidence of the comet and the arrival of the *Beaver* may have had on the Lekwungen. To the Coast Salish, the heavens were a world parallel to their own. Indeed, the Lekwungen origin story, like those of many of their neighbours, told of the first human falling to earth from the sky as a meteor. The "Transformer," who had brought them salmon and cedar, travelled through the sky like a comet, and they knew instances of the "star" men coming to earth to seek after women.[65]

By this time, the Lekwungen had been in intermittent contact with Europeans for fifty years and had, no doubt, sized them up as something other than heaven-sent. Still, Lekwungen cosmology was largely intact when James Douglas was rowed ashore after a brief cannonade from the steam

The Great Comet of 1843, painted by astronomer Charles Piazzi Smyth

Stupendous Spectacle

Saw a luminous streak in the heavens this evening, which lasted from dusk until 9 o'clock when the moon rose and obscured it ... forming an arc of about 90 degrees ... We cannot account for this phenomenon.

James Douglas, "Diary of a Trip to Victoria," March 17, 1843

The Indians suppose the stars to be little people and the region they live in to be much the same as this world down below. As one of the girls looked up at the little people twinkling overhead, one of them said to the other ... "That's the little man to my liking; how I would like him for my lover!" When the girls awoke in the morning it was in Starland, with their lovers by their sides.

A Lekwungen story told by Tomo, a Métis, as related by Robert Brown, 1864

By far the most remarkable comet, however, which has been seen during the present century, is that which appeared in the spring of 1843, and whose tail ... a great beam of nebulous light ... the head and nucleus appeared with extra-ordinary splendour, exciting in every country where it was seen the greatest astonishment and admiration. Indeed, all descriptions agree on representing it as a stupendous spectacle, such as in superstitious ages would not fail to have carried into every bosom.

John Herschel, astronomer, *Outlines of Astronomy,* 1849

ship, so speculation about the comet and the newcomers must have been rampant in the Lekwungen village.[66] The coincidence of the two arrivals must have affected the reception of Hudson's Bay Company (HBC) factor James Douglas and his party. It certainly signalled a new era in the social relations of the Lekwungen.

The fur traders were expecting the worst. Sir George Simpson had written the governor and committee of the HBC in March 1842, "there is a very large population of daring fierce and treacherous Indians on, and in the neighbourhood of the Southern Shore of Vancouver's Island." Douglas, a little over a month before arriving to establish the post, wrote a friend that the Aboriginal People whose land he was to occupy are "numerous and daring having as yet lost no trait of their natural barbarity so that we will have both trouble and anxiety in the first course of training."[67]

Lekwungen Chief Chee-
ah-thluc (later known as
King Freezy) as painted
by Paul Kane in 1847

But the anxiety was misplaced. The next morning canoes arrived from every side and surrounded the steamboat. "All shook hands, and the Chief, a young man about twenty years of age," escorted James Douglas, the senior HBC officer, Captain McNeil of the *Beaver*, and Jean Baptiste Bolduc, a Roman Catholic missionary, on a long walk "into the interior of the island." These men were seeking the most favourable location to build the fort that would become the HBC's headquarters on the west coast and, ultimately, Victoria, the capital of a colony.[68]

On the third day after his arrival Douglas spoke to the "Samose" (Songhees/Lekwungen): "and informed them of our intention of building in this place which appeared to please them very much and they immediately offered their services in procuring pickets for the establishment, an offer which I gladly accepted and promised to pay them a blanket ... for every forty pickets of 22 feet by 36 inches which they bring."[69]

There is an aboriginal account of this meeting from David Latasse. He recollected, in 1934, speaking partly in the Wsanec (Saanich) language and partly in Chinook jargon:

> Off Laurel Point stood a tall ship, the sails were braided up and she was anchored. For two days nothing happened that I know of, though the whites may have been having talks with tribal leaders. Then there was action which terrified we youths, though I believe the elders knew what was coming. The ship changed her position, wide runways were let down, huge animals armed with horns, charged down into the sea and came on shore. Men in four boats came around the other side of the ship and drove the monsters to Mud Bay where they came ashore, close to the Songhees village. We youngsters were terribly frightened when those great beasts came snorting through the water.

Latasse continued, noting that "Indians brought the logs [for the fort] and Douglas paid the chiefs for such work."[70] The missionary Bolduc reported that, except for Sunday, a day of rest, nearly all the Lekwungen men "were working to cut stakes for the new fort," and another HBC witness estimated that three hundred to four hundred men worked on the fort. None of the accounts mentions the language through which this transaction was negotiated. It was likely Chinook jargon.[71]

The construction of the fort resumed in June, when the staff and the effects of the just-closed northern forts (Taku, Stikine, and McLoughlin) were delivered to the site of the new Fort Victoria. The Lekwungen continued supplying pickets, firewood, salmon, berries, and other foodstuffs, all without any need for "training" or coercion.[72]

Do You Want to Work?

Mika tikeh mámook?
Do you want to work?

Iktah mika mámook?
To do what?

Mámook stick.
Cut some wood [pickets].

Newitka.
Certainly.

John Gill, *Gill's Dictionary of the Chinook Jargon* [1909]

In light of the consequences for the Lekwungen, it seems ironic that they welcomed, and assisted with, the building of Fort Victoria. But in the context of the time, the history of the Lekwungen, and the knowledge that was available to them, this was consistent with their own priorities. In the Coast Salish world, house construction was a cooperative endeavour. Although ownership of the house and land remained with the sponsor, there was still a sense of collective ownership on the part of those who contributed wealth and materials. The Lekwungen likely viewed their assistance as giving them a stake and an interest in Fort Victoria, the most elaborate "house" on their territory.

The Lekwungen likely saw the arrival of the Europeans as proof of their own spiritual power to bring wealth. For the first time, the abundant food and forest resources, which they already harvested for their own use, were directly convertible into rare wealth goods. That the Lekwungen wanted to be paid in blankets was also understandable since blankets were the main measure of wealth in their economy.

Lekwungen blankets were made of the wool of dogs and mountain goats, and so their production was limited by several factors. The dogs had to be specially bred and isolated from other breeds as well as shorn, probably once a year in the spring; mountain goat wool was a rare commodity and was acquired in trade from the Squamish and Stó:lō on the mainland. Once acquired, the wool had to be cleaned, carded, and spun, then woven on a warp of cedar fibre by women who had been specially trained in this art. Given the Lekwungen response to the import of blankets, it seems likely that a large, wealthy family might have produced a few blankets a year before the coming of Europeans.

One measure of the value the blankets had for the Lekwungen may be seen in the fact that Bolduc bought a forty-two-foot long, three-foot wide canoe, with a six foot bow capable of carrying thirty people, for four blankets. In this transaction the Lekwungen were in a good bargaining position relative to Bolduc as the latter needed transportation. It is hard to imagine they did not charge at least the going rate, yet Bolduc also thought he made an excellent deal. I paid, he said, "the modest sum [in blankets] of seven and one-half piastres. I am certain a similar model could not be bought for less than ten pounds in Canada." When he engaged the "chief" of the Lekwungen, "Tsamics" (or "Tsumishs"), and a crew of ten to take him to Whidbey Island – a trip that took two days each way – the price was one blanket. At a minimum, the blanket was seen as equivalent to the labour of eleven men for four days (and possibly much longer).

To build Fort Victoria, Douglas offered the Lekwungen one wool blanket (of standard quality, i.e., two and one-half points) for each group of

Do You Want an Indian to Work for You?

Mika tikka ikt Siwashe mamook copa mika.
Do you want an Indian to work for you?

Mika kumtax mamook lehash.
Do you understand how to use an axe?

Nowitks, hyas kloshe mika kumtux.
Yes, very well.

Konsick chickamen mika tikka?
How much pay do you want?

Mika tum tum.
You name a price.

Abba, spose mila mamook kloshe konaway sun nika maish copa sitkum dollar pi potlatch muckamuck sitcum sun.

Well then, if you work hard all day, I'll pay you ½ dollar and give you dinner.

Harry Guillod, *Chinook Dictionary* [1862-88]

Lekwungen canoe of style purchased by Jean Baptiste Bolduc, sketched by Franz Boas

forty logs, twenty-two feet long and three feet in diameter, brought several miles. This event was not just an exchange, it was a transformative process that linked two value systems. In the hands of the Lekwungen, the trader's machine-woven woollen blankets were not the "trade goods" that they were to the HBC; rather, they were "potlatch goods," with all the associated prestige and spiritual qualities associated with the potlatch. The Lekwungen might easily have driven the traders away, as the Tsilhqot'in did elsewhere, but they accepted the offer. It allowed them to transform something abundant in their territory for something rare. For their part, the HBC transformed relatively cheap goods into what would otherwise have been very expensive labour and building materials.

The fort was 150 yards square, so the palisade alone (before the construction of any buildings) required six hundred three-foot-wide pickets and, therefore, injected fifteen blankets into the Lekwungen economy (perhaps several times the normal, annual increment of hand-made blankets).[73]

These "negotiated" exchanges between the Lekwungen and the fur traders were accompanied by exchanges that were not negotiated, and the latter produced friction. The fur trade records contain two incidents of open and general confrontation. The first of these arose from different understandings of property rights and agriculture. The traders used *Meeqan*, the very prairie where the Lekwungen had for generations cultivated their own "root vegetables," camas and lily bulbs, to graze their cattle. At first, not surprisingly, the Lekwungen people did not understand or accept the newcomers' agricultural system, particularly animal husbandry, which involved the "great beasts" devouring their food supplies. To the Lekwungen, cattle must have been classed as game, like other such large mammals, and so were fairly "harvested."

The Lekwungen became pointedly aware of the sense of ownership the Europeans felt towards these cattle in the spring of 1844, when the fort's chief factor, Roderick Finlayson, announced that "unless the cattle killed were paid for [he] would demolish all the [Lekwungen] huts and drive them from the place" with his cannons. Initially, the Lekwungen resisted the demands and, with the help of their Cowichan neighbours, laid siege to the fort. But after a demonstration in which an empty aboriginal house was destroyed with one cannon shot, the Lekwungen opted to pay restitution. Secure in their fort, with its bastions and cannons, the fur traders had introduced the Lekwungen to the new regime of property relations. The chief factor thought that they "learned that it was wisest to be submissive and we made farmers and bull drivers of them."[74]

The next incident revealed a further incentive the Lekwungen may have had for welcoming the fur traders into their territory: the Lekwungen

fully expected to maintain their historic right to control access to their
territory. By controlling access to the fort, the Lekwungen would become
"middlemen" and thus profit from both ends of the exchange with the
HBC. Attempts by the "home guard" Aboriginal People to control access
to the fort were common throughout what is now British Columbia and
western Canada.

To accomplish this, in 1843-44 the Lekwungen abandoned their previous village sites, one at Swhaymalthelth (Esquimalt Harbour) and the other
(the main village) at Sungayka (Cadboro Bay), for a site immediately adjacent the new fort.[75] Finlayson recalled that, during the construction of the
fort, a large number of Lekwungen men camped in the vicinity and looked
on. After that "the natives for some time after our arrival kept aloof and
would not come near ... however [they] soon got rid of their shyness [and]
began to remove from their village at Cadboro Bay and erect houses for
themselves along the bank of the harbour." Sometime thereafter, probably
in 1844, the wood behind the aboriginal village caught fire and threatened
the fort. Finlayson used this as his rationale "to remove them to the other
side of the harbor, which at first they declined to do, saying that the land
was theirs." After "a great deal of angry parlaying" the Lekwungen agreed
to move to a point four hundred yards across the harbour if Finlayson and
his men would assist them.[76]

From their location on the harbour, the Lekwungen were in a good
position to police their monopoly. When the Bellingham Bay Lummi came
to trade in 1845, the Lekwungen allowed them in but robbed them of their
newly traded goods as they left the harbour. Having the Lekwungen control the trade was antithetical to HBC interests. Finlayson decided that
"this was a clear case in which I was bound to interfere to protect the friendly
Indians coming to trade with us."

Finlayson's account of this incident is interesting for how it differs
from another observer's. Finlayson recalls sending "his interpreter" to get
the Lekwungen "to restore the goods they took from these friendly Indians,
as otherwise I would have to take action on their behalf." After considering
the matter "these robbers came to the fort and delivered up the goods." In
Finlayson's words, "thus these wild savages were taught to respect British
justice."[77]

A different explanation for the free passage granted other aboriginal
groups is offered by Berthold Seemann, who visited the fort in 1846 and
noted that "certain supplies to the chiefs keep them in good humour with
their intruding visitors."[78] James Deans, who arrived in 1853, offered a
perspective that supports Seemann's earlier conclusion:

Chee-ah-thluc (also known
as King Freezy), Chief of the
Lekwungen (Songhees), in
February 1864

The celebrated King Freezy chief of the Songhish tribe was completely under the control of the Hudson Bay Company to whom he rendered himself valuable by being at all times ready in consideration of a small donation of blankets etc ... to exert his authority in quelling any disturbance that broke out or was impending among his subjects. He also possessed considerable influence over surrounding tribes and was frequently in the service to the company in staying hostilities among them.[79]

When, in 1847, the Lekwungen assisted the company by "taking up arms against a body of Cape Flattery Indians, who threatened to attack the Fort in retaliation for a whipping of one of their number," Douglas interpreted this as "convincing proof" of their loyalty to the company. For their part, the Lekwungen may well have been using the opportunity to re-establish a measure of control over their own territory and to establish themselves as intermediaries between the fort and the Makah of Cape Flattery. On the other hand, they may have expected to be financially rewarded, as Deans suggested, for assisting the traders.[80]

While the HBC began to refer to the Lekwungen as "our Indians," the Lekwungen seem to have regarded the traders as "our whites." Whereas their previous village at Cadboro Bay had been pallisaded, the new Lekwungen village on the Victoria harbour was not. The Europeans, within their barricades, were evidently more afraid of the Lekwungen than the Lekwungen were of them. The Lekwungen likely saw the HBC fort as their protection against attacks by northern peoples, against whom their previous village had been fortified. When Salish John Fornsby made his first visit to Victoria, he was given a tour of "our white community" by Lekwungen chief Michael Cooper, illustrating this proprietary feeling.[81]

The move from their former village sites to Victoria harbour occurred for another reason besides the one mentioned above: access to employment. After the fort was built, Chief Factor Finlayson wrote that he employed his men to clear the land around it in order to raise vegetables and cereals. "Gradually," Finlayson recalled, "we got some of the young natives to assist, paying them in goods, and found them very useful as ox drivers in ploughing the land." By 1847, "some of these wild Indians" were also employed as assistant dairymen carters and sheep shearers. As herders, their new duties included protecting the cattle from other aboriginal groups that had not yet accepted the immigrants' concept of cattle ownership. Walter Colquhoun Grant, the first surveyor, employed aboriginal labour on his farm and for his surveys along the south coast of the island, reporting that "those who are able to work are all anxious to be employed." The Lekwungen were also hired as canoe-express people, transporting mail and passengers between Fort Victoria and Fort Nisqually. A mixture of Lekwungen sense of ownership and willingness to be employed was captured by Captain Courtenay of HMS *Constance* on his visit to Victoria in 1848: "they will not do you a hand's turn or give you a drink of water without payment."[82]

HBC officials were most interested in the availability and quality of the local labour supply. At other posts, the journals often commented on the unwillingness of Aboriginal People to work, but the HBC deputy governor wrote that the Lekwungen were "very well disposed, and seem more inclined to agriculture than most I have seen. They raise a good many potatoes on their own account, and are always willing to work for the company."[83] For the Lekwungen, working for goods was not dissimilar to working for a share of the catch at the reef nets or being hired by another family to assist with a funeral or a feast.[84]

After 1849 and the establishment of the Colony of Vancouver Island, with its capital at Fort Victoria, the Puget Sound Agricultural Company, a subsidiary of the HBC, established four farms around the fort and "a force of men and Indians were employed to clear land and cultivate it." Finlayson recalled: "[Aboriginal] labour was cheap in those days hence the facility with which those operations were carried out." The actual numbers of Lekwungen hired by the traders is rarely recorded, but in April 1851, before large numbers of other aboriginal groups began migrating to the fort, Douglas reported "about 100 Indians employed in clearing Brush and trees and bringing new land into cultivation." James Douglas, who succeeded Finlayson as chief factor, repeatedly remarked on the use of Aboriginal People as "rough carpenters" who built or helped build many of the early structures, including his own house. The company's doctor also noted that "the Indians at this time made shingles," which they sold to the new colonists for their roofs.[85] Henry Charles, a twentieth-century elder from the Beecher Bay band, told Wayne Suttles that his people were Clallam from across the Strait of Juan de Fuca who had "moved over to Victoria when the whites came in order to make shingles and plant potatoes for them."[86]

In addition to performing farm work and engaging in clearing and construction labour, the Lekwungen provided the fort with the majority of its food requirements. The Fort Victoria journals, which survive from 1846 to 1850, show the Lekwungen to be the fort's largest trading partner. Unlike other nations, which brought furs or oil, the Lekwungen traded primarily in food. In 1849 alone, the fort salted five hundred barrels of salmon for overseas markets. According to Douglas, "We could not take one half of the fish brought in by the Indians for sale." Surveyor Grant gave another

You Don't Understand

"Chā-ko, hiac, chā-ko,"
"Come quick! Come," said a settler one day to an Indian who was very busy.

"Wicht nika chā-ko,"
"I will come directly," said the Indian.

But the white man understood him to say, "Wake nika chā-ko,"
"I will not come," consequently got angry.

"You don't understand Indian talk; I did not say I would not come," said the Indian.

James Swan, *The Northwest Coast*, 1857

Work Conversation

Chim, nika tika mahsh konaway stick copo nika illahee.
Jim, I want taken (away) all timber from my land.

Konce chickamun ict sun tika spose mamook mahsh konaway stick spose mamook copo lasee pe lahash pe mamook hual copo kuitan copa nika house?
How much money (per) one day you want if make taken away all timber (and) if make good for fire with saw and axe and make haul by horse to my house?

W.S. Phillips, *The Chinook Book*, 1913

Sister of James Sqwameyuks with basket of fish for sale

Necessity of Employing Indians

As all immigrants and new settlers are more or less under the necessity of employing Indian service in one way or another, a publication of the "wawa" used has been frequently called for, and regarded as highly necessary in facilitating the knowledge of the language.

British Columbian, January 15, 1853

I Have Slaves Who Work for Me ...

I asked [George Bennett, the Kaigani chief] if he would like to go to America or England? He answered "No!" as he considered we were slaves – even our chiefs ... as we were always at work for a living.

"I have slaves who hunt for me – paddle me in my canoes, – and my wives to attend upon me. Why should I wish to leave."

John Dunn, *History of the Oregon Territory and British North American Fur Trade*, 1844

example of the extent of the provision trade in 1851: "On one day a few canoes brought as many as 3000 salmon to trade."[87] The Lekwungen also supplied the fort and growing community with potatoes, clams, oysters, lathes, and baskets.[88]

The Lekwungen became still more valuable to the company after 1849, when the discovery of gold in California induced large numbers of non-aboriginal company employees to desert. In the spring of that year, Finlayson acknowledged, "even our ships were left with insufficient crews. This state of affairs was partly remedied by employing Indians on board in the Coast shipping" and by employing Aboriginal People to replace the labourers on the land. Lekwungen workers were not only available and eager for work, they were also a bargain compared to non-aboriginal labour. When, in 1853, aboriginal labourers were paid eight dollars per month, white labourers could not "be procured under the rate of $2 and $2½ dollars a day so that we cannot afford to employ them on public works."[89]

The Lekwungen's willingness to participate in the European economy did not imply sacrificing their own cultural priorities or relationships. On the contrary, when the Lekwungen welcomed the European fur traders, they were inviting them into an existing social network that placed great importance on saving for a potlatch. Ethnologist Robert Brown remarked in the 1860s: "I had often commiserated a poor-looking man lounging about, his only covering a threadbare tattered blanket, and on inquiry be surprised to learn that he was one of the wealthiest men in the tribe, and had several hundred blankets stored up in air tight boxes, of native manufacture, in his lodge."

Slavery was also a part of the system. Slavery was the fate of captives (and their descendants) taken in inter-village raiding. It was a long-standing way of organizing labour among the Coast Salish and among the people of the West Coast in general. Once captured, slaves were often traded to distant groups to make escape more difficult. In addition to being bought and sold, slaves might also be won through gambling or received as a "gift" at a potlatch.[90]

In Lekwungen society slaves had economic value, as they laboured for their owners, and they also brought prestige. An 1839 rough census of one family of Songhees headed by Cheethulm showed 12 married men with 14 wives, 22 sons, 9 daughters, and 70 "followers," which included slaves and the low-class descendants of slaves and their masters.[91]

The Aboriginal People, visiting different HBC forts, thought that their day-to-day treatment of slaves was not that different from the HBC's treatment of its employees. The Nisga'a who visited Fort Simpson and the Chinook who visited Fort Vancouver observed that employees were subject to harsh and sometimes arbitrary discipline. The "servants," as the HBC called its employees, performed all the hard physical labour and lived in poverty compared to the "officers." This looked like a slave/owner relationship to these Aboriginal People, who offered at different times to buy one of the HBC men. Fur trader William Tolmie recalled that "Tshinooks of the Lower Columbia and the Indians thence to Puget Sound would not work for new-comers, any individual so-doing being reproached as placing himself on the level of a slave." The same was evidently true of upper-class Nisga'a and Tlingit from the north.[92]

The Lekwungen found that they could transform their slaves' labour into wealth by renting them to the Europeans. In a few cases we have specific details. The Lekwungen *siem ci'lem* rented or sold a Twana captive named Peter Solomon to Fort Victoria in the mid-1840s. When emissaries from the Twana came to Fort Victoria, they recalled that the traders told them: "Oh no, this is a good boy. We want him here working for us. He says he does not want to go home and when he does we'll take him back. He wants to stay here and work for us and we'll pay him."

The Twana were apparently satisfied by this explanation, but in order to smooth relations, the HBC gave each of the Twana a blanket and the group was given two boxes of biscuits. In what seems to be a similar arrangement, the HBC bought a Cowichan slave from the Makah, with the offer of redemption once he worked off his purchase price.[93]

The fur traders told the Twana that they would have no more slaves working for them, but many of the commodities purchased by the fort must have been gathered and manufactured, in part or in full, by slaves.[94] Louie Pilkey remembered that the Wsanec chief "Lesceum" had ten slaves whom he put to work raising potatoes to sell to the whites. Charles Jones reports that his grandfather, a Nuu-chah-nulth from Port San Juan, had sixteen slaves engaged in the manufacture of dog fish oil. Five male slaves fished, while six female slaves dressed and rendered the catch. The remaining slaves shuttled Jones' grandfather and canoe, loaded with barrels of oil, to and from Victoria. Certainly, as late as 1860, some of the nearby Salish made "a great deal of money" by sending their slaves to work for the whites, and appropriating their wages. A 'Chilukweyuk' man, like Captain John of Soowahlie, whose slave was employed for several months by the [Boundary] Commission pocketed a large sum of money in this way. "The money was of course paid to the slave, but his master was always near at hand on pay-day to look after the dollars."[95]

In other parts of the coast, it was primarily slaves who first worked for the whites, but ordinary "free" Lekwungen took up paid work within days of the fur traders' arrival. Bolduc reported that "all the men" cut pickets for the

Not Vicious, Avaricious

These coast Indians are very avaricious in the acquisition of property ... Though muskets, canoes etc ... are all carefully collected, yet most of these articles owe their acquisition to blankets, and an Indian, in describing the wealth of another, will indicate this by telling how many *pessise* [Chinook jargon for blankets] he has. This hoarding up of blankets is the engrossing passion of these people.

Robert Brown, journal account, 1864

Robert Brown, leader of the Vancouver Island Exploration Expedition and author of *The Races of Mankind: Being a Popular Description of the Characteristics and Manners and Customs of the Principal Varieties of the Human Family*, 1873.

fort. The particular history of the Lekwungen and their systems of labour subordination meant that the exchange relationships that developed at Fort Victoria differed from those in other parts of the Northwest Coast. The reef net production system meant that, among the Lekwungen, there had been a previous history of labour subordination that was separate from slavery. This explains their being willing to work for pay at an earlier date than, for example, the Chinook or Nisga'a.[96]

At the other end of the Lekwungen social scale from slaves were *siem*, "chiefs," as the newcomers usually called them.[97] Prior to the arrival of Europeans the *siem* would organize work crews for the reef net fishery and other projects. When the steamship *Beaver* arrived, laden with new work opportunities, the Lekwungen *siem*, accordingly, organized and supervised the labourers. Father Bolduc wrote of his experience hiring Lekwungen workers: "I engaged Tsamics ... who is chief of the tribe to conduct me to Whidby Island ... I gave him a blanket on the condition that he give me ten men for a crew." In 1855, when James Douglas wanted to ensure an orderly process for hiring aboriginal workers, he "called the chiefs together ... exacted a pledge for the good behaviour of their respective tribes" and gave them permission to hire their people out as labourers. Similarly, at other locations along the coast, the *siem* were labour brokers for their extended families.[98]

The brokerage system worked well for the HBC in the early years of the fort, when it was not unusual to have forty to one hundred people working on a single project, building or clearing land.[99] The system also worked for the *siem* who maintained control over access to the new wealth goods. In addition to arranging labour for the fort the *siem* were also provisioning it by intensifying their workers' reef netting and duck netting and converting this food into wealth.

At the same time, the Lekwungen system of property rights allowed for the harvest of such food resources as deer, clams, and oysters by whomever gathered them, *siem* and commoners alike. This new provision trade enabled individuals, for the first time, to accumulate wealth independent of the *siem*. As the settlement grew, the potential to circumvent the *siem*'s near-monopoly on accumulating surplus wealth increased as a growing number of employers wanted only one or a few employees. The ability of the *siem* to manage people and the main resources was further weakened over time by the settlers' appropriation of many of their resource-gathering sites.[100]

In some cases the appropriation of Lekwungen land came without any form of compensation, as when the traders grazed cattle on the camas patches. But in 1850, Governor Douglas moved to formalize the relationship with the Lekwungen "whose land we occupy" through a treaty.[101] Douglas wrote that he "summoned to a conference, the chiefs and influential men of the Songees tribe ... After considerable discussion it was arranged that the whole of their lands, forming ... the District of Victoria, should be sold to the Company, with the exception of Village sites and enclosed fields, for a certain remuneration, to be paid at once to each member of the Tribe. I was in favour of a series of payments to be paid annually but the proposal was so generally disliked that I yielded to their wishes and paid the sum at once."

According to Douglas, the Lekwungen exchanged their land for a sum of three blankets for each male head of family, with additional blankets to the "chiefs," for a total price of 371 blankets plus a cap.

Within three weeks of making the treaty, Douglas wrote to the HBC: "I informed the natives that they would not be disturbed in the possession of their Village sites and enclosed fields, which are of small extent, and that they were at liberty to hunt over the unoccupied lands, and to carry on their fisheries with the same freedom as when they were the sole occupants of the country."[102]

There is a single Lekwungen-Wsanec account of the treaties from David Latasse, who recounted it in 1934, reportedly aged 105. Latasse recalled that, for weeks in advance, the "party" was the talk of all the encampments within eighty miles of Victoria. On the appointed day, May 24, 1850, the Lekwungen and their neighbours assembled on Beacon Hill overlooking Fort Victoria and Meeqan. The HBC men distributed hard biscuits smeared with molasses and gave away other food. Governor Douglas, dressed in a coat of blue with gold shoulder pieces and gold trimming, gave a salute to the queen, and then:

> He stressed the desire of the white men to be friends with the tribes. He assured the chiefs that trade in furs with peaceful use of enough land to grow food, were the only reasons for establishment of the settlement. His statement was welcomed by the peace-loving tribes, whose view of the settlement, had it been voiced at all, would have been that there was lots of land and no harm could come from letting the whites use some of it ... We all understood that similar gifts would be made each year, what is now called rent.[103]

Chief Latasse added that the "Indians were great bargainers" and would not have consented to a once-only payment.

The accounts differ regarding whether an annual rent or a lump sum was understood, and they differ on the question of who was letting who use the land. But both accounts stress that the Aboriginal People were guaranteed their village sites and fields. They were also guaranteed fishing rights,

Not for a Few Blankets

To-day (reverting to the Chinook jargon), why should the white people treat us so? We never fought them, yet they took away our property. This land is ours. It was as I knew it when a boy and it should be ours today. Never, never, did the Indians sign away title to their land just for a few blankets.

Chief David Latasse, *Victoria Daily Times*, July 14, 1934

I Like Work

"Chief," asked the white man, "what is the secret of your long life?" "I like work" answered the centurion Chief David Latasse.

Victoria Colonist, May 3, 1936

Chief David Latasse in the early 1930s

Saanich Make Signs of Cross

Douglas invited all the head people into Victoria. When they got there all these piles of blankets plus other goods were on the ground. They told them these bundles of blankets were for them plus about $200 but it was in pounds and shillings. They saw these bundles of blankets and goods and they were asked to put X's on this paper ... One man spoke up after they discussed it, and said ... "I think these are peace offerings. I think Douglas means to keep the peace. I think these are the sign of the cross" ... It wasn't much later they found out actually they were signing their land away by putting those crosses out there.

Dave Elliot, Wsanec elder, *Saltwater People,* 1990

and fishing was the mainstay of their subsistence economy as well as a new route to wealth (i.e., through supplying the fort with fish). Moreover, most of the Lekwungen fishing sites were off San Juan Island, across Haro Strait, and were unaffected by the occupation. The Lekwungen were guaranteed hunting and, it would seem, gathering rights on all "unoccupied" lands. In 1850, even the most prescient among the Lekwungen (and the fur traders) would have had a hard time imagining the extent of "occupation" that would prevail forty or fifty years later. Probably the Lekwungen thought they were being compensated for the lands, particularly the camas patches, that had already been occupied. Since this land had been taken, and it did not look like the Lekwungen could get it back, some payment was probably accepted as better than none.

Moreover, Douglas's formal declaration of ownership of the land mirrored the potlatch – a public ceremony in which rights were proclaimed and gifts distributed. Each individual was called by name and given his gifts. The gifts took the form of the potlatch standard – the HBC blanket. By attending the potlatch and accepting the gifts, the Lekwungen were acknowledging the HBC's claim to the small patch of land that it used. Like other claims to ownership, in the Lekwungen worldview, this one would need to be periodically revalidated with a feast and gifts. Like other potlatches, it put the givers and the receivers in a moral obligation to continue a reciprocal gift-giving cycle. And the gifts given were very valuable.

It is easy to trivialize this exchange from a present-day perspective, but the blankets received were, as we have seen, a princely sum in the economy of the Lekwungen. This new concentration of wealth goods among the Lekwungen was probably unprecedented. David Latasse, who was there, remembers the "sense of wealth" shared by the Lekwungen when they received their settlement from Douglas.[104]

In the months following, Douglas signed treaties with the Wsanec bands to the north of the Lekwungen, with the Clallam and TSou-ke [Sooke] bands to the west, and with the Nanaimo and the Fort Rupert Kwakwaka'wakw. Whatever the Aboriginal Peoples thought they were agreeing to, in the treaty ceremonies they did it willingly. The Cowichan even sought Douglas out and asked him to sign a treaty with them, an invitation that Douglas declined, saying that no whites wanted to settle there yet so the land was not needed.[105]

How did this payment for land, work, and the resulting infusion of hundreds of blankets and shirts affect Lekwungen society? In the hands of the Lekwungen, blankets were transformed into measures of wealth and status. Most likely, the treaty payment of 1850 was the main source of gifts for the potlatch hosted by the Lekwungen three years later. This potlatch, hosted by Chee-ah-thluc, brought two thousand guests to their village and was probably the largest event of its kind ever to have taken place among the Lekwungen or their neighbours.[106]

Albert Westly, a Nanaimo who potlatched with the Lekwungen, observed that "in the days before the white man came, fifty blankets or fifty goat skins were a tremendous accumulation, and very few men ever amassed so many." When an appropriate sum was finally accumulated, a few guests from one or two villages would be invited to potlatch. Subsequently, however: "Hudson's Bay blankets were bought in bales of fifty and distributed by tens and twenties."[107]

While documentation of Lekwungen potlatches is fragmentary, the events themselves were, by those rare accounts, increasingly frequent and grand. Artist Paul Kane was told of a potlatch that occurred prior to his visit in 1846, and he said that such events, hosted by the Lekwungen or their neighbours, took place every three or four years. Already, by 1846, HBC blankets were the main currency in which potlatches were measured. In the feast described by Kane, twelve bales – six hundred blankets – were distributed.[108]

Every year it seemed that more goods were given away. John Fornsby was at a wedding potlatch hosted by the Lekwungen in the late 1850s in Puget Sound, and he mentions a return potlatch at the Lekwungen village a short time later. This may have been the same potlatch described in the *Victoria Gazette* in October 1858 or by Charles Wilson in 1859 when he watched as several Lekwungen "chiefs" each "gave away between 3 & 400 blankets." The *British Colonist* and the *Port Townsend Register* newspapers note wedding potlatches among the Lekwungen in 1860 and in 1861; MacFie, in 1863, describes the gifts as consisting of "cotton cloth by the hundreds of yards, blankets to the value of hundreds of pounds" and says that these potlatches are annual events. The *British Colonist* records two potlatches that year. The newcomers triggered a tremendous inflationary spiral in the Lekwungen's prestige economy, and it guaranteed them an eager labour force.[109]

The *British Colonist* estimated that at another potlatch in April 1869 an astounding $20,000 in goods and cash were given away by the Lekwungen to seven hundred assembled guests. In April 1874, "the grandest affair of that kind that has been held upon Vancouver Island for many years, came off ... at Victoria," hosted by Chief Sqwameyuks (Scomiach) of the Lekwungen. Sqwameyuk personally distributed over $1,000 worth of blankets to the two thousand assembled, and, during that week, the total value of goods given away by all the families amounted to between $8,000

Potlatch of 1853

The Old Tyee [Chee-ah-thluc] invited us in the camp to see his friends ... they were very proud to see us, so they honoured us with a dance and a song it was quite amusing to see them all with their Knifes, Pistols, Swords, & Guns in their hands, holding them above their heads, now and then firing a Gun or two out of the Roof, then we saw about 9 more Canoes come in then they shoot and the Canoes come up in a Row the Indians that are in the canoes singing and Dancing all the time they are coming, when they get near the Beach one Man goes to the edge of the water and makes a speech, to the Indians that are in the canoes, Saying, that his heart is very good towards them, and hopes theirs are towards them, and that he had invited them to come to this feast and share with some Blankets that they had to give away.

Martha Cheney Ella, "Diary," 1853

and $10,000. The next year a week-long potlatch saw a similar distribution among a crowd of the same size. Two years later, at a potlatch given by the neighbouring Wsanec people, the Indian superintendent saw "three members of one family (brothers) give away 3,500 blankets, no doubt the savings of many years ... Goods to the value of $15,400 were distributed ere the affair ended."[110] Such sums would be considered large if they were given away today, given the current value of the dollar. In the mid- to late nineteenth century, when aboriginal workers made fifty cents to a dollar per day and white labourers made two dollars per day, these sums represent an incredible accumulation of wealth. A sum like $15,000 in 1870 would be the equivalent of more than $315,000 today.[111] There was abundant wealth for redistribution in the South Island aboriginal communities.

The late 1850s to 1880s was a time of catastrophic population decline for the Lekwungen, yet potlatches not only persisted but increased, both in number and amount of wealth distributed. In a sad irony, the high death rate among the Lekwungen contributed to the frequency of potlatches as, with more deaths, more ceremonies were required to mark inheritance and the names and privileges that went with it. That commoners could also now accumulate wealth within the wage-labour system added to the increase in potlatching. George Mitchell of the Comox Salish, who potlatched the Lekwungen, noted that, in prior times, only people with special powers could "hold the people," or potlatch. Now, even "clam diggers," as he called poor men, could do it.[112]

The early capitalist economy fit well with the existing Lekwungen economy. Much of the new work that required many labourers – agriculture, fishing, and, later, fish canning – was seasonal, being particularly demanding in the summer and fall. There was only a slight demand for labour in the winter, the main potlatch-ceremonial season, so it was possible for the Lekwungen to participate fully in both economies. In year-round industries, the Lekwungen often worked until they had accumulated the sums required for potlatch goods and then quit. The Fort Victoria Journal for December 23, 1846, noted that the Lekwungen "are now busy with their annual 'Madigans' [?] ceremonies and we have consequently much difficulty to get the hired hands to attend their work." I.W. Powell, in 1883, described how difficult it was to keep aboriginal deck hands in the winter, despite the high (fifty-dollar) monthly wage. In fact, the high wages may have caused a faster turnover as it made accumulation easier.[113]

It seems clear that, until at least the 1880s, the main reason that so many Aboriginal People participated in the capitalist economy was to enable them to participate more fully in their own. Their wages were converted into goods, which were then given away to renew claims on resource sites, to pass on names, and to commemorate the dead.

Few non-aboriginal immigrants could reconcile the motivations that led Aboriginal People into the workforce with their own work ethic. When George Walkem observed a Wsanec potlatch in 1875, he was struck by the incompatibility of the Salish system of social elevation with that of his own culture. He said that never, before or since, had he witnessed "a man transform himself so rapidly from a state of plenty to one of poverty."[114] Reverend George Grant, accompanying Sanford Fleming on his cross-country inspection of possible Canadian Pacific Railway (CPR) routes thought that the Salish custom of potlatching "to the Anglo-saxon mind borders on insanity."[115]

More thoughtful white observers recognized the potlatch for what it was: the central institution of Lekwungen culture. For the Lekwungen it was the nexus of the prestige, subsistence, and new capitalist economies. Wage work, though useful as an adjunct to the prestige economy, was precisely that: an adjunct.

The primacy of the non-capitalist economy among the Salish in particular and Northwest Coast Aboriginal Peoples in general reinforced white attitudes about aboriginal work habits. Robert Brown's 1864 account of the Cowichan talks about "a very lazy set, only labouring to get a bare sufficiency of fish food." They were lazy, he said, because they "only car[ed] to work if they got high wages." Brown described how Indians in the remotest locations had refused to sell him fish if they thought the price not high enough, even though they had no other potential purchasers. He found the Cowichan would rather attend a potlatch than work for wages, and so he had to wait until they were ready to work. Douglas previously noted, with regard to the coal mines in Nanaimo and Fort Rupert, that when it was time to engage in their seasonal subsistence or prestige economies, Aboriginal People would quit working for pay and would only return to paid work when their own economic cycle permitted.[116] Colonist W.C. Grant's words, "Their labour is not to be depended on for any continuous period," are echoed repeatedly throughout the period.[117] Employers' difficulties in coping with an independent aboriginal agenda helps to explain why the aboriginal workforce was simultaneously described as "unreliable," "indolent," and "indispensable."

The Lekwungen enjoyed a virtual monopoly on work contracted by the colonists until their grand potlatch of 1853 brought thousands of Aboriginal People to Victoria for the first time. The visitors saw the new wealth of the Lekwungen and the opportunities for paid work. The following year

How Marked the Contrast

How marked the contrast between the ideas of these natives of the uses of wealth, and those of their pale faced brethren, who hoard up money in order to become great, while the untutored savage gives it away for the same end.

British Colonist, April 20, 1869, 3

Victorian Hannah Maynard took this photo of her aboriginal washerwoman, Mary, ca. 1860s

The Steamer's Arrival

High prices rule, and fierce competition ensues between the boatmen and the Indians ... Ambitious and economical individuals hurl phrases from Chinook vocabulary at the aborigines, and are rewarded by the utter failure in being comprehended ... Of those unwary enough to embark without inquiry, fabulous prices are demanded.

Chinook conveyance is found to be less cheap than was anticipated at the start; the compensation eagerly accepted in promise at the steamer is disdained in reaching the shore, and persistent individuals who will pay no more than they agree to, are followed into the woods by denunciation and objurgation in an unknown and expressive tongue.

Victoria Gazette, July 3, 1858, 2

many returned. Governor Douglas reported two thousand aboriginal visitors to Victoria in 1854, most of whom were looking for work. Every year thereafter, until the 1880s, two thousand to four thousand Aboriginal People from all over the coast congregated seasonally in Victoria.[118]

These aboriginal sojourners from the north and from Puget Sound increasingly competed for work with the Lekwungen, particularly with regard to seasonal labour.[119] The Lekwungen apparently began to specialize in more permanent jobs, including working as domestics for the colonists. J.S. Helmcken "had Dick, my Indian for a servant and cook," whom he paid two blankets and a shirt per month. Dick was later married, and his wife joined him at the Helmcken house as a domestic. Other Aboriginal People were hired for "chopping wood, carrying water and doing odd jobs."[120] In 1852 Reverend Staines wrote that he was busy teaching his aboriginal cooks how to prepare venison, beef, and mutton and that he was supervising the "Indian" servants who were responsible for "trading venison, partridges, salmon, mats, berries, etc" that they acquired from other Indians.[121]

The gold rushes that swept the territory between 1858 and 1866 brought the Lekwungen people new opportunities for work as Victoria temporarily grew to the point where it contained ten thousand to fifteen thousand non-Aboriginal People. This influx also brought a cash economy to British Columbia. Whereas previously both Aboriginal People and company servants had been paid in goods from the company storehouse, increasingly they were paid in cash. Wsanec-Lekwungen David Latasse was in his mid-twenties when this invasion hit. He noted that, at the time of the gold rush to the Fraser River, "all the ... Songhies removed to the Inner Harbor reserve, to share in the wealth to be earned by transporting the miners and their supplies to the Fraser River ... the Indians were profiting largely ... There were many potlatch parties."[122]

Lekwungen men supplied venison, firewood, and building materials to the booming city; ferried passengers and freight from ship to shore; and worked as unskilled and semi-skilled labourers. They also worked extensively loading and unloading ships. Women expanded their subsistence work into commercial production. At a time when skilled tradesmen were earning $4.85 (see Table 6.2), the *British Colonist* newspaper asked: "Need any be idle, when the very squaws are making four and five dollars a day, in bringing in oysters from Victoria Arm, So[o]ke or Cowichan and peddling them around town? They monopolize the whole trade; not a white man or a civi[li]zed man enters the field against them." Lekwungen women also worked as domestics, seamstresses, and laundresses for the thousands of miners who passed through town. Edgar Fawcett remembered that "the men and the young women went out washing by the day, from seven to six o'clock, at fifty cents." They also sold fish, eggs, potatoes, berries, and mushrooms door-to-door. Their calls "as they passed the doors might be heard at all hours."

The language sung out in the streets of Victoria was Chinook jargon.[123] In April 1862, the *British Colonist* reported that "the Indians have free access to the town day and night. They line our streets, filling the pit in our theatre, are found at nearly every open door during the day and evening in the town; and are even employed as servants in our dwellings, and in the culinary departments of our restaurants and hotels."[124]

More Than Was Bargained For ...

Trading and paid work had been something the Lekwungen had sought for reasons of their own. But they could not anticipate all that would accompany these explicit exchanges. While material exchange enriched the ceremonial life of the Lekwungen, non-material dimensions took a major toll on them as European society introduced many more new ways to die than it did new ways to live.

Unlike other exchanges, the epidemiological exchanges between the Lekwungen and the newcomers was almost totally one-sided. Before the arrival of Europeans, the Northwest Coast, like the rest of the Americas, seems to have been free from lethal density-dependent infectious diseases. All of the epidemic diseases that are documented on the Northwest Coast in the first century of contact – smallpox, malaria, measles, influenza, dysentery, whooping cough, typhus, and typhoid fever – were part of the cargo brought by European visitors or immigrants, as were venereal diseases and tuberculosis.[125]

The first epidemic of new diseases – smallpox – probably hit the Lekwungen in 1782, before they even met a European. Vancouver noted the tell-tale pock marks on the skin of many of the Lekwungen's Georgia Strait neighbours in 1792 as well as abandoned villages full of skeletal remains. Several studies of the effect of smallpox on populations with no immunity have concluded that a one-third mortality rate is a conservative estimate. A story that most likely relates to the arrival of smallpox tells of the Lekwungen commoners fleeing the advance of the deadly winds. The family of the *siem* locked themselves in their fortified village on what is now Finlayson Point. When the winds had passed, the people returned and the family of the *siem* were all dead. They were buried in cairns on the slope below the observation point on Beacon Hill.[126]

Thereafter, historical and ethnographic evidence confirms that the Lekwungen suffered epidemics every twenty-four to thirty years as new generations with no immunity grew up. Smallpox may have reappeared in 1801, and it or measles swept the area in 1824. There is evidence that the

"Ah, Culla Culla"

"Ah, Culla Culla" (grouse and ducks), "Mowich" (venison), "Oolally" (berries), "Sooke Oysters," "Salmon," and "Cowichan potatoes" ... "Ick quarter" or "King George Quarter" (twenty-five cents) bought almost anything.

Edgar Fawcett, *Some Reminiscences of Old Victoria*, 1912

Smallpox the Terrible Sill-kous

A very long time ago a terrible sickness visited this part of the world from which ninety out of every one hundred died. This sickness ... known to this day as the Terrible Sill-kous ... was caused by piercing northeast ... winds ... chilling people to the bones. Soon they felt sore all over, as if beaten with a stick; next their faces begin to swell, and the eyes to feel as if they would drop out; next their throat was so sore that the neck swelled up, many unable to swallow died through want of food; next came the last symptom, a violent dysentery and then death.

Lekwungen story about smallpox as told to James Deans, *Victoria Daily Times*, December 22, 1900

Stó:lō artist Stan Greene's interpretation of smallpox

Lekwungen were struck by some epidemic in 1841-42 as they associated the sickness to their baptism at Fort Langley by Father De Smet in 1841.[127]

When James Douglas and the Reverend Bolduc visited the main Lekwungen village at Sungayka in 1843, they met the remnants of a large population that had concentrated here. Bolduc counted 525 individuals "and many were absent." A few days later, 1,200 Aboriginal People assembled at Sungayka for a service led by Bolduc, though some of these are stated to have been "Kawitskins" (Cowichan) and "Isanisks" (Wsanec) in addition to Lekwungen. Measles swept their villages in 1848.[128]

The first real census of the Lekwungen was conducted by Douglas as he made his treaties with them and other south Island groups in 1850. His careful count revealed a population of 1,649 Aboriginal People on southeast Vancouver Island, and this after the measles and influenza epidemic that "made great havoc" in 1848. Douglas's census of the six "Tribes or Families" that comprised the people he called "Samose" (Songhees or Lekwungen) accounted for 122 "men with beards, 134 women, 221 boys and 223 girls which sums to precisely 700."[129]

By applying the uncertain methods of disease demography, Douglas's census provides us with an opportunity to re-examine the accepted estimates of precontact populations on the south Island. Two scholars who have estimated the pre-epidemic population of southeast Vancouver Island, including that of the Lekwungen and Wsanec, agree on a population of between 2,600 and 2,700.[130] However, if we use their own formulas in relation to Douglas's careful census (and taking into account Bolduc's observation of some mortality in 1841), what is suggested, as a conservative estimate, is a population of 3,825 for the southeast Island, of which 1,624 would have been Lekwungen.[131]

The presence of Fort Victoria in their territory meant that the Lekwungen had more regular contact with carriers of exotic diseases than did most aboriginal groups, but it also gave them earlier access to vaccinations. In 1853, Douglas reported that, as a result of vaccination, the Lekwungen were spared the smallpox epidemic that was devastating aboriginal populations across the Straits of Georgia.[132] Vaccination and the speedy removal of the Lekwungen to their Discovery Island village site meant that the 1862-63 smallpox epidemic, which had disastrous effects on the northern coast, only had a small impact on the Lekwungen.

Yet, despite the meliorations that reduced the impact of smallpox, the Lekwungen population still plummeted from the 700 Douglas counted in 1850, to 285 in 1864, and to 182 in 1876.[133] Venereal diseases and tuberculosis evidently accounted for a large number of the deaths. In 1849, surveyor Walter Grant thought that, among the Lekwungen's neighbours,

Smallpox and Songhees, 1862

Strange to say the tribe whose language I have learned [Songhees], has not been attacked with any violence by the disease. But 3 died from their whole number. Then under my advice they left for an island and the pestilence has not spread among them.

Rev. A.C. Garrett, Letter to the Secretary of the United Society for the Propagation of the Gospel, from Victoria, June 6, 1862

the T'sou-ke (with whom he was most familiar), "at least two thirds of the population were diseased either with scrofula or syphilis. The annual mortality is considerable."[134] In taking his census in 1872, the new superintendent of British Columbia Indians concluded that "Consumption, Bloody Flux, Syphilis and various cutaneous eruptions are common" to the Straits Salish, including the Lekwungen.[135] Reports by the Indian Agents also show that measles, smallpox, and influenza continued to take their toll on the younger and older members of the Lekwungen throughout the nineteenth century, while tuberculosis and venereal disease struck at those who were in the prime of life.

Out-migration, which for some aboriginal groups contributed to population decline, was not a significant factor in the decline of the Lekwungen. Although many Lekwungen women married into the non-aboriginal community and ceased to be counted as Lekwungen, this was more than compensated for by non-Lekwungen women marrying Lekwungen men. Douglas's 1850 count, the 1876 census conducted by the reserve commission, and the federal censuses of 1881 and 1891 all show more adult women among the Lekwungen than adult men.[136] Some cases of non-aboriginal men moving onto the Lekwungen reserve to live with a Lekwungen women are also recorded; often these men, or at least their children, were "adopted" into the band. It was also common for Lekwungen women to return to the reserve with their children after having lived with a non-aboriginal partner off the reserve for some time.[137]

A significant portion of the population decline is accounted for by alcohol-related deaths. Alcohol became widely available during the gold rush. The trade in alcohol was technically illegal but was so profitable that the law was easily evaded; the illicit nature of the trade also meant that the spirits sold to Aboriginal People were "of the vilest and most destructive kind, manufactured on the site from pure alcohol ... diluted with *salt* water, and flavoured [with] ... camphine, creosote, and even sulphuric acid ... to give strength and flavour." The Lekwungen's urban location gave them easy access to alcohol, increasing their mortality rates in several ways. Alcohol poisoning (or poisoning by the other substances added to liquor sold to Aboriginal People), deadly fights, and accidents, particularly since the journey from the Lekwungen village to the rum shops was made by small canoe, account for some of the population decline. Chief Freezie of the Lekwungen, who met his death crossing the harbour in 1864, was one of these victims.[138]

The *British Colonist* estimated in February 1859 that four hundred Aboriginal People in the Victoria area had died from the use of alcohol in the previous eighteen months, and, even if this is exaggerated, other evi-

Whiskey Kills My Friends

Whiskey memaloos Tillicum (x3)
Whisky Kills [my] friends.

Pe alta mika mash,
But now I throw it Away.

Ahncuttie mika ti[ky] whisky (x3)
Formerly I liked whiskey,

Pe alta nika mash,
But now I throw it Away.

Recorded by Mary Bourque at Neah Bay, 1908, to the tune of "The Bear Went over the Mountain"

All Our People Are Dead

Colloquial phrases, written down as they
were heard from the natives and others
versed in the [Chinook] idiom:

Kántshiak maika tílikŬm?
How many are thy people?

Nawítika kanawē nŬsaike tílikŬm
mémelust.
Truly all our people are dead.

Horatio Hale, "The 'Jargon' or Trade-
Language of Oregon" [1846]

dence suggests alcohol-related deaths were a real problem. Aboriginal leaders were asking for help for their people. An 1872 petition for the chiefs of
Nanaimo, north of Victoria, asked that the "poison" be kept from their
people. "We look around and ask where are the hundreds of our people?
They are gone and most of them by the white man's rum."[139]

By the time Franz Boas visited the Lekwungen in the 1880s, the
"drunken Indian" stereotype was already a part of the white image of Aboriginal People. His dismissal of the Lekwungen as "terrible drunkards"
who are "always full of whiskey" has to be understood within this context, as
does the Indian Agent's 1882 comment that "the Lekwungen village is one
of the most degraded on the coast."[140] As Bishop Hills pointed out, alcohol
abuse and alcohol-related deaths were endemic in the non-aboriginal gold
rush community as well, only the effect on the small Lekwungen population was more visible.[141]

"Whiskey may have killed its tens," observed J.S. Helmcken, the best
known doctor in Victoria from 1851 through to his death in 1920, "but
imported diseases its hundreds."[142] Indeed, the popularity of alcohol among
the Lekwungen may have been a way of coping with, and escaping from,
the personal anguish and cultural disruption caused by repeated deadly
epidemics and persistent chronic diseases.

Disease, drunkenness, and prostitution – all exchanges with the newcomers – were the reasons offered by a faction of the Victoria business
community to justify ridding the city of Aboriginal People. As the city
grew, the Lekwungen harbour-side village site became the most commercially valuable property in the city. After 1858, the Victoria City Council,
the *British Colonist* newspaper, and prominent citizens regularly called for
the removal of the Lekwungen from the city core. Objections to their removal were twofold. First was the legal difficulty. Douglas' 1850 treaty
granted the Lekwungen the reserve in perpetuity; this was confirmed by
the Indian Act, 1876, which declared that the majority of eligible Indians
in a band must consent to any surrender of reserve land, and the Lekwungen
did not want to move.[143]

The second problem was the value of Aboriginal People to Victoria as
employees and consumers. Not only did the Lekwungen depend on the
town, the town depended, at least to some extent, on the Lekwungen.
When the smallpox epidemic hit, the Songhees left for Discovery Island,
and other visiting Aboriginal People were driven away. The Victoria press
complained that the lumber yards were forced to hire white men at $2.50 a
day instead of aboriginal workers, who worked for two dollars. Moreover,
if the Lekwungen were moved, the commissioners of the Indian reserve

wondered in 1864, "what [was] to be done" with the visiting Aboriginal People who came to work and trade? There were eighty-five licensed public houses in Victoria in 1866, numerous unlicensed ones, and twenty wholesale, or "gallon," houses, many depending on the "Indian trade." The supplying of goods for potlatches was big business, and in the 1860s and 1870s Aboriginal People were among Victoria's best customers: "many traders among us realise very large profits from their dealings with the Indians – indeed it is stated that one street in our town is almost entirely supported by them." Traders along Victoria's Johnston Street told the *British Colonist* that they would be ruined if the Indians were driven out. "I see no present necessity for removing them," advised Dr. Tolmie in 1883. The men and women perform valuable work, he said, earn much and spend it all in the city: "This money might otherwise go to Chinamen who would spend but a fraction of it in the province."[144]

The *makúk* with Europeans had mixed consequences for family and gender relations as, when individuals became able to earn an income independently of the *siem*, household production was rearranged. In addition to doing farm and construction work, supplying foodstuffs and firewood, men were hired on steamboats, in the sawmills, and on the docks. Women, too, had expanded work opportunities, particularly as launderers, domestics, and as suppliers of provisions and sexual services. Opportunities for out-marriage also increased for women.[145]

Yet, for all its disruption, the gold rush left the household basically intact as a production unit, and *siem* were enriched beyond their previous experience. This was due to the increasing value of the *siem*'s resource sites – reef net locations in particular – as the demand for fish among the immigrant community escalated. Many of the Lekwungen continued to engage in the reef net fishery at their sites along the San Juan Island through the 1860s.[146] Long-standing Lekwungen domestic products, canoes, paddles, and baskets were in high demand in gold rush society, as were carved miniature "curiosities." The rush mats that Bishop Hills saw being produced by women in King Freezie's household in 1860 were highly sought after by the miners as bedding. Francis Reinhart, a 59'er, described them as "just the thing to spread on the ground under our blankets and roll them up in when we travel. We bought several, some colored and quite nice."[147]

The Lekwungen continued to live in extended families despite deaths from disease and alcohol abuse and a drastically reduced birth/infant survival rate. In 1887, Indian Agent Lomas reported that there was only one child for every two adults among the Lekwungen.[148] In the face of the shrinking populations, households maintained their basic structure by consolidating. Slaves were still a part of the household economy, though their function changed to bringing in cash from harvesting natural resources, and there were new outlets through which they could escape their status.[149]

Potlatches continued to be the focus of household production, occurring with increased frequency and with more wealth being distributed to larger numbers of people. As previously discussed, the decimation by disease of high-born families probably meant that distant "common" relatives would be next in line to inherit "noble" names and positions. And the increased wealth available to non-nobles meant that they, too, could participate more fully.[150]

When the composition of the Lekwungen household began to shift in the 1870s, this had more to do with intensified evangelization than it did with the changing economy. Although Catholics and Anglicans had been working with the Lekwungen from 1843 and 1851, respectively, and the former had baptized and married several of the Lekwungen, it was with Shee-at-ston's 1870 conversion to Methodism that the new lifestyle called for by the Christians gained a foothold. According to the missionary accounts, which have to be read within their own evangelizing context, Shee-at-ston, a *siem*, apparently saw in the Methodists an alternative to the widespread drinking that was consuming his community. If Shee-at-ston saw the missionaries as an ally in coping with his rapidly urbanizing world, this would be consistent with the active approach many Aboriginal People took with respect to approaching missionaries.[151]

Christianity impinged on Lekwungen household structure in several ways. For one thing, the prohibition on polygyny changed household composition. Pressure from the missionaries was reinforced by the sex imbalance in the immigrant population. Any woman who preferred to have a man of her own could easily get one. The shift away from polygyny, according to the missionary Thomas Crosby who ministered to the Lekwungen, was gradual: "It was a matter that could not have been forced upon them, but gradually they arranged it. The oldest one, perhaps, was put away with an ample dowry. Another, who had no family ties, married another man who had no wife ... The one whose growing family of little ones laid heavy responsibilities upon her was usually retained."[152]

It seems doubtful that the process worked as smoothly as Crosby described, but available statistics do suggest a decline in polygynous marriages. The 1876 census, conducted by George Blenkinsop of the Indian Reserve Commission, was the first to enumerate the Lekwungen by "family." In that year, as in 1850, the number of adult women (162) exceeded the number of adult men (155), and female youths (9) exceeded male youths

(7). Of the adult men, eight apparently had two wives, and two, including Chief Sqwameyuks (Scomiach), had three.[153] By 1891, according to the census, no man, Sqwameyuks included, had more than one wife.[154]

The missionaries' encouragement of new forms of social organization probably had even more impact than is indicated above. First, their religious sects offered the Lekwungen new ways to define themselves, separating from the households that, previously, had been the largest social unit. In adopting Methodism, Shee-at-ston set himself apart from the nominal Catholicism of the other Lekwungen; and in taking the temperance pledge, he set himself apart in terms of temporal activities. Thereafter, a new wedge separated the increasingly atomized Lekwungen households from one another. Second, the missionaries encouraged converts to build houses in the Euro-American style – houses that would hold only one conjugal family. The missionary Thomas Crosby reported with pride that, as soon as Shee-at-ston became a Christian, he "built himself a neat little house, and moved out of the old lodge with all its associations of heathenism." Amos, as Shee-at-ston was christened, was joined by his wife Sarah, and their home became the Methodist meeting place for fourteen of the Lekwungen who subsequently broke from Catholicism.[155]

Thomas Crosby preaching to an unidentified man in a staged photo by Hannah Maynard, ca. 1860s

Studies of the relationships between Aboriginal People and missionaries in British Columbia and elsewhere help to put Shee-at-ston's conversion into perspective. In the face of a rapidly changing world, one way that Aboriginal People could make a place for themselves and protect their economy was through seeking the assistance of missionaries. By offering a spiritual world attuned to the industrializing world around them, missionaries presented something appealing and useful to many Aboriginal People. Far from being a one-sided process, the conversion of Aboriginal People was like trade – a dialogue in which meaning was transformed.[156]

Through the 1870s and 1880s, Department of Indian Affairs (DIA) officials reported the Lekwungen erecting "modern" houses that held only one family, so that when Franz Boas visited the reserve in 1886, "only a few old houses [were] still inhabited. The Indians ha[d] built themselves others according to the European plan." A few "longhouses" were maintained as separate dance and potlatch houses.[157]

The nuclear family idealized by the missionaries was economically feasible in the altered circumstances of the 1880s in a way that it had not been before. Previously, a large household ensured the labour force necessary to harvest resources like camas and salmon, which were abundant but only for short periods. By the mid-1870s, a small household could earn enough at wage labour to purchase subsistence goods that were more and more difficult to get from the land. Abundant wage labour opportunities meant that even small families, with both parents and elder children working, could accumulate sufficient wealth to hold their own potlatch – something that would have previously required the combined effort of a large household.

Although Victoria's economy slowed through the 1870s as the impact of the gold rushes diminished, the mid- to late 1870s and early 1880s saw the opening of two new seasonal industries – salmon canning and hop farming – that, at first, seemed to offer an inexhaustible demand for aboriginal labour and, with it, opportunities for the economic independence of women as well as children and the elderly. The new canneries appropriated the gendered division of work already established in aboriginal societies: aboriginal men fished and aboriginal women mended nets and processed the catch. Older men worked alongside women mending nets. The infirm looked after the infants, while even young children could get work cleaning cans. In peak seasons, every available person would be brought in and infants would be placed in a corner where they could be watched. In this way, the canneries perpetuated a modified system of family-based production.[158]

By the 1880s some, if not most, Aboriginal People had relaxed the prohibitions against women handling fishing equipment, and some women fished with their husbands (the boats required a puller and a fisher). In 1883, the Indian Agent for the Fraser River records an aboriginal husband and wife fishing team (the wife pulling the boat and the husband handling the net) making $240 in fourteen days.[159]

Initially, the canneries hired more aboriginal men as fishers than they did women as processors, but by the 1890s competition from European and Asian fishers eroded the demand for aboriginal men, while demand

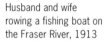

Husband and wife rowing a fishing boat on the Fraser River, 1913

for aboriginal women workers continued to grow into the twentieth century.[160] This high demand for female cannery labour was, in many cases, the main reason the men were employed as fishers. According to canner F.L. Lord, "The real reason that you want to have ... [cannery-owned boats] and get Indian fishermen is they bring their families around and you have Indian women and boys, and some of the men, not fishermen to work in the canneries."[161]

Family-based production was also the norm for the hop fields, which began demanding large amounts of labour in the late 1870s. Moreover, the hop picking season closely followed the canning season, allowing families to participate in both. "Indian women and children are always the most eager to go to the hop fields, where they always earn considerable sums of money," noted the Lekwungen agent. This wage economy paralleled the prestige economy. In contrast to subsistence production, in which Aboriginal People pooled their resources, in the wage economy the Indian Agent noted that, "among these Indians, the wife's purse is generally entirely separate from the husband's."[162]

When Johan Jacobsen first visited Victoria in 1881, he was surprised that "the streets of this town swarmed with Indians of all kinds." At the reserve he visited, "most of the young people had gone to the Fraser River to fish for the canneries." That year the Indian Agent for the Lekwungen was reporting that "the great bulk of these Indians are really well off this winter," and the following year he commented, "Indian labor is much in demand at higher wages than has ever before been paid."[163] Referring to the Lekwungen in the mid-1870s, a federal official, James Edgar, wrote, "he often has hoarded many hundreds of dollars of wealth in coin or kind, which he delights to gamble or give away ... he can easily make a round sum each year above his actual needs." Edgar concluded: "To imagine that a West Coast Indian is poor, is a great mistake."[164]

They Honour Hops as Their Grandparents, 1885-1970

The arrival of the first steam train on Canada's west coast on November 7, 1885, was not accompanied by any great celestial event; however, like the arrival of the steamship *Beaver* forty-two years earlier, it signalled a major change for the Lekwungen. The completion of the Canadian Pacific Railway was the start of a massive invasion of their wage economy by competing labourers. If this were not enough to make 1885 a notorious year, it was compounded by a new law, effective January 1, prohibiting potlatches.

The anti-potlatch regulations were the result of a strong lobby of missionaries, Indian Agents, and the first Indian superintendent, I.W. Powell, to the Department of Indian Affairs (DIA) in Ottawa. Powell considered

When we apply for work people tell us we do not pay taxes and so cannot get work, as all the public work is kept for the poor white men just now.

George Chictlan, Lekwungen, 1894

Although on account of the influx of labourers of all nationalities, and from other causes ... there has been a gradual falling off in the earnings of Indians for some years past.

A.W. Vowell, Indian Superintendent, 1903

Fie on the Tribes

At Steveston all the tribes were fishing.
I went there to invite them for immediate
response and I found that they were
going to make hops. "You are too late,
were are going to the hop (fields)," they
told me ... My heart was sore at having
failed to get the different tribes at
Victoria, the Saanitch, the Cowichan,
and the Hikwihltaath ...

"Fie on the tribes," said the chief, "I
wonder if hops are their grandparents,
since they consider them more
important [than their real] grandparents."

Sayach'apis, Nuu-chah-nulth, ca. 1888

Sayach'apis (Tom), ca. 1920s

that "potlatches, not only retard civilizing influences, but encourage idleness among the less worthy members of the tribe." Missionary Duncan,
who had worked among the Songhees and was considered, in the 1870s, to
have had the most success in "civilizing Indians," argued that "there [could]
be no progress in civilization" while potlatches were allowed to continue.
Another Protestant missionary working among the Lekwungen, Thomas
Crosby, concurred: "of the many evils of heathenism, with the exception of
witchcraft, the potlatch is the worst."[165]

The intent of the anti-potlatch law was to hasten the assimilation of
Aboriginal People by striking at the institution that held their society together. Crosby concluded that "the potlatch relates to all the life of the
people, such as giving of names, the raising into social position, their marriages, births, deaths." In banning the potlatch the government was, in
effect, banning the whole prestige economy as well as the hereditary ownership of the subsistence economy's key resource sites, which could only be
validated through potlatching.[166]

What the missionaries and government agents did not see was that,
for the Lekwungen, paid work and potlatching were complementary. The
Lekwungen, in large part, accumulated goods in the paid-labour economy
so that they could use them within the potlatch and the prestige economy.
Without the potlatch complex, there was little incentive in Lekwungen
culture to engage in paid work.

At first, both the Lekwungen and Victoria merchants resisted attempts
to enforce the anti-potlatch laws. Moreover, the initial legislation proved
to be unenforceable because "potlatch," like other Chinook jargon words,
had multiple meanings, including "gift" and "gift giving" as well as a "gift-
giving ritual."[167] Nonetheless, agents and missionaries continued to use the
threat of prosecution to suppress the potlatch as they lobbied the government to revise the law. In 1895, the law was strengthened to prohibit the
giving away of anything at a congregation of "Indians," (presumably including Christmas gifts) thereby forcing many of the potlatches underground, especially after a series of successful prosecutions was mounted
between 1907 and the 1920s.[168] Nonetheless, potlatches and dancing continued, more covertly, and in 1936 the minister responsible for Indian affairs introduced amendments that would have made accumulation of any
property that *might* be used for potlatching illegal. This latter amendment
was dropped in the face of public opposition, but it illustrates both an
ongoing aboriginal desire to accumulate goods and the department's frustration at not being able to stamp out this barrier to "civilization."[169]

The potlatch culture of the Lekwungen was coming under pressure
from a variety of sources. The reserve school that was operated on and off,

Field boss "Captain John" Swah-lis (centre, with bowler hat) and Soowahlie hop pickers, ca. 1895

first by Anglicans and then by Catholics, taught against the potlatch. The same message was preached at the services of other denominations. The increasing ability of individuals to sell their own labour power independent of the *siem* put pressure on the aboriginal system of authority and governance, and all around them was the example of a growing population that celebrated individual accumulation.

Another indication of a shift away from the primacy of the prestige economy may be seen in an account by Sayach'apis, a Nuu-chah-nulth who invited the Lekwungen to a potlatch in the mid-1880s. Sayach'apis called upon the nations of southern Vancouver Island to celebrate his daughter's maturation in the fall of the year. The Snuneymuxw [Nanaimo], Comox, the Tla-o-qui-aht [Clayoquot], the Ditidaht [Nitinat], and many others replied and attended. However, the Lekwungen, whom Sayach'apis's messengers found working at the canneries at the mouth of the Fraser River, along with the Makah, Wsanec, Cowichan, and some others, turned down the invitation. They told Sayach'apis that "he was too late." They were on their way to harvest hops in Washington State. In contrast to Robert Brown's experience twenty years earlier, when the Cowichan refused work to attend a potlatch, in the 1880s the Cowichan, Lekwungen and others declined the potlatch to go to work. Sayach'apis was distressed to see them all forsaking

Indians Were Then What John Chinamen Is Now

Indians performed all the manual labour – in fact were to that day [1860s] what John Chinamen is to this [1910s].

Edgar Fawcett, *Some Reminiscences of Old Victoria*, 1912

their obligations and the traditions of their grandparents, and he told them that they had "hops for grandparents," whom they honoured instead of their real ones.[170]

As important as the pressures on the potlatch were, the most immediate impact on the Lekwungen's economy came from the lay-off of Chinese labourers after railway construction hit its peak in 1883. When thousands of Chinese labourers hit the labour market at the same time, the wages paid to unskilled labour fell by 50 percent.[171] In the 1860s, "Chinese were almost as rare in Victoria as Turks," but by 1881 the census for Victoria showed 1,344 Chinese; and the 1891 census showed 2,080. An Indian Agent observed that even "the poor Indian women and old men, their boys and girls, [who] used to make considerable money every summer picking berries" had been "ruined [by] large numbers of Chinamen." In 1884, at the canneries, Aboriginal People found that "their places had been taken by Chinamen in cleaning and canning the fish." Around Victoria, many of the unemployed Chinese "of the poorer classes" were attempting to make a living by bootlegging liquor to the Lekwungen.[172]

The laid-off Chinese railway navvies were only one part of the massive wave of immigration that began to flow along the new railway line. Between the completion of the railway in 1885 and the census of 1891, some forty thousand people immigrated to British Columbia, more than doubling the non-aboriginal population, while the Lekwungen population continued to decline through to the 1930s as a result of an extraordinarily high death rate due primarily to disease.[173]

The sharp population declines in 1892-93, visible in Figure 4.1, are attributable to an influenza epidemic that not only caused "a high death rate" on its own but also contributed to the deaths of many of the young men already suffering from "lung disorders" as well as children previously afflicted with "mesenteric disease." Through the 1890s, the Indian Agent noted that "the young men between the ages of 16 and 30 seem particularly liable to lung disease" – in other words, tuberculosis. Influenza struck again in 1895 and was responsible for killing nearly one hundred Aboriginal People in the Cowichan Agency, and it probably accounts for the deaths of twenty Lekwungen. The 1888 measles epidemic, with its "high mortality," was brought back to Vancouver Island by aboriginal workers returning from the Washington State hop fields. Measles spread at the canneries in 1898, apparently accounting for most of the thirteen deaths among the Lekwungen that year.[174]

The 1891 census takers have left a clear snapshot of the Lekwungen population and economy as it was when Victoria was at the tail-end of a

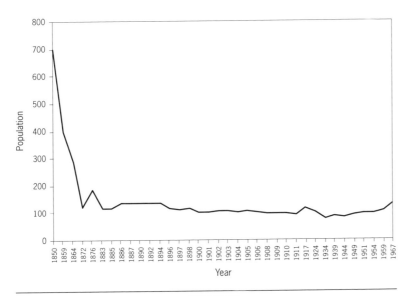

FIGURE 4.1 Songhees band population, 1850-1967

Sources: **Estimates for 1858:** Captain Wilson, "Report on the Indian Tribes Inhabiting the Country in the Vicinity of the 49th Parallel of North Latitude," *Transactions of the Ethnological Society of London* (new series) 14 (1866): 278. Wilson says the estimate was made in 1858-59, "since which time the native population has greatly decreased." **1864:** "Report of the Commissioners of Indian Reserve at Victoria," May 27, 1864, BCA, CO 305/23 10589; **1872:** LAC, RG 10, vol. 11213, file 1; **1876:** LAC, RG 10, vol. 11213, file 1; **1883-1959:** Department of Indian Affairs Annual Reports; **1967:** Capital Region Planning Board of BC, *Indian Communities and Land Use Planning* (Victoria: Capital Region, 1968), appendix 1.

railroad-induced economic boom.[175] Of the forty-seven Lekwungen men between the ages of fifteen and sixty-five who were enumerated in 1891, all but seven have their occupations listed. Six of the seven with no occupations were young men in their teens or early twenties. Of the fifty-one Lekwungen women between the ages of fifteen and sixty-five, only ten have their occupations listed. The occupations listed and the numbers employed are seen in Table 4.1.

The census provides a snapshot of paid work but suggests more permanence than the economy actually provided. The enumerator listed only one occupation per person, but we know from oral accounts and other evidence that only those in skilled trades (like the baker) and professions (like the police officer) had a single job all year. Fishing, farming, sealing, and gardening were all seasonal work, and sawmill and longshoring work was volatile, depending as it did on the business cycle. The work in the other seasons, such as the autumn migration to the hop fields (which involved most of the Lekwungen not permanently employed) or cannery labour (which probably employed most of the women during the late summer), is not hinted at in the census.

TABLE 4.1

Lekwungen occupations for men and women (aged 15-65), 1891

Men		Women	
Fisherman	12	Charwoman	9
Sawmill hand	10	Washerwoman	1
Sealer	3	No occupation	41
Carpenter	3		
Longshoreman	3		
Farmhand*	3		
Policeman	1		
Baker	1		
General labourer	1		
Soap factory	1		
Messenger boy	1		
Gardener	1		
No occupation	7		
Total	47	Total	51

* In the Annual Report of the BC Department of Agriculture for 1891, the local correspondent, J.W. Tolmie, remarked that around Victoria experienced farmhands were scarce, wages were high, and "natives seldom condescend to work on farms" (*BC Sessional Papers*, 1891, 795).
Source: Census of Canada, 1891.

When the worldwide depression of the early 1890s hit Victoria and combined with the influx of white and Asian labour, the new order became visible. Indian Superintendent Vowell remarked in 1892 that, owing to the depression, "combined with the increase of white labour, the native cannot now so readily obtain work or get as high wages as they did in former years." Lekwungen Joe Etienne told the agent at an 1894 band meeting: "Times have been very bad in Victoria and nearly all of us who used to get work in the town cannot now get a day's work." The Indian Agent's own observations confirmed the Lekwungen's gloomy reports. In 1894, according to the Cowichan Indian Agent, "The depression in trade has affected all the bands to a greater or less degree ... Employment in the saw-mills, coal-mines and municipal works has been closed to them, and their employment on farms has also been limited."[176]

The Indian superintendent described the situation in 1901:

Every year, as time advances, proves that the days when Indians had, to all intents and purposes, a monopoly of the work to be done each season at the canneries and hop fields are rapidly disappearing. These sources of employment, at which large earnings are gathered in by the Indians (men and women), are being gradually closed against them owing to the advent of peoples of all

Chinese and Whites Take Their Places

A few years ago most of the [Songhees] men ... found employment in the saw-mills, on steamers and along the wharves, but the Chinese sawmill hands and the white longshoreman have taken their places. Now they make a living by fishing and doing odd jobs.

Victoria Colonist, December 20, 1898

nationalities, who flock into the country seeking such employment periodically. The most formidable rivals that the Indians have to contend with, numerically, are the Chinese and the Japanese. The former have been co-labourers
in the canneries for years, and did not so very much interfere with the natives
as they found employment chiefly within the canneries, whilst the latter, who
have of late been entering the country in hordes, and who compete with the
Indians as fishermen are reducing the earnings by over-competition, etc, to
such an extent as to make it no longer a source of profit to the Indians, the
latter having to travel distances from their homes and to meet considerable
expenses attendant thereupon.[177]

Aboriginal People were being partly or wholly replaced with white or
Asian labour in the industries in which they had earlier comprised the
largest component of the labour force. In examining the main employers,
one by one, the Indian Agents observed: "The employment of oriental
labour has displaced the Indians in certain lines such as farm work, cutting
of cord wood," and as domestics, launderers, and charworkers. Cannery
and agricultural jobs were also under assault by immigrant competitors:
"The earnings of the Indians at the canneries, hop fields and other pursuits, have not been as great as in the past: the competition in the labour
market continues to be greater each year." Even in the fishery at the mouth
of the Fraser River, where aboriginal men had dominated as late as 1891-94,
by 1901-4 they were the smallest ethnic group of fishers.[178]

In the long run, even more significant than losing part of their seasonal occupations and part-time work to low-wage Asian labour, was the
loss of more permanent jobs to white labour:

> Less than a score of years ago many Indians along the sea-coast of the prov-
> ince found profitable employment working as deck-hands, and at other
> such labour on the passenger and freight steamers plying to and fro; of late
> years however, white labour has almost wholly supplanted that previously
> employed.[179]

Even on the docks, where they had always found work, "now white
men are being hired first." Taken together, the agents' and newspaper reports suggest a steady decline in the economic condition of the Lekwungen
after 1890. In 1897, sixteen years after his appointment as Indian Agent,
Lomas described the Lekwungen as in "the poorest condition ever."[180] A
temporary shortage of white labour in 1899 and 1900 meant better years
for the Lekwungen, but by 1902 the Indian affairs officials were back to

Never Again Make as Much

They cannot now, or ever again, expect
to make as much money as formerly
when they were about the only people
available to carry on the limited
industries of the country.

A.W. Vowell, Indian Superintendent, 1902

what had become a familiar theme in the reports: "Whitemen, Chinamen and Japanese and others, are daily increasing in the province and are, naturally, doing much of the work that fell to Indians in the past."[181]

After a decade of declining employment, there was a considerable improvement in the Lekwungen's paid-work possibilities. Things picked up in 1905, when J.H. Todd and Sons established the Empire Cannery on the nearby Esquimalt Indian Reserve. For the Lekwungen, work at the Empire Cannery was close to home and, though it was seasonal, it was reasonably dependable. For the employers, the Lekwungen provided a local labour force, and they adapted one of the Lekwungen's long-standing forms of labour organization. While publicly announcing a "whites only" hiring policy, the Empire Cannery employed Lekwungen chief, Michael Cooper "to secure labour and to look after the Indian Help." Cooper's role as labour broker, or "Indian boss," continued through to 1933, when he wrote to the DIA: "I look after employment of Indians at Empire Cannery, see that they receive employment and proper pay and living conditions."

The *siem*'s role in managing the labour of his group may have diminished, but it had not disappeared. Cooper was also appointed supervisor of the crew for DIA road work on the reserve.[182] As intermediary between the white economy and the prestige economy, Cooper's experience was common to many high-status "Indian bosses" and recruiters, particularly at the canneries and hop fields, which required a guaranteed number of workers for a specified season.[183]

In his different roles, Chief Cooper symbolized both continuity and adaptation. Although he was a chief, and *siem*/chiefs were the customary organizers of labour among the Lekwungen, he did not inherit his right to be head of a family group. In 1896, Cooper became the first Lekwungen chief to be elected according to the Indian Act, which only recognized one "chief" in a band, though there had been several *siem*. Mary Kamia, granddaughter of Cooper's predecessor, hereditary Chief Sqwameyuks (Scomiach), suggested that Cooper was elected for his ability to serve as intermediary between the Lekwungen and the non-aboriginal community: Cooper's mother was Lekwungen, while his father was a British soldier stationed on San Juan Island in 1864, near where the Lekwungen conducted their reef netting. According to Kamia, Cooper was elected over his competitors, both of whom were high-born "hereditary" leaders, because "Willie and James didn't no [sic] how to talk English very well."[184]

The Indian Agent was happy with Cooper's election, reporting that he "has always been a steady, sober and industrious man," even though, he added, it was rumoured that he had "white blood in his veins." It would appear that industriousness and the ability to serve as a mediator between

Songhees Are Eminently Satisfied

Nothing but praise of the men who brought about the settlement is to be heard from the Indians, who describe the arrangement as a:

Delate cloosh hoy-hoy kina mox Boston-man pi Songhees [Chinook jargon meaning "very happy with the agreement].

Victoria Colonist, November 6, 1910

the Lekwungen and non-Aboriginal People, rather than high birth, made Cooper a chief to the majority of the Lekwungen. With the exception of an interval between 1916 and 1922, he remained the elected chief until his death in 1935.[185]

In its early years of operation, the cannery required about one hundred employees for a two-month season, many more than the Lekwungen could supply. So aboriginal women from all over southern Vancouver Island were recruited. In its first season the cannery manager wrote the Cowichan Indian Agent, asking him to send

> 10, 15, or 20 more Indian women or grown up girls who would assist in washing fish, filling cans etc. You know that the Empire Cannery at Esquimalt is a very desirable spot for them as they can come down by rail, there is good camping ground at the reserve and good water etc. Please advise if you could pick up this quantity for us around Duncans or Somenos etc at short notice ... The Empire Cannery is very busy and we have a general shortage of labour.[186]

Labour shortages in the canning industry continued through to 1909, when "large numbers of Indians coming from the west coast and other places" came to work at the Empire Cannery, and then became more general between 1907 and 1913 as Victoria's economy experienced a boom the likes of which had not been seen since the gold rush.[187]

Songhees Chief Michael Cooper and Premier Richard McBride at the ceremony to transfer the Songhees Reserve

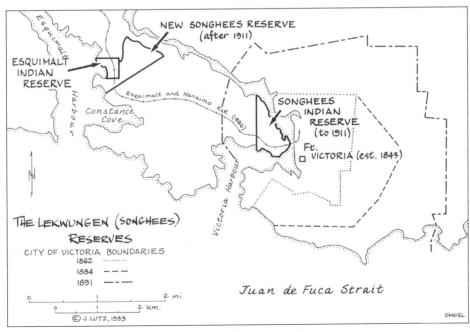

MAP 4.3 Lekwungen (Songhees) reserves and City of Victoria boundaries

Coinciding with the boom, the Lekwungen agreed to exchange their inner-city reserve for a suburban one adjacent to the Esquimalt reserve (see Map 4.3). For fifty years, the Lekwungen had resisted all the offers and threats used to relocate them from the heart of the city. For his first fifteen years as chief, Cooper's major preoccupation was the pressure from the City of Victoria, the province, and the Department of Indian Affairs to relocate. Finally, in 1911, he negotiated, on terms agreeable to the majority of the band, the exchange of the city-centre reserve. Although the negotiations for the move were conducted in English, this land transfer was explained to the band members in Chinook jargon. Ironically, the new reserve had formerly been the Puget Sound Agricultural Company's Craigflower Farm, which the Lekwungen had cleared as one of their first jobs in the wage economy.[188]

The relocation suddenly placed the Lekwungen among the richest Aboriginal People in the country. As part of the settlement, the forty-one heads of families received $10,000 in cash, plus the value of their "improvements," including houses, barns, stables, fences, and fruit trees. In 2008 dollars this was more than $230,000. Chief Cooper, it was later revealed, was paid an additional $28,000 (in today's terms, half a million dollars) for his assistance in negotiating the deal. The Lekwungen insisted that the money be paid to them directly, not, as was required by the Indian Act, held in trust for them by the DIA. This condition of sale was so extraordinary that it required the federal government to pass a special piece of legislation.[189]

Two years later, Indian Superintendent Ditchburn was asked by the DIA to account for how the Lekwungen had spent their nearly half-million dollars (approximately $8.5 million in 2008 dollars). The nature of the request and the response both suggest the racialization of Aboriginal People within the DIA. After collecting their receipts, examining their bank accounts, and interviewing individuals, Ditchburn concluded that, although a few had "squandered their money," overall, "the Songhees ... have done as well, if not better, with their money than the same number of white people, in a much higher stage of civilization, would have done."[190] Of the total money received in 1911, 19 percent remained as cash on hand. About 40 percent of the total could be accounted for in the value of assets purchased: mainly houses, furniture, horses, buggies, implements, and stock. Another 19 percent was invested in interest-bearing deposits, loans, or real estate. The remaining 22 percent had been spent or given to relatives.

While Ditchburn was examining the personal finances of the Lekwungen, the McKenna McBride Royal Commission on Indian Land Claims was conducting its own hearings in Victoria. The commissioners concluded that the Lekwungen were generally "prosperous, virtually all have money in the bank and good homes well furnished." Of the Chatham and Discovery Island bands of the Lekwungen, they wrote: "Fishing, sheep raising and working for wages etc, also weaving sweaters, and selling seaweed to Chinese" were their sources of income, and in all they, too, were "comfortable and prosperous."[191]

The commission mentioned sweater making as one of the principal sources of income for the Lekwungen. Sometime prior to 1872, aboriginal women adapted their long-standing knowledge of spinning wool and weaving decorative blankets to the preparing of knitted woollen items, having learned knitting from the newcomers. The Lekwungen may have been the first to knit what came to be called "Cowichan sweaters" and this cottage industry later grew into a major source of income for women.[192]

With the new capital provided by the reserve settlement, several of the Lekwungen moved into entrepreneurial endeavours. Charlie Gunion and Johnny Gabriel started stores on the reserve, and Robbie David started a chicken farm. Austin Albany, the butcher, established his own shop – which, according to the agent, failed by 1913 "owing to keen competition and giving too much credit." Several of the men bought express wagons and teams of horses, yet, despite the influx of cash, most of the Lekwungen continued their work as usual. In his 1913 report, the agent confirmed the general prosperity of the Lekwungen as well as of the other Aboriginal People in the agency: "On the whole they have all done much better during the past year than in any previous year, as times have been good and all classes of unskilled labour have been in great demand. Any Indian who was desirous of obtaining employment could easily have his wants fulfilled at good wages."[193]

The same year, however, the federal fisheries department introduced new salmon fishing regulations, making it more difficult for Aboriginal People to make a living from fishing. The new rules prohibited "Indians" from obtaining "independent" fishing licences, a privilege only allowed to whites. Non-whites who wanted to fish had to do so under a limited number of less lucrative special "cannery licences" controlled by the canneries.[194]

The fishing regulations and the next depression, which swept the country in 1914, affected the Lekwungen pool of unskilled labour severely. In his report for that year, the Indian superintendent for British Columbia reported: "the principal sources of income of these Indians are hunting, fishing, working at canneries, hop-picking, stevedoring, boat and canoe building and general day labour." But, he added, "the amount of revenue obtained from the last named source was not as great as has been the case for some years as the period of depression affected the Indians in this respect to

Old People Want Muckamuck

Old Dick from Discovery Island and Joe Thaselock from the same place came to my office wanting "muckamuck." Dick or Joe has a paralyzed arm. Will await your responses. They say they have not had an order for 3 months.

W.E. Ditchburn to the Secretary of the Department of Indian Affairs, February 16, 1911

quite an extent."[195] The DIA attributed the general inability of Aboriginal People to get employment outside the resource industries to widespread racism: "When applying for work outside of the reserve he is often refused because white men are as a rule unwilling to work alongside of Indians."[196]

The pattern was increasingly obvious. In times of depression and labour surplus, Aboriginal People were excluded from employment on the basis of being "Indian," with all its racialized associations, and left to fend for themselves through their subsistence economy or through relief from the state. In times of labour shortage they were welcomed back into the workforce. The Lekwungen, and Aboriginal People in British Columbia in general, were being placed in a functional role that Karl Marx referred to as the "reserve army of the unemployed." Only in this case, "reserve" had a double meaning.[197]

By 1917, the expansion of war industries turned a labour surplus into a shortage, and Aboriginal People were again drawn into the labour force. "The past year has been one of great prosperity for the Indians of southwestern British Columbia," according to Indian affairs officials, due to "the extraordinary high prices paid for all kinds of fish, and the great scarcity of unskilled labour. Never in the history of the province have such high prices been paid for fish as in the past year. Even the poorer variety, known as dog salmon, sold for as high as 67 cents each. On the west coast some Indians are known to have earned as much as $1,000 in a single week."[198]

The following year the DIA's annual report stated: "The prevailing wage paid for farm labourers and for work in the saw mills and logging camps was higher than at any time previous ... In the lumbering industry wages were exceptionally high and Indians engaged in that work earned from five to eight dollars per day."[199]

Through the good times, and the not-so-good, and despite legal prohibitions, many Lekwungen continued to hold and attend potlatches. The agent's diary shows the Lekwungen potlatching in 1898, and the newspaper reports a winter dance initiation that year. The *British Colonist* reported Lekwungen Thomas George's potlatch in January 1901, and compared its three hundred guests favourably to Willie Jack's potlatch of the year prior "even though the expense was not as great." The Lekwungen attended other local potlatches in 1903, 1906, and 1907. Lekwungen Ida Jackson's family hosted a memorial potlatch for her in 1908.[200]

Although the potlatch persisted through this era, it was also transformed. Sometime between the first prohibition in 1885 and the 1920s, perhaps to avoid persecution, its name was changed. Events previously associated with "potlatches" began to be performed under the auspices of the other main Salish winter ceremonial, the "spirit dance," or simply the "winter dance." Instead of a four- or five-day potlatch, a winter dance could take place over the course of one night. Whereas previously, thousands of dollars were redistributed to thousands of guests, after the turn of the century only hundreds of dollars were given, and this at much smaller gatherings. The smaller potlatches were, perhaps, a reflection of the Lekwungen's diminished economic circumstances, the prohibitions against the potlatch, and a new preoccupation with personal accumulation through paid work. Still, dance or potlatch, the "main work" of giving gifts remained for all the old reasons – except one. The main economic incentive for the potlatch, the need to pass on the rights to valuable resource sites, diminished as the sites were lost to urbanization and new state regulations, which appropriated control over hunting and fishing. Hereditary names continued to be passed down, but the focus had shifted to spiritual accomplishments and the winter dance.[201]

Potlatching and winter dancing were still important enough that, in 1911, nine of the forty-one family heads who had received the $10,000 cash settlement as part of the relocation package, built two houses each, one for living in and one, at a cost of between $500 and $1000 each, for potlatches and spirit dances. According to Suttles' informants, after 1911 there was a "glorious potlatch" where "the greater part" of the cash distribution was spent. Although "greater part" is certainly an exaggeration, Peter George described how one family, wanting to commemorate a member lost at sea

We Let the White People Have Theirs ... We Expect to Have Ours

We like the white people want to have some fun. We know they have their dances – they have their celebrations during which lots of money is spent ... Therefore we humbly petition the government not to interfere with our celebrations – we let the white people have theirs therefore we expect to have ours. We are oppressed from all sides we never have any satisfaction given to our many petitions sent in – We notice that all times the white people are listened to but we seem forgotten. Now our patience is coming to an end.

Cowichan Chiefs, to Superintendent of Indian Affairs, 1914

Cowichan chiefs at a potlatch in Duncan, 1899

on a commercial sealing trip, threw coins by the handful along the muddy shore; another threw silver coins into the crowd "like a man sowing grain."[202] This may be the same event described in the *Vancouver Sun*:

> [Lekwungen] Willie Jack, on this great occasion filled his plug hat with silver half dollars and walked proudly around between two rows of his admiring tribesmen. To each one he handed a shining new half dollar. This has remained the record for generous giving ever since ... Other gifts in the shape of canoes, blankets, and many things were distributed besides by this generous chieftain, who added to his reputation for generosity.[203]

In the face of strong resistance from Aboriginal People and some vocal opposition from the public, from 1884 to 1914 the DIA was reluctant to prosecute potlatchers.[204] The Lekwungen's Indian Agent generally turned a blind eye to the events until a 1914 potlatch at Cowichan, after which Agent Robertson announced that there were to be no more. This prompted southern Vancouver Island chiefs and councillors, Michael Cooper and William Roberts of the Lekwungen among them, to send a letter of protest to Ottawa.

The protest pointed out that those who participated in the potlatch at Cowichan were well-off and well-equipped with lands and houses as well as stock and other property. The government had "put a stop to their catching fish or hunting game on their lands and they desire[d] to know what [would] be the next step to limit their liberties."[205]

Mr. W.E. Ditchburn of the DIA responded that, although the department had been endeavouring to use moral suasion to end potlatching, "of late years this practice had been increasing among some tribes. There had been a tremendous waste of money, which the Indians should have saved and used in developing their holdings. The physical and moral effect of such celebrations had been shown beyond a doubt to be pernicious. The practice had a degrading influence, which among some tribes had proved a serious matter." Statistics showed, according to Ditchburn, "that, in the past twenty years, among those tribes in which the practice of holding potlatches had been most prevalent, the Indian population had seriously declined. While this might not be wholly due to the practice, it was certain that it was to a great extent the outcome of the custom."[206]

Despite government admonition and pressure, the prestige economy continued. In August 1916, the *Vancouver Sun* reported: "When the Indian families come down from their reservation villages to work in the salmon canneries of the Fraser River they look forward to the potlatches which will take place when they return home with the money they have earned."[207]

During the First World War, the DIA resituated its argument around resources required for the war effort and the "wasteful" nature of potlatches. In 1918, the Indian Act was amended to enable agents to try potlatchers without a judge. Staff members were instructed to "carefully observe the movements of your Indians and check any tendency in the direction of preparing for one of these ceremonies."[208] In 1921, after Agent W.R. Robertson tried but failed to keep the Lekwungen from a potlatch in Cowichan, charges were laid against the principals.[209]

There are a few indications that the 1920s were reasonably prosperous years for the Lekwungen. One is that little relief was given out by the agent. Several references in the correspondence remark that, in the summer, "most of the people" were away working. For women, a variety of work was available. Some worked at the Empire Cannery in season, Mrs. Hutty Dick worked at the Cold Storage Plant at Ogden Point, and Mrs. Andrew Tom and her daughters worked at the herring reduction works at Cowichan Gap. Jimmie Freezie, one of the Lekwungen migrants, wrote Agent Lomas in 1923: "I left Victoria in July to pick berries and worked for four months at Puyalup and made so much money I bought a car that cost $225." Unfortunately, he lent the car to his boss, who wrecked it in a traffic mishap. Various indications suggest a continuation of the pattern of seasonal work in the canneries and hop or berry fields as well as occasional work longshoring. The men also benefited from occasional on-reserve public works, paid for by the DIA.[210] Only one Lekwungen, Louie Kamia, held down a skilled position: "I am employed in Victoria City as a baker," he said in 1919. In order to be close to his work, he purchased a house in the city with his share of the reserve settlement. Even if their current income did not sustain them, based on an examination of their estates, most families still had something of their cash settlement to fall back on.[211]

The Great Depression, like the 1892 and 1914 depressions, hit the Lekwungen harder than it did their non-aboriginal neighbours. Four years into the Depression, when the average Canadian income from wages and salaries was 61 percent of its 1929 level, the average for registered Indians was down to 37 percent of the 1929 level. In explaining this, the DIA pointed to racism: "The Indian was the first to be thrown out of work when the depression started and evidently will be the last to be again absorbed when the conditions improve."[212]

By 1932, the Indian Agent was getting an unprecedented number of letters asking for help: "We have nothing to eat. I will ask your assistance please for supplies, for food for my family is necessary I could not get anny [sic] work no where." One man, Charles, wrote that he needed food "for I have no work to do, the cannery is working but I can't get in to[o] many workers so please."[213] By January 1933, Frank George wrote, "I'm the only one on the reserve that is not getting any relief which I need as much as the rest."[214]

Despite the lack of work, potlatching continued, though secretly, in the repressive climate that had developed after the First World War. References to potlatches/dances only occur on those infrequent occasions when the agent and police found out about them, such as in February, 1933. According to police informants, Chief Cooper himself distributed money and otherwise took "a very prominent part" in a dance-potlatch ceremony at the Cole Bay Reserve in Saanich, attended by over eight hundred Aboriginal People. When the police reported this to the Indian Agent, Cooper's thirty-dollar-per-month chief's allowance was permanently cut off.[215] A decade later, another police report documents an "Indian dance" on the Lekwungen reserve, attended by 350 people from the reserves south of Nanaimo, in which an unspecified amount of money was given away.[216]

Relief payments were paid to Indians in kind to a value of four dollars per month, less than one-quarter of the $16.50 non-Indians were getting from the province and municipalities.[217] The agents, aware of the inadequate relief rates, encouraged Aboriginal People to return to subsistence activities or home-manufactures as supplements. The importance of this non-wage income was highlighted by Dora Ross, a non-aboriginal woman

The Charlie family (Cowichan) knitting sweaters in a 1946 BC government photo

who acquired the legal status of Indian upon marriage to an Indian man: "I can't possibly make out on the $4.00 [per month] grocery order and I can't get any other help as I live on the Reserve. The Indians here might make it do but they can do other jobs, also make sweaters etc ... I have no means of adding anything to the allowance."[218]

Women's home production, a consistent supplement to employment income since the establishment of the cash economy, took on primary importance in the Depression.[219] Sweaters were traded to storekeepers for food, until supply outstripped demand. Susan Cooper wrote the Indian Agent in March 1933: "I owe a great deal to the store which I will pay by making sweaters[,] but the store keeper will not let me trade with sweaters for groceries any more after I pay him all because he has to[o] many sweaters on hand right now so that is why I am asking you for some groceries." Later in the year, Elsie Kamia wrote the agent: "I understand you are buying Indian sweaters I have one made – the stores in town offer small money for them so I wondered if you could help us – many women in this reserve make them." According to one knitter, a sweater in 1935 could bring in as much as $4.50; with wool costing only three cents a pound, the net payment to the knitter would have been close to the four-dollar monthly grocery order available through relief.[220]

Knitting fit well with the other elements of the aboriginal economy because it could be done in the evenings and when there was little other work. It also allowed parents, particularly women, to work at home and provide their own child care, and it was an enterprise in which most of the family could contribute. In recalling the early 1930s, one knitter from southern Vancouver Island said: "I was eight years old when I started knitting with my mother. Our dad went fishing once in awhile but it was seasonal. My dad used to card the wool, my mom would spin and knit." Another knitter, interviewed by Sylvia Olsen, recalled learning to knit from her mother before she was a teen: "We were like contractors – we knit sleeves for mom – but we never got paid for it."[221]

Another means of supplementing relief was clamming, for food and for sale, but this required transportation. "Everybody is digging clams except me," wrote Robbie Davis in 1934, "I have no boat or canoe." As a result, "I wish you would give me relieve [sic] for it is about three weeks from the time I did went out of grocery ... please hurry."[222]

Hop picking continued throughout the 1930s, but wages were so low that, in 1932, many who went south did not even make enough to pay for their passage home and so were stranded. Still, in 1933, the Inspector of Indian Agencies, who had previously tried to dissuade Indians from this annual migration, wished them well: "Unfortunately there is nothing else

Suffering from Want of the Necessaries of Life

We would point out that no member of the Tribe at the present time, with the exception of one man, is employed and that one man is only engaged in part-time employment. Owing to the conditions prevailing with regard to employment generally, it is impossible for any of the members of the band to obtain employment. In consequence members of the Band and members of their families are suffering from want of the necessaries of life.

Memorial of the Songhees Band, 1935

for them in the way of employment in BC, with the exception of those who may get work in the canneries."[223] Berry picking, locally and in Washington State, took some Aboriginal People off the relief rolls in the summer, but they were back on in the fall.[224]

By 1935, band members were forced to write a memorial to the agent asking for an immediate distribution from the Lekwungen band trust account. The Esquimalt band took the extraordinary step of consulting a law firm to force the DIA to make an interest distribution from band funds.[225] The records do not indicate whether a distribution was made, but the department continued to issue its four dollars per month to virtually every family in the band.

By this time, the main focus of Chief Cooper's liaison work between the Lekwungen and the DIA related to matters affecting the welfare of the band and the provision of relief to the indigent. "Apart from my duties as Chief of the Songhees," Cooper wrote, he was "frequently called upon not only by Chiefs of other bands from various parts of this Island, but also from members of the Tribes for advice on matters affecting themselves personally and sometimes effecting [sic] the welfare of the Tribe." Cooper wrote the agent, saying that he gave his time and services freely "because, in the first place they have no other Indian adviser than myself, and in the second place it is very difficult and sometimes it is expense prevents them from going to call on you personally and as your time is very much taken up with the Tribes under your jurisdiction I am frequently called to act and do things for them, which, under ordinary circumstances, would be performed by yourself."[226]

In some cases, the agent asked for Cooper's advice as to whether an individual needed relief, while in others cases, Cooper initiated measures to get relief to elderly and/or destitute Lekwungen. In recognition of the value of his role as intermediary, the DIA put Cooper on salary until his potlatch participation was noted.[227] After Cooper's death in January 1936, his successors did not assume his role as labour broker for the cannery, nor were they salaried; however, they did carry on the ambiguous role of cultural/economic mediator between the Lekwungen and state via the Indian Agent (this revolving largely around welfare).[228]

Judging by what the Lekwungen owned at death, the Depression had wiped out whatever was left of the liquid assets from the 1911 settlement. Of the thirteen band members who died between 1929 and 1958, and for whom the estate records survive, none left more than $300 worth of assets, over and above their house and lot on the reserve; most left barely enough to pay for their funerals, and several did not have that.[229]

There was some optimism in the DIA's annual report for 1937: "The re-employment of Indians in industrial activities showed some improvement." However, it candidly pointed out, "preference largely continues to be given to unemployed whites."[230] The work situation started to change with the beginning of the Second World War in 1939; by 1940 the relief list was down to twelve, and in 1943 it was down to four "old widows and invalids," according to the new Lekwungen chief Percy Ross. Lekwungen men were all employed by 1942-43, many of them by the local shipyards, which were trying to meet the wartime ship-building demand.[231]

Aboriginal worker, Inverness Cannery, Skeena River, 1947

The war also increased the value of Lekwungen land for leasing and brought applications from "Oriental" market gardeners for unused reserve acreage. While the local agent wished to accept these applications, particularly for aged Indians who would otherwise be on relief, D.M. McKay, the Indian commissioner for British Columbia, requested that "he discourage the leasing of Indian lands to Orientals as much as possible." After much correspondence, the head office of the DIA overruled the BC commissioner's wishes and allowed the leases.[232]

Expanded wartime demand and the government's removal of Japanese-Canadians from coastal areas combined to increase the requirement for Lekwungen labour in the fishing and canning industries. In 1944, the Empire Cannery near the Lekwungen Reserve added four herring canning lines to its three salmon lines, more than doubling its labour force and expanding the work season from the two summer months to include the four fall months. The annual payroll at the Empire Cannery jumped tenfold from its 1941-43 levels to $59,250 in 1944.[233]

From 1944 to the cannery's closure in 1951, the cannery employed fifteen to twenty aboriginal women through July and August on the salmon lines and forty to eighty aboriginal women from September to December on the herring lines. The expanded demand drew aboriginal women from all over the south island as well as a few elderly Lekwungen men.[234] The men who continued to fish made good incomes owing to high prices and the absence of competition from ethnic Japanese.[235]

A couple of Lekwungen men enlisted in the military early in the war, and a few others were drafted later on, making a total of six who did military service.[236] Compared to a four-dollar monthly relief cheque, the pay of an enlisted man looked pretty good. Mrs. Frank and Mrs. Dick received between eighty-five dollars and ninety-three dollars per month, which included a portion of their husband's pay plus a wife's and child's allowance.[237]

The Second World War drew women and children back into the workforce, just as the First World War had done a generation before. The

Indian Agent's report for 1946 noted that "women and elderly people, as well as the older children worked in the canneries and berry and hop fields, both in British Columbia and the State of Washington ... Conditions were good and work plentiful for Indians of all ages." Berry pickers earned an unprecedented eighty-five cents an hour, and the hop companies paid pickers five cents a pound. "Crops were good and the returns to the Indians were most satisfactory," reported the agent. Even knitting sweaters became dramatically more profitable during the war, as prices leapt from $4.50 in 1935 to $25 to $40 per sweater in 1943.[238]

Although the Lekwungen economy was strong during the war, several factors came together in the immediate postwar period to once again re-shape the Lekwungen economy. First, the return of demobilized soldiers and ethnic Japanese (who were released from the detention camps) allevi-ated the wartime labour shortage. Second, and even more important in the long run, was an overall slackening in the demand for low-skill seasonal labour, which, since the depression of the 1890s, had been the mainstay of the Lekwungen economy. In the meantime, the ongoing process of limit-ing access to subsistence food resources meant that the alternative econ-omy was less and less viable. Finally, the state began a dramatic expansion of welfare payments to Aboriginal People.[239]

In 1945, family allowance payments were extended to all Canadians. The new injection of cash income was particularly important to aboriginal communities, given that the allowance came year-round regardless of weather, strikes, or other factors that often limited seasonal employment. There was a catch, however. The $5.94 per child per month was conditional on school-age children regularly attending school for the ten months that it was in session. Family allowance was withheld for any child not in at-tendance all month, and the July and August cheques were not issued if children were not in school all of June and all of September. Moreover, families were not technically eligible while working in the United States. Accepting family allowance meant that school-age children could no longer accompany their parents in their work rounds and, for most of the year, could no longer contribute directly to the family economy.[240]

Indian Agents were positively gleeful about this additional tool that they could now use to put a stop to "the Indian wandering habits." Accord-ing to the agents: "A marked improvement in school attendance and enrolments stems in part from the emphasis on education in the Family Allowances legislation." School attendance increased 35 percent in 1946, following the introduction of family allowances the year before.[241]

While more children stayed behind to attend school, the family allow-ance policy did not initially deter many Aboriginal People from taking

advantage of the exceptionally high wages being paid to hop pickers as the booming Washington economy produced its own labour shortages.[242] At its postwar peak in 1949, the hop and berry yards of Washington State drew nine hundred people from the Cowichan Agency alone, over one-third of the agency's population, from June to September inclusive. Thereafter, the numbers dwindled until 1957, when none of the Lekwungen, and none of the people from the Cowichan Agency, made the trip. The introduction of mechanical hop pickers and the northward migration of Filipino and Mexican farm workers into the American Pacific Northwest reduced the demand for aboriginal labour.[243]

The Empire Cannery operated its herring line for the last time in 1951; it then closed its salmon line in 1952 and shut down completely. Like so many other canneries on the coast, the Empire Cannery fell victim to financial consolidation and technological change. Improved refrigeration techniques meant fish harvested at the firm's traps in Sooke could be transported to a cannery on the Fraser River and processed more cheaply there than at a separate cannery in Esquimalt. With its closing, Lekwungen women, in particular, lost their most regular source of employment. In 1953, only twenty-six Indians in the entire Cowichan agency found work in fish processing, and most of these went to herring packing and salting plants on the Gulf Islands rather than to their major historical employers, the salmon canneries.[244] That year, the federal and provincial governments extended old age security allowances to Indians. Four Lekwungen over the age of seventy were eligible for the forty-dollar-per-month payment.[245]

While the number of cannery jobs was shrinking, aboriginal fishers were also under increasing pressure. The Cowichan Indian Agent (now called superintendent) remarked in 1954 that, "With the return of numerous Japanese fishermen to the Pacific Coast, Indians are again finding it difficult to negotiate contracts with the fish canners who prefer to deal with the Japanese because of their dependability in paying accounts. Poor fishing conditions last year also resulted in the majority of Indian fishermen being financially 'broke' during the winter months." With the closure of work opportunities and the opening of social welfare programs to Aboriginal People, the importance of the wage economy fell relative to an increasingly robust welfare economy. In his December quarterly report for 1955, the Cowichan Indian Agent noted that "requests for relief assistance have been unusually heavy ... Fortunately ... the Indian women of this agency derive a very considerable income from knitting sweaters."[246]

By the time unemployment insurance benefits were extended to the fishing industry in 1958, the superintendent reported that there was only one Lekwungen left fishing, and, as he fished only part-time, he was ineligible. In that year, the agent conducted a rough employment review and found that the majority of Lekwungen men earned their living in unskilled intermittent jobs "in neighbouring booming grounds and sawmills, and in various jobs in Victoria such as contracting, coalyards, etc." Their neighbours, the Esquimalt, were benefiting from the harbourfront location of their reserve: "Most derive their livelihood from leases on the Reserve. At present three large sawmills are located there."[247]

In 1960, the DIA undertook a "labour force survey" of the young men on southern Vancouver Island, with a view to helping them find employment. The survey found fourteen Lekwungen men between the ages of sixteen and twenty-four, all "unskilled." Five were listed as being in school and one in prison. Of the other nine, four were listed as casual labourers and five as unemployed. In August 1960, the director of the DIA wrote a local member of Parliament to say that "the economic situation on Vancouver Island (and indeed in BC generally) is extremely poor." He added that, under the circumstances, there was no point in continuing the labour survey since there was no work to be found. Two months later, the Victoria newspaper headlines read: "Indians Face Starvation as Winter Approaches."[248]

A more precise view of the lack of employment opportunities for Lekwungen men and women is captured by Kathleen Mooney's survey of Victoria directories for the two decades between 1952 and 1971. Directories

Disturbingly High Rate

In spite of the proximity of industries and businesses including farming, fishing, logging, sawmilling, wood processing and shipbuilding, a disturbingly high rate of unemployment exists with its attendant low living standards and demoralization, and excessive food relief expenditures.

Cowichan Agency, Quarterly Report for the period ending August 31, 1962

tend to enumerate only the more successful and permanently located of economically marginal groups, so Mooney's study tends to overemphasize the successful. In 1961, she found that 106 aboriginal men from southeast Vancouver Island, including the Lekwungen, had occupations. Of these, thirty-four (32 percent) were engaged in the forest industry, thirty (28 percent) were general labourers, and twenty-four (22 percent) were in skilled trades. Only six men (5.6 percent), on southeast Vancouver Island, were fishers while five were farmers, one was a dentist, one was an armed forces officer, one was a bookkeeper, and another was a clerk. She noted that "in practice many men were only seasonally employed and with little stability at that."[249]

Relief records reveal the seasonal nature of the cash economy and the compensating value of welfare payments. Complete relief records survive for the Cowichan Agency, which included the Lekwungen, for the year April 1, 1960 to March 31, 1961. During the peak employment season, one-quarter of the Indians in the agency were receiving relief; over the winter, when seasonal employment was scarce, just over 50 percent were receiving relief. In addition, 145 families received family allowance in the Cowichan Agency, and 106 individuals received old age or disability pensions.[250]

In 1962, the relief load was higher still, and it continued to worsen over the decade. Even in peak employment season – August – the Indian Agent was reporting that 50 percent of Indians in the Cowichan Agency, 1,600 individuals, were on full relief, requiring an annual expenditure of $150,000.[251] In 1971, only ninety-two men could be identified in Mooney's directory survey as employed (15 percent less than a decade prior), and more were in low-skill occupational classes. Thirty-five men (38 percent) were listed as forest industry workers, twenty-four (26 percent) as labourers. Only twelve, half the number of a decade before, were in skilled trades, while six were in professions, five were fishers, and one was a farmer. The occupational status of Victoria-area Indians is confirmed by the 1971 federal census, which showed 73 percent of Indian men in the unskilled occupational category, compared to only 19 percent of non-Indians living in similar "blue-collar" neighbourhoods.[252]

Low-skill and low-wage occupations characterized over three-quarters of Victoria-area aboriginal men, who evidently bore a disproportionate share of unemployment. Mooney's census statistics show that aboriginal men were unemployed, on average, eight times more frequently than were non-aboriginal men. In 1971, she found a 36 percent unemployment rate among Indian men aged twenty to fifty-nine. Two different studies focusing on the Lekwungen showed unemployment rates of 22 percent in both 1967 and in 1969, but, on the basis of interviews, it was apparent that only

20 percent of those showing occupations in 1969 were actually steadily employed. The Lekwungen appear to have been faring better than the rest of the members of the Cowichan Indian agency, 48 percent (1,617) of whom were on relief.[253]

The statistics were notoriously poor when it came to enumerating work by women. Domestic labour, seasonal cannery work, home production of knitted goods for sale are all missed in income and occupational statistics. To some extent, these gaps can be filled through other sources. In her 1971 interviews, Mooney found that aboriginal women were less likely to be employed than were non-aboriginal women: "Seasonal, unsteady and part-time berry, potato and weed picking or bulb sorting was said to be almost the only source of employment available for women, children and older people, involving the adults in twelve sample households." Directories for 1951-71 produced a list of 101 aboriginal women on southeast Vancouver Island. Of those, Mooney could only find fourteen women who had listed employment information for at least five years.[254]

She found that "even the knitting of Cowichan sweaters, long an important source of supplementary income has become increasingly unprofitable. Although an Indian owned and operated sweater store is located on the reserve, and people in ten of the 15 sample households used to knit regularly, only four continued to do so." Other evidence suggests the diminished earning power of women. In 1972, Marjorie Mitchell estimated that the median income from all sources for Indian women was $975 per year, compared to $3,400 for Indian men. Not only did a registered Indian's chance of unemployment greatly exceed that of his non-Indian neighbour in 1971, but an Indian family was also much less likely to have the advantage of a second income.[255]

Comparing the 1891 and 1910 censuses with the surveys from the late 1960s highlights the important transformations that had taken place in Lekwungen economic lives. The population of the Lekwungen band, 134 in 1890, was almost identical to the 131 in the band in 1967; however, the percentage of the population in the workforce had dropped dramatically. In 1891, the census showed 35 percent of the adult Lekwungen with occupations, while the 1967 survey showed only 15 percent with occupations. A more precise comparison would examine the segment of the Lekwungen that had the highest rate of persistence in the labour force: adult males. In 1891, 84 percent of Lekwungen males (on reserve) aged fifteen to sixty-five were employed, but in 1967 only 58 percent of the males (on reserve) aged fifteen to fifty-five were listed as employed. In the twentieth century, the Lekwungen had become increasingly unemployed and impoverished.

When, on October 16, 1960, the readers of the *Colonist* saw that the local aboriginal population was in danger of starving, most did not stop to think of the tragic irony: they were hungry in a land that had fed them well for centuries. Few knew that Lekwungen poverty was a reversal of the wealthy position they and other Aboriginal Peoples had in the 1880s, when "hops had become their grandparents"; in 1911, when they received payment for their downtown reserve; and even from the end of the Second World War, fifteen years earlier, when they were fully employed. The newspaper article caught many Lekwungen in the process of a steep slide into poverty. "We're going through bad times now, really bad times," said Wsanec elder Dave Elliot.[256]

We Are Living in the Shadow

My people today know too much poverty, chaos, destruction. We are living in the shadow of rubble, the destruction of a beautiful land.

Dave Elliot, Wsanec elder, ca. 1981

Wsanec (Saanich) elder
Dave Elliot, ca. 1981

FIVE

The Tsilhqot'in

You cannot spend too long in Tsilhqot'in country before you hear of the "Chilcotin War." To hear local people discuss it, it might have happened a few years back instead of in 1864, so vivid are the memories, so precise the details. Much less known to Canadians than the other violent western confrontations – the Cypress Hills Massacre, the Red River Rebellion (which it preceded by five years), and the Northwest Rebellion – the Chilcotin War was an uprising of Tsilhqot'in (Chilcotin) people aimed at driving whites off the Chilcotin Plateau and out of the core of what is now British Columbia. The Royal Navy was enlisted to assist in putting it down, an army of over a hundred was raised and sent into the field for over a hundred days, led, for most of the time, by the governor himself.

It was not one of imperialism's finest moments. There was dissension in the ranks, ineptitude bordering on cowardice, and no hope of engaging the elusive Tsilhqot'in or winning the war. The only way the colony captured any Tsilhqot'in was by luring them to a peace talk and then clapping them in irons and trying them as murderers – a practice so unethical it made the presiding officials squirm. Having caught six of the participants at the cost of $80,000, the colony of British Columbia withdrew and left the Chilcotin Plateau to the Tsilhqot'in people.

The history of the colonial settlement of the west involves a series of discontinuous settlements – islands of Euro-Canadian culture in a landscape already owned and occupied by Aboriginal Peoples. The Lekwungen territory was an early island of European settlement, and now it is the Lekwungen community that is a small island in a sea of European settlement. Today, the Chilcotin remains largely "unsettled" by Euro-Canadians, whose few communities still have the character of islands. This is not an accident of history or geography. The remoteness of the Chilcotin Plateau in the twenty-first century is a result of the actions of the Tsilhqot'in in the nineteenth century: they did their utmost to prevent settlement and to keep a road from being built through their territory.

Today the main entrance to the traditional territory of the Tsilhqot'in requires climbing a series of steep switchbacks up from Sheep Creek Bridge

When we are talking about the Tsilhqot'in War, we are not talking about only the past. We are talking about the future.

Ray Hance, Tsilhqot'in National Government, 1994

The Chilcotin had a bad reputation at one time, and were noted as ruthless, turbulent and roguish people, inclined to take advantage of strangers, and bad to deal with. There is no doubt that they were of a bolder and more restless disposition than the Carrier.

James Teit, *The Shuswap*, 1909

James Teit and his Nlaka'pamux wife Lucy Antko, ca. 1910

◄ Detail of attack on Alexander McDonald's pack train (see p. 135)

over the Fraser River on Highway 20 west of Williams Lake. From this deep canyon, which is also the eastern boundary of the Chilcotin Plateau, you crest onto a rolling tableland veined by the deep ravines of the major rivers and streams carrying snowmelt from the coast mountain range on the western border of Tsilhqot'in territory. The Tsilhqot'in people live in a string of communities accessible from Highway 20, paved now but only completely so in the past few years: from east to west, one encounters Toosey (Tl'esqoxt'in), Stone (Yunesit'in), Anaham (Tl'etinqox), Redstone (Tsi Del Del), and the mixed Tsilhqot'in-Carrier community of Ulkatcho at Anahim Lake. South from Highway 20 an hour and a half along a gravel road is the Nemiah Valley, home of the Xeni Gwet'in.

Aside from the aboriginal communities, there are only two small un-incorporated towns in the whole region: Alexis Creek and Anahim Lake, the largest, with 522 people. Turn off Highway 20 almost anywhere else and you will travel hundreds of miles north or south and not run across a paved road or more than a handful of habitations.

There is a mountain range and an ocean strait between the Tsilhqot'in and the Lekwungen and a world of difference in their cultures. From ancient times the Lekwungen were organized into distinct classes, while the Tsilhqot'in were classless; the Lekwungen had large permanent villages, while the Tsilhqot'in lived in smaller semi-sedentary bands; the Lekwungen put a premium on acquiring and storing wealth for major feasts, while the Tsilhqot'in carried everything on their backs and had little use for status goods; the Lekwungen culture was built around the acquisition of status, while the Tsilhqot'in idealized self-derogation.[1] Owing to their distinctly different cultures, these two groups formed different relationships with the Europeans infiltrating their lands.

Stone, Grease, and the Great Road

If the Lekwungen were located on the "Great Thoroughfare" of the coast – the north-south ocean route from Johnstone Strait to the Strait of Juan de Fuca – the Tsilhqot'in were located alongside the "Great Road," as Alexander Mackenzie called it, one of a network of east-west trails that linked the coast to the Prairies and eastward: the precursor to the Trans-Canada Highway. It was along this "great road" that Mackenzie, the first European to cross North America by land, made his famous journey, – passing along the top of Tsilhqo'tin country in 1793.[2] Mackenzie and his men were guided from one family to the next until he reached the Ulkatcho, called by their Carrier (Dene) neighbours, the *Nechowt'en*, meaning "Carrier people mixed with Tsilhqot'in."[3] As he left the Fraser River on the trail westward, MacKenzie noted an example of how European goods had passed along

Before Europeans came we were quite well off. We had obsidian rock and traded all over North America. We used to control the arms race.

Joe Alphonse, Director of Government Services, Tsilhqot'in National Government, 2000

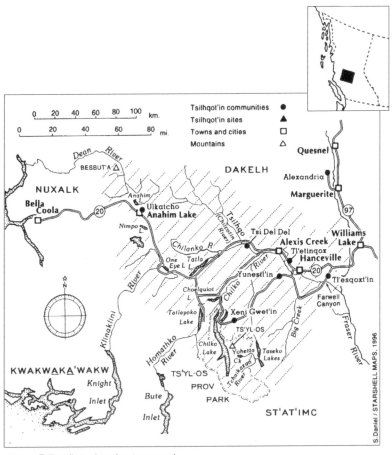

MAP 5.1 Tsilhqot'in territory (contemporary)

this route and how they were transformed in an aboriginal setting. Dangling from the ears of a child were two coins, two halfpennies, one British, the other minted in 1787 by the State of Massachusetts (which had just thrown off the British yoke).[4]

The "great road" was a trade route. Eight to ten thousand years ago, before the rise of the great empires of the Nile, long before the rise of the classical Chinese or Greek civilizations, and millennia before Marco Polo travelled the spice road across Asia, Aboriginal Peoples had a trade route that linked the Pacific coast to a vast portion of North America.[5] For these traders on the great northern plateau between the Rocky Mountains and the Coast Range, the most valuable condiment was not salt, nor pepper or cloves. Prior to the arrival of Europeans, the two most valuable commodities from the coast were eulachon grease – the rendered oil of the eulachon fish (so rich in fat that, once dried, it is said to burn like a candle if lit at one end) and dentalia shells.

Nuxalk Pat Schooner with a boat full of
eulachon on the Bella Coola River, April
1935

The eulachon arrive early in the spring in coastal river mouths – often the hungriest time of year. So welcome were these finger-sized fish that the Nisga'a called them the "little saviours." Caught in vast quantities, the eulachon would be rendered and their oil allowed to congeal. In the summer, the grease would be packed into cedar boxes and carried over mountains on "grease trails," so called because of the importance of this trade and, perhaps, because the trails were marked by stains of oil spilled along the route. Eager Tsilhqot'in and Carrier customers used the grease as a calorie-rich addition to their other meals, in the way that Thai cookery uses "fish sauce" or North Americans use congealed cow grease on their bread. Eulachon grease, though still a delicacy in many coastal aboriginal communities, did not suit the pemmican-eating Plains man: the smell of this "stinking oil," as Mackenzie put it, "was sufficient to sicken me without tasting it." It was, and is, also used to soften hides for tanning.[6]

Dentalia are white, talon-shaped seashells, which were harvested from depths of more than one hundred feet by a few coastal peoples. Traded as far inland as the Great Plains, these shells operated much as did gold in the European world. They were valuable because of their scarcity. They were ornamental, and, being light and portable, they could act as a currency in transactions. The Tsilhqot'in, who wore dentalia ornaments in their ears and noses, were the conduit for dentalia from the coast to the Secwepemc, and from them into the interior of the continent. The trade in dentalia was such an important part of their relationship with the Secwepemc that the word for Tsilhqot'in in the language of the Secwepemc was *Pesê'xEnen*, meaning dentalia people.[7]

In return for the oil and dentalia from the coast, many commodities flowed west over the coast range. Among these, Mackenzie noted "beaver coating and parchment, as well as the skins of the otter, the marten, the lynx, and dressed moose skins."[8]

Among the trade items that we know flowed west, and perhaps even more prized than moose-hide armour, was obsidian. Obsidian is a black volcanic rock that is so shiny it reflects images in a mirror-like fashion. It can be chipped so that it has an edge so sharp that today some surgeons prefer it to any blade modern science has produced.[9] Obsidian occurs naturally in only a few locations, but, because of its value, it is the most widely dispersed of the trade goods found in archaeological sites. The Tsilhqot'in territory abutted or included three of the best sources of obsidian in the entire west of North America, all of them near Besbut'a, shown on current maps as Anahim Peak. Each deposit is distinct, with the result that a chemical analysis can trace the source of obsidian found at any archaeological site. Besbut'a obsidian found its way to the west coast at least as long ago as

9500 BP, and it found its way east into the Alberta prairies no later than 3500 BP to 3000 BP.[10]

It is probably no coincidence that the greatest of the grease trails, the Great Road, ran just to the north of Besbut'a. Obsidian was likely one of the key items of exchange, and so the Great Road, in a sense, linked the Tsilhqot'in and Besbut'a to the rest of the Americas. The western terminus of the Great Road was just to the west of the Tsilhqot'in, in the territory of the Nuxalk, where there was a major greenstone quarry (greenstone was used throughout the northern interior for adzes and chisel blades). Just to the south of the Tsilhqot'in, in the territory of the St'at'imc, was the major source of jade (nephrite) and soapstone (steatite), also traded throughout the inter-montane west.[11]

Exchange was clearly a part of the Tsilhqot'in culture thousands of years before Europeans arrived, but it played a dramatically different role in the lives of the Tsilhqot'in than it did in the lives of the Lekwungen and other coastal peoples. As a highly mobile society, the Tsilhqot'in were little inclined to acquire goods that were not small, light, and useful.

The Tsilhqot'in economy, and so their social structure, derived largely from their environment. The precontact homeland of the Tsilhqot'in is one of the "roofs of the world." The Chilcotin Plateau is sandwiched between several mountain ranges. The wide, undulating plateau slopes eastward from the Coast Mountain Range and is framed in the north by the Netchako Range and the Fawnie Range, and on the south by the Chilcotin Range and the Camelsfoot Range. The highest mountain in British Columbia, Mount Waddington (at 13,168 feet [4,016 metres]), marks the western boundary of Tsilhqot'in territory.

Despite its general eastward slope, the Chilcotin Plateau has major rivers draining off it in all directions. The Chilco River and the Chilcotin River drain west to the Fraser River; the Nazko River flows north into the Blackwater, or West Road, River; the Dean River flows northwest into Bentinck Arm at Bella Coola; the Kleena Kleene River flows southwest into Knight Inlet; and the Homathco River flows south into Bute Inlet. The latter three rivers perform the remarkable feat of cutting right through the Coast Range Mountains. The boundary on the east, at the time of Mackenzie's journey, was Big Creek and its tributary Groundhog Creek (see Map 5.2); however, since the arrival of the Europeans, Tsilhqot'in territory has spread eastward to the Fraser River.

Much of the plateau region ranges from 1,000 to 1,200 metres in elevation, and the winters are long and harsh. At Big Creek in the eastern part of the territory, the coldest recorded temperature is -50° F (the same in Celsius), and the mean winter temperature is well below freezing, at 17° F (-8.3° C).

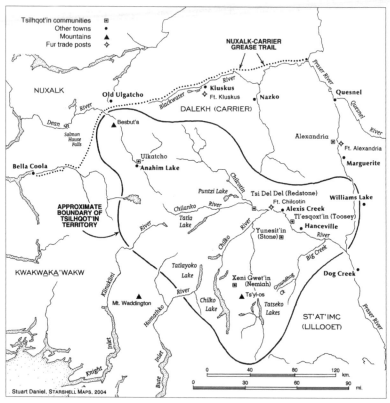

MAP 5.2 Tsilhqot'in territory (historical)

The mean annual temperature is just above freezing, at 37° F (2.8° C). The plateau is in the rain shadow of the Coast Range, so precipitation is not great, thirty centimetres (twelve inches) a year at Big Creek, but one-third of it falls as snow and lingers for a long while on the ground.[12] There is still ice on most of the lakes in June.

The Chilcotin Plateau is dotted with lakes but has only two salmon rivers, the Dean and the Chilcotin, and in both cases the Tsilhqot'in live at the headwaters, where the catches are not reliable. More fish were taken from the lakes than salmon from the rivers. As a result, most of the Tsilhqot'in differed from their piscatory coastal neighbours, deriving more of their food from hunting than from fishing. Archaeological evidence shows that caribou were the primary game animal but that beaver, groundhogs, hoary marmots, hares, and deer as well as ducks were hunted.[13]

The Tsilhqot'in were superbly adapted to their environment. People lived in family groups that travelled from hunting to gathering to fishing to trading sites within the seasonal cycle. In the spring, the lakes would be fished and sap would be collected from pine trees; also in the spring and summer the inner bark of the pine and other trees would be gathered and

Homathco River where it cuts through the Coast Range, southwestern boundary of Tsilhqot'in territory.

eaten. Mackenzie notes the use of the "wild parsnep," as he calls it (*Heracleum lanatum Michx.*), which was harvested in the spring and then roasted, at which time the outer stem was peeled off. Ducks and geese were clubbed during their spring-summer moult.

Summer trips into the local subalpine, including the aptly named Potato Mountains, would yield "mountain carrots" – water parsnip (*Sium suave Walt*), mountain potatoes (*Clatonia lanceolata Pursh*), rice root (*Fritillaria camschatcensis*), and a limited amount of camas. This might coincide with a gathering with other families at Tanya Lake (or elsewhere) or a meeting with the Nuxalk from the coast and/or the Carrier from the north, during which various items would be traded.

In the fall, the men might go hunting while the women and children picked berries in the uplands. In the winter, families settled into regular lakeside locations and built or reinhabited A-frame cabins made of poles covered with bark or brush and insulated with soil. Nets were set under the ice to catch whitefish. Until the eastern movement to the mouth of the Chilcotin River after the arrival of Europeans, the Tsilhqot'in obtained much of their salmon in trade from the Nuxalk and the Secwepemc. Afterwards, many would travel to salmon-fishing sites on the Chilcotin River or Dean River systems. The Hudson's Bay Company men described the conical salmon traps of the Tsilhqot'in as "ingenious" and noted that, with a good salmon run, they might catch between eight hundred and nine hundred fish daily.[14]

Tsilhqot'in fish trap, sketched by James Teit in 1900

Theirs was a relatively harsh environment, and attention was always focused on preparing for the long winter. In 1827, the salmon and the berries failed, and this was not a rare event. The Tsilhqot'in told the Hudson's Bay Company trader William Connolly "that their resources for subsistence were so extremely scanty and precarious that when the salmon failed ... they were reduced to the necessity of deserting their lands and flying for relief to some other quarter near the sea coast."[15] This is probably an exaggeration as salmon were not a staple of most Tsilhqot'in. The account probably came from the several Tsilhqot'in families that married into the coastal Nuxalk and that may have spent parts of their winters in the gentler, and more abundant, climate of Bella Coola.

The variability of the resources, and the small scale of the family units, meant that there was no strict gender division of labour. Although it was the men who tended to hunt, fish, and make the traps and weapons associated with these activities, women also performed these tasks if widowed or if their husbands were absent. While women tended to cook, make clothes and nets, gather roots and berries, and trap small game, some men also performed these chores, either out of preference or necessity.[16]

The Tsilhqot'in sat astride one of the greatest trading networks in North America. They were the intermediaries between two of the major sources of soapstone and jade – not to mention having access to eulachon grease, dentalia shells, and moose hide – and they had unlimited access to obsidian, a trade commodity that was both rare and valuable. Despite the wealth in their territory and the wealth that they exchanged through it, the Tsilhqot'in did not amass wealth. In an environment and economy like theirs, there was no incentive to build caches of material possessions. To feed themselves, the Tsilhqot'in ranged over their territory on foot and carried most of their possessions on their backs. They developed a society similar to that developed by other cultures with similar environments: there was little attempt to acquire status goods, differences of wealth were negligible, interpersonal relationships were egalitarian, and there were no class distinctions. Productive resources were in the public domain and were available to all Tsilhqot'in.[17]

Instead of the elaborate public dance societies and ceremonies of the cultures of the Northwest Coast, the Tsilhqot'in developed their spirituality more privately and personally. Individuals went on quests for "spirit helpers," who only presented themselves to those who were worthy and vulnerable. One way to seek a spiritual guide was to leave the village and lay uncovered for several nights under a spruce tree. Youths were naturally more vulnerable than adults, and it was easier to acquire a spirit helper when young. Once acquired, these helpers assisted as their powers permitted. For example, some had the power to hunt effectively, others to heal. The primary medium through which healing medicine was practised was language. Spirit helpers present themselves in song.[18]

In the 1940s, the Tsilhqot'in contrasted themselves with the Carrier, whom they regarded as stingy and as sharp dealers. Anthropologist Robert Lane believed that this was a result of the Carrier's having adapted the potlatch system from the coast but without its ranking system. "Since anyone could participate in the quest for status, everyone was a potential competitor for such status"; thus, the Carrier were always anxious to earn a dollar. "The Chilcotin ha[d] no such system and therefore lacked the values" endemic to materialism. Irving Goldman, who did ethnographic work among the Carrier in the 1930s, found that their attitude towards the Tsilhqot'in mirrored this. The Tsilhqot'in, he says, were regarded as reckless "spendthrifts" with "[very little] interest in accumulating wealth."[19] When the Europeans arrived with their hordes of status goods, the Tsilhqot'in were not much interested.

Spirit carvings on trees near Anahim Lake, 1900

They Do Not Know a Word of Chinook

The Tsilhqot'in were, and still are, mysterious to outsiders. In earlier times, their seasonal rounds meant that they were elusive, dangerous enemies since one never knew where to find them in order to retaliate. In colonial times, they appeared and disappeared just as easily as they had in earlier days, avoiding a small army sent to hunt them down in 1864. By virtue of their resistance, they were circumvented by provincial transportation corridors until the latter half of the twentieth century and, consequently, were little visited by Indian Agents and little studied by anthropologists. Even today, you can cross the Chilcotin Plateau and, if you stay on the paved roads, you will miss three of the six Tsilhqot'in communities.[20]

Before the arrival of Europeans, the Tsilhqot'in did not live in big villages, as did their neighbours to the east and west. The Tsilhqot'in bands had a looser social organization than did their ranked, potlatching coastal neighbours, yet they had distinct communities, each with recognized chiefs and territories. You might imagine that this would put them at the mercy of their more numerous, better organized enemies; however, the reverse was often the case. The Tsilhqot'in seemed better able to cooperate with each other than did many other groups.

The conditions were not particularly favorable to the work, for the Indians were by no means cordial at the outset, and good interpreters were not to be had. That great resource of ethnological work in the Northwest, the Chinook jargon, was also not available in this tribe.

Livingstone Farrand, *Traditions of the Chilcotin Indians*, 1900

We are still considered the fiercest Indians around. That's because we speak our mind. Why not? We are speaking the truth!

Chief Leslie Stump, Tl'etinqox, September 1999

Tsilhqot'in cradle, sketched by James Teit in 1900

Two stories illustrate the nature of warfare on the plateau, the best known of which is the story of the Tsilhqot'in raid on the Carrier village at Chinlac and its reprisal. About 1745, the Tsilhqot'in attacked the village at the confluence of the Stuart River and the Nechako River in revenge for the killing of one of their leading men. The Tsilhqot'in killed every villager on whom they could lay their hands and left a grisly warning: "hanging on transverse poles resting on stout forked sticks planted in the ground, were the bodies of the children, ripped open and spitted through the out-turned ribs in exactly the same way as salmon drying in the sun." It took three years for the Carrier to mount a revenge attack. They succeeded in locating a Tsilhqot'in camp near present-day Anahim Lake and struck it at dawn. The Carrier killed everyone they could and spitted the bodies of the Tsilhqot'in children.[21]

The Carrier say the Tsilhqot'in were trying to seize the productive salmon fishery site at Chinlac. If true, this would fit the pattern of most of the hostile interactions on and around the plateau. Battles, both defensive and offensive, often seem to have been fought over resource sites or large hunting areas. Examples include the Tsilhqot'in raiding down the Homathco River to Bute Inlet to claim salmon-fishing sites, and the Homalco people raiding upriver and occupying Chilco Lake.[22]

A second example of a dispute of this kind arose in the winter of 1826, when four Lhakot'en (Talkotin) hunters were found in Tsilhqot'in territory. Three were killed and one escaped (or was deliberately allowed to escape) to take the story home to his people. A round of retaliatory attacks proceeded. On one occasion, a party of twenty-four Lhakot'en embarked on a raid, and, on another, eighty Tsilhqot'in attacked the Lhakot'en village at Stella. Scalping and mutilation was practised on both sides. When a Tsilhqot'in woman who lived at Fort Alexandria slipped away to tell her people that the fort was resupplying the Lhakot'en, the fur trade factor reported that the Tsilhqot'in "pronounced vengeance against us, and threatened to cut off all white men that might thereafter fall in their way." This and several other of the battles between the Tsilhqot'in and their Secwepemc and Carrier neighbours are recorded in the Fort Alexandria and Fort Chilcotin post journals for the 1820s and 1840s.[23]

The Tsilhqot'in and Kwakwaka'wakw have stories of the latter raiding up the Kleena Kleene River into Tsilhqot'in territory for slaves and of the former engaging in retaliatory raids "for women."[24] Skirmishes between hunting parties in the St'at'imc borderlands to the south were not uncommon; nor were periods of hostility with the Secwepemc to the east and other Athapaskans to the north, as is demonstrated by the Chinlac story. The oral histories of warfare likely exaggerate the hostilities on the plateau as peacetime generates few dramatic stories. There was, for example, a long history of peaceful and cordial relationships with the Nuxalk to the west, and, in most cases, it is likely that Tsilhqot'in relations with their other neighbours were characterized by long periods of peace punctuated by brief periods of war. Still, there is no doubt that, when Europeans arrived, most of the Tsilhqot'in's neighbours regarded them as fierce and combative.

Newcomers

Given that the Tsilhqot'in were protective of their territory and were no shrinking violets, how did they receive their first European visitors? When Alexander Mackenzie crossed along the top of Tsilhqot'in territory in the summer of 1793 he recorded his observations of the people and the country and his puzzlement at how he was treated. The Tsilhqot'in have left little in the way of accounts of their meetings with Mackenzie, but their initial response may have been similar to that of their neighbours to the west and the south. The Aboriginal People Mackenzie met regarded him suspiciously – as though he and his seven men were a threat. The Nuxalk, to the west, have several accounts that suggest that the prevailing view was that Mackenzie was a man who had returned from the dead, although there were some who thought that he had descended from the land of the star people in the sky. His association with the dead – some have suggested as the result of his pale face – meant that he was potent with spiritual power but also taboo in certain respects. The Nuxalk and their Tsilhqot'in/Carrier contacts took great pains to divert him around their salmon fishing sites, and the only salmon they would allow him to touch or eat were cooked and had had the bones removed. The salmon could easily be offended, and the Nuxalk feared that certain actions of the strangers might prompt the salmon to desert the Nuxalk altogether.[25]

On the other hand, the neighbours to the south had their first encounter with a European when Simon Fraser travelled down the river that bears his name in 1808. The Nlaka'pamux around Lytton interpreted Fraser and his party as a visit by Coyote, the transformer and trickster, and his companions, Sun and Moon. The Secwepemc people, just to the east of the Tsilhqot'in, called the first Europeans *Spetêkł*, meaning the "ancients" from mythological times. The Carrier and the Tsilhqot'in called the Europeans *midugh*, the root of which means "above," perhaps referring to celestial origins.[26]

The suspicion/awe that Aboriginal Peoples showed the first Europeans makes it clear that the novelty of these lighter-skinned, bearded men with strange accoutrements was viewed through the lens of spiritual beliefs. Mackenzie, Simon Fraser, and their men were unpredictable, potentially malevolent spirits who could not be offended.

I Shall Sell My Life Dearly

Everything quiet and not an Indian coming to the Fort ... a conduct very unusual. I am beginning to think they contemplate a blow upon the fort and I am badly prepared to receive them as my Fort is not fortified and destitute of a single bastion. Nevertheless I shall endeavour to sell my life as dearly as I can.

Fort Chilcotin Journal, December 25, 1838

Painting of Alexander Mackenzie, by Thomas Lawrence, ca. 1800

After Mackenzie had gone west and returned east through their territory, it was a long time before the Tsilhqot'in saw any more Europeans. By this time they had determined that, whoever they were, the Europeans had valuable items that were worth trading furs for. Soon after the establishment of Fort Fraser at Fraser's Lake north of their territory in 1806, the Tsilhqot'in began to trade with it through Naskotin intermediaries. In 1808, they probably learned of Simon Fraser's passage to the east of their territory. In 1815, they were visited by a party of fur traders from the North West Company. Then, in 1821, a post was established on the Fraser River, just east of their territory, at what the North West Company and, after the 1824 merger, the Hudson's Bay Company called Fort Alexandria.[27]

The Tsilhqot'in visited the fort to trade and to satisfy their curiosity about the traders, and the fur traders made expeditions into Tsilhqot'in lands. The Europeans found the Tsilhqot'in men, women, and children clothed in beaver pelts, and, in 1825, a trading party returned with between three hundred and four hundred excellent beaver pelts. The trading party reported that the Tsilhqot'in "[were] extremely fond of iron works, and appear[ed] to be well acquainted with the use of firearms." One had a gun marked "Barrett, 1808," which he had purchased from Indians who came from the sea coast. According to Tsilhqot'in accounts, it took six days from the end of Chilco Lake, travelling over mountains, to reach a river (the Homathco) in the south that discharges into the ocean at a place where Indians carry on traffic with Europeans: "From their general behaviour we were led to imagine they must have had frequent intercourse with the whites and a peculiar kind of blanket, resembling a rug, which was in common use among them, we supposed had been obtained from Russian traders."[28]

So much of Fort Alexandria's furs came from the Tsilhqot'in that, as early as 1823, the traders resolved to establish a trading post in the heart of Tsilhqot'in territory. Warfare between the Tsilhqot'in and the Lhakot'en home guard at Alexandria caused friction with the Hudson's Bay Company and so they feared Tsilhqot'in furs were being diverted to the coast. A collapse of the salmon fishery, and other misadventures, delayed the establishment of Fort Chilcotin until 1831, when a post was built on one of the Tsilhqot'ins' ancient campsites at the junction of the Chilco River and the Chilcotin River.[29]

The Tsilhqot'in took (and take) pride in their hospitality – a characteristic that was acknowledged and remarked upon by the earliest fur traders. Despite this general tradition, the Tsilhqot'in never did welcome the fur traders who set up a post in their territory. A trading expedition in the Chilcotin in 1831-32 was turned back, "having met a very rough reception, that tribe behaved with much insolence and used some Menaces towards them."[30] The fort was closed in 1836 because traders found the Tsilhqot'in had been "troublesome and disorderly" but reopened in the spring of 1837. In the summer of 1839, the Tsilhqot'in apparently attempted to starve the fort into submission by blockading the Chilcotin River with a salmon weir built below the fort so that the traders could catch no fish. That year a wall and bastions were erected around the post.[31]

In 1841, it appears that Donald McLean took over the post, and he wrote that, "one and all of" the Aboriginal People around Chilco Lake "appear inclined to mischief. The keeping of such a paltry establishment is in my humble opinion a dead loss to the HB Co and risking the lives of people placed at it – who are little better than slaves to the Indian, being unable to keep them in check." If anyone was calculated to increase the enmity of the Tsilhqot'in it was McLean. Historian Father Morice described him as having "the most perfect antipathy [for Aboriginal People]" whom he treated "with superb disdain." McLean was an enforcer for the Hudson's Bay Company, carrying out brutal reprisals for attacks on company personnel. Finally, in September 1844, the post was relocated north of Tsilhqot'in territory in the territory of the Naskotin Carrier owing, said HBC factor A.C. Anderson, "to the evil disposition of the Chilcotin Indians." The people around the new Fort Kluskus, as it was called, were, by contrast, "well disposed and industrious."[32]

In Tsilhqot'in society, no one needed goods that were not portable. The Tsilhqot'in did not follow the path of their northern neighbours, the Carrier, who adopted coastal potlatch practices during the contact era. Beyond the trade in ammunition, guns, and some iron ware, which were obtainable by trade from any of their neighbours, the Tsilhqot'in were not much interested in trading with, or working for, the Europeans. At this early date, they held that Europeans were interlopers, like the Secwepemc, the Lakhot'en, and others who infiltrated their territory. Instead of being cowed by the HBC, the Tsilhqot'in worked to hold it, and European society, in check.

Chilcotin War

Fourteen years after driving off the HBC, the Tsilhqot'in met a whole new breed of Europeans. A gold rush had developed along the lower reaches of the Fraser River in 1858, and it was not long before a vanguard of prospectors and miners worked its way north up the Fraser and began exploring its tributaries. One of these tributaries, Williams Creek, north and east of the Chilcotin Plateau, proved to be gold-rich, and the Tsilhqot'in's "Great Road" turned out to be the shortest direct route between Victoria and the new "Cariboo" mines.

The Chilcotin River cutting through the Chilcotin Plateau west of the junction with the Fraser River

I Feared the Smallpox

I had a row with [the Nuxalk] a few days ago. On sending them away from my camp, they refused to go ... They came back with muskets cocked, and were going to shoot me ... They wanted to know why I had ordered them away, did I suspect them of stealing? I told them I wouldn't suspect them of such a thing for the world ... but that I feared the smallpox ... down down with the muskets, "capit wa wa" was "the word" and peace was declared.

Letter from Lieut. H.S. Palmer, R.E., entering the Chilcotin, July 16, 1862

With miners filtering into their territory from the west via Bute Inlet and Bentinck Arm, and from the south up the Fraser and over the watershed dividing the Bridge and Chilcotin rivers, there were new conflicts. One of these, which comes to us through a somewhat fictionalized reminiscence, suggests that, in 1858, Peter Dunlevy attended a meeting of some Tsilhqot'in and Secwepemc at Lac La Hache. Dunlevy recounts that the Tsilhqot'in advocated driving all the whites out of the Chilcotin-Cariboo but were frustrated by two Secwepemc chiefs, William and Lolo, who refused to participate in an uprising. This account may be partially or entirely fictional, but it does fit with Tsilhqot'in actions both before and after this alleged conference.[33]

In 1860, while recovering from a bout of gout, Alfred Waddington, a civic-minded but impractical businessman, whom John A. Macdonald later described as "a respectable old fool," decided, on the basis of an incomplete map, that he could shave 175 miles off the journey to the Cariboo by building a road from Bute Inlet on the coast, up the Homathco River Valley, through Tsilhqot'in territory, to Alexandria near the Cariboo. He commissioned a surveyor, Robert Homfrey, in 1861 to look over the route. Homfrey barely returned alive as a result of the physical difficulties of the journey, and he turned back before reaching the half-way point. Part of the route was also crossed in 1862 by Royal Engineer, Lieutenant H.S. Palmer.

Waddington was not to be daunted. He had a townsite, named after himself, laid out at the mouth of the Homathco River. Waddington received a charter from the Colony of British Columbia to build a road from the coast to the goldfields in exchange for the right to levy tolls. The timing was inauspicious. Ten days after the charter was issued, a major smallpox epidemic broke out in Victoria.

Waddington sent workers to begin the clearing and blasting of the trail from Bute Inlet along the route used by the Tsilhqot'in to communicate with the Homalco people on the coast. By the time his party left Victoria in August, the city was in the midst of the deadliest smallpox epidemic of the century. Six Tsilhqot'in met the party at Bute Inlet. Sometime that same spring or summer, the most lethal smallpox epidemic since the start of European settlement entered the Chilcotin Plateau.[34]

The coincidence of the arrival of the road party and the smallpox was not lost on the Tsilhqot'in, though the route of infection may have come from a party of whites crossing through from Bella Coola. That party left several of its members, who were ill from smallpox, in the Tsilhqot'in village of Nacoontlon for the native people to take care of. The disease could also have come from the Bella Coola, who were infected at this time, or it could have had more than one source. In any case, its effect was devastating. In some communities, one-third were killed; in others, all apparently died from the disease or the effects of starvation (as they had been too weak to put away a winter's supply of food). Many estimates suggest that half the population of the Tsilhqot'in was killed in this epidemic.[35]

The members of the road construction party returned to Victoria for the winter but were back at Bute Inlet in the summer of 1863 to carry on their work. At the end of the season, they built a storehouse and left some supplies for the next season. When they returned in the spring of 1864, the Tsilhqot'in anxiously awaited them. It had been a hungry winter, and some Tsilhqot'in families, including that of an influential man named Klatsassin, had spent it in the Homathco Valley.[36] Not normally eager to work for the whites, these people must have thought they could at least get some food and perhaps earn enough for a musket and ammunition by packing for the road crew.

The road builders found that, over the winter, someone had broken into the storehouse and had stolen food. The road crew assembled the Tsilhqot'in, and, as Klatsassin told the judge at his trial: "A white man took all our names down in a book ... & told us we sho[ul]d all die, whose names were there of small pox. Tyorkell told us this wo[ul]d certainly happen unless we killed every white man."[37] Judge Begbie noted: "The threat acquired substance and force from the circumstance that the same threat is said to have been made to them previous to the small pox of /62-/63 when half their numbers (on a moderate computation) perished [and] that this same threat had been made by a white man in 1862."[38] According to the inquest into the death of the members of the road crew, and based on interviews with European and aboriginal witnesses, there were other aggravating factors: "the Indians were little removed from a state of starvation yet not the lightest effort was made to obtain the good will of the Indians or to guard against their enmity. When they worked they complained that Brewster [the foreman] paid them badly and gave them nothing to eat ... They begged food or stole it and if those means failed them they hunted or fished." And if this insulting treatment were not enough to provoke the Tsilhqot'in, there was more: "Their women particularly the younger ones were better fed than the men as the price of prostitution to the hungry wretches was enough to eat ... The Indians have I believe been most injudiciously treated. If a sound discretion had been exercised towards them I believe this outrage would not have been perpetrated."[39]

The abuse of the women is remembered today in Tsilhqot'in territory. Ervin Charleyboy, chief of the Redstone band, whose grandfather packed for the road crew, believed that this, combined with the fact that the Tsilhqot'in workers "were treated like slaves," touched off a war. Patrick

Surely Improbable That They Are All Dead

Two Indians from Kluskus ... report the Indians of Kluskus all dead of the smallpox. Geltess went there in search of his wife visited two villages but found nothing but dead lodges [with bodies] in rows on each side of the fireplace. In one lodge there was still fire but the occupants were already locked in death's cold embrace. Surely improbable that they are all dead, some of them perhaps has escaped & gone somewhere else. I hope so anyways.

Fort Alexandria Post Journal, December 12, 1862

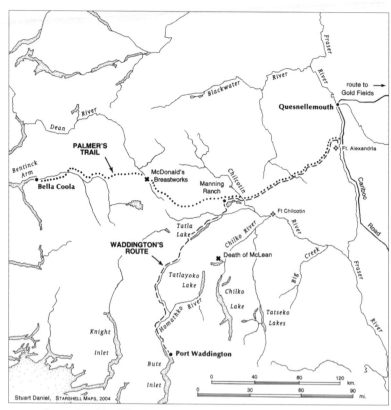

MAP 5.3 Geography of the Chilcotin War

Lulua, from Nemiah and a worker for the Tsilhqot'in National Government, says that what occurred was rape, not prostitution, and that Klatsassin's
thirteen-year-old daughter was one of the victims.

As Patrick Lulua was told, Klatsassin wanted to take his time getting
revenge, but other men provoked him to settle the score immediately. The
members of the road crew were attacked while most of them were in their
tents: "They snuck up to the crew – so close that they could smell them.
Holes were cut in both ends of the tents and cottonwoods dropped on
them ... they were clubbed to death."[40] Of the seventeen men on the crew
on April 29-30, 1864, only three escaped into the woods and made their
way back to Bute Inlet. According to the inquest, the foreman's "belly was
ripped up." According to the Tsilhqot'in, his heart was cut out.[41]

From Bute Inlet, the Tsilhqot'in party headed to the home of the only
white settler in Tsilhqot'in territory (see Map 5.3). William Manning had
settled on Puntzi Lake with a Tsilhqot'in wife. There was some resentment,
according to Patrick Lulua, because he had fenced off a track to the lake
that the Tsilhqot'in used for fishing. According to the trial notes of Judge

Begbie, "It appeared to have been formerly a constant camping place of Tahpit & his tribe, but Manning had driven them off, & taken possession of the spring." On being warned of danger by his wife, Manning told her that he felt himself to be on good terms with the local people. It was a member of the local people, Tahpit, who, in May, after the arrival of Klatsassin's party and in the company of the Chief Anahim, shot Manning and then hacked at him with a hatchet. His possessions were looted and his farm equipment broken up.

In the meantime, a pack train consisting of forty horses, eight white men, and one woman (Klymtedza, the Tsilhqot'in wife of the teamster Alexander McDonald) was working its way towards Anahim Lake from Bella Coola on Bentinck Arm with supplies for the road crew. When they reached Anahim Lake, Klymtedza heard of the uprising and warned her husband to flee to the coast. Instead, the packers climbed a promontory (still visible along Highway 20), dug in, and made a mini-stockade. After holding up for a couple of days they decided to retreat to the coast and were ambushed. McDonald, Klymtedza, and two other whites were killed by Klatsassin's party, while five fled on foot, one hundred miles (160 kilometres) back to Bella Coola. The local chief, Anahim, did not participate in the killings but took advantage of the situation to appropriate much of the pack train.[42] A party of Tsilhqot'in then headed down to the Bella Coola Valley and attacked the home and store of a white trader, who fled unharmed.[43]

Attack on Alexander McDonald's pack train; painting by Brian Seymour

They Do Not Know Chinook

I trust you will excuse the imperfections of this communication I am writing in the open air pestered by mosquitoes people talking all around me and to me and I am conscious that I have made many mistakes. I keep no copy. I send this by the gunboat as it will be in N.W. sooner than a Canoe could be ... I found it most difficult to examine the Indians here as they do not know a word of chinook.

Chartres Brew to the Colonial Secretary, May 23, 1864

Governor Seymour, who had arrived in the colony less than a month before, wrote London that "an Indian insurrection existed, extremely formidable from the inaccessible nature of the country over which it raged. It seemed that the whole Chilcoten tribe was [either] involved in it [or sympathetic to it]." "The country had been so thinly settled by Europeans," he wrote, "that [settlement] had ceased from the sea to the Fraser."[44]

The Chilcotin Plateau had been rid of Europeans, but their absence was temporary. When the word of the deaths reached Victoria, and then New Westminster (capital of the Colony of British Columbia), two expeditions were mounted to respond to this "war." A force of fifty men, under Magistrate and Gold Commissioner William Cox, was sent westward from Fort Alexandria. This volunteer army was described by Governor Seymour as "mostly natives of the United States, & not much disposed to relish the restraint which I put on them in carrying on operation against the Indians." Second-in-command of this force was Donald McLean, the former keeper of Fort Chilcotin. A naval ship took a party of thirty-five volunteers, including former Royal Engineers from New Westminster, to Bute Inlet. When they could not follow the Tsilhqot'in, they returned to New Westminster and increased their force to fifty. Nominally commanded by the superintendent of police, Chartres Brew, the party was accompanied by Governor Frederick Seymour, to whom Brew reported. At Bella Coola, they disembarked and enlisted the aid of twenty Nuxalk.

The party under Cox attacked the camp of Anahim on Puntzi Lake from the east and, having driven the occupants away, burnt the lodges and food caches. Nearby, the Cox party built a log fort and barricaded themselves in, where they remained "virtually besieged by an invisible enemy" for three weeks until united with the force from the coast. The other party under Brew spent two weeks marching around the Chilcotin Plateau, being followed and harassed. The Tsilhqot'in were so confident that, on one occasion, they warmed themselves by the fire of the field force before the latter had marched two hundred metres from camp. The only casualty was the former HBC man in charge of Fort Chilcotin, Donald McLean, who, the Tsilhqot'in say, was deliberately singled out. He took a bullet through the heart.[45]

The governor reported on July 20, 1864 that Mr. Brew and Mr. Cox, his commanding officers, "looked upon the case as hopeless," at least until winter set in and the Tsilhqot'in settled into their winter camps.

I found myself, after reaching the heart of Chilcotin Country advised to direct the two bands of volunteers ... simply to return home, leaving matters worse than we found them ... The return ... after the death of McLean would spread the notion throughout the Indians of the whole Colony that we had been beaten, and in point of fact, this was not far from being the case.[46]

The volunteers under Mr. Cox were on the verge of open rebellion and the whole party was "in dread of famine," according to Governor Seymour.

Then, at the eleventh hour, Tsilhqot'in chief Alexis came into the camp of the field force. Seymour told Alexis that he was determined to "shoot down or catch" the Tsilhqot'in war party, to which Alexis "enquired with something approaching a sneer, how long I meant to remain." The governor had tired and probably despaired of success and opted to leave immediately, though he left the volunteers in the field. He told the Colonial Office that his role had been to "obtain moderation from the white men in the treatment of the Indians." That time had now passed: "But there was no use any longer shutting my eyes to the fact; this was a war merciless on one side, and in which we were engaged with the greater part of the Chilcotin nations and must be carried on as a war by us." When Mr. Brew's party, with the assistance of the Nuxalk, adopted a scorched earth policy, driving the Tsilhqot'in from their fishing grounds, burning their lodges and their winter supplies of food, the governor wrote London that it was "a little short of marvelous." Should the war spread, Seymour told the Colonial Secretary in London: "I may find myself compelled to follow in the footsteps of the Governor of Colorado ... and invite every white man to shoot every Indian he may meet."[47]

Alexis brokered a meeting between Klatsassin and the governor under a flag of truce to discuss a settlement to the war. But when Klatsassin came into camp with seven of his group, they were told that the governor was no longer there and that he and his men were prisoners – not prisoners of war but criminals who would be tried and hanged for the murders they had committed. Klatsassin and his companions were tried in Quesnelle Forks by Judge Begbie through the intermediary of Chinook jargon; five were hanged immediately and one was sent down to New Westminster for trial, where witnesses could link him to the murderers. Among the hanged were Klatsassin; his teen-aged son Piell (who was only convicted of shooting McDonald's horse); Telloot, whom Begbie said would have been convicted but not executed by an English court; Tahpit; and Chessus. A year later, another Tsilhqoti'in, Ahan, was hanged in New Westminster for his part in the attack on the McDonald pack train.[48]

Judge Begbie was uncomfortable with the trick used to lure the Tsilhqot'in into their capture and secretly interviewed Klatsassin in his cell, where the latter made it clear that he would not have come into camp had he known that it was not for a peace parley. Klatsassin said that he had

They Meant War, Not Murder

The prisoners received us well, and after some preliminary conversation, we set about our proper task. I spoke now Chinook, now French, and Baptiste interpreted in Chilcoaten.

We spoke of Law and of Sin, and of wrath consequent upon Sin. They received all this quietly, but when, in our next visit, I applied the subject, and, speaking of the law against murder, said they had broken it, and incurred the Divine displeasure, they resented this.

They had only killed the white men, they said, because otherwise the whites would have destroyed them (alluding to the small-pox story), and they could not see that they had done wrong. I said we were all in one way or other sinners, needing salvation.

Supposing, for a moment, the Indians had not committed murder in what they had done, had they not sinned in other ways? ... Even supposing they were justified in murdering the foreman, Brewster, was it becoming to eat his heart? But, indeed, they were not justified in destroying those men. The law was, "Thou shalt not kill." They said, "They meant war, not murder."

R.C. Lundin Brown, *Klatsassin and Other Reminiscences of Missionary Life in British Columbia*, 1873

Multiple Meanings

Chinook [has a very] scanty vocabulary [where] one phrase may convey five or six meanings to as many different interpreters.

Matthew B. Begbie to the Governor of British Columbia, April 8, 1869

Klatsassin

He Fired at His Head

I saw Lutas fire at him. He fired at his head (Mamooked poo lopo latete). I saw Yahooslas shoot Higgins and Alick ... Ahan said to me that I was scared (hiyou quass).

Testimony of Ach-pie-er-mous, Special Assize, New Westminster, July 3-4, 1865

received a gift of tobacco from Mr. Cox via Alexis and had come to smoke the pipe of peace with him. Even the *British Colonist* newspaper in Victoria commented that "the means by which Mr. Cox obtained possession of the eight prisoners ... does not look very well." The fine points of justice did not weigh too heavily on Begbie, however, as he said: "It seems horrible to hang 5 men at once, especially under the circumstances of the capitulation. Yet the blood of 21 [sic] whites calls for retribution."[49]

Begbie concluded his letter with the cause of the war: "I was particular in inquiring into the name of the individual who as they all assert & I have not the least doubt, truly, was by his rash threat [of sending smallpox] the cause of all this uproar, and of the death of 21 white men & 3 Indians already, & nobody can say how many more by the hand of the executioner & famine in the fall & winter."[50] That individual has never been identified.

The plans for a road died with the road crew. Even today, the prehistoric trails remain the only link between Bute Inlet and the Chilcotin Plateau. By blocking access to a road that would have placed them on a main transportation artery, the Tsilhqot'in found themselves bypassed for nearly a century. Alfred Waddington, who pushed so hard to have the road constructed in the 1860s, only to have the process sabotaged by the threat of a smallpox visitation, was himself visited fatally by smallpox in Ottawa in 1872.[51]

Their attack, and their subsequent ability to elude their pursuers, gave the Tsilhqot'in a reputation in the late nineteenth century for being "dangerous and blood-thirsty," and this also gave them a certain measure of respect. In 1872, the *British Colonist* wrote: "Of all the tribes in the Province, probably the Chilcoten is at once the most formidable and the least civilized. The terrible massacre at Bute Inlet in 1864 will still be fresh in the public mind ... scarcely surprising that there is a feeling of uneasiness lest the railway scheme should meet some opposition from that source." The federal surveyor Marcus Smith, who worked among them in the early 1870s, thought the Tsilhqot'in "the manliest and most intelligent Siwashes in the province." Ranchers, who were eyeing the Chilcotin Plateau in the 1870s, were worried that "a number of [Tsilhqot'in people] concerned in the massacre of the Waddington Party are living there and express their constant hostility to the Whites."[52]

That same year, federal surveyors were approaching Tsilhqot'in territory with the goal of surveying another road – this time a railroad. Peter O'Reilly was sent as a government representative to meet with the Tsilhqot'in and to assure them that they would not be dispossessed. O'Reilly wrote:

I explained to them the purpose of the surveys and should the line come
through to Bute Inlet they would be materially benefited and that they would
be fully and regularly compensated for any assistance they might afford. They
expressed themselves satisfied at the prospect of the road being made, but
they did not evince the least disposition to engage in any occupation of any
kind, which was probably due to the fact that they do not understand the
value of money and that they are at present fully occupied in fishing and
gathering berries for the support of their families during the winter.[53]

The plateau people's lack of interest in working for the whites is also
evident in the records of the Western Telegraph Company, which built a
line from the Fraser River along the West Road (Blackwater River) in 1863-
64. Charles Buckley, the engineer in charge, wrote: "no dependence whatever can be placed on Indian labor. They will work, when they are out of
food, but prefer being idle, as long as they have sufficient to keep them
alive."[54]

Ranchers tentatively occupied the west bank of the Fraser River, which
the Tsilhqot'in had moved into earlier in the century. The ranchers complained that the Tsilhqot'in were quite clear that it was their land and that
the former were only there because they allowed them to be. As one of the
pioneers, L.W. Riske, wrote to the government:

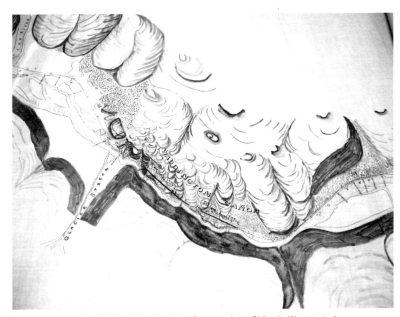

CPR survey map (1875-76) of Waddington's Canyon where Chilcotin War started

The Indian Races Should Go to the Wall

My packers are "semi-Civilized. Like most Indians their capacity for food is about double that of white men, & their capacity for work about one half. Who can wonder that under these circum-stances the Indian races should go to the wall in the "struggle for existence" ... The Indians about here belong to the Chilacotin [sic] bands ... & many of them are so barbarous as not to understand Chinook Jargon.

George M. Dawson, Tatlayoko Lake, September 5, 1875

George Mercer Dawson, later director of the Geological Survey of Canada

In our coming to this place the Indians have professed themselves friendly and agreeable to our settling here, and on the whole they have acted so far towards us very peaceably. They have always however, considered the land theirs, [and that we are] beholden to them for it and occupy it on sufferance. We have always avoided arguing it with them till someone in authority could come and explain to them their duties and rights. Our all being invested here, we have been anxious to conciliate them, and to that end we enclosed and ploughed land for them giving potatoes to plant and water to irrigate – as also potatoes to plant out back and the privilege of gleaning in the fields in harvest.[55]

One rancher, named Salmon, married to an Nlaka'pamux woman, de-cided to push the limits and settle up the Chilcotin River Valley close to the camps of Alexis. According to L.W. Riske, "[Salmon] was told by the Indi-ans that he must leave, that was their land and they did not want whites to live on it. They had for sometime expressed unfriendliness to any going in there but Salmon, having moved in there at a large loss and expense deter-mined to stay, till fully satisfied of eminent [sic] danger to himself and stock."

Chief Alexis had formerly offered Salmon protection, but the latter's erratic and rude behaviour caused him to revoke it, and "now [he] has told Salmon he must go ere so many days or expect to be killed and have his stock run off." The other white man in the valley 15 miles lower down got the same warning and helped Salmon get his stock out.[56]

Not surprisingly, four other ranchers who had planned to preempt in the valley changed their minds, and the province put a freeze on pre-emptions until reserves could be surveyed, "lest collisions of a more serious character should occur." Chief Justice Begbie investigated the case and de-cided that Salmon deserved what he got. Begbie noted that there "is still extant some dissatisfaction at the memories of 1864." He advised pacifying the Tsilhqot'in, not Salmon: "A little soothing language and tobacco, the intimation of power without any threats, might be a very cheap way of procuring quick [settlement] without any loss of dignity but rather on the contrary, as well as greatly for the good of the 'bad Indians' themselves."[57]

The Tsilhqot'in reputation for hostility to outsiders was confirmed in 1865, with the death of a Chinese miner in their territory, and again in April 1879, with the murder of the Poole family being attributed to a Tsilhqot'in named Emia (sometimes rendered "Tamio" or "Nemiah"). A one-thousand-dollar reward was posted for the capture of Emia, and at least one bounty hunter went into the Chilcotin to track him down. But Emia eluded justice. Then, in 1891, he disemboweled another aboriginal man and was seized by his band. Emia escaped before the police arrived and was pursued by a constable. Finally captured, he was held in jail, but two witnesses to the murder of the Chinese had also been implicated in the 1864 war and had fled with fourteen supporters to avoid capture. The two police officers sent to bring them in to testify returned empty-handed, and Emia was freed.[58]

In 1882, two Chinese miners were murdered at Dog Creek along the Fraser River, and the Tsilhqot'in were implicated. Father Morice, who had just visited the Tsilhqot'in, recorded:

> Some days only after the first visit that I made to them in the month of April last, two savages, found themselves one night at the mouth of the Chilcotin River, entered a tiny cabin where two Chinese men lived. After having eaten that which they were offered in good grace by the Chinese, who refused to accommodate them for the night because of the small size of their dwelling, my Chilcotins seized their rifles, and without hesitation, sent off two bullets at the hosts which put them out dead on their feet. Then, not content with that exploit, they traveled the country, pillaging the houses of the whites that they could knock down under their hand.

Morice goes on to relate that they and several other individuals had developed a plan "to clear out all the whites" but that before this could be executed a local white militia seized one of the murderers, and, two months later, the second was arrested. They were brought to Clinton to be tried, and, on being questioned repeatedly, one of the accused, Taratsiltinat, declared: "'Why so many questions? I told you and I repeat: It was I that murdered the Chinese. My father was killed by the rope, by the rope I wish to die.' He was the son of one of the principal authors of the massacre of 1863 [sic] ... You see, my revered Father, my savages are not saints."[59]

At the same time five settlers, including L.W. Riske, who had written earlier asking for someone to put the Tsilhqot'in in their place, again wrote about the "depredations" of the Tsilhqot'in, including cattle killing and house robberies: "There is an existing state of lawlessness among them that makes it all but impossible for us to remain in our places."[60] At several points between 1877 and 1883, settlers wrote to the government claiming they feared that the Tsilhqot'in intended to drive all the whites out of their territory.[61]

The fears were rekindled in 1898, when a white storekeeper, Louis Elkins, was killed by Tsilhqot'in Sami'hi'u when he refused the hungry traveller food and shelter on a cold winter's night. On account of this, the deceased's brother, Ed Elkins, the only white living in the Nemiah Valley, fled to Bella Coola, leaving that portion of the Chilcotin once again empty of whites.[62]

We'll Give You Lots of Money

That fella you know, he steals cattle all the time. Pretty soon that Lejab [devil in Chinook] started bothering him ... First he say, "We are going to give you lots of money [if] you keep going like that. We'll be your friend." Pretty soon *Nentsen* [evil in Tsilhqot'in] start to talk to him and he say "You keep going like that and we'll give you lots of money. Give you so much you can't run out any money no more." So [that fella] got scared and then he took off [and stopped stealing].

Leonard Johnson, Tsilhqot'in, in David Dinwoodie, "Reserve Memories"

Klahowya Far Chilcotin

Farewell to far Chilcotin and goodbye to Tatla Lake.

The throughfare that Waddington was not allowed to make ...

Goodbye! Good folks ... I leave you with a sigh,

My heart aches as I say it, but "Klahowya" and "Goodbye."

William L. Fernie, a Chilcotin Cowboy in the 1890s, on his retirement from the RCMP, 1934

These Indians do not throw away their money on useless luxuries of food or dress, but invest it in wagons, harness, and such like. They are still contented with the food which they can raise on their land or obtain by hunting, and they do not hanker for the expensive dainties of the whites.

Indian Agent William Laing-Meason, 1892

The young people all want to live like white people.

Xeni Gwet'in elder, Henry Solomon, 1999

A young Henry Solomon and friends

The Damaging Effect of Welfare

The Fraser River, which defines the eastern boundary of the Chilcotin Plateau and modern Tsilhqot'in territory, was not bridged until 1904. From that point on, a small web of wagon roads spread westward in a tentative manner. By 1925, to give one example, Hugh Bostock took two days to reach the town of Williams Lake by train and boat from Vancouver. The centre for the whole of the Cariboo-Chilcotin, Williams Lake, was home to a few hundred people. Then it was a day by truck to Chilanko Forks on the Chilcotin Plateau and nearly another to the end of the road at Tatla Lake. Even in early summer, the one-ton truck was stuck in the mire three times and had to be dug out. To get to either Anahim or Tatlayoko Lake was another couple of days further travel by horse and wagon. Not until 1934 did a summer road that could be driven by an automobile snake its way west to Anahim Lake near the western reaches of Tsilhqot'in territory. By the time the road cut through the Coast Range and connected Williams Lake to Bella Coola in 1955, the Yukon and Alaska had been connected to the continental highway system for over a decade. It was not until 1961 that the Chilcotin Road (now Highway 20) was cleared in the winter. North or south of the main road, horse-pulled wagons were the main form of transportation, remaining common right into the 1970s, when a car bridge was built into the Nemiah Valley, which was home to the last handful of aboriginal communities in the province not linked by land or water to the urban south.[63]

Remote to outsiders, it was the centre of the world to the Tsilhqot'in, who, if they were beginning to lose control in other ways, still dominated the plateau numerically. At the beginning of the twentieth century, there were fewer than one hundred non-aboriginal settlers on the entire plateau, compared to some five hundred Tsilhqot'in. In 1970, Tsilhqot'in still outnumbered *Midugh* (as they called the whites) on the plateau 1,271 to 802.[64]

The isolation of the Tsilhqot'in from whites meant that they were one of the last aboriginal groups to acquire the language of the in-between – Chinook jargon. Chinook jargon infiltrated the Chilcotin Plateau with the surveyors and then the ranchers who slowly started to take up the prime grazing and haying lands on the plateau. Their isolation meant that they were also among the last to give up the jargon. Where English schooling displaced the need for an intermediary language in much of the province, the first of the Tsilhqot'in only started school in 1907, and it was not until the 1960s that there were either schools in every Tsilhqot'in community or that Tsilhqot'in students were integrated into provincially run schools in nearby white communities. It has only been in the last two decades that Tsilhqot'in has ceased to be the first language of many families, and even today there are still elderly Tsilhqot'in who can speak Chinook but not English.

Chinook wawa or jargon took root in the Chilcotin in the late nineteenth century and still maintains a grip there. The Tsilhqot'in Nation's annual celebration in late August is referred to as "Siwash Days," and it is held at an ancient and contemporary fishing site known as Siwash Rock. "Siwash" is the Chinook jargon word for "Indian" (derived from the French *sauvage*). Chinook jargon has become part of the cultural and physical landscape.[65]

BC Indians had become a federal responsibility in 1871, and in 1872 the province made the lower Chilcotin Valley a Tsilhqot'in reserve in order to prevent clashes between the Tsilhqot'in and the settlers. The Tsilhqot'in considered this to be an agreement between them and the Crown, a treaty that guaranteed them this land. The reserve was withdrawn two years later.[66] It was a full decade later before an Indian Agent found the Tsilhqot'in. In September 1883, the Indian Superintendent for British Columbia, I.W. Powell, and the new Indian Agent for the region, retired army officer Captain William Laing-Meason, responded to settler complaints about depredations and crossed the Fraser River at Soda Creek, where they were met by the Tsilhqot'in chiefs Anahim and Toosey.

Despite the apparent urgency in the 1870s to lay out reserves, the first reserve in the Chilcotin Plateau was not established until 1887, when Indian Reserve Commissioner P. O'Reilly laid out reserves for the Stone, Toosey, and Anaham bands. Anahim asked O'Reilly to reserve two thousand acres of swamp meadow, saying that these bands had been cutting hay on them for twenty years, but "this [O'Reilly] refused to do, as [he] considered it would be in excess of their requirements, [he] therefore marked off six hundred and forty acres for their use." Anahim's answer was: "if you do not give us all the meadow I will not accept any part of it." Neither backed down. Anahim organized a meeting of his people and called on the premier, who was visiting Quesnel at the time. Premier Davie told Anahim to go ahead and use the meadow, which meant pulling up the stakes of a settler preemption. In relating these events, Indian Agent Laing-Meason writes: "You, Sir, and the Government know this Country well [and] what trouble these Chilcotin Tribes have given and how carefully they have to be handled; and the ill will of Anahim would likely cause him to allow his Indians to follow their lawless actions as formerly."[67]

As late as 1909, anthropologist James Teit noted that the remote Nemiah band of the Tsilhqot'in were not under the supervision of any agent since none had been able to visit. The next year Ashdown Green became the first surveyor to make it into the valley to lay out reserves for the Nemiah. He reported that, "until recent years [the Nemiah] have had the valley to themselves. Now Americans have taken up areas for hunting. Two settlers, Robertson and Anderson have taken up land with [a] view to cattle raising and the former has acquired the only dry meadows in [the] valley in which the Indians have cut hay for 25 years."[68]

It took another three years before an Indian Agent included the Nemiah band in an annual report.[69] The first non-aboriginal settlers in the Anahim Lake area arrived in the 1920s, and in the Blackwater Region it was not until 1934 that Pan Phillips and Rich Hobson, author of the book-cum-TV series *Nothing Too Good for a Cowboy*, became the first whites to settle there.[70] As whites were migrating westward, the Tsilhqot'in were migrating eastward.

The decimation of the Secwepemc, who had lived near the confluence of the Chilcotin and Fraser rivers, especially from the smallpox epidemic of 1862, led to their abandoning the territory on the west bank of the Fraser. The area left vacant consisted of rich hunting grounds for bighorn sheep, deer, and moose (the latter were just beginning to migrate into the territory at this time), and it included the productive salmon fishery at Farwell Canyon. Here the Tsilhqot'in could have a predictable salmon run as the foundation of their subsistence economy.

The opportunity for the Tsilhqot'in to gain access to the rich subsistence resources in this area coincided with the demand for seasonal labour on the ranches on both sides of the Fraser River as well as an opportunity to earn money by selling cattle and freighting for the mining and farming population of the Cariboo. These opportunities also coincided with the desire of the church, federal, and provincial authorities to have the Tsilhqot'in close to the Fraser River, where they could be administered and ministered to. Between 1885 and 1933, reserves were laid out for the Tsilhqot'in at Toosey near Riske Creek, at Stone and Redstone, and at Anaham Flats near Alexis Creek. Anahim (or Nacoontloon) Lake, the former homeland of the Tsilhqot'in, was practically deserted by 1870, and only the Nemiah people stuck close to Chilco Lake, the other centre of pre-1860s Tsilhqot'in territory. By 1910, probably only one in five Tsilhqot'in lived in their former territory.[71]

Along with the migration eastward came the acquisition of horses. By 1887, the sixty-eight members of the Stone band of Tsilhqot'in had 168 horses. The horse assisted rather than displaced their traditional economy, facilitating their movement into hunting, trapping, and gathering territories. The Indian Agent opined: "These Indians have had but little intercourse with whites, they are wild, uncivilized, and have hitherto maintained themselves almost entirely by hunting, trapping and fishing." Even the more settled bands continued a life dominated by seasonal rounds: they continued to trap, hunt, and fish but added farming to their subsistence economy. In 1887, the Anaham people, with two hundred horses, also had one hundred acres that they were cultivating with peas, potatoes, and wheat. The Toosey people had added livestock to their economy and now had 121 horses, twenty head of cattle, and seventy-one pigs.[72] Five years later, the agent noted that the Tsilhqot'in still "follow the outdoor life much of the year ... The nature of the Indian is still like that of the wild animal in one respect – confinement is soon followed by premature sickness and death." He observed that they had not yet become acquisitive consumers: "they do not hanker for the expensive dainties of the whites."[73]

From the 1880s, the Tsilhqot'in modified their precontact seasonal rounds to take into account the raising of root crops like potatoes, carrots, and turnips. Cattle were incorporated into their economy but were largely left to forage for themselves from spring to fall and were fed hay in the winter. Otherwise, the horse facilitated their longstanding seasonal rounds. Now, they often camped in tents instead of brush shelters. A few of the young men took seasonal work as cowboys or farm hands on the ranches that were spreading into their territories.

Haying on a swamp grass meadow near Anahim Lake, August 1934

It is from this date that the Tsilhqot'in "Indian" identity became linked to a "cowboy" identity. Wealth began to be measured in cattle and horses, so successful Tsilhqot'in were, in effect, ranchers. The experience they had gained working with cattle, their familiarity with the country, and their preference for seasonal employment made the Tsilhqot'in ideal workers for the white ranchers who were slowly infiltrating their territory. One of these ranches, the Gang Ranch, the largest ranch in Canada, grew up on the eastern fringe of the Chilcotin. As communities organized "stampedes" – gatherings focused on rodeo and ranching expertise – cowboy skills became an intense source of pride for the Tsilhqoti'in. In the 1930s, the Carrier to the north of the Tsilhqot'in generally looked down on them as quick-tempered and warlike, as reckless gamblers, drinkers, and spendthrifts; however, they were "respected for one trait – they [rode] like demons and [won] prizes in the rodeos."[74]

The priests visited the Tsilhqot'in once a year, and, during these "priest times," the people would congregate at their village sites. Although the Tsilhqot'in had been contacted by Roman Catholic missionaries as early as 1842, it was not until the 1880s that their missionaries paid regular visits. The priests seem to have had a profound early impact. In 1875 and 1876, geologist George Dawson noted that many Tsilhqot'in wore church medals, that they abstained from eating flesh on Fridays, that they made the sign of the cross before eating (some even before taking a sip of tea). By 1891, this enthusiasm had evidently waned. The Indian Agent noted that "they do not as yet 'take much stock' in religion. Their nature is of a practical kind, and until they find that religion helps them in their mundane affairs, they will never become very zealous converts to any form of religion." It must have been an intermittent relationship because "priest time" remained important to the Tsilhqot'in right up through the 1950s.[75]

The white settlers brought seasonal work opportunities but they also precluded, in some cases, more independent economic activities. The Toosey band lost its water rights when a white settler preempted the headwaters of the creek that ran through their settlement four days before the Indian reserve commissioner arrived to create a reserve and to secure water. Without water, the Toosey could not irrigate, and without irrigation, they could not raise crops or hay to keep their cattle through the winter. In many areas, the inability of the federal government to secure water rights from the province effectively kept Aboriginal People out of commercial agriculture.[76]

Tsilhqot'in who wanted to secure the land that they had ranched or farmed were prohibited by law from preempting land. In the Indian affairs files for British Columbia there is a letter about "Capoose, an Indian who is trying to live a white man's life, and who is enterprising, has improved a piece of land at Anaham [probably Anahim Lake], and having been in peaceful occupation of the same for about fifteen years, desires to obtain title to it. People are flocking to that part of the country now and some are threatening to take his lands and improvements away from him." A few like Capoose were able to find white neighbours who would take out a preemption on their behalf, but this was obviously fraught with difficulty.[77]

Agriculture was the DIA's rather simple-minded strategy for "civilizing" Aboriginal Peoples. Whether on the Prairies, in the rock scrabble earth of Cape Breton, on the rocky coast of British Columbia, or in the subalpine of the Chilcotin, the department had a uniform strategy of encouraging Aboriginal Peoples to be farmers. This would teach them work habits, would require little education, and would keep them at home, where they could be guided by priest and Indian Agent. Agents made their annual reports on forms that asked them about the amount of peas, hay, and so on that had been harvested, the number of acres fenced, the amount of farm equipment purchased. Never mind that frost (or even snow) is not unheard of in the Chilcotin in July, the agents encouraged the Tsilhqot'in to farm. As a result, they had to regularly report that an "early frost at a dozen reserves destroyed grain and root crops necessitating relief to quite a number of destitute Indians." And if it was not the cold that was a problem, it was drought.[78] The Tsilhqot'in knew their land and its climate and quickly discerned the limits of agriculture. Where we, in retrospect, would see as prudent their reluctance to clear forests, divert streams, and plough and fence land for little return, the wheat-blind Indian Agents interpreted this as a lack of cooperation.

As isolated as the Tsilhqot'in were, by the 1910s they were falling within reach of the provincial government as it attempted to limit access to their traditional economy. In 1908, a game commissioner had been appointed for the district by the province, and in 1911, a revised Provincial Game Act limited the hunting season for deer to mid-September to December. And no "Indian" was permitted to kill more than three deer per year. Although there was an amendment made to the act in 1913 to allow provincial game wardens to issue Indians permits to hunt deer for food, wardens were often far away when food was needed, and they were not inclined to give permits to anyone but those too old to work and, presumably, to hunt.[79] As Indian Agent McLeod pointed out to the Game Board: "In outlying places where there is only weekly mail service this means that three or four weeks may elapse before the applicant gets permission to stop starving."[80]

A good picture of the economy of the Tsilhqot'in and their reliance on hunting is provided by the McKenna-McBride Royal Commission, which toured the Chilcotin in 1914 and heard from the chiefs of most of the

Inclined To Be Lazy

These Indians are inclined to be lazy, preferring to hunt and fish for a living rather than cultivate their lands.

Ewan Bell, Williams Lake Indian Agent, 1906

Tsilhqot'in Tsulin and
party with pack horses
in the Bella Coola Valley,
July 19, 1924

communities between 1914 and 1916. At Toosey, on the eastern edge of the
plateau, Chief Toosey told the commission that, in the past, they hunted
and trapped but that now game animals "are getting very scarce," and said
that some of the good hunters go out in the fall but they get very little." He
added that they depend on their fifty-two cattle for milk and the sale of the
steers for money. The fishery was also important: "Every fall we go fishing
on the Chilcotin River (reserve 3) and dry the catch." Asked if they worked
for the whites, Toosey replied that in the past they had freighted but that
now they only made two to three cents a pound to haul freight from
Ashcroft. Moreover, most of the people on his reserve were not much interested in wage labour: "they are all pretty lazy, so they don't work."

At the largest Tsilhqot'in community, Chief Anaham Bob told the
commission that his people raised one hundred tons of hay plus oats for
use and sale. They did some freighting, though prices were low, and they
had had a small sawmill but could not now keep it running so sold it off.
His comments show that the traditional economy was still vital. He said
that they picked a lot of berries, got a lot of lake fish for food, and that
"when the season is open [they] do quite a lot of trapping. Sometimes
[they] don't make much, sometimes [they] make a little on it." A single
black fox skin was worth between $250 and $300 and could set a family up
for the winter.

South of Anaham, at the Stone village, Chief Louis said that, in his
community: "Our living comes from hunting and fishing and what we get

off the land. There is not trapping much at all. [The] land is too poor."
Deer were the main animals hunted, and lake trout was the fish staple.
Further west, at Redstone, Captain Tobie told the commission that fishing
in Penisk [Puntzi?] Lake provided his community with its main source of
food. For cash, they did some trapping for fox, fisher, mink, and beaver:
"Some years [were] good, some bad." They also had 183 head of cattle, but
Tobie did not consider them to be important economically. A Nemiah and
Ulkatcho delegation told the commission that their livelihood came en-
tirely from fishing, trapping, and hunting.[81]

It was clear from the Royal Commission and the annual Indian Agent's
reports that all the Tsilhqot'in, even the more agricultural Anaham band,
still lived an itinerant life. If they lived in their villages at all, it was only on
a few occasions a year – Christmas and "priest time" (i.e., the annual spring
visit of the Roman Catholic priest) and sowing and harvest times. Otherwise, they were on their hunting, fishing, or gathering grounds, their range
lands or hay meadows, camped in traditional sites on what the government
regarded as Crown land.

Surveyor Hugh Bostock gave an account of the seasonal rounds of
Tsilhqot'in Henry Alexis (Eagle Lake Henry) and his brother-in-law Billy
Dagg in 1925, when they were reputed to be the wealthiest men in the
region, aboriginal or white. In the fall and winter the two of them trapped
and hunted coyotes for bounty, making fifteen dollars per pelt and selling
sixty-four pelts in 1924-25. In the spring they worked at their ranch, where
they had about two hundred cattle and the same number of horses. In the
summer, Henry guided for the Geological Survey or BC Land Branch survey parties (he received four dollars per day for himself and $2.50 for each
of twelve horses, which he rented to the survey) and Billy put up the hay at
the ranch. In the fall each guided for hunters, and when hunting season
was over it was time to round up the cattle, drive some to Williams Lake
for sale, and feed the stock.[82]

The longevity of the subsistence economy was a thorn in the paw of
the provincial game department. It harboured a particular dislike for the
Tsilhqot'in people, who, in carrying on traditional practices, had flouted
the province's game laws. In 1918, the local game warden wrote that the
"Chilcotin are an annual source of trouble." That year the province imposed a ban on trapping beaver in order to conserve stocks.[83]

The hunting closures coincided with fishing closures, which dramatically affected the Tsilhqot'in. The same year, two hundred and seventeen
miles (350 kilometres) to the south, the construction of the Canadian Northern Railway caused a dramatic decline in the Tsilhqot'in subsistence economy. The construction, which went through Hell's Gate in the Fraser

Talking in Broken English, Local Indian, and Chinook

When we got back to camp I was delighted to find that Henry Alexis and his wife had arrived with 14 horses, 12 rented to the survey ... Henry had killed a deer along the way and about the first thing he said to me was "Me saddlem horse, me see'em mowich, me shootem, me kipem, heap fine" ... Henry liked to talk and told us many useful things in his mixture of broken English, local Indian and Chinook.

Hugh Bostock, "Pack Horse Tracks," June 1925

Eagle Lake Henry (Henry Alexis), possibly the richest man in the Chilcotin, and his wife Alietta

More Trouble than Other Indians

The Chilcotin Indians have caused us
more trouble than any other Indians.

BC Game Commissioner M.B. Jackson to
Indian Agent E. McLeod, June 10, 1925

Canyon, temporarily blocked the Fraser River and then narrowed it, speeding up the flow of water through this already narrow channel so that salmon could not make it back to the Chilcotin River to spawn. The slide wiped out the major portion of the salmon stocks of the entire province, and the government moved to protect the commercial fisheries by limiting the aboriginal fishery. In the three years between 1919 and 1921, food fishing was banned entirely on the Fraser River and its watershed, depriving the eastern Tsilhqot'in of the main item in their subsistence economy.[84] To give an indication of what this meant to the Anaham, Toosey, and Stone peoples, a decade later the Indian Agent estimated that the average Tsilhqot'in ate fifty to sixty salmon per year. If the average sockeye weighed five pounds dried, then the average Tsilhqot'in (including those who did not fish for salmon) ate 250 to 300 pounds of fish per year, or over three-quarters of a pound per day. The closing of this fishery had to have created enormous hardship.[85]

Nearly simultaneous with the early attempts to limit subsistence hunting and the fishing closure was the demise of the packing industry, which had employed people from the eastern Chilcotin, especially Anaham, including Henry Solomon's father. This, too, was the result of a railway, the Pacific Great Eastern (now Canadian National Railway), which ran up the coast from Vancouver to Squamish and through the Coast Range through Williams Lake to Prince George. The railway, which was completed to Quesnel in 1921, killed the freighting industry and also brought prairie grain to the edge of the Chilcotin Plateau, where it was cheaply brought. The fall in the price of oats and hay helped the ranchers but it hurt the farmers.[86]

Then, in 1925 the Game Board unilaterally closed the trapping industry, declaring that the whole "Eastern District" of the province, including the Chilcotin, would be subject to an indefinite ban on the harvest of fur-bearers. Agent McLeod thought that the policy was calculated to drive Aboriginal People out of a subsistence economy and onto relief in order to benefit the white trapper and sport hunter: "Many of the Indians can eke out a living from wild life without the need of getting government relief, if left free from persecution. Such a policy will sap their self-reliance and drive them more than ever to look for government aid." Moreover, he added, "the white settlers, almost without exception are commonly known to live practically the year round on wild game, yet one never hears of them being prosecuted." The Game Branch was not sympathetic and proceeded with the closure.[87] In effect, the province was diverting the game and fish to white sports hunters and fishers, and forcing the Tsilhqot'in onto federal relief. Agent McLeod complained that his relief costs had shot up to five hundred dollars per month in 1925 as a result of provincial action.[88]

When the salmon runs appeared to be down in the late 1930s, the aboriginal fishery on the Chilcotin system was again closed. To fish in 1938, 1939, and 1942, the Tsilhqot'in had to apply to the federal fisheries inspector and then travel down to the Fraser River. Since there are only a few good fishing spots on the Chilcotin and Fraser River System, this area was easier to police than might otherwise have been the case. Since the Chilcotin River was a much more productive fishery than was the Fraser River, given the narrow channels the fish had to pass through, the closure of the former cut the aboriginal catch by between 83 percent and 95 percent (see Table 5.1). In 1940, James Kew, the fisheries inspector for the region, proudly declared that, "in 1936 Indians took approx 26 percent of the run and this year only four percent."[89]

The great economic events of North America, the Depression and the Second World War, were transmitted to the Chilcotin Plateau through fur prices and the local demand for labour. The 1930s Depression was noticed in the low fur prices and the virtual disappearance of wage labour. The Indian Agent estimated that wages paid to Indians in the Williams Lake Agency fell by 75 percent, from $55,000 in 1930 to $12,350 in 1933. With the loss of a cash economy, the Tsilhqot'in people relied more on their subsistence economy; however, as has just been noted, in the late 1930s, the fishery was largely denied to them. Thanks to the new hunting and fishing regulations, they had little alternative but to ask for relief.[90]

Regulating the Chilcotin into Their Graves

I cannot too strongly emphasize upon the fact that this closed season is going to create a hardship on the majority of the bands, greater than any law or regulation heretofore passed by any government and if rigidly carried, will no doubt be the means of putting a number of them in their graves, more especially the Chilcotin tribe which have been depending on fur for most of their living.

Indian Agent E. McLeod to M.B. Jackson, Chairman of the Game Conservation Board of BC, May 20, 1925

Nuxalk boys bringing salmon home, 1920

TABLE 5.1

**Food fishery salmon caught in the Williams Lake Indian Agency/
Quesnel Fisheries District, 1933-47**

Year	Sockeye salmon	Spring salmon	Total caught	Total permits to fishermen*
1933	16,700	4,600	21,100	n/a
1938	475	50	525†	n/a
1939	675	165	940†	59
1940	14,717	224	14,941	n/a
1941	18,204	230	18,434	100
1942	2,472	77	2,549†	70
1943	n/a	n/a	n/a	93
1944	13,310	171	13,481‡	87
1945	8,606	165	8,771	n/a
1946	1,982	64	2,046†	96§
1947	n/a	n/a	n/a	86

* For those years where permits were issued separately for the Chilcotin and Fraser Rivers, the higher figure for the Fraser River is given, assuming that the lower number who took permits for the Chilcotin also took them for the Fraser.
† Chilcotin River closed to Indian salmon harvest.
‡ Fishing permitted only on the north side of the Chilcotin River.
§ Fisheries agent estimates that only half the permits used.
Sources: This includes the Sugar Cane band and the Alexandria band (who are not Tsilhqot'in) and seems to exclude the Nemiah band (who are). Estimates from Report of James E. Kew, Fisheries Inspector, Quesnel Subdistrict, Library and Archives Canada, RG 23, vol. 662, file 712-2-72, pts. 3 and 4; and for 1933, C.C. Perry to Secretary of DIA, March 2, 1933, RG 10, vol. 11298, file 34-38.

Although among the most isolated Aboriginal Peoples in the county, the Tsilhqot'in also felt the impact of the Second World War. Few Tsilhqot'in went to war for Canada – a country that existed for the Tsilhqot'in only in the form of Indian and fishery agents – but the war came to them. Fur prices went up, and even the lowly squirrel could provide them with a livelihood. According to the Indian Agent, "Many are making as high as $20 a day hunting squirrels with skins worth 25 cents each." The price on squirrel skins climbed from five cents in 1939 to one dollar per skin in 1946. This was a big raise when compared to ranch work, which was paying only fifty cents per day.[91]

The war also brought a new industry to the eastern Chilcotin: logging and sawmilling. Small sawmills popped up to meet wartime demands for lumber, and this demand carried on beyond the war. In the 1950s, "little mills popped up like mushrooms after a rain" so that, at one point, there were twenty-five of them strung out between Riske Creek and Tatlayoko Lake.[92] Another new industry had come to the Chilcotin as the road network snaked its way westward: Christmas tree cutting. With the labour shortage during the war, prices went up and the Indian Agent reported that Christmas tree cutting provided lots of work for some Tsilhqot'in, with some families earning between two hundred and three hundred dollars for a little more than one month's work: "There is a dearth of labour in the district and the Indians reap the benefit."[93]

Wartime employment gave Fisheries Inspector James Kew an opportunity to further limit fishing permits. In 1941, he reported: "All these natives are not dependent on salmon for their winter food supply and an effort was made to limit fishing privileges to those individuals who are or may become destitute during the year." In 1942, he only issued seventy permits to the 1,500 Indians in his district. The next year he proudly proclaimed: "The total landing of salmon would not amount to more than one fish an individual considering the whole Indian population of the Cariboo [and Chilcotin] area."[94]

Ironically, the Tsilhqot'in's nineteenth-century move eastward to take advantage of the rich hunting and salmon harvesting sites close to the Fraser River put them in closer contact with the twentieth-century state's attempt to limit aboriginal access to these resources. The Nemiah people, who remained in their isolated valley, still lived beyond the vision of the state, and, at the end of the salmon migration when the fish are in poor condition, they still fished as much as they wished even as late as the 1970s, when road access opened them up to supervision as well.

In fact, the decade and a half after the war were boom times for the eastern Chilcotin, for the same reasons that they were boom times for the rest of North America. The Second World War had ended, but the economy of North America remained on a war footing as the world moved into the Cold War. This undeclared war came to the Chilcotin in 1951, when a location near Puntzi Lake was chosen as the site for a military radar base – part of the Pine Tree Line of radar installations meant to warn Americans (and only incidentally, Canadians) when they were about to be attacked by Russian bombers or intercontinental ballistic missiles.

Eighty-seven years after the colonial militia established a base near Puntzi Lake during the Chilcotin War, the Canadian and American military reoccupied the area to fight the Cold War. Access to the Chilcotin had not improved dramatically in the years in between, so the first stage was to link Puntzi Lake to the rest of North America. The dirt and gravel seasonal road that linked Puntzi Lake to Williams Lake became the Cariboo Highway, which was maintained year-round. The second longest airstrip in British Columbia was built to accommodate the transport planes that brought the base into being. Before the base was established, you could not get a bulldozer to Puntzi Lake to begin road work; after the base appeared, thirteen D8 bulldozers were available year round to maintain the runway and to keep it clear of snow.[95]

More Work So Less Fish

With the labour shortage and the high wages to be obtained on ranch work, the need for fish-food supplies has been greatly lessened and more or less confined to a few of the older and indigent natives in the reserves.

James Kew, Fisheries Inspector, Quesnel Subdistrict, 1941

Puntzi, as the base was called, became the biggest community in the whole Chilcotin, with one hundred American, and a smattering of Canadian, servicemen living on the base, a few with families. Road and base construction improved access to the mills at Williams Lake and to provincial lumber markets more generally. That, plus some wage labour on the base, made the period between 1951 and 1965 one of the most prosperous the Chilcotin region had ever seen.

Yet, few of the Tsilhqot'in experienced the boom. For a few young men, the logging and milling operations added some wage labour to their seasonal rounds. But even with regard to these twin "bush" activities, the Tsilhqot'in were only hired when there was not enough white labour in the area. In the more lucrative construction or service jobs provided by the base, only whites were hired. Despite the claims by the Indian Agent that there was little racism in the region, other reports are rife with indications of racist hiring and other practices.[96]

If the logging industry brought a few jobs to the Tsilhqot'in in the 1950s, many more livelihoods were lost by the decline in the trapping

Trading coyote pelts at Bert Lehman's store at Anahim Lake, 1938

industry. Fur prices fell off dramatically after the war and were down to Depression-era prices by 1953, while the prices of supplies, driven up by wartime inflation, stayed high, necessitating the issuance of relief. The communities that had been sustained by trapping, especially Nemiah and Redstone, turned to small-scale stock raising and relied more heavily on seasonal haying and fencing contracts with plateau ranchers. The DIA reports for 1955-56 were typical for the decade:

> Below average financial returns from trapping resulted from lower market prices and severe weather conditions. Many Indian families in the northern and coastal areas who had previously derived their livelihood from trapping have now changed their locations to points where advantage can be taken of part-time employment to augment their income from trapping.[97]

Likewise, the Ulkatcho people (a mix of Carrier and Tsilhqot'in) were gradually shifting southwest into the former heart of Tsilhqot'in territory to establish a community around the school and church at Anahim Lake.

Logging also had the effect of destroying some wildlife habitat. Logging opens up browsing areas for ungulates like deer, but this is offset by the deep snow that drifts off the trees into the clear cuts and makes the deer more vulnerable to wolves. The network of logging roads also had the effect of opening the diminished traditional hunting grounds of the Tsilhqot'in to anyone with a pick-up truck.[98]

The postwar cash opportunities started to come off the rails in the late 1960s. The Puntzi military base closed in 1965. The small sawmill operations closed as economies of scale and transportation improvements meant that logs were trucked to Williams Lake for milling. Even the century-old practice of hiring Tsilhqot'in crews to hay and fence came to an end as ranchers turned to mechanical reapers and balers to cut and store hay and began to use barbed wire and post hole diggers attached to tractors to do fencing. They were no longer hiring people to make split-rail fences. Fur prices had remained low but as late as the early 1960s there were still Tsilhqot'in communities who depended on this for their main livelihood. The trapline, for many Tsilhqot'in and their Carrier neighbours, meant independence. One Carrier man explained it this way: "My trapline is like money in the bank. When I need something, I just go out and get it." By 1970, even those communities had to give up trapping as unprofitable. No trapline, no bank account. When the land could not provide, people turned to the government.[99]

Catherine Brow studied the nearby Secwepemc community of Alkali Lake in 1967 and found that, of 209 people resident on the reserve, only

Chief William Charleyboy and his wife Elaine of Redstone, 1910s. Their grandson, Ervin Charleyboy, is the current chief.

eight had wage-earning jobs: "Potatoes and salmon, which is smoked and preserved, constitute the basic food supply of every family. Although the diet is supplemented with some purchased goods, especially balogna, cookies and eggs, most meals consist of bread, potatoes and salmon."[100]

The changing economy affected aboriginal and non-aboriginal residents of the Chilcotin differently. When times were good, whites used their land as capital to mortgage or sell to start another business or invest in a pension plan. When times were bad, whites had a simple economic strategy: they left. For the Tsilhqot'in, the situation was different. This was their home, and they stayed.[101]

Obviously, the territory of the Tsilhqot'in is strongly intertwined with their culture. Unlike most of the immigrants, whose culture encouraged them to relocate for better economic opportunities, the Tsilhqot'in prefer location over economic advancement. While, historically, the Tsilhqoti'in have been migratory, this movement occurred within specified owned territories. Although there was a prehistoric and historic movement of home territories, these moves have always been to contiguous territories. Tsilhqoti'in history is written onto the landscape in the place names that are associated with the stories of a distant, communal past as well as a more immediate, individual past: "the land itself becomes the map of human experience by which 'telling one's life' is remembered."[102]

Even had they wanted to leave, it was not easy for the Tsilhqot'in to do so. Unlike the white ranchers who moved into the Chilcotin from elsewhere and so had kin networks elsewhere – networks that might support them while they re-established themselves, the Tsilhqot'in kin networks are largely in the Chilcotin. Since most live on reserve or vacant Crown land, they cannot sell or mortgage property to start a new business or finance a relocation. In fact, the reserve is the one place where their housing is subsidized. Moreover, the educational levels of the Tsilhqot'in were dramatically lower than were those of their non-aboriginal neighbours, with the result that they had fewer employment options and less mobility.[103]

An indication of the Tsilhqot'in's attachment to their land may be seen in a 1971 survey, which shows that 75 percent of the Aboriginal People surveyed in the Fraser River drainage system (including the Chilcotin Plateau) lived in the same village as did their fathers, and 61 percent lived in the same location as did their grandfathers. Eighty-six percent said that they had lived in their current location for most or all of their lives and that they did not want to move anywhere else. Of these, 96 percent said that they did not want to move because this was their home and they liked it.[104]

Schooling came much later to the Tsilhqot'in communities than it did to their white neighbours, and transportation difficulties delayed the enrolment of Tsilhqot'in youth in the residential school that had been established at Williams Lake in 1891. Not until 1907 did the first of the Tsilhqot'in children go to the school, and then only from the closer communities of Anaham and Toosey. By 1914, the parents told the McKenna-McBride Commission that they were anxious to have their children educated but that they were not going to send them to the residential school at Williams Lake. Chief Louis from Stone told the commissioners that they tried sending children to school "but they all died on us so we stopped." Other chiefs complained about the children being whipped and worked too hard in the fields. Henry Solomon, interviewed in 1999, said he ran away from the school shortly after he got there as the people were too mean.[105]

The difficult and sometimes brutal life of children at the residential school, combined with the difficulty of travelling through the Chilcotin and the dependence on an economy based on the land, meant that there was little incentive for Tsilhqot'in parents to send their children away for schooling. Not until the 1940s was the first school established for aboriginal children in the Chilcotin, and this was founded by the Sisters of Christ the King at the Anaham Reserve. The lack of formal schooling meant that Tsilhqot'in kids grew up speaking their own language and being schooled in their own culture long after most aboriginal children in British Columbia were being force-fed English and a foreign culture. It meant that there was a continuing need to keep Chinook jargon alive as a means of communication between Tsilhqot'in speakers and white immigrants. It also limited the Tsilhqot'in people's ability to leave the plateau to get work.

When the DIA finally established schools in the Chilcotin communities in the 1950s and 1960s, there was no culture of schooling in these communities (as had developed elsewhere over the previous one hundred years). Moreover, the teachers that could be hired in these very remote schools were, in the words of Indian Agent Demerais, "no credit to our educational program."[106] The educational opportunities for most of the Tsilhqot'in lagged far behind those of their non-native counterparts who had attended provincially funded schools since the 1920s.

The reports of the Indian Agents, which, seventy years previously, had spoken to the relative prosperity of the Tsilhqot'in now reported the opposite:

> We are faced with both a very low standard of living amongst the Indians and also a serious unemployment problem. If we were to provide a decent living for the Indians of this Agency without developing every resource that we have, it would cost thousands and thousands of dollars annually in welfare assistance, along with the damaging effect welfare has on people.[107]

Outliving the Coyotes

"Chee Whit, I presume?"

"Would you like to go to the old people's home?"

"She say she don't want to go anywhere," says John Quilt, translating ... The talk on the meadow is in a mishmash of English-Chilcotin and the old Chinook trade lingo.

"She told the people all the coyotes die before I'm going to die."

Dave Stockland, "Ageless Cheewhit Spurns a House, Prefers Nomadic life in Chilcotin," *Vancouver Sun*, June 26, 1973

Tsilhqot'in Cheewhit lived on and from the land into the 1970s.

We Live Like We're Indian

Henry Solomon: Yeah. We got a pension
now.

John Lutz: Do ya?

HS: Yeah, me and my wife.

JL: Yeah? Is that enough to get by on?

HS: Ah, some.

JL: Some?

HS: Every month we get a pension,
yeah.

JL: Uh-huh. Do you still hunt and fish?

HS: Yeah, we still do, yeah. Sometimes
(?) like you buy in store, you know,
not enough. Maybe go fishing and
stuff like that and then we live like
we're Indian long time ago.

Henry Solomon, Xeni Gwet'in, September 5,
1999

For the Tsilhqot'in, the decline of the cash economy after the Second
World War coincided with the rise of the welfare economy. In 1945, the
Tsilhqot'in were eligible for family allowance, as were all other Canadians.
For the Santa Lulua family of Nemiah, with nine children, for example,
this meant an additional fifty-four dollars per month. In 1948, a DIA old
age allowance of eight dollars per month was issued to Indians over seventy
years old, but in 1953 they became eligible for the national old age security
allowance of forty dollars per month. The national programs were far more
generous than were the DIA relief payments, and they came in cash rather
than in food.[108] Then, in 1965, the DIA increased the welfare rates to bring
them close to provincial rates, and in the Chilcotin it shifted from giving
out welfare in kind to giving recipients cash payments.

A dramatic transformation took place after these 1965 changes, according to Tsilhqot'in observers. Ervin Charleyboy, chief of Redstone, noted
that trapping collapsed between 1960 and 1965 and that welfare "totally
changed the lifestyle" of the Tsilhqot'in. In an interview at the Tsilhqot'in
National Government Office in August 2000, Orrey Charleyboy, Manager
of the Traditional Resource Use Survey, put it this way: "When welfare
came in the 1970s people did not leave the reserve, people stopped trapping." Joe Alphonse put it succinctly, "The reliance on the land decreased.
Reliance on Overwaitea [a supermarket in Williams Lake] increased."[109]

The Nemiah people, the Xeni Gweti'in, witnessed the change more
dramatically than most, since a road connection to Williams Lake and cash
welfare payments arrived at almost the same time. Patrick Lulua of Nemiah
noted: "The road to Nemiah and welfare made all the difference. Before
people used to trap, ranch, taking haying and fencing contracts for large
ranches. [After] people do not like to get their hands wet and frozen trapping; instead they go to the warm band office and collect a cheque." In a
separate interview, Gilbert Solomon, also in Nemiah, remarked: "When
social assistance came people did not hustle enough. Welfare made it so we
do not go as far into the bush."[110] In 1967, the Indian Agent commented:
"There are some disadvantages resulting from the welfare rates being more
than many could earn on ranches and a reluctance to resume work does
crop up."[111]

In the Chilcotin, all of these changes were accompanied by the arrival
of television and a shift to a consumer mentality among the young. Young
men were the most employable of the Tsilhqot'in, and they were the most
vulnerable to enthusiasm for the brand new sports car that swept young
men across North America. Don Wise remembered that the desire to own
vehicles like the Ford Mustang took young men off the reserves and ranches
to work in Williams Lake and adversely affected the operation of small-scale

family ranches, which had depended on that labour. Nemiah elder Henry Solomon put it this way: "The young people all want to live like white people."[112]

John Hall captured the employment/unemployment patterns of all the families living in the mixed aboriginal and non-aboriginal Chilcotin community of Anahim Lake in 1969-70. He surveyed all the households and found that, of the fifty-two white households, none relied wholly or even partially on government income assistance (beyond the universal family allowance program). By contrast, thirty of the thirty-five aboriginal households depended wholly or partially on income assistance. Of these thirty, eight relied completely on income assistance, while the remaining twenty-two households used government payments to supplement trapping, ranching, or logging income or income from other odd jobs. The traditional and modern economies, which had fused in the late nineteenth century into a "moditional economy," now had the added component of the welfare economy. When work was available, people took it; when it was not, they turned to the bush, the rivers, and the state.

The occupations of the employed tell us much about rural employment. Twenty of the fifty-two white households relied on jobs with the public sector, with the police, school, highway maintenance, or the government-owned BC Hydro. Given racist hiring practices and educational limitations, these jobs were largely restricted to whites. Only four of the aboriginal households were supported by public sector work: three were involved in road maintenance and one in welfare work.[113] A 1971 employment survey that sampled the Tsilhqot'in suggests that, while 69 percent expressed a preference for year-round employment, less than 29 percent were employed all year. One-third (31 percent) of the respondents expressed a preference for seasonal labour only.

The poverty of many Tsilhqot'in was inscribed in their bodies. A survey of the nutrition on the Anaham reserve, published in 1971, showed that iron deficiency anaemia was well above standard rates for adult and teenage Tsilhqot'in women. Since organ meats obtained from hunting are an excellent source of iron, the presence of this condition suggests a decline in the use of these foods as well as a lack of an affordable store-bought alternative. Low levels of vitamins C and E were found in the blood samples, as were elevated levels of cholesterol, suggesting a switch to the consumption of fat and refined sugars.[114]

In 1971, the Fraser River aboriginal respondents to the survey were virtually unanimous in their opinion that fewer people fished, hunted, and gathered berries than had done so in their grandparents' time. Over three-quarters attributed this to the fact that their grandparents had no access to

We Used to Live a Long Time

Henry Solomon: We got no welfare nothing long time ago.

John Lutz: No welfare? No.

HS: No. Now everybody getting welfare.

JL: Yeah?

HS: Yeah. Like every month they get welfare.

JL: Is that a good thing or a bad thing do you think?

HS: Uh, maybe a long time ago, we used to live for a long time.

JL: Uh-huh.

HS: With different kind of food, you know, and now you buy sodas, buy, you know, what the hell you buying! [laughing]

Henry Solomon, Xeni Gwet'in, September 5, 1999

Ulkatcho woman scraping moose skin
near Bella Coola, 1922

wage labour or welfare payments. Another 8 percent attributed the decline
in the subsistence economy to a decline in resources, and another 8 percent
attributed it to an increase in regulation.

Yet, the survey established the persistence of the subsistence economy.
Representatives from the Tsilhqot'in estimated that 42 percent of their people
actively engaged in food fishing. Given that few children under sixteen
engage in the fishery, this suggests that almost every family fished. The
eight Tsilhqot'in representatives each spent an average of forty-seven days
fishing per year – an estimated 275 hours. They estimated that they ate fish
between three and four times a week throughout the year. The researchers
calculated that the per capita consumption of salmon among the Tsilhqot'in
was 85 pounds (38 kilograms) per year. Without salmon, most thought that
there would be some families in their communities who would not have
enough food to eat.

The subsistence economy was not limited to fish. The Tsilhqot'in representatives estimated that 29 percent of their communities hunted for food.
Eleven percent of the Tsilhqot'in still engaged in wild berry picking, while

7 percent had gardens or animals that they raised for food. In 1971, the Tsilhqot'in rated fishing as equally important to game and wild plants in their subsistence economy.[115]

The integration of the subsistence and cash economies into a mixed moditional economy is illustrated by a 1969 community study of the Chilcotin community of Anaham. That year, the eighty families in that community consumed the meat of ninety-six moose, 480 deer, and some 3,500 fish. Some families had gardens for root crops and continued to pick wild berries. This accounted for almost half of their caloric intake. It was the country foods that provided the bulk of protein, calcium, and vitamins, and the researchers concluded that the persistence of the subsistence economy was essential to the health of the community. The other half of their food calories came from store-bought foods, of which bread, cookies, cereal, candies, soft drinks, sugar, and flour topped the list.[116] These were bought with cash from wage work or with relief vouchers from the state.

By the early 1970s, the employment and welfare situations of the isolated Tsilhqot'in and the urban Lekwungen were very similar, but while their urban counterparts were in danger of starving, the Tsilhqot'in still gathered a fundamental part of their diet from the land and rivers around them. In some respects, this can be attributed to choices that the Tsilhqot'in made in the nineteenth century. Instead of welcoming settlers and fully engaging in the capitalist economy, the Tsilhqot'in had resisted settlement and kept the European economy at arm's length. They resisted the building of a road that would have put them on the main thoroughfare to the south, with the result that, when a road was finally built, it avoided their territory, passing along the opposite side of the Fraser River. Their insistence, in the nineteenth century, that Europeans enter their territory on Tsilhqot'in terms meant that the Chilcotin Plateau was one of the least settled areas in British Columbia.

The different responses of the Tsilhqot'in and the Lekwungen to the Europeans have, with 160 years of perspective, advantaged neither with respect to wealth or power, at least as measured in Canadian society. They have, however, made a major difference in cultural wealth. Tsilhqot'in resistance meant that their language and culture came under less pressure from the capitalist economy, from the state, from missionaries, and from white society in general than did the languages and cultures of other First Nations peoples. While there are no living native speakers of Lekwungen, for instance, all adults in Nemiah are native speakers of Tsilhqot'in, and the language retention rate among the rest of the Tsilhqot'in is also high. If their early resistance to capitalist relations did not protect their economy in the long run, it would seem that it did protect their culture.

SIX

Outside History:
Labourers of the Aboriginal Province

The contradictions and mixed messages connecting Aboriginal People and paid labour are well illustrated in the quotes from the *British Colonist* in the 1860s (see sidebar). Written only sixteen months apart, one article suggests that Aboriginal People were "valueless in the labour market" and the other suggests that, as an abundant source of labour, they were a threat to white workers. The inconsistency is typical of sources from the period: Indians were "lazy" *and* "hard working." One view seems to echo the settler characterizations of the Tsilhqot'in, who avoided working for whites, and the other the Lekwungen. Looking at aboriginal work across the whole region that became British Columbia, this chapter explores whether the Lekwungen or the Tsilhqot'in experience with paid work was more common. Such an overview allows us to see the extent to which the economy depended on aboriginal labour, the peak years of aboriginal wealth in the post-contact period, and the decline of that affluence.

The time frame with which I am concerned in this section is usually described as BC's "settlement" period. It starts with the establishment of Fort Victoria in 1843 and includes the creation of the Colony of Vancouver Island in 1849, the gold rushes, the founding of the giant export sawmills, Confederation, the development and spread of the salmon-canning industry, and the completion of the Canadian Pacific Railway in 1885 – an event that tied the Province of British Columbia to the North American continental economy. What is remarkable about this chronology is that it only follows the activities of the whites, who were, after all, a small minority of the population.

We usually think of the coming of Europeans to BC as the peopling of an area, but the first century of European "settlement" was, in fact, a period of depopulation. Yet, despite introduced diseases and a dramatically reduced population, Aboriginal People remained in the majority long after the first white settlement. In 1855, of the 34,600 or so inhabitants of the Colony of Vancouver Island and the adjacent islands and shores, all but 774 were aboriginal. There were probably an additional thirty thousand to forty thousand Aboriginal People living in the remainder of what became

Their habits of indolence, roaming propensities, and natural repugnance for manual labour, together with a thievish disposition which appears to be inherently characteristic of the Indian race, totally disqualifies them from ever becoming either useful or desirable citizens.

British Colonist, February 19, 1861

For years Victoria has suffered to an extent unknown in any civilized town in the universe from the residence of an Indian population ... "cheap" labor at the expense of a white immigrant population.

British Colonist, June 17, 1862

◀ Aboriginal navies (railway construction crew) working on the Canadian Northern Railway between Yale and Spuzzum in the Fraser Canyon, ca. 1912

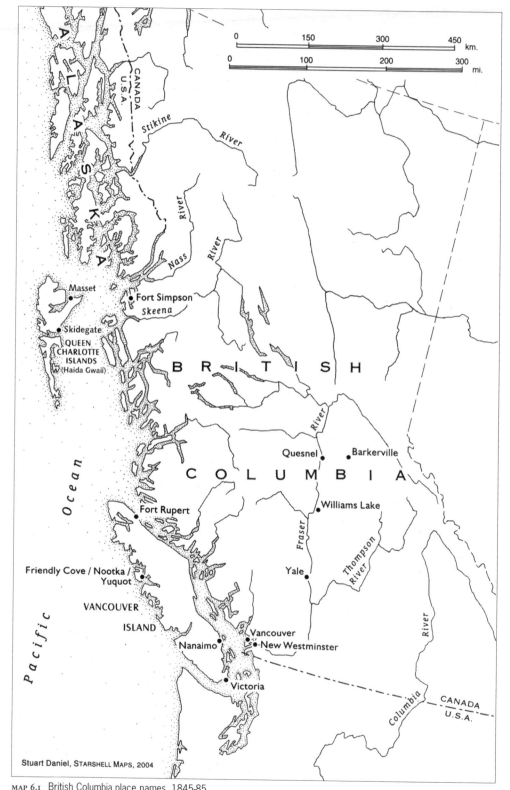

MAP 6.1 British Columbia place names, 1845-85

British Columbia. When BC joined Canada in 1871, there were three times as many Aboriginal People as "settlers" living there. In fact, until 1885, BC was, by population at least, an "aboriginal province."[1]

This vast aboriginal population was extremely heterogeneous, both culturally and in terms of its history with non-Aboriginal People. It was comprised of at least thirty "nations," or ethnic groups, speaking twenty-six distinct, and largely mutually unintelligible, languages. Each nation had its own customary laws that defined property rights and social relations so by 1843 each village had its own "history" of exchange with non-Aboriginal People or their trade goods.[2] This history is available to us, in many cases, in the words of Aboriginal People themselves.

This period has been seen as a watershed, a time when European power was established and Aboriginal Peoples displaced. One of the historians who has taken this view, Martin Robin, puts it this way: "Not being a serious competitor to the white capitalist, landowner or labourer, the Indian was neither feared nor despised; he was rather ignored, patronized or romanticized." Robin Fisher thought Aboriginal People had become irrelevant.[3] A closer look challenges this evaluation.

"Useful, Indeed Necessary," 1843-85

From the closing of the Spanish fort at Yuquot (Nootka) in 1792 until the establishment of the Colony of Vancouver Island in 1849, diverse aboriginal nations accommodated twenty-three small European "settlements" in what is now BC.[4] Until 1824, these "settlements" were fur trading posts that were connected by trails and waterways to England, where furs were sent and from which provisions were obtained. In that year, Governor George Simpson of the Hudson's Bay Company embarked on a tour of the company's posts, acquired from the North West Company three years previously. Few of these posts were making any profit, and Simpson soon discovered why. He wrote in his diary that the staff of the Columbia District "have shewn an extraordinary predilection for European provisions ... all this time they may be said to be eating gold; such fare we cannot afford in the present times." Given the cost of transportation, he ordered the staff to cultivate a taste for local salmon.[5]

By halving the number of staff and ordering the remainder to become self-sufficient, Simpson's orders produced a fundamental reorientation among the fur trading posts. On his return trip in 1828, Simpson found that, in contrast to their previous practice of importing food, HBC people were now dependent upon Aboriginal People "for the means of subsistence and for various duties about the establishments."[6] As a result of expanding into subsistence activities, the settlements came to embrace activities other

I Am Good Company Man Today

Today I was in the store the Hudsons Bay Company take me in Fort to employ. Also to help them in Trad ship. I had company man today. I am good trader.

Arthur Wellington Clah, Ts'msyen, February 26, 1868

A Perfect Babel

Fort Vancouver is the largest of all posts in the Hudson's Bay Territory, and has frequently upwards of two hundred voyageurs with their Indian wives residing there, besides the factors and clerks. A perfect babel of languages is to be heard among them. [H]ence the growth of a patois by which they can hold intercourse together ... There are Canadian and half-breeds married to Chinook women, who can only converse with their wives in this speech; and it is the fact, strange as it may seem, that many young children are growing up to whom this factitious language is really the mother tongue.

Horatio Hale, "The 'Jargon' or Trade-Language of Oregon" [1846]

than the fur trade; correspondingly, the "various duties" that Aboriginal People were hired to perform expanded as well.

The company's labour shortage worsened in 1849, when the California gold rush prompted the desertion of many non-aboriginal employees. The acting governor, on his 1849 visit to the west coast, wrote that "at [Fort] Vancouver there is not one white man employed about the establishment, and I think it will be necessary to break in Indians at the different posts to a great part of the work now done by white men."[7]

At Fort Vancouver and other fur trade posts, historian Richard Mackie has documented the wide-scale employment of Aboriginal People to cut shingles and spars, pick cranberries, and harvest ice as well as to garden, fish, preserve food, and engage in general construction.[8] The comments in the Fort St. James journal for 1853 reflect a common situation: "The few hands available at this Post are insufficient for the duties of the fall and without the assistance of the Indians we could not get through with the work."[9]

Another historian, James McDonald, systematically evaluated the importance of aboriginal labour at Fort Simpson by examining its daily journals. In the early 1830s, there were occasional references to Aboriginal People

TABLE 6.1

Aboriginal and non-aboriginal population estimates for British Columbia, 1835-1901

Year	Aboriginal population	Non-aboriginal population	Aboriginal (% of population)
1835	70,000	350	99.9
1851	65,000	750	98.8
1856	62,000	1,000	98.4
1861	60,000	13,624	81.5
1871	37,000	13,247	73.6
1881	29,000	23,798	54.9
1885	28,000	–	–
1891	26,000	72,173	26.5
1901	25,488	153,169	14.3

Sources: Aboriginal population from Wilson Duff, *Indian History of British Columbia: The Impact of the White Man* (Victoria: Provincial Museum, 1980), 39-35; and for 1901, from the *Census of Canada*. Non-aboriginal population is taken from Douglas' census of Vancouver Island in 1854, which gave 774 whites on Vancouver Island, plus an estimate for the mainland. The 1861 population estimate is from Paul Phillips, "Confederation and the Economy of British Columbia," in *British Columbia and Confederation*, ed. W. George Shelton, 43-66 (Victoria: University of Victoria, 1967), 59. Other estimates are from the *Census of Canada* for 1871, 1881, and 1891. Since racial information was not tabulated in 1891, the non-aboriginal population given here is the total population less Duff's estimate for the aboriginal population. See also Douglas to Labouchere, October 20, 1856, Colonial Office Records 305/7, 11582, and Douglas to Russell, August 21, 1855, Colonial Office Records 305/6, 10048.

being engaged as guides, hunters, and fishers. But by 1838, the journal mentions hiring 240 person-days of aboriginal labour, and the numbers tend upward to 1857, when a peak of more than 3,345 person-days of aboriginal labour were explicitly recorded in the post accounts.[10]

The Great Migrations

While some work was available locally for Aboriginal People living close to the HBC forts, others looked further afield. Victoria, the west coast HBC headquarters since 1846, became the capital when the Colony of Vancouver Island was established in 1849. As the largest community of non-Aboriginal People north of Oregon, it became "the great emporium" for the Pacific Northwest, from Russian America down.[11]

Since the establishment of the post in 1843, distant aboriginal groups had made trading visits to Victoria, but mass seasonal migrations only began in the summer of 1853. At that time, Governor Douglas reported a gathering of three thousand "Indians" at a "potlatch" hosted by the Songhees people, who lived across the harbour from the fort.[12] The next year, Aboriginal People from "all parts of the mainland coast south of Cape Spencer, in north latitude 59 degrees" came, not for a potlatch, but to visit Victoria itself.[13] From 1853 through to the 1880s, two thousand to four thousand Aboriginal People canoed up to eight hundred miles to spend part of the year in Victoria.

Five to 10 percent of the whole aboriginal population north of Puget Sound sometimes spent more than a month each way, paddling hundreds of miles to visit a community that, in 1855, numbered only 232. Why? Trading was a major attraction. As Roderick Finlayson recalled, "So much better was the stock of goods kept" in Victoria than elsewhere, and the prices better than at closer trading posts, that "latterly Victoria interfered a good

What Work Do You Want Me to Do?

Iktah míka mamook?
What do you want me to do?

Lólo ókoke lacasett kopa piah ship.
Carry this box to the steamer.

Iktah mika potlátch?
What will you pay?

Ick kwatah?
A quarter?

Kloshe kahkua. Pee tenas muckamuk?
Very well; and something to eat?

John Gill, *Gill's Dictionary of the Chinook Jargon* [1881]

Aboriginal family packed for long-distance travel

deal with [the allocated trading areas of each fort]." "Because time was to them no object, [they] came to Victoria to trade, where there was a large quantity, and a greater variety of food from whence to choose." As Douglas explained in his dispatches to the Colonial Office, he was not alarmed about being outnumbered ten-to-one during these seasonal visits by "ignorant and barbarous people ... For the object of the Indians in visiting this place is not to make War upon the White man, but to benefit by his presence, by selling their Furs and other commodities."[14]

Curiosity was no doubt another reason that Aboriginal People came to Fort Victoria. H.H. Bancroft, having interviewed many of the early white residents of Victoria, thought that "the natives were quite curious as to what was going on among the white men, and would come from a distance, and in large numbers to see the strangers."[15]

The third and key reason that Aboriginal People returned to Fort Victoria year after year was, as Douglas reported in 1853, that they were "attracted to the colony by the reported high price of labour."[16] Already, he said, "a great part of the agricultural labour of the colony, is at present performed by means of the Natives, who though less skilled and industrious than the white men, work at a comparatively much cheaper rate, so that on the whole, they are exceedingly useful to the colonists."[17]

Douglas had been a career fur trader with the HBC and jointly held the post of HBC chief factor at Fort Victoria and governor of Vancouver Island until 1858, when he relinquished his post with the company. He had a reputation for being an acute observer of aboriginal behaviour, and he used this knowledge to advantage when dealing with the indigenous population. He is often credited with formulating and maintaining an "Indian policy" that made harmonious relations with Aboriginal People *the* priority, and so he is credited for the relatively peaceful nature of British Columbia's settlement process. Certainly, as an observer of Aboriginal People, he was less critical than were many of his contemporaries. He believed that, although Aboriginal People were in their natural state "barbarous," they were capable of "civilization," and he instituted a policy that accorded Aboriginal People and settlers the same rights to acquire land.[18]

Like Douglas, nearly all of the early colonists who left records mention the hiring of aboriginal labour. One of the first colonists, W.C. Grant, hired Aboriginal People on his "farm" and reported, in 1853, that Aboriginal People "with the proper superintendence are capable of being made very useful. They all live by fishing but take kindly to any kind of rough agricultural employment, though their labour is not to be depended on for any continuous period." Colonist J.S. Helmcken used Indians "chiefly from the north" to clear land for his home, and the colony paid "scores of

Indians" in HBC blankets to clear the land around the surveyor's office. From 1849 and throughout the 1850s, the Puget Sound Agricultural Company hired Aboriginal People on its farms as herders, sheep shearers, and ploughmen; the colony employed them to build roads, and individuals hired them to farm and clear land. Missionary William Duncan noted in 1857 that, around Victoria, "most of the Farm Servants employed ... by the settlers are Chimsyan [Ts'msyen] Indians – and they all give them a good character."[19]

The enthusiasm of the coastal Aboriginal People for these seasonal work migrations literally overwhelmed the small colony. In 1854, Douglas reported that "the settlements have in fact been overrun by those wild migrations."[20] These migrations seemed wild to Douglas and the colonists partly because of the battles that flared up between encampments of different Aboriginal Peoples. Many of the aboriginal groups who visited Victoria had unfriendly relations with each other – relations that sometimes erupted into warfare on the outskirts of the town and that were aggravated by the easy access to alcohol in Victoria.[21]

What was, in fact, occurring was that Aboriginal People were combining two economic modes on their trips to Victoria: engaging in the new economy and continuing the raiding excursions that were part of their traditional economy. On their way to and from Victoria, some aboriginal groups would raid others, taking slaves, heads, and portable goods. These hostilities might well be carried on adjacent to Victoria, as both raiders and victims found themselves camped near one another. This is an early example of a modified traditional, or moditional, economy. Capturing slaves while on one's way to engage in wage labour is one of many examples of how two distinct economies could be complementary and "confound our definitions of tradition and modernity."[22]

Because of the frequent violence between aboriginal groups, Douglas, at the start of the 1855 seasonal visit, called the chiefs together and "spoke to them seriously on the subject of their relations with the whites, and their duties to the public, and after exacting a pledge for the good behaviour of their respective Tribes ... [he] gave them permission to hire themselves out as labourers to the white settlers, and for the public works in progress." At the end of August, he reported that "the greater number of those people have lately departed with their earnings to their distant homes, and will not return to Vancouver's Island, before the spring of 1856; those who still remain about the settlements will spend the winter here."[23]

Here, Douglas points out a central feature of these migrations – the "greater number" came to Victoria for a work season that lasted from early spring to late summer. Although the economies of the Aboriginal Peoples

Drawn by the Prospect of Employment

The Natives ... have congregated in large bodies this season in the settlements, to which they have been drawn from almost every part of the coast between this place and 57th degree of north latitude by the prospect of obtaining employment as labourers and procuring by their industry supplies of clothing for themselves and families.

James Douglas, Douglas to Barclay, June 15, 1854

Four Months' Work in Victoria

Harry started for Victoria and Clah going
with him ... in one canoe to Hydahs
Indians an 7 Tsimshen indians. one half
breet. We had one month and half
[travelling]. We Shew Victoria in January-
1856. February March April May I had
four months as I working in Victoria ...
and I am done working in Victoria ... an
in May 1856.

Arthur Wellington Clah, Ts'msyen from Fort
Simpson, 1859

varied between nations and even between villages, depending upon their
access to resources, they all followed a distinct seasonal work cycle. The
coastal groups had "permanent" winter villages, and from these they moved
to seasonal camps for harvesting bulbs and berries in the spring and summer, and to fishing sites in the summer and fall. Winter was the season for
hunting and trapping, and, most important, it was the ceremonial season.
But from 1853 onwards, a spring and summer working visit to Victoria
became part of the seasonal cycle for west coast people from as far away as
Russian America. The route from the Alaskan panahandle, along the inside passage to Johnstone Strait and the Strait of Georgia, became so well
travelled it became known as the "Great Thoroughfare."[24]

An account of this modified seasonal round, given by William Duncan
in 1857, describes the melding of "subsistence" and wage economies among
the Ts'msyen at Fort Simpson:

> In mid Feb about 200 go to Victoria or American ports about 500 miles [south].
> Of those that remain they disperse where they make canvas and boxes etc ...
> gathering in March to harvest and preserve small fish [eulachon], trading
> many to Fort. Then they go hunting and trading and large numbers of other
> Indians come here to trade. At the latter end of April about another 100 go to
> Victoria. At the latter part of the year the Indians who went south return
> bringing great quantities of rum and various kinds of property.[25]

Arthur Wellington Clah and William Pierce were two of the Ts'msyen to
whom Duncan referred, and they have left brief accounts of these jour-
neys.

Other accounts confirm that it was common for Aboriginal People
who could not find work in Victoria in the 1850s and 1860s to continue
south into the American territory of Puget Sound. John Fornsby, a Coast
Salish living in Puget Sound, first saw "Northern Indians" when forty to
fifty of them came to work at a Puget Sound sawmill around 1865. From
Port Townsend, at the head of Puget Sound, James Swan wrote that the
northern Indians "yearly come to Victoria and whenever they get a chance,
come over here to work – the men at our mills or among the farmers,
where they prove themselves faithful and efficient; and the women, by
their cleanly habits, their bright dresses and hoop skirts ... winning the
hearts or purses of the bachelors." A Puget Sound newspaper noted in 1858
that "many areas of work – lumber mills, logging camps, farming and shipping – would have been unable to get along without Indian labour."[26]

While the summer migrants from the north laboured on the farms
and on public projects around Victoria, there was also year-round employ-

ment for Aboriginal People whose homes were close to the other settlements – employment as servants and cooks for the richer colonists. Aboriginal People also supplied immigrants with venison, partridges, salmon, potatoes, and berries as well as shingles, lathes, mats, and baskets. At Nanaimo, for example, the colonial surveyor reported that "the inhabitants are principally dependent on the Indians who sometimes bring as many as 63 deer in a day from Sechelt or Jervis Inlet."[27]

The Coal Tyees

The economy of the territory expanded beyond fur and food when the Aboriginal People of northern Vancouver Island brought coal to the attention of the fur traders, and it expanded again in 1846, when the traders directed the Royal Navy vessel *Cormorant* to the coal: "With the assistance of the Indians they collected about 60 tons."[28] The Kwakwa̲ka̲'wakw at the mines told the HBC that "they would not permit us to work the coals as they were valuable to them, but that they would labor in the mines themselves and sell to us the produce of their exertions." They were, however, only prepared to work the mines seasonally, when it did not interfere with their subsistence and ceremonial activities.[29]

Between 1849, when the HBC established Fort Rupert at the coal mines, and 1851, when the seam was exhausted, the Kwakwa̲ka̲'wakw people mined 3,650 tons of coal, for which they were paid "one blanket 2½ pt.s or equivalent in Grey Cotton for every two tons delivered at the Fort." In the summer of 1849 alone, an estimated eight hundred Kwakwa̲ka̲'wakw surface-mined the coal, and, in Douglas's opinion, "the industry and perseverance they exhibited in that pursuit [was] truly wonderful and astonished every person

I Am One of the Ten Who Discovered Coal

I feel sorry that I am the only one of the 10 Indians who discovered the coal, who is still alive. "Coal Tyee" and the others died without being rewarded, and I do not want to be like them. I want some compensation before I die.

Dick Whoakum, Snuneymuxw, May 28, 1913

Called the "Coal Chief" in Chinook Jargon, Coal Tyee (centre) told the Hudson's Bay Company where to find coal in the Nanaimo area

who visited that spot." If Douglas was right, about three-quarters of the local people were engaged in mining.[30]

In Nanaimo, starting in 1852, the Fort Rupert experience was repeated after trader Joe McKay, and then Governor Douglas, were led to various seams of coal by the local people. Douglas sent the HBC's *Cadboro* to the spot "and succeeded in procuring, with the assistance of Indians, about 50 tons of coal in one day." He wrote: "The natives, who are now indefatigable in their researches for Coal, lately discovered a magnificent seam over six feet in depth ... Such places are left entirely to the Indians, who work, with a surprising degree of industry, and dispose of the coal to the Agents of the Hudson's Bay Company for clothing and other articles of European manufacture." In 1853 "nearly all" of the Snuneymuxw (Nanaimo) people were among "a great number of Indians" engaged in coal mining. They were "conveying Coal from the shafts, working at the Bores, hewing and drawing timber for the buildings, and other operations carried on at the Establishment, all of who are paid at the rate of 2 Blankets per month." They "display[ed] a high degree of zeal and industry, in advancing the work of the establishment." An able man, reported McKay, could earn a shirt a day in 1852 or two blankets a month in 1853. This was high pay. At the time, a blanket was worth six pounds at the company store, and a company servant only made twelve pounds a year.[31]

Once the surface coal had been removed and there was a need to dig shafts and use pumps, the Hudson's Bay Company brought skilled miners from Great Britain. However, as Douglas noted in 1857, Aboriginal People remained crucial to the mining operations: "The want of Indian labor is certainly a great inconvenience for the miners but really they must learn to be independent of Indians for our work will otherwise be subject to continual stoppage."[32] In 1858, the *Victoria Gazette* reported that "there are some thirty or forty miners, mostly Indians, constantly employed in getting out the coal, and the lead has now been worked a quarter of a mile."[33] In addition to work in the mines, "Hundreds of natives, mostly women, [were] employed who conveyed the coal alongside the ships in canoes which was paid for by tickets so many representing a Ton or its proportion. The same rule was applied to the removal of goods or building material as we had no roads or carts to convey the same, and it was a curious sight to see the string of Natives of both sexes working like Ants in one continuous line over the trail to where they deposited their loads."[34]

Although partly displaced by Chinese labour in the various coal mines that subsequently sunk shafts around Nanaimo, in 1877, the Indian reserve commissioner noted that "the Nanaimo Indians ... have hitherto been chiefly employed about the coal mines as labourers."[35] Figure 6.1 shows the number

Nanaimo Coal

I was at that meeting. I can remember all the people in that house, and lots outside, but I was only a small boy standing beside my father ...

Then the Hudson's Bay men talked to the Indians. "This coal that is here," they said, "it is no good to you, and we would like it, but we want to be friends, so if you will let us come and take as much of the black rock as we want, we will be good to you." They told my father, "The good Queen, our great white chief, far over the water, will look after your people for all time, and they will be given much money so that they will never be poor."

Told by Quen-Es-Then (Joe Wyse) and interpreted by Tstass-Aya (his wife, Jenny Wyse), Snuneymuxw, to Beryl Cryer in the 1930s

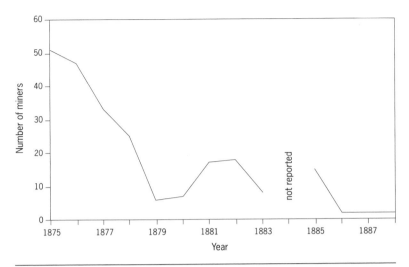

FIGURE 6.1 Number of aboriginal coal miners in Nanaimo mines, 1875-88
Source: BC Department of Mines, *Annual Reports.* Does not include miners' assistants.

of aboriginal miners in the underground coal mines around Nanaimo according to the British Columbia Department of Mines.[36]

The government statistics stop reporting "Indian" miners after 1887, but the reports of Indian Agents and others suggest that they had not disappeared from the mines. The very next year the Indian Agent for Nanaimo noted that "many Indians are again working at the coal mines at Nanaimo, taking the place of the Chinese; the fear of accident by explosions deterred them for some time, but now the high wages paid has attracted them again to the mines." Nearly fifty years since the commencement of coal mining, in 1897, the Yearbook of British Columbia listed wages at the mines, suggesting that Aboriginal People were making the same wages as were whites: "Roustabouts: $2.50-3.00/day; Miners: $3-3.50/day; Japs and Chinese: $1-1.25/day; Indians: $3.00/day."[37] In 1900, the agent again noted that the Snuneymuxw and Chemainus people "derive[d] quite a bit of employment in the coal mines." As late as 1913, the McKenna-McBride Royal Commission on Indian Affairs noted that the coal mines were a major source of employment for the Snuneymuxw people.[38]

Gole Illahee: Mining for Gold

Gold, like coal, was first offered to the HBC in trade by Aboriginal People, initially, in 1851, by the Haida of Haida Gwaii (Queen Charlotte Islands) and, in the mid-1850s, by the Interior Salish of the Fraser and Thompson valleys. In both cases, these exchanges started small gold rushes, but the white miners were "obstructed by the natives in all their attempts to search

Nlaka'pumx gold miners at the confluence of the Thompson and Fraser Rivers: from left Meshkt' Naxaxalhtsi (Antoine McHalsie, the grandfather to Sonny McHalsie), his wife Katherine McHalsie, one of their sons, Ch'et', Minnie Smith (Katherine's sister), and three unidentified women, early twentieth century

Buying an Indian Canoe, 1858

American: Chako six, nika tikke waw waw copa mika. Nika tikka makook kanim pe lackat issick.
Come here, friend. I want to talk to you. I want to buy a canoe with four paddles.

Indian: Kloshe.
Very good.

American: Konsick dollar mika tikke?
What is your price?

Indian: Klone totilum dollar.
Thirty Dollars.

American: Wake six, nika marsh copa mika mox totilum dollar.
No Sir, I'll give you $20.

Indian: Klonass, nika nanitch.
I don't know. I'll See.

A.C. Anderson, *Hand Book and Map to the Gold Region of Frazer's and Thompson Rivers*, 1858

for gold," and "when [the whites] did succeed in removing the surface and excavating to the depth of the auriferous stratum, they were quietly hustled and crowded by the natives who ... proceeded to reap the fruits of their labours." James Douglas reported in April 1858 that a thousand Aboriginal People had been working for ten months, mining gold along the Thompson River up from its confluence with the Fraser. He thought that, "as far as the Company interests are concerned it is desired that the Indian population alone should be employed in working of gold."[39]

However, before these very words reached London in the mail, some thirty thousand non-aboriginals surged into the Fraser Valley and up the Thompson River, completely overwhelming the few thousand aboriginal inhabitants, who, nonetheless, continued to work alongside them. In late March or early April 1858, James Moore reported that the "whole tribe of Yale Indians moved down from Yale and camped on Hill's Bar, about three hundred men, women and children, and they also commenced to wash for gold"; and Governor Douglas reported that "it is impossible to get Indian labor at present, as they are all busy mining, and make between two and three dollars a day each man."[40] A May 1858 letter from Fort Hope noted that "the Indians are getting plenty of gold, and trade with the Americans. Indian wages are from three to four dollars a day," the rate for a skilled tradesman in Victoria. In 1860, at Lillooet, aboriginal labourers were paid $5.25 per day and could earn much more mining on their own account.[41]

In addition to mining, many aboriginal groups along the Fraser, Thompson, and Nicola rivers took up packing supplies as a vocation. Bishop

Hills, who ventured into the gold fields in 1860, remarked on the ubiquity of aboriginal packers – men, women, and youths: "The traffic between Yale and the upper country ie. to Lytton about 80 miles is carried on the backs of Indians." Chief Justice Begbie, who regularly travelled this circuit, recalled that "no supplies were taken in [to the gold districts] except by Indians ... Without them ... the country could not have been entered or supplied in 1858-1860."[42] Aboriginal accounts confirm aboriginal involvement in the packing trade. The Secwepemc still tell stories of their neighbours, the Lillooet, passing through Alexandria on the Fraser River en route to the gold fields of the Cariboo with their pack trains. There is also an account from Swah-lis, a Stó:lō known to the miners as Captain John, who piloted river boats up the difficult stretch from Hope to Yale and freighted supplies upriver from Yale, saving, by his own account, some two thousand dollars. Bishop Hills thought he was witnessing a major transformation: "There is now an abundance of work for the Indians. So much so as to make many give up their former method of living and live as the whites."[43]

Edgar Dewdney engaged Aboriginal People to pack supplies over the Hope Mountains for the building of the Dewdney Trail to the Kootenay mines:

I picked out 18, some men and some women. The old Indians were quite as good, if not better than the young ones. One couple, "Polalee," which means powder [in Chinook jargon], and his wife, each at least 60 years old, were two of my best. The old woman packed a barrel of sugar, which weighed 125 pounds, and she was a small woman, and weighed very little more, if as much as the

Plenty of Money

Hyou Pack – Hyou Chechamen, Siwash Hyou Muckamuck.

Plenty of packing – plenty of money – Indians plenty of food.

Chief Spintlam, Nlaka'pamux, July 1, 1860

Wet'suwet'en packers at Moricetown, 1910s

Hiring Indian Canoe Men

American: Mika klapp klone alloyama
siwash pe klatawa copa
nesika mamook kanim
sockally Frazer River copa
gole ihale?
*Will you find three more
Indians and go with us to
work canoe up Frazer River
to the gold land?*

Indian: Nawitka, coqua nika tum tum
spose mika marsh hiyou
chickaman.
*Yes, thats my mind, if you
pay plenty money.*

A.C. Anderson, *Hand Book and Map to
the Gold Region of Frazer's and Thompson
Rivers*, 1858

We Soling Bread

In February 1859 ... Clah went in the
Spring for Victoria and he arrived at
Victoria in the June 1859. and after that
time. Clah begin working in the Store in
July 1859. John Charly, Smith. an Clah 3
men in one Store. We soling Bread. flour.
Rice. molasise. Sugar. Butter and Clah
been working in one month and he will
Doning 15 Dollars pay.

Arthur Wellington Clah, Ts'msyen,
November, 1859

sugar ... I shall never forget what pleasure and enjoyment I had when walking over the frozen summits on a bright sun shiny early morning.[44]

Aboriginal labourers also worked on building the Cariboo Road through the Fraser Canyon and along the Thompson River.[45]

With the 1858 gold rush and the consequent growth of Victoria came even more opportunities for paid work in the city and even larger migrations of aboriginal labour; soon thereafter, whole aboriginal villages were seasonally deserted by wage-seekers. Making for Haida Gwaii on board HMS *Alert,* James Cooper met the whole population of Masset, heading for Victoria. At Skidegate, meanwhile, Chief "Estercana" asked the officers of the *Alert* to "tell Mr Douglas and the man-of-war to send my people home; I wanted to build a house this summer [but] nearly all my people are away at Victoria."[46] That summer, Douglas reported over four thousand Aboriginal People visiting Victoria for the purpose of exchange, double the number of non-aboriginal inhabitants in the town.[47]

Despite the large increase in the non-aboriginal population after 1858, Douglas reminded the Colonial Office in 1860 that, "When not under the influence of intoxication [the Aboriginal People] are quiet and well conducted, make good servants and by them is executed a large proportion of the menial, agricultural, and shipping labour of the Colony. Besides their value as labourers they are of value commercially as consumers of food and clothing."[48]

Others made similar observations. Remembering his first sight of Victoria's James Bay, Colonel Wolfendon saw "a gang of Indians – it may be one hundred – under Grizzly Morris, a contractor ... with pick, shovel, and wheelbarrow making Belleville Street along the water." Between 1859 and 1864, Aboriginal People were employed on all the major public projects in the colonies, from building roads to laying out the Collins Overland Telegraph and performing the Boundary Survey.[49]

In 1861, a visitor to Victoria recorded that "Indians are seen everywhere throughout the town – in the morning carrying cut wood for sale; the women, baskets of oysters, clams etc ... fish being generally sold by Indians." In his eye-witness account of Victoria in the 1860s, Edgar Fawcett emphatically stated: "Indians performed all the manual labor."[50]

So prevalent was aboriginal labour that, in 1862, the *British Colonist* and the letters to the New Westminster *British Columbian* actually complained that cities were suffering from an abundance of "cheap" Indian labour "at the expense of a white immigrant population." Aboriginal People worked in construction, in stores, in domestic service, in brickyards, at farm labour, and in hospitals as well as selling their own products. In addition to monopolizing manual, menial, and temporary labour positions, some Aboriginal People were entering more skilled trades. A letter to the editor added that, while hundreds of whites remained unemployed, capitalists "employ Indian Men to do not only common labourer's work, but tradesmen's work, such as painters and carpenters."[51] Other observers noted Aboriginal People steering and working as engineers on steamships, earning the same wages as white employees.[52]

In addition to gathering in and around Victoria, Aboriginal People were relocating to the gold-mining communities at Fort Hope, Lytton, Yale, Wild Horse Creek, and New Westminster, the capital of the new colony of British Columbia. Judge Begbie told the governor in April 1860 that, with regard to Hope, "Indians are useful, indeed necessary for the trade of the town."[53] Christine Quintasket joined this migration. Her family moved to Fort Steele at Wild Horse Creek from their home in the Washington Territory to cut wood and labour at the North West Mounted Police post. Like other aboriginal families, they relocated seasonally, and sometimes for longer periods, to work in the new communities.[54]

In spite of the suggestions to the contrary, Aboriginal People were not made redundant by the influx of immigrants, just less visible in the cosmopolitan society of the gold-rush colonies. When the gold rushes had passed and most of the immigrants had abandoned the diggings, Aboriginal People, their numbers reduced by disease, were still on their ancestral lands. Gold mining remained an addition to their modified seasonal cycle and economy. In 1871, Alfred Selwyn of the Geological Survey of Canada remarked that "nearly all the Indians of the Fraser above Yale have now become gold washers. They return to the same spot on the river year after year, at the season of lowest water, to wash the sands, and, it is asserted, can almost always earn for a day's labour from one to two dollar's worth of gold." The next year the *British Colonist* reported that "from $15,000-$20,000 is annually contributed to the wealth of the Province by mining on the Thompson and Fraser Rivers, which is carried on almost exclusively by the Natives at low water." In 1876, a local storekeeper estimated the aboriginal harvest of gold on the Thompson River to be between $20,000 and $30,000 annually. In 1886, it was estimated that the bands around Lytton made $10,000 from gold panning alone.[55] Aboriginal People, Indian Agents, and the mining department regularly recorded the bands along the Fraser and Thompson rivers panning gold into the twentieth century.[56]

Besides mining and packing, the Aboriginal People of the southern Interior took up farming, both on their own behalf and for others. In 1874, the Roman Catholic missionary C.J. Grandidier wrote from Kamloops that "the Indians in this part of the country are now quite awake to the

Brick Houses

There are several kilns in the vicinity of Victoria, now busily engaged in burning brick ... Laborers in the yards are paid $30 per month and board. Most of the rough work however, is performed by Indians, who receive $20 per month.

British Colonist, June 5-6, 1860, 3

I Begin working with Mr. Carroll. Him Built new Bricks store. Clah an Mr. Roch Builting brick house. Clah had ten Days and half working in Yat[e]s street. one Dollar a Day.

Arthur Wellington Clah Diary, March 6, 1860

Indians to the Gold Fields

That was big cloud of dust 'way down
to the south in the spring yes,
It was the Lillooet Indians coming north,
coming north to the goldfields
up by Barkerville.

They go north into that country to work.
To work all the time, hard.
Horses and wagons, women and children,
and dogs, *hiyu* dogs, all going up by
Barkerville.

Mary Augusta Tappage, Secwepemc
(Shuswap), ca. 1971

Group of Interior Salish on their way to diggings near Gladwin, BC, ca. 1899

necessity of working, of following the examples of the whites, they look to the future and are afraid for their children's sake if they do not work." Writing on behalf of the people of the Fraser Valley, Alexis, Chief of Cheam, asked the Indian Agent for advance warning of his visit "in order to unite our people who are now a little dispersed as they are working for the whites." Both the missionary and the chief used "work" to refer to paid work.[57]

The attorney general of British Columbia, George Walkem, was also referring to paid labour when, in 1871, he reflected on the period before Confederation:

> Every Indian therefore who could and would work – and they were numerous – was employed in almost every branch of industrial and domestic life, at wages which would appear excessively high in England or in Canada. From becoming labourers, some of the Natives ... engaged on their own account in stock breeding, in river boating, and in "packing," as it is termed, as carriers of merchandise by land and water; while others followed fishing and hunting with more vigour than formerly to supply the wants of the incoming population. The Government frequently employed those living in the interior as police, labourers, servants, and as messengers entrusted with errands of importance.[58]

Admittedly, the attorney general was involved in a case of special pleading. He was justifying the former colonial government's lack of a clear Indian policy and its stingy allocation of reserves by suggesting that Aboriginal People were primarily wage workers rather than agriculturalists. Yet, in spite of its partiality, Walkem's statement is born out by an abundance of other evidence: aboriginal labour was widely employed.

Selling Sex

Another source of income that expanded with the gold rush was what contemporary observers referred to as "prostitution." However, the exchange of sex for payment, like other cross-cultural exchanges, had room for different understandings from each side. Prostitution may describe the relationship that non-aboriginal men thought they were engaged in, but it is unlikely that it accurately describes the relationship as viewed by participating aboriginal women. Within the context of the sale of sex, what was sold was not the same as what was purchased.[59]

It seems certain that a portion of what the Europeans called prostitution was, in fact, the coerced "rental" of female slaves. Slaves, according to the social relations of aboriginal society, could be prostituted by their owners. From the first appearance of Europeans on the coast, the hiring out of slaves to the fur traders/sailors had been a sideline venture. With the gold rush, slave-prostitution became an industry.

The best estimates available for the gold rush influx suggest that over thirty thousand people, almost all of whom were men, headed to the gold fields in 1858 alone, and many of these passed through Victoria. The miners provided an enthusiastic market, actively seeking out and purchasing sexual services. The small city was, moreover, the site of the Pacific's major British naval base, and, in the words of Reverend Matthew MacFie, "the extent to which the nefarious practices referred to are encouraged by the crews of Her Majesty's ships is a disgrace to the service they represent."[60] Aboriginal women greatly outnumbered non-aboriginal women in Victoria and were represented in like proportion in the sex trade.

The exchange of sexual services for goods or cash provides another illustration of how the Lekwungen and their neighbours adapted their own form of social organization – in this case slavery – to the capitalist economy in order to expand their own prestige economy. In 1859, a "chief" of the Toquat (a Nuu-chah-nulth group) replied to Captain Prevost's question about slaves: "All they captured were now sent to Victoria and bought by the Indians there because they fetched a higher price than anywhere else," up to $200 each, and the reason, according to Prevost, was "too apparent."[61]

William Banfield, trader and government agent, one of a handful of non-Aboriginal People living on the west coast of Vancouver Island in 1859, remarked on the trade:

> The Cape Flattery Indians are the principals of this vile traffic, they are rich in material wealth – they taunt, intimidate and wheedle the Vancouver Indians, taunt them with poverty, intimidate them by superiority of wealth and numbers and wheedle them by false promises into a cowardly onslaught on small

That's How It Started

The only thing my people could do at that point in time was hop-picking ... and chambermaid to Europeans, washerwomen ... and what we consider prostitution today. That was not the norm. I want that perfectly clear. I'm squeamish about talking about prostitution because a lot of people forget we didn't institute that industry. That was brought over by the Europeans, encouraged by the Europeans, encouraged by the government. They set up houses for European women to service the European settlers that came over here. So it was not part of our world until the smallpox broke out and for many of our woman to try and save their children came into the city ... That's when some of them got into prostitution to get medication for their children. So that's how that started. But there was a very small percentage of my people that went into that industry.

Daisy Sewid-Smith, Kwakwa̱ka̱'wakw, October 19, 2000

tribes; a number of slaves will be the result which will be readily exchanged at Cape Flattery or Port San Juan for Blankets or muskets ... The poor creatures when they get into the hands of masters about such places as Victoria or Ports in Puget Sound, the females are appropriated to the vilest purposes.

Between 1855 and 1859, on the short stretch of western Vancouver Island between Clayoquot and Ahousat, Banfield estimated that hundreds of slaves changed hands. Northern peoples heading to Victoria seeking wage work would engage in slave-raiding missions en route. That the new value of slaves led to increased intertribal warfare and slave trafficking was an ironic outcome of the new capitalist economy – given the aliens' "civilizing impulse."[62]

Victoria was the "Indian capital of the coast" as well as its slave-trade capital. Nations from up and down the coast congregated at the Lekwungen reserve to buy, sell, and prostitute slaves. In 1861, Bishop Hills found among the Cowichan people a Haida woman who had been sold in Victoria for $300 and "let out to the depraved whites" for the purposes of prostitution. A few months later, he recounted how a twelve-year-old Heiltsuk (Bella Bella) girl, prostituted by her Ts'msyen owners, had escaped in Victoria and was returned, by the police, to her owners.[63]

The sale and pimping of slaves comprised a significant part of the sex trade in Victoria, but in other cases, the transactions are more complex, particularly in the 1860s and later when slavery had dwindled in importance. There is little to go on, but one account from an aboriginal source raises enough questions to suggest that something other than prostitution was transpiring. This account was collected by George Hunt among the Kwakwaka'wakw, and it puts a different perspective on the exchange of sex for pay. It tells of

a commoner HawasElal' who was a "clay face" as they call those who never give a feast to their tribe. He was instructed by his wife that they should go down to Victoria with her three pretty girls [by an earlier marriage] that they should become prostitutes among the whites, for none of them had a husband ... Now they went to Victoria, five in a long nosed canoe. Now they arrived in Victoria and became prostitutes, the three pretty sisters and their mother. They staid one winter in Victoria and then they went home. Now HawasElal' obtained much money from this and immediately they bought an expensive copper, "Dry-Mouth-Maker-Cause-of-Shame." Then [his wife] and her three daughters bought the copper and gave it to HawaSElal'. Now the youngest of the three daughters became sick and she was sick in bed before she died. And then the second of the children dies, and then the eldest one also died.

HawasElal's brother-in-law said that his nieces had been bewitched on account of the fact that HawasElal' was a common man and that real chiefs do not allow common men to buy coppers. So he returned the copper and, not long after that, HawasElal' died himself.[64]

What is problematized is not the exchange of sex for goods but, rather, common people trying to acquire status like chiefs. The story lends credence to accounts by non-aboriginal observers that some Haida, Tlingit, and Kwakwaka'wakw women used what the whites referred to as prostitution to earn wealth independently of men in order to potlatch and to enhance their own status with their communities.[65] Kwakwaka'wakw historian Daisy Sewid-Smith emphasizes the impact of disease on aboriginal culture and suggests that, after the smallpox epidemic, some destitute widows and orphans had little recourse except the sex trade, which allowed them to buy necessities, including medicine for their children.[66]

Copa Molla: Come to the Mill

Aboriginal men had a range of new possibilities, including industrial occupations. A re-examination of the early factory system in the colonies shows that Aboriginal People were among the region's first factory workers and that they dominated the early factory labour force. The "modern" factory arrived on Vancouver Island in 1861, when Captain Stamp commenced operation of the largest sawmill on the west coast of North America, a steam-powered mill that cost $120,000 to build and that was eventually capable of cutting 100,000 feet of lumber a day. For the Tseshaht people of Alberni Inlet, where the mill was located, the industrial revolution arrived at the end of a cannon. The Europeans chose to establish the mill on the site where the local people had their winter village. The mill's operators "bought" the site from the local people for "Some 50 blankets, muskets, molasses and food, trinkets etc." Obviously, however, the local people had a different idea of the exchange than did the mill owners: they refused to leave. They were introduced to capitalist property relations when the mill managers trained their cannons on them.[67] Ultimately, they agreed to move, and when they returned to the mill site it was as workers.

The mill manager recorded: "When I first employed Indians at Alberni, the price of their labour was two blankets and rations of bisquits and molasses for a month's work for each man, if he worked the whole time." Piecing together the workforce from various accounts of visitors to the mill during its three years of operation, it seems likely that over half of the two hundred employees were aboriginal.[68] Two more giant export sawmills were established on Burrard Inlet between 1863 and 1867. Both rivalled the Alberni Mill in size, and unlike their predecessor, they continued to operate into

Indian Fireman

I was dead broke, and went over to
North Vancouver in a small canoe to the
sawmill and asked the manager if he
could give me a job. He told me I could
be a fireman in the sawmill. I says, "I
never did it before, but I will try and do
my best." He says there is another
Indian there who has been working there
for two years and will tell me what to do.

Charley Nowell, Kwakwaka'wakw, ca. 1895

the next century. Together, these were the largest industrial operations in
the colonies.[69]

Whole aboriginal communities relocated to the Burrard Inlet sawmills,
and evidence from the 1860s and 1870s, buried in a number of disparate
accounts, indicates that the majority of the workers inside and outside these
factories were aboriginal. Recalling this period, mill manager R.H. Alexander wrote: "Our mill hands were largely composed of runaway sailors and
Indians," but it is clear the runaway white sailors were a minority.[70]

In 1875, when the two mills were employing between 60 and one hundred men each, Walkem wrote: "our lumber mills alone pay about 130
Indian employés over $40,000 annually. Each individual receives from $20
to $30 per month and board ... In the present infancy of British Columbia,
the Indian of this [labouring] class have proved invaluable in the settled
portions of this province." Another estimate, this one from the Indian Reserve Commission's census taker in 1879, placed their income considerably
higher: "from the saw mills and other concomitant interests ... a sum variously computed at from $80,000 to $100,000 finds its way annually into
the hands of the natives." Although it does not provide an exact comparison, the total payroll for the nine sawmills in the Burrard Inlet-Fraser River
District, according to the 1881 census, was $126,950, paid to 252 employees.[71]

At the same time as the Burrard Inlet sawmills were hiring aboriginal
workers, sawmills in Puget Sound, just south of the Canadian border in
Washington State, employed "hundreds and sometimes thousands of the
Northern Indians," who, according to ethnologist and Indian Agent James
Swan, congregated every spring at Port Townsend looking for wage work.[72]
Who were these northern Indians? One of them, William Pierce, remarked
that, in the mid-1870s, his co-workers in a Puget Sound sawmill included
Haida from the Queen Charlottes, Ts'msyen like himself from the north
coast and Skeena River, and Nisga'a from the Nass River, Bella Bella
(Heiltsuk), Bella Coola (Nuxalk), Kitamaat (Haisla), Kwakwaka'wakw from
the central coast, and Tlingit from Alaska.[73]

In the late 1890s, another of the "Northern Indians," Charles Nowell,
a seventeen-year-old Kwakwaka'wakw from Fort Rupert, recalled arriving
in Burrard Inlet after returning empty-handed from seeking work in Washington State. Nowell found working as a fireman too hot, so he switched to
loading lumber onto the ships for two dollars per day, then he became a
tally man for $7.50 per day.[74]

As Nowell's reference to "firemen" suggests, these mills were large industrial operations, operated by steam power, complete with high risk of
industrial accidents. A nearby sawmill in New Westminster, worked by a

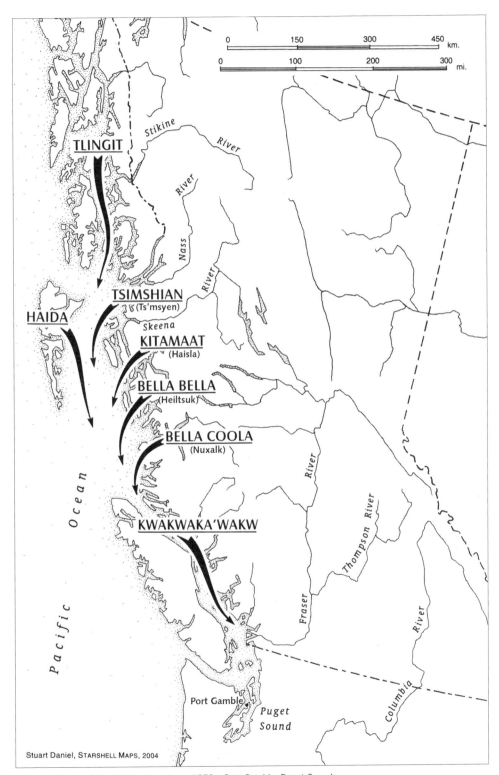

MAP 6.2 Origins of aboriginal mill workers, 1870s, Port Gamble, Puget Sound

handful of whites, "Indians, half-breed and Chinamen" was described by Morley Roberts, a non-aboriginal labourer, a few years later:

> in the half-open mill, one storey up in the air, I passed the days with the whir of the belts above and below, the scream of the circular saws as it bit the advancing log ... with the strips of bitten-wood thrown out in a stream, and

Mike Trains a Fireman

In 1865 there was a scarcity of white labor on Puget Sound and Mike Drew, Foreman of the Puget Mill Company at Port Gamble ... opened negotiations with an aboriginal man as helper and fireman:

Mike: Mika tickee mamook?
       Do you want to work?

Indian: Icta Mamook?
       What work?

Mike: Mamook pire keekwillie copa kittle.
       Making a fire underneath the kettle (boiler).

Indian: Konsict mika pay?
       How much will you pay?

Mike: Ict dollar ict sun.
       One dollar a day.

Indian: Hyas kloshe.
       Very good.

Mike: Well, kiack chaco copa molla.
       Well, hurry up and come to the mill.

When Mike and the Indian arrived at the mill the steam was down and the boilers needed water. This being remedied, Mike gave the Indian the following instructions:

Mike: Mika cumtux mamook delate hyas skookum pire?
       Do you understand how to make a very strong fire?

Indian: Nowitka.
       Yes.

Mike: Mika cumtux pump?
       Do you understand a pump?

Indian: Clonass nowitka.
       Very likely. Yes.

Mike: Mika nanage ocook glass?
       Do you see that glass?

Indian: Nowitka.
       Yes.

Mike: Mika nanage chuck mitlite?
       Do you see the water in it?

Indian: Nowitka.
       Yes.

Mike: Well, kyah kloshe spose mile quansome mamook delate skookum pire, pe quansome kloshe nanich pump, pe quansome kloshe nanich glass. Hyas kloshe spose chuck quansome mitlite sitkum copa glass. Spose shuck chahco saghalie, halo steam, spose chuck klatawa keekwillie delate hyas mamook poo poo contaway hyas kokshut, pe mika go to Hell in a minute. Mika cumtux?
       Well, it will be good if you always make a strong fire and always watch the pump and always watch the glass. It will be good if the water stays half way in the glass. If the water goes up, no steam. If the water goes down there will be a big explosion, everything will be broken and you will go to hell in a minute. Do you understand?

Indian: Nowitka.
       Yes.

Mike: All right, damn you, hyak mammok.
       All right, damn you, hurry up and work.

Dialogue between foreman and aboriginal man at a sawmill, 1865

Puget Mill Co. sawmill and log pond, Port Gamble, WA, ca. 1882

the clouds of smaller sawdust, with the smiting of mallets on wedges in the cut, and the heavy fall on the greasy skids of the divided tree. And then, in the pool below, stood a long figure with a pole balancing on a round log, pushing it into its place, then hammer driving in iron clamps or dogs, and the chain revolving on the drum, dragging the ponderous tree to the saw, and then its rolling over and over on to the carriage, and afterwards more saw screaming and saw-dust and wedge driving. So hour after hour, till the trees, rude and huge, fall into planks and boards and squared timbers ... and the sawdust burning in the gaping furnaces to drive the saw again. Then sudden whistle screaming, and hurrying figures ... then dinner devoured, not eaten, and a smoke, and the whistle, and the saws turn quicker and quicker, and all is to do again till dark and supper and rest.[75]

Dick Isaacs (Que-yah-chulk), a Squamish from North Vancouver lost one arm working in the Hastings sawmill in 1886. Isaacs, like other aboriginal workers, moved into a skilled job, as a sawyer, as did Alex Tom, who ran saw carriages in the late 1880s, and Jim Franks who was working at the Hastings Mill the day Vancouver burnt down in June 1886.[76]

Nonetheless, the majority of the aboriginal workers, like the majority of non-aboriginal workers, were unskilled. August Khahtsahlano and his half-brother Dominic Charlie were two of the many Aboriginal People who cut wood for the mills. In 1876, among these loggers were most of the men of the Sechelt people from the Sunshine Coast north of Burrard Inlet. Skagit John Fornsby recalled that he got his first paid job at age ten, in 1865, when he was hired to grease the "skids" of the skid roads over which the logs were hauled from the forest to the sawmills. Combining all these accounts, we know that, in the 1860s and 1870s, Aboriginal People made up a significant part of the logging crews, constituted most of the sawmill labour, and numerically dominated the longshoremen and longshorewomen who loaded the timber onto the ships.[77]

Mika, Mammok, Mika: Fishing and Canning Fish

While the sawmills of Burrard Inlet were getting into full swing, the second major factory-based industry – salmon canning – was in its infancy. First attempted in 1867, it was not until 1870 that continuous production began. Within a decade, the canneries were large, "modern" factories employing hundreds of people each and using steam boilers and retorts to heat and cook the salmon and seal the cans.[78] The sawmills may have employed hundreds of Aboriginal People, but the canneries employed thousands.

From the first arrival of Europeans on the coast, Aboriginal People supplied them with fresh fish. In the 1840s, the Hudson's Bay Company

The First Commercial Fishermen

The commercial fishery started at Fort Langley and our fishermen supplied all the salmon ... They were entrepreneurs, that's exactly what they were. Once they saw a need for labour they just stepped in and gladly did it. They paddled canoes to come up [to the Fraser Canyon] to get salmon and it was a natural thing for them to paddle people up here for the gold rush.

Albert (Sonny) McHalsie, interviewed in the film *A Forgotten Legacy: Spirit of Reclamation* (2002)

Stó:lō Sonny McHalsie, 2006

even began a small export business in salted salmon, using aboriginal men as fishers and aboriginal women as processors.[79] When advances in technology and a European demand for canned fish encouraged the establishment of salmon canneries, aboriginal men continued to supply the canneries with fish; aboriginal women, alongside Chinese men, processed the fish inside the canneries.

There is little concrete evidence as to the size and composition of the commercial fishery in the 1870s, but in 1881, the census estimated that there were 1,045 fishers in British Columbia. We know from two different observers that Aboriginal People comprised the vast majority of these. In 1882 and 1883, they calculated 1,200 to 1,300 aboriginal men comprised the fishing fleet for eleven canneries on the Fraser River alone.[80]

In 1884, the fisheries officer for BC described the labour force employed at the salmon canneries as composed of 1,280 Indians (men and women), 1,157 Chinese, and 273 whites: "The white men are generally employed as foremen, mechanics and fishermen, Indians fish for and clean salmon, and Chinamen make the cans ... fill them and solder them up, etc."[81] Farther north, at the canneries on the Skeena River: "Chinamen are employed at the fishery, but the much greater part of the work is now done by Indians. The men enter into contract to supply salmon, and the women and the children are handy workers and most useful in the various steps necessary to prepare fish for market."[82]

Cannery work differed from sawmill labour in that it provided jobs for the whole family. Alfred Carmichael, the foreman in charge of the aboriginal women workers at the Windsor Cannery on the Skeena River in 1891, wrote a detailed description of the labour force. Aboriginal men fished, while women made nets and worked inside the cannery, sometimes cleaning fish and often filling the cans. Children were hired for light work such as labelling, stacking, or cleaning fish oil off the cans.[83]

In the late 1880s, the ethnologist Franz Boas, who had travelled extensively along the coast, observed: "The fisheries on the coast are operated chiefly with Indian help. The owner is at the same time the trader from whom the Indians buy the European goods they need. The salmon fisheries and the canning plants are all situated in the larger Indian villages because the Indians do the fishing. They are paid in script with which they pay the trader for their necessities. This makes it possible to operate the fisheries with a minimum amount of capital."[84]

The censuses of 1881 and 1891 provide interesting points of comparison. The 1881 census shows that the 1,264 men, 114 women, and two boys (under sixteen years of age) employed in fourteen canneries along the mainland coast from the Fraser to the Nass, were paid a total of $243,456. The

*K lootchman filling
a chuamau chechirs
full bay.*

Carmichael sketch of Aboriginal women at work at Windsor Cannery, Skeena River Cannery, ca. 1885

1891 census shows thirty-one canneries on the mainland employing 4,115 men, 970 women, 232 boys, and 127 girls under the age of sixteen, for total wages of $525,215.[85] Evidence from workers, from employers, and from fisheries inspectors concurs: women and children cannery workers were virtually all aboriginal, while the largest ethnic group of men was Chinese, followed by aboriginals and a few white overseers.

Based on the census figures, the average income per cannery labourer in 1881 was $176, or $58.66 per month, for the three-month season. This coincides exactly with the observation by ethnologist Johan Jacobsen, who wrote, in the same year, that most of the young people from the Saanich (Wsanec) reserves north of Victoria were at the Fraser River canneries, earning between fifty and sixty dollars per month. He was astounded at the high wages.[86] A comparison with Table 6.2 shows why. This average monthly wage compares favourably with that of a skilled tradesperson. Of course, the tradesperson might have work for most of the year; but, on the other hand, an aboriginal family of four working in the canneries for three months might earn the same annual wage as the tradesperson before moving on to their other income-earning and subsistence activities.

The best province-wide survey of aboriginal seasonal employment in the early 1880s comes from the 1881 annual report of the Commissioner for Indian Affairs. Starting on the north coast and chronicling the activities of the aboriginal bands he met as he travelled south, I.W. Powell remarked that, in the Cassiar region (close to what became the Yukon border), where gold had been mined since 1874, the Tahltan "are honest and trustworthy and exceedingly industrious, being most useful as packers and labourers ... A good many [Ts'msyen] and [Haida], as well as natives from some of the more northern tribes of Alaska find remunerative occupation in the district, canoeing and packing along the various mining creeks."[87]

Mammook Mika – You Work!

It was my duty to see that [the aboriginal women] did not squash the salmon or put in nothing but back or skin [in the cans]. I would of course point out to them their mistake if too full I would say, "Nase hhhal," if not enough I would say "Hase hhal slouch," too much skin, "itstiha," and so on. I remember correcting one a dozen times for the same mistake, she got awfully angry and throwing the can on the floor, said "Kahta mika halo mammuk. Mika, Mammook, mika" in Chinook, she wanted to know why I did not fill the cans, "*you* work," putting another mika at the end, accents it in a way.

Alfred Carmichael, "Account of a Seasons Work at the Salmon Cannery, Windsor, Cannery, Aberdeen, Skeena," 1885

TABLE 6.2

Average rates of pay for various professions in British Columbia, 1860-90 (dollars per day unless specified)

Occupation	1860*	1864*	1883	1890
Indian Agent			$200/month	
Indian Department constable			$40/month	
General labourers	$2.50	$3.00-4.00	$1.75-2.00	$1.25-2.50
Coal miners			$3.00-4.00	
Gold miners				$1.75-3.00
Colliery labourers			$2.50	
Skilled tradesmen	$5.00	$4.85	$3.50-4.00	$4.00-6.00
Laundresses		$2.10/dozen shirts		$10.00-18.00/month
Longshoremen				50¢/hour
Lumbermen	$48.50/month	$60-75/month		$1.50-2.25
Millhands	$60/month	$1.25-2.50		
Farm labourers		$1.00 and board		

*   The figures for 1860-64 are converted to dollars at the rate of one pound to $4.85.

Sources: **1860 wages:** Bishop Hill to the Secretary, Society for the Propagation of the Gospel, May 8, 1860, Anglican Diocese of British Columbia, Bishop Hill Collection, text 57, box 3, file 3, courtesy of Ira Chaikin; **1864 wages:** Matthew MacFie, *Vancouver Island and British Columbia* (London, 1865), 499-500; **1883 wages:** Canada, *Province of British Columbia, Information for Intending Settlers* (Ottawa, 1883), 23, and G. Sproat "Cost of Labor on Farms," *The Resources of British Columbia* 1, 9 (November 1, 1883): 14; **1890 wages:** *Canada Sessional Papers*, 1891, "Immigration Agents' Reports," 95-97. Longshoreman rate from Biggar, *Canadian Handbook* 20; farm labour from M.C. Urquhart and K.A.H. Buckley, *Historical Statistics of Canada* (Toronto: Macmillan, 1965), series D196-207; Indian Agent's salary from Department of Indian Affairs Annual Reports.

On Haida Gwaii, where a fish-oil refinery was established in 1876, "the past summer has been a very successful one for the [Haida] ... who have made considerable money in supplying the oil company here with dogfish, and those who chose to work had little difficulty in making five or six dollars per diem." In ten days, they could earn the monthly wage of a skilled worker in Victoria. At Kincolith on the Nass River "the Indians were all – men, women and children, employed at the Fisheries ... making a little pocket money at the cannery in order to supply themselves with other comforts." Further south, among the Ts'msyen on the Skeena River, "there are two large canneries, consequently Indians from all the tribes within a hundred miles visit the place, both with a view of obtaining lucrative occupation, as well as taking their own winter's supply of salmon for home consumption."[88] The Alert Bay Kwakwaka'wakw found work fishing for, and working in, the cannery located there, while the Fort Rupert Kwakwaka'wakw travelled to the Fraser River fisheries to find work.[89]

On the west coast of Vancouver Island, an Indian Agent had just been appointed for the Nuu-chah-nulth (Nootka) in 1881, and he described their seasonal round, which consisted of making fish oil for sale to white traders in December and starting to fish for seal in February: "In the month of June, or as soon as sealing is over, they begin to travel, some to potlatches, some to Victoria, New Westminster or the American side for goods or work; others are scattered along the coast fishing until it is time to get their winter supply of dry salmon up the rivers; this secured, they settle at their villages in November."[90]

Six years earlier, the Indian superintendent had declared the Nuu-chah-nulth the richest of any Indians he had met: "Were a proper disposal made of their immense gains they could without a doubt, live independently, and furnish themselves with every comfort, and even luxury to be wished for ... it is not uncommon for any Indian to realize $500 to $1,000 per annum." In the mid-1880s, when the off-shore sealing industry was underway, each Nuu-chah-nulth "would make almost twice as much in one sealing season as the average white man would make in a year."[91]

The Indian Agent on southern Vancouver Island reported that several of the villages in his agency had been almost deserted, "men, women and children having found paying employment at the salmon canneries on the Fraser." The agent for the Fraser Valley made similar comments: "All the Indians included within these extensive limits have enjoyed a golden harvest by having the most lucrative employment at the various canneries on the Fraser ... all who chose to work could net $4 or $6 a day without exertion." Within a few years, this was also true on the north coast.[92]

The superintendent's claims that Aboriginal People could earn wages of four to six dollars per day "without exertion" may reflect local labour shortages; the daily wages most frequently mentioned from 1879 to 1887 (between $1.75 and $2.50 per day) agree with other estimates of aboriginal monthly wages as well as the 1881 average cannery income from the census.

Chinook Recruiting Letter

Mr. Smis,
Tenas alka klones ick moon pe sitkum, nika klatawa kopa Queets pe Ho, iksum kopa siwash lolo kopa Quileute mamook sealskin.

Mr. Smith,
In a little while maybe six weeks, I'll go to Queets and Hoh River to get some Indians there to bring back to Quileute to work at sealing.

Letter from Jack to Mr. Smith, dated February 7, 1881

Fort Rupert Kwakw<u>a</u>ka'wakw people en route to Steveston canneries, ca. 1898

These wages attracted aboriginal migrants from the northernmost coastal village in the province to the Fraser River in increasing numbers. In each of the years between 1885 and 1887, from a total provincial aboriginal population of around 25,000, the Indian Agents estimated 3,000 to 3,500 Aboriginal People, some 15 percent of the total population, were camping on the Fraser River and working (or looking for work) at the canneries. An additional number were employed in the northern canneries.[93]

Historian Robin Fisher has argued that "the effect of frontier settlement was to diminish Indian wealth," but Powell finished his overview with the observation that "there was never a time in the history of the Province when the Indians have been so prosperous as during the present year." A comparison with the provincial standard wages (see Table 6.2) lends credibility to Powell's assessment.[94]

Indispensable on the Labour Market

In the late 1870s or early 1880s, Aboriginal People also expanded their wage-work migration beyond the fish canning season into the autumn to pick hops and fruits in the Fraser Valley and Puget Sound. This annual migration took on huge proportions. One Indian Aagent reported that, following the 1885 canning season, six thousand Aboriginal People – one-quarter of the aboriginal population of British Columbia – travelled to the Washington Territory hop fields. Like the canneries, the hop fields were a source of wages for whole families: men, women, children, and the elderly.[95]

Given these numbers, it is no surprise that, in aboriginal accounts of this period, salmon canning and hop picking loom large. John Fornsby's narrative from the 1880s describes his work as the foreman of a hop-picking crew in Puget Sound; Charles Nowell tells of following his girlfriend to the hop fields of Washington State; Sayach'apis tried to recruit the tribes from southern Vancouver Island and the Fraser Valley to come to a potlatch but found them en route from the canneries to the hop fields; and August Khahtsahlano was interviewed by J.S. Matthews while his wife was hop picking.[96]

Not only did Aboriginal People work in the farms, canneries, mills, and mines, but Indian Superintendent Powell also noted in 1884 that "the river steamers all prefer Indian crews, from the fact that the natives are found to be the most willing and active. During the previous seasons no difficulty was experienced in obtaining native deck hands at $15 or $18 per month, now the steamers were glad to get them for $45 and $50 and even at this rate with difficulty." The local Indian Agent pointed out that, in addition to working on steamer crews, "there are a good many men also who make a considerable money at getting out cord wood and selling it at $2.50 per cord to the river steamers ... There is no class of labour to compete with them at the fisheries or at steamboating on the Fraser River." George Swanaset and Harry Mussel, both Stó:lō [Salish] from the Chilliwack area, and Arthur Wellington Clah, a Ts'msyen, were among the many Aboriginal People who worked as deckhands on the run from New Westminster to Victoria and who cut wood for the steamships and locomotives.[97]

Moving inland up the Fraser Valley, Powell reported that "railroad construction has enabled the inland natives in this part of the province to do quite as well as their brethren on the Lower Fraser, from other industries." In 1882 alone, Andrew Onderdonk, one of the main CPR contractors, estimated he paid at least $40,000 for aboriginal labour.[98]

In addition to paid labour, these aboriginal accounts also highlight aboriginal entrepreneurs. The *British Colonist* noted as early as 1860 that "several of the Northern women have established small trading posts at the villages and sell to their friends at a small advance on Victoria prices." Some, like Sayach'apis and Arthur Wellington Clah, were active traders, who bought furs, fish, and fish oil and took them to Victoria, exchanging them for goods they would resell up the coast. Charles Jones was heavily engaged in the process of catching dog fish and refining the oil for sale in the Victoria market. Others, like Haida carver Charles Edenshaw, turned their artwork into a profession. Edenshaw's cousin, Henry Edenshaw of Masset, and the Ts'msyen Dudoward family at Port Simpson were among those who owned their own trading vessels. Others established stores, including the following families: Dudoward at Port Simpson, Constance at Hesquiat, Mack at Ohiat, August at Ahousaht, John at Kyuquot, Jim at Chicklesaht, Cook at Alert Bay, and Clifton at Hartley Bay. There were also others at Aiyansh, Kincolith, Lakalsap, Masset, Skidegate, Hazleton, Anidmaul, Bella Bella, Village Island, and Kyuquot.[99]

Aboriginal People also ran several smaller sawmills that were scattered throughout the province, most of them first established by missionaries to encourage their parishioners to adopt capitalist-Christian ethics. Missionary William Duncan had established a sawmill and a soap factory at Metlakatla by 1871, and other mission-mills followed at Alert Bay, Glen Vowell, Hartley Bay, and Kispiox. The Anglican mission at Masset also helped the local people establish a clam cannery.[100]

To what extent were Aboriginal People involved in the capitalist economy of British Columbia? Prior to 1849, Aboriginal People provided the furs that were the foundation of the capitalist economy and much of the food upon which the fur traders depended. After the 1849 founding of

This house of the Ts'msyen Chief A.S. Dudoward of Port Simpson was chosen in 1905 by the Department of Indian Affairs to show the affluence of coastal Aboriginal People.

The Man of British Columbia

Arrived Clah. Arrived at Fort Simpson ... with 7 passenger Mr. Clah Constable. The man of British Columbia. $500.00 Brought of home for myself. $130.00 I Sole [sold] at Victoria.

Arthur Wellington Clah, Ts'msyen, July 15, 1864

Without Them the Province Would Suffer

The Indians who live close together here [Victoria] belong to the various language groups of the coast. And since they do not speak any English, they used a mixed language, the Chinook [jargon], in which conversation goes along easily. The visitor who leaves the much traveled tourist round in British Columbia has to depend completely on this means of intercourse.

...

Certain Indian tribes have already become indispensable on the labor market and without them the province would suffer a great economic damage.

Franz Boas, June 1889

Almost All the Labour

Almost all the labour of the province is done by Indians and Chinese. All the steamboats in which we travelled were manned by Indians – the Stevedores and longshoremen and the labourers you find about the streets are for the most part Indians. All the fishing for the canneries is done by them and in all these occupations they compare favourably with the labouring classes elsewhere.

Franz Boas, September 1886

Aboriginal cook on west coast trading schooner, ca. 1880s

the Colony of Vancouver Island, Aboriginal People continued to play a major role in the expanding economy. Aboriginal workers cleared the first farm fields in British Columbia and helped build many of the early structures. Coal was the key to making steam, and steam powered the industries and transportation of BC as elsewhere. Coal was also the province's most lucrative industry in the nineteenth century. Aboriginal People were the original labour force in the coal mines, and they continued to work as miners throughout the 1800s. Gold, some have said, created British Columbia; certainly the gold-mining industry serves as a metaphor for the riches of the province. Aboriginal People were the first to mine gold here and were the most enduring of the miners. Aboriginal labourers also dominated the early labour force of the provinces' other great industries, including sawmills and canneries, as well as the workforce on the docks and steamships. The public works of the colony and the province, from the boundary survey to the building of the Canadian Pacific Railway, all relied on aboriginal labour.

The census of 1881 reveals that the manufacturing establishments in British Columbia, primarily canneries and sawmills, were, on average, the biggest enterprises in Canada, in terms of both numbers of employees and capital invested. In 1881, the proportion of BC's population working in the manufacturing sector ranked fourth in Canada, after Ontario, Quebec, and New Brunswick. BC had become one of the most industrialized provinces in the country, and it did so by relying on a workforce dominated by Aboriginal People.[101]

How widespread was aboriginal involvement in paid labour? A rough estimate based on the reports of Indian Agents suggests that, of the 28,000 Aboriginal People in British Columbia in 1885, over 85 percent belonged to bands that earned substantial incomes through paid labour or entrepreneurial activity. The remaining 15 percent, although not wage labourers, continued to participate in the economy as fur traders.[102]

The paid work of Aboriginal People fit a specific pattern: it was largely seasonal. Most Aboriginal People in BC did not decide whether to engage in paid labour or subsistence work: they did both, at different times of the year. Moreover, much of the work was organized along family lines. As George Blenkinsop noted in 1879, "the various numerous industries on the [Fraser River] requiring a large number of working hands, there is no want of employment for [Indians] both young and old, men, women and children."[103]

While the histories of coal mining and gold mining, and many of the extant records of sawmilling, have "vanished" Aboriginal People from the workforce, they were working in all these industries and more. If

Aboriginal People are invisible to us now, contemporary observers saw them everywhere. It seems clear that the response of most Aboriginal People in British Columbia to the newcomers was closer to that of the Lekwungen than that of the Tsilhqot'in.

These accounts all contribute to a reappraisal of the early labour force in British Columbia. Twenty-five years after the gold rush, despite a dramatic population decline, Aboriginal People remained at the centre of the region's capitalist economic activity. What was obvious everywhere was not "Lo, the poor Indian" but, rather, they can "furnish themselves with every comfort and even luxury."[104] They were prosperous according to the incomes they earned, and these substantial incomes were added to a subsistence economy that provided them with food and shelter.

Chinook jargon was the language of exchange and the workplace, of the "middle ground" between Aboriginal People and immigrants, a place where meanings moved across cultures and were frequently transformed. So central was Chinook to the life of British Columbia that numerous publishing houses put out their own dictionaries. The provincial directory for 1877-78 included a Chinook-English dictionary, and the federal government published a Chinook dictionary in the national parliamentary papers when BC joined Canada. It did this because the wawa was "the language of commerce." Chinook jargon created a space that allowed for just enough comprehension to get exchanges going; however, it was clear that miscommunication was built into these exchanges.

Preconceptions Overturned

The preconceived ideas about the Indians visited in British Columbia were rapidly dispelled upon coming into contact with them ... In fact many of them appeared to be in better circumstances than a large percentage of white settlers resident in the country.

Deputy Superintendent of Indian Affairs, 1895

Tag Throws Sense to the White Man

This is the narrative of Tagwɔx (house of la.n Kispayaks).

Tagwɔx was living at laanndil-g.on.

And a white man met Tag and his wife in this place.

This was during the summer.

There were three white men coming over from the Nass.

And the white man said: payumamakxa (lots of work) [haiyu mamook] in Chinook.

But the Gitcan term for muku [mamoolk] was a species of small birds (ducks).

Tag spoke to them saying – We have no birds here.

So he cannot give you any.

So the white man said – what is the matter?

Tag thought he was then saying fr matix – goat.

And he said – we do not have any mountain goat so we cannot give you any.

So the white man said you are crazy.

So Tag thought he asked for the village of g.áinis the dog salmon.

He said – we have none here. So then the white man called him – you are a real siwash –.

So Tag thought these people were talking in Ts'msyen to him.

He said – I am very sorry even if you talk Ts'msyen I cannot understand you. I can only understand a little for parts you said – haiwas there – big rain.

So the white man laughed at him and he laughed at the white man.

Then Tag said to the man: I will address you people now.

I will show you people how to speak.

So he took off all his garments and was then all naked.

Then he said pointing to his wife – my wife is partaking of my flesh indicating his penis.

So then the white people ran away from him.

And then T[ag] started to throw sense to the white man.

Story told by John Brown, which came from his uncle nieɔalibos, to Marius Barbeau, ca. 1917

The Indians do not now, nor can they expect to in the future, make as much money as formerly in any line of industry or business.

A.W. Vowell, Indian Superintendent, 1894,

If you don't own your own boat, the only way to make a living is to rent the boat from the packers and fish all year round. We didn't have to work that way before. In the old days there was time for commercial fishing, a time for oolichan fishing and processing, a time for mountain goat hunting, a time for berries. The Nass River people have always traded their oolichan oil. If you don't fish oolichan, you're not Nisga'a.

Murphy Stanley, Nisga'a, c. 1977

Vanishing the Indians, 1885-1970

So completely had Aboriginal People vanished from the historical record of the nineteenth century that, in the twentieth century, historians hardly looked for them at all. However, if Aboriginal People were, in the late nineteenth century, labouring "in the sawmill, the logging camp, the field, the store in fact in every department where labour is required," as the Superintendent of Indian Affairs told Parliament, then what became of them? Did they continue to work in these enterprises into the twentieth century? If they vanished from the workforce, when did this happen? This section charts the changing patterns of Aboriginal paid work in the twentieth century by examining the main industries in which Aboriginal People were employed.[105]

For this more recent period, the record of Aboriginal work is more accessible. The stories in this section come from interviews with more than four dozen Aboriginal People from across much of British Columbia as well as from other accounts that include significant discussions of paid work. Each story offers a kind of "thick description" of one life as it was lived in a particular place and time, and within a particular set of circumstances. They suggest some of the individual triumphs and crises common to Aboriginal People across the province, and they do so in the compelling words of those who experienced them.

For all their immediacy and power as stories, each interview, autobiography, or auto-ethnography poses a question to the historian: how typical were the experiences of the author? The mere fact that these narratives have been recorded makes their authors exceptional. Three of them – James Sewid, Simon Baker, and Harry Assu – were chiefs of their bands. Sewid was specifically chosen as a subject of an "autobiography" because of his success in the "non-Indian world." Assu, who actively sought a collaborator to write his auto-ethnography, was also proud of his success in both "worlds." Baker prided himself on his role as a cultural ambassador of his people. Mary John and Florence Davidson became informal leaders in their own communities. The subjects of the other auto-ethnographies are exceptional individuals who stand out due to their longevity, memory, and/or storytelling ability; however, their life stories were collected and presented because of their apparent typicality. None of these people could be called exceptional in terms of economic success. All but three (Mary Augusta Tappage, Mary John, and Beth White) belonged to coastal groups, so interior people are not as well represented.[106]

The best way to determine how the individual histories range on a scale from typical to unique is to compare them to the aggregate statistics gathered by various agencies for different routine purposes between 1885 and 1970. Foremost among these agencies was the Department of Indian Affairs (DIA), which, from the mid-1880s to the 1940s, expanded the types of information it was gathering about registered Indians, especially between 1900 and 1946, when it estimated annual incomes. So extensive is the DIA documentation that Bill Russell called it the "the white man's paper burden." This collection was explicitly linked to the DIA's goal of assimilation: "The Department would like to know more of the domestic life of the natives, with a view to remedying, if possible, undesirable habits. It would also like to have a more detailed description of the Indian's house, stables, and other buildings, the conditions in which the houses are kept, and the employment that usually occupies the attention of women."[107]

Other government departments started to keep records on "Indians." From the late 1870s, the federal Department of Fisheries expanded its collection of data on matters relating to fur sealing, fishing, and canning, with a view to regulating access to marine resources. In 1926, the Province of British Columbia established a game branch, with wardens around the province enforcing hunting and trapping regulations. During the Second World War, due to a labour shortage exacerbated by the internment of Japanese Canadians, the provincial labour department began an annual count of Aboriginal People involved in wartime industries.

Due to inconsistent coverage of aboriginal employment, incomplete enumeration, and (lately) non-participation, the federal census is only of partial utility. For example, in 1901, Aboriginal People were enumerated on a separate schedule from other Canadians – one that did not ask about employment. In 1951, "On Reserve Indians" were considered to be neither in nor out of the labour force. In 1961, this "census apartheid" was rescinded, but the coverage is such that the utility of the census is limited.

The statistics and the stories put each other in context, showing, through comparison, the range and mean of experience. The two sets of evidence are complementary in another fashion, as they focus on different elements of the aboriginal economy. The statistics focus on the formal capitalist economies, while the life stories accord major places to informal work as well as work for the subsistence and prestige economies. The auto-ethnographic works also inject into the historical conversation a subjective and experiential dimension that is definitely lacking in the extant data. All of the sources are partial in their own way and have to be understood in dialogue with each other and within the context of the racialization and the social construction of race (see Chapter 3).[108]

The history of aboriginal-white relations also needs to be put within the context of falling aboriginal populations. The year 1885 marked the end of a long century of steep decline in aboriginal population levels, but a

Neither In Nor Out of the Labour Force

Due to their unique economic circumstances, Indians living on reserves at the time of the 1951 Census were classified as a separate group from those "in the labour forces" and those "not in the labour forces."

Census of Canada, 1951

Died Like Flies

It must have been about 1860, that smallpox time. My grandmother told me. She lived through it. Not many did ... They died like flies, yes ... Then the 'flu came, yes. Years, after the flu came. It was when the soldier boys were coming home [1918-19]. My grandmother was old then, old and weak, I guess ... She lived through the smallpox, but not the flu.

Mary Augusta Tappage, *The Days of Augusta*, 1973

Waking to the Sound of Caskets Being Made

When I was a young man and TB was still running like wildfire, our people were dying so often it seemed like every week we were taking somebody up to the cemetery. In the morning when you'd get up the first thing you would hear somebody crying or wailing. Amid this ... you would hear saws and hammers going. We used to make our own caskets ... This is what we lived through. It lasted up into the fifties. If you can understand this and feel a little better about us maybe we won't look just like lazy people. We won't look like people that don't know or don't care what we are doing or where we are going. We lived through hell and we survived it.

Dave Elliot, Wsanec elder, *Saltwater People*, 1990

slow decline continued until the nadir was reached with the 1918-19 flu epidemics.

Population Decline: Living through Hell

Phillip John, of the Ehhatteaht band (Nuu-chah-nulth) put it this way: "We had a lot of people living in the other places before the measles came around with that civilization. Our medicines didn't work for those European diseases. And the injections and liquid stuffs we were given didn't seem to help too much. Our people got sick and stayed sick and died. The Asian flu in 1918 took lots of them. They were just packing the dead into the [burial] caves."[109]

The accounts of William Pierce, John Fornsby, Dave Elliot, Mary John, Harry Assu, Clayton Mack, and Florence Davidson all tell of the personal effects of the epidemics.[110] After 1919, a slow increase in the registered Indian population began, despite high rates of tuberculosis and other illnesses. By the decade 1949-59, the aboriginal population began a rapid growth, which has not yet slowed.

Ironically, the levelling of the aboriginal population decline in 1885 coincided with the historical moment when they became a minority population. Even slowly declining aboriginal populations were in marked contrast to the catapulting immigrant population. In 1881, Aboriginal People comprised 55 percent of the population of British Columbia, by 1901 only 12 percent, and by 1961 a mere 2.3 percent.[111]

Railway Navvies and Powder Monkeys

The year 1885 was important to Aboriginal People for another reason. That year the last spike of the Canadian Pacific Railway was driven into British Columbia soil, directly linking the province to the Canadian economy and labour market. Besides opening BC to massive immigration, the

TABLE 6.3

Working-age aboriginal population (aged 16-64) in British Columbia, 1880-1959

	1800	1885	1911	1929	1939	1949	1959
Men, 16-64*		6,862	6,464	6,413	7,755	9,403	
Women, 16-64		6,871	6,114	5,817	6,657	8,054	
Total, 16-64		13,733	12,578	12,230	14,412	17,457	
Total aboriginal	200,000	27,994	25,149	22,607	24,276	27,936	36,229

* For 1939, age range for men, women, and total is 17-65 inclusive, while in 1949 it is 16-69.

Sources: Canada, Indian Affairs Branch, *Annual Reports* and *Census of Indians in Canada*. The estimates for 1929 do not include 2,500 "nomadic Indians" whose existence was apparently apocryphal. The estimate for 1800 is from Robert Boyd, "Demographic History, 1874-1874," in *Handbook of North American Indians*, vol. 7 (Washington, DC: Smithsonian Institution, 1990), 135-48. The 1885 estimates are from Wilson Duff, *Indian History of British Columbia: The Impact of the White Man* (Victoria: Provincial Museum, 1980), 35-40.

last spike of the CPR signalled an end to a major source of employment for Aboriginal People along the Fraser and Thompson rivers. Although recent histories of the railway's construction have focused on the contribution of Chinese labourers, Aboriginal People made up a significant part of the navvies who laid the tracks. George Swanaset, a Salish from the Lower Fraser area, was only ten years old in 1884, but he remembered that "all the Indians worked on the railroad at that time."[112]

From 1879 through to 1885, the Indian Agents along the line reported that large numbers of aboriginal men were employed in construction or in packing supplies for the railway. Commissioner Powell was told by just one railway contractor, presumably Andrew Onderdonck, "that he had paid out nearly $300,000 for Indian labour alone" over the course of the railway's construction.[113]

The completion of the railway not only ended construction work but also cut out much of the work of the freighters and packers, who, since the gold rush, had moved goods along the Fraser and Thompson rivers into the interior. In 1882, Newton Chittenden reported "hundreds of pack animals filing by, driven by Indians, carrying supplies into the interior" through Lytton. After the completion of the railway, freight was moved to Lytton, Ashcroft, or other interior points by rail; the freighters' work was limited to linking the rail line to more remote communities.[114]

My Uncle Was a Powder Man

[My uncle] was a powder man, and he always makes the holes where they are going to blast ... he put the caps in, and he pound it ... The blast went off, and he went up in the air ... He was lucky to get away ... others died.

Annie York, Nlaka'pamux, from Spuzzum, September 13, 1973

Aboriginal railway labourers between Yale and Spuzzum in the Fraser Canyon, ca. 1912

The railway's completion in 1885 also threw over 6,500 Chinese labourers out of work.[115] Prior to the early 1880s, the Chinese had competed with Aboriginal People mostly in placer mining and in domestic service. With the ending of railway construction, these workers moved immediately into many of the industries that had been the nearly exclusive domain of aboriginal labourers.

By 1884, the Indian Agent for the Fraser Valley was noticing that his charges were being displaced "in the labor market by Chinamen, especially in all kinds of light work ... Day by day they come to find that the large influx of Chinese into this country is a great misfortune to Indians."[116] The depression of the early 1890s temporarily closed many employment opportunities, but the Indian superintendent noted that, in the longer run, it was because of an increase in competition that "the native [could not] now so readily obtain work or get as high wages as they did in former years."[117]

Sealing

The regional economies of Aboriginal People varied considerably, both before the arrival of immigrants and after. While employment was falling off dramatically along the route of the CPR in 1885, on the west coast of Vancouver Island, employment was expanding as an old activity – sealing – took on a new form. The Nuu-chah-nulth had traded fur seal skins with Europeans since the eighteenth century, hunting the seals in their canoes

Aboriginal sealers and their equipment aboard the *Forward*, ca. 1894

from the shore. In the 1870s, the rise in demand for seal-skin coats in Europe pushed prices up, and European entrepreneurs outfitted deep-sea sealing schooners, which followed the migrating seal herds from Panama to the Aleutian Islands. Aboriginal men signed on in large numbers as hunters.

There is considerable information available for the number of sealers, sealing vessels, and seal skins harvested from the early 1880s to 1911. Shipping regulations required that the crews be recorded, and the Department of Fisheries took a particular interest in the seal harvest. This interest was due to the fact that the fur seals migrated along the British Columbia coast to their breeding rookeries in Alaska. Which country had the right to harvest the seals became a major international issue, and American authorities began to seize Canadian ships. Because of these seizures and claims for compensation, as well as declining seal populations, these meticulously kept statistics were offered as evidence in international tribunals.

The first of the pelagic vessels took on an aboriginal crew in 1866. From the 1860s to mid-1883, aboriginal hunters were the only sealing labour. By 1890, the industry was well under way when 293 Indians were listed by the Department of Fisheries as crew on sealing boats, and the federal Census (conducted by the Indian Agent), of 1891 showed that 40 percent of Nuu-chah-nulth men claimed sealing as their main occupation. At the industry's peak, in 1896, 848 Aboriginal People participated in the sealing fleet, the majority drawn from the Nuu-chah-nulth population of the West Coast Indian Agency. That year the population of this agency – men, women, and children – was estimated at 2,800. Non-aboriginal sealers began to be taken on in 1884, and, for a short interval (1890-94), they comprised the majority of sealers. From the mid-1890s onward, a ban on shooting seals meant that aboriginal hunters using spears comprised the majority of seal hunters, fluctuating between 51 percent and 73 percent of the total sealing workforce.[118]

Charley Nowell and Charles Jones were among the Aboriginal People who worked on the sealing schooners and who left a record of their experience.[119] Sealing was a lucrative occupation while it lasted, though the level of income for any one hunter was highly variable from year to year. Charley Jones recalls sealers earning $1,000 in a good year, and Alex Amos's father used to come home with $700. In 1892, one of the best years, sealers from Ahousat earned an average of $1,200 each. Other sealers made between $200 and $600 that year, while those who were on schooners seized by American authorities and were put in the "skookum-house" only took home $40 to $60 for the season. The routine statistics generated by the Department of Fisheries give a better indication of the average sealing income. These suggest that, in 1892, an average income for all hunters, white and

Sealers Fear Skookum-House

[Captain Cox] hunted out "Old Jim," who had been the headman or tyee of the crew the previous cruise. Jim was pleased to see him and, of course, to receive the cultus potlatch, or gift, that he gave him. But when it came to the matter of hunters for the year, the old man shook his head, and in Chinook told the captain there would be no hunters ... "The people are afraid of the Bostonman's skookum-house [American jail] Some of those who were put in the skookum-house from other villages did not return."

Bruce McKelvie, "Saga of Sealing," from the recollections of Captain Ernst Jordan, ca. 1940

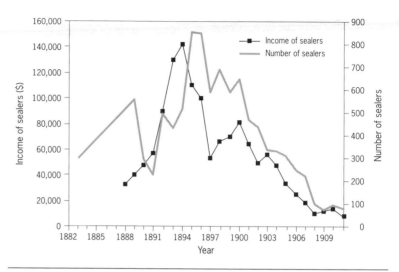

FIGURE 6.2 Number and income of Aboriginal People in the BC sealing industry, 1882-1911

Sources: **Number of sealers:** LAC, Vancouver, RG 10, Acc. 1984-85/316, box 22, file 998-37-7, and Annual Reports of the Department of Fisheries and Marine; **sealing income:** from prices per skin multiplied by aboriginal catch, given in D.G. Patteson and J. Wilen, "Depletion and Diplomacy: The North Pacifc Seal Hunt, 1886-1910," *Research in Economic History* 2 (1977): 99.

aboriginal, was closer to $94. However, it is clear that, after 1900, when comparable figures from the Department of Indian Affairs become available, aboriginal hunters earned twice the income of all seal hunters taken together (see Figure 6.2).[120]

The sealing industry offers another example of how pre-European forms of labour organization interacted with capitalist labour practices to produce a workplace and an economy that was neither Aboriginal nor European. Nuu-chah-nulth chiefs organized the people from the community and bargained with the sealing schooner companies for the prices they would receive per seal. There is abundant evidence that the Nuu-chah-nulth had enormous bargaining power. There are several reports of the sealers striking for higher pay, refusing to sail, and only sealing on a timetable that fit with their other pursuits in the prestige economy. The aboriginal "boss," "captain," or chief was kept apprised of the alternative work possibilities at the Fraser River canneries and was also kept informed of the price of seal skins on the Victoria and London markets, and he/she bargained accordingly.[121]

Around the same time that Saycha'apis was telling the Lekwungen that they honoured the hops more than they did their culture, he and his fellow Nuu-chah-nulth were making the sealing schooners wait for several weeks until potlatch ceremonies were concluded. The sealing season would end, as Victor Jacobsen noted, "As soon as the salmon season started, [at which time] the Indians would quit sealing and go to the salmon fishing and then hop picking." Alex Amos told how his father lived ultra-frugally and used his sealing income to host potlatches: "He was a good man, but too much potlatch in his head, yeah."[122] In the middle years of the industry, frustration over the continuation of the prestige and subsistence economies led many schooner owners to use less productive non-aboriginal labour.

Figure 6.2 shows that the industry had a thirty-year life, until over-hunting and the consequent international prohibition of pelagic sealing effectively killed one of the most lucrative coastal occupations and the Nuu-chah-nulth's main employer. The dramatic effect of this decline has been documented by historian Cairn Crockford, who uses Indian affairs statistics to suggest that the total income for Aboriginal People in the West Coast Agency fell by over 75 percent, from $181,000 in 1900 to just over $41,000 in 1916. No longer would they make in a season what a white man made in a year.[123]

Trapping

It was trapping that first brought most Aboriginal People into contact with the economy of non-aboriginals. James Sewid's father trapped in the 1840s

Nuu-chah-nulth Sealer's Song

Haiias lele naika sick tumtum
A long time I felt unhappy

Pe okok sun elip haias k'al
But today is the hardest day,

Kada Entelplaize yaqka leave naika.
For the [ship] Enterprise has left me.

Franz Boas, "Chinook Songs," 1888

Aboriginal sealers on Victoria-based sealing schooner, *Favorite*, ca. 1894

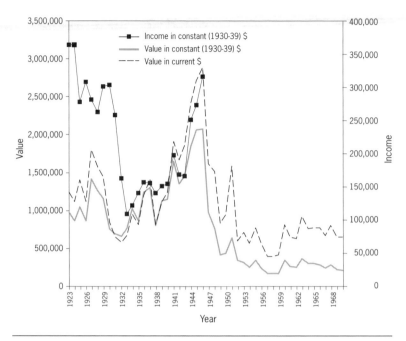

FIGURE 6.3 Value of fur trapped in British Columbia, 1923-70, and Registered Indian income from trapping, 1923-46

Sources: Dominion Bureau of Statistics, *Fur Production* (Ottawa, 1919-61); Department of Indian Affairs Annual Reports.

and 1850s to finance potlatches. Mary John's stepfather and husband in the Vanderhoof area, Beth White's father in the Atlin area, Florence Davidson's husband in the Queen Charlottes, Ruth Cook's grandfather at Village Island, Clayton Mack in Bella Coola, Harry Assu at Cape Mudge, and Ed Sparrow in the Lower Mainland were all trappers at some time in their lives.[124] Like sealing, fishing, and other industries employing concentrations of Aboriginal People, trapping, too, was a seasonal industry.

Although trapping took place in much of the province, by the 1920s, it remained the main source of income only in the north and the Chilcotin Plateau. Figure 6.3 takes a closer look at the trapping economy of the province from 1922 to 1970. It is apparent that the fur industry, like sealing, was quite volatile, with prices and supply fluctuating widely from year to year. Although the fluctuations continued, during the Second World War, prices and trapping incomes rose dramatically, making it the most lucrative trapping period in the twentieth century (see also Figure 6.7).

Although the Second World War was a boom time for trappers, by then, the aboriginal share of the industry had seriously declined. Starting in his annual report for 1892, the Superintendent of Indian Affairs wrote that Aboriginal People were facing significant competition from non-aboriginal trappers. This was exacerbated in 1912, when the provincial government required the registration of traplines. Many Aboriginal People found that the traplines their ancestors had worked for generations had been registered by non-aboriginals. As the inspector of Indian agencies noted in 1924, "The almost universal complaint by the Indians is that *their lines* are seized upon by the white men, under the cover of law ... I am referring to the trapping lines ... which an Indian and his family may have trapped all their lives, and has been handed down from mother or father to the children from time immemorial." He remarked that, if excluded from their traplines, "the Indian in the North and other outlying wild districts, has not got agriculture to fall back on, and will either starve or become a total charge on the public purse, if deprived of his British right to live." In 1926, the registration system was further tightened by the mapping of trapline territories.[125]

The effect of this loss of traplines is conveyed to some extent by the lower line in Figure 6.3, which shows aboriginal trapping and hunting income in constant (1930-39) dollars. The percentage of the traplines run by Aboriginal People fell from near 100 percent in the 1880s to 53 percent in 1947 to only 10 percent in 1956.[126] James McDonald's study of Kitsumkalum Ts'msyen maps part of this displacement in an important trapping region of the province along the Skeena River, and studies of the Carrier and Nisga'a support his findings.[127]

After the war, the fur industry went into a steep decline from which it has not recovered, and total incomes and employment from trapping have fallen accordingly. A decade after the peak year of 1945-46, the real value of

Furs being unloaded in Prince Rupert. ca. 1910

Ban on Trapping

Each year the Indians are more and more
proscribed from their natural way of life
and what game they take from the woods
is all eaten and properly used, even to
the hide and sinews, and does not
decrease the supply ... We have not yet
placed our interior and Northern Indian
on his feet yet. Employment such as an
Indian can get on the coast is not to be
had here and since the Grazing Commission is chasing the Indian horse off the
Crown Ranges and he has no land that
can be cultivated to any great extent
owing to climate and lack of irrigation in
places. I think, and he thinks and feels,
that to stop him from trapping so
suddenly is expecting too much from him.

Indian Agent E. McLeod to M.B. Jackson,
Chairman of the BC Game Conservation
Board, May 20, 1925

furs trapped in British Columbia had fallen by a catastrophic 92 percent.
While fur prices were falling, expenses were increasing. In 1870, one could
outfit a fall hunt for twenty-five dollars, but by 1950, this had risen to
ninety-six dollars, about half of which went to gasoline and kerosene.
Moreover, to compete with white trappers, an outboard motor was required,
and this involved an investment of $560 in 1940 and substantially more by
1950. In 1954, a survey of BC Aboriginal People showed that only 401 derived their primary income from trapping and that another 409 supplemented their income in this manner. Aboriginal People and communities
who had depended on trapping had to turn elsewhere to survive.[128]

Fishing and Cannery Labour

While the decline of the trapping industry was felt most in the north,
where aboriginal communities like the Nak'azdli at Fort St. James found
themselves without alternatives, on the coast the commercial fishing industry was changing in ways that affected much larger numbers of people.
Commercial fishing was concentrated in coastal regions, but people from
as far inland as Lillooet (on the Fraser River), Kispiox (on the Skeena River),
Telegraph Creek (on the Stikine River), and into the Chilcotin Plateau as
far east as Kluskus Lake migrated seasonally to participate.[129] Coupled with
the existing concentration of Aboriginal People on the coast, these migrations meant that the fishing industry was the largest employer of aboriginal labour from the 1880s through to the 1960s.

From the 1,400 fishers employed in fishing in 1882, the fleet grew to
employ 12,675 by 1929. Between the years 1925 and 1940, the fishing fleet
was 30 percent to 40 percent aboriginal. One Indian Agent wrote the federal fisheries commissioner: "As you are aware, the fishing industry on this
coast to a great extent is largely composed of Indian labour, both men and
women, and it [is] the major means of their livelihood." The cannery labour force, largely consisting of aboriginal women, grew as well, and, by
1929, the Department of Indian Affairs estimated that, of the 27,720 Indians in British Columbia, 11,488, or 41 percent, "engage in the several branches
of the commercial fishing operations."[130]

The importance of the fisheries is reflected in both published auto-
ethnographies and interviews. All the coastal men interviewed, with the
exception of Henry Pennier, fished commercially. James Sewid, Harry Assu,
Charles Nowell, Charles Jones, Ed Sparrow, and Gilbert Joe owned their
own fish boats.[131] The aboriginal cannery workforce was heavily dominated by women. Rose Sparrow, Florence Davidson, Mary Hopkins, Emma
Nyce, Elizabeth Spalding, Dorothy Young, Rosie Temple, Hazel Stewart,
and Theresa Jeffries all worked in the canneries, as did a few men such as

Charles Nowell and James Sewid. Children also found employment in the canneries and contributed to the family income: Florence Davidson recalls starting work in the canneries at age eleven, Clayton Mack at nine, James Sewid and Ed Sparrow at eight. Mack was one of many children born at the canneries.[132]

The fishing industry and the canneries, which employed such a large percentage of Aboriginal People, were, however, in decline after the 1920s. Several factors contributed to this decline, among them technological change and financial consolidation. The introduction of gas-powered boats in the 1920s meant that greater distances could be travelled faster. This meant that canneries could be further apart, with the result that many closed. Later, in the 1930s and 1940s, the introduction of refrigeration allowed the transportation of fish over longer distances before processing. Previously, it had been necessary for fish to be processed within a day of being caught, requiring many small canneries close to the prime fishing sites – sites that Aboriginal People had identified centuries before and established as village locations. The ability to keep fish fresh for longer periods of time meant that canneries could be consolidated into a few large operations, which were finally located in two main centres: Vancouver and Prince Rupert. Figure 6.4 shows the rise and fall of the cannery industry.[133]

Song of a Traveller

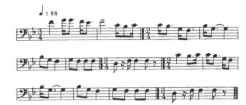

Free translation.—Ridden Cannery is a happy place, they have electric lights; Swell Cove is a happy place, and Tabishin and Church House.

Sung by Sophie Wilson from Church House, Homalko, at the Columbia Hop Company Hop Yards in 1926

Sophie Wilson, Homalco, and her song of a traveler

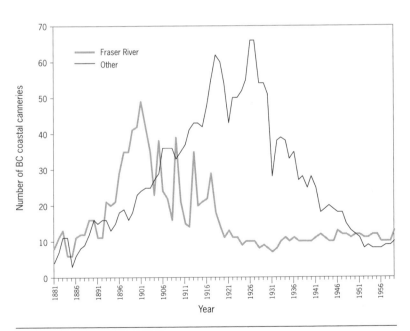

FIGURE 6.4 Number of BC coastal canneries, 1881-1959

Sources: Department of Fisheries Annual Reports; Fraser River Canners Association Annual Reports; British Columbia, *Report of the Provincial Fisheries Department,* as compiled in Cicely Lyons, *Salmon Our Heritage* [S.l.: s.n.], 1969.

When the Canneries Closed ...

All the women were working. When the canneries closed, there were no more jobs for us. All the women have time. We were really sad when we heard it; some of them cried. Now we only get welfare. I get old-age pension.

Mary Hopkins, Klemtu, ca. 1977

The dramatic effect of the consolidation of the canneries, on the number of aboriginal women and children employed in the canneries is illustrated by the workforce of Anglo British Columbia (ABC) Packers, variously the second or third largest operator of canneries on the BC coast. ABC Packers, at its peak in 1917, operated twelve canneries; however, by 1965, it operated only four. As the *Colonist* noted as early as 1948, mechanization was also reducing the demand for labour in the remaining canneries: "Hand labor has almost entirely disappeared and the cannery is a plant where ingenious machinery operates with wonderful efficiency and cheapness." Figure 6.5 shows the number and percentage of Aboriginal People (overwhelmingly women) employed by ABC. The graph exhibits two trends, the closing and consolidation of canneries and a declining proportion of Aboriginal People in the remaining operations.

Whereas in 1892, sixteen Fraser River canneries employed between 640 and 800 aboriginal women, by 1953 that number was down to ten canneries employing a total of 91 aboriginal women and men.[134] A different comparison illustrates the same trend. Province-wide in 1970, less than one-third, only 1,500 of 3,700 shoreworkers in the BC fishing industry, was aboriginal.[135] Many fewer Aboriginal People were employed in the canneries than had been the case ninety years before.

Mary Hopkins, Klemtu, retired cannery worker, ca. 1977

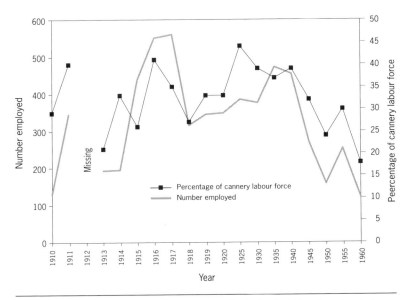

FIGURE 6.5 Aboriginal cannery workers employed in the Anglo-British Columbia Packing Company, selected years, 1910-60

Source: Bell-Irving Papers, Vancouver City Archives, mss 485, file 5.

The timing of the changes in the fishing sector differs from the cannery experience and aboriginal fishers faced different pressures. From the turn of the century a flow of Japanese immigrants into the fishery displaced some aboriginal fishers. Cannery managers who held the licences gave preference to the Japanese as "it [was] well known that Japs work harder."[136] As early as 1913, Jim Pollard, chief of Kimsquit, and others were telling the McKenna-McBride Commission about being displaced by the Japanese. Another Kimsquit man, Wilson, told the commission:

> *Wilson:*   This is our country, but in spite of that, because I have no right to work in the cannery, I cannot get a boat to fish with, and therefore I can get no money. The Japanese and the white man came here and they have no wives, but they are given work whenever they want it. I have no wife to work in the Cannery and because I have no wife to work inside they will not give me a boat to fish.
>
> *Commissioners:*   Why have you no wife?
>
> *Wilson:*   Because I have no money to keep one with.[137]

When a federal fisheries commission toured the province in 1922, it heard the same complaint from Aboriginal People.[138] A long-term decline in the number of fishing licences is discernable from 1925. It was temporarily reversed by the Second World War when aboriginal fishers benefited

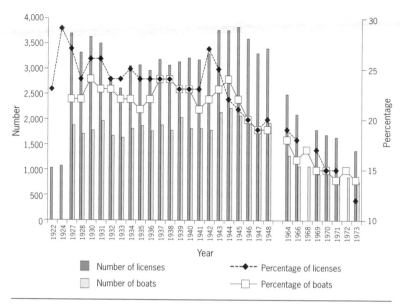

FIGURE 6.6 Number and percentage of fishing licenses and boats held by Aboriginal People, selected years, 1922-73

Sources: **1922-45**: Department of Fisheries Annual Reports; **1964-73**: M.J. Friedlaender, *Economic Status of Native Indians in British Columbia Fisheries,* **Technical Report Series PAC/T-75-25** (Vancouver: Environment Canada, Fisheries Operations Branch, 1975).

Our People Lost Out

The number of our native people fishing in their own waters here on the coast has fallen off with poor harvests and the restrictions on fishing. While our people lost out in many places, the number of non-Indian "fishermen" buying seiners on these waters built up.

Harry Assu, Kwakwa̱ka̱'wakw, *Assu of Cape Mudge,* 1989

Kwakwa̱ka̱'wakw James Sewid (left) and crew of his seiner *Twin Sisters,* 1963.

from high prices and reduced competition. After the Japanese Canadians were interned in 1942 there was a brief labour shortage and a surplus of fishing boats (confiscated from the Japanese), which allowed many Aboriginal People back in. After the war the decline continued. The numbers of aboriginal fishers fell between 1948 and 1953 – even though the total number of fishers increased (see Figure 6.6).

Cannery closures affected fishers as well as the cannery labour force. Many canneries provided boats to aboriginal fishers on a share basis, and these boats were no longer available when the canneries closed. At Klemtu, George Brown noted: "We have about sixty families in the village; only nine or ten people own a fishing boat. When the cannery was still open, our men fished on company boats. The ones that didn't go fishing worked in cold storage. All the women worked during canning season. But the plant closed in 1968. For forty years we had got used to working all the time. Then they closed her down, quit operating. That's when things went from bad to worse ... Prices here are about double Vancouver's. Many people are on welfare; that's why it hits us so much."[139]

Table 6.4 shows that, although fishing's contribution to aboriginal income rose during the war years, by 1954 it was declining. Aboriginal fishers held their relative position a decade longer in the northern fishing district, but after 1964, the share of licences going to Aboriginal People in

TABLE 6.4

Relative importance of sources of income (%) for Aboriginal People in British Columbia for selected years, 1900-54

Year	Wages	Agriculture	Fishing	Trapping/ hunting	Other industries	Rents/royalty payments	Relief/ welfare
1900	23.2	16.9	28.0	10.1	21.4	0.0	0.3
1905	29.5	18.4	20.9	13.2	17.6	0.0	0.5
1910	28.3	25.0	22.3	11.5	12.1	0.1	0.6
1915	18.5	39.8	21.7	7.0	10.5	0.8	1.6
1921	20.6	32.3	25.4	8.1	10.2	2.3	1.1
1925	23.1	29.3	19.8	12.8	8.7	5.1	1.2
1930	31.6	22.7	18.9	12.5	7.0	3.4	3.8
1935	19.2	25.3	23.9	8.3	6.5	5.7	8.6
1940	25.3	23.4	24.1	7.9	7.9	6.2	5.1
1945	35.5	18.2	31.0	7.0	5.3	1.3	1.6
1954	62.6	4.2	10.3	1.2	3.0	1.7	16.9

Sources: The amount spent in direct relief is taken from the "Appropriation Accounts" in the Department of Indian Affairs Annual Reports and added to total income from the tables, "Sources and Values of Incomes" (also in the Annual Reports). The figures for 1954 are from a survey of a sample of 5 percent of BC Indian males and 1.5 percent of females reported in H.B. Hawthorn et al., *Indians of British Columbia: A Study of Contemporary Social Adjustment* (Toronto: University of Toronto Press, 1959), 221.

this district also fell off.[140] The year-to-year decline was often small, but the long-term effect was striking. In 1883, the Fraser River fisheries alone employed 1,000 to 1,200 aboriginal fishers; seventy years later, fewer than one hundred were employed in fishing in the whole lower coast area.

Fishing was still important to communities, particularly up-coast, despite declining numbers, because those who stayed in the business, like the Assu family (who owned seven boats), prospered through this period.[141] The peak years, for those able to keep their fishing licences and boats, were the twenty years between 1958 and 1978. Namgis fisher Art Dick remembered that period: "Whereas in the old days, you get 200-300 thousand pounds of fish, you're looking at $200-300,000 gross. And everybody would walk off with $50-60,000 crew-share. Now, you can't do that. I remember one week I loaded this boat up three times. I came home and I had $15,000 apiece for my crew. Can't do that anymore in one week. And I walked off with $150,000 for my dad."[142]

The windfalls likely had a relationship to the declining participation in the industry. The federal government's policy was to drive small operators out of the fishery by purchasing fishing licences. Small operators with less efficient boats were targeted in two boat buy-back schemes that privileged the corporate ownership of fishing licences.[143]

John Pritchard's examination of the economy of Kitimaat, a Haisla community on the mid-coast, provides a local account of the declining aboriginal participation rate in the commercial fishery. At the turn of the

Today There Is Not One Boat There

I'll speak particularly about one village I know of, and that's Gilford – every single person in that village had a gillnet boat ... So, of course, they could roam wherever they wanted to. They'd go to Charles Creek, or Echo Bay, or to Knight's Inlet, Kincome Inlet, or come out here, or anywhere. But when the Davis Plan came into place ... what they [big companies] were doing at that time was they were going around and collecting, maybe 10-12-14 licenses from the gillnetters and paying them very little money. People didn't know they were worth money. I've heard stories about people getting paid 200 bucks for a license ... And what happened is they stacked them on and they built these big seine boats. And then everybody in Gilford Island soon lost the ability to eke out a living, to travel, to collect their own food, and go to the places they used to go to. It's like that today. There's not one boat there.

Verna Ambers, Namgis, Alert Bay, July 7, 2003

century, the whole village went to the canneries to fish and to can fish; in
1953, only 223 people (half the village) went, while 228 stayed. In 1954,
there were seventy-seven men fishing, but in 1977 only twenty-six continued to fish.[144] This local study, the statistics, and the auto-ethnographies all
show similar trends. Since the Second World War, aboriginal employment
in the fishing sector, which had provided the most employment, was in
relative and absolute decline.

Agricultural Industries

Aboriginal People were involved in agriculture in two distinct ways: some
raised crops and stock on their own account as farmers and ranchers for
both the commercial and domestic economies, while most provided waged
or piece-rate labour for other farmers.

The source that best suggests the extent of aboriginal farming is the
Department of Indian Affairs income estimates.[145] Despite the characterization of BC Aboriginal People as non-agricultural, at the beginning of the
century and between 1910 and 1926, this sector supplied more income to
BC Indians than any other (Figure 6.7). In the latter part of the period
studied, farming declined in importance as a source of income for Aboriginal People, though, as Table 6.4 suggests, it remained, even in 1961, the
third largest source of income after fishing and forestry.

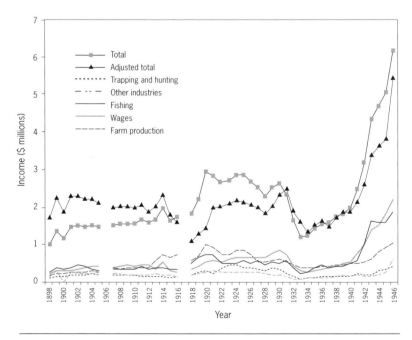

FIGURE 6.7 Income of BC Aboriginal People, 1898-1945
Source: DIAR, 1898-1946. See also Appendix 2, this volume.

Christine Quintasket's account of her family's ranching experience offers one window into aboriginal farming. Born around 1885, Quintasket was Interior Salish from the Colville people. Her family ranched just south of the Canadian border in eastern Washington and pastured their horses in the Kettle Valley on the Canadian side. Making a living meant moving regularly, and Christine spent a considerable part of her life on the Canadian side of the border.

In order to finance the ranch, her parents both worked on pack trains taking supplies from Walla Walla (in American territory) to Fort Steele (in Canada), and Quintasket herself was born on one of these packing trips. When cash was needed, the family moved to Fort Steele, and Quintasket's father worked cutting wood for the North West Mounted Police. To supplement his farming income, he tried (unsuccessfully) to run a road house and (also unsuccessfully) to be a gambler. He also worked as a freighter.[146]

The Quintaskets ranched in the 1910s and 1920s, when agriculture contributed the largest share to aboriginal income in the province, up to 39 percent. From that time through to the early 1950s, agriculture comprised a declining share, accounting for less than 5 percent of aboriginal income in 1954. Despite this small share, agriculture was the main employer of Aboriginal People in three of the eighteen Indian agencies in the province in 1954, when the wealthiest registered Indian in the province was said to be a rancher in the Okanagan Agency, with assets of over $500,000.[147]

Although agriculture was concentrated in the southern and central interior of the province and in the coastal river valleys, many Aboriginal People from other parts of British Columbia expanded their seasonal migrations to take in seasonal farm labour in the Fraser Valley and Puget Sound.[148] Seasonal migration to the hop fields of the Fraser Valley and Puget Sound were part of Charley Nowell's and John Fornsby's experience in the 1880s. John Wallace was born "to be a hop picker" at Hulbert's Hop Yard in the Fraser Valley on September 25, 1905, when his family was there picking.[149] Around the same time, Henry Pennier worked nearby at a hop farm that employed seven hundred "Indians from all over the [province] ... They'd bawl me out in their own languages and I'll bet my last bale of hay that there were seven or eight different Indian languages there."[150] More than half of the work histories of Aboriginal People describe this (see Appendix 1).

Estimates of the numbers involved in these migrations remain sketchy. In 1912, a Vancouver newspaper estimated that 1,500 aboriginal hop-pickers were employed in the Fraser Valley alone, and in 1915 the Indian Agent told the McKenna-McBride Commission that the average number was more like three thousand. A 1912 description suggests the family involvement, as well as the racialization, current at the time:

Aboriginal hop pickers at Hulbert's hop
fields in Agassiz, ca. 1896

Today [the summons] came and they sailed out, old and young, with their
baskets to gather in the hops. The vines cut down, they separate the hops
from the leaves. The foreman is all watchful that the work be cleanly done
and that only the hops go into the baskets, by the number of which are pickers paid. Few are too old or too young to go hop picking. The wrinkled old
dame approaching senility can sit in the field and use her fingers in the work
and the children, whose chubby cheeks, at least, afford no evidence of race
decay are eager to join in the same task. The pay is usually $1 a box of 100
pounds of green hops.[151]

In 1926, the Columbia Hop Company, just one of half-a-dozen hop
companies, employed around one thousand Aboriginal People. They came
from the west coast of Vancouver Island, from the Skeena and Nass rivers,
from Babine Lake, from Port Simpson on the north coast, from Powell
River and Bute Inlet on the central coast, as well as from up the Fraser
River as far as Lytton and as far east as Kamloops. In 1934, the *Chilliwack
Progress* estimated that five thousand aboriginal pickers would be employed
in the hop fields that year.[152]

Indeed, the foregoing citations may refer to some time after the peak
years as it seems that by the 1920s the peak migrations to the hop fields had
ceased.[153]

Indian Agents' reports reveal that, while seasonal agricultural labour
remained a source of aboriginal income, its importance was dwindling by
the early 1950s.[154] This was also true for the migrations to the American hop

Indians Better than Whites

The Indians were better pickers than the
whites. They were faster, and much
cleaner pickers. They could make more
money than the white people at picking.
A family in many cases would take home
several hundred dollars, if they were
good pickers ... That was not
uncommon.

Ernest Pearson, storekeeper, Columbia Hop
Yards, Sardis, interviewed by Mr. Charlie,
June 29, 1976

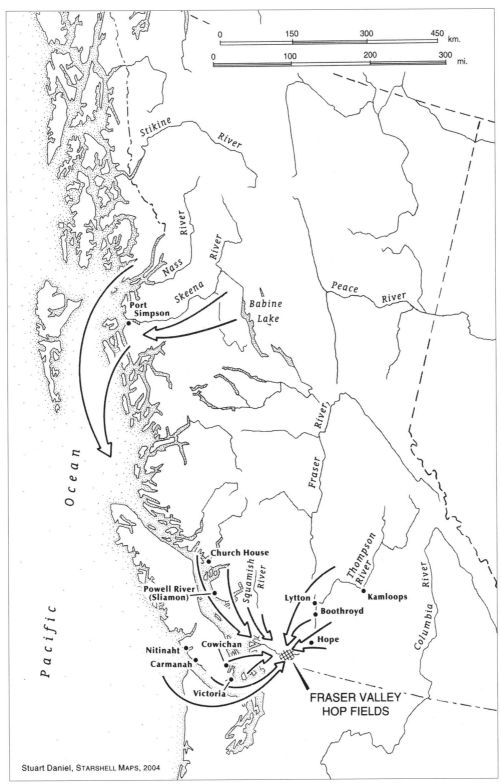

MAP 6.3 Origins of aboriginal hop pickers, 1926, Fraser Valley

and berry fields, which had once involved one-quarter of all BC Aboriginal People. As late as 1953, the Canadian Regional Employment Offices placed the average number of Aboriginal People migrating to the United States at 1,800 men and 1,555 women, primarily agricultural labourers from British Columbia. They estimated that another 3,000 to 3,500 migrated within BC itself to engage in seasonal agricultural labour. However, by 1957, only three hundred BC Aboriginal People participated in the hop harvest in BC and the United States.[155]

The Indian Agents' observations are supported by a detailed community study. Michael Ames's work on the Xaxli'p (Fountain) community near Lillooet shows that, in 1951, thirty-eight of their forty-one families went hop picking; four years later, only four families and six women (whose husbands stayed to work construction) participated in the migration. Ames's study, with the diminishing references to this form of labour in the auto-ethnographies and the statistics, demonstrates that many fewer Aboriginal People participated in seasonal harvesting in the 1950s than had done so seventy years earlier. Stó:lō Peter Peters put it this way: "I went to the hopfields every years ... [but] the machines took over ... It was finished in the 1950s."[156]

Forest Industry

It is clear from the evidence presented in the last section that aboriginal men were a major part of the sawmill labour force in the nineteenth century, comprising over half the workers at the first industrial mill at Port Alberni and its successors in what became Vancouver. In 1897, the Yearbook of British Columbia noted that the sawmills "are principally worked by Indians, half-breed, Chinese and Japs." In 1916, the Indian Agent for Vancouver told the McKenna-McBride Royal Commission that "I have known some of these men," referring to Squamish, Musqueam, and others near Vancouver, "who have been working for over twenty years in the saw mill and at other occupations of a like character."[157]

Stó:lō Leonard Point, when interviewed in 1951, had been working in sawmills since 1929 and in logging camps before that, but he noted that he was the only Aboriginal Person employed at the Universal Box Company mill in Vancouver. He also stated that, since the Second World War, few Aboriginal People had worked in the mills but more worked in the bush as loggers, since the latter gave them more flexibility to fish and engage in traditional activities.[158]

It is difficult to get an overall picture of the harvesting part of the forest industry. We do know that all twelve of the aboriginal men who left work histories, from all parts of the province, worked at one time or

Working in the Mill

Once I young, strong, work Hastings Mill, two and one half years' work on carriage [ca. 1886], good man, then I work Faber Bros. Sawmill; but now I get old, have no money, have to sell basket. When white-mans call me Siwash I say "Go to hell."

Chil-lah-minst [Jim Franks] Squamish, to Major Matthews, November 20, 1932

another as loggers, wood-cutters, boom men, sawmill labourers, and/or pole cutters. Charles Jones became a logger at the turn of the century, when the sealing industry shut down, and he remained a logger for the rest of his life; however, "when the jobs in the logging industry were scarce, [he] often went fishing."[159]

Although logging was widely distributed throughout the province, it was most intensively pursued in the coastal regions. Codere's study of the Kwakw̱aka̱'wakw and Pritchard's of the Haisla found widespread involvement in hand-logging in the early part of the twentieth century. This is probably true for many of the other coastal aboriginal communities as well. We know, for example, that Gilbert Joe's Sechelt father, Florence Davidson's Haida husband, and Nuu-chah-nulth Charles Jones were among those who participated in this industry.[160]

When legislative changes forced an end to hand-logging in 1910, in several cases, Aboriginal People formed their own logging companies; however, they soon found that the provincial forestry branch did not want to give licences to Aboriginal People. In 1913, Wilson, a Nuxalk, told the McKenna-McBride Commission: "When an Indian wants work at logging he cannot always get a licence. In fact we have great difficulty in getting these licences." The discrimination against aboriginal loggers is born out by Chief Julian of Sechelt, who told the commission: "A few years ago we used to make our living by logging; that is hand logging, but we had to buy a license to do so but now in these late years we cannot do that. The only thing we do now is to make our living by fishing." John Pritchard, who studied the economy of the Haisla, found that their logging peaked by 1924, although they were also logging during the Second World War and the immediate postwar period.[161]

One indicator of the relative importance of the forest sector to Aboriginal People is the decennial census; another is a survey of aboriginal occupations conducted by Harry Hawthorn in 1954 (Table 6.5). Both suggest a relative increase in the importance of the forest industry between 1931 and 1961. There are, however, serious questions about the reliability of the federal census, which, in 1931, began tabulating occupational category according to race.

It is possible, from the auto-ethnographies and agents' reports, to say that the forest industry has continued to be a major employer of Aboriginal People in the province, but it is difficult to chart changing patterns after 1954. Amy O'Neill interviewed Stó:lō loggers and found that, in the last half of the twentieth century, logging was a key source of livelihood for Aboriginal People in the Fraser Valley and a source of pride and identity for many Stó:lō men.[162] One of the best histories of an aboriginal logger

Stó:lō logger Hank Pennier

Indians Will Work Then Quit

A lot of Indians will work for a couple of months and then quit. They could get away with this during war-time but now employment is tightening up. The mills will hire only experienced men ... As a rule, logging is a more seasonal employment than mill work. Because it is easy to enter this industry, with its fluid labour force, it makes it a convenient source of employment for the native fishermen in the off-season. For these two reasons, there are considerably more Indians in logging than in other phases of the lumber industry.

Leonard Point, Stó:lō, interviewed by Frances Thompson, March 4, 1951

was written by Stó:lō Hank Pennier.[163] Interviews with aboriginal men in the coastal towns of Queen's Cove, Kingcome, and Owikeno suggest that logging has employed a part of the male labour force formerly engaged in fishing, but they also indicate that, once the local area has been logged, even this form of employment becomes tenuous.

The only study of an aboriginal economy based on logging is Douglas Hudson's of the Carrier people in north central British Columbia. Based on interviews with an employer, Hudson argues that the period between 1946 and 1964 marked the boom years for logging operations in that area and the peak years of aboriginal employment in that sector. After that, the "gypo" logging operations and local sawmills, which employed most of the aboriginal forest workers, were displaced by multinational firms that brought in workers from "outside." George Jolliffe, Namgis fisher and former logger, confirmed the same pattern for the coast: "My dad did that census – I forget what year it was – at that time he said there was 110 Gypo camps in this area. Now there's none. Just 4 logging camps. Big ones."[164]

This pattern seems to hold for the whole province. In 1910, Aboriginal People were denied harvesting permits in their own right and so became employees. So long as the logging industry was made up of many small operations that hired locally, Aboriginal People could integrate it into their seasonal rounds. Art Dick describes the pattern: "We started fishing about this time of year [July] and we didn't get finished until sometime in the middle of October. And after that ... you could either go logging or working in the pulp mill or collect UI [Unemployment Insurance, now called Employment Insurance]." All but two of the fourteen aboriginal men interviewed for the Coast under Stress Project in Alert Bay worked seasonally in logging as well as in fishing.

When the smaller "gypo" operations were replaced by large corporations, employment became more regular and hiring was concentrated in union halls in Vancouver rather than conducted by owners scattered across the province. This, of course, meant that local people were left out.[165] Also, many aboriginal loggers only wanted seasonal work and, in Billy Wasden's words, "quit logging with the first sockeye run." Employers wanted year-round labour, so "the pattern was the native people were the first to be laid off." Namgis fisher and community leader Chris Cook Jr. recalled: "Before the fishermen got unemployment insurance, we looked for jobs, logging, you know we did all kinds of different things. You know, since then, with the automation of the logging industry ... there's been a big change." Government employment insurance arrived just as it became more difficult for aboriginal workers to combine a range of seasonal jobs. Government transfer payments supplemented income from one seasonal job and the traditional subsistence economy, and the three merged to form a new, "moditional," economy.

Other Occupations

When it comes to Aboriginal People, the decennial census has to be treated with more than the usual degree of skepticism. It does, however, hint at the importance of domestic service as a long-standing employer of aboriginal women. Visitors to nineteenth-century British Columbia commented on the ubiquity of aboriginal washerwomen and domestics, and the biographies are emphatic about this. Of the seven women for whom we have work histories, six mention that, at different times in their lives, they were paid to do laundry and domestic work or to cook in camps, restaurants, or on fish boats (see Appendix 1).

Two biographies from the interior, Tahltan Beth White's and Carrier Mary John's, extend to the 1960s, when both women left their previous seasonal occupational activities and found year-round work in the service industry. Mary John started work in the Vanderhoof hospital in 1959 and in 1972 taught the Carrier language and history at the local school. Beth White owned and operated a gas station in Atlin from 1960 to 1967.[166] From the census, it appears that, in the 1960s, they were representative of a small but growing group of Aboriginal People who were finding employment outside the resource industries. Since the late nineteenth century, a few Aboriginal British Columbians have found employment in the professions, particularly in the clergy, which attracted a small but influential group (e.g., W.H. Pierce and Peter Kelly), or in teaching (e.g., Christine Quintasket).[167] Although the numbers remained small, the 1960 and 1970 censuses document definite aboriginal employment increases in the professional, government, and service sectors. By the 1991 census, Aboriginal People were 30 percent more likely to be employed in the hospitality industry and were twice as likely to be employed in government service as non-Aboriginal People. Almost 30 percent of registered Indian workers were in government service.[168]

The census, and Hawthorn's survey, records a continuing involvement of Aboriginal People in the transportation sector. Longshoring, mentioned as employing Lekwungen men in Victoria and the Squamish in Vancouver in the 1860s, continued to provide occupations for the Lekwungen until the Second World War and, through the 1970s, for the Squamish, although aboriginal participation declined overall. In the 1930s, aboriginal workers comprised about 40 percent of the membership in the International Longshoreman's Union, which served all BC ports, but by 1951 only 3 percent. According to Frances Thompson, who investigated aboriginal

I Was Worth over $100 a Month

It was a big house where I cooked and they had little bathrooms, tiny, just big enough for their bath and they had this water running in. Oh, it was nice to work toward the end you know with water running in.

I like it although it was hard work and I was paid forty-five dollars a month, yes. She told me I was worth over a hundred as far as was go for cooks – but she [told] me, I can't afford it.

Mary Augusta Tappage, Secwepemc (Shuswap),
c. 1971

Aboriginal girls trained to be servants at All Hallows School,
Yale, 1902

longshoring in 1951, "the decline in membership seems to be in inverse
ratio to the degree of stabilization of employment in the longshoring industry." The union strove to decasualize longshoring by formalizing labour
relations with seniority rights and call-up lists. These provided more hours
of work for those with seniority, but to maintain standing, longshoremen
had to work when their names came up. This adversely affected aboriginal
workers, who had taken advantage of the casual labour market to fish in
the summer and to engage in ceremonial activities in the winter.[169] There
was an additional reason. One informant on the Capilano reserve said in
1951 that the younger men on his own and Mission reserves do not take to
longshoring as older men do. "There seems to be a feeling among the
younger men that the Indian Affairs Branch will look after them."[170]

The railways employed several hundred Aboriginal People as section
hands and trackmen in the 1940s, but the censuses suggest that this employment has been dropping ever since, reflecting, perhaps, the effect of
technological change on railway maintenance. The growing numbers employed in the transportation sector capture the effect of provincial highway
expansion in the 1950s and the resulting highway maintenance work. Both

Mary John's and Beth White's husbands found full-time jobs working for the highways department in the 1960s.

As recreational hunting expanded in the 1920s, some aboriginal men became guide-outfitters. Clayton Mack was successful at this. Clayton, who had logged, ranched, fished, and just about everything else spent fifty years of his life guiding American and German hunters in search of grizzly bear. All in all, his hunts accounted for the deaths of over three hundred grizzlies: "I made a good living grizzly bear guiding. Get a new pickup truck every two years." But Mack may never have received his guiding licence if it were not for influential American hunters, who supported his application.[171]

A snapshot of the multifaceted economy of Aboriginal British Columbia comes from the testimony of the twenty-six Sheshaht men from the west coast of Vancouver Island who made claims to the Royal Commission on Pelagic Sealing for income lost as a result of the international ban on sealing. In 1912-13, they had an average of three different paid "occupations" each before they went to work in the "subsistence" economy. Three-quarters of them (20) included a trip to the Fraser River canneries as part of their income, and about half (12) followed that with work in the hop fields. A little under half (12) sold fish locally, and between five and six trapped or worked in one or another of the local canneries, local whaling station, or sawmills. Others logged (1), sold cordwood (3), made canoes for sale (3), guided (1), worked in off-shore sealing (1), or as local agricultural labourers (1).[172]

It is clear that, as far as paid work goes, all the men and many of the women did not have an "occupation," as such. In common with rural people in British Columbia, in the Saguenay region of Quebec, and no doubt in many other places, people shifted jobs with the seasons and with the economic and political cycles that directed or redirected employment dollars to their region (see Chapter 2 and Postscript). What made aboriginal workers distinct is that they had a subsistence economy that persisted well past those of other Canadians, and this supplied them with food when other work did not. The availability of fish and game in season, and a strong cultural preference for harvesting these foods, meant that they struggled to create a wage-work cycle that allowed the other modes of production, including gathering food, potlatching, and the rest of the prestige economy.

Aboriginal Entrepreneurs

Archaeological and other evidence make it clear that Aboriginal People were "traders" long before Europeans ever came into their territory. It is not surprising, then, that European goods were added to these trading networks and that Aboriginal People continued to act as traders, intermediaries, and, eventually, retailers. Sayach'apis and Arthur Wellington Clah

Learned English When I Worked with Whites

My mother teach us Nuxalk language and she teach us how to speak Chinook language too. She can't speak English but she speak Chinook real good. My dad, too, he speak Chinook language. Chinook language was something like English language in them days. Everyone know that language on the coast. My dad, when he meet guys from Bella Bella or Alert Bay or Rivers Inlet they all speak Chinook language ... my mum she sing songs in Chinook too. So I learn Nuxalk, then I learn Chinook, then I learn English. I didn't really learn English at that day school, I learn it most when I work for and with white people.

Clayton Mack, Nuxalk, *Grizzlies and White Guys: The Stories of Clayton Mack*, 1993

Mrs. Willie Mack, Nuxalk, mother of Clayton Mack, 1923

I've Been Everything

I've been everything. The only thing I haven't done is logging. I tree planted, I worked on a fish farm, oyster plant on an oyster farm ... Worked in a processing plant here. Labourer. Everybody's been a labourer at some time or another.

Art Dick, Namgis, Alert Bay, July 6, 2003

are excellent examples of businesspeople who took aboriginal-produced/harvested goods to capitalist markets and brought back consumer goods, which they then sold to other Aboriginal People.

In the nineteenth century, aboriginal entrepreneurs were considered success stories and were highlighted by Indian Agents wishing to illustrate Indian "progress." As a result, there are occasional reports like that from the Indian superintendent in 1892, noting that, in the Northwest Agency, "the Indians own saw-mills, and dog-fish oil manufactures, they also have many stores and have commenced in a small way to can salmon and clams." Some Heiltsuk operated their own trading company by 1888, and by early in the twentieth century there were five Heiltsuk-owned businesses in Bella Bella. There is also a clear entrepreneurial element to small-scale commodity production, like fishing, farming, and logging, that engaged large numbers of aboriginal men and women before and after the turn of the century.[173]

Some Aboriginal People continued to work their own farms and fish boats in the 1970s, while those like Beth White opened gas stations or other small businesses. Nonetheless, the relative importance of small-scale commodity production and entrepreneurial enterprises in general seems to have been shrinking. Relative income figures show that the proportion of aboriginal-earned income gained through wage labour climbed at the expense of commodity production such as fishing, farming, and trapping (see Table 6.4).

Other Non-Wage Income

Statistical records are silent on a number of other activities that loom large in the auto-ethnographies. One of these is home-based production of items for sale – something that is mentioned in all the sampled work histories of aboriginal women. Florence Davidson recalled her mother weaving baskets, placemats, and hats all winter long, "from the time she finished picking and putting up berries until spring." Her weaving "she sold in June when we went to the mainland to work in the canneries." Davidson learned how to weave and knit, and she sold baskets to the local store owner for $1.25 each. According to Mary John, "the families depended on wives and mothers and grandmothers to make moccasins, jackets and mitts out of hides." All over the province, aboriginal women worked on home production to provide income for their families. For Mary John's family, selling home-manufactures door to door in Vanderhoof was often the only source of cash income during the Depression.[174] Rose Sparrow, Florence Davidson and her mother, and many other women knitted "Cowichan Indian Sweaters" in the evenings and off-season. Some men, like Florence Davidson's father, also earned part of their living as carvers.[175]

Jessie Wilson, Nuu-chah-nulth, selling her baskets, Yuquot (Friendly Cove), 1930s.

The Klootchman Are Laughing at Us

You know the time we had the meeting at Cape Mudge school house for to keep the clotchmen [klootchman] at home but they have broken the law they are staying at Rock Bay [logging camp] staying with white men and drinking whiskey. The clotchman are laughing at you and me and they say we cannot stop them from going to the logging camps.

Chief Jim Chackidl, We Wai Kai (Cape Mudge), to Indian Agent G.W. Debeck, December 28, 1903

The Department of Indian Affairs thought that "Indian handicraft, although only a part-time activity in most families, represent[ed] an important source of income." The DIA set up a branch to encourage and market these home-manufactures.[176] The importance of handicraft production has been illustrated with regard to the Lekwungen economy, described earlier.

The gender imbalance in the settler population created a steady demand for female partners and the purchase of sexual services. In coastal British Columbia, where there were many logging camps, the only single women for hundreds of miles were aboriginal. Up until the First World War, the DIA and missionary correspondence as well as other records suggest that aboriginal men were seeking help from government officials to keep some aboriginal women from engaging in this kind of entrepreneurship.[177]

Everybody Used to Have a Boat

I bet you that the meals that are –
everyday meal within the First Nations
people, I believe that 75-80 percent of
it is non-traditional. I think one reason
here for us is that for us here to go and
get stuff, like abalone, mussels, clams,
salmon, halibut and all those different
things, you can't just go out in a boat
anymore. Everybody used to have a
boat to go out and catch them.

Billy Wasden, Namgis, Alert Bay, May 19,
2003

The Subsistence Economy

The auto-ethnographies and interviews also stress that, from the 1880s
through to 1970 and to today, many aboriginal men and women continued
to work at subsistence activities or to enjoy the food-gifts of others who
still did so.[178]

Initially, the subsistence economy determined when Aboriginal People
were available to work in the capitalist economy. As we saw in the previous
section, the Kwakwaka'wakw of Fort Rupert and the Nanaimo people were
only willing to dig for coal, for example, when it fit into their subsistence
economy; likewise, the Ts'msyen from Port Simpson and the Nuu-chah-
nulth from Barclay Sound all came to Victoria when doing so was compatible with their food fishery.

In the 1890s, game and fishing regulations began to prescribe when
Aboriginal People could participate in subsistence activities, and several
aboriginal observers have noted a connection between these laws and a
new dependence on wage labour. According to Charles Jones: "If we get
caught hunting out of season, we get into trouble. After they had passed
this law, we had to start eating white man's food, as that was the only way
to stay alive. So, to pay for the white man's goods, we had to make money,
and the only way we could do that was to work for the white man's companies."[179] The Quintaskets planted their crops in the spring and then left the
ranch to gather native foods, "which were always relished more than potatoes and vegetables. We never missed the annual fall hunt until it was forbidden by the state game department."[180]

Still, a wide range of studies, including Hawthorn's 1954 provincial
examination and more detailed and contemporary studies of the Ts'msyen,
Carrier, Nisga'a, Haisla, Musqueam, Wsanec, and Stó:lō, all show that food
gathering continued in most aboriginal communities through the 1970s
and up to the present day. The most comprehensive of any survey of aboriginal subsistence harvesting was conducted jointly by the BC Union of
Indian Chiefs and the federal fisheries department in 1972, and it covered
all the bands in the Fraser River watershed from the headwaters near Fraser
Lake, northwest of Prince George, to the mouth at Vancouver. The survey
sampled key members from eighty-five bands, whose membership totalled
17,548 people. Aboriginal respondents thought that about one-third of all
registered Indians – men, women, and children – engaged in the food fishery, while about one-quarter engaged in berry picking and nearly one-fifth
in hunting. Given that the Indian population was disproportionately made
up of children, these are very significant numbers. With food fishing, the
estimates varied from 2.8 percent participation for the most urban bands to
over 58 percent. Among the respondents surveyed in each band, 94 percent

fished for food. If the food fishery were to be outlawed, only 17 percent thought that no one in their community would go hungry, while one-quarter thought that everyone in their community would go hungry.

The community studies, the biographies, and the survey data also suggest that, while still significant, there has been a decline in the economic importance of the subsistence economy since the Great Depression. Only 12 percent of those surveyed thought that they fished as much or more than their grandparents, less than 8 percent thought they hunted as much or more than their grandparents, and only 6 percent thought they harvested as many berries. Seventy-seven percent attributed the decline in fishing to the availability of employment or social services.[181] Sixty-four percent said they caught enough fish for themselves and their families, and 85 percent reported that their preserved fish lasted them throughout the winter. The yearly per capita consumption of salmon was estimated to be sixty-one pounds (27.7 kilograms), an average of just over a pound (half a kilogram) per week.[182]

Where capitalist work opportunities opened up for men, subsistence activities fell increasingly to the women. Jo-Anne Fiske has shown that these activities remained vital to the economy of the Carrier. She found that, in recognition of their increased importance as providers, Carrier women began to take on expanded roles in the political life of their communities.[183]

Income Patterns, 1898-1945

The Department of Indian Affairs was intensely concerned with the involvement of Aboriginal People in the capitalist economy. In written reports, agents took great pains to describe the range of work opportunities available to Aboriginal People. Beginning in 1877, they were also asked to report on the income of the bands in their respective jurisdictions. For reasons discussed in Appendix 2, the estimates do not appear to have been very reliable until 1898, when more precise categories were established for income reporting. Even if the post-1898 figures cannot be accepted as exact records of Indian incomes, given the alternatives, they appear to be reasonable indicators of relative levels of income from various sources as well as accurate reflections of relative changes of income levels over time.

Figure 6.7 shows the income of registered Indians according to the estimates of the Indian Agents from 1898 to 1945. The income is divided into categories: farming, fishing, hunting and trapping, wages, and "other industries," a residual category that includes home-manufactures, canoe-making, self-employed logging, and other entrepreneurial incomes. It suited the DIA's agenda to combine estimates of subsistence food with goods sold under the categories of agricultural produce, hunting, and fishing, with

Being Mortals, They Rest

Most of the Bella Coola are fairly well-to-do, they fish for the cannery in the summer, if energetic, work for a few months logging and are able to earn in about 5 months all the money they need for the year. Being ordinary mortals they rest for the other seven months of the year.

Thomas McIlwraith, anthropologist, in letter to Dr. Haddon, August 29, 1922

Anthropologist Thomas McIlwraith with Nuxalk Willie Mack and son, Bella Coola, 1922

the result that actual cash income is considerably inflated within these categories. In Figure 6.7 income from each of these categories is shown in the dollar values recorded at the time. Total income has also been converted into constant dollars to allow comparison over time.

These relative changes are expressed in Table 6.4, which considers work income and the amount of annuities, rent, trust payments, and welfare payments distributed to British Columbia's registered Indians as a percentage of total income for selected years from 1900 to 1954.

Figure 6.7 and Table 6.4 indicate that wage work has generally been increasing in importance to the incomes of Aboriginal People over time, except during the depressions that accompanied the First World War and that preceded the Second World War. Agriculture's contribution rose to a peak in the 1920s and has subsided since then. Fishing income was most important at the beginning of the century and during the Second World War and has dropped off since. Relief and welfare payments comprised an insignificant part of aboriginal incomes until the Depression of the 1930s, when many Canadians turned to the government for assistance. State payments to Aboriginal People begin to be a real presence only after the Second World War.

Through the 1890s, the agents noted the continuing desire of Aboriginal People to work and the decreasing options open to them. "Most of the Indians of the superintendency have a fondness for the earning of money ... Where there is money to be made, the Indians are eager to earn it," wrote Indian Superintendent A.W. Vowell in 1901. But "as time advances, they find many of the channels closed against them through which in former times, when white settlers were few and the extent of country open to them almost limitless, they obtained all the necessaries of life."[184]

There was another common factor that affected most aboriginal incomes. Based in resource industries, they were vulnerable to fluctuating resource prices and, in the case of the fishery, to supply. The resource industries in British Columbia also had volatile labour relations, and strikes could shut down the fishery during the short season, as happened in 1935. In that year, aboriginal families not only did not earn a cent from the fishery but they also accumulated a debt of up to $150 while living at the

Tlingit woman applying labels to salmon cans, Sitkoh Bay Cannery, Alaska, ca. 1907-13

cannery waiting for the strike to end. The aggregate figures also hide enormous variability in incomes. In 1935, for example, Kwakwaka'wakw families returned from the cannery season with incomes that ranged from $300 to $1500. The agent thought their cannery earnings generally sufficient "to provide for their families for the rest of the year."[185]

Putting aboriginal income into constant dollars (Figure 6.7) and thereby showing "real income" or purchasing power sheds more light on the matter. Figure 6.7 shows that the real income of BC Aboriginal People was greater when the statistics first become available (between 1899 and 1914) than at any other extended period up to the Second World War.[186] The first section of this chapter shows that, prior to 1899, Aboriginal People's incomes had been even higher. Indian Agent reports, starting in 1892 and continuing through to the turn of the century, consistently state that "there has been a gradual falling off in the earnings of Indians."[187] It appears that Aboriginal People's incomes were already on the decline when consistent estimates first became available.

Cyclical Patterns: Depression and War

From Figure 6.7, it is apparent that Aboriginal People shared the increase in wartime employment, from 1914 to 1919, alongside other Canadians. Yet, despite the rising dollar income, wartime inflation caused real income (constant dollars) to plummet. In the 1920s, real income rose until it hit the prewar levels in 1929-30, then it plummeted again.

Mary John described the effect of the 1930s Depression on her community: "Our hard life became harder ... Employment for our men became scarce and finally non-existent. By the end of the Depression the only work available for the men was relief work ... Many times relief money was the only cash which was circulating on the reserve."[188] Figure 6.7 indicates that her experience was probably widely shared among registered Indians in British Columbia. Aboriginal People, like other Canadians, rode the roller-coaster of the national and international economy. They experienced sharp dips in 1914, 1924, and 1927, and then they experienced the full impact of the Great Depression.

Similarly, the rise in wages and employment that Florence Davidson recalls during the Second World War is dramatically reflected in the income statistics and in the information gathered by the provincial Department of Labour.[189] From 1939 to 1945, the Department of Labour added an "Indian" category to the annual surveys it sent to all major industrial firms. These surveys asked about the ethnicity of employees, hours worked, and rates of pay. Table 6.5 provides a summary of this enumeration, which indicates that, during the war years, Aboriginal People were hired in industries

Quit When First Salmon Jumps

During the depression the logging companies [on Haida Gwaii] wouldn't hire Indians because they said that when the first salmon jumped in the inlet the Indian would quit his job and go fishing ... But in the Second World War some of our men started working ... [and] today about 70 per cent of our able-bodied men are hired by MacMillan Bloedel [logging company].

John Williams, Haida, 1969

Okanagan men wearing World War I uniforms

and occupational categories other than those in which they had previously
been concentrated. Employment in these enumerated industries doubled
between 1940 and 1941, and they almost doubled again to peak in 1942.
The detailed figures from which Table 6.5 is drawn show that these record
employment levels were caused, in part, by hirings in such industries as explosives and chemicals, the metal trades, utilities, and, notably, shipbuilding,
which, in 1942, employed 107 aboriginal men.[190] R.W. McLeod, federal
fisheries supervisor for British Columbia, stated that, during the war, a
"large percentage of male Indians, physically fit, found remunerative employment in the logging industry, auto highway upkeep, railroad track re-
pair, and agricultural pursuits." As a result, he added, aboriginal subsistence
fishing was much reduced.[191] The Department of Labour figures also suggest that the movement of Aboriginal People into these industries was only
temporary. After 1942, employment declined steadily through to 1945.

TABLE 6.5

Aboriginal People employed in BC industries (excluding fishing, trapping, and agriculture), 1940-45

Industry		1940	1941	1942	1943	1944	1945
Canning/food processing	Men	316	715	650	1,636	1,549	1,488
	Women	525	1,081	1,775	1,767	1,479	1,423
Logging/wood processing	Men	195	339	1,045	703	721	698
	Women	0	0	3	15	10	11
Oil reduction plants	Men	54	65	89	164	97	86
	Women	0	0	14	4	2	3
Longshoring/coast shipping	Men	129	137	45	0	6	15
Shipbuilding	Men	0	76	107	60	51	35
Construction/building materials	Men	20	50	216	244	119	81
Mining	Men	11	20	13	20	18	15
Other industries/utilities*	Men	36	26	806	204	170	188
	Women	0	2	1	5	16	5
Total	Men	761	1,428	2,971	3,031	2,731	2,606
	Women	525	1,083	1,793	1,791	1,507	1,442
	Both sexes	1,286	2,511	4,764	4,822	4,238	4,048

* Includes explosives, building supplies, garment manufacturing, fur and leather manufacturing, laundries, printing and publishing, metal trades, miscellaneous manufacturing, and utilities. No Aboriginal People are reported as being employed in brewing, tobacco, household furnishing, jewellery, paint manufacturing, or smelting.

Source: BC Department of Labour, Annual Reports, in *BC Sessional Papers,* 1940-45.

The industries not included in the Department of Labour surveys – fishing, trapping, and agriculture – also employed record numbers of aboriginal workers. Figure 6.3 shows that this was a period of record high incomes for trappers, and Figure 6.6 illustrates that it was also a period of high employment in the fisheries.

In addition, 270 BC registered Indians had enlisted in the armed forces by 1945.[192] All the statistical evidence confirms the wartime recollections of Florence Davidson: that, for Aboriginal People, the Second World War was a time of economic prosperity unprecedented since the 1880s. After the war, opportunities shrunk as the Japanese and service personnel returned to the coast, followed by a growing wave of postwar immigration. Gitga'at Helen Clifton from Hartley Bay recalls that the new immigrants "displaced a lot of our workers, you know, they went back to being the second class citizens they were before the war."[193]

Occupational Concentration by Region

The statistical evidence gathered on a provincial basis reveals provincial trends, but the personal accounts in the auto-ethnographies illustrate that the economies in which Aboriginal People worked varied from region to region.

They Were Treated Special

For a while during the war years, Native people and Native labour, they were treated far better. The housing they had at the canneries, they got the bigger, getting the bigger boats, they were treated special, they had better treatment, yeah.

Helen Clifton, Gitga'at, Hartley Bay, June 9, 2004

The auto-ethnographies of coastal people like James Sewid, Charley Nowell, and Harry Assu (Kwakwaka'wakw); Florence Edenshaw Davidson (Haida); W.H. Pierce (Ts'msyen); and the biographies and/or short sketches of Simon Baker, Theresa Jeffries, Ed and Rose Sparrow, George Swanaset, Gilbert Joe, and John Fornsby (Coast Salish); and Sayach'apis and Charles Jones (Nuu-chah-nulth) all stress the importance of the fishing industry. On the coast, men typically fished, in their own boats or in cannery-owned boats, and women, children, and the elderly worked in the canneries. Supplementary activities such as logging, trapping, and home-manufacturing were usually combined with fishing as sources of income.[194] From the biographical accounts, we know that many Salish, Nuu-chah-nulth, and Kwakwaka'wakw of both sexes and all ages migrated in the late summer to work in the hop and berry fields of the Fraser Valley and Puget Sound. In addition, Cowichan men like Albert Westly, who lived between Chemainus and Nanaimo, specialized in working in the neighbouring coal fields as well as in the sawmills and on the docks. On Vancouver Island, the Salish, the Kwakwaka'wakw, and, particularly, the Nuu-chah-nulth, worked the sealing fleet as long as it flourished.

The accounts of Mary John, Mary Augusta Tappage, Christine Quintasket, Harry Robinson, Clayton Mack, and Henry Pennier recall that, in the south and central interior, as well as up the Fraser Valley, farming,

Aboriginal Canadian Pacific Rail section crew on Speeder, at Mile 183, 1909

We Never Felt the Hungry '30s

We were very rich people. Very rich people, I am not talking about money wise. What we have surrounding, like berries, salmon, clams – name it. Everything was there. We never went hungry. They talk about the hungry thirties we never felt that. Cause we had lots ... you know today we are poor people now.

Chief Adam Dick (Kwaxsistala), Kwakw̱aka'wakw, Victoria, October 23, 2001

Hereditary Chief Adam Dick (Kwaxsistala), Kwakw̱aka'wakw

ranching, agricultural labour, and (for the men) logging were the most important industries. A 1972 survey of one member from each of eighty-four bands in the Fraser River watershed showed that nearly 60 percent considered logging to be their principal occupation, 13 percent sawmill work, and 12 percent ranching. Aboriginal men also worked on railroad construction, cut railway ties, and worked as section hands. Here, earlier in the century, clearing land, cutting firewood, and placer mining for gold were occupations that almost every family turned their hand to when cash was needed.[195]

In British Columbia's far north, where there had also been mining-related work opportunities in the late nineteenth century, trapping was the main cash-earner in the twentieth century. Beth White, a Tahltan woman who trapped with her husband, recorded that cash-earning opportunities remained limited to trapping through to the Second World War. Her husband supplemented their income with occasional work in mining camps, packing, and guiding. Trapping was also a major source of income for the Carrier people in Mary John's community of Stoney Creek in north central BC.[196]

Yet, within this diversity, there are strikingly common patterns. All but two of the auto-ethnographies suggest that Aboriginal People were concentrated in seasonal occupations, primarily fishing, canning, trapping, agricultural harvesting, and logging, as well as other low-skill work (e.g., cutting wood, and domestic service).[197] Community studies and surveys bear this out.[198] Within these limited occupational choices, they were extremely mobile, often working three and even as many as five different occupations in a "normal" year – in addition to participating in subsistence and prestige economies. In all parts of the province, the aboriginal economy involved whole households. Finally, between 1885 and 1970, most of their paid work shared one of two characteristics, and sometimes both: either the industries themselves were in decline or aboriginal participation in the industries was declining. The railway construction ended, the sealing and trapping industries collapsed, and mechanization pushed Aboriginal People out of seasonal agricultural labour. Eighty percent of the canneries, the biggest employer of aboriginal women, closed while, in fishing, the largest employer of aboriginal men, their participation shrunk relatively and absolutely.

From the end of the First World War to the present, the aboriginal population has been increasing against a backdrop of declining employment opportunities. "In terms of their economic performance," economist W.T. Stanbury concluded in 1970, "the Indians of British Columbia have barely been touched by the affluent society."[199]

TABLE 6.6

Occupations of Aboriginal People, 1931-61

	1931			1941			1954		1961		
	Male	Female	Total	Male	Female	Total	Primary	Supp.	Male	Female	Total
All occupations	6,886	778	7,664	7,077	641	7,718	7,293	1,637	4,567	1,134	5,701
All agriculture	2,167	152	2,319	2,042	142	2,184	1,203	221	611	102	713
Farmers	1,191	97	1288	1,025	73	1,098	689	134			
Labourers	976	55	1,031	1,017	69	1,086	514	87			
All fishers/hunters/trappers	3,724	29	3,753	3,725	24	3,749	2,565	640	413	14	427
Fishers	2,576	15	2,591	2,355	7	2,362	2,164	240			
Hunters/trappers	1,148	14	1,162	1,370	17	1,387	401	400			
Logging*	189	0	189	594	0	594	1,353	330	880	13	893
Mining	18	0	18	55	0	55	43†	17	55	1	56
All manufacturing	122	481	603	113	259	372	1,082	207	1,583	339	1,922
Fish canning	46	452	498				1,076	205			
Food products				55	248	303			648	319	967
Wood products				15	0	15	1		867	4	871
Construction	20	0	20	38	0	38	117	19	125	2	127
All transportation	240	0	240	311	0	311	205	9	363	22	385
Railway	237	0	237	299	0	299	112	1			
Trade/commerce	32	2	34	35	3	38	51	4	65	47	112
Retail							47	4	44	40	84
All service	18	83	101	29	204	233	110	27	137	513	650
Domestic	8	78	86	0	199	66	5		46	259	305
Education							6		46	66	112
Health/welfare							8	45	45	188	233
Clerical				2	1	3	9	1			
Other labour	353	31	384	135	9	144	551	160	176	60	236
Public administration							2	1	159	21	180

* Including forestry work but not sawmilling, except in 1954 when sawmilling is included.

† Includes smelting, which employs 25 as primary occupation and 15 as supplementary.

Other Sources: Census of Canada, 1931, Table 49; *Census of Canada,* 1941, Table 12; *Census of Canada,* 1961, Bulletin 3.2-10, Table 11.

SEVEN

The White Problem

Few Aboriginal People in the province were as favourably located as were the Lekwungen when it came to access to an urban market.[1] Moreover, the Lekwungen were unique in that the head of each family received a large cash settlement – $10,000 – in 1911 as part of their agreement to exchange their urban reserve for a suburban one. So it is puzzling that the particular experience of the Lekwungen mirrors the provincial patterns of increasing involvement in the capitalist economy in the nineteenth century and the decreasing involvement in the twentieth century. By 1960, the Lekwungen were apparently worse off than were the Tsilhqot'in, for example, who had no advantages when it came to joining the modern capitalist economy.

Aboriginal Peoples around British Columbia had different access to subsistence resources and paid work. Their cultures, histories, and experiences with immigrants varied dramatically. Yet, in spite of this diversity, which is evident in the comparison of the Lekwungen and the Tsilhqot'in and is drawn out in other local studies[2] – there was one key feature that was held in common: the "state" played a primary role in shaping aboriginal access to the capitalist, subsistence, prestige, and welfare economies. Moreover, the government's role was complicated by the fact that the various arms of the state were often at war with each other. This conflict was physically enacted in 1929, on the steps of the legislature, when the superintendent of Indian Affairs for British Columbia and the Commissioner of the Game Branch had a shouting and shoving match, practically coming to blows over the latter's limitation of aboriginal trapping and hunting.[3]

The Tsilhqot'in harassed the fur traders until they left their territory and generally kept European settlement at bay, but they were at one end of the scale of responses. More common were the Aboriginal People who relocated their village sites so as to be close to the centres of European commerce. When Fort Simpson was established at its present location in 1834, ten Ts'msyen villages relocated to the site to benefit from trading with, and working for, the European newcomers.[4] The four Kwakwaka'wakw villages that relocated to be close to Fort Rupert when it was established in 1849 did so for similar reasons. Several Heiltsuk villages amalgamated around

When applying for work outside of the reserve he is often refused because white men are as a rule unwilling to work alongside of Indians.

Department of Indian Affairs Annual Reports, 1912

In that House of Commons in Ottawa, there's a couple of hundred white men, and sometimes I think that all they do is dream up new laws against the Indians! They've pushed the old ways out so we can never go back.

Charles Jones, Nuu-chah-nulth, 1976

◀ Secwepemc waiting to meet game warden, 1891 (see p. 250)

After the Money, the Potlatch

After 1900, when we got gas boats and money was coming in from fishing and logging, we called all the fourteen tribes of our Kwagiuth people to Cape Mudge for potlatches more often.

Harry Assu, Kwakwaka'wakw, *Assu of Cape Mudge*, 1989

the site of Fort McLoughlin after its establishment in 1833, and the Kwantlan people moved their village adjacent to Fort Langley after its construction in 1827.

In the mid- and late nineteenth century, many aboriginal groups asked that fur posts or settlements be established among them. After the Haida on Haida Gwaii had dug as much gold as they could without having access to explosives, they invited the Hudson's Bay Company to establish a fort among them; the Cowichan also asked that a fort be established in their territory; while the Haisla of Kitamaat and the Nisga'a of Kincolith on the Nass River asked for a sawmill to be built in their respective areas.[5]

The Aboriginal People who were eager to participate in the foreign economy tended to be those who had well-developed prestige economies of their own. When these aboriginal workers joined the capitalist economy, they, like the Lekwungen, did so for purposes integral to their own priorities. Helen Codere's study of the Kwakwaka'wakw shows that, for them, work for wages and production of goods for sale increased the frequency of potlatches as well as the number of guests and the wealth distributed. She calls the period between the founding of Fort Rupert in 1849 and 1921 "the potlatch period."[6]

Codere charted the increasing number of blankets given at Kwakwaka'wakw potlatches, going back over a century (numbers that were well remembered by her informants owing to the importance of establishing relative prestige levels). The number of blankets distributed gives an indication of the striking increase in wealth, both available and distributed. The following list shows the peak number of blankets distributed at the single greatest potlatch of a twenty-year period:

1829-48	320 blankets
1849-69	9,000 blankets
1870-89	7,000 blankets
1890-1909	19,000 blankets
1910-29	14,000 blankets
1930-49	33,000 blankets[7]

Billy Assu, a Kwakwaka'wakw from Cape Mudge, wrote that his first memories were of his father's 1911 potlatch: "My father worked for the money to give that potlatch for many years. He gave away goods and money to the value of more than $10,000 [over $230,000 in 2008 dollars]."[8]

Among the Haida, increased work and trade meant that the number of new totems being raised with the accompanying gift-giving ceremonies reached a peak between 1860 and 1876. In 1884, a delegation of Nuu-chah-

nulth chiefs expressed their views about the purpose of work, saying "We work for our money and like to spend it as we please, in gathering our friends together; now whenever we travel we find friends; the 'potlatch' does that."[9] Like the Lekwungen, Aboriginal People in many parts of the region made wage labour work for them, not the other way around.

These Aboriginal People entered the workforce on their own initiative; however, where and when work opportunities opened up was something they could not control. Nor did they have control over the process whereby they were "racialized" as "Indians" and assigned a particular role in the hierarchy of wage relations. As Europeans settled among Aboriginal People and began working alongside them, some were willing to admit that "Indians" worked "better than many whitemen," that they were "equal, if not superior to a man of our own race."[10] But there were those in prominent positions, like the editors of Victoria's *British Colonist* newspaper, who, even while Aboriginal People were performing the bulk of the labour in the city, could say: "though they are possessed of 'bone, muscle, energy and intellect,' their habits of indolence, roaming propensities, and natural repugnance for manual labour, together with a thievish disposition which appears to be inherently characteristic of the Indian race, totally disqualifies them from ever becoming either useful or desirable citizens."[11]

British Columbia was to be "a White Man's Province," where employers were publicly chastised for hiring "Indians."[12] When the other Victoria paper, the *Gazette*, called for a dispassionate examination of "whether it

Potlatch at Alert Bay, 1910-12. Chief Johnnie Clark is in the centre (in white shirt, right hand in pocket)

Indians versus Whites

Scores of Indians are employed by the Executive at the expense of the country to improve the grounds around the surveyor's office ... Now we are disposed to employ whitemen in order to retain population in the country. If public monies are to be dispensed let it be given to those who are bone of our bone and who will thereby remain with us to build up the country with the proceeds of their labour. The Indians will remain anyhow.

British Colonist, June 1, 1859, 2

would not be better for us as a colony to encourage white labor, and discourage Indian, as far as lies within our power," it came down heavily on the side of discouraging Indian labour.[13] And this is just what the laws of the colony, and subsequently the provincial and federal governments, did.

Aboriginal People all over the province experienced the effects of laws explicitly aimed at limiting their economies as well as other laws, which, in the process of their administration, had the same effect. These severely limited the kinds of work that Aboriginal People could do, but even more fundamental were the laws and regulations that defined "Indians" and established a set of race-based privileges and limitations.[14]

In 1872, the Act to Amend the Qualification and Registration of Voters removed the right of Aboriginal People to vote in provincial and federal elections. One of the impacts of this act was that, not being voters, Aboriginal and Chinese people were legally prohibited from the professions of law and politics.[15] Worse, the aboriginal majority of the population (about 73 percent of the population at that time [see Table 6.1]) was thereafter at the legislative mercy of the white minority, who used the state to further disadvantage Aboriginal People.

This single act put Aboriginal People outside the political process. They would have no say in who governed them, even in those places and periods in which they were the majority. They could not elect anyone to represent them municipally, provincially, or federally. When unfairly treated, they had no political voice. Their only access to politicians was through the Indian Agent, up the chain of command in the federal bureaucracy, to the Minister of Indian Affairs and then possibly through him to other federal, provincial or municipal officials. Of course, this rarely worked, and it was often the case that it was the Indian Agent himself who was the problem they wanted to complain about.[16]

When the federal Indian Act, 1876, pathologized Indians as legal minors, it prohibited them from buying, selling, or consuming alcoholic beverages. The prohibitions against alcohol had a far-reaching effect with regard to limiting aboriginal employment as it kept Aboriginal People out of the hospitality industry. While fortunes were made in Victoria by supplying Indians with liquor (a crime), and a tavern operated on the Songhees reserve in Victoria from 1862 to after 1879, it was against the law for Indians themselves to engage in the extremely profitable liquor trade.[17]

The Indian Act made it illegal for Aboriginal People to own or to be employed in establishments that served liquor. In rural British Columbia, the few viable service enterprises included stores and hotels. Since hotels had to sell liquor in order to compete and survive, Aboriginal People were essentially excluded from the hospitality industries until after 1956, when the last federal laws restricting "Indians" from consuming alcohol were withdrawn. Hotels and saloon/beer parlours were among the most common forms of rural enterprise, and one of the most profitable urban ones.

Many Aboriginal People did take up another common form of rural enterprise – the general store. Though there were no prohibitions against running a store, there were limits on what Indians could sell, and not being able to sell liquor put them at a distinct disadvantage. Moreover, any products containing alcohol were also prohibited to them. As the Pharmaceutical Society of British Columbia pointed out, no products containing alcohol, including medicines, cod liver oil, hair oil, vanilla and other extracts, and even perfume, could be legally stocked by aboriginal merchants.[18]

Being legally defined as minors had another far-reaching effect on aboriginal entrepreneurs: Indians did not own their own land. Non-Indian entrepreneurs could borrow, using their house and land as collateral, and use these loans to invest in stock, boats, logging equipment, or more land. Indian reserves were owned by the Crown and held in trust for Indians: they could not be mortgaged. This lack of borrowing power disadvantaged Aboriginal People in every enterprise that required capital investment. In the fishing industry in particular, it meant that Aboriginal People were more dependent on canning companies than were white fishermen, who could mortgage to raise capital and buy their own boats.

The Voter Registration Act and the Indian Act may have been the most significant individual pieces of legislation affecting Indians, but they were accompanied by a long stream of legal enactments that had two consistent aims. First, the state alienated control over resources that had previously rested with the indigenous inhabitants; and, second, it gave whites preferential access to these resources. This pattern of alienation of aboriginal control of resources, and then the denial of access on the same terms as whites, is visible in every major economic resource: fish, timber, fur, and minerals. But the first and most important alienation came in the form of land.

The full impact of the alienation of land from aboriginal to colonial, provincial, and federal control lies beyond the scope of this discussion, but certain elements are important in the context of aboriginal economies.[19] By limiting the size of the reserves allocated to less than twenty acres per family (compared to the 160 acres allocated to aboriginal families on the Prairies), and by preventing Aboriginal People from pre-empting land (whites could pre-empt 320 acres [160 acres west of the Cascade Mountains]), the colony and the province effectively transferred most of the land owned and used by Aboriginal People in southern and central British Columbia to white farmers, loggers, and ranchers.[20]

It Was a Big Deal

My dad started a sawmill to create employment for people on the reserve. So what's the big deal about? Anybody can go and start up a business – unless you are a native Indian during that time you couldn't go to a bank and borrow money because you were considered a ward of the government and you had no assets that the bank could claim if you weren't able to pay back your loan. So it was a big deal that he started the sawmill and employed all the able bodied men in the village.

Doreen Jensen, Gitksan, interviewed in the film *A Forgotten Legacy: Spirit of Reclamation* (2002)

Busteling Sons of Civilization

The indolent, contented savage must give way to the busteling [sic] sons of civilization and toil.

James Bell to John Thomson, February 27, 1859

Although federal Indian policy and the Indian Agents made a concerted effort to turn Aboriginal People into agriculturists, the size, soil, and location of most the land left to Indians made that an impossible task. In the remaining areas, where conditions were favourable for agriculture, Aboriginal People did take up farming, but against enormous odds. When the Department of Indian Affairs applied to the province on behalf of Indians for grazing land, which was regularly leased to whites, Indian Superintendent Vowell reported "that all such applications have been invariably refused." The Indian Agents complained that "the provincial authorities will not sell or lease lands to Indians," are "chasing the Indian's horse off the Crown Ranges," and have denied them water rights necessary for irrigation. Thus, through its control over pre-emptions, reserve allotments, grazing, and water rights, the province curtailed the ability of Aboriginal People to move into commercial agriculture.[21]

Aboriginal People were also denied other assistance that provincial and federal departments of agriculture offered white farmers. In 1913, noting the relative success of non-aboriginal fruit farmers, the commissioners of the McKenna-McBride Commission addressed the Cowichan Indian Agent as follows: "You know as a matter of fact that the fruit growing industry of this province has been developed largely by the efforts of the Agricultural Departments of both the federal and provincial governments in sending out experts who lecture at different places and which have started such things as Farmers' Institutes. Have the Indians been able to avail themselves of this instruction?" "No Sir," was the response. In fact, the only

Threshing machine owned and operated by the Cowichan at Somenos, 1901

trained agricultural "assistance" provided to aboriginal farmers in British Columbia was through a single inspector whose job was to ensure that aboriginal orchards were sprayed with pesticides – not to improve the aboriginal crop but, rather, to prevent pests from spreading to nearby white orchards.[22]

The pattern of alienation and discriminatory regulation is also apparent in the federal government's attempt to make fishing a "white man's" industry. Until Confederation, Aboriginal People controlled access to the fisheries and managed them according to their own complex system of customary law.[23] After 1871, the federal government claimed the sea and the resources in it, by virtue of the British North America Act and the agreement that brought British Columbia into Confederation. In 1877, the federal Fisheries Act was extended to BC.[24]

From before the arrival of Europeans to the expansion of salmon cannery operations in the late 1870s, aboriginal men comprised the fishing fleet in British Columbia and aboriginal women processed the fish.[25] The large sums earned by Aboriginal People in fishing and canning as the commercial fishery expanded in the 1880s drew competition from whites, Chinese, and, later, Japanese. This inundation of immigrant fishers put pressure on the fish stocks, and the federal government responded by imposing a licence system for fishers that was in force between 1888 and 1892. Thereafter, the canneries agreed on a voluntary quota system, which set an upper limit on the number of Aboriginal People and Asians that would be allowed to fish.[26]

When the voluntary system proved unstable, the state intervened in 1913 with a "white-preference" system of licensing. White fishers were granted independent licences and were able to sell their fish at higher prices than were non-white "attached fishermen." Aboriginal and Asian fishers could only get a licence by applying through individual canneries, where they had to sell their fish at the offered price. The government's stated intention was to increase the share of whites-only licences in the industry by 10 percent per year at the expense of Aboriginal People and Asians.[27]

The canning companies argued that they, too, wanted a "white man's" industry: "We have always been loyally anxious to employ white fishermen and have in every instance given good and competent white fishermen the preference," wrote the president of the largest cannery corporation on the coast, BC Packers. His company "voluntarily offered to employ a steadily increasing proportion of white fishermen [commencing at 20 percent of the total number] which we believe the only method calculated to attain the desired result, viz, the settlement of a large number of white fishermen on the coast."[28] It appears that the Department of Fisheries agreed.

Independent Indians Liable to Be Difficult

The issue of [independent] fishing licences to Indians is especially to be depreciated. They are wards of the Dominion Government and specially treated and protected ... It is not deemed advisable to grant Indians "Independent" licences as they are liable to misinterpret the reason and become difficult to manage by the authorities.

William Henry Barker, BC Packers, to the Hon. J.D. Hazen, Minister of Fisheries, August 19, 1913

David Moody, Nuxalk, rows a gillnetter toward the BC Packers Wharf at Bella Coola in 1934

These new regulations prompted eighty aboriginal fishers from northern British Columbia to protest to the fisheries department:

> During the present season we were told by the officials of your department that we could not purchase an Independent Licence as it was only for white men ... We have fished on the various rivers of Northern British Columbia for a good many years and many of us have our own boats and fishing gear and we think we are entitled to have an independent licence to catch salmon, provided we comply with the regulations laid down by your department. We are natives of this country and as fishing is one of our means of livelihood, and we are loyal British Subjects, we think that it is only right and fair that if we have the money to purchase a licence, and the other qualifications necessary, we be allowed to have these independent licences.[29]

In 1916, William Halliday, Indian Agent at Alert Bay, pointed out the effect of the licence system: "No Indians at present in District No. 2 can get an independent licence and as the number of attached licences are limited many of them can get no chance whatever to fish."[30] One aboriginal witness told a 1917 Fisheries Commission: "The Indians always get smaller licences every year ... We are liable to not fish in some years. There is very few Indians fishing now to-day compared with before. Q. But do they want to fish? A. Sure they want to fish, but lots of fellows just stay home; can't get no licence."[31]

Without any elected legislators to advocate on their behalf, Aboriginal People depended on the Indian Agents to intercede with the Department of Fisheries, which they often did. In comparison to the lobbying of the cannery companies and the voting white fishers, the agents had little

Forced Out of Fishery onto Relief

Graham: I think it is a great hardship that the Indian is not allowed to sell his salmon in order that he might be able to buy sugar, tea and flour and other ordinary necessaries of life ... Take, now for Indian at Yale. There are great numbers – in fact all the Indians living at Yale are the old Indians who have never worked out. They have made a living by catching the odd salmon and selling them in the town and they have complained very bitterly on account of their being prevented from selling fish in order to provide themselves with sufficient money to purchase the ordinary necessities of life.

Commissioners: Have many of them been imprisoned for that object?

Graham: Yes, and in cases like that I have to supply the old people with relief because they are not allowed to sell fish.

Indian Agent Graham, Lytton Agency, to McKenna-McBride Commission, October 27, 1915

---

effect. In 1919, Agent Halliday told his superiors that fisheries officers had arbitrarily decided not to give licences to Indians who had not fished the year before. Since there had been a high demand for spruce wood in 1918 for wartime airplane construction, forty-six Indians from Halliday's Kwawkewlth Agency who normally fished had logged instead, and now they could not get back into the fishery. In turning down their applications, the inspector of fisheries was prepared to admit that he had "a great reluctance in granting salmon gillnet licences to Indians" because, he said, "they are so persistent in going up streams" and fishing in their traditional territories, "where they are not permitted."[32]

While disadvantaged compared to whites when it came to gillnet licences, Aboriginal People were absolutely prohibited from holding a licence to operate the more profitable purse seiners. Beginning in 1886, seiners appeared in the Pacific salmon and herring fishery. Bigger than other fish boats, and requiring a larger crew and more technology in the form of power winches, seiners, under most conditions, were the most efficient harvesters. Purse-seine licences, the Indian Agents were told, were limited to "persons of the white race." When applying for a seining licence for Banks Island, Ts'msyen Amos Collison was told by the fishery inspector that the area was "already covered by licenses." Joshua Sebeshaw heard a similar story, while Henry Watt was told that independent licences were only granted to enfranchised Indians or half-breeds not living on a reserve. Not until 1923 did the combined pressure from Aboriginal People and Indian Agents persuade the Department of Fisheries to allow Indians to purchase seine licences on the same basis as whites – a rare example of the fisheries department backing down.[33]

The link between salmon fishing and the well-being of most Aboriginal British Columbians related both to the commercial and the subsistence fisheries. In the 1908 view of the Department of Indian Affairs: "In British

No Indian Has Ever Yet...

You know that no Indian has ever yet
been given a purse seine license and
that they have not changed their policy.

Agent W.M. Halliday to Johnny Scow, May
20, 1922

Columbia the character of the salmon run very much determines the question of the year's prosperity for the majority of Indians, since they depend upon the salmon to furnish the main staple of their winter's food, and upon the earnings at the canneries for the purchase of other necessaries."[34]

While barriers were being placed in front of Indians engaged in the commercial fishery, between 1894 and 1911 their rights to fish for their own food purposes were also increasingly circumscribed. First, the federal government made it illegal for Aboriginal People to catch fish in the traps, weirs, and reef nets they had used long before Europeans arrived. The fisheries inspector for the North Coast District 2, John Williams, rationalized the prohibitions on traditional food fishing this way: "The trouble is that the Indians are so lazy and idle that they will not do anything at all ... Let them come down to the cannery and work as all other Indians do, they cannot be spared."[35]

Then, the regulations stipulated that Aboriginal People had to obtain a permit from fisheries officers before they could catch fish for food by any means whatsoever. In theory, any (registered) Indian could get one of these; in practice, the fisheries officials limited the number of licences issued and the times and places they could be used. In certain periods, such as the three years between 1919 and 1921, food fishing was banned entirely on the Fraser River and its watershed, depriving over eight thousand Aboriginal People of the main item in their subsistence economy.[36] Referring to the proliferation of fisheries laws, Nuu-chah-nulth Peter Webster thought: "All of these things made it easy to get into trouble with the law. I think a lot of us became 'criminals' without really knowing the reason."[37]

In the 1950s, aboriginal fishers received "I" licences and were only permitted to fish in designated areas. Alternatively, they could purchase a non-aboriginal "A" licence that would allow them to fish in a broader area, as they had traditionally done, but this licence prohibited them from receiving any help from the Indian Fisheries Assistance Board. Since aboriginal fishers could not borrow money from a bank to buy a boat (because, as mentioned, they could not use their homes to secure a loan), in order to remain competitive, people like Johnny Clifton had little choice but to accept an "I" licence and to forego the advantages associated with the non-aboriginal licences.[38]

In addition to laws that were explicitly "racial" in their design, there were also state policies that disproportionately affected Aboriginal People. The so-called "Davis Plan," unveiled by the federal government in 1968, is an example. Intended to reduce the number of fishers and to raise average fishing incomes by eliminating the smaller and technologically less efficient part of the fleet, it targeted precisely that category that included the majority of aboriginal fishers. The effect on aboriginal fishers who had remained in this industry is reflected in Figure 6.6.

The Davis Plan froze the size of the fishing fleet and issued permanent licences to large producers who had caught over 10,000 pounds (4,540 kilograms) in either of the previous two years. To the smaller boats, the government issued temporary licences, two or more of which could be converted into permanent licences if combined and attached to one new boat. Licences immediately became costly and difficult to obtain. Small boat owners required new, bigger boats and another temporary licence just to stay in the industry. Small operators, who could not afford to expand, had to sell to those who could.[39]

The cost of licences, new boats, and the increasing amount of electronic gear needed to compete with the now over-capitalized fleet, accounted for some of the decline in the number of aboriginal fishers, as did the decline in fish stocks, which was accelerated by the high-tech fleet. The Davis Plan was also intended to promote a leaner canning industry, in which fewer plants operated at maximum efficiency. Larger fish boats, with the capacity to stay at sea longer than smaller boats, assisted in this plan; however, more significant was the federal government's offer to buy and scrap the older fishing vessels owned by the canneries in order to reduce the size of the fleet. Most of these cannery-owned vessels were used by aboriginal men who could not afford to buy their own boats.[40]

As the state began to limit entry into specific fisheries, many aboriginal fishers felt that they had not been given the same notice as had whites

All Fishboats Gone But One

Thirty years ago, fishing was our people's life, and everyone had a boat; today there is only one boat in Kingcome.

Dave Dawson, Kingcome, ca. 1978

Hartley Bay wharf with band-owned seine boats, 2004

and so were too late to apply for the licences that would allow them access to the closed fisheries. In Hartley Bay, the abalone and halibut licences were cited as examples, while in Alert Bay it was the halibut, herring roe, and clamming licenses.[41]

In 1979, Dave Dawson from Kingcome Inlet summarized the impact of the changing fishery regulations on his community: "There are many reasons why we no longer fish, but I think that the licensing that came in after the war, that probably had a lot to do with it. Before the war the majority of fishermen on the coast were Indians with small boats. Licensing pushed the small boats out– you had to fish a minimum every year to keep a license."[42]

Kwakwaka'wakw fisher Harry Assu makes a similar point, which is born out by Friedlaender's 1975 quantitative study of the fishing fleet. Friedlaender demonstrated that the Davis Plan, in particular, forced a significant number of aboriginal fishers from the industry between 1964 and 1973.[43]

Aboriginal workers and entrepreneurs in other industries had to deal with informal, racialized policies that limited aboriginal labourers and entrepreneurs, though these are difficult to find in the written record. The logging industry provides one such example. The appropriation of aboriginal control of the forests was clearly laid out in law, but thereafter the discrimination against Aboriginal People with regard to the forest industry took place at a staff level.

When James Douglas arrived to build Fort Victoria in 1843, it was quite apparent that Aboriginal People had control over the forests in their territory. The local Lekwungen supplied cedar pickets from forests in their territory for the construction of the fort. When the Hudson's Bay Company sent fallers to cut timber at Cordova Bay, the Saanich people would not let them proceed until they paid for the right to do so.

As far as the colony was concerned, Aboriginal People surrendered their rights to the timber around Victoria when they signed the 1850 Fort Victoria Treaties (interestingly, the Wsanec believed the treaty payments were to smooth over the theft of wood by white loggers). The colony formalized its claim over all the forests with a land ordinance in 1865, which declared that timber belonged to the Crown and that people had to obtain leases before harvesting it. Yet, the power of the state to enforce these regulations, and its interest in doing so, was still limited. Despite the timber ordinances, aboriginal men continued, without molestation, to supply wood from their ancestral lands to the growing settlements.[44] In 1888, British Columbia required that a person have a "hand-logger's licence" to cut timber on land anywhere in the province that had not already been "alienated."

Cut No More Trees

I don't know how long they had been cutting this timber when our people became aware of it. Actually it wasn't in our territory, it was Songhees territory but the Songhees weren't doing anything about it.

Our people got together and they said "What are we going to do about these people falling those beautiful trees? Are we just going to sit here and just let them do it?" ... So they loaded up four big canoes with warriors, with their fighting equipment and battle dress, painted faces and they paddled around the peninsula and right to where those people were working.

"Tell your boss to take his men and his tools and go back to Victoria and cut no more trees" ... When he took a look and saw what they were faced with, he told his men to gather up their tools and they went back to Victoria.

Dave Elliot, Wsanec, *Saltwater People,* 1990

Also at this time the government began to enforce its claims over timber, with the result that many Aboriginal People on the coast took out handlogger's licences.[45]

At its turn-of-the-century peak, hand-logging provided a major part of the income of non-urban coastal Aboriginal People throughout British Columbia, including the Kwakwa̱ka̱'wakw, Haisla, and Ts'msyen, and, among the Coast Salish, the Sechelt, Sliammon, and Semiahmoo.[46] The year 1904 saw the beginning of a three-year timber rush, which alienated over 11.4 million acres of the best forest land, handicapping hand-loggers, who could only cut in areas not already under some form of timber lease or sale.[47] The provincial government contributed to the industry's demise in 1907, when it stopped issuing hand-loggers' licences altogether. Although this halt was temporary, when sales resumed the new conditions, according to the Kwakewlth agent, made them difficult for aboriginal men to obtain licences: "Until recently many of the younger men have been engaged in hand-logging operations, but the recent action of the government of the province in not renewing hand-logger licenses did away with that means of livelihood. The licences are again being issued, but the conditions of issue are so difficult, necessitating a special trip to Victoria, that it is questionable whether many of them will be in a position to avail themselves of the opportunity."[48]

In 1915, Chief Julian of the Sechelt told the McKenna-McBride Royal Commission: "A few years ago we used to make our living by logging; that

Logging, Not Potlatching

I am hand logging at Seymours narries [Seymour narrows] ... I did not go to the potlatch at Salmon River because I wanted to finish my boom.

Chief Jim Chackidl of Cape Mudge to G.W. Debeck, Indian Agent, December 28, 1903

When an Indian Wants Work ...

I have been refused work at Ocean Fall Company Camps, at the saw mills and other places as well ... When an Indian wants work at logging he cannot always get a licence. In fact we have great difficulty in getting these licences.

Wilson, a Nuxalk from Kimsquit, to the McKenna-McBride Royal Commission, August 22, 1913

Log drivers Joe Christian (left) and Adrian Alexander of the Spallumcheen band compete in a log-rolling contest at a Victoria Day celebration, Enderby, BC, ca. 1930

The Destruction Is Easy to See

The lumber people like MacMillan Bloedel seemed to own the entire forest. This made it illegal to get trees for canoes and cedar bark for weaving except from our tiny reserves. When the loggers moved in the animals that we hunted and trapped disappeared. Their destruction of the forest is easy to see. Our use of the woods was hardly noticeable.

Peter Webster, Ahousat, *As Far as I Know: Reminiscences of an Ahousat Elder*, 1983

Nuu-chah-nulth Peter Webster with wife Jessie and grandchild, ca. 1980

is hand logging, but we had to buy a license to do so but now in these late years we cannot do that." Codere's study of the Kwakwa̱ka̱'wakw documents their declining employment after this change.[49]

Some displaced Aboriginal People found work as wage labourers for logging companies, while others invested in the power equipment necessary to bid on the smaller timber sales. The legal status of "Indian" made it difficult for Aboriginal People to obtain credit and, therefore, to raise logging capital. John Pritchard's research into the economy of the Haisla revealed that there were other "extra-legal" obstacles as well. By definition, it is difficult to find written evidence of "unwritten policy," but Pritchard has produced interesting inferential evidence suggesting that the British Columbia Forest Service had a "policy" of allocating only marginal timber lands to Aboriginal People.[50]

When Aboriginal People applied for prime areas, it appears they were either turned down outright or the Forest Service forced the sale to go to public auction (something they rarely required for applications from white firms). In one such case, in 1924, the assistant district forester wrote on the rejected application of Haisla Ed Gray: "There is a good body of timber in here and we do not want it alienated by any Indian Reserve Applications."[51] The Forest Service also used the "lazy Indian" stereotype to deny Aboriginal People access to the forest. On Haisla Fred Woods' application one forester wrote: "Applicant (an Indian) will employ his fellow men which speaks for itself regarding the output to be expected."[52]

With access to the "publicly owned" forest being increasingly denied them both by regulation and alienation, Aboriginal People found they did not even have access to the forests on their own "reserves." This policy was articulated in the following exchange between the McKenna-McBride commissioners and Indian Agent William Robertson:

Commissioners: You heard a good deal from the Indians that owing to the practical prohibition from cutting timber that they were impeded in clearing the land?

Robertson: Well, the department won't stop any Indian from cutting timber for bona fide clearing purposes.

Commissioners: But the Indians are not allowed to log for the purpose of selling?

Robertson: No sir.

Commissioners: In other words they are not allowed to do what a white man could do on his own land?

Robertson: That is so.[53]

While limitations on aboriginal participation in the forest industry increased, the non-aboriginal logging industry was expanding at a rapid rate. In areas where big logging companies were engaged in clear-cutting, they were also devastating another main industry of Aboriginal People – trapping. Nuu-chah-nulth Charles Jones remembered: "Ever since the logging came, there's been no more deer or wolf or elk or beaver. They've all disappeared. Maybe they've been killed off, or maybe they've just moved on to somewhere else."[54]

By the time logging started to have a major effect on game populations, the animals too belonged to Her Majesty. The Crown claimed wildlife for the first time in the Colony of Vancouver Island's Act for the Preservation of Game, 1859, which was amended and expanded in 1862. Both acts limited aboriginal use of wildlife and commercial hunting (conducted to supply urban butcher shops) in favour of the "sportsman."[55] In 1865, the separate Colony of British Columbia prohibited the sale of deer, elk, grouse, or

Remote Indians Better Off

Indians living away from the settlements are much better off in this respect than those whose reserves are surrounded by white settlers, for they can always procure venison, which is still plentiful, and there is no one to enforce the game acts of the Province; whereas in the settlements the laws relating to game and salmon are rigidly enforced, and the Indian who formerly lived by fishing and hunting may not shoot a deer eight months out of twelve.

W.H. Lomas, Cowichan Indian Agent, 1888

Mathilda Joe of Alexandria, known as an excellent hunter who provided meat for her family and community

Doesn't Much Care for Indians

Lots of Indians around here have their traplines taken by white men ... and my own trapline I registered but I went there last spring and found whitemen still trapping there ... The Indians are natives to here you know and then a white come along and says "this is my place" and the Game Warden believes them. He never listens to Indians. Mr. Muirhead, the Game Warden here, is a straight man, but he doesn't much care for Indians. He prefers white men to Indians.

Chief Louis Prince and Councillors, Secwepemc (Shuswap) Kamloops, to J.H. Pragnell, Indian Inspector, January 1, 1929

Secwepemc Chief Louis Prince of Kamloops, ca. 1920

partridge from March through August, even in unsettled areas, and in 1869 it made the *intention* to sell game illegal: the mere possession of animal carcasses could be considered prima facie evidence of intention to sell, except in the case of "bona fide settlers."[56]

The province assumed control of wildlife after Confederation and increased limitations on access to game by extending the closed season. In 1896, the Game Act prevented Aboriginal People from selling deer in any season, and it applied the closed hunting season to Indian subsistence hunters. By 1911, deer could only be hunted three and a half months each year, and Aboriginal People were limited to harvesting three deer per year. An amendment in 1913 allowed the provincial game warden to give permits to Aboriginal People to kill additional deer for food, but under restrictive circumstances, specifying the number of deer and the length of time the permit was in effect. Amendments to the Game Act in 1927, coupled with the federal Migratory Bird Act, meant that by this date there was hardly an animal, bird, or fish that was not regulated by the provincial or federal government.[57]

A circular letter issued to Indian Agents by the provincial game warden in 1913 emphasized the paternal and discretionary nature of the control over food permits: "I do not intend to grant any permit to any Indian except under the recommendation of the Indian Agent ... In considering such applications I would require to know ... the age of the Indian, number in his family and other information which would be of assistance to me in deciding whether he is entitled to such a permit or not." The rationale for the policy was also expressed in the circular: "Young Indians who are capable of obtaining work are not entitled to them, it is for the more older class of Indians who have been in the habit of hunting all their lives and feel more severely the enforcement of the present games laws." The warden also expressed his interest in whether the applicant was "sober and industrious" and warned that any abuse of the permits "would simply result in all such permits being cancelled."[58]

The provincial game warden deliberately stated his goal of eliminating the subsistence economy in favour of wage labour. He told the McKenna-McBride Royal Commission that Indians did not need to hunt deer in the fall because "in many places there is work for Indians haying and harvesting and giving Indians permits to hunt deer at this time of year simply encourages them to do nothing else."[59]

Provincial laws also targeted the trapping industry. First the province legally limited the trapping seasons,[60] then, in 1921, it assumed the right to allocate trapline territories. Not recognizing provincial authority, many Aboriginal People refused, at first, to register and, as a result, their traplines were open to being registered by whites. Even when Aboriginal People accepted provincial authority and applied for traplines, there is strong evidence – from Aboriginal People, from Indian Agents, and even from the game wardens themselves – that the provincial game department gave preference to whites.

After a year-long survey of trapping in the province, Inspector of BC Indian Agencies George Pragnell found, in 1924, that the "almost universal complaint by the Indian is that *their lines* are seized upon by white men under cover of the law." Pragnell pointed out to the Game Board that, according to an aboriginal system, most of the province's traplines had already been allocated: "For all time ... his trapline has always been immune from molestation, or theft ... from his fellow tribesmen. They have always, and even do now, respect each other's rights, even though said trap line might not be in use for many years."[61]

The effect of discriminatory trapline registrations was felt all over the province. From near 100 Mile House, George Archie, secretary of the Canim Lake band, wrote the Department of Indian Affairs for help restoring traplines registered by whites (see sidebar). From Fort St. James in

White People Are Taking Our Traplines

The white people are taking Indian traplines and the Indians cannot trap ... This is a pity for the Indians to lose their traplines and only way to get their food in winter ... I have my trap line taken away from me from Mahood Lake whom I trap now for twenty-five years ... I would like you to help me on that case and get back my trap lines and so I can support my family and them other Indians also.

George Archie, Secwepemc, Secretary Canim Lake Band, to W.E. Ditchburn, December 1, 1927

Daniel Wigaix (Big Wings), Gitksan, with winter's catch of furs, 1923

Too Much Logging

Kah míka klop ókoke opalo?
Where did you catch that trout?

Kopa Skamikoway ikhál.
In the Skamikway River.

Nah, hiyú lepish yáhwa?
Are there many fish there?

Wake Klaska mamook hiyu stick alta.
Not many. Too much logging.

John Gill, *Gill's Dictionary of the Chinook Jargon*, 1881

Secwepemc people waiting to meet the game warden coming to remove their fish weirs, 1891

north-central British Columbia, the non-aboriginal matron of the hospital wrote: "It appears to me that in this district, there has been a systematic lopping off of Indian lines, in favour of white men, and in the case of Louis Billie has rendered it necessary for him to be put on the ration list."[62] Not only was the Game Board unwilling to entertain arguments about prior aboriginal trapping rights but it was also prepared to deny Aboriginal People any rights to fur-bearing animals. In 1925, for conservation purposes, the Game Board closed indefinitely the whole "Eastern District" of the province to the harvest of fur-bearers. This made it illegal for most Aboriginal People to pursue their livelihoods.[63]

From the far northwest of the province, Indian Agent Harper Reed wrote that "Swedes" had taken most of the best traplines from the Indians, with the result that "Chief John Jack with most of his band are now in town and it is reported that the Indians have come into Teslin also, and now they are sitting around doing nothing at a time when in years gone bye, they used to go out ... for the Beaver hunt."[64]

In 1928, the Game Branch banned the sale of tanned moose, deer, and elk hides, threatening the livelihood of many aboriginal women who subsisted on this industry. The DIA made a direct appeal to the BC attorney general, who overruled the restriction.[65]

As the turnover of aboriginal trapping grounds continued, the relationship between the federal DIA and the provincial Game Branch became

openly hostile. When W.E. Ditchburn, Indian commissioner for British Columbia, met Bryan Williams, the provincial game commissioner, on the steps of the legislature in 1938, a shouting match broke out in which Williams told Ditchburn "the applications for Indian trap-lines filed by our Indian Agents on behalf of the Indians throughout British Columbia were not worth the paper they were written on."[66]

The BC game department's hostility towards Aboriginal People stemmed from three sources and may suggest the motives underlying other provincial policies. From its inception, the game department resented aboriginal claims to ownership of wildlife resources and made a determined effort to station "wardens" throughout the province to enforce provincial regulation over aboriginal practice: "Many of the Indians are raising their old story of rights to the land and rights to the game and fish ... In consequence it has been necessary to take a firm stand with them, as they quite refused to listen to reason ... some of them not only being sent to gaol, but also losing some valuable furs."[67]

There were also financial reasons for the province's refusal to give native trappers "an even break." The province earned income from the trapline registration fees of white trappers but not from Indians.[68] The third, and perhaps most fundamental reason, for the game department's antagonistic attitude towards Aboriginal People appears to be its belief that "the Indian, could, if he chose, make his living by the sweat of his brow, just as well as anyone else ... [and] if he were forced to do so it would tend towards the general prosperity of the country. Everybody knows how scarce labour has been during the past summer ... and what an aid the Indian might have been had they chosen to get down to steady work."[69] Trapping, hunting, and fishing were considered to be the opposite of work.

Letters from aboriginal trappers, asking for help in getting their traplines back, filled many DIA files in the 1920s.[70] Nonetheless, the reallocation of traplines to white trappers continued through the 1930s, the 1940s, and the 1950s over the protests of Aboriginal People, Indian Agents, and the Native Brotherhood of British Columbia.[71] By 1956, according to the game commissioner' figures, only 10 percent of BC's traplines were operated by Aboriginal People.[72]

Aboriginal employment in other areas was also circumscribed by provincial laws and policy decisions. One of the most important of these was the provincial government policy not to employ Aboriginal People on public works projects, especially roads – a policy that Lekwungen George Chictlan criticized in 1894. It was still in force ten years later, when provincial government agent John Baird told the DIA: "I am unable to give Indians work

White Settlers Hired First

To: Premier Richard McBride
July, 1909

We the undersigned "bona fide" settlers and residents of Ootsa Lake in view of the difficulty we find in getting a market for our produce and owing to the unorganized condition of the country do earnestly request that white settlers and taxpayers be given preference of work on government roads. In connection with our settlement, a number of us have expended considerable time and money during these last three years for which we have never received any remuneration only to find that Indians are given preference at high wages for doing the work we are able and willing to do hoping that this will receive your earnest attention, we remain.

George Lewis and 14 others

To George Lewis
July 6, 1909

Have instructions issued to our officials [that] white settlers must be considered first.

Premier Richard McBride

Correspondence between George Lewis and Premier Richard McBride, July 1909

Tsilhqot'in entrepreneurs (left to right) Joe Elkins, Baptise Elkins, and Willie Long Jimmie, who were barred from getting a licence to purchase fur, Quesnel, 1910s

Refused Government Work

The Indians were refused from the government to labour on any government roads and to let only white men work.

George Archie, Secretary of the Canim Lake band, to W.E. Ditchburn, Indian Superintendent for British Columbia, December 1, 1927

as I received orders from the works department not to employ Indians if white men were available." DIA officials were also being pressured to hire whites to work on Indian reserves. Federal MP Ralph Smith wrote the local Indian superintendent: "I understand that there are works to be done this season and so I want to appoint the white labour."[73] The provincial premier himself confirmed this policy in 1909, and evidence from Aboriginal People indicates that, in some areas at least, this policy was in effect throughout the Depression.[74]

The province stymied aboriginal entrepreneurial activity in other ways. Joe Elkins, a Tsilhqot'in man from the Williams Lake Agency, tried to obtain a provincial licence to purchase fur in 1936; however, "being an Indian he was barred from getting the necessary licences." When he bought a truck and tried to buy beef from local farmers to sell to butchers, the province would neither permit him to buy or lease the meadow lots needed to graze the cattle, nor, because he was an Indian, would it issue him with a provincial trucking licence.[75]

Ironically, given the statutory exclusion of Aboriginal People from so many fields of employment, employers often used their "favoured status" as a rationale for not giving them jobs. The DIA noted this "tendency on the part of employers of labour to refuse employment to Indians considering that they are a public charge and it is not necessary to give them employment where there are white applicants for the job." The provincial and city governments also argued that, given that Aboriginal People did not pay property taxes, they were not entitled to jobs that were paid with taxpayers' money.[76]

It was another Catch-22. In times of labour surplus, like during the depression just prior to the First World War, the Department of Fisheries argued that, as Aboriginal People had access to a subsistence fishery, they should not have equal access to the commercial fishery. When there was a labour shortage, the subsistence economy was attacked because it enabled Aboriginal People to stay out of the wage-labour force. In the 1907 annual report of the BC Game Branch, one warden commented: "As long as they could hunt, or put in weirs to trap trout or salmon on their way up streams to spawn, and do the occasional day's work to get enough money to buy a little tea and sugar, they were contented, and the idea of steady work scouted [avoided]. It must be admitted that this state of things is most unsatisfactory."[77]

And when the labour shortage was over? Aboriginal People found themselves squeezed out of both the capitalist and subsistence economies. In the eyes of the DIA: "The policy of the Game Branch is now to handle [food hunting] permits very sparingly, the argument being that if an Indian is destitute enough to need deer meat, the Department can give him relief rations."[78] All over the province, aboriginal trappers and hunters were forced out of both the cash and subsistence economies and onto relief.

Aboriginal choices took place within a framework of laws and regulations established by "the state." But it was a state that neither spoke with one voice nor moved in one direction. There were numerous conflicts between the federal DIA and Department of Fisheries, on the one hand, and the provincial Game Branch, on the other, as well as between departments on the same level. Alongside their better-known efforts to suppress aboriginal ceremonies and reorder political life within aboriginal communities, the DIA did carry Indian protests to other state agencies and did

Give Up Their Land

They [Indians] should either give up their land or be made to respect the game laws.

M.B. Jackson, Provincial Game Warden, 1917

I Don't Think So ...

And now that Canadian society has inherited what the White Man calls the Indian problem, most people like to think it's up to the Indian to straighten it out. But is it an Indian problem? I don't think so.

Chief John Albany, Songhees (Lekwungen), from the 1961 CBC radio program, *The Way of the Indian*

sometimes succeed in amending discriminatory laws (e.g., those allocating fishing licences according to race) and changing racist policies. Nonetheless, without a voting constituency, the minister of Indian affairs had limited power with which to fight, for example, the vocal voting constituency of the minister of fisheries. At a provincial level, the federal DIA had even less influence than it did at the federal level.

The end result of interdepartmental and intergovernmental struggles was a set of laws – a framework imposed on Aboriginal People with the full coercive force of the state's police power. Laws and policies, emanating from different levels of the state and enshrined in legislation, did more than limit where and when Aboriginal People could participate in the capitalist and subsistence economies. The Indian Act, voters registration acts, fisheries acts, game acts, land acts, timber legislation, and agricultural policy all helped define what it meant to be Indian and what it meant to be white. And, of course, they did this by defining the rights associated with each category. With every act that affected Indians and non-Indians differently, governments redefined race to the disadvantage of Aboriginal People.

It would be an exaggeration to say that the legislative factors outlined here were solely responsible for the declining participation of Aboriginal People in the wage economy. Other factors were also at work. Employers did not hire aboriginal workers either because of their own racist attitudes or because of their perception of their customers' attitudes. More than 90 percent of the Aboriginal People whom Salim Aziz surveyed in the Victoria area in 1969 felt that they were regularly discriminated against with regard to employment and that they were not offered jobs even when they were the most qualified. Racism was particularly effective in keeping Aboriginal People out of the retail sector owing "to the prejudice of buyers against being served by Indians."[79] Indeed, as Mary John recalled, in Vanderhoof, Aboriginal People were not allowed in restaurants or other public facilities up to the 1960s. Racism was so intense in parts of British Columbia that there was a virtual apartheid, with Aboriginal People not welcome, even as customers, in businesses that served whites. Helen Clifton remembers when in the late 1950s, in Prince Rupert, the Capital Theatre had an Indian section and when "Indians" were barred from the Rupert Hotel.[80]

White workers held racialized views of Aboriginal People and objected to working alongside them. Nuu-chah-nulth Charles Jones met with resistance from white-dominated unions. He was kept out of the International Woodworkers of America until the 1950s solely because he was "Indian." One aboriginal man from the Musqueam Reserve, who had apprenticed and become a plumber, was asked by the McKenna-McBride Commission why, if he could learn a trade, other Indians could not. He answered: "The conditions I had to go through I would not like to mention them." To the commissioner's query, "You mean that the white man does not give you a fair show?" the witness broke down in tears and said he would sooner not be asked to recall the hardships he had had to undergo.[81]

The education offered to Aboriginal People was well below that offered to non-aboriginal students. The federally sponsored, missionary-run schools left Aboriginal People ill-equipped for the postwar world and its technological changes. Moreover, compulsory schooling broke up elements of the family economy.

Because of the early settlement around Victoria, the Lekwungen were the first Aboriginal People to be affected by racist legislation and attitudes. However, as federal and provincial legislation and enforcement expanded to regulate fish and wildlife even in the remotest parts of the province, other aboriginal groups began to feel the same kind of pressure. And, as their protests suggest, individuals like Lekwungen Joyce Albany recognized this form of state racism for what it was: "Believe me," she told the *Colonist* in 1973, "we very often sit down and talk about the White Problem."[82]

EIGHT

Prestige to Welfare:
Remaking the Moditional Economy

Even a welfare payment has a genealogy. The first welfare payment to the Lekwungen occurred in 1888. In December that year, the leaders of the Lekwungen people in Victoria petitioned the Department of Indian Affairs to provide "relief" from the band's own funds to destitute old people, including seven women (Gleeacweeah, Tolayuk, Swasseeah, Tolass, Annick, Clakamah, and Cockquasseeah), one old man (Lapulauwah), and one orphan (Annie). In passing on this petition a few days later, H.M. Moffat, acting Indian superintendent, asked "to be authorized to supply at intervals, if necessary, a sack of flour and a few groceries to each of the applicants until spring sets in," meanwhile assuring the department "that economy in distribution will be strictly enforced." The department did authorize relief – too late for one woman, who died in the interim – which consisted of one blanket per person plus one sack (twenty-five pounds, or 11.3 kilograms) of flour, one pound of tea, five pounds of sugar, one tin of yeast powder, and ten pounds of rice per month.[1]

British Columbia was booming in 1888. Aboriginal People were working everywhere, especially around Victoria. Moreover, the Northwest Coast had supplied the Lekwungen and their neighbours with an abundance of food and material wealth for centuries. Why, all of a sudden, was it necessary for the government to step in to stop the starvation of a few dependent individuals? When Fort Victoria was established in 1843, no one thought it was the responsibility of Europeans to provide sustenance to Aboriginal People, who, in any case, did not appear to need help. In fact, if anything, it was the immigrants who needed the labour of Aboriginal People to provide them with food.

The Victoria newspapers of the late 1850s and early 1860s are full of accounts of the local people bringing products of the land (especially deer) and of the sea (especially fish, oysters, and clams) into Victoria to sell to the urban settlers. No doubt the added population and the commercial demand for these products put pressure on the local resources, but these "country foods" remained available both for food and for sale.[2]

Indians were rich many years ago before the white man came. They didn't have money but they were never, never hungry. When the white man came the whole story changed. Indians are always hungry.

Leslie John, Snuneymuxw, 1948

Our people were prosperous in the old days. There was no welfare ... We had no what we call DIA housing in those days because everybody built their own house. We were a prosperous people. [We] didn't depend on the government for anything, or, very little. You know, we even built our own roads in Bella Bella, and board walks. We had our own sawmill with our own money. We didn't ask the government for money. We had access to all the resources.

Edwin Newman, Heiltsuk, July 6, 2003

◄ Songhees woman awaiting relief, 1880s (see p. 259)

Great Provisions

The Indians have great provision on this Island. In winter and spring are innumerable wild fowl – in the summer 5 or 6 sorts of delicious wild berry fruit – and in the Autumn the salmon. They have also abundant fish of other kinds and herring and oysters always – also deer. In the Salmon season they cure large quantities of dried salmon for consumption in the rest of the year.

Bishop George Hills, February 6, 1860

Anglican Bishop George Hills, ca. 1870s

Sap Self-Reliance

Many of the Indians can eke out a living from wild life without the need of getting government relief, if left free from persecution. Such a policy will sap their self-reliance and drive them more than ever to look for government aid.

Indian Agent E. McLeod, Lytton, to M.B. Jackson, Chairman of the Game Conservation Board, May 20, 1925

The ability of the Lekwungen to harvest and sell fish and game over the "unoccupied lands" in their traditional territories had been guaranteed in the 1850 treaties, but piece by piece, starting with Vancouver Island's Act for the Preservation of Game in 1859, these guarantees were slowly eroded.[3]

The colonial acts formed the foundation for British Columbia's game acts. By the 1880s, the Indian Agent observed that the Lekwungen people had been severely affected by having had local subsistence resources removed from their control. Agent W.H. Lomas explained in 1887 that "the lands that once yielded berries and roots are now fenced and cultivated, and even on the hills the sheep have destroyed them." Twenty-five years after the establishment of Fort Victoria, G.M. Sproat, a sympathetic observer of Aboriginal People, wrote of the Lekwungen: "One of the bitterest regrets of the natives is that the encroachment of whites is rapidly depriving them of their crops of [camas] this useful and almost necessary plant."[4] Occupation of resource-gathering sites was not the only effect of the "settling of the land" for even where there was no settlement, "game laws restrict the time for the killing of deer and grouse, and the fishery regulations interfere with their old methods of taking salmon and trout." Lomas thought that this had little effect on the young people, who had wage work and who could buy food, but "the very old people who formerly lived entirely on fish, berries, and roots, suffer[ed] a great deal through the settling up of the country."[5]

The following year, Lomas emphasized that it was the game laws, not lack of game, that was causing hardship: "Indians living away from the settlements ... can always procure venison, which is still plentiful, and there is no one to enforce the game acts of the Province; whereas in the settlements the laws relating to game and salmon are rigidly enforced, and the Indian who formerly lived by fishing and hunting may not shoot a deer eight months out of twelve."

Lomas specifically noted that "the strict Provincial Game Acts and Fishery Regulations make the food supply for the old people a very serious matter."[6]

The prosperity of the young and the destitution of the old is explained, in part, by the separation of the wage economy and the subsistence economy. According to Agent Lomas, "with the younger men the loss of these kinds of food is more than compensated for by the good wages they earn, which supplement what they produce on their allotments." He observed that "Indians are often generous with the food they have taken in the chase, but begrudge giving what they have paid money for, without suitable return." The game laws, combined with more younger people moving into the wage economy, meant that there was less subsistence food to be shared,

Discovery Island woman, 100 years old, possibly one of the seven Songhees for whom relief was requested in 1888

and this forced the Indian Agent to dispense relief in order to alleviate "many cases of extreme destitution."[7] In the midst of abundance, new laws passed by the colony, and then by the province, caused starvation, which had previously been unknown among the Lekwungen, who used to have access to the largest range of resources on the entire Northwest Coast.[8]

In the 1890s, a worldwide depression hit British Columbia and resulted in widespread unemployment among aboriginal workers. Many were forced to live entirely through the subsistence economy. The winter of 1892-93 was particularly hard because, as Cowichan agent Lomas reported, "sawmills ha[d] been closed for some time, thus throwing many young men out of employment." They might have been all right, he added, but the extremely long winter and its deep snows prevented many from obtaining fish in bays and rivers as well as from hunting and hauling firewood. As a result, relief costs went up.[9]

Lomas's supervisor, A.W. Vowell, wrote him in November 1893 to warn him that the budget for relief had been exhausted, with the result that no one could be paid "at present": "Relief should only be given where there is a danger of starvation, or in the case of extreme old age or sickness ... In the future, before rendering assistance, Agents should assure themselves that every effort has been put forth towards support, both by the applicant for relief and such of his friends or relatives as could reasonably be expected to assist him."[10] Agents were warned not to promise any relief, "even to the

Entitled to Her Potlatch

Dear Sir:-

Indian Mrs. Louisa Mckenzie wishes me to write you. Shes been getting potlatched every month at the Quathiaski Cove Store which she understands last month that [the Indian Agent] has stopped her potlatch at the store ... She got advise to ask you that she is entitle to get her potlatch from the Department of Indian Affairs. Will you please look in to the matter ... as soon as possible as Louisa are in need.

Yours truly
James Smith, Indian

Correspondence to Indian Agent F.G. Newnham from James Smith for Louisa McKenzie, September 14, 1931

Relief in Lieu of Fish

I have been instructed to supply those Indians with the absolute necessities of life in lieu of the fish that they are prevented from taking.

Indian Agent O'Byrne to McKenna-McBride Royal Commission, January 27, 1916

old and destitute; because, although the Department may recognize the propriety of helping destitute aged and sick Indians when in absolute want ... to make such promises in advance ... is simply to assure other Indians ... that they need not exert themselves in the matter as the Government will look after them."[11]

However, as discussed in the last chapter, the aboriginal subsistence economy was under pressure at the same time as the DIA was cutting off relief. The most significant interference with the subsistence economy came in the form of restrictions on how Aboriginal People could fish. For the Lekwungen, for example, in 1916 the reef nets they had used since long before the arrival of Europeans were outlawed as "fish traps." Only one fish trap was permitted, and that belonged to J.H. Todd and Sons, who owned the Empire Cannery. The Lekwungen were invited to process the trapped fish in the cannery but were not permitted to catch them.[12]

Aboriginal People were also told when and where they could and could not fish. In the colonial period, the Lekwungen had been prohibited from fishing along the Victoria inlet gorge, one of their prime fishing sites. By 1890, regulations prevented any aboriginal person from selling fish outside of a specified season.[13] In 1921, Simon Johns wrote the Indian Agent, saying: "The Esquimalt and Songhees [Lekwungen] Indians have always fished at Goldstream for their winter's food, but this year they have been forbidden." He added that he had a copy of the Indian Act, which gave Indians the right to fish at any time for their own use: "You know the run of salmon is only for a short time, so please advise me at once. Should we be prosecuted, would the department engage a counsel to defend us?" There is no response on file to Johns' request. The next year, the Indian superintendent for British Columbia told a Royal Commission that, despite the Douglas Treaties, which guaranteed that aboriginal fisheries would carry on as formerly, Indians had been prohibited from fishing in their traditional fishing area, Saanich Arm, for several years.[14]

New restrictions in 1917 required Aboriginal People to obtain permits from fisheries officials or Indian Agents in order to fish for food. In 1928, George Pragnell, inspector of Indian agencies, commented: "There seems to be a general complaint amongst the Indians that the more generous policy in fishing for food purposes as promised has not materialized. Permits are hard to get and the presumption seems to be that the Indians will necessarily break the law regarding the sale of fish." Pragnell noted that Indians were no longer allowed to fish at the sites where they had previously located their villages (expressly for the purposes of the fishing). The DIA recognized that relief was necessary only because the Department of Fisheries had denied Aboriginal People access to fish. The Indian Agent for the lower Fraser Valley told the McKenna-McBride Commission that relief payments were to be in lieu of subsistence food, which could no longer be obtained.[15]

The 1930s Depression had a devastating effect on the wage employment of Aboriginal People and again threw them back upon their subsistence economy – only this time the tightening web of laws severely limited what they could harvest. By the 1930s, in the south of the province, the land over which they had formerly hunted and harvested wild foods had largely been settled and farmed. Hunting was restricted to a limited season in the fall and winter. Aboriginal People who needed to hunt out of season had to apply to the nearest game warden for a permit, and as this was often done by mail it could take weeks to get a reply.[16]

In 1933, Aboriginal People were further restricted by the provincial game department, which demanded that, even when hunting in season, Indians had to get another set of permits for game shot for food purposes. This, according to one of the agents, referring particularly to the Kwawkewlth Agency on northern Vancouver Island (but clearly reflecting a more general situation), had a dramatic effect: "In the past Indians have been accustomed to procure game and fish for food without interference, but this last year the regulations have been strictly enforced which has worked a hardship on the Indians *and thrown them more or less on relief.*"[17]

Yet another Catch-22: squeezed out of the subsistence economy by regulation and appropriation of the subsistence resources, Aboriginal People

Frank Kibbie, game warden at Bowron Lake, ca. 1890, appears to have an Aboriginal wife but prohibited her relatives from hunting in the Lakes area.

Relief Will Increase Out of Proportion

There is no work for wages to be had for many Indians this year, and if we have to feed the deer killers our relief will increase out of all proportion. The white settlers, almost without exception are commonly known to live practically the year round on wild game, yet one never hears of them being prosecuted ... I think your honourable Board will agree that the Indians who are in need should get certain privileges and consideration when it comes to the natural resources of their native land.

Indian Agent E. McLeod, Lytton, to M.B. Jackson, Chairman of Game Conservation Board, May 20, 1925

were forced onto relief; however, that relief was based on the principle that it would be supplemented by subsistence foods, which they could no longer obtain! An examination of relief paid to Aboriginal People shows that they were expected to gather part of their food, including all their protein requirements, from nature, while non-Aboriginal Peoples were not.

In 1880, the Province of British Columbia first established an indigent fund for non-Aboriginal People living outside municipalities (municipalities were responsible for looking after the poor). Aboriginal People were not eligible for the provincial fund and continued to receive assistance from the federal government. For the first three decades, the provincial payments were made on a case-by-case basis so it is hard to make direct comparisons between provincial payments to whites and federal payments to Aboriginal People. However, by 1912, thanks to the increasing bureaucratization of the provincial civil service, a standard list of provincial monthly relief was promulgated, with the result that some comparisons are possible. The following table compares provincial relief to that given by the DIA.[18]

Non-Indians (single person, 1912-16)	Indians (single person, 1910-16)
25 lbs of flour	25 lbs of flour
3 lbs rice	4 lbs of rice
8 lbs sugar	4 lbs sugar (only to sick)
1 lb tea	1/2 pound tea (only to sick)
1 pack of yeast cakes	
3 lbs salt	
6 lbs salt bacon	
5 lbs of white beans	
4 lbs dried apples	
3 lbs lard	

There is a dramatic difference in relief payments between Indians and non-Indians. Given that relief was meant only to stave off starvation, why did assumptions about minimum sustenance for Aboriginal People differ from those for whites? Was it a simple matter of racism?

As an explanation, "racism" does not tell us very much; it is simply another way of saying that the difference in the allocation of resources was race-based (see Chapter 2). Aboriginal People came to be seen (i.e., to be racialized) as people who needed less relief than did whites largely because many of them continued to practise a subsistence economy.[19] The federal authorities, in providing Indians only with carbohydrates and tea, assumed that protein and the necessary vitamins and minerals found in fruit and vegetables, as well as salt, would come from the aboriginal subsistence economy. Even though many Aboriginal People, like the Lekwungen, lived in urban areas beside non-Indian neighbours, and even though the state was limiting their access to wild foods, there was a racialized expectation that, as Indians, they would get protein from fishing and hunting and that they would get other necessities from gathering.

This two-tiered system was made very explicit in 1922, when provincial relief for whites began to be paid in cash at the value of fifteen dollars per person per month, increasing in 1924-25 to twenty dollars per month, and in 1926 to twenty-five dollars per month. Indigent white mothers were also eligible for the Mothers' Pension, which the province introduced in 1920. Single white mothers and mothers with disabled husbands were eligible for monthly payments of $42.50 if they had one child, plus an additional $7.50 for each child under the age of sixteen. Starting in 1927, elderly indigent white British Columbians were eligible for an old age pension of twenty dollars per month.[20] By contrast, aboriginal families, of whatever size, had to make do with the standard four dollars per month paid by the federal government "in kind" from a list of goods provided to storekeepers.

In 1931, when the Depression was in full force, municipalities bore the brunt of relief payments. Non-Indians (at this point, legal status as a registered Indian became very important) around Victoria were supplied with relief by the city to the value of $16.50 per month. For their Lekwungen neighbours and other registered Indians, the standard relief remained at provisions worth four dollars per family per month, substantially unchanged from the rations provided to the destitute Lekwungen elderly in 1888.[21] The rations in 1931 were as follows:

> 49 lb. [22kg] flour
> 6 lb. sugar
> 3 lb., 7 oz. rolled oats
> 12 oz. baking powder
> limited quantities of tea, rice, beans, and salt pork.[22]

Mary John, Carrier, from Stoney Creek west of Prince George, must have had the Depression rations imprinted on her memory for even in the 1980s she could recite them: twenty-four pounds (approximately ten kilograms) of flour, five pounds of rice, a bag of salt, half a pound of tea, two pounds of lard, and a bag of rolled oats for a family of eight for a month.[23]

Aboriginal People were expected to make up the difference between relief and their minimum food requirements from their gardens, the land, and the sea. The secretary of the DIA made this explicit in asking agents to

The Welfare Indian Comes True

Now the prediction of the non-Native saying all Indians are on welfare looks like it's going to come true and not because we want it to. Our people want to work. It's because of what has happened. We're not going to pick up and move away! It's not part of our DNA to do that! We stay put. The big companies that rape and reap our land are gone. So most of my people have now had to turn to welfare but when the Europeans look at it, welfare, they think, "Oh the big money they're making on welfare just sitting at home." That's not true. The welfare people get on reserve is far less than what they get off-reserve.

Daisy Sewid-Smith, Kwakw̲a̲ka'wakw, Victoria, October 19, 2000

Daisy Sewid-Smith (Mayanilth), right, and Chief of the Qualicum Band, Kim Recalma-Clutesi (Ogwilogwa), both Kwakw̲a̲ka'wakw

reduce relief costs by encouraging Aboriginal People to do more fishing and gardening. In describing the Cowichan, the Inspector of Indian Agencies said: "as whole [they] should not be too bad off during the depression as many can grow their own food if they want and have fish at their door."[24]

The importance of subsistence and household production is poignantly illustrated by the case of a family that relied entirely on relief. Left on her own with a young son when her husband was imprisoned in 1935, Dora Ross had no extended family among the Lekwungen with whom she lived. Her husband was an orphan with no siblings, and she was a non-aboriginal woman with no family in the community. Unconnected to the other Lekwungen families, unskilled in the knitting of Cowichan sweaters (which sustained many families), and not knowledgeable about "country foods," Dora Ross and her son had no options but relief. She petitioned both the DIA and the British Columbia Department of Social Welfare: "I can't live on four dollars groceries a month, no meats, vegetables, the necessities of clothing, lights, soaps, face and washing. We'd be rotten with scurvy or some sort of thing and be public charges."[25] She wrote the Indian Agent as follows: "I have no means of adding anything to the allowance. The boy and I have both been sick and we haven't fully recovered. I can't be expected to go out to work. I have the boy to take care of ... I have to have meat and vegetables and other things. Also something must be arranged for my lights. Surely I'm not to sit around in the dark."[26] Even firewood, which could have been obtained from Lekwungen land, was difficult to obtain for this family as they had no kin connections in the community.

Ross was particularly galled because she had become an "Indian" through marriage. Unmarried, she would have been entitled to the $16.50 that the city offered to indigents, and married to an imprisoned white husband she might have been eligible for the Mothers' Pension, which had been reduced during the Depression but still amounted to thirty-five dollars per month.[27] The agent was embarrassed by this situation, particularly when Ross described her situation in the letters section of the Victoria paper. He ensured that Ross received a little more than "regular Indians" by allocating a further $3.50 per month for a milk order for her son. However, when Ross's case came to the attention of the DIA in Ottawa, the agent was told that she was to be treated the same as any other Indian.[28]

Some young Indians responded to the low relief rates allocated to "families" by getting married and starting their own families. In 1933, the DIA responded to this tactic with a circular advising agents that "any Indian marrying while unable to support himself and wife will be given no separate allowance for a period of at least one year from date of marriage" and that newly married couples would have to continue to share in the allowance already provided for their families.[29] Faced with spiralling welfare costs and pressure on its own budget, the DIA, in 1936, issued "definite instructions" that able-bodied Indians were not to be given relief.[30]

In the face of the crisis produced by the Depression, the federal government increased per capita welfare spending from 1931 to 1934 by 367 percent. For Aboriginal People, the per capita spending declined by 16.5 percent. By 1936, per capita relief spending for registered Indians was one-third of that for other Canadians.[31]

The increase in employment brought by the Second World War led most aboriginal men and women back to paid work, and, as the Department of Fisheries noted, the increase in war work meant there was less of a demand for food-fishing permits: "The majority of the local Indians are working in the shipyards doing war work, consequently a very small number of food fishing permits were required." The fisheries inspector at Squamish expressed the general condition: "Most able-bodied Indians were making good wages as labourers in various wood harvesting camps, and as railway section hands; this sub-district being practically drained of all its young men eligible for military training. Indians are getting much higher prices for their field crops and farm animals and it does not pay them to neglect these matters for the time taken up in catching and curing salmon."[32]

The Department of Fisheries used the plentiful supply of work as an excuse to further reduce aboriginal access to food resources. Since so many were employed in commercial fishing during the war, the chief inspector of fisheries wrote to one of the Indian Agents to say: "It is felt that Indians engaged in the commercial fishing during the height of the season do not require food permits."[33]

Despite the increase in work for the able-bodied, and despite wartime inflation, the elderly and infirm still had to get by on a relief payment of four dollars per month. Mary Quocksister, a Kwakwaka'wakw from Quadra Island, wrote "I am an old Indian great-grandmother, too old and infirm to work for my bread any more ... If I were a German born galvanized Canadian ... I should now be getting the old-age pension of twenty dollars a month. Instead ... I am brought to the brink of my grave by the lack of necessities of life."[34]

For the elderly who had the skills and knowledge to live off the land and sea, increasing infirmity and state prohibition made relying on the subsistence economy less and less viable. For the young, there was another problem. Since the 1920s, schooling had been compulsory. Even those children attending day school could no longer travel, trap, and hunt with their parents, except for two months in the summer. Well over one-third of aboriginal students who attended residential schools, where they were away

$4 a Month

The Indian agent used to give us only $4 a month and all we were allowed was a package of matches, and tea ... sugar, and salt, and things like that ... Then we had to wait 'til the next month to make another bigger supply to increase these that we already had. And that's what we had to do.

Tilly Gutierrez, Stó:lō, May 26, 2005

Tilly Gutierrez, Stó:lō elder, 2005

Begging for Relief

I just spent time in the archives in Ottawa – I was busy reading just from my granny's old files, they had to beg for relief cheques ... just to be able to put food on the table when they were old and really disabled, right up until the '50s. It was just horrible the process they went through.

Daisy Sewid-Smith, Kwakwaka'wakw, Victoria, October 19, 2000

from their families for long periods, could not assist in the processing of harvest foods. Schooling, which brought some advantages with regard to one's ability to participate in the capitalist economy, definitely involved sacrifices with regard to one's ability to learn skills necessary to the "bush" economy. Mary John, a Carrier woman, recounts her embarrassment at not knowing how to tan hides and to preserve game when she returned from residential school. By the 1940s, several generations of families had been in residential schools, and people's knowledge of how to hunt, fish, harvest bulbs and berries (and how to preserve all of these foods) was becoming quite attenuated.[35]

The DIA tacitly recognized the declining access to subsistence food in 1946 when it included some fresh meat, beans, peanut butter, and tinned vegetables in its monthly relief package. The value of this monthly relief, which was still paid in kind, rose to $10.10 for a family of three (which included a two-month-old baby); however, the Indian Agent himself admitted that this was less than half of what such a family needed in order to survive, and he unsuccessfully petitioned Ottawa to increase this allowance.[36]

When, in the 1950s, the economy again declined for Aboriginal People and increased numbers returned to the relief-subsistence mode of survival, they protested the new limitations on subsistence fishing. In 1955, Andy Paull, editor of the magazine *Indian Voice*, said that conditions had been better earlier in the century: "at least then a hungry Indian could go down to the creek and hook a salmon – now they have to watch the salmon swimming by."[37]

Clam digging remained one of the few means by which Aboriginal People could still harvest food without restriction. Clams were gathered both for subsistence use and for sale, and clam digging became an increasingly important source of casual employment for coastal Aboriginal People, especially on southeast Vancouver Island. In 1960, when the federal fisheries department instituted a closed season for the commercial harvesting of clams between June and November, Lekwungen chief Albany considered this to be yet another step in the federal government's appropriation of aboriginal resources. He pointed out that, at one time, they had a full open season for digging clams: "Now through regulations, it is only seven months. They tell us the clams are no good from June to November, but Indians feel the clam is really at its prime then. Those are the months Indians used to put up their food for the winter. For many hundreds of years Indians were eating clams in those months." Albany noted that, since the Lekwungen could not sell clams, which, by this time, accounted for 80 percent of their livelihood, clams were about all they would have to eat. As the Lekwungen

Clams were a mainstay of the Gitga'at commercial economy. Charles Robinson opened a clam cannery at Lachljeets near Hartley Bay around the time of the First World War.

were faced with having to rely principally on relief, it was probably not too much of an exaggeration for the *Colonist*, in October 1960, to run the headline: "Indians Face Starvation."[38]

A decade later, when Katherine Mooney surveyed the Lekwungen and other aboriginal groups on southeast Vancouver Island, she found the use of subsistence foods further curtailed by increasing population densities. As one Wsanec (Saanich) woman put it, "Clams are hard to get now – pollution." Some men continued to harvest crabs and sea urchins, while "in most households the women and children [dug] clams and sometimes collect[ed] oysters." However, she found that, although "the males in most households frequently hunt game or ducks or fish or do both ... [they] have done less hunting in the past several years with the growing observance of legal restrictions and the disappearance of hunting areas."[39]

There was still a lot of support among the Salish people Mooney interviewed in 1971 for the ideal of sharing food; however, she was told that this was becoming less and less the case: "Its not the same now the old people are passing away. We don't have big cooks on the beach – crabs and so on ... It used to be one big family like. For example if someone came home with fish, he'd invite everyone." Items like game, ducks, and shellfish "are frequently shared only with the family ... for the simple reason that they are scarce and not obtainable in any great quantities at once. 'Others get their own game in the hunting season – on the island, there's not much anymore.'"[40]

In 1970, the collection of wild berries continued, but most people waited until the commercial berry fields were opened up for free picking at the end of the season. Then, large numbers of aboriginal women, children, and the elderly from southeast Vancouver Island reserves picked large quantities of berries for freezing or, less commonly, canning. With the assistance

Caught in the Middle

Our people are caught between two ways of life. The old way is gone and we haven't gotten into the new way. We still don't understand. Many of us still don't want to, but what do you do when you are forced into it? You have to.

Everything is gone from the past. The hunting's gone, the fishing's gone, the land is gone, the timber, the streams are spoiled, the lakes are spoiled.

Forbidden, outlawed, legislated away, harassed away. My people are caught in the middle.

Dave Elliott, Wsanec

of men, many women also picked free potatoes at the end of the potato season. Many households also had their own kitchen gardens and fruit trees.[41]

Some subsistence foods, like sea urchin, continued to be harvested because they were unavailable commercially and were considered a delicacy. More often, however, Mooney found that subsistence foods were harvested not out of preference but, rather, simply out of need. Interfamily sharing networks maintained along the lines of traditional kin relationships were in fact cultural adaptations crucial to ameliorating "the long term prevailing uncertainties of Indian life."[42]

In 1971, Mooney found another continuity in the boundaries separating the subsistence economy from the prestige and capitalist economies: "an omnipresent distinction exists between home-grown, baked, gathered, hunted, [and] fished delicacies and store bought goods." The former were given away freely, but the latter (like a century before), were given only to close family or on specific ceremonial occasions.[43]

Although Mooney found an overall decline in the extent of sharing foodstuffs, chiefs and "high-born" people in the 1960s still provided for community functions such as the potlatch/winter dances and gave food to needy people. In the 1960s, community functions focused on the "winter dances," which combined elements of the potlatch and of spirit dancing. After the anti-potlatch laws were removed in 1951, the winter dances increased in frequency, as did the number of participants. In this way the subsistence economy was still connected to the prestige economy: in order to gain respect and to be a *siem*, or "leader," it was necessary to be generous with food as well as with goods and cash.

Wayne Suttles described one of these "modern" potlatches in the Cowichan Agency in March 1960. The main work involved passing on hereditary names from deceased relatives. Dancing preceded the naming, and the dancers were paid by the host family. Those in attendance, official witnesses to the naming, were also given "gifts" – ranging from a mountain goat wool blanket to flannel blankets and kerchiefs to fifty-cent pieces. Two families were primarily involved in the naming, but other families used the opportunity to make announcements of their own, and they also paid their witnesses.[44]

The work and the accompanying meals for the six hundred to eight hundred people in attendance (provided by the hosts) lasted from 9:00 PM until 3:00 AM, when the dancing – which lasted until well past daybreak – began. Each time a dancer moved out onto the floor, some member of his or her family moved around the crowd distributing fifty-cent pieces to selected members of the audience in order to "help" the dancer.

Meanwhile, the dancers passed fruit to the crowd, and, as a final act, the host community distributed three hundred pounds of sugar. Suttles estimated that, in the Coast Salish area, there was a dance like this one every Saturday night throughout the winter, that smaller dances were held every night in many locations, and that Salish spiritual life was flourishing. Although different in form from the potlatches of a century earlier, the dances and, particularly, the gifts, affirmed the persistence of a non-capitalist economy in which one's stature was measured by how much one gave away.[45]

Participation in the rituals of the winter dance societies sometimes involved extended periods of cleansing, training, and isolation. In former times, the community would have supported the "initiates" or people would have saved money earned in the wage economy in order to buy necessities during training. From the 1960s, spiritual "work" could be subsidized by stepping out of the capitalist economy and collecting employment insurance or welfare – a practice that some people continue today.[46]

According to Douglas Hudson's work on the Carrier and Hugh Brody's on the people of the Treaty 8 area, in the interior of British Columbia, where the potlatch was not part of the culture, the non-capitalist economy melded with welfare and intermittent wage work to create a distinctive "bush economy" or what I call "moditional" economy. Both these studies show Aboriginal People using state transfer payments (family allowance, old age pension, unemployment insurance, and relief/welfare) to purchase those items they could not acquire through hunting, trapping, and/or seasonal wage labour. This mixed economy gave many Aboriginal People an alternative to being totally dependent on wage labour, which often necessitated their having to leave their communities and miss culturally important activities. There was no stigma attached to combining relief with the subsistence economy.

Brody did some calculations based on a study of three communities in the Treaty 8 area: East Moberly, Doig, and Blueberry. Whereas in 1978 the DIA calculated that the annual per capita cash income of these people was in the neighbourhood of $161 per year, Brody found that, when the full bush economy was considered, their income was more than twelve times that high. They were still poor people by Canadian standards (their income being about 30 percent of the Canadian average), but they were poor people "whose tables [were] always laden with meat."[47] Ken Coates's study of Aboriginal People along the Yukon River and south into northern British Columbia also describes this kind of bush economy as a way of keeping a modified traditional culture viable.

The provision of "relief," or state welfare assistance, to Aboriginal People as a substitute for subsistence was an innovation that the federal government

Please Give Me My Potlatch

I hereby apply for potlatch. I am a man of sixty-seven years of age and have no relatives and if I should take sick I have no one to look after me. I hear that you give some of the people food and you will not give any to me ... If you do not give me potlatch I will write to Mr. Perry [Chief Commissioner].

Letter from Johnny Galakawmei to Indian Agent E.G. Newnham, August 1, 1933

brought to BC after Confederation, adding a new dimension to aboriginal economies. The pre-Confederation policy had been, in the words of the new Indian commissioner: "let the Indians alone ... Money payments by the Government, on account of the native race, have been restricted to expenses incurred by Indian outrages."[48] The provincial government's game and land laws pushed Aboriginal People out of their subsistence economy, and, after 1871, the federal government assumed responsibility for preventing starvation. State relief was explicitly described as a substitute for a subsistence economy that was no longer accessible. The DIA resented the limitations on the aboriginal subsistence economy for budgetary, if for no other, reasons and conducted a long-standing battle with the provincial game department and the federal fisheries department, with very limited success. White fishers, trappers, and sport hunters had more political influence than did the disenfranchised Aboriginal People, and the subsistence economy continued to erode.

At the turn of the century, Indian Agents estimated that less than 1 percent of aboriginal income came from the government. During the Depression this rose to 4 percent. By 1954, that figure was 17 percent. In 1966, 25.4 percent of the on-reserve Indian population in British Columbia received financial assistance, more than eight times the provincial average. By 1972-73, the percentage of BC Aboriginal People dependent on social assistance had increased to 47 percent.[49]

While "relief" was a new addition to their multiple economies, there were elements in the provision of relief that had parallels in the aboriginal subsistence economy. Relief payments came in the form of "gifts," principally food and blankets. In the Coast Salish economy, like that of other Northwest Coast cultures, food circulated separately from wealth, and anyone who was in need received food if it was available. *Siem*, or leaders, had a responsibility to provide for the indigent, and this is what they understood the Indian Agent to be doing. The Lekwungen word for Indian Agent was: *si?éms t^ ?^xwélng^xw*, which translates roughly to mean, "*siem*/ leader of the Indian people." "Relief" was transformed as it became incorporated into the Lekwungen worldview. They would ask the agent for "muckamuck" ("food" in Chinook jargon) or they would ask for their monthly "potlatch" ("gift" in Chinook jargon).[50] There was no shame attached to accepting relief. On the contrary, it was seen as part of the *siem*'s responsibility with regard to providing for his/her people.

The agents were not the only ones who saw the relief potlatch as *makúk* for the limits that had been placed upon their subsistence economy. Certainly, Stó:lō Rena Peters made this connection in the 1970s:

When I used to be on welfare, I used to think that the government owed it to me. That's what I thought. They haven't given us anything for coming here and saying this is their country and they've never treated us like we're of any value to this country. So I put it in my head as they owed it to me. They're not going to do me anything else. They don't give me pride in who I am, they don't give me a home, they don't give me a place to respect myself, to respect First Nations People – they think of us as in the way. "If you guys were gone, we wouldn't have to think about what we did!" ... So I think, "Hey, they owe it. I have two little kids here, I can't go to school. I'm going to take the welfare but I'm not going to call it welfare, I'm going to call it spirit money![51]

Stó:lō Herb Joe (*Tíxwelátsa*), a former manager of the Chilliwack Area Indian Council's Social Development Program, commented: "There wasn't a notable stigma attached to applying for and receiving social assistance. It was a new term to our people, a term that people didn't understand, you know ... I don't think initially the [social welfare] programs were delivered in such a way as to make the people understand really what social assistance is all about. You know, like "social" and "assistance," when you put the two words together, what does it really mean? Well, to our people it didn't mean "social assistance." What it meant was another source of income."[52]

Helen Clifton and her daughter Chief Pat Sterritt of the Gitga'at in Hartley Bay made the same observations. As soon as children were old enough to collect welfare payments, they were encouraged by their parents to visit the local welfare agent rather than to seek employment. Pat Sterritt thought that, around 1968, when welfare hit Hartley Bay, "[it] changed the way people related to each other. That's when things really started to go bad."[53]

Verna Ambers, director of community development with the Namgis First Nation at Alert Bay, tied the rise of welfare dependency to the decline of the fishery, which, in that community, occurred only in the last twenty years:

A lot of people migrated into welfare state, income assistance, and I think that there's been people who have been on income assistance for ever ... There's no where else to go. And I think people's self esteem and all that, was again eroded by going on welfare. And fishermen – you know when you're born into that, in this community or any other, you start fishing when you're eleven or twelve. So what kind of education do you have? And then you come down the road fifty years later and you're sixty-three or sixty-one or fifty-six and you've never had any education, what else can you do?[54]

New Lifestyle

Then we had this new lifestyle that you had to be – when you became nineteen years of age, you were eligible to get welfare on your own ... And so all of a sudden, I started to see this trend starting up in this community. And as I go out and meet with other social workers and centres, I see that the birthday present when you get nineteen is to go up to the welfare office and apply for social assistance.

Helen Clifton, Gitga'at, former social worker, Hartley Bay, June 9, 2004

Helen Clifton, Gitga'at, elder and former social worker, 2004

Aboriginal Right to Welfare

And so we need to find a way of breaking through that aboriginal right to welfare mentality. A big part of that is esteem. There's value in who we are and where we come from.

Doug Kelly, Stó:lō, Soowahlie Band Office, May 27, 2005

Employment Insurance (EI) fit well with aboriginal patterns of seasonal employment and, in effect, subsidized the non-wage part of the moditional economy. Chris Cook Jr., Namgis councillor, observed: "before the fishermen got unemployment insurance, we looked for jobs, logging, you know we did all kinds of different things." Afterwards, "Whether it's a good thing or a bad thing, I think that it has been a ... crutch for a lot of our people over the years." Heiltsuk Ed Newman thought that EI and welfare undermined the traditional ethic of hard work: "Some of our people work just long enough to collect EI. A lot of our people do that. I'd never do that because my grandmother used to tell me when you get too comfortable you get lazy. A lot of our young people now don't want to get work because it's easier to collect welfare."[55]

The result, according to many aboriginal observers, has been that a culture of welfare has developed in many First Nations communities. According to Stó:lō Doug Kelly, "what was intended as a safety net has become a way of life. We've gone from where there was one generation dependent on income assistance, now we're up to three or four families where it's generational. And so that's going to be a difficult thing, breaking that belief."[56]

Welfare payments have a genealogy that goes back even before the arrival of Europeans when the *siem* took care of their people. Charting the history of *makúk* exhibits a complex pattern of distinct but linked economies changing and shifting in relative importance. Whereas at first Aboriginal People were able to add the capitalist wage economy and social welfare programs to their long-standing prestige and subsistence economies, for many coastal people, over time the latter has given way to the former.

The experiences of the 1880s, the early 1900s, and the Second World War demonstrate that, when there was a wage alternative to the subsistence economy, most Aboriginal People took it. Yet, as long as a viable subsistence economy existed, it had important implications for the aboriginal relationship to the capitalist economy. In contrast to immigrant labourers, both Asian and European, Aboriginal People did not *have* to sell their labour: they could move in and out of wage economy according to how it best fit with their prestige and subsistence economies.

Beginning in the 1880s in southwestern British Columbia, aboriginal access to subsistence resources has been squeezed out of their economy as settlement and industrial activity reduced the productivity of the land and sea, and laws have prohibited harvesting what is left. By the mid-twentieth century, this two-pronged attack on the harvest of traditional foods was felt throughout the province. The government's response to starvation or hardship caused by its own regulations was to substitute "welfare" – state transfer payments. Welfare has ensured that Aboriginal People did not starve and that they continue to have an alternative to wage work – but at a very high price.

NINE

Conclusion:
The Outer Edge of Probability, 1970-2007

In 1785, James Hanna, commanding the first European vessel to approach the West Coast after James Cook's ship, observed one of the most astonishing phenomena described in this book. Aboriginal People on the Northwest Coast, on the whole, welcomed Europeans, were eager to trade with them, and later to work for wages. For the Nuu-chah-nulth who met Cook and Hanna, and for most other Aboriginal Peoples, *makúk* with the newcomers offered a way to enrich themselves in their own economies.

Today's relationships between Aboriginal and non-Aboriginal People are derived from these early contact experiences, and these, in turn, were products of very old histories negotiated differently in different contexts. Comparing the Lekwungen and Tsilhqot'in responses to Europeans shows that "History," as it worked itself out in the bays and valleys of British Columbia, was an intensely local process. The Lekwungen, as a result of their history and how it shaped their culture, welcomed Europeans. The Tsilhqot'in, whose own history was quite different from that of the Lekwungen, drove the Europeans away. The comparison between these two peoples shows us that the history of aboriginal/non-aboriginal relations did not start with contact: it started, both in the Americas and in Europe, centuries before.

The people described here are ordinary people by their own reckoning but are extraordinary with regard to how they have been treated in history, literature, and public policy, and how they feature in the current perceptions of mass society. When the Europeans first arrived on the west coast of what became Canada, Aboriginal Peoples owned the entire territory, a sovereignty that has never been acquired by the nation-state.[1] In Canada, they were called wards of the Crown – a status also given to orphans and run-away children. This status, which deprived them of their lands as it deprived them of the right to buy land, denied them the right to vote in elections and ensured that no peoples in Canada would be more controlled by the government than would Aboriginal People, despite the fact that, in British Columbia, they dominated the population until the late 1800s.

At nine o'clock in the evening three canoes approached; as the night was dark, the arms were got up. And they hallowed at a distance "Maakook" – this was asking to trade. We soon got them alongside.

James Hanna, August 9, 1785

The Outer Edge of Probability

Hiyu (many), *skookum* (strong), *mesachie* (bad), *cultus* (worthless) and other Chinook words spot conversations but all is fading, fading, fading fast in this land that once occupied a position on the outer edge of probability.

Paul St. Pierre, "The Past Frontier," *Vancouver Sun*, December 5, 2000, A13

◀ Detail of John Webber painting depicting Cook's ship, *Resolution*, in Nootka Sound

Prior to the establishment of white settlement, the Aboriginal Peoples of present-day British Columbia were among the richest and best-fed societies in the world. When the industrial revolution arrived in their inlets and valleys, these extraordinary people did a very ordinary thing: they went to work for white employers and many prospered. Yet, as the newcomers' economy grew and employed more and more people, it employed fewer and fewer Aboriginal People. The high unemployment and social problems widespread in today's aboriginal communities are relatively recent phenomena – the legacy of a history of ordinary events and everyday racism. That such a history has transpired puts this place, in Paul St. Pierre's words, "on the outer edge of probability."

The writing of this book has spanned more than a decade – a decade during which Canadians have constantly been reminded of the importance of the past. I began my research in 1991, the year British Columbia

A Tin Ear

Chief Justice Allan McEachern: I don't want to be skeptical, but to have witnesses singing songs in court is, in my respectful view, not the proper way to approach this problem.

Mr Grant: Well, my Lord, with respect, the song is what one may refer to as a death song. It's a song which invokes the history of and the depth of the history of what she is telling.

McEachern: I have a tin ear, Mr. Grant, so it's not going to do any good to sing it to me.

Transcript, *Delgamuukw* v. *The Queen*, 1997

Mary Johnson (Antgulilibix), Gitksan, sings her history into the court record in front of Chief Justice McEachern at the *Delgamuukw* trial, 1987

Supreme Court justice Allan McEachern delivered his decision on the Gitksan-Wet'suwet'en's claim to 54,000 square kilometres of the province. The fifty-four hereditary chiefs (representing seventy-six houses of the Gitksan and Wet'suwet'en peoples) and the battery of lawyers (representing the governments of Canada and BC) all appealed to history to justify their positions.

It was a remarkable case because the stakes were so high, because the three-year trial was so long and complex, and because the success or failure of the claimants rested on the acceptability of different kinds of historical evidence. McEachern rejected the *adaawk*, or "orally transmitted" history presented by the aboriginal plaintiffs, thus rejecting their case in favour of the written sources of the Crown. On the other hand, the "marvellous collections" of manuscripts generated by the immigrants, he said, "largely spoke for themselves."[2]

The manuscripts, records of white fur traders, missionaries, and government officials do "speak for themselves," but only for themselves. They are one side of, or one account of, a conversation held between two cultures. They are *partial*, in both meanings of the word: biased and fragmentary. Like many who have written about aboriginal/non-aboriginal relations, McEachern was misled by his sources. Relying exclusively on texts written by white observers – texts that incorporated notions of indolence and dependence into the very definition of "Indian" – he heard only one side of a long exchange. It is not surprising then that, with respect to aboriginal involvement in paid work (a crucial issue in the case), McEachern reached the conventional conclusion: since the fur trade Aboriginal Peoples have been left outside the developing capitalist economy.[3]

Makúk: A New History of Aboriginal-White Relations attempts to show that, with more effort, the historic conversation between Aboriginal and non-Aboriginal People in British Columbia is accessible. Listening to aboriginal accounts along with those of non-aboriginal ethnologists, employers, missionaries, government agents, and travellers reveals a rich and complex series of interactions that call for a reinterpretation of our shared history.

First, the inadequacy of the standard ways of understanding the interaction of colonizers and colonized is immediately apparent. Aboriginal People flocked to the colonizers' factories to work not because they had "acculturized" to the ways of the Europeans but because they saw this as a way of enabling them to engage more fully in their own "traditional pursuits." Second, the stereotype of the "lazy Indian" has to be discarded in the face of a history of hard work and aboriginal cultures that emphasized

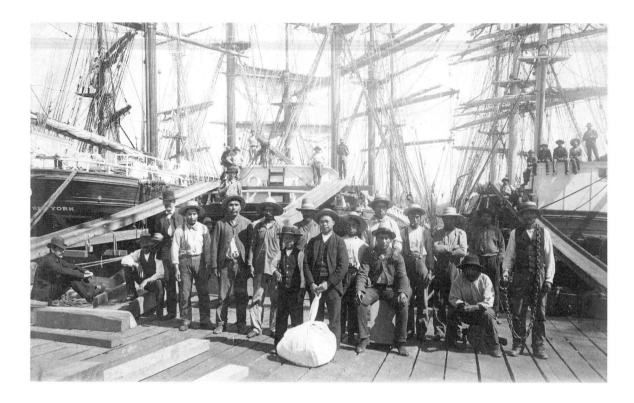

Aboriginal longshoremen at Moodyville,
1889

industrious behaviour. Despite a European predisposition to believe that
all indigenous peoples were lazy, the traders and settlers saw them working
"with a remarkable degree of industry." In the 1850s, Governor James Douglas called them "exceedingly useful to the colonists"; in the 1860s, Chief
Justice Begbie described their work as essential to supplying the gold fields;
in the 1870s, the BC attorney general described them working "in almost
every branch of industrial and domestic life, at wages which would appear
excessively high in England or in Canada"; in the 1880s, Franz Boas, father
of modern anthropology, described them as "indispensable on the labour
market." In spite of cultural disruption and disease, aboriginal economies
grew in the nineteenth century and Aboriginal People in British Columbia
were, on the whole, "independent and prosperous."[4]

Listening to more than one side of the conversation puts to rest the
thesis that Aboriginal Peoples were made irrelevant by the coming of the
gold rush and settlement. There is abundant testimony from the early 1850s
into the twentieth century, from Aboriginal and non-Aboriginal People,
that whole villages emptied to participate in paid work and that whole
families participated. The gold rush recedes as the great divide in BC history. The contact era, in which Aboriginal Peoples were enriched, and the
conflict era, in which Aboriginal Peoples were marginalized, are not easily
divisible. There was no fatal collision of cultures but, rather, a process that

enriched as it displaced, that impoverished Aboriginal People even as it made them the centre of state attention. Non-aboriginal historians, however, have accomplished what disease, violence, and social disruption could not: by basing history on the impressions of immigrant groups, we have made Aboriginal People "disappear."

Aboriginal writers have also contributed to a misleading periodization. As Maori Linda Tuhwai Smith notes, in writing against colonial writing there has been a tendency to idealize the precontact past and to miss the links between indigenous cultures and the history of colonialism. Aboriginal scholars, she says, have too easily accepted the binary of colonized/colonizer, without looking at the layerings and internal contradictions on both sides. Not unexpectedly, aboriginal writers and storytellers have tended to focus on what made their cultures different from the new cultures rather than on what made them the same.[5] If we can step outside the traditional patterning of traditional-modern, colonist-colonized, lazy-industrious, the history of British Columbia appears in a new frame.

Aboriginal People were, in fact, essential to the development of new industries and to the spread of capitalism in the province-to-be. Coal would not have been mined in British Columbia in the 1840s and 1850s, export sawmills would have been unable to function in the 1860s and 1870s, and canneries would have had neither fishing fleet nor fish processors in the 1870s and 1880s without the widespread participation of Aboriginal People. Until the late 1880s, Aboriginal People constituted the majority of BC's population, and it was their labour that allowed the rapid creation of an economic base, from the fur trade, to coal mining, sawmilling, and salmon canning. This was the regional economy that kept the Hudson's Bay Company on the Pacific coast, that persuaded Britain that its colonies could be profitable as well as strategic, and that ultimately ensured that British Columbia would be *British* Columbia.

The Aboriginal population did not succumb to the assault of capitalism, Christianity, or a technologically superior culture. They used or adapted parts of European culture, incorporating various aspects of it into their own societies. Most, like the Lekwungen, made industrialization work for them in the nineteenth century. Where they saw their interests threatened, particularly by the appropriation of their resource base, they protested and even took up arms. The Tsilhqot'in hostility towards Europeans, illustrated in the nineteenth century by their threatening actions and occasional deadly attacks, ensured that they lived a life that was little disrupted by Europeans for nearly a century longer than did the Lekwungen.

The twentieth century has for Aboriginal Peoples been a century of impoverishment. The steepest decline in aboriginal economies, and the

We Cannot Sell Fish and We Cannot Work

We used to have at one time great fishing on the [Sproat] river and we used to sell our salmon; but when the white people came in here they stopped us from selling our salmon. The Whites brought tea, sugar and flour here and we have to eat it, but where are we going to get the money to buy all these things? We cannot sell the fish and we cannot work because the white people won't employ us. We want to know if we have the right to catch and sell fish in season and out of season."

Tatoosh, Opetchesaht, to the Royal Commission on Indians Affairs, 1914

consequent dependence and social disruption, occurred between 1950 and 1970, when many Aboriginal Peoples, if the Lekwungen are an indication, were measurably poorer than they had been a century earlier. These years ushered in an era of widespread unemployment and growing dependence on state support.

By comparing the Lekwungen (who welcomed the traders) and the Tsilhqot'in (who drove them away), we can see the impact of different cultural responses to the Europeans on the place of indigenous peoples in British Columbia, both historically and today. The results are mixed. Despite Tsilhqot'in resistance in the nineteenth century, by the early 1900s many were participating in seasonal wage work, and, by the 1970s, the

Suggesting resistance: (left to right) George Jimmy, Tsilhqot'in Peelas, and Tow-hu-quam-kee, 1891, photographed at Snauq (False Creek), now Vancouver

Tsilhqot'in were in a similar position to the Lekwungen: displaced from many of their subsistence resources; apparently marginal to the capitalist economy; experiencing high rates of unemployment, alcohol, and other abuse; and increasingly dependent on state welfare payments. Economically, the Tsilhqot'in were in much the same dependent position as were the Lekwungen. No matter what strategy Aboriginal People adopted to deal with the Europeans, accommodation, resistance, or a combination of both, two centuries after the first Europeans arrived, the Lekwungen, the Tsilhqot'in, and the vast majority of Aboriginal People in British Columbia were impoverished and dependent.

Culturally, their self-imposed isolation meant that the Tsilhqot'in experienced much less dislocation than did other aboriginal groups. In 1970, in the Nemiah Valley, everybody, old and young, still spoke the Tsilhqot'in language, whereas the Lekwungen had to rely on a few elders to compile a dictionary of a language that was no longer spoken at all. Wilfully remote, the Tsilhqot'in still had access to hunting grounds for moose, deer, and caribou, and they also had access to a rich salmon river. With the help of a generator and a freezer, these country foods could last a family a long time.

The two examples of the Lekwungen and the Tsilhqot'in remind us of the complexity and variability of these innumerable interactions and the danger of broad-brush theoretical approaches to them. The simplicity of the progression from "traditional" to "modern" suggested by modernization theorists was lost on the Lekwungen, who used the modern to buttress their traditional economy. Likewise, the predictions of the dependency theorists are confounded by the agency and independence of the Tsilhqot'in. Aboriginal Peoples created an economy that linked their own prestige and subsistence economies to a capitalist economy and, later, a welfare economy. Capitalism is often hailed for its versatility and ability to change shape as circumstances require, but these economies have been equally flexible and equally long-lived. Neither fully European nor Aboriginal, neither traditional nor modern, Aboriginal British Columbians have an economy that combines wage labour, capitalist investment, prestige, subsistence, and welfare. This is a distinctive economy, and it needs its own name. "Bush economy" has been proposed as an appropriate term, but since this economy is practised in urban as well as rural British Columbia, I suggest "moditional": it captures both the modern and the traditional as well as the "modes of production" that connect them.[6]

This book has been framed to encourage comparison and, ultimately, to facilitate a fuller understanding of the global process that incorporated Aboriginal Peoples into a world capitalist system. Some aspects of what has been described have affected indigenous peoples everywhere. What is very

A Confounding of Tongues

[Chinook jargon] is an attempt on a small scale to nullify Babel by combining a confusion of tongues into a confounding of tongues – a witches cauldron in which the vocable that bobs up may be some old familiar Saxon verb, having suffered a Procrustean docking or elongation, and now doing substantive duty; or some strange monsters, evidently nurtured within the range of tomahawks and calumets.

Theodore Winthrop, *The Canoe and the Saddle*, 1913

Canadian about the variant discussed here is how the displacement of Aboriginal Peoples was (and is) conducted through "peaceable subordination." The work-for-pay exchange with the Euro-Canadian economy was and is a key part of this process.

When Aboriginal People welcomed Europeans, or simply permitted them to set up shop in order to engage in trade, they became part of a dialogue. By engaging with the newcomers first in the form of trade and then in the form of paid work, Aboriginal Peoples unwittingly gave the newcomers both the incentive and the means to build a new economy – one that would ultimately dislodge their own. Although never fully captured by the capitalist system, Aboriginal Peoples incorporated many of its features into their own lives. Work, and later welfare, were both means of including Aboriginal Peoples in the new state while excluding them from their land and resources.

Origins of Impoverishment

Why, if Aboriginal Peoples were so eager to trade and work for wages from the 1780s to the 1880s, and so many were "prosperous" in the nineteenth century, were so many of them unemployed and on welfare by the 1960s and 1970s? Why were Aboriginal People working in fewer occupational categories, with a lower workforce participation rate, in 1970 than in 1870? The answer involves the intersection of several factors – competition, the deliberate erosion of some elements of aboriginal culture and the persistence of others – racism, educational opportunities, technological change, and restrictions on subsistence economies – all of which came together as Canada undertook to dramatically expand the welfare state.

Many of the early interactions between non-Aboriginal and Aboriginal People could be summed up in the Chinook jargon word *makúk*, loosely translated as "exchange." The accounts of Captain James Cook and Captain George Vancouver, and the extensive examinations of the Tsilhqot'in and Lekwungen, show that the motivation for engaging in any transaction was varied, as was the whole meaning of the exchange process. Even the meaning of the items exchanged transformed as they moved from one culture into another. The encounter of Cook, followed by that of Hanna, started a history of dialogue, of *makúk*, and from that time onward it is possible to chart and make visible a long history of misunderstanding.

When we consider work-for-pay as part of the dialogue between Aboriginal and non-Aboriginal People, it becomes obvious that there was enormous room for "slippage" with regard to the nature of what was being exchanged and to the mutual obligation between an employer and the employee. Although it seems ironic, given the unintended consequences, to think that most Aboriginal People were so welcoming to whites, it is understandable in context. The Lekwungen, like other Northwest Coast peoples, worked to acquire goods that were then transformed into potlatch gifts and given away. By gathering and distributing wealth in this fashion, Aboriginal People met their obligations and raised their status in their own society.

Aboriginal People worked according to a logic that was based in their own economies, but they were hired by Europeans who worked according to a logic based in a capitalist economy. As far as the newcomers were concerned, Aboriginal People were workers with a difference: they had a different relationship to land and work, different ideas about what was being exchanged, and different notions about the hierarchy of obligations as it applied to employer, community, and family. It is not surprising that the European saw this difference as "laziness" and lack of dependability.

The racialization process that defined Aboriginal Peoples in British Columbia was complicated by the ethnic mix of the workforce. In the more skilled jobs on steamships and in sawmills, and in more lucrative work on the docks, Aboriginal People were largely displaced by white labour. In low-skill labour, like agricultural, domestic, or cannery work, Aboriginal People were partially displaced by Chinese immigrants. Aboriginal fishers were displaced by Japanese fishers. Employers explained that the Asians were harder working and more dependable. If we probe those perceptions, we find that Aboriginal People and Asians had completely different relationships to the European economy.

Chinese and Japanese labour brokers supplied the required number of labourers to employers, took care of recruitment, replaced those who quit or got sick, provided food and shelter, and exercised enormous authority over the workers. Asian workers came as single men. They needed to pay the labour brokers for their passage and earn lots of money as quickly as possible so that they could return home and live in a relatively well-off manner. These workers were entirely dependent on wage work to survive, and when wages were low, they accepted a mere subsistence wage in preference to starvation.

Aboriginal People originally entered the capitalist economy knowing that they could fall back on a subsistence economy. They already had a sophisticated exchange economy that was highly seasonal. They turned to wage work when there were no major conflicts in their own economic and cultural cycles. At salmon time, many quit to make sure they could lay by enough salmon to feed them through the winter. During the winter, many quit to participate in the winter ceremonials. For Aboriginal People, work was only advantageous if it helped them in their own economies. If the

We Ask Whiteman's Wages

Bailey: We used to try several times to get work outside of the Reserve and the whites used to turn us off …

Shaw: Why can't they get that work now?

Bailey: Because we ask the Whiteman's wages, and the Whiteman says it is a little bit too high, and the Whitemen wants to give the Indians just the same as they pay the Chinamen, Japs and Hindoos, and the Indians won't stand for it.

Chief David Bailey of the Coquitlam Band and Commissioner Shaw, McKenna-McBride Commission Transcripts, January 8, 1915

Indians Compete with Our Own People

We are educating Indians to compete industrially with our own people. Which seems to me a very undesirable use of public money.

Clifford Sifton, Superintendent of Indian Affairs, *House of Commons Debates*, June 14, 1897

Clifford Sifton, Superintendent of Indian Affairs

wages were too low, the work too dangerous, or the discipline too harsh, they left the European economy. In claiming that aboriginal labourers were not dependable enough, what employers really meant was that aboriginal labourers were not dependent enough on the capitalist economy.

In 1885, the completion of the Canadian Pacific Railway linked British Columbia to the rest of Canada. Before the railway, large and small employers were dependent on aboriginal labour. The end of construction released some 6,500 Chinese railway labourers into the wage-labour economy. The beginning of passenger service from eastern Canada brought another thirty-five thousand people into the province over the next six years. Aboriginal People were washed out of the capitalist economy by a flood of low-wage labour.

The immigrants that rode the rails into British Columbia were competitors for aboriginal jobs, and "white preference" became the order of the day. At work sites around the province, on the docks, on steamships, in the mills, even in public works, as the non-aboriginal population increased, whites were "naturally doing much of the work that fell to Indians in the past." This seemed natural to the white observers because whites were "our countrymen" and "our people." In the nineteenth century, this attitude came down from the top levels of government.

Indians were not one of "us," not citizens, not Canadian.[7] As the population of immigrants grew, and the aboriginal population shrank, the newcomers established legal frameworks that ensured that Aboriginal People remained within the definition established for them. Increasingly, federal, provincial, and municipal regulations limited the extent to which Aboriginal People would be allowed to integrate into the capitalist economy.

The very missionaries and government agents who wanted to make Aboriginal People into capitalists began undermining their success in the capitalist economy at an early date. In 1885, the long-standing campaign by missionaries against the potlatch system was taken up by the federal government, which banned the potlatch, the central element of the west coast prestige economy. Missionaries and government agents correctly identified the potlatch as the centrepiece of the *non*-capitalist economic system that formed the foundation of Northwest Coast society. They incorrectly identified it as *anti*-capitalist. The potlatch was what had motivated the Lekwungen and other coastal people to accept the capitalist economy, and it continued to be their main reason for working for pay.

In fact, the anti-potlatch laws were not immediately effective. Although the number and size of potlatches diminished soon after the laws were imposed, coastal people continued to potlatch on a smaller scale. After the turn of the century, more vigorous enforcement of the laws drove the potlatch underground, further diminishing the vitality of the prestige economy. The more successful the colonizers were in breaking aboriginal culture, the more they eroded Aboriginal People's cultural reasons for working.

In the nineteenth century, Aboriginal People could work seasonally at skilled or well-paid jobs. In the twentieth century, Aboriginal People were increasingly confined to an economic niche consisting of low-wage seasonal labour. Restricted by a variety of state policies from entering agriculture, the hospitality industry, or public works; disadvantaged vis-à-vis whites in the fishing and logging industry; and, due to racism, the last hired in the expanding retail and white-collar sectors, Aboriginal People were limited to taking jobs no one else wanted. Employers, while reluctant to hire Aboriginal People as permanent employees, were delighted to have a labour pool that could be called upon a few months a year. Obviously, Aboriginal People did not choose to be paid low wages and to have access only to the jobs associated with a low socioeconomic niche. But seasonal labour did have some advantages for Aboriginal People, allowing them to be free of the capitalist economy for much of the year and so be able to pursue their own economic and cultural goals.[8] In the late twentieth century, even this niche was disappearing.

In the socioeconomic niche inhabited by Aboriginal People, schooling was of no great advantage. The work open to them did not require education, and children, as subsistence and agricultural harvesters and fish canners, were valuable contributors to the family economy. Education, for

Work, for the Night Is Coming

Mamook, polatkely chaco,
Work, for the night is coming,
Mamook miltite sitcum sun;
Work through the sunny noon;
Pahlt t'waugh sun kopa mamook,
Fill brightest hours with labor,
Kopet mamook tenas alki.
Rest comes sure and soon.
Potlatch conaway kawok sun.
Give every flying minute
Mitlite, wake potlatch pee mika.
Something to keep in store.
Mammok, polatkely chaco,
Work for the night is coming,
Konsi man kopet mamook.
When man works no more.

Laura B. Downey-Bartlett, *Chinook-English Songs*, 1914

Aboriginal boys learning trades at St Mary's residential school, Mission, BC, 1905

most Aboriginal families, meant sending their children far away to schools that were culturally foreign and often abusive. The DIA- and church-run schools operated well below provincial schools with regard to budget, teacher training, and curriculum. Moreover, the training that was provided was directed towards low-skill jobs rather than what was needed to ensure success in the new economy. It should be no surprise that, in 1970, only 14.7 percent of Aboriginal People had completed their high school education. Most were in no position to take advantage of white-collar job opportunities.[9]

The low-skill sectors of the economy occupied by aboriginal workers in the mid-twentieth century were among the most vulnerable to technological change. The 1950s saw the closure of numerous fish canneries around the province, including the Empire Cannery (which had sustained the Lekwungen), as freezing technology and economies of scale resulted in the industry being consolidated into a few large canneries in Vancouver and Prince Rupert. The 1960s saw mechanization close the hop fields to seasonal labour, and by the 1980s, they were all gone. Large industrial logging operations, with union labour hired in Vancouver, displaced the small-scale gypo loggers, who relied on local labour; and mechanization displaced the haying and fencing crews that had injected cash into the Tsilhqot'in economy.

Throughout the fur trade era, and when the province was sparsely settled by newcomers, Aboriginal Peoples had a viable alternative to the European economy. However, between 1870 and 1970, depending on the proximity to growing urban and agricultural settlement, the subsistence economy became less and less viable. The first Northwest Coast group to be affected was the Lekwungen, who saw the city of Victoria overtake their lands and bays. In 1887, the Indian Agent began informing his supervisor that the settlement of Lekwungen territory and, more important, the enforcement of new game and fishing laws meant that the subsistence economy was no longer a full-time option. Urban Aboriginal People would face starvation if they could not get work. In 1888, the DIA began issuing relief to the elderly and destitute among the Lekwungen, a "temporary measure" that initiated a new, parallel, and long-term "welfare economy."

By the 1940s and 1950s, with the expansion of settlement and the enforcement of fishing and game regulations, along with the growth of industrial activity like logging, mining, and the building of hydro-electric dams, even Aboriginal People as isolated as the Tsilhqot'in found that their subsistence economy could no longer support them. Squeezed from their niche in the wage economy and faced with severe limitations on their subsistence economy, many turned to the only option that was expanding in the 1950s and 1960s – the welfare economy. In fact, there is a lot of government correspondence acknowledging that welfare was a substitution for food they formerly harvested from the land and sea.

In looking back over nearly a century of aboriginal work history, it is evident that, since the 1880s, Aboriginal People had become, in several senses of the phrase, "a reserve army of the unemployed" for the capitalist economy of southern British Columbia and northern Washington State. Although, at any given time, some worked in skilled trades or the professions and a few became wealthy, the majority were drawn into the capitalist economy once it boomed, as it did in the period between 1907 and 1913 and 1940 and 1949; otherwise, they were only involved in it for short seasons of the year. When the economy slumped, preference was given to "the poor whites" and "Indians" were let go. Given this, many Aboriginal People created a moditional economy that consisted of a mixture of low-wage seasonal employment for the whole family, subsistence harvesting and intra-village sharing, and, later, relief and welfare.

Through the aboriginal experience, we can see that the "state" was not a single entity but, rather, a hydra-headed being that pursued many different policies at once, some of which were at odds with others and some of which, at least on particular issues, supported Aboriginal People. The objectives of the federal DIA, when contrasted with the objectives of the more powerful federal Department of Fisheries and the provincial Game Branch, explain much about the extension of a welfare economy to Aboriginal People. "Welfare colonialism" was not something the state moved into willingly.[10] Relief was paid to Aboriginal People by one state agency, the DIA, primarily because the regulations of the other state agencies limited aboriginal access to both the subsistence and the cash economies.

When we consider the complex notions of welfare and relief, we see in the historical conversations numerous examples of how the understandings of the government and of Aboriginal Peoples clearly diverged. In aboriginal communities in British Columbia, food was a resource that had to be shared. In the coastal cultures, where wealth was unevenly distributed, the wealthy were obliged to take care of the poor. To maintain one's high status meant regularly delivering food and wealth to other people. State relief was initially given as food to the old and infirm, whose families had died or could no longer support them. Relief was easily assimilated into the aboriginal version of a subsistence/prestige economy, in which those who had food, like the Indian Agent, were obliged to share it with those who did not. When an Indian Agent distributed food as relief, this action was referred to by the Chinook jargon word "potlatch" and was compatible with the aboriginal view that this was the agent's responsibility — something he had to do in order to maintain his status. Add to this the feeling

We Would Work All the Time

No matter if there is work, wherever he goes an Indian is called a Siwash and suppose he is a Siwash he is not given the work. We would work all the time if they would give us work.

Wilson, a Nuxalk from Kimsquit, to the McKenna-McBride Royal Commission, August 22, 1913

that non-Aboriginal People had deprived Aboriginal People of the ability to harvest their country food, and the obligation of the government to provide and the entitlement of the First Nations to receive increased. Clearly, Aboriginal People had a different understanding of state support payments than did the government and most non-Aboriginal Canadians.

Even in the welfare economy, the preference for "poor whites" persisted. Job preference was given to whites because "Indians" were said to be a public charge and so eligible for state support. In fact, the welfare state supported Aboriginal People to a lesser degree than it did other Canadians. For example, non-Aboriginal People started receiving old age security more than twenty years before registered Indians, and, until 1965, relief and/or welfare rates paid to Aboriginal People were considerably lower than were those paid to their non-aboriginal neighbours. Aboriginal People in Canada found themselves squeezed between the racist notion that they were a public charge, declining employment opportunities, and a shrinking subsistence economy.

Weeping Woman Totem, at Anspayaxw, showing a woman clutching a grouse caught too late to save her brother from starvation, 1994

Changes since 1970

In many ways, Aboriginal Peoples in British Columbia hit bottom around 1970. Although their numbers had been growing since the 1930s, their economies had been shrinking and their dependence on government welfare had been increasing, as had social problems. At the end of the 1960s, Aboriginal People in BC were eight times more likely to be dependent on government welfare payments than were members of the general population. Over 60 percent of aboriginal families in BC lived below the poverty line, compared to 21 percent of non-aboriginal families living in comparable communities. The average family income for registered Indians was only 58 percent that of non-Indians. Off-reserve Indians did not fare much better, with an unemployment rate of 46.5 percent. This was the time when the chief of the Lekwungen, on the outskirts of Victoria, warned that his people were facing starvation.[11]

Culturally, aboriginal communities were also at a low ebb. Up until 1970, there had been no support for aboriginal languages, no cultural centres, no formalized artist training. Alcoholism was probably at its peak, along with all the social disorganization and dysfunction that followed the deliberate attempt to erase aboriginal culture in residential schools and that goes with being poor. It was a time when Aboriginal People were embarrassed or ashamed to be "Indians," when they watched western movies and pretended they were the cowboys.[12] In the social sciences, the dominant model for cultural change had been "acculturation," which translates into the undermining and replacing of aboriginal cultures. In everyday life all over rural British Columbia, signs indicated that no "Indians" were allowed in restaurants and stores.[13]

Aboriginal Canada has changed considerably in the last thirty to forty years. One of the most significant changes involves the fact that Aboriginal People have organized and joined a dialogue with Canadians and that they are speaking with powerful, confident voices. The spark that pushed the disparate Aboriginal Peoples in Canada to come together was the infamous White Paper, which was introduced by the Liberal government of Pierre Elliott Trudeau in 1969 and which proposed legislation to wipe out Indian status and rights. Aboriginal groups formed nationally, provincially, and regionally to protest this action and to pressure for the acknowledgment of aboriginal rights.

The 1970s saw a cultural revival spread through Aboriginal Canada, partly inspired by the Black Power Movement and the Civil Rights Movement in the United States as well as by international decolonization movements. The American Indian Movement (AIM) gained a high profile and encouraged a positive self-image for Aboriginal Peoples, and in the

I Wouldn't Employ One

Well, I for one wouldn't trust an Indian. As far as employing one, I wouldn't have any confidence at all. They're shiftless ... they're not capable of punching a time clock, they are willing to stay on the reserve and just be lazy and self indulgent.

Anonymous white woman, interviewed for the 1961 CBC radio program, *The Way of the Indian*

1970s AIM came to Canada. This process was fostered by new government programs designed to encourage a soft multiculturalism. The DIA responded with attempts to encourage self-sufficiency through rebuilding cultural pride by funding language and cultural programs. At the same time, federal employment initiatives (e.g., the Winter Works Program, the Local Employment Program, the Youth Employment Program) directed funding into cultural projects. Further, Canada and British Columbia formally acknowledged the problem of a continuing systemic racism by implementing human rights legislation that strengthened laws (and the enforcement of laws) against racist practices. When the Canadian Constitution was codified in 1982, aboriginal rights were specifically protected by Section 35.

Aboriginal People began to speak through the courts after decades of being prohibited by the Indian Act from hiring lawyers. In 1973, a major watershed was reached with the Supreme Court decision on the *Calder* case, where the judges split evenly on the question of whether the Nisga'a in northwestern British Columbia still had aboriginal title over their ancestral land. This launched the federal government into land title negotiations with groups across Canada, including the Nisga'a (a negotiation that BC joined in 1989). Treaties acknowledging those aboriginal rights were signed in the Yukon, in the Northwest Territories, by the James Bay Cree, and, finally, by the Nisga'a in 1999. Just a year earlier, a new federal territory, Nunavut, was created, with a population and government dominated by indigenous people.

Other court-based dialogues have shifted the basis of discussion between Aboriginal and non-Aboriginal Peoples. The *Delgamuukw* case launched by the Gitksan-Wet'suwet'en was referred to the Supreme Court, which decided in 1997 that the case should be reheard, with aboriginal oral history being given more weight by the courts. This is a hopeful sign that aboriginal voices will be heard in the courts and that the courtroom will be a space for a renewed dialogue. The courts also established that Aboriginal Peoples still have title to all land that was not surrendered by a specific treaty, and this includes practically all the land in British Columbia. Makúk, as I have said, refers to an exchange that can go either way. Some of the power, land, and resources that have flowed from Aboriginal Peoples to non-Aboriginal People in the last two centuries are on the verge of flowing back.

Public attention has been drawn to title issues by high-profile civil disobedience at Oka, Quebec; Ipperwash, Ontario; Gustafson Lake, British Columbia (in Tsilhqot'in territory); and at Burnt Church, New Brunswick. There was also a high-profile Royal Commission on Aboriginal Peoples that ran from 1991 to 1996.

Real change has been brought to aboriginal communities by an amendment to the Indian Act known as Bill C-31, which aimed to eliminate gender discrimination and resulted in 100,000 women and children successfully applying to have their status and federal rights as Indians reinstated. We have also seen the elimination of the position of "Indian Agent" and the transfer of the administration of most government, education, and social welfare services to bands, tribal councils, and other aboriginal organizations.

Educational levels have risen dramatically. In the 1970s, residential schools were phased out, the last one closing in 1988, and aboriginal children have been integrated into provincial schools. By 1991, only one-third of Aboriginal People did not have a high school education (compared to one-quarter of all Canadians), while university completion attendance rates were almost on par with the Canadian average.[14] Increased education and the transfer of the control of administration to band and tribal council levels meant that employment in government services has shot up. Government services employ six out of every ten employed Aboriginal People on-reserve – twice the rate for all Canadians.[15]

On a cultural level, potlatching has been reestablished in most coastal aboriginal communities in British Columbia. To give one example, a recent potlatch in Alert Bay reportedly involved the redistribution of $250,000 worth of goods from one family to its extended community. In Coast Salish communities, sacred winter dancing occurs every weekend of the season, and the summer pow wows, a cultural import from the Prairies, attract many Aboriginal People. Aboriginal-run cultural centres and museums now exist throughout the province, as do language training programs and sporting events. Not only do Aboriginal People want to be "Indians" today, so do many "wannabees" – people with few cultural or biological ties to indigenous communities.[16]

Today

In the last three decades, the economic and cultural situation of Aboriginal Peoples has improved dramatically. The legislative and other visible traces of racism have diminished, and the dialogue between Aboriginal and non-Aboriginal Canadians has been given much more prominence. However, the history and the misunderstanding chronicled in this book are still very much with us.

Economically, Aboriginal People are still the poorest people in Canada, poorer even than other "visible minority groups." In 1996 (the most recent data available), the on-reserve population had an average annual income of $12,245, just under half of the $25,196 average of Canadians in general. Other indexes reflect their relative impoverishment. At least 44

Education Has Largest Impact

There has been change for the better in the last 30 years. The largest single impact has been education. The federal vote in 1960 was the turning point.

The Honourable Leonard (Len) Marchand, Okanagan, in the film *A Forgotten Legacy: Spirit of Reclamation* (2002)

percent of the aboriginal population and a full 60 percent of aboriginal children under the age of six, and 85 percent of those over sixty-five, lived below Statistics Canada's poverty line. There are also gaps in terms of family and housing arrangements. The homes of Aboriginal People on-reserve are over six times more likely to be overcrowded than are the homes of Canadians as a whole (31 percent compared with 5 percent). Dependency on government support is still a major issue. In 1991 (the most recent comparison available), government transfer payments made up 19 percent of on-reserve income compared to 4 percent of the average Canadian's income.[17]

In 1996, the unemployment rate among Aboriginal People, on- or off-reserve, was more than two and half times the average for all Canadians. Health Canada notes that "unemployed people have a reduced life expectancy and suffer more health problems than people who have a job." This is borne out in a 1999 study linking unemployment with a "pervasive and pernicious impact on health," including premature mortality, high levels of psychological distress, and emotional and behavioural childhood problems. The health of Aboriginal People in their home communities is ranked sixty-second in the world, compared to Canada's overall second place. On-reserve Indians live lives that were, on average, ten years shorter than those of non-Aboriginal Canadians.[18]

Although there have been gains in some areas, a study for the Royal Commission on Aboriginal Peoples showed that, overall, "Aboriginal Canadians experienced a lower level of economic well being in 1990 than in 1980 and that the income gap between aboriginal and non-aboriginal populations grew during the period." Other reports show the same decline between 1986 and 1996. Robin Armstrong's 2001 study suggests a relative erosion in the circumstances of coastal regions of British Columbia over that period.[19]

Average incomes underrepresent both poverty and wealth in aboriginal communities as, since 1971, there has been a growing disparity in income and wealth among registered Indians. Generally, off-reserve Indians have higher earnings and lower unemployment than do their on-reserve counterparts, but here, too, there is a vast disparity. Half of all registered Indians living in urban areas in 1995 fell below the poverty line, compared to one-quarter of other Canadians. Moreover, there is a great disparity between aboriginal communities. Armstrong identified 154 "better off" communities, located primarily in northern Quebec, mid- and southern Ontario, and in British Columbia's southern and coastal regions. These show quite different profiles than do 213 "typical communities" and 124 "high disparity" poor communities. Yet, even the best of these communities, Armstrong says, "compare only with the poorest regions of non-aboriginal Canada."

While Canada tops the United Nations index for the highest quality of life in the world, on-reserve Indians rank sixty-fifth on the same index, on par with Brazil.[20]

It is hard to isolate data for British Columbia from that for Canada. A study conducted by the Caledonian Institute using 1996 data shows that, despite pockets of better-off communities, BC Aboriginal People had the fourth highest unemployment for Aboriginal People in Canada. The aboriginal unemployment rate in British Columbia (at 27 percent) was three times the rate for all British Columbians. In Vancouver, half of all Aboriginal People lived below the poverty line compared to one-quarter of non-Aboriginal People. In rural communities it is even worse. In 1999, Chief Archie Pootlas of the Nuxalk estimated that 80 percent of his people were unemployed and that the band's biggest budget item was welfare. "This is criminal," he said, "when you look at the resource rich region we live in."[21]

The last thirty years have affected the Straits Salish and Tsilhqot'in differently. The Straits Salish on Saanich Peninsula and in Victoria have benefited economically from the increased value of their land as the City of Victoria and suburbs have expanded. The two urban bands, the Lekwungen and the Esquimalt, have been able to lease their lands to industrial, commercial, and residential users, and this has provided a steady stream of income into the communities. Due to the lands having been subdivided into "locations," with the rights to each location held by individuals in the bands, this wealth is not shared equally but, rather, flows to specific families.

Lekwungen voices are increasingly being heard in local decisions. The Lekwungen have two seats on the new Harbour Authority, which has assumed federal responsibilities for land- and water-use decisions around the Victoria and Esquimalt harbours. The Songhees and Esquimalt bands have cooperated to purchase urban land for joint tourism ventures and launched a lawsuit to reclaim the land upon which the Legislative Buildings sit (land that was promised them in the Douglas Treaty). The two bands settled out of court in 2006 for $31.5 million.[22]

The changes have been more dramatic for the Tsilhqot'in than for the Lekwungen. The Chilcotin, in 1970, may have been the last part of Canada where horses and horse-drawn carts were still the major form of transportation. The last thirty years have seen a shift from horse culture to truck culture as roads reached the last of the Tsilhqot'in communities in the 1970s, and telephones reached them in 2000. In the 1970s, it was still possible for a few individuals, like Chiwid, to live in the bush, totally independent of government and largely independent of other people. According to her biographer, Sage Birchwater, "Chiwid couldn't live in the Chilcotin today."[23]

We Claim the Legislative Buildings

The Defendant, Her Majesty the Queen in Right of British Columbia (the "Province") is the occupier of the British Columbia Legislative Buildings which are located on lands to which the Plaintiffs hold treaty rights.

Songhees and Esquimalt Bands, "Statement of Claim," Supreme Court of British Columbia, August 23, 2001

The last three decades have also seen a shift away from hunting and ranching to wage work and the increasing presence of state welfare assistance. Gilbert Solomon, a Nemiah band councillor, suggested that when social assistance came people "did not hustle enough" to get their own food nor did they "go so far into the bush." People stopped gardening and, instead, would make an hour's drive into Williams Lake to buy potatoes and carrots. As mentioned in Chapter 5, Joe Alphonse, director of government services for the Tsilhqot'in National Government, put it this way: "Reliance on the land decreased. Reliance on Overwaitea increased."[24] At Redstone, Chief Charleyboy thought that the arrival of welfare in the 1970s contributed to the demise of trapping: "People just did not leave the reserve. It totally changed the lifestyle of the Chilcotin." Today, there are still sixty traplines registered to Aboriginal People in the Cariboo-Chilcotin District, but few are used, and these comprise only one-quarter of all registered traplines. According to Gilbert Solomon, "It was like we put a blanket on our heads. We all zeroed in on this path DIA put us on. People became more dependent."[25]

The decades of dislocation were also decades of despair. The opening of the Chilcotin allowed easier access to alcohol. At one point, alcoholism rates reached 90 percent in neighbouring Alkali Lake, and it was not much below that in many other communities.

Roads have given the Tsilhqot'in access to the rest of the world, but they have also given the rest of the world access to the Tsilhqot'in. New transportation corridors have made the Chilcotin forests accessible to multinational forest companies based in Williams Lake. With a "blanket" over their heads, the Tsilhqot'in have not been able to mount any effective opposition to industrial logging, which stretched to the west Chilcotin in the 1980s. With logging came environmental degradation as well as roads that gave non-local hunters access to game. One-fifth of the big game guiding operations in the province are now located in the Cariboo-Chilcotin area.

The seeds of revival were planted in 1979-80, when, in a statement of independence, the Kluskus band, just north of Tsilhqot'in territory, refused welfare payments and federal government support payments. In the 1980s, the Alkali Lake band gained national prominence for its sobriety campaign, which dried up the village; and in 1989, the Xeni Gwet'in issued the Nemiah Declaration, proclaiming their ownership of traditional territories and their opposition to industrial logging. In 1992, this was backed by a roadblock at Henry's Crossing to prevent logging. In 1993, the Xeni Gwet'in signed a co-management plan that brought into being Ts'il?os Provincial Park, which protected a large swath of their territory from logging. In 1998, they began to work with the David Suzuki Foundation on ecologically sustainable forestry and development, and they have pulled out of timber-sharing negotiations with major timber firms. The Xeni Gwet'in led the Tsilhqot'in in a court case claiming full title to their traditional land. In November 2007, BC Supreme Court Justice David Vickers agreed with them and accepted their title claim, although he left the definition of title to future negotiation or litigation.[26]

Other bands were also undergoing an economic and cultural revival. In 1994-95, the Ulkatcho band at Anahim Lake took a different approach from the Xeni Gwet'in, buying a one-third share in a sawmill and industrial logging operation in their territory. The arrangement saw employment levels jump from 35 percent to 85 percent, although, according to Chief Cassidy Sill, this brought its own social problems. Increased cash circulating in the community, some of it passed on to extended family, increased access to alcohol and drugs. As a result, there are more funerals in Ulkatcho, he said, than in all the other Tsilhqot'in communities combined.[27]

Other bands have started their own logging, ranching, or retail businesses and have taken over their own administration, providing some stable jobs in their communities. The Ulkatcho Band, for example, owns a logging company that in April 2005 signed a land use agreement with the Province of British Columbia and local stakeholders covering 700,000 hectares that protects cultural, wildlife, and tourism values, and allocates timber to the forest industry.[28]

The economic improvements have been accompanied by a cultural and political revival. The past three decades have seen the construction of new local schools at most of the Tsilhqot'in communities, and the latter have considerable control over the former, where the Tsilhqot'in language is now being taught. In the mid-1980s, a shift began to be visible as women became the stable income earners in the family, often working in government-sector administrative or social programs.[29]

Several political events have galvanized the Tsilhqot'in. In 1993, the Cariboo-Chilcotin Justice Inquiry toured Tsilhqot'in communities and listened to aboriginal complaints about how they had been treated. The commissioner, Judge Anthony Sarich, concluded that one of the key problems was a lack of communication between non-Aboriginal People (especially the police) and Aboriginal People. One of the many recommendations to emerge from the inquiry (besides more dialogue) was to pardon the Tsilhqot'in chiefs hung in 1864 for defending their territory. In October 1999, the provincial government officially apologized for the hangings and erected a commemorative plaque, describing the injustice and honouring the hanged.

Part-Time Capitalists, Part-Time Hunter-Gatherers

Within the span of a couple of months [Tsilhqot'in] individuals help cousins with fencing contracts, work as teaching assistants, hunt, take temporary welfare, receive dried salmon from siblings, sell cows, substitute at the local post office and drag neighbor's hunted game out of the woods. Part-time capitalists, part-time peasants, part-time hunter-gatherers.

David Dinwoodie, "Reserve Memories: Historical Consciousness on the Nemiah Valley Indian Reserve," 1996

Talking...

Talking. Twenty years go by and we are still talking.

Gilbert Solomon, Nemiah [Tsilhqot'in] councillor, Nemiah Band Office, August 23, 2000

View of James Douglas's Indian Policy

The best reply is given by the Indians in their own words in the classical "Chinook": – "*Hiyu closh wawa pe wake consick mamook coqua,*" which, being rendered into English, would read – "He gives many good words but never performs."

Columbian, June 8, 1864

The Dead Are Not Powerless

At night, when the streets of your cities and villages are silent, they will throng with the returning hosts that once filled them and still love this beautiful land. The White Man will never be alone. Let him be just and deal kindly with my people. For the dead are not powerless.

Attributed to Chief Seattle, Duwamish, likely erroneously, in a column by Dr. Henry A. Smith, *Seattle Sunday Star,* October 29, 1887

Between the commission of inquiry recommending more police sensitivity to Aboriginal People and the apology for the conduct of the 1864 Chilcotin War, the Canadian military and RCMP mounted a second paramilitary invasion of Tsilhqot'in territory in 1995 to counter the occupation of a campsite at Gustafson Lake. A small aboriginal group of between ten and fifteen had used a lakeside campsite for seasonal religious ceremonies for years, but in 1995 decided to stay on. A local rancher claimed rights to the campsite and obtained an injunction to force them to leave. This launched the biggest RCMP operation in Canadian history, involving over a hundred officers, about the same number dispatched to the Chilcotin in 1864, as well as the modern accoutrements of war: military advisors, helicopters, and armoured personnel carriers. Thousands of rounds of ammunition were expended, one gun battle lasting forty-five minutes. Miraculously, there were only slight injuries. The incident concluded with a brokered surrender and a trial in which the police were widely excoriated for their conduct and for their manipulation of the media. The principal aboriginal participants received minor convictions. Although the main aboriginal figures were from other First Nations, the events played out in Tsilhqot'in territory and showed how little state attitudes had shifted from 1864, and they emphasized just how much dialogue is needed.

Final Words

Makúk: A New History of Aboriginal-White Relations documents the arrival of a European capitalist economy in aboriginal territory and the transformation of aboriginal subsistence and prestige economies into "moditional" economies that included wage labour and welfare. The current features of that economy – high unemployment and high rates of welfare dependency – have arisen only in the last fifty years. This is something that has slipped out of public consciousness, out of the awareness of those who make policy affecting Aboriginal Peoples, and out of the memories of the younger generations of British Columbia's Aboriginal Peoples themselves.

"Indians" have been vanished from our history books and, in many cases, from our communities. In Victoria, as Robin Ward observed, the Lekwungen "seem a phantom presence in land that was once their own." Perhaps that is because, as Avery Gordon observes, "to write stories concerning exclusion and invisibility is to write ghost stories." Canadians are haunted by the unfinished business of colonization and a collective guilt over historic injustices and our contemporary relationships with Aboriginal Peoples.[30]

Although Aboriginal Peoples comprise only 3 percent of the people in Canada and many live in relative poverty, isolated on small pockets of land, they are not marginal to Canadian society. Aboriginal Peoples have been and continue to be at the centre of what it means to be Canadian. The state has placed them at the centre of a vast bureaucracy, first, to effect the transfer of their land to other Canadians. The country's very legitimacy, or lack of it, depends on the justice of that transfer and now to revitalize the aboriginal economies it has so effectively handicapped.

This book starts by asking about the "Indian problem" and concludes by identifying "the white problem." Having removed Aboriginal Peoples from their resource base, labelled them "lazy" or difficult employees, and relegated many of them to the bottom of the occupational scale, our treatment of them has become a standard by which, as Canadians, we measure ourselves. The poverty and attendant social problems on aboriginal reserves has been an international embarrassment for this country for over a century. It is repeatedly brought up by the press as a national scandal, a sobering reminder to Canadians who like to think of themselves as a "generous people" living in a "just society."[31]

Makúk was the word that Aboriginal People on the Pacific Coast used to draw Europeans into a conversation, and together they parlayed it into a new language: Chinook jargon. Chinook is no longer the universal intermediary between Aboriginal and non-Aboriginal Peoples in British Columbia, but it has not disappeared. Like the people who are intermingled, the words of the jargon are a mixture of English and aboriginal languages. Linguist Kyle Campbell notes that dictionaries of most regional aboriginal languages include a smattering of Chinook jargon "loan words," while the *Oxford English Dictionary* lists eighteen words of Chinook jargon (including Siwash, muckamuck, potlatch, skookum, cheechako, and salt-chuck). Chinook jargon has become part of all of us.

Linguists can discern a distinctive regional dialect in British Columbia and the Pacific Northwest in the use of Chinook words. From Siwash Rock at the entrance to Vancouver Harbour to Wawa Creek in Haida Gwaii, the jargon (*wawa*) is also inscribed on our landscape: hundreds of lakes, rivers, and mountains are named in that language. Chinook jargon is part of a regional identity that is neither fully Aboriginal nor fully European.[32]

In Chinook jargon, *mamook* means "to do" and "to work." The aboriginal communities under consideration evidently attached a different meaning to the idea of work than did the newcomers. In our present era, where hard work for long hours is defined as our salvation and our duty, where workaholics are hailed as role models, and where books such as *High on Stress* are on the bestseller list, perhaps Canadians should consider the history of alternative definitions. Aboriginal culture encourages work and the accumulation of wealth, but that wealth has no meaning unless given

Rain Language

Leland mitlite
The language lingers,

Halo chako, halo mahsh
not arriving, not leaving

kopa ole shanites
In old songs

pe kopa nems
and in names

tzum kopa illahie
written on the country

Tzum Point, Boston Bar, Chikamin Bay, Snass Creek ... Kopa nems tzum kopa illahie
In the names written on the country

tsaiko cooley chako halo kah
ghosts walk out of nowhere

pe mammok tuletule kopa nesika laboos
and touch our lips.

Leloo Island, NaitchPea, Lebahdo Station, Illahee meadow.

Excerpt from Terry Glavin's Chinook-English poem, "Rain Language," in Charles Lillard and Terry Glavin, *A Voice Great within Us*

Terry Glavin

Wisdom in Sustaining a Conversation

To see wisdom as consisting in the ability to sustain a conversation is to see human beings as generators of new descriptions rather than beings one hopes to be able to describe accurately.

Richard Rorty, *Philosophy and the Mirror of Nature*, 1979

away. Aboriginal economies saw "leisure time" as economically productive since it was through recreation that family relationships and community were recreated and extended, and this was vital to economic as well as to cultural well-being. Immigrants succeeded in making individual acquisitiveness for selfish purposes the ideal for North America, but it may be that the alternative model that tied work to need, and wealth to redistribution, is needed now more than ever.

There are hopeful signs for a new dialogue in some legal decisions (such as *Haida Nation v. B.C. and Weyerhaeuser*, 2002; *Regina v. Marshall*, 1999; *Delgamuukw v. B.C., 1997*; and *Regina v. Sparrow, 1990*), some non-governmental organizations (such as the David Suzuki Foundation), the Royal Commission on Aboriginal Affairs Report, the treaty process, and a new generation of indigenous leaders (including Taiaiake Alfred, Matthew Coon Come, and Mary Ellen Turpel-Lafond, for example). But there are also signs that there is not yet a will among non-Aboriginal Canadians to listen across the boundaries that so clearly exist, to hear alternative ideas. Racism has not gone away. Though there are many signs that it has diminished, in a 1995 survey almost one-fifth of Aboriginal People reported that racism limited their ability to get work. Progress in combatting racism has recently been undermined by the elimination of state-financed human rights agencies and the elimination of budgets for anti-racism education.[33]

The recommendations of the Royal Commission on Aboriginal Peoples have not been addressed or implemented by the Canadian government, which is still unilaterally revising the Indian Act over the objections of aboriginal political organizations. And governments are not honouring the 1997 Supreme Court *Delgamuukw* decision.[34] In 2002, the BC government, backed by the Forest Council of British Columbia, the BC Cattleman's Association, the British Columbia Chamber of Commerce, and the Business Council of British Columbia, argued that it had no legal or moral duty to consult with Aboriginal Peoples when they infringed upon aboriginal title.[35] There are powerful forces aligned against the redistribution of wealth in Canada, and "consultation" or "dialogue" will not occur without enormous judicial, state, and public pressure. Moreover, the courts and the state are not neutral in this process. The unevenness of the playing field is demonstrated in the *Delgamuukw* decision, which recognized aboriginal title at the same time as it reserved the power to legitimate what would count as acceptable translations of aboriginal history and testimony. We are reminded that dialogue does not mean that both parties speak from the same position of power, and that "dia-logue" is sometimes no more than "double talk." Today, when we *makúk*, we speak the same language and use the same words, but words such as "sovereignty," "title," "surrender," "taxes," "tradition," "environment," "obligation," "work," and "welfare" can have very different meanings for Aboriginal and non-Aboriginal Canadians, respectively. As a starting point, all of us, both Aboriginal and non-Aboriginal, need to shift to a place of creative understanding – a place that can only be approached through dialogue.

Alki nesika kunamokst wawa.

Postscript:
Subordination without Subjugation

We adjust what we say, and how we say it, in order to make ourselves better understood. We often try to enter into another's mood, or even worldview, to try to ensure that she or he hears what we say in such a way that it will produce the response we seek.

The observation that all deliberate communication takes the intended recipient into account is the essence of Mikhail Bakhtin's concept of dialogism, and Chinook jargon is an elaborate expression of dialogism. The jargon is an intentional hybrid language built by both sides of an exchange, the point being to enter into the worldview of another in order to be able to communicate with her/him. Initially a language of trade, it became a language of work, welfare, law, spirituality, love, loss, and poetry. It was the medium of communication, and, in important respects, Marshall McLuhan was right: "the medium is the message."

The existence of Chinook jargon and the notion of dialogism help us wrest the historical focus from the white explorer, trader, missionary, and entrepreneur, where it has largely rested, to the interaction between aboriginals and newcomers. This helps us to understand that the two sides of this dialogue were actively communicating, actively participating in a variety of exchanges, though they seldom had control over all aspects of it (and certainly not over the long-term direction of the interaction).

Cross-cultural dialogue is fraught with spaces of misunderstanding, of the "systematic misrecognition" of signs and meanings, and this leads to different understandings living within the same words. Objects, as they move from one culture to another, are transformed; and complex concepts, like wage labour and the economy, live different lives in different cultural contexts.

The trickster-like nature of exchange – where an item is, and is not, what it appears to be – helps explain much of the miscommunication and misunderstanding that has governed aboriginal/non-aboriginal relations (and the written history of those exchanges) through to the present day. Of all the examples one might point to, the Chinook jargon word "potlatch" is perhaps the best. Derived from a Nuu-chah-nulth word meaning "to give,"

◀ Painting of an aboriginal railway labourer with hops growing in the background, by Stó:lō Stan Greene

it came to mean, in Chinook jargon, "a gift, to give," to "give a speech" (*potlatch wawa*), and "wages" (*potlatch dolla*). It also came to mean any of the wide range of celebrations, feasts, or gatherings in which Aboriginal Peoples of the Northwest Coast gave gifts.

The fact that "potlatch" subsumes a wide range of community events – from marking deaths, to weddings, to the onset of a daughter's menstruation, to the passing on of names or privileges, and to the wiping away of shame – already suggests that there was lots of room for Europeans to misunderstand the goals and ideas behind potlatches. Northwest Coast peoples had joined the capitalist economy in order to acquire wealth so that they could host feasts at which they could give away wealth to those who attended and thus affirm the business of the potlatch. Europeans misunderstood the potlatch, seeing it as anti-capitalist because it was an occasion on which wealth was shared in and between communities, with the highest status being achieved by the one who gave away the most. Missionaries and government agents worked hard against "the potlatch," and in 1885, they were successful in having it banned by law. The ambiguities of Chinook jargon, however, frustrated this effort. When the first case was prosecuted, the judge, Matthew Baillie Begbie (who sentenced the seven Tsilhqot'in chiefs to death for their role in the Chilcotin War), threw it

Throwing blankets to crowd at Lekwungen Ches-lum George's potlatch, Songhees Reserve, 1895

out, noting that no definition had been provided for "potlatch" and, as the law was worded, any gift giving (perhaps even paying wages) would be rendered illegal. The winter dancing had been prohibited in the same statute, being referred to by the Chinook jargon word *Tamananawas*, but Begbie said what that meant "was utterly unknown here."[1]

The law against the gift-giving feast known as the potlatch was tightened in the 1890s through specific use of the English language (the language of the court), and prosecutions were then more successful. Around this time another meaning of the word "potlatch" appears: when Indian Agents distributed "relief," Aboriginal People thanked them for the "potlatch." In making this link, we see language undergoing dialogization and become aware of "competing definitions for the same things."[2] These competing definitions have existed – and still exist – side by side in the dialogue between Aboriginal and non-Aboriginal Peoples.

Another word that needs to be dialogized is "economy." Europeans, Canadians, statisticians, and historians have often seen Aboriginal People as existing outside the economy. We have applied a liberal, capitalist, and gendered idea of economy, using it with reference only to items exchanged in the capitalist market. This definition implies that people who have alternative economies – be they based on hunting and gathering, prestige gift-giving, welfare, or domestic production – are outside the "real" economy, that they are engaged in inferior activities and, therefore, are inferior people. If we move the liberal-capitalist notion of economy off centre stage and understand it as a particular socially and culturally constructed category that privileges the autonomy of the individual, disinterested exchange relationships, male labour, objective remuneration, and a distinctly Protestant work ethic, we make room to see different, and equally valid, alternatives. Aboriginal Peoples in British Columbia had such an alternative, fully elaborated economy in the eighteenth century, as they do today. In this alternative economy, personal relationships are privileged, exchange is not disinterested (as it occurs with relations and friends), remuneration is situational, and leisure constitutes valuable economic time. In such an economy, which is based on interpersonal relationships, it is in shared leisure activities that the community and interpersonal linkages necessary for individual and collective success are built.

Today, most Aboriginal People in British Columbia engage in the capitalist economy and participate, to some degree, in a subsistence economy through the community sharing of fish, meat, berries, labour, and/or other items. Many continue to participate in prestige economies while others participate in a welfare economy. This ability to integrate different economic systems has characterized Aboriginal People across North America for over two centuries. As David Dinwoodie, an anthropologist who worked among the Tsilhqot'in, affirms: "Native Americans typically put together their lives by doing a little bit of this and a little bit of that."[3]

Some people see today's Aboriginal Peoples as "caught between traditions that have not yet gone and a modernity that has not yet arrived"; however, as anthropologist Néstor García Canclini points out, Aboriginal Peoples have not failed to modernize or to choose between the modern and the traditional: they have chosen both. Capitalism has not replaced the traditional and the ancient but, rather, has been added to them. Both have been transformed in the process, resulting in what he calls "an apparent multi-temporal heterogeneity of modern culture."[4]

Charley Nowell, Kwakw̱aka'wakw mill worker, hop picker, sealer, fisherman, and performer, at World's Fair in St. Louis, 1904

One key feature that sets Aboriginal People apart in Canada concerns the fact that they have always had a non-capitalist alternative: the subsistence and prestige economies and, in the past five decades, the welfare economy. Although in the last century this has not brought them personal financial independence – as I have pointed out, more Aboriginal People than non-Aboriginal People are dependent on the welfare state – their alternative economies have ensured a cultural distinctiveness. While Aboriginal People have entered the capitalist-modern economy, they have not been totally captured by it.[5] It is this non-capitalist element in aboriginal culture that drove missionaries to reform them, that prompted employers to label them lazy, and that drives some of the anti-aboriginal racism that persists today. Another part of the paradox is that, when Aboriginal People do enter the capitalist economy, they are judged to be "inauthentic," assimilated, "just like white men," corrupted, and not deserving of any recognition or protection for their alleged distinctiveness. For Aboriginal Peoples it is a lose-lose situation: they are expected to choose between their culture and our economy, but economy *is* culture.

What is central is that Aboriginal Peoples have built themselves a new, distinctive economy out of the available options, choosing independence over any one of wage labour, state support, or "living off the land." This economy has yet to be named, and without a name we have not been able to clearly speak of it or, indeed, even "see it."[6] We have thought of it only as a hybrid economy, as something caught somewhere between a pure "traditional" economy and a pure "modern" or "capitalist" economy. It is far better to think of this economy as a novel creation – one that is as flexible and responsive to change as are capitalism and welfare capitalism. It is this economy within which aboriginal families everywhere operate, within which work and family intertwine. Such an economy needs to be named, and I have suggested the term "moditional."

The moditional economy, with its focus on families' choosing or emphasizing different modes as conditions change, covers indigenous peoples as well as rural and urban settler populations, historically and today. We all live within the moditional economy. The key modes of production and reproduction may be wages, state transfer payments, capitalist profit, family labour, or hunting and gathering. To say we are engaged in a moditional economy is to say that we are always engaged in more than one of these modes at a time and that the choices we make with respect to one are always dependent on our relationship to the others.

One of the "modes" in "moditional" was capitalist, and by linking up with that mode, Aboriginal People unwittingly stepped into a process that would subordinate them and their economies to capitalism and

Not in Picturesque Attire

Among the others who came to interview us was the son of the chief of the Achwilgate Hagwilget tribe. He was not dressed in the traditional picturesque attire of an Indian chief; one sees little of that phase of Indian life outside of Cooper's novels; nor had he come to question our right of way through the country. He was anxious simply to hire as one of those who should "pack" for us.

Daniel Gordon, *Mountain and Prairie*, 1880

Canadianism. Aboriginal People worked for wages, but wage labour also worked on them in many ways, both subtle and gross. Ritual changed as new items were incorporated into old forms. Ideas changed as the exposure to alien cultures created a critical distance, enabling Aboriginal People to reflect upon their own. Bodies were transformed, as when Northwest Coast Aboriginal Peoples gave up the practices of tattooing and cranial shaping. Aboriginal Peoples surely entered the European economy for reasons of their own, but they were transformed in the process.[7]

The moditional economy has been captured by neither neoclassical nor neo-Marxist models. In Canada, historians studying rural cultures have come closest to capturing it.[8] Priorities are set by the "maximization of culture" as well as by the "maximization of profit," and "profit" may accrue as much to the family or community as to the individual. Choices are not so much determined by the different modes of production within which people engage as they are by a dialogue between what people have to do and what they want to do. We all make our economic choices for reasons that are only explainable by reference to history and culture. Aboriginal history and culture embraces an economy and choices that are much wider than what is covered by mainstream "economics."

Dialogue is an imprecise art. We know from the vast postmodern literature that the words that are spoken are not necessarily the words that are heard, that each of us will understand the same words (the connotations, the intonation, the stresses) in our own way. But dialogue is not random. Most of our daily conversations are not idle ramblings but purposive acts. We may have a discussion with our boss about our work performance, with a colleague about another whom we want to promote or demote, with a salesperson trying to get the best deal. In each, one may have more power than the other to set the agenda, while the other may be able to derail it.

On a societal level, individuals or groups may succeed in derailing the agenda in one conversation with representatives of certain structures of power; however, the state, church, and corporations have powerful rewards and sanctions with which to constantly set the terms of conversation. Even putting aside their coercive power, the sheer longevity and human mass of the state, church, and corporations will outlast the individual, family, tribe, and community. A dialogic relationship does not imply an equal relationship; on the contrary, power operates through dialogue to benefit some at the expense of others.

Capitalist work, Christian teaching, public education through residential and/or day schools, and the regulation of aboriginal life through legislation were all key elements in the "peaceable subordination" of Aboriginal

Peoples in Canada. The new European social system held labourers in low esteem (even as it gave primacy to labour as the source of value) and considered Aboriginal People to be lazy and unproductive (even as these people provided the workforce in all the early industries). Aboriginal men, women, and children were constantly found wanting when assessed by the measures of capitalism. As the supply of white labour grew, "white preference" pushed Aboriginal People out of the skilled and semi-skilled jobs, and they were increasingly confined by racialized European beliefs, which held that "Indians" were barely suitable for menial work. Discursively, Aboriginal Peoples were vanished from "the economy"; practically, their participation provided the resources that enabled it to expand, and their land provided the resources upon which it was based.

At an ontological level, capitalist work introduced Aboriginal People to the values of newcomer society – values that were both selectively incorporated and destabilizing. At first, wage work was of benefit to Aboriginal People, but their inclusion in capitalist work places brought them into a social system that valued subordination, industrial time-discipline, individualism, and private property – all of which were ideas that clashed with those embedded in their subsistence and prestige economies.[9]

To the extent that wages and cash came to be considered individual property, wage work reinforced the message of the church and state: the autonomy of the individual, which was promoted but never fully offered to Aboriginal People. Wage work also privileged the young, strong, and malleable and reversed the wealth-power pyramid that had historically favoured the old, knowledgeable, and traditional.

Aboriginal People were subordinated to the immigrant state through the regimes of wage work, missionization, education, and supervision but – and the terminology is important here – they were not subjugated. "To subordinate" derives from "*ordain*: to put and keep in order, to regulate, govern, direct, manage, and conduct." Ordain has another meaning: to raise up and bring into a religious order, where one's will comes second to that of the order. The stated goal of the Canadian relationship to its indigenous peoples combined both senses of the term "subordinate."

"Subjugation," on the other hand, means "to bring under the yoke of." The history of aboriginal/non-aboriginal relations shows that, while this was the realpolitik side of the loftier pronouncements regarding the inclusion of Aboriginal Peoples, the state has failed to harness them to the plough. And it has failed both in the literal sense of making farmers of a non-agricultural people and in the metaphorical sense of bringing them under complete control. The confusion of dominance with hegemony, and the confusion of hegemony with collaboration, is widespread in the literature,

A World That Demands We Hoard

It became unlawful for the Indians to give away their worldly possessions to their fellow man, or to engage in any manner whatsoever in any festival, dance, or other ceremony ... That urge to give is still in his blood. Just as it is in yours to save and store away for the morrow because it has been hammered into your very soul for centuries and more. That is why he (the Indian) is in a quandary this day. He feels the old teaching in a world that demands one to grab, to take and to hoard.

George Clutesi, Nuu-chah-nulth, "The Viewpoint of the Native Indian," ca. 1950

Invisible Peoples

As we live through our daily lives as Indians, eventually we become accustomed to the fact that non-native people can see right through us ... We simply mean that the majority of non-native people view us as Invisible Peoples who really should not exist outside museums.

Ruby Dunstan, former chief of the Lytton Band, 1986

but these terms are not synonymous. Aboriginal Peoples have been subordinated but not subjugated. As Ranajit Guha puts it, the state has achieved dominance without hegemony.

So long as we keep the silence, so long as we continue to "vanish," or, in literary scholar Renée Bergland's, words, "ghost" Indians, we will continue to be doomed to revisit the site of our haunting – the history of aboriginal/non-aboriginal encounters – over and over again. The creation and the perpetuation of this haunted national space are proof, she says, of the existence of the "unsuccessfully colonized."[10]

The moditional economy offers one concrete example of subordination without subjugation, but there are many. Aboriginal Peoples' referring their grievances to the courts is another, as is the negotiation of treaties that recognize pre-existing rights. The notion in law that the Crown has a fiduciary responsibility to protect the interests of Aboriginal Peoples also encapsulates the idea of subordination without subjugation. Finally, that there has been no subjugation, no capitulation, is clear in the artistic, political, and spiritual expressions that are widespread in aboriginal communities across Canada today.

Auto-Ethnographic Sources and Interviews

In Chapter 2, I describe texts recorded or joint-authored with non-aboriginals as "auto-ethnographies"[1] because, although in these works aboriginal authors tell their own stories, they often do so in an idiom that has been strongly influenced by non-aboriginal editors/collaborators. Several of these nineteenth-century texts survive, and they force us to re-examine accounts given by government officials, missionaries, travellers, and employers. The auto-ethnographies upon which I have drawn include all the published and unpublished atuobiographical accounts (including oral histories) of nineteenth-century BC Aboriginal People that I was able to locate in Library and Archives Canada, British Columbia Archives, Yukon Archives, University of British Columbia Special Collections, University of Washington Special Collections, and some local collections, including the Chilliwack and Esquimalt Municipal Archives. Among them are the four volumes cited in David Brumble III's *An Annotated Bibliography of American Indian and Eskimo Autobiographies*,[2] which relate to this time and place.

All of the above are collaborative works in which the voices of Aboriginal People have already been in dialogue with an anthropologist or editor before we get to join the conversation. It is useful to know how much the voice of the author-subject has been determined by the setting. Thus, in this section, I examine how each was collected and then place it within a comparative setting, with the purpose of focusing on paid and unpaid work.

This book draws heavily on a series of dialogues I had with contemporary Aboriginal People, and it also benefits from dialogues that were carried on by research assistants who interviewed on my behalf or who worked on joint projects. Not all the interviewees are directly quoted, but I include them because they corroborate and expand upon my findings. Most are available for other researchers to consult. I have also been lucky to gain access to dialogues recorded by earlier researchers. I have drawn on all of these dialogues, which are listed below, for information, verification, and context (although only those from which I have directly quoted are listed in the bibliography).

Published and Manuscript Auto-Ethnographies

Nineteenth Century

Arthur Wellington Clah (1831-1916), a Ts'msyen from Lax Kw'alaams (Fort Simpson, later Port Simpson), has left a remarkable account. Clah's journal spans the years between 1860 and 1910 and provides the only day-to-day description of aboriginal life that I was able to locate. It is a rich and detailed document that he seems to have kept for his own use, and it is written in an idiosyncratic phonetic English.[3]

Sayach'apis (born ca. 1840-42), a Nuu-chah-nulth from Alberni Inlet, had his stories collected and transcribed by Edward Sapir and Morris Swadesh. Sayach'apis, who knew no English, was interviewed between 1910 and 1914 and between 1921 and 1922. Though Sapir knew some Nuu-chah-nulth, this material was collected with the aid of interpreters, particularly Alex Thomas.[4]

Charles Jones (b. 1876), a Nuu-chah-nulth from Port Renfrew, "co-authored" his biography with Stephen Bosustow. Jones and his wife were interviewed in English by Bosustow, a film producer, over a few days in 1976. The text shows signs of considerable rewording.[5]

Captain John Swah-lis (born ca. 1810-13), a Stó:lō from Chilliwack, told his life history in Chinook jargon to a missionary. The intent was to highlight Captain John's conversion to Christianity.[6]

Other biographical accounts, ranging from a few pages to book length, have been compiled for a few others, most within an ethnographic context. These include:

John Fornsby (b. 1855), Skagit-Coast Salish. Fornsby was interviewed in English in 1942 and in 1947 by anthropologist June Collins, who tried unsuccessfully to direct the questioning. Fornsby frequently followed his own threads, which Collins decided to arrange into a loosely chronological life history, deleting some details and translating Fornsby's Salish words into English.[7]

William Pierce (born ca. 1855), Ts'msyen, set his story down in 1910, and described his life to that time. His editor, J.P. Hicks, combined this with an account of Pierce's later life (taken from Pierce's notes). Both sections suggest that the material is shaped to highlight Pierce's transition from heathen to Christian.[8]

August Khahtsahlano (b. 1877), Squamish, was interviewed in English by Oliver Wells in 1965 and by Major J.S. Matthews at various intervals between the 1930s and the 1950s. In both cases, the material is presented in a question-and-answer format.[9]

George Swanaset (b. 1874), originally Stó:lō, was interviewed by Paul Fetzer in 1951, but I have no information on how this was accomplished.[10]

Charley Nowell (b. 1870), a Kwakwa̱ka̱'wakw from Fort Rupert,[11] was interviewed in 1940. He spoke English, and so it was "possible to take down the story of his life exactly as he told it," though Ford rearranged the events into a more chronological sequence. Ford substituted some of the names of the women with whom Charley had affairs and altered some syntax, but he left much of Nowell's non-standard English intact. Brumble, in his annotated bibliography, suggests that Nowell was guided by Ford's questions.

Mrs. Moses Knight (born ca. 1870), Heiltsuk from Bella Bella, had her biography recorded through the use of the interpreter Mrs. William Grant; the biography was "slightly modified" by anthropologist Ronald Olson, who has put all of it in the first person.[12]

Christine Quintasket (born ca. 1885), Plateau Salish, wrote an autobiography. She was a writer and translator of aboriginal traditions in her own right; however, editor Jay Miller had to reassemble the manuscript from a variety of sources, and he "rewrote each sentence to achieve agreement of subject and verb, a uniform past tense, and appropriate use of pronouns." He offers the manuscript as "my sense of her work."[13] Other ethnographic sources, not intended as biographic, include incidental references to aboriginal work.

There are inevitably limitations to these sources too. All but one of the auto-ethnographies, Quintasket's *Mourning Dove,* are from coastal groups. In part, this unbalanced representation reflects the population distribution of Aboriginal People, approximately 80 percent of whom belonged to coastal groups. It is also a reflection of ethnographic interest. The coastal groups had permanent winter villages, more elaborate rituals, and more material goods than did the interior groups, and so they have drawn more scholarly attention.

Four of the men – Jones, Nowell, Swah-lis, and Pierce – were the subjects of auto-ethnographies largely due to their prominence as chiefs (or, in the case of Pierce, as a missionary). These are accounts of "successes" as determined by distinctly Euro-American criteria. On the other hand, the remaining eight auto-ethnographies emphasize success in the "traditional" economy. Ethnographers sought people with as much understanding as possible of "traditional life," so age and knowledge were the main criteria. Those people whose stories were recorded stood out because they had not "assimilated" and so were not "successful" in the white world. All but two of the accounts are from male informants. Moreover, since one of the accounts from an aboriginal woman, Mrs. Knight, is very brief, our knowledge of nineteenth-century paid and unpaid work is definitely skewed towards males. This is reflected, to a degree, in the language used. "Work," in both the aboriginal and non-aboriginal accounts, means paid work and is distinguished from subsistence activities such as hunting or fishing, gathering plants or preserving foods – activities that involved the expenditure of much labour (particularly that of women) but no pay.[14] Taking into account their partial nature, these aboriginal voices, along with those captured in letters to government and church officials and residing in archives, allow us to lay a foundation for a renewed discussion of the early years of aboriginal paid labour in British Columbia.

Twentieth Century

The record for the twentieth century is richer than is that for the century before. I have used the following biographies or autobiographies of Aboriginal British Columbians, whose lives have been lived primarily in the twentieth century (though some of them continue to make history in the twenty-first century). The publication details or manuscript locations are given in the bibliography.

Florence Davidson (b. 1896), Haida, had her life story recorded by anthropologist Margaret Blackman, who spent weeks living with Florence. Blackman wrote the biography, which she reviewed with Davidson.

Ed Sparrow (b. 1898), Musqueam, and Rose Sparrow (b. 1902), Musqueam, left the best account of aboriginal work in this century in Leona Marie Sparrow, "Work Histories of a Coast Salish Couple."[15] In 1976, Sparrow interviewed her grandparents about their work histories and recorded their answers. Much of the transcript is available in the thesis.

Mary Augusta Tappage (b. 1899), Secwepemc, shared some of her memories with Jean Speare shortly before they were published in a photo-essay in 1973. Tappage's stories are told in her words as arranged by Speare.[16]

Henry Pennier (b. 1904), Stó:lō-French, hijacked an attempt by linguistics professor E. Wyn Roberts to collect some "Indian Stories" in Halkomelem. Henry (Hank) wanted to tell his life story, and he so captivated Roberts that he connected him to publisher Herb McDonald and together they published this series of stories in 1972. It was reissued in 2006.[17]

Harry Assu (b. 1905), Kwakwa̱ka̱'wakw, worked extensively with Joy Inglis to produce his memoirs. The two met regularly through the fall of 1982 and the spring of 1983 and again for seven weeks in 1984. Interviews were taped and transcribed. Inglis "expanded the phrases Harry Assu used in ordinary conversation ... into sentences that clarify meaning and permit the narrative to flow." The text was then reviewed by Harry and his family.[18]

John Wallace (b. 1905), Stó:lō, was interviewed by historian Oliver Wells. He was recorded on October 2, 1967, as well as at other times, while he and Wells worked on a canoe and the latter kept notes. Both the transcript

and the notes are in Wells' *The Chilliwack and Their Neighbours*.[19]

Beth White (born ca. 1905), Tahltan, was interviewed for the Yukon Women's Sound Recording Project in 1974. The name is a pseudonym, in accordance with the access agreement made for the right to use material from this collection.[20]

Clayton Mack's (b. 1910) Nuxalk stories were recorded and edited by his physician, Harvey Thommasen, when Clayton was in his seventies. These stories emphasize extraordinary occurrences while including basic biographical information.[21]

Simon Baker (b. 1911), Squamish, co-wrote his life story with Verna Kirkness, a professor in UBC's education faculty who, with others, recorded interviews with him between 1986 and 1992.[22]

Mary John (b. 1913), Carrier, related her account in her voice in the book edited by Bridget Moran, although the process of capturing that voice is not recorded. Moran met John in 1976, though it seems that the material was recorded in the mid-1980s.

James Sewid (b. 1913), Kwakwa̱ka̱'wakw, was chosen as the subject of a biography by anthropologist James Spradley, who saw him as an example of an Indian "who has made ... an exceptional adjustment to culture conflict." Sewid was interviewed in English between 1966 and 1968, and the manuscript was read back to him. Changes were made for grammatical consistency and to place events in chronological order, then the manuscript was cut down.[23]

Joyce Albany (b. 1919), Lekwungen, was interviewed as part of an oral history project initiated by the Esquimalt City Archives in 1990. She was likely recruited because she was a prominent member of the local community.[24]

Earl Maquinna George (b. 1926), Nuu-chah-nulth, authored his own history in 2003 after completing his master's degree. His book offers an unfiltered aboriginal voice but is still heavily influenced by the ethnographic idiom.[25]

Both Theresa Jeffries (b. 1932), Sechelt, and Gilbert Joe (b. 1933), Sechelt, were interviewed for a special issue of the *Labour History* journal in 1980. Theresa, the first aboriginal woman in Sechelt to graduate from secondary school, was interviewed by Colleen Bostwick at the United Native Nations Office in Vancouver on 26 June 1980. Gilbert Joe, owner of the fishing and research vessel *Artic Harvester*, was interviewed by his friend (and president of the Labour History Association) Frank Fuller, also in 1980.[26]

In the twentieth century, there are more diverse aboriginal voices available than can be found in the nineteenth century. Half of the sixteen works mentioned come from women, and three, including the accounts of Mary Augusta Tappage, Beth White,[27] and Mary John,[28] come from interior nations. However, the better studied and better known coastal peoples still account for the largest part of the record.

The work histories of those for whom we have biographies show striking parallels over time, across nations, and between places. Comparing Charley Nowell's biography with that of his contemporary, Ed Sparrow, is instructive because, although these men came from different parts of the coast and from different cultural groups – Kwakwaka'wakw (Fort Rupert) and Coast Salish (Musqueam), respectively – there are many similarities. Both logged, fished, picked hops, worked in sawmills, sold firewood, and trapped. Nowell also worked for the Indian agent, helped ethnographers Franz Boas and C.F. Newcombe collect artefacts, recruited cannery labour, and worked as a sealer. For his part, Sparrow worked as a market gardener, net mender, civic employee, and beachcomber. George Swanaset, also a contemporary, fished, cut wood for steam locomotives and steamships, cut shingle bolts, ran logs downriver to the mills, worked in mills, kept sheep, cut hay, and worked as a deckhand.

Women, within a similarly limited range, experienced almost the same degree of mobility between occupations as did men. Rose Sparrow, a Coast Salish from the Fraser Valley, at different times mended nets, worked in canneries, picked hops and berries, prepared pelts, wove baskets, knitted sweaters for sale, gardened, and harvested and preserved fish and berries for home use. Florence Davidson, a Haida from Haida Gwaii, worked at exactly the same income and subsistence activities as did Sparrow, with the exception of hop picking and sweater knitting; instead, Davidson worked as a cook and a baker and ran a small restaurant.

Interviews

Contemporary

The following is a list of people I interviewed for this book:

Adam Dick, Kwakwaka'wakw, interviewed October 19, 2003, at the University of Victoria (tape and transcript in the University of Victoria Special Collections).

Adam Dick and Daisy Sewid-Smith, Kwakwaka'wakw, interviewed October 23, 2001, at the University of Victoria (tape and transcript in the University of Victoria Special Collections).

Joe Alphonse, Tsilhqot'in, Director of Government Services for the Tsilhqot'in National Government, interviewed at the Tsilhqot'in National Government Office, Williams Lake, August 24, 2000.

Cameron Beck, Economic Development Officer, Carrier Chilcotin Tribal Council, interviewed in Williams Lake, August 30, 1999.

Chief Ervin Charleyboy, Tsilhqot'in, interviewed at Tsi Del Del (Redstone) Band Office, September 1, 1999.

Orrey Charleyboy, Tsilhqot'in, interviewed at Tshilqot'in National Government Office, Williams Lake, September 1999.

Patrick Lulua, Tsilhqot'in, interviewed August 31, 1999, at Toosey.

Chief Robert Sam, Lekwungen, interviewed at Songhees Band Office, 2000.

Sammy Sam, Saanich, interviewed at Songhees Bighouse, 2000.

Chief Cassidy Sill, Ulkatcho, interviewed August 31, 1999, at Toosey.

Gilbert Solomon, Tsilhqot'in, interviewed at the Nemiah Band Office, August 2000.

Henry Solomon, Tsilhqot'in, interviewed at his home in Nemiah, September 5, 1999. Tape and transcript at the University of Victoria Special Collections.

Chief Leslie Stump, Tsilhqot'in, interviewed at the Band Office at Anaham, August 31, 2001.

Don Wise, interviewed at the Tsilhqot'in National Government Office, Williams Lake, September 1999.

The following is a list of interviews conducted as part of the Ethnohistory Field School with the Stó:lō Nation for this book or for joint projects. (Copies of the tapes and

TABLE A.1

Paid and subsistence work described in auto-ethnographic sources

Name	Birth year	Subsistence	Sealing	Trade	Fishing	Canning	Logging	Trapping	Hop picking	Freighting	Ship's crew	Agriculture	Public works	Sawmill	Service	Handicrafts
Arthur W. Clah[1]	1831	•	—	•	•	—	—	•	—	•	•	—	—	—	•	—
Sayach'apis[2]	1841~	•	•	•	•	—	—	—	—	—	—	—	—	—	—	—
John Fornsby	1855	•	—	—	•	—	•	—	•	—	—	—	•	•	—	—
William Pierce[3]	1855~	—	—	—	—	—	—	—	—	—	—	—	—	—	—	•
Charley Nowell[4]	1870	•	•	—	•	•	•	•	•	—	—	—	—	—	•	—
George Swanaset	1874	—	—	—	•	—	•	—	—	—	—	•	•	—	•	—
Charles Jones[5]	1874	•	—	—	•	—	•	•	—	•	—	—	•	—	—	—
A. Khahtsahlano	1877	•	—	—	•	—	•	—	—	—	—	—	•	—	•	•
Mr. Quintasket[6]	1885	•	—	•	—	—	•	—	—	—	—	—	•	—	•	—
Mary A. Tappage	1888	•	—	—	—	—	—	•	—	—	—	—	•	—	•	—
Florence Davidson	1896	•	—	—	—	•	—	—	—	—	—	—	•	—	•	•
Ed Sparrow[7]	1898	•	—	—	•	•	•	—	—	•	—	—	•	—	•	—
Rose Sparrow	1902	•	—	—	—	•	—	•	•	—	—	—	—	—	—	•
Henry Pennier[8]	1904	•	—	—	—	—	•	•	—	—	—	—	•	—	—	—
Harry Assu	1905	•	—	—	•	—	•	•	—	—	—	—	—	—	—	—
Beth White[9]	1905~	•	—	—	—	—	—	•	—	—	—	—	—	—	•	•
Mary John[10]	1913	•	—	—	—	—	—	•	—	—	—	—	—	—	•	—
James Sewid[11]	1913	•	—	—	•	•	•	•	—	—	—	—	•	—	•	—
Joyce Albany[12]	1919	•	—	—	—	—	—	—	—	—	—	—	—	—	•	—
John Wallace[13]	1925	—	—	—	•	—	•	•	•	—	—	—	—	—	—	—
Theresa Jeffries[14]	1932	—	—	—	—	•	—	—	—	—	—	—	•	—	•	—
Gilbert Joe	1933	—	—	—	•	—	•	—	—	—	—	—	—	—	—	—

1 Also preached and was a healer.

2 Also did theatrical performances and was a healer.

3 Main career was as a minister.

4 Also worked for Indian Agent, assisted ethnographers, and was a labour recruiter.

5 Also worked as a railway brakeman.

6 Christine Quintasket provides more information on her father's occupation than her own. He also earned his living as a gambler, and she was a teacher.

7 Also was band business manager and secretary.

8 Also bootlegged liquor.

9 Also ran a gas station with her husband.

10 Also worked in the local hospital and became a teacher.

11 Also did performances for tourists.

12 Had a career as office worker, band manager, and bookkeeper.

13 Also construction worker, carpenter, and guide.

14 Worked for the Department of Indian Affairs coordinating craft-training programs and then for the BC Association of Non-Status Indians as a field worker.

transcripts are available from the Stó:lō Nation Archives, Sardis, BC.)

Tilly and Al Gutierrez, Stó:lō, interviewed by Liam Haggarty and Heather Watson, Chilliwack, May 26, 2005.

Herb Joe, Stó:lō, interviewed by Liam Haggarty and Heather Watson, Chilliwack, May 20, 2005.

Doug Kelly, Stó:lō, interviewed by Liam Haggarty and Heather Watson at the Soowahlie Band Office, May 27, 2005.

Dennis Leon, Stó:lō, interviewed by Liam Haggarty and Heather Watson, Chilliwack, May 25, 2005.

Rena Peters and Joanne Jefferson, Stó:lō, interviewed by Liam Haggarty and Heather Watson, Chilliwack, May 24, 2005.

The following is a list of interviews conducted for the Coast under Stress Project for this book and for joint projects. (Copies of the interviews and questions have been deposited with the Namgis Tribal Council in Alert Bay as well as at the University of Victoria Special Collections).

Chief Pat Alfred, Kwakwaka'wakw, interviewed by Chris Cook III, 2003.

Elizabeth Alfred, Kwakwaka'wakw, interviewed by Byron Plant and Chris Cook III at the Chris Cook Jr. residence, Alert Bay, July 6, 2003.

George William Alfred, Kwakwaka'wakw, interviewed by Byron Plant and Chris Cook III at the Chris Cook Jr. residence, Alert Bay, May 19, 2003

Verna Ambers, Kwakwaka'wakw, Office of Community Development, interviewed by Byron Plant, Alert Bay, July 7, 2003.

Stevie Beans, Kwakwaka'wakw, interviewed by Chris Cook Jr. and Byron Plant, Alert Bay, July 8, 2003.

Pete Cook, Kwakwaka'wakw, interviewed by Byron Plant and Chris Cook, Alert Bay, July 8, 2003.

Gloria Cranmer Webster, Kwakwaka'wakw, interviewed by Byron Plant at Gloria Cranmer-Webster residence, Alert Bay, July 8, 2003.

Roy Cranmer, Kwakwaka'wakw, interviewed by Chris Cook III at St. Michael's Residential School, Alert Bay, July 8, 2003.

Chris Cook Jr., Kwakwaka'wakw, interviewed by Chris Cook III at the Chris Cook Jr. residence, Alert Bay, May 18, 2003.

Adam Dick, Kwakwaka'wakw, and Kim Recalma Clutesi interviewed at the University of Victoria by John Lutz, October 23, 2001.

Adam Dick, Kwakwaka'wakw, and Daisy Sewid-Smith, Kwakwaka'wakw, interviewed by John Lutz at the University of Victoria, October 18, 2003.

Art Dick, Kwakwaka'wakw, interviewed by Byron Plant and Chris Cook III, Alert Bay, July 6, 2003.

George "Porgie" Jolliffe, Kwakwaka'wakw, interviewed by Chris Cook III, Alert Bay, July 6, 2003.

Edwin Newman, Heiltsuk, interviewed by Byron Plant and Chris Cook III, at the Namgis Band Office, Alert Bay, July 6 2003.

Jack and Dot Nolie, Kwakwaka'wakw, interviewed by Chris Cook III and Byron Plant at the Nolie residence on Whe-La-La-U Reserve on Cormorant Island, May 21, 2003

Arnie Wadhams, Kwakwaka'wakw, interviewed by Byron Plant and Chris Cook III at his residence in Alert Bay, July 7, 2003.

Greg Wadhams, Kwakwaka'wakw, interviewed by Byron Plant, Alert Bay, July 2003.

Billy Wasden, Kwakwaka'wakw, interviewed by John Lutz, Byron Plant, and Chris Cook III, Alert Bay, May 19, 2003.

The following is a list of Ts'mysen interviews. Copies of interviews have been deposited with the Gitga'at Nation and with University of Victoria Special Collections.

Wally Thompson, Ts'msyen, Prince Rupert, interviewed by John Lutz and Nancy Turner, Prince Rupert, June 2004.

Bruce Reece, Gitga'at economic development officer, interviewed by John Lutz, Hartley Bay, June 10, 2004.

James (Jimmy) and Annetta Robinson, Gitga'at, interviewed by John Lutz at their home in Hartley Bay, June 2004.

Edward (Eddie) Robinson, Gitga'at, band councilor, interviewed by John Lutz, Hartley Bay, June 2004.

Pearl Clifton, Gitga'at, interviewed by John Lutz, Nancy Turner, and Liam Haggarty at her home in Hartley Bay, February 2005.

Margaret "Goulie" Reece, Gitga'at, interviewed by John Lutz and Liam Haggarty at her home in Hartley Bay, February 2005.

Merle Reece, Gitga'at, interviewed by John Lutz at the Gitga'at Development Corporation Offices, Hartley Bay, June 2003.

George Clifton, Clyde Ridley, and Fred Ridley (all Gitga'at), Reynold Grant (Kitamaat), Vernon Skog (Gitkxaahla), interviewed by John Lutz and Liam Haggarty in Prince Rupert, December 2, 2005.

Interviews from Existing Collections

Stó:lō Nation Archives

Pat Campo, Stó:lō, interviewed by Sarah Eustace, November 20, 1997, December 15 1997, and February 2, 1998.

Jimmie Charlie and Dean Louie, Stó:lō, interviewed by Sarah Eustace and Keith Carlson, December 8, 1997.

Rosaline George, Stó:lō, interviewed by Sarah Eustace, November 18, 1997.

Sweetie Malloway, Stó:lō, interviewed by Sarah Eustace, November 14, 1997.

Ed Nelson, Stó:lō, interviewed by Sarah Eustace, November 12, 1997.

Chief Peter D. Peters, Stó:lō, interviewed by Larry Commodore, July 21, 1985.

Aggie Victor, Stó:lō, interviewed by Sarah Eustace, November 13, 1997.

BC Archives

Annie York, Nlaka'pamux, interviewed by Imbert Orchard in the Imbert Orchard Oral History Collection, tape 678:1+2.

John Williams, Haida, interviewed by Imbert Orchard 1969, Aural History Program, acc. no. 2428, tape 1, tract 1.

British Columbia Indian Language Project

Felicity Walkus, Agnes Edgar, and Orden Mack, all Nuxalk, interviewed by Randy Bouchard and Dorothy Kennedy, fieldnotes, 1971-77.

Coqualeetza Resource Centre (Sardis, BC)

Ernest Pearson, shopkeeper, Columbia Hop Co., Sardis, interviewed by Mr. Charlie, June 29, 1976, tape 1, 971.hop/1/1.

Esquimalt Municipal Archives

Joyce Albany, Lekwungen, Oral History Project, interview, August 17, 1990, file 990.16.1.

Yukon Archives

Beth White (pseudonym), Tahltan, interviewed for the Yukon Women's Project Sound Recording 1974 (transcripts) file 13-5.

Eva Thompson (pseudonym), Tagish, interviewed for the Yukon Women's Project Sound Recording 1974 (transcripts) file 13-6.

Reliability of Department of Indian Affairs Estimates

Aside from the accounts of aboriginal workers themselves, one of the best available sources for a study of aboriginal working lives is the annual reports of the Indian Agents published in departmental annual reports. Until 1946, these reports included agents' estimates of aboriginal earnings. It is not clear whether these estimates bear any relation to reality, and so we do not know how much credibility to attach to them. Anthropologist Helen Codere has closely examined the income figures for the Kwawkewlth Agency from 1903 to 1939, and, although she found a few anomalies, overall thought them to be reliable indicators of economic activity.[1] Historian James Burrows has examined the figures and the worksheets used by the agent in the Kamloops-Okanagan Agency. He also considers them to be reliable estimates.[2]

Although agents began reporting band incomes in 1877, the detail and quality of the estimates do not appear to be very reliable until 1898, when total income was disaggregated into more precise categories. That year the Department of Indian Affairs sent a flurry of circulars to agents, clarifying what was to be included in each category. Precise instructions on how to estimate aboriginal income were included in a letter from the British Columbia Indian superintendent to Indian Agent W.H. Lomas, August 4, 1898. The relevant part of the letter reads as follows:

> [Regarding the] 3rd column[,] wages earned, you can get at this for the present approximately only by estimating the number of your Indians and their time whilst employed for the canneries, otherwise that when taking fish, work at the sawmills other than contracts[, plus] any other work for which they were paid wages. [Regarding the] 5th [fishing] and 6th Columns [trapping and hunting] add to the monies earned for fishing at the canneries and fishing for the markets the following estimates, say half the food or any other proportion you may think correct is the product of hunting and fishing, [say] 1/6 hunting and 2/6 fishing[, then] estimate the fish at 4¢ per lb and meat @ 8¢ per lb. Say each adult consumes 2lbs of meat or 3lbs of fish each day reckoning for this estimate 180 days in the year hence adults x 120 [days] for fish x 3lb + 60 [days] for meat x 2 lbs + children at half rations = lbs fish @ 4¢ = lbs meat @ 8¢ = earned by hunting and fishing to which you must add earned by fishing for canneries [and] earned by fishing for market. By questioning the Indians closely on your rounds you can get sufficient data to enable you to make a very close estimate of the quantities required by the department. The proportions which I have given you above are merely arbitrary for illustration but you can readily obtain from the Indians the kinds of food on which they subsist and where they procure it.[3]

For some categories of income the agent was probably able to obtain precise figures. Local traders could supply the value of furs that had been purchased from Indians, and perhaps the local canners could state the wages paid. It is clear from the letter above, however, that a large part of Indian income was estimated rather than precisely recorded.

The agents could not survey every Indian in their agency every year; they could not even visit every reserve in remote parts of the province. And it is true that sometimes the income figures are simply repeated verbatim over a period of a few years. Agents were, however, in a position to know what prices were being paid for furs, fish, logs, and labour; the length of the season; and the overall prosperity of the bands relative to previous years. More-over, the gathering of these statistics was of considerable importance to the DIA and the agents because it was a key indicator of the so-called "progress" of Indians.

An internal check of the post-1898 data shows con-sistency between the conditions the agents were record-ing in their written reports and the statistics that they provided. Perhaps a more interesting test would involve comparing the overall income patterns with the particu-lar comments in aboriginal biographies and against some of the other statistical series such as fur prices. Certainly the income crashes recorded in the biographies during the Depression are reflected in the income levels reported in the annual reports, as are the boom years of the Second World War. The changing relative share of income from different industry categories is also consistent for the in-dependent evidence we have for numbers of fishers, can-nery employees, wartime manufacturing employees, and trappers.

In sum, it seems that, although these figures cannot be accepted as exact records of Indian incomes, they do appear to be reliable indicators of relative levels of income from various sources as well as accurate reflections of rela-tive changes to income levels over time.

Glossary of Chinook Jargon Terms

Where Chinook jargon is used in the book it is usually paired with its English equivalent. Included below are definitions for terms that are not always translated. They are based on Edward Harper Thomas, *A History and Dictionary of the Northwest Coast Trade Jargon* (Portland: Binfords and Mort, 1970).

The letter in parentheses following the term indicates language of origin: c = language of Chinook people, n = language of the Nuu-chah-nulth, e = English, f = French, and j = word original to the Chinook jargon.

alki (c): in the future, soon, presently, directly, in a little while, hold on, not so fast, shall, will.

capit [also kopet] (c): stop, quit, leave off, enough, only.

chako [copa] (n): to come, to approach, to be or become.

cultus (c): worthless, good for noting, bad, dissolute, filthy, foul.

cultus potlatch: a present of free gift – not a potlatch item.

cole [pil chikamin] (e): gold.

haiyu [haiyou, hiyu] (n): much, many, plenty, abundance.

hiyu muckamuck: plenty of food, rich person, one's social superiors.

illahee (c): country, land region, district, soil, farm, field.

klahowya (c): hello, how do you do? good morning, good evening, good bye.

klootchman (n): woman, women, wife, female.

kunamokst (c): together, both, with, amid, among, beside, besides.

latete [letete] (f): head.

lejab [deaub] (f): devil.

mahsie (f): thanks, thank you, praise.

makúk [makook, mahkook, ma-kuk, maá-kuk] (n): buy, sell, trade, exchange, barter.

mamook (n): to work, work, to make, to do, the act of doing, action, labor, job, task.

mesachie (c): bad, wicked, evil, vile, sin, vice, inequity.

moola [molla] (f): a mill or factory.

mowich (n): deer.

muckamuck (j): food, meal, feast, to eat, relief.

nesika (c): us, we, ours.

poo (j): to shoot.

potlatch (n): gift, to give, festival in which gifts are given, relief payment.

potlatch dolla: pay, to pay.

quass [kwass] (c): to be afraid.

siwash (f): Indian; today often pejorative but not historically or now in the Chilcotin when used by the Tsilhqot'in themselves and where Siwash Days is celebrated at a traditional campsite called Siwash Bridge.

tamananawas [tahmahnawis] (c): a guardian spirit, medicine power, magic, supernatural.

tumtum (j): heart, purpose, will, intentions, disposition, belief, memory, mind, thought.

tyee [tayee, tayi] (n): chief, head man, boss, master, gentleman, important person.

wawa (c): talk, converse, conversation, speech, dialogue, language, jargon, story, tale.

Notes

Abbreviations

BCA   British Columbia Archives

BCSP   *British Columbia Sessional Papers*

CO   Colonial Office Records, Great Britain Public Record Office (records are at the Public Record Office, in Kew, UK, but copies of much of it are available at the BCA and LAC)

DIA   Department of Indian Affairs

DIAR   Department of Indian Affairs Annual Reports, published in *Canada Sessional Papers* the year following the date on the report (also at http://www.collectionscanada.ca/indian affairs/index-e.html)

DIAND-CR   Department of Indian and Northern Affairs, Central Registry Office

HBC   Hudson's Bay Company

HBCA   Hudson's Bay Company Archives, Manitoba Provincial Archives

LAC   Library and Archives Canada

Preface

1 There is a debate among linguists concerning whether or not the language existed before contact as a lingua franca between Aboriginal Peoples. For a summary of the debate see Henry B. Zenk and Tony A. Johnson, "Uncovering the Chinookan Roots of Chinuk Wawa: A New Look at the Linguistic and Historical Record," *University of British Columbia Working Papers in Linguistics* (*Papers for the International Conference on Salish and Neighbouring Languages* 39) 14 (2004): 419-51.

2 Franz Boas, *The Ethnography of Franz Boas: Letters and Diaries of Franz Boas Written on the West Coast from 1881-1931,* ed. Richard Rohner, trans. Hedy Parker (Chicago: University of Chicago Press, 1969), 9. Others who made the same point include: Ernst von Hesse-Wartegg, "A Visit to the Anglo-Saxon Antipodes (Chapter 18 of *Curiosa aus der Neuen Welt,* 1893)," trans. John Maass, *BC Studies* 50 (1981): 38; T.N. Hibben, *Guide to the Province of British Columbia for 1877-78* (Victoria: T.N. Hibben, 1877), 222-49; J.A. Jacobsen, *Alaskan Voyage, 1881-83: An Expedition to the Northwest Coast of America,* translated from the German text of Adrian Woldt by Erna Gunther (Chicago: University of Chicago Press, 1977), 5.

3 Gary Geddes, *Skookum Wawa: Writings of the Canadian Northwest* (Toronto: Oxford University Press, 1975), xiii; Lewis Hyde, *Trickster Makes This World, Mischief, Myth and Art* (New York: Farrar, Straus and Giroux, 1998), 299. There is also a Lushootseed version of the story told in 1923 by Chief William Shelton at Tulalip and recorded in Vi Hilbert, *Haboo: Native American Stories from Puget Sound* (Seattle: University of Washington Press, ca. 1996), 75.

4 C.M. Buchanan, "Elementary Lessons in the Chinook Jargon as Used by the Indians of Puget Sound," mss. Tulalip Washington, 1900B; cited in Edwin Harper Thomas, *Chinook: A History and Dictionary of the Northwest Coast Trade Jargon* (Portland: Metropolitan, 1935), 4.

5 Bishop George Hills Diary, 16 February 1860, Archives of the Ecclesiastical Province of British Columbia; Thomas Crosby, *Among the An-ko-me-nums or Flathead Tribes of Indians of the Pacific Coast* (Toronto: William Briggs, 1907), 54.

6 For creolization see Henry B. Zenk, "A Chinook Jargon and Native Cultural Persistence in the Grand Ronde Indian Community, 1856-1970: A Special Case of Creolization" (PhD diss., University of Oregon, 1984).

7 Alfred Carmichael, "Account of a Season's Work at a Salmon Cannery, Windsor Cannery, Aberdeen, Skeena," ca. 1885, BCA, add. mss. 2305, records the widespread use of Chinook in the Skeena canneries in the mid-1880s. Peacock describes its use in the Fraser canneries, and Knight refers to its use on the docks and in the sawmills. See Catherine Kirby Peacock, "Salmon Canning in British Columbia," *Good Words* 35 (1894): 605-9; Rolf Knight, *Indians at Work: An Informal History of Native Indian Labour in British Columbia, 1858-1930* (Vancouver: New Star, 1978), 114.

8 Most of the Hudson's Bay Company's relations with Aboriginal People were conducted through Chinook, and some traders who married aboriginal women conversed with them and their children in Chinook. Bishop Hills preached and taught in Chinook, as did most of the Roman Catholic priests, including Father Bolduc at Fort Victoria. Roman Catholic Father Le Jeune published a Chinook jargon monthly journal, the *Wawa*, in a script improvised from French business shorthand. The sale of the Songhees land to the province in 1910 was conducted with the help of Chinook.

9 Several of these songs were transcribed by Franz Boas in "Chinook Songs," *Journal of American Folk-Lore* 6 (1888): 220-26; Laura B. Downey-Bartlett, *Chinook-English Songs* (Portland, OR: Kubli Miller, 1914); Charles Lillard and Terry Glavin, *A Voice Great within Us* (Vancouver: New Star, 1998).

10 Harry Assu, with Joy Inglis, *Assu of Cape Mudge: Recollections of a Coastal Indian Chief* (Vancouver: UBC Press, 1989), 69; H.S. Bostock, "Pack Horse Tracks: Recollections of a Geologist's Life in British Columbia and the Yukon, 1924-1954," Geological Survey of Canada Open File 650 (Ottawa: Geological Survey of Canada, 1979), 13-27.

11 Richard White calls these "creative and expedient misunderstandings" in *The Middle Ground: Indians, Empires and Republics in the Great Lakes Region, 1650-1815* (Cambridge: Cambridge University Press, 1991), x.

Chapter 1: Introduction

1 This story was told on May 3, 1932, by Joseph Morton about his father, and was recorded in J.S. Matthews, *Early Vancouver: Narratives of Pioneers of Vancouver, BC* (Vancouver: Brock Webber, 1933), 78-79.

2 Ibid.

3 See Canada, Department of Indian Affairs and Northern Development, Corporate Services, Information Quality and Research Directorate, *Socio-Economic Indicators in Indian Reserves and Comparable Communities, 1971-1991, Departmental Statistics* (Ottawa: Department of Indian Affairs and Northern Development, 1997), cat. no. R32-181/1991E.

4 For biological exchanges see, particularly, Alfred Crosby, *Ecological Imperialism: The Biological Expansion of Europe, 900-1900* (Cambridge: Cambridge University Press, 1986); and Alfred Crosby, *The Columbian Exchange: Biological and Cultural Consequences of 1492* (Westport, CT: Greenwood, 1972).

5 John Locke, *Second Treatise of Government*, EBook #7370, January 2005, http://www.gutenberg.org/dirs/etext05/trgov10.txt.

6 Cole Harris, *Making Native Space: Colonialism, Resistance and Reserves in British Columbia* (Vancouver: UBC Press, 2002), x.

7 Max Weber, *The Protestant Ethic and the Spirit of Capitalism* (New York: Scribner, 1958); James Tully, *A Discourse on Property: John Locke and His Adversaries* (Cambridge: Cambridge University Press, 1980); Elizabeth Povinelli, *Labor's Lot: The Power, History and Culture of Aboriginal Action* (Chicago: University of Chicago, 1993); Emmerich de Vattel, *The Law of Nations: Or, Principles of the Law of Nations: Applied to the Conduit of Nations and Sovereigns* (Philadelphia: T. and J.W. Johnson, 1861), 36-37.

8 Cardell Jacobson, "Internal Colonialism and Native American Indian Labor in the United States from 1871 to World War II," *Social Science Quarterly* 65 (1984): 168-69; Noel Dyck, *What Is the Indian 'Problem': Tutelage and Resistance in Canadian Indian Administration* (St. John's: Institute of Social and Economic Research, 1991), 29, 165n. See also David McNally, "Political Economy without a Working Class," *Labour/Le Travail* 25 (1990): 220n; Robin Fisher, *Contact and Conflict: Indian European Relations in British Columbia, 1774-1890*

(Vancouver: UBC Press, 1977; reprinted 1992), 96; H. Craig Miner, *The Corporation and the Indian: Tribal Sovereignty and Industrial Civilization in Indian Territory, 1865-1907*, 2nd ed. (Norman: University of Oklahoma Press, 1989).

9 See Chapter 2, "Pomo Wawa," for an elaboration of these ideas.

10 Contemporary studies confirm that the labour force participation rates of Aboriginal British Columbians are lower, while unemployment and welfare dependency rates are higher, than are those of non-Aboriginal People. See Michael Mendelson and Ken Battle, *Aboriginal People in Canada's Labour Market* (Ottawa: Caledon Institute of Social Policy, 1999); Katie Cooke, *Images of Indians Held by Non-Indians: A Review of Current Canadian Research* (Ottawa: Research Branch, Department of Indian Affairs and Northern Development Canada, 1984); Elizabeth Furniss, *The Burden of History: Colonialism and the Frontier Myth in a Rural Canadian Community* (Vancouver: UBC Press, 1999).

11 N. Redclift and E. Mingione, *Beyond Employment: Household, Gender, and Subsistence* (Oxford: Blackwell, 1985); Phillip Wood, "Barriers to Capitalist Development in Maritime Canada, 1870-1930: A Comparative Perspective," in *Canadian Papers in Business History*, ed. P. Baskerville (Victoria: Public History Group, 1989), 33-58.

12 E.P. Thompson, *The Making of the English Working Class* (Hammondsworth, UK: Penguin, 1968). For American examples, see Anthony Wallace, *Rockdale: The Growth of an American Village in the Early Industrial Revolution* (New York: W.W. Norton, 1978); Merrit Roe Smith, *Harpers Ferry Armory and the New Technology* (Ithaca: Cornell University Press, 1977).

13 Here I build on the work of Gérard Bouchard and Ruth Sandwell and place it within a framework that also includes the welfare state and the aboriginal economies of British Columbia. See Gérard Bouchard, *Quelques Arpents d'Amérique: Population, Économie, Famille au Saguenay, 1838-1971* (Montreal: Boréal, 1996), and his "Marginality, Co-Integration and Change: Social History as Critical Exercise," *Journal of the Canadian Historical Association* New Series 8 (1997), 19-38; Ruth W. Sandwell, *Contesting Rural Space: Land Policy and the Practices of Resettlement on Saltspring Island, 1859-1891* (Montreal and Kingston: McGill-Queen's University Press, 2005).

14 George Vancouver, *A Voyage of Discovery to the North Pacific Ocean and Round the World* (London: G.G. and J. Robinson, 1798; reprint ed. W. Kaye Lamb, London: Hakluyt Society, 1984]), 581-82. Vancouver indicates that the two groups communicated "with hand signals" and gives details of the signals used with other Salish groups on p. 551.

15 August Jack Khahtsahlano in J.S. Matthews, *Conversations with Khahtsahlano, 1932-1954* (Vancouver: Vancouver City Archives, 1933), 11 (spelling and grammar from Matthews transcription).

16 Both stress the encounter with the unknown: Vancouver mentions his inability to comprehend the meetings held by the local people, and the latter mention their inability to understand the nature of the ship, the crew's clothing, and the items traded. Both were willing to participate in the exchange of goods, and both stressed what they received over what they gave, as though what they gave was of little consequence to them.

17 See the account of this encounter told by Squamish Andrew Paull in Matthews, *Early Vancouver*, 49-50; and the account based on Joe Miranda's account in Robin Fisher and Hugh Johnston, eds., *From Maps to Metaphors: The Pacific World of George Vancouver* (Vancouver: UBC Press, 1993).

18 In recording aboriginal traditions of the first arrival of the Dutch at New York, John Heckewelder heard a similar story. The local people suspended the axes and hoes on their breasts as ornaments and used the stockings as tobacco pouches. A story from the Pacific Island of Vanuatu tells how Europeans left tobacco on the shore to entice the locals, who, mistaking the sticky black knobs for pig feces, were offended and attacked the ship. See John Heckewelder, "Indian Tradition of the First Arrival of the Dutch at Manhattan Island, Now New York," *Collections of the New York Historical Society*, 4 vols. (New York: I. Riley, 1841), 1: 71-74; Margaret Jolly, "The Forgotten Women: A History of Migrant Labour and Gender Relations in Vanuatu," *Oceania* 58, 2 (1987): 132. The Skidegate and Masset stories are recorded in Collison, *In the Wake of the War Canoe*, 120. There are several accounts of the Nuu-chah-nulth story, including one recorded by C.M. Tate in Matthews, *Early Vancouver*, 306.

19 The best exposition of this transformation process is Nicholas Thomas, *Entangled Objects: Exchange, Material Culture and Colonialism in the Pacific* (Cambridge, MA: Harvard University Press, 1991). The fur trade expression of this phenomenon is discussed in Christopher Miller and George R. Hammell, "A New Perspective on Indian-White Contact: Cultural Symbols and Colonial Trade," *Journal of American History* 73, 2 (1986): 311-28. For the use of Chinese and British objects in Lekwungen ceremonials in 1847, see Paul Kane, *Wanderings of an Artist: Among the Indians of North America: From Canada to Vancouver Island to Oregon, through Hudson's Bay Company's Territory and Back Again* (1859; reprinted Edmonton: Hurtig, 1968), 153. For Chinese coins as part of Northwest Coast ceremonial objects, see Grant Keddie, "The Question of Asiatic Objects on the North Pacific Coast of America: Historic or Prehistoric?" *Contributions to Human History* 3 (1990): 1-26.

20 Wendy Wickwire is able to date precisely when certain Nlaka'pamux people began exchanging items they had previously refused to sell. See her "Women in Ethnography: The Research of James A. Teit," *Ethnohistory* 40, 4 (1993): 542-43. See also Joanne Macdonald, "From Ceremonial Object to Curio: Object Transformation at Port Simpson and Metlakatla, British Columbia, in the Nineteenth Century," *Canadian Journal of Native Studies* 10, 2 (1990): 193-217; Aldona Jonaitis and Richard Inglis, "Power, History and Authenticity: The Mowachaht Whaler's Washing Shrine," *South Atlantic Quarterly* 91, 1 (1992): 193-213; Michael Ames, *Cannibal Tours and Glass Boxes: The Anthropology of Museums* (Vancouver: UBC Press, 1992).

21 H.F. Nater, *A Concise Nuxalk-English Dictionary*, Mercury Series no. 115 (Ottawa: Canadian Museum of Civilization, Canadian Ethnology Service, 1990), 25; Thomas, *Entangled Objects*, 123.

22 As exotic as the Northwest Coast and its peoples were to Europeans, the transformations I am suggesting were not in themselves limited to the intersection of offshore cultures. Other important but more general treatments that look at how consumers transform the meaning of value in everyday life include Michel de Certeau, *The Practice of Everyday Life*, trans. Stephen Randall (Berkeley: University of California Press, 1988); Grant McCracken, *Culture and Consumption: New Approaches*

to the Symbolic Character of Consumer Goods and Activities (Bloomington: Indiana University Press, 1988); and the essays in Arjun Appadurai, *The Social Life of Things: Commodities in Cultural Perspective* (Cambridge: Cambridge University Press, 1986).

23 Here I am appropriating the words of Barbara Babcock, "Arrange Me into Disorder," in *Rite, Drama, Festival, Spectacle: Rehearsals toward a Theory of Cultural Performance*, ed. Ron MacAloon (Philadelphia: Institute for the Study of Human Issues, 1984), 107.

24 Four other communities were studied in detail for the book but are not specifically written up: the Kwakwa̱ka'wakw community of Alert Bay, the Ts'mysen community of Hartley Bay, the Tahltan community of Telegraph Creek, and the Stó:lō communities centred around Chilliwack.

25 The other case was the "Fraser River War," a series of skirmishes between mostly American gold miners and the Aboriginal People of the Fraser Canyon in July and August 1858. See Daniel Marshall, "Claiming the Land: Indians, Goldseekers, and the Rush to British Columbia" (PhD diss., University of British Columbia, 2000).

26 Giovanni Levi, "On Microhistory" in *New Perspectives on Historical Writing*, ed. Peter Burke, 93-113 (University Park: Penn State Press, 1991); Carlo Ginzburg, "Microhistory: Two or Three Things That I Know about It," *Critical Inquiry* 20 (1993): 10-35; Georg G. Iggers, "From Macro- to Microhistory: The History of Everyday Life," in *Historiography in the 20th Century: From Scientific Objectivitiy to the Postmodern Challenge* (Hanover, NH: University Press of New England, 1997). Dorothy Smith also argues for this approach in *Texts, Facts and Femininity: Exploring the Relations of Ruling* (London: Routledge and Kegan Paul, 1990).

Chapter 2: Pomo Wawa: The Other Jargon

1 Quoted in Greg Dening, *Performances* (Chicago: University of Chicago, 1996), 105.

2 Linda Tuhiwai Smith, *Decolonizing Methodologies: Research and Indigenous Peoples* (London: Zed Books, 1999), 34.

3 Although there is a range of terms used in aboriginal communities, I use the term "Aboriginal Peoples" to describe the descendants of the pre-European population in the Americas. I capitalize "Aboriginal" when

it is part of the proper name "Aboriginal People," but not when it is an adjective, e.g., aboriginal labour. The term "Indian" is used in two senses: (1) in quotes to refer to stereotypes of Aboriginal People, and (2) without quotes to refer to the legal category of Registered Indian (i.e., a person who is on the register of an Indian band). I use the term "Native" (with regard to pre-European populations) to contrast with "newcomer." See, for one suggested usage, Greg Young-Ing, "Talking Terminology: What's in a Word and What's Not," *Prairie Fire* 22, 3 (2001): 130-40.

4 John Lutz, "Myth Understandings," *Myth and Memory: Stories of Indigenous-European Contact,* ed. Lutz, 1-14 (Vancouver: UBC Press, 2007).

5 Studies of science indicate that historians are not alone in this interactive, reflexive relationship with their research subjects. See Bruno Latour and Steven Woolgar, *Laboratory Life: The Social Construction of Scientific Facts* (Beverly Hills: Sage, 1979); and Michael Lynch and Steven Woolgar, eds. *Representation in Scientific Practice* (London: MIT Press, 1990).

6 Julie Cruikshank, with Angela Sidney, Kitty Smith, and Annie Ned, *Life Lived Like a Story* (Vancouver: UBC Press, 1990); Harry Robinson, *Write It on Your Heart,* ed. and comp. Wendy Wickwire (Vancouver: Talonbooks/ Theytus, 1989); Wendy Wickwire, "To See Ourselves as the Other's Other: Nlaka'pamux Contact Narratives," *Canadian Historical Review* 75, 1 (1994): 1-20.

7 In particular, I wish to thank the Stó:lō Nation Archives as well as the Coqualeetza Cultural Centre, the BC Archives, the Yukon Archives, Special Collections at the University of British Columbia, the University of Washington Special Collections, the Simon Fraser Special Collections, and those authors who interviewed on related themes.

8 Appendix 1 gives an indication of the available auto-ethnographies.

9 The diary of Arthur Wellington Clah (a Ts'mysen from Fort Simpson), covering the years between 1860 and 1910 and preserved at the Wellcome Institute in London, is an important example.

10 These are discussed individually in the chapters where they are cited and listed in Appendix 1.

11 David Murray, *Forked Tongue: Speech, Writing and Representation in North American Indian Texts* (London:

Pinter, 1991). These are the same points made by Ian MacLaren (with respect to explorers' accounts) in "Exploration/Travel Literature and the Evolution of the Author," *International Journal of Canadian Studies* 5 (1992): 39-67.

12 Brian Swan and Arnold Krupat, *Recovering the Word* (Berkeley: University of California Press, 1987); Jerry L. Clark, "Thus Spoke Chief Seattle: The Story of an Undocumented Speech," *Prologue* 17, 1 (1985): 58-63.

13 Including Marius Barbeau, Ruth Benedict, Philip Drucker, Diamond Jenness, Claude Levi-Strauss, Edward Sapir, and Morris Swadesh.

14 The topic of "vanishing" Indians is taken up in the next chapter. For example, there is much more about aboriginal work in Boas's few personal letters home than in all of his published writings. Fortunately, some of his correspondence has now been published in Franz Boas, *The Ethnography of Franz Boas: Letters and Diaries of Franz Boas Written on the Northwest Coast from 1886-1931,* ed. Ronald Rohner, trans. Hedy Parker (Chicago: University of Chicago, 1969). See also Patricia Albers, "From Legend to Land to Labor: Changing Perspectives on Native American Work," in *Native Americans and Wage Labor,* ed. Alice Littlefield and Martha Knack (Norman: University of Oklahoma, 1996), 271-73; Murray, *Forked Tongue,* 101-4.

15 The list is now too long to mention. Several of these works are listed in the bibliography.

16 Mary Louise Pratt, *Imperial Eyes: Travel Writing and Transculturation* (London: Routledge, 1992), 7; Keith Thor Carlson, ed., *A Stó:lō-Coast Salish Historical Atlas* (Vancouver: Douglas and McIntyre/University of Washington Press/Stó:lō Heritage Trust, 2001); and Keith Thor Carlson, ed., *You Are Asked to Witness: The Stó:lō in Canada's Pacific Coast History* (Chilliwack, BC: Stó:lō Heritage Trust, 1997), are exceptions that largely escape this trap.

17 See, for example, *Gazette,* May 18, 1860; *British Columbian,* July 11, 1861; *British Colonist,* June 17 and September 24, 1862. Many of the upper-class settlers, who authored most of the surviving accounts, also demean working-class *white* labour as well. See, for example, Matthew Baillie Begbie, "Journey into the Interior of British Columbia," *Journal of the Royal Geographical Society* 31 (1861): 243.

18　See, for example, Reverend Collison, *In the Wake of the War Canoe* (London: Seeley, Service, 1915), 58.

19　John Lutz, "Relating to the Country: The Lekwammen and the Expansion of European Settlement, 1843-1911," in *Beyond the City Limits: Rural History in British Columbia*, ed. Ruth W. Sandwell, 17-32 (Vancouver: UBC Press, 1999).

20　The reliability of income figures is discussed in Appendix 2.

21　Michel Foucault is the best known of those who have written about the expansion of state knowledge through surveillance. See Michel Foucault, *Discipline and Punish: The Birth of the Prison* (New York: Vintage, 1979). Some of these concepts are applied to the Lekwungen in Lutz, "'Relating to the Country,'" 17-32.

22　T. Todorov, *Mikhail Bakhtin: The Dialogical Principle* (Minneapolis: University of Minnesota Press, 1984), 72.

23　Ibid., 60.

24　Jean and John Comaroff, *Of Revelation and Revolution: Christianity, Colonialism, and Consciousness in South Africa* (Chicago: University of Chicago Press, 1991); Michael Harkin, *The Heiltsuks: Dialogues of Culture and History on the Northwest Coast* (Lincoln: University of Nebraska Press, 1997), viii.

25　Sergei Kan, "Shamanism and Christianity: Modern-Day Tlingit Elders Look at the Past," *Ethnohistory* 38, 4 (1991): 382; Mikhail Bakhtin, *The Dialogic Imagination: Four Essays,* ed. Michael Holquist, trans. Caryl Emerson and Michael Holquist (Austin: University of Texas, 1996), 427.

26　Nicholas Thomas, *Entangled Objects: Exchange, Material Culture and Colonialism in the Pacific* (Cambridge, MA: Harvard University Press, 1991), 123; Renato Rosaldo, "Foreword," in Nestor Garcia Canclini, *Hybrid Cultures: Strategies for Entering and Leaving Modernity* (Minneapolis: University of Minnesota Press, 1995), xv. This theme is developed in Chapter 1.

27　Alexandra Harmon, *Indians in the Making: Ethnic Relations and Indian Identities around Puget Sound* (Berkeley: University of California Press, 1998), 35; Homi Bhabha, "Frontlines/Borderposts," in *Displacements: Cultural Identities in Question*, ed. Angelika Bammer (Bloomington: Indiana University Press, 1994), 270.

28　Nestor Garcia Canclini, *Hybrid Cultures: Strategies for Entering and Leaving Modernity* (Minneapolis: University of Minnesota Press, 1995), 47; Karl Marx, *Grundrisse*

(Hammondsworth, UK and Boston: Penguin, 1973), 410; Ranajit Guha, *Dominance without Hegemony: History and Power in Colonial India* (Cambridge, MA: Harvard University Press, 1997), 6.

29　John Lutz, "Work, Sex, and Death on the Great Thoroughfare: Annual Migrations of 'Canadian Indians' to the American Pacific Northwest," in *Parallel Destinies: Canadian-American Relations West of the Rockies*, ed. John M. Findlay and Ken Coates (Seattle: Center for the Study of the Pacific Northwest and University of Washington Press, 2002), 80-103.

30　Ruth W. Sandwell, *Contesting Rural Space: Land Policy and the Practices of Resettlement on Saltspring Island, 1859-1891* (Montreal and Kingston: McGill-Queen's University Press, 2005), xx; Daniel Samson, ed., *Contested Countryside: Rural Workers and Modern Society in Atlantic Canada* (Fredericton: Acadensis, 1994); Gérard Bouchard, *Quelques Arpents d'Amérique: Population, Économie, Famille, au Saguenay 1838-1971 (*Montreal: Boréal, 1996); José E. Igartua, *Arvida au Saguenay: Naissance d'une Ville Industrielle* (Montreal and Kingston: McGill-Queen's University Press, 1996). See also Ruth W. Sandwell, "The Limits of Liberalism: The Liberal Reconnaissance and the History of the Family in Canada," *Canadian Historical Review* 84, 3 (2003): 423-50.

31　Gérard Bouchard, "Marginality, Co-Integration and Change: Social History as a Critical Exercise," *Journal of the Canadian Historical Association* New Series 8 (1997): 19-38.

32　The phrase "peaceable subordination" is inspired by Mary Louise Pratt's "anti-conquest" and includes the strategies of representation that she refers to as well as the broader meaning that I describe. See Pratt, *Imperial Eyes, 7.* Elizabeth Furniss uses the phrase "conquest by benevolence" in "Pioneers, Progress and Myth of the Pioneer: The Landscape of Public History in British Columbia," *BC Studies* 115/116 (1997/98): 7-44.

33　Guha, *Dominance without Hegemony,* 6. Recent court decisions, which have argued that the government has not lived up to these ideals and is obliged to make remedies, suggest that there may be a belated reckoning.

34　The term "enframement" is inspired by Timothy Mitchell's *Colonizing Egypt* (Cambridge: Cambridge University Press, 1988); however, true to Foucault's advice, I have distorted and expanded the term. I develop this further in Lutz, "Relating to the Country." See Cole Harris, *Making Native Space: Colonialism, Resistance and Reserves in British Columbia* (Vancouver: UBC Press, 2002); Douglas C. Harris, *Fish Law and Colonialism: The Legal Capture of Salmon in British Columbia* (Toronto: University of Toronto, 2001); Paul Nadasdy, *Hunters and Bureaucrats: Power, Knowledge and Aboriginal-State Relations in the Southwest Yukon* (Vancouver: UBC Press, 2003); Harkin, *The Heiltsuks*.

35 Guha, *Dominance without Hegemony*, 19-24; Stuart Hall employs a variant of Gramsci's concept of hegemony that is close to this. In Hall, hegemonic power is negotiated between the subject, whose identity remains fluid, and dominant society, itself unstable and constantly shifting. See Stuart Hall, "Gramsci's Relevance for the Study of Race and Ethnicity," *Journal of Communication Inquiry* 10, 2 (1996): 123-27.

36 Roy Miki, "Unclassified Subjects: Question Marking 'Japanese Canadian' Identity," paper presented to the Making History: Constructing Race conference, University of Victoria, 1998; M. Taussig, *Shamanism, Colonialism and the Wild Man: A Study in Terror and Healing* (Chicago: University of Chicago Press, 1987); Renato Rosaldo, "Foreword," in Canclini, *Hybrid Cultures*, xv; Kirin Narayan, "How Native Is a 'Native' Anthropologist?" *American Anthropologist* 95, 3 (1993): 673, 681; Nicholas Thomas, "'Partial Texts': Representation, Colonialism and Agency in Pacific History," *Journal of Pacific History* 25, 2 (1990): 139-58. Christopher Bracken makes this point in an interesting way in *The Potlatch Papers: A Colonial Case History* (Chicago: University of Chicago, 1997).

37 Clifford Geertz, "Thick Descriptions: Toward an Interpretive Theory of Culture," in *The Interpretation of Cultures: Selected Essays* (New York: Basic Books, 1973), 13.

38 Bakhtin in Todorov, *Mikhail Bakhtin*, 109.

39 Gayatri Chakravorty Spivak, "Can the Subaltern Speak?" in *Post-colonial Studies Reader*, ed. Bill Ashcroft, Gareth Griffiths, and Helen Tiffer, 24-28 (New York: Routledge, 1995).

40 Rey Chow, "Where Have All the Natives Gone?" in *Displacements: Cultural Identities in Question*, ed. A. Bammer (Bloomington: Indiana University Press, 1994), 130-34; Gayatri Chakravorty Spivak, "The New Historicism: Political Commitment and the Postmodern Critic," in *Post-colonial Critic: Interviews, Strategies,*

Dialogues, ed. Sarah Harasym (London: Routledge, 1990), 158.

41 Homi Bhabha, "Signs Taken for Wonders: Questions of Ambivalence and Authority under a Tree outside Delhi, May 1817," in *Europe and Its Others: Proceedings of the Essex Conference of the Sociology of Literature*, ed. Francis Barker, Peter Hulme, Margaret Iverson, Diana Loxley (Colchester: University of Essex, 1985), 89-106; Benita Parry, "Problems in Current Theories of Colonial Discourse, *Oxford Literary Review* 9, 1-2 (1987): 27-58. For critiques of hybridity, see A.S. Caglar, "Hyphenated Identities and the Limits of Culture," in *The Politics of Multiculturalism in the New Europe: Racism, Identity and Community*, ed. T. Modood and P. Werbner, 169-85 (London: Zed Books, 1997); R.J.C. Young, *Colonial Desire: Hybridity in Theory, Culture and Race* (London: Routledge, 1995).

42 Jean François Lyotard, *The Differend: Phrases in Dispute*, trans. Georges Van Den Abbeele (Minneapolis: University of Minnesota Press, 1988).

43 The phrase is from Chow, "Where Have All the Natives Gone?" 133.

44 Bakhtin, *Dialogic Imagination*, 360.

45 "Exotopy" (literally, "finding oneself outside") is Todorov's translation of Bakhtin's *vnenakhodimost*. See Bakhtin in Todorov, *Mikhail Bakhtin*, 30, 109.

Chapter 3: Making the Lazy Indian

1 One can find other references, going back to the mid-nineteenth century, that make the same point. Robin Fisher quotes Admiral Arthur Cochrane, who, in 1874, made the following comment about the industrious Metlakatla Indians: "I say these are not Indians. These are white men." See Robin Fisher, *Contact and Conflict: Indian-European Relations in British Columbia* (Vancouver: UBC Press, 1977; reprinted 1992), 134; W.H. Lomas, in Canada, Legislative Assembly, "Department of Indian Affairs Annual Report" (DIAR), *Canada Sessional Papers* (Ottawa: Canada, 1887): 105-7.

2 George Vancouver, *A Voyage of Discovery to the North Pacific Ocean and Round the World* (London: G.G. and J. Robinson, 1798; reprint ed. W. Kaye Lamb, London: Hakluyt Society, 1984), 236.

3 See, for example, John Scouler, "Observations of the Indigenous Tribes of the N.W. Coast of America," *Journal*

of the Royal Geographical Society of London 11 (1841): 218; James Cook, *Captain Cook's Voyages of Discovery*, ed. John Barrow (London: J.M. Dent and Sons, 1967), 347; Herbert K. Beales, trans., *Juan Perez in the Northwest Coast: Six Documents of His Expedition in 1774* (Oregon: Oregon Historical Society, 1989), 78.

4 Phenotypical differences are not prerequisites for racial differentiation. One only has to look at the English/Irish conflict during Vancouver's own lifetime or, more recently, the Nazi persecution of Jews. For a fuller examination of this, see John Lutz, "Making 'Indians' in British Columbia: Power, Race and the Importance of Place," in *Power and Place in the North American West*, ed. Richard White and John Findlay (Seattle: University of Washington Press, 1999), 61-86.

5 Agnes Smedley, *Race in North America: Origin and Evolution of a Worldview* (Boulder, CO: Westview, 1993), 36-72; Robert Berkhofer Jr., *The White Man's Indian: Images of the North American Indian from Columbus to the Present* (New York: Vintage, 1978), 3-22 ; Nancy Stepan, *The Idea of Race in Science: Great Britain, 1800-1960* (London: Macmillan, 1982).

6 For a provocative discussion of the role of explorers and travellers in "creating" the rest of the world for Europeans, see Mary Louise Pratt, *Imperial Eyes: Travel Writing and Transculturation* (London: Routledge, 1992), 32.

7 Carl Linnaeus, *Systema Naturae*, quoted in Pratt, *Imperial Eyes*, 32.

8 Renato Rosaldo, "Utter Savages of Scientific Value," in *Politics and History in Band Societies*, ed. E. Leacock and Richard Lee (Cambridge: Cambridge University Press, 1982) 319; Pratt, *Imperial Eyes*, 45.

9 Gaspar Mollien, *Travels in the Republic of Columbia in the Years 1822-23* (London: C. Knight, 1824), 57, quoted in Pratt, *Imperial Eyes*, 151.

10 Timothy Mitchell, *Colonizing Egypt* (Cambridge: Cambridge University Press, 1988), 109.

11 Nicholas Thomas, "Sanitation and Seeing: The Creation of State Power in Early Colonial Fiji," *Comparative Studies of Society and History* 32 (1990): 156.

12 For examples, see Cook, *Captain Cook's Voyages of Discovery*, 350; Alexander Walker, *An Account of a Voyage to the North West Coast of America in 1785 and 1786*, ed. Robin Fisher and J.M. Bumsted (Toronto: Douglas and McIntyre, 1982), 84.

13 Brown was one of the earliest ethnographers to work in British Columbia. See Robert Brown, *The Races of Mankind: Being a Popular Description of the Characteristics, Manners and Customs of the Principal Varieties of the Human Family* (London: Cassell, Petter and Galpin, Belle Savage Works, 1873), 3:31 (emphasis mine).

14 Ruth W. Sandwell, "Negotiating Rural: Policy and Practice in the Settlement of Saltspring Island, 1859-91," in *Beyond the City Limits*, ed. R. Sandwell (Vancouver: UBC Press, 1999), 83-101; M. Hunt, "Racism, Imperialism, and the Traveler's Gaze in Eighteenth Century England," *Journal of British Studies* 32 (1993): 333-57.

15 Elizabeth Povinelli, *Labor's Lot: The Power, History and Culture of Aboriginal Action* (Chicago: University of Chicago, 1993), 6.

16 Aboriginal Americans depended partly or largely on agricultural production in eastern and central North America down through Central and South America when Europeans arrived. On the northwest coast of America, one could find evidence of agriculture if one looked, but it was not as apparent as elsewhere on the continent. For northwest coast agriculture, see Brenda Beckwith, "'The Queen Root of This Clime': Ethnoecological Investigations of Blue Camas (Camassia leichtlinii, C. quamash; Liliaceae) and Its Landscapes on Southern Vancouver Island, British Columbia" PhD diss., Department of Biology, University of Victoria, 2004; for mariculture, see Judith Williams, *Clam Gardens: Aboriginal Mariculture on Canada's West Coast* (Vancouver: New Star, 2006), and N. Alexander Easton, "The Archaeology of Straits Salish Reef Netting: Past and Future Research Strategies," *Northwest Anthropological Research Notes* 24, 2 (1990): 161-77; for silviculture, see Robert Boyd, ed., *Indians, Fire, and the Land in the Pacific Northwest* (Corvalis: Oregon State University, 1999), and C. Cwynar, "Fire and the Forest History of the North Cascade Range," *Ecology* 68, 4 (1987): 791-802.

17 Simpson quoted in Frederick Merk, ed., *Fur Trade and Empire; George Simpson's Journal Entitled Remarks Connected with the Fur Trade in the Course of a Voyage from York Factory to Fort George and back to York Factory 1824-25* (Cambridge, MA: Belknap Press of Harvard University Press, 1968); Dugald McTavish in G.P.T.

Glazebrook, ed., *The Hargrave Correspondence* (Toronto: Champlain Society, 1938), 307-8. McLeod quoted in Elizabeth Vibert, *Traders' Tales: Narratives of Cultural Encounters in the Columbia Plateau, 1801-1846* (Norman: University of Oklahoma Press, 1997), 125-26.

18 Gabriel Franchère, *Narrative of a Voyage to the Northwest Coast of America, in the Years 1811, 1812, 1813, and 1814, or, The First American Settlement on the Pacific*, trans. and ed. J.V. Huntington (New York: Redfield, 1854), 261 (emphasis mine).

19 Mary Black Rogers, "Varieties of 'Starving': Semantics and Survival in the Subarctic Fur Trade, 1750-1850," *Ethnohistory* 33, 4 (1986): 353-83; Vibert, *Traders' Tales*, 120-31.

20 There is evidence that this meaning of indolent also became widespread in other colonies. See, for example, M. Taussig, *Shamanism, Colonialism and the Wild Man: A Study in Terror and Healing* (Chicago: University of Chicago Press, 1987), 56.

21 A thoughtful discussion of the importance of leisure as economic time can be found in Povinelli, *Labor's Lot*, 185-92.

22 The traders' journals show that they only actually traded furs a fraction of the year, that they complained of boredom and had little actual work. A fictional description of traders' lives based on actual accounts may be found in Fred Stenson, *The Trade* (Vancouver: Douglas and McIntyre, 2000).

23 Barnett, *Coast Salish*, 87, 248.

24 Ibid., 141; Edna Bobb from an interview with Keith Carlson, contained in Carlson, personal communication, October 2004; Irving Goldman, "The Alkatcho Carrier of British Columbia," *Acculturation in Seven American Indian Tribes*, ed. R. Linton (Gloucester, MA: Peter Smith, 1963), 370, 383; Frederica de Laguna, *Under Mount Saint Elias: The History and Culture of the Yakutat Tlingit* (Washington: Smithsonian, 1972). See also Chapter 4.

25 Barnett, *Coast Salish*, 243-45; Wayne Suttles, *Economic Life of the Coast Salish of Haro and Rosario Straits* (New York: Garland, 1974), 169-73.

26 Brian Dippie, *The Vanishing American: White Attitudes and US Indian Policy* (Middletown, CT: Wesleyan University Press, 1982); Berkhofer, *The White Man's Indian*; Daniel Francis, *The Imaginary Indian: The Image of the Indian in Canadian Culture* (Vancouver: Arsenal Pulp, 1992).

27 Emmerich de Vattel, *The Law of Nations: Or, Principles of the Law of Nature: Applied to the Conduct and Affairs of Nations and Sovereigns* (1758; reprinted Philadelphia: T. & J.W. Johnson, 1861), 36-37; *British Columbian*, June 1, 1869; quote from BCA, James Bell to John Thompson, February 27, 1859, add mss 412, Box 8, File 5.

28 Charles Forbes, *Vancouver Island: Its Resources and Capabilities as a Colony* (Victoria: Colony of Vancouver Island, 1862), 25; *Gazette*, May 18, 1860, 3.

29 A.A. Harvey, *A Statistical Account of British Columbia* (Ottawa: G.E. Desbarats, 1867), 9; George A. Walkem, Attorney General, August 17, 1875, in British Columbia, *Papers Connected with the Indian Land Question* (Victoria: R. Wolfenden, 1875; reprinted 1987); Matthew Baillie Begbie, Bench Books, November 17, 1885, cited in David Williams, *The Man for a New Country* (Victoria: Sono Nis, 1972), 13: 102.

30 W.C. Grant, "Report on Vancouver Island," BCA, A/B/20/G76,; W.C. Grant in William Carew Hazlitt, *British Columbia and Vancouver Island* (London: G. Routledge, 1858), 179; James E. Hendrickson, ed., "Two Letters From Walter Colquhoun Grant," *BC Studies* 26 (1975): 13.

31 Robert Brown, *Robert Brown and the Vancouver Island Exploring Expedition*, ed. John Hayman (Vancouver: UBC Press, 1989), 47 and 52; *British Colonist*, 5 June and 23 October 1860, 19 February 1861, and 17 June 1862.

32 The quote is from Governor James Douglas, commenting on aboriginal coal miners at Nanaimo, in Great Britain, Colonial Office, Original Correspondence, Vancouver Island, 1846-1867 (CO) 305/3, 10199, 12345, Douglas to Pakington, August 28, 1852; also CO 305/3, 933, November 11, 1852.

33 W.H. Lomas, in DIAR, 1887, 105-7.

34 Dorothy Blakey-Smith, ed., *The Reminiscences of Doctor John Sebastian Helmcken*, by J.S. Helmcken (Vancouver: UBC Press, 1975), 187; Arthur Bunster, testifying to the Select Committee on Oriental Immigration, 1879, cited in James Morton, *In the Sea of Sterile Mountains: The Chinese in British Columbia* (Vancouver: J.J. Douglas, 1974), 69. In 1885, the Royal Commission on Chinese Immigration conducted what appears to be a very

thorough census of Chinese in British Columbia, identifying towns in which even only one or two Chinese lived, and it counted seventy Chinese prostitutes. See Canada, *Sessional Papers*, 1885, no. 54a, appendix C.

35 Commission on the Salmon Fishing Industry in BC 1902, 14th sess., BCA, GR 213, evidence of C.F. Todd, quoted in Dianne Newell, *Tangled Webs of History: Indians and the Law in Canada's Pacific Coast Fisheries* (Toronto: University of Toronto Press, 1993), 84.

36 *Lumberman and Contractor*, quoted in Morton, *In the Sea of Sterile Mountains*, 201.

37 See the comments in the Report of the Royal Commission on Chinese Immigration, in Canada, *Sessional Papers*, 1885, no. 54a. A description of the racialization of Chinese in British Columbia may be found in Kay Anderson, *Vancouver's Chinatown: Racial Discourse in Canada, 1875-1980* (Vancouver: UBC Press, 1991). A detailed history of the relationship between whites and Asians may be found in Patricia Roy, *A White Man's Province: British Columbia Politicians and Chinese and Japanese Immigrants, 1858-1914* (Vancouver: UBC Press, 1989).

38 The Alberni mill, costing $120,000 to build and eventually capable of cutting 100,000 feet of lumber per day, commenced operation in 1861. The following accounts ignore the aboriginal workers in the first mill and ignore or underplay their subsequent involvement in the industry: W. Kaye Lamb, "Early Lumbering on Vancouver Island, I and II," *British Columbia Historical Quarterly* 2 (1938): 31-53 and 95-144; Myrtle Bergen, *Tough Timber: The Loggers of British Columbia – Their Story* (Toronto: Progress, 1966; reprinted Vancouver: Elgin, 1979); Thomas Cox, *Mills and Markets: A History of the Pacific Coast Lumber Industry to 1900* (Seattle: University of Washington Press, 1974); G.W. Taylor, *Timber: History of the Forest Industry in British Columbia* (Vancouver: J.J. Douglas, 1975); James Morton, *The Enterprising Mr. Moody and the Bumptious Captain Stamp: The Lives and Times of Vancouver's Lumber Pioneers* (Vancouver: J.J. Douglas, 1977); Ed Gould, *Logging: British Columbia's Logging History* (North Vancouver: Hancock, 1975); Jan Peterson, *The Albernis* (Lantzville, BC: Oolichan, 1992).

39 Matthew MacFie, *Vancouver Island and British Columbia* (London: Longman, Roberts, and Green, 1865), 51;

R.C. Mayne, *Four Years in British Columbia and Vancouver Island* (London: John Murray, 1862), 228; Frederick Whymper, *Travel and Adventure in Alaska* (London: J. Murray, 1868), 68. Whymper adds that Sproat was "a large employer of native as well as white labour ... at his sawmill settlement of Alberni" (37). And Sproat himself speaks of when he "first employed Indians at Alberni." See G.M. Sproat, *The Nootka: Scenes and Studies of Savage Life* (London: Smith, Elder, 1868; reprinted Victoria: Sono Nis, 1989), 40. One could make the same case for the Burrard Inlet mills.

40 Martin Robin, *The Rush for Spoils: The Company Province, 1871-1933* (Toronto: McClelland and Stewart, 1972) 30. See also Paul Phillips, "Confederation and the Economy of British Columbia," *British Columbia and Confederation*, ed. W. George Shelton (Victoria: University of Victoria, 1967), 59.

41 Statistics Canada, *Census of Canada* (1871) (Ottawa: Canada, 1871-1971), 4: 376-77.

42 An example of the under-enumeration is suggested by observers' reports that in 1881 the streets of Victoria thronged with Indians, while the census showed only 71 Indian men and 144 Indian women in the city. See Peter Baskerville and Eric Sager, *The 1881 Canadian Census: Vancouver Island* (Victoria: Public History Group, 1990). For other estimates of under-enumeration, see Robert Galois and Cole Harris, "Recalibrating Society: The Population Geography of British Columbia in 1881," *Canadian Geographer* 38, 1 (1994): 37-53.

43 Meeting at Fort Fraser, McKenna-McBride Commission, BCA, MS 1056, box 1, June 7, 1915.

44 *Census of Canada* (1951), 4: 14. See Nancy Shoemaker, "The Census as Civilizer: American Indian Household Structure in the 1900 and 1910 US Censuses," *Historical Methods* 25, 1 (1992): 6.

45 British Columbia, Legislative Assembly, *Annual Report of the Minister of Mines* (Victoria: British Columbia, 1874-1920); T.A. Rickard, "Indian Participation in the Gold Discoveries," *British Columbia Historical Quarterly* 2 (1938): 3-18; Dan Marshall, "Rickard Revisited: Native 'Participation' in the Gold Discoveries of British Columbia," *Native Studies Review* 11, 1 (1996): 91-99. A discussion of aboriginal gold miners is taken up in Chapter 6.

46 See Chapter 6.

47 "Irrelevant" quote from Eric Newsome, *The Coal Coast: History of Coal Mining in British Columbia* (Victoria: Orca, 1989), 33; Lynne Bowen, *Boss Whistle: The Coal Miners of Vancouver Island Remember* (Lantzville, BC: Oolichan, 1982) does not mention Aboriginal People at all. On the Scottish miners not raising any coal, see Hendrickson, "Two Letters," 12; "Trip Up the Fraser," *Victoria Gazette*, July 21, 1858, 2.

48 Turner first read this paper in 1893, and it was published in his collection of essays, *The Frontier in American History in 1920* (New York: Holt, Rinehart and Winston, 1962). See also Richard Slotkin, *Regeneration through Violence: The Mythology of the American Frontier, 1600-1860* (Middleton, CT: Wesleyan University Press, 1973). For BC variants, see H.H. Bancroft, *History of British Columbia, 1792-1887* (San Francisco: History, 1887); F.W. Howay and E.O.S. Scholefield, *British Columbia from the Earliest Times to the Present* (Vancouver: S.J. Clarke, 1913).

49 In his April 1991 decision on one of the largest land claim cases in Canadian legal history, *Delgamuukw v. BC*, Justice McEachern took this position in denying the claim. See the special issue of *BC Studies* (Anthropology and History in the Courts) 95 (1992), particularly Robin Ridington's "Fieldwork in Courtroom 53," for a discussion of how the judge used the work of historians and anthropologists. See also Dara Culhane, *The Pleasure of the Crown: Anthropology, Law, and First Nations* (Vancouver: Talonbooks, 1998).

50 If all aboriginal/non-aboriginal encounters were only variations on the same theme, then how do we explain, for example, why the Haida survived and the Beothuk did not? See Michael Harkin, "Dialogues of History: Transformation and Change in Heiltsuk Culture" (PhD diss., University of Chicago, 1988), 24; Nicholas Thomas, *Entangled Objects: Exchange, Material Culture and Colonialism in the Pacific* (Cambridge, MA: Harvard University Press, 1991), 10. A recent example of this perspective can be found in Peter Carstens, *The Queen's People: A Study of Hegemony, Coercion and Accommodation among the Okanagan of Canada* (Toronto: University of Toronto Press, 1991).

51 Fisher, *Contact and Conflict*, 111, 211. The enrichment thesis originated with Joyce Wike's doctoral dissertation, written at Columbia University. The thesis was published in her "Problems in Fur Trade Analyses: The Northwest Coast," *American Anthropologist* 60, 1 (1958): 1086-101. See also Wilson Duff, *The Indian History of British Columbia: The Impact of the White Man* (Victoria: Provincial Museum, 1964); Rennie Warburton and Stephen Scott, "The Fur Trade and Early Capitalist Development in British Columbia," *Canadian Journal of Native Studies* 5, 1 (1985): 27-46.

52 Sarah Carter, *Lost Harvests: Prairie Indian Reserve Farmers and Government Policy* (Montreal and Kingston: McGill-Queen's University Press, 1990). For a more contemporary analysis see also Helen Buckley, *From Wooden Ploughs to Welfare: Why Indian Policy Failed in the Prairie Provinces* (Montreal and Kingston: McGill-Queen's University Press, 1992); Leo Waisberg and Tim Holzkamm, "'A Tendency to Discourage Them from Cultivating': Ojibwa Agriculture and Indian Affairs Administration in Northwest Ontario," *Ethnohistory* 40, 2 (1993): 175-211; Ellice B. Gonzalez, *Changing Economic Roles for Micmac Men and Women: An Ethnohistorical Analysis* (Ottawa: National Museums of Canada, 1981).

53 Kenneth Coates, *Best Left as Indians: Native-White Relations in the Yukon Territory, 1840-1973* (Montreal and Kingston: McGill-Queen's University Press, 1991) 49, 52, 56, 64-65, 69.

54 Frank Tough, *As Their Natural Resources Fail: Native People and the Economic History of Northern Manitoba, 1870-1930* (Vancouver: UBC Press, 1996).

55 Knight's book, which I first read three decades ago, planted the seeds that resulted in this book. See Rolf Knight, *Indians at Work: An Informal History of Native Indian Labour in British Columbia, 1858-1930* (Vancouver: New Star, 1978). It was reissued, slightly revised, in 1996.

56 Knight, *Indians at Work*, 189. Fisher, in his 1992 re-issue of *Contact and Conflict*, flays Knight for his use of "impressionistic evidence and isolated examples" as well as for his lack of "systematic or statistical analyses" (19). Ironically, Fisher's own work relies on similar "impressionistic" evidence, offering no statistics in support of its position.

57 Knight, *Indians at Work*, 10, 22.

58 Alicja Muszynski, "Class Formation and Class Consciousness: The Making of Shoreworkers in the BC Fishing Industry," *Studies in Political Economy* 20 (1986): 85-116;

Muszynski, "Major Processors to 1940 and the Early Labour Force: Historical Notes," in *Uncommon Property: The Fishing and Fish Processing Industries in British Columbia*, ed. Patricia Marchak, Neil Guppy, and John McMullan (Toronto: Methuen, 1987), 46-65; Muszynski, "Race and Gender: Structural Determinants in the Formation of BC's Salmon Canning Labour Forces," *Canadian Journal of Sociology* (1988): 110. I find these earlier works more helpful than her more theory-driven *Cheap Wage Labour: Race and Gender in the Fisheries of British Columbia* (Montreal and Kingston: McGill-Queen's University Press, 1996). Quote from Evelyn Pinkerton, "Competition among BC Fish-Processing Firms," in Marchak, Guppy, and McMullan, *Uncommon Property*, 256.

59 Pinkerton, "Competition among BC Fish-Processing Firms," 261; Pinkerton notes that some cannery owners preferred Indian labour even when other cheap sources of labour were available. Other evidence shows that aboriginal women continued to constitute the main labour force in rural canneries until technological change and economic consolidation closed these institutions in the 1950s. See Newell, *Tangled Webs*; Douglas C. Harris, *Fish Law and Colonialism: The Legal Capture of Salmon in British Columbia* (Toronto: University of Toronto Press, 2001). See Chapter 6.

60 Richard Mackie, *Trading beyond the Mountains: The British Fur Trade on the Pacific, 1793-1843* (Vancouver: UBC Press, 1997); and Richard Mackie, "Colonial Land, Indian Labour and Company Capital: The Economy of Vancouver Island, 1849-1858" (MA thesis, University of Victoria, 1984).

61 Michael Harkin, *The Heiltsuks: Dialogues of Culture and History on the Northwest Coast* (Lincoln: University of Nebraska Press, 1997); M.M. Bakhtin, *The Dialogic Imagination: Four Essays*, ed. Michael Holquist, trans. Caryl Emmerson and Michael Holquist (Austin: University of Texas, 1981), 25-30, 427.

Chapter 4: The Lekwungen

1 Originally called the *British Colonist*, "British" was dropped in 1893 so that colonists of all origins could find themselves reflected in the paper.

2 W.H. Lomas, in Canada, Legislative Assembly, "Department of Indian Affairs Annual Report" (DIAR), *Canada Sessional Papers* (Ottawa: Canada, 1882), 160-62; William Fraser Tolmie to Sir Alexander Campbell, Federal Minister of Justice, August 21, 1883, BCA, A E O13 C15.

3 Aziz found an earned income of $31,385 in a survey of 80 members of the 156-member labour force. I have extrapolated his sample, which was supposed to be representative, in order to estimate the total income of the Indian labour force ($61,201) and divided by the total south island Indian population of 1,075. The 1881 figure of $15,000 has been inflated in accordance with the wholesale price indexes in Table K33 of F.H. Leachy, ed., *Historical Statistics of Canada*, 2nd ed. (Ottawa: Statistics Canada, 1983), to its value in 1969 dollars ($61,118). Divided by the 1881 south island population of 661, this yields a per capita income of $92.46. The real 1969 income could have been 40 percent higher before it would have exceeded the 1881 value. Moreover, we know that the 1881 figure only accounts for one of the income sources, so the total 1881 income was undoubtedly higher. See Salim Akhtar Aziz, "Selected Aspects of Cultural Change among Amerindians: A Case Study of Southeast Vancouver Island" (MA thesis, University of Victoria, 1970), 33-35.

4 John Kendrick, *The Men with Wooden Feet* (Toronto: NC, 1986), 17-18. These acts of possession have been analyzed by Patricia Seed, *Ceremonies of Possession in Europe's Conquest of the New World, 1492-1690* (Cambridge: Cambridge University Press, 1995).

5 The Mitchell Bay Aboriginal People on San Juan Island claim descent from the Lekwungen, who had villages at Open Bay on Henry Island and at Taleqamus Bay, Garrison Bay, and Wescott Bay, all of which are on San Juan Island. See Robert H. Ruby and John A. Brown, *A Guide to the Indian Tribes of the Pacific Northwest* (Norman: University of Oklahoma Press, 1986), 133, and Map 3.2.

6 Henry R. Wagner, *Spanish Explorations in the Strait of Juan de Fuca* (New York: AMS, 1933), 206. It is possible that the Lekwungen saw the vessel the *Washington* in 1789, when Robert Gray entered the strait for fifty miles before "finding he did not meet with encouragement as a trader" and turned back. Gray was looking for sea otter pelts, which were not found in the Straits of Juan de Fuca. See George Vancouver, *A Voyage of Discovery to the North Pacific Ocean and Round the World* (London: G.G. and J. Robinson, 1798; reprint ed. W. Kaye

Lamb, London: Hakluyt Society, 1984), 581-82.

7 Cecil Jane, *A Spanish Voyage to Vancouver Island and the North-West Coast of America* (London: Argonaut, 1930), 34, 38. Kendrick's translation of the story has the incident occurring in Haro Strait (also Lekwungen territory) and reports that the longboat fired, "killing some of them." See John Kendrick, "The End of the Northern Mystery: The Spanish in Juan de Fuca and Beyond, 1790-1792," in *Spain and the North Pacific Coast*, ed. Robin Inglis (Vancouver: Vancouver Maritime Museum, 1992), 105. Richard Inglis points out in his article, "The Spanish on the North Pacific Coast: An Alternative View from Nootka Sound," in Inglis, *Spain and the North Pacific Coast*, that Spanish sailors, in contrast to their officers, were often brutal in their behaviour towards Aboriginal People at Yuquot. Similar behaviour may have precipitated violence in Lekwungen territory.

8 Marjorie Mitchell, "A Dictionary of Songish: A Dialect of Coast Salish" (MA thesis, University of Victoria, 1968), 102. Martinez bought a boy and a girl in 1789, Malaspina bought twenty-two children in 1791 in Nootka Sound (for one or two copper sheets each), and Eliza purchased a total of fifty-two children on the coast in 1792. Apparently the children were intended to be taken to Mexico to be instructed in Christianity. See Warren L. Cook, *Flood Tide of Empire* (New Haven: Yale University Press, 1973), 118, 306-14.

9 Jane, *A Spanish Voyage*, 34-35. That same year Captain Vancouver passed through the Straits of Juan de Fuca, and his tender, the *Chatham*, explored the San Juan Islands and bought venison from some Aboriginal People who may have been Lekwungen. See J. Neilson Barry, "Broughton's Reconnaissance of the San Juan Islands in 1792," *Washington Historical Quarterly* 21 (1930): 55-60.

10 Jane, *A Spanish Voyage*, 34-35. The Lekwungen had no sheep but used the wool of dogs to make their cloaks. The transformation from bulb to fig probably occurred because the Lekwungen dried the bulbs, as the Spaniards dried figs, on a string. The resemblance is clear in the Hesquiaht and Manhousaht word for fig, which may be translated as "looks like camas bulbs." See Nancy J. Turner, John Thomas, Barry F. Carlson, and Robert Ogilvie, *Ethnobotany of the Nitinaht Indians of Vancou-*ver Island, Occasional Papers no. 24 (Victoria: Royal BC Museum, 1983), 142. For the "molasses sticks legs" story, see Introduction.

11 Another "transformation," since mulberries (*moraceae*) are not native. More likely they were given salmonberries (*rubus spectablis*), a significant part of the Lekwungen diet and the only berries that were ripe at the time of Quimper's June visit.

12 Jane, *A Spanish Voyage*, 35; Kendrick has analyzed this journal, trying to understand how they communicated with one another. He concludes, from internal evidence, that some communication definitely transpired but that Galiano may have exaggerated the extent of it to impress upon his superiors his success in establishing friendly relations with the local people. See Kendrick, "The End," 107.

13 The major anthropological sources on the Lekwungen are: Franz Boas, "The Lku'ñgen," *Report of the British Association for the Advancement of Science* 59 (1890), 563-82; Wayne Suttles, *Economic Life of the Coast Salish of Haro and Rosario Straits* (New York: Garland, 1974); Homer Barnett, *Coast Salish of British Columbia* (Eugene: University of Oregon Press, 1955); and Charles Hill-Tout, *The Salish People*, vol. 4, ed. Ralph Maud (Vancouver: Talon, 1977). Other important material on the relationship of the larger group of Coast Salish people to the spirit world is found in Diamond Jenness, *The Faith of a Coast Salish Indian* (Victoria: BC Provincial Museum, 1986). See also Diamond Jenness, "The Saanich Indians of Vancouver Island," National Museum of Canada, mss no. VIIOG-8M, p114ff; and June Collins, "John Fornsby: The Personal Document of a Coast Salish Indian," in *Indians of the Urban Northwest*, ed. Marian Smith (New York: Columbia University Press, 1949), 287-341.

14 Chief David Latasse describes the Lekwungen-Wsanec spirit quest in N. De B. Lugrin, "Chief David's Saga," *Daily Colonist*, May 17, 1936, 6, and it appears in the Lekwungen "Story of Sematl" recorded by Hill-Tout, *The Salish People*, 135-55; Wilson Duff, "The Fort Victoria Treaties," *BC Studies* 3 (1969): 8-9; Grant Keddie, "Legend of Camosun," *Discovery* (Autumn 1991): 3; Suttles, *Economic Life*, 33; Wayne Suttles, "Post-Contact Culture Change Among the Lummi Indians," *British Columbia Historical Quarterly* 18 (1945): 52. The importance

of place names in oral cultures is well illustrated by Keith Basso, *Wisdom Sits in Places: Landscape and Language among the Western Apache* (Albuquerque: University of New Mexico Press, 1996); and Fernando Santos-Granero, "Writing History into the Landscape: Space, Myth, and Ritual in Contemporary Amazonia," *American Ethnologist* 25, 2 (1998): 128-48.

15 The Fornsby account is transcribed in a narrative style little influenced by Europeans. See Collins, "John Fornsby," 322; Suttles, *Economic Life*, 327-31, 448. See also William W. Elmendorf, *Twana Narratives: Native Historical Accounts of a Coast Salish Culture* (Seattle: University of Washington Press, 1993), 165-98; Jenness, *Faith of a Coast Salish Indian*, 48.

16 Hill-Tout notes that the Lekwungen were distinguished from their neighbours by a highly refined sense of ownership of specific resources. See Charles Hill-Tout, "Report on the Ethnology of the South-Eastern Tribes of Vancouver Island, BC," 1907, in Maud, *Salish People*, 130; Suttles, *Economic Life*, particularly 325-425; Suttles, "Private Knowledge, Morality, and Social Classes among the Coast Salish," in *Coast Salish Essays*, ed. Wayne Suttles (Vancouver/Seattle: Talonbooks/University of Washington Press, 1987), 3-14; Homer Barnett, "Culture Element Distributions: Gulf of Georgia Salish," *Anthropological Records* 1, 5 (1939): 221-95; Jenness, "The Saanich Indians," 50-95. For a discussion of the concentric rings of ownership, see Keith Thor Carlson, "Stó:lō Exchange Dynamics," *Native Studies Review* 11, 1 (1996): 5-47; Bruce Miller, "Centrality and Measures of Regional Structure in Aboriginal Western Washington," *Ethnology* 28, 3 (1989): 265-76.

17 Suttles, "Private Knowledge," 3-14.

18 Suttles, *Economic Life*, 381.

19 Barnett, *Coast Salish*, 250-51; Marian W. Smith, *The Puyallup-Nisqually* (New York: Columbia University Press, 1940), 143-45.

20 Suttles, *Economic Life*, 50.

21 Ray F. Verne, *Lower Chinook Ethnographic Notes* (Seattle: University of Washington, 1938), records that chiefs appropriated food in times of shortage. Carlson, "Stó:lō Exchange Dynamics," and Miller, "Centrality and Measures," propose the idea that the more two groups were separated spatially and socially the less reciprocity there was between them. People distant enough to trade food for wealth were also distant enough to steal from, or even to attack and rob, so exchange at this level had its own risks.

22 The strongest case for two separate but connected economies is found in Suttles, "Affinal Ties, Subsistence and Prestige among the Coast Salish," in Suttles, *Coast Salish Essays*, 15-25; and Carlson, "Stó:lō Exchange Dynamics." See also Homer Barnett, "The Nature of the Potlatch," in *Indians of the North Pacific Coast*, ed. Tom McFeat (Toronto: McClelland and Stewart, 1966), 81-91.

23 Carlson notes that, in the Halq'eméylem language of the Stó:lō, blankets and currency (or dollars) were the only items that shared the same counting word. See Carlson, "Stó:lō Exchange Dynamics," 41. Haiqua shells were another medium of exchange. See Robert Galois and Richard Mackie, "A Curious Currency," *The Midden* 22, 4 and 5 (1990): 1-3, 6-9; Suttles, *Economic Life*, 325; Barnett, *Coast Salish*, 257.

24 Collins, "John Fornsby," 304; Kane, *Wanderings of an Artist*, 152. Others noted blankets, canoes, horses, watches, guns, ammunition, clothes, and slaves as gambling stakes. See Lynn Maranda, *Coast Salish Gambling Games*, Mercury Series no. 93 (Ottawa: National Museums of Canada, 1984), 26-27, 44-46.

25 Boas, "The Lku'ñgen," 569.

26 For an elaboration of this, see Carlson, "Stó:lō Exchange Dynamics."

27 Robert Brown, "On the Vegetable Products Used by the North-West American Indians," *Transactions of the Botanical Society of Edinburgh* 27 (1868): 393; Collins, "John Fornsby," 319, 325; Kane, *Wanderings of an Artist*, 149, 151; Boas, "The Lku'ñgen," 570, 572, 575, 578-9; Suttles, *Economic Life*, 492-94.

28 Carlson, "Stó:lō Exchange Dynamics," 23-25; Barnett, *Coast Salish*, 253; Wayne Suttles, *Coast Salish Essays* (Vancouver/Seattle: Talonbooks/University of Washington Press, 1987), 8, 17.

29 For a personal account from this area, see N. de. B. Lugrin, "Aged Indian Princess Recalls Childhood," *Victoria Sunday Times Magazine*, May 3, 1952, 5. See the stories collected by Hill-Tout, *Salish People*, 4: 135-55; and those recorded by Robert Brown and printed in Robert Brown, *Robert Brown and the Vancouver Island Exploring Expedition*, ed. John Hayman (Vancouver: UBC Press, 1989), 179-96.

30 Although the male party would humble himself in this way to obtain his wife, the rough equivalence of the marriage gift and the return gift from the bride's family suggests that acquiring a good son-in-law was at least as valuable as was acquiring a good daughter-in-law.

31 Since these marriages were unions between households, not villages or nations, a visiting party of in-laws might still be victims of predatory attacks on the part of their neighbours.

32 Carlson, "Stó:lō Exchange Dynamics," 23-25; Barnett, *Coast Salish*, 253.

33 This description is from Collins, "John Fornsby," 302, 317, 320. Fornsby also described his own marriage (ca. 1875), which was a simple affair between two "common people." Another marriage of a high-ranking Lekwungen (ca. 1840-45) is described in Elmendorf, *Twana Narratives*, 39-40. For a Lekwungen account of marriage that ended hostilities between the Squamish and the Lekwungen, see Hill-Tout, *Salish People*, 4:142.

34 The marks on the ends of blankets refer to the "points" that the HBC used on blankets to mark their quality. Two and one-half points was the standard, although blankets may have as many as four points. When Fornsby said that the Swinomish had never seen caps or shirts before, he apparently meant that they had never *had* caps or shirts before. Presumably he meant that these were not common rather than unknown. See Collins, "John Fornsby," 309. A parallel description of an 1873 Lekwungen potlatch, from a non-aboriginal perspective, can be found in J.D. Edgar, "A Potlatch among Our West Coast Indians," *Canadian Monthly and National Review* 6, 2 (1874): 93-99.

35 This may be the "wedding ceremony" described by Wilson in 1858 in Charles Wilson, *Mapping the Frontier: Charles Wilson's Diary of the Survey of the 49th Parallel, 1858-1862*, ed. G.F.G. Stanley (Toronto: Macmillan, 1970), 29. Jenness describes a Lekwungen wedding, as does Hill-Tout. See Jenness, "The Saanich Indians," 83-84; Hill-Tout, "Report on the Ethnology of the South-Eastern Tribes," 132-34.

36 This relationship between gift giver and receiver has been analyzed in detail in other social settings in C.A. Gregory, *Gifts and Commodities* (London: Academic, 1982), 41-69.

37 Barnett, *Coast Salish*, 257-58.

38 Mitchell, "A Dictionary of Songish," 87, 89; Suttles, "Private Knowledge," 6-9; Barnett, *Coast Salish*, 141, 243-45, 248. This disdain was generally similar throughout the Northwest Coast.

39 A fuller description of the gendered nature of Lekwungen life can be found in John Lutz, "Gender and Work in Lekwammen Families, 1843-1970," in *Gendered Pasts: Historical Essays on Femininity and Masculinity in Canada*, ed. Kathryn McPherson, Cecilia Morgan, and Nancy M. Forestell (Don Mills, ON: Oxford University Press, 1999), 80-105.

40 The Lekwungen were divided into three classes according to Suttles: "Good People" or nobles, from which the headmen would be drawn; "Worthless People," or commoners; and slaves. Boas and Hill-Tout believed that there were four classes, including a separate middle *nitcnanit* (parvenu) class, which was not of the nobility but had acquired considerable wealth. See Wayne Suttles, "Private Knowledge," 3-14; Hill-Tout, *Salish People*, 4: 130; Boas, "The Lku'ñgen," 569

41 J.M. Yale's 1839 census included one of the Lekwungen extended families. He records twelve families, which included fifty-seven "people" plus seventy male and female "followers," which seems to include slaves and the offspring of slaves and masters (Keith Carlson, private communication). The large number of slaves may have been a recent adaptation. See BCA, B/20/1853, James Douglas, Private Papers, 2nd series, 5-31. For the impact of the European economy on slaves, see Leland Donald, *Aboriginal Slavery on the Northwest Coast of North America* (Berkeley: University of California Press, 1997).

42 Kane, *Wanderings of an Artist*, 152; Gary J. Morris, *Straits Salish Prehistory* (Lopez Island: Morris, 1993), 11; Jean Baptiste Zacharie Bolduc, *Mission of the Columbia*, ed. and trans. Edward J. Kowrach (Fairfield, WA: Ye Galleon, 1979), 108; the interior of a longhouse is described in 1861 in Sophia Cracroft, "Letters, Vancouver and British Columbia: 1861," BCA, add. mss. 227.

43 Chee-al-thluk was generally known to the whites as King Freezie. He was "chief" of the Lekwungen until his death in 1864. See Grant Keddie, *Songhees Pictorial: A History of the Songhees People as Seen by Outsiders, 1790-1912* (Victoria: Royal BC Museum, 2003), 93.

44 Barnett, *Coast Salish*, 241-44; James Robert Anderson, "Notes and Comments on Early Days and Events in

British Columbia, Washington, and Oregon," BCA, add mss 1912, box 8/18.

45 Suttles believes that, while women made the twine, most reef and other nets were made by men. See Suttles, *Economic Life*, 235-40.

46 Suttles, *Economic Life*, 57, 69. Vancouver, visiting a Salish village in 1790, commented: "nearly the whole of the inhabitants ... about 80 or 100 men, women and children, were busily engaged ... rooting up this beautiful verdant meadow in quest of a species of wild onion." See Vancouver, *Voyage of Discovery*, 545.

47 Myron Eells, *The Indians of Puget Sound: The Notebooks of Myron Eells,* ed. George Pierre Castile (Seattle: University of Washington Press, 1985), 122; F.W. Howay, "The Dog's Hair Blankets of the Coast Salish," *Washington Historical Quarterly* 9, 2 (1918): 83-91. One of Paul Kane's paintings (see page 63) shows a Lekwungen woman weaving such a blanket and another spinning dog's wool with a sheared dog in the foreground. See also Erna Gunther, *Indian Life on the Northwest Coast of North America* (Chicago: University of Chicago Press, 1972), appendix 2; Erna Gunther, *Klallam Ethnography* (Seattle: University of Washington Press, 1927) 221. Suttles, *Economic Life*, writes that hunting dogs were owned by men; Jane, *A Spanish Voyage*, 34-35; Vancouver, *A Voyage of Discovery*, 524.

48 Concerning the Coast Salish group the Duwamish and their adoption of potatoes, the Indian Agent wrote: "Each head of family plants his own; the quantity being regulated by the number of his women." See United States, Governor Stevens, "Report of the Commissioner of Indian Affairs," November 25, 1854, Senate Exec. Doc., 33rd cong., 2nd sess., no. 746 211.

49 Boas, "The Lku'ñgen," 571. Boas notes that this custom was found all along the Northwest Coast. See O.B. Sperlin, "Two Kootenay Women Masquerading as Men? Or Were They One?" *Washington Historical Quarterly* 21 (1930): 120-30. An aboriginal transvestite was castrated by British sailors on the Columbia River in the 1840s, according to Lorne Hammond, "Adulterers, Murderers, Orphans and Transvestites: A Look at the Periphery of Fur Trade Masculinity," paper presented to the Columbia Department Fur Trade Conference, Victoria, 1993. Charles Nowell mentions transvestites among the Kwakwaka'wakw in Clellan S. Ford, *Smoke*

from Their Fires: The Life of a Kwakiutl Chief (Hamden, CN: Archon, 1968), 68-69.

50 Brian Chisholm and Toshio Nakamura, "Prehistoric Diet at DgRl 5 (Esilao Village) and DjRi 46," report prepared for Stó:lō Nation, August 9, 1994, Stó:lō Nation Archives.

51 Earl Claxton Jr. and John Elliot Sr., *Reef Net Technology of the Saltwater People* (Saanich, BC: Saanich Indian School Board, 1994); Dave Elliot, Sr., *Saltwater People*, ed. Janet Poth (Saanich: BC School District 63, 1990); Erna Gunther, "A Further Analysis of the First Salmon Ceremony," *University of Washington Press Publications in Anthropology* 2, 5 (1928):129-73.

52 The description of reef netting is from Claxton and Elliot, *Reef Net Technology of the Saltwater People*; Suttles, *Economic Life*, 152-222; and N. Alexander Easton, "The Archaeology of Straits Salish Reef Netting: Past and Future Research Strategies," *Northwest Anthropological Research Notes* 24, 2 (1990): 161-77. See also Daniel Boxberger, *San Juan Island National Historical Park: Cultural Affiliation Study* (Seattle: National Park Service, n.d.).

53 Boas, "The Lku'ñgen," 568. Suttles' aboriginal informants used the word "hire" to describe the engagement of captain and crew. Quote from Suttles, *Economic Life*, 31 (see also 219, 485-89).

54 Suttles, *Economic Life*, 221.

55 Collins, 1892, quoted in Boxberger, who accepts the estimate that, on average, the Straits Salish consumed just under two pounds of fish per day, or six hundred pounds per person per annum. Estimating a normal daily catch to be one thousand fish at five pounds (dried weight) per fish, the product of one normal day at one reef net would feed almost nine people for a year. See Daniel L. Boxberger, *To Fish in Common: The Ethnohistory of Lummi Salmon Fishing* (Lincoln: University of Nebraska Press, 1989), 15-16. For another estimate that "under exceptionally favourable conditions ... a single net may secure as many as 2,000 fish in a day," see Richard Rathbun, "A Review of the Fisheries in the Contiguous Waters of the State of Washington and British Columbia," *Report of the US Commissioner of Fisheries for 1899* (Washington: United States Government Printing Office, 1900), 231.

56 Quoting Father P.J. De Smet, *Oregon Missions and Travels over the Rocky Mountains in 1845-46* (New York:

Edward Dunigan, 1847), 117; Suttles, *Economic Life*, 58-63, 488-89.

57 De Smet, *Oregon Missions*, 117; Charles Wilkes, *Life in Oregon Country before the Emigration*, ed. Richard Moore (Ashland: Oregon Book Society, 1974), 45; Vancouver, *Voyage*, 262.

58 Bernhard Stern, *The Lummi Indians of Northwest Washington* (New York: Columbia University Press, 1934), 42-43.

59 Report of the first colonial surveyor, W.C. Grant, "Report on Vancouver Island, 1849," BCA, A/B/20/G76. See also Brenda Beckwith, "'The Queen Root of This Clime': Ethnoecological Investigations of Blue Camas (Camassia leichtlinii, C. quamash; Liliaceae) and Its Landscapes on Southern Vancouver Island, British Columbia" (PhD diss., University of Victoria, 2004).

60 In the 1940s, Mr. and Mrs. Tom James of the Lekwungen (Discovery Island) told Suttles that the camas beds around Victoria were open to anyone; however, the evidence of the treaties and his other Salish informants suggest that it was more likely that the camas prairies and islands were "owned" but that relations or others were permitted to use them. See Suttles, *Economic Life*, 59-64.

61 Duff, "Fort Victoria Treaties."

62 See John Lutz, "Preparing Eden: Aboriginal Land Use and European Settlement," paper presented to the Canadian Historical Association Annual Meeting, Montreal, August 25-27, 1995. All over the Straits area the first choice of European settlers was the cleared camas fields of the Salish. See Richard White, *Land Use, Environment, and Social Change: The Shaping of Island County, Washington* (Seattle: University of Washington Press, 1980).

63 James Douglas to James Hargrave, February 1843, in G.P.T. Glazebrook, ed., *The Hargrave Correspondence* (Toronto: Champlain Society, 1938), 420-21; James Douglas to John McLoughlin, July 12, 1842, printed in "The Founding of Fort Victoria," *The Beaver*, March 1943, 4; G. M. Sproat, *The Nootka: Scenes and Studies of Savage Life* (London: Smith, Elder; reprinted Victoria: Sono Nis, 1989), 42.

64 European observers declared this comet to have the longest tail ever observed. See Fred L. Whipple, *The Mystery of Comets* (Washington, DC: Smithsonian, 1985), 84.

65 In addition to the stories mentioned above, see Ella E. Clark, "George Gibbs' account of Indian Mythology in Oregon and Washington Territory," *Oregon Historical Quarterly* 56, 4 (1955): 319. Y.F. Tuan suggests that, instead of knowing the world horizontally as the moderns do (i.e., as part of a curved plane that connects us to the imperial centres/rest of world), tribal peoples knew it as a vertical column in which the stars and the deep sea were as much a part of the world as was the ground. See Y.F. Tuan, *Topophilia* (Englewood Cliffs, NJ: Prentice-Hall, 1974), 130-31.

66 Europeans also interpreted the spectacular comets as major events. We know that another comet, visible in the daytime in 44 BC, was interpreted by Romans as the ascension of Caesar to heaven (thus resulting in the mantle of succession being conferred upon his son) and that the comets of 1577 and 1618 were instrumental in overthrowing the Aristotelian world view. See T. Van Nouhuys, *The Age of the Two-Faced Janus* (Leiden, Netherlands: Brill, 1998); J.T. Ramsay and A.L. Licht, *The Comet of 44 BC and Caesar's Funeral Games* (Atlanta: Scholars, 1997). The great comets of 1664 and 1665 were thought to have presaged the London plague of 1665 and the great fire of 1666. Milton wrote the following year, echoing the nineteenth book of Homer's *Illiad* in speaking of the helmet of Achilles, which shone "Like the red star, that from his flaming hair, Shakes down disease, pestilence and war." In New England in 1843, fifty thousand followers of the prophet William Miller believed that the earth would end in a fire in April 1843, and the comet of that year seemed to be a sign that he was right. See Donald K. Yeomans, *Comets* (New York: John Wiley and Sons, 1991), 78, 178-79.

67 Simpson, quoted in "The Founding of Fort Victoria," *Beaver* Outfit 273 (1943): 3; James Douglas to James Hargrave, February 5, 1843, in G.P.T. Glazebrook, ed., *The Hargrave Correspondence, 1821-1843* (Toronto: Champlain Society, 1938), 420-21.

68 Bolduc, *Mission of the Columbia*, 107.

69 James Douglas, Diary of a Trip to Victoria, March 1-21, 1843, BCA, A/B/40/D75.4A.

70 David Latasse was born Lekwungen, but at age eight he went to live with the neighbouring Wsanec people. He is quoted in Frank Pagett, "105 Years in Victoria and Saanich! Chief David Recalls White Man's Coming;

80 Years Rent Unpaid," *Victoria Daily Times,* July 14, 1934, Features 1. Later censuses suggest that Latasse may not have been old enough to witness the event himself and that this may be a secondhand account.

71 Douglas certainly spoke Chinook, and Bolduc was in the process of acquiring the jargon. When Bolduc went to the Songhees' camp, he was accompanied by a "Canadian" named Gobin, an interpreter. It is not clear whether Gobin translated Bolduc's French into Chinook or into a dialect of Straits Salish. Chinook jargon was not widely spoken among the Lekwungen at this time, but a few individuals likely understood some of it. See Bolduc, *Mission of the Columbia,* 93, 109; Thomas Lowe, quoted by John Walbran, in J. Walbran, *British Columbia Coast Names* (Vancouver: J.J. Douglas, 1971), 512.

72 The log of the HBC vessel *Camosun,* from August and September 1843, records this employment. Printed in *Beaver,* 22, 4 (March 1943): 8-9. Douglas wrote to Simpson on November 16, 1843, that "the resources of the country in fish, are only known as yet through the supply procured in trade from the Natives, which was abundant after the arrival of the salmon in July, other kinds of fish were not regularly brought in, a proof of their being, either, less sought after or not so easily caught." See HBCA, D.5/9, printed in W. Kaye Lamb, "Founding of Fort Victoria," *British Columbia Historical Quarterly* 7 (1940): 90; Roderick Finlayson, "History of Vancouver Island and the Northwest Coast," BCA, A/B/30/F49.1, describes the construction of the fort.

73 Bolduc, *Mission of the Columbia,* 110; Roderick Finlayson, "Biography," BCA, A/B/30/F49A.

74 Finlayson, "History of Vancouver Island."

75 The concentration of most Lekwungen at these two sites was itself a recent adaptation. Previously, each of the Lekwungen family groups had occupied its own winter village. See Duff, "Fort Victoria Treaties."

76 Finlayson, "Biography" and "History of Vancouver Island."

77 Ibid. Finlayson says the visitors were from Whidbey Island.

78 Berthold Seemann, *Narrative of the Voyage of HMS Herald during the Years 1845-51* (London: Reeve and Co., 1853).

79 James Deans, "Settlement of Vancouver Island," BCA, 1878, E/B/D342.

80 Finlayson, "History of Vancouver Island" and "Biography"; Douglas to Governor and Committee, November 6, 1847, in Hartwell Bowsfield, *Fort Victoria Letters: 1846-1851* (Winnipeg: Hudson's Bay Record Society, 1979), 16.

81 Collins, "John Fornsby." The date must have been in the 1890s or first years of the twentieth century, when Cooper was chief.

82 Finlayson, "Biography"; Finlayson, "History of Vancouver Island"; William Fraser Tolmie, "Utilization of the Indians," *The Resources of British Columbia* 1, 12, February 1, 1884, 7; James Douglas to W.F. Tolmie, August 13, 1857, country letterbook, BCA, 171; W.C. Grant, "Report on Vancouver Island, 1849," BCA, A/B/20/G76; Great Britain, Colonial Office, Despatches about Vancouver Island, William Miller to H.A. Addington, October 23, 1848, quoting a letter of Captain Courtenay dated September 12, BCA, GR-0328.

83 Eden Colville to Sir George Simpson, October 15, 1849, in E.E. Rich, *London Correspondence Inward from Eden Colvile, 1849-1852* (London: Hudson's Bay Record Society, 1952), 181.

84 Keith Thor Carlson, "Stó:lō Exchange Dynamics," *Native Studies Review* 11, 1 (1996): 5-47.

85 See, for examples, Douglas to Barclay, September 1, 1850, Douglas to Barclay, April 16, 1851, in Bowsfield, *Fort Victoria Letters,* 17, 115, 170, 174; Dorothy Blakey-Smith, ed., *The Reminiscences of Doctor John Sebastian Helmcken,* by J.S. Helmcken (Vancouver: UBC Press, 1975), 127; Finlayson, "Biography." When Kane was at Fort Victoria in 1847, he saw forty Lekwungen with ten non-Aboriginal People building a new warehouse. See Kane, *Wanderings of an Artist,* 145.

86 Later, when the young people started drinking, the Clallum moved some distance away to Witty's Beach and then to Beecher Bay. See Suttles, *Economic Life,* 11. When Paul Kane visited the fort in 1847, he called the local people Clallum rather than Lekwungen. His confusion may have stemmed from the temporary cohabitation of these two peoples.

87 He added, though, that "the only fisherman as yet being Indians their supplies are precarious and uncertain," suggesting perhaps that Aboriginal People used provisions as a lever in their disputes with the immigrants. The estimate is quite plausible, given that a single net

could likely catch about two thousand salmon per day. See W.C. Grant to Brodie, August 8, 1851, in J.E. Hendrickson, ed. "Two Letters from Walter Colquhoun Grant," *BC Studies* 26 (1975): 12.

88 Douglas to Governor and Committee, October 27, 1849, in Bowsfield, *Fort Victoria Letters*, 63. Cairn Crockford has quantitatively evaluated the trade at Fort Victoria in "Fort Victoria Journals," paper presented to Columbia Department Fur Trade Conference, Victoria, October 1-3, 1993.

89 Finlayson, "Biography," 16; Finlayson, "History of Vancouver Island," 35-36; Douglas Letters to the Hudson's Bay Company, August 26, 1853, BCA, A/C/20Vi2A.

90 Suttles, *Economic Life*, 305-06; Barnett, "Culture Element Distributions," 267; Collins, "John Fornsby," 303. A female slave was given to one of the participants in an 1863 potlatch in the Lekwungen village, according to Matthew MacFie, *Vancouver Island and British Columbia: Their History, Resources, and Prospects* (London: Longman, Roberts, and Green, 1865), 431. MacFie was a very biased observer; however, descriptions of slavery in west coast societies can be found in: Donald, *Aboriginal Slavery*; Donald H. Mitchell, "Predatory Warfare, Social Status and the North Pacific Slave Trade," *Ethnology* 23, 1 (1984): 39-48; and Donald Mitchell and Leland Donald, "Some Economic Aspects of Tlingit, Haida, and Tsimshian Slavery," *Research in Economic Anthropology* 7 (1985), 19-35. A more anecdotal study may be found in Robert H. Ruby and John A. Brown, *Indian Slavery in the Pacific Northwest* (Spokane, WA: A.H. Clark, 1993).

91 In his journal Paul Kane claims that he saw a Lekwungen slave killed by her owner in 1846. See Kane, *Wanderings of an Artist*, 149. But see MacLaren's analyses of Kane's journal in Ian S. MacLaren, "The Metamorphosis of Travelers into Authors: The Case of Paul Kane," in *Critical Issues in Editing Exploration Texts: Papers Given at the Twenty-Eighth Annual Conference on Editorial Problems, University of Toronto, 6-7 November, 1992*, ed. Germaine Warkentin (Toronto: University of Toronto Press, 1995), 67-108. The census of the Lekwungen is in James Douglas, Private Papers, 2nd series, 5-31, BCA, B/20/1853; Keith Thor Carlson, "The Power of Place, the Problem of Time: A Study of History and Aborig-

inal Collective Identity" (PhD diss., University of British Columbia, 2003).

92 Throughout the 1840s, it was common to have slaves owned either by the employees of the fort or their aboriginal wives at HBC forts. See Tolmie, "Utilization of the Indians," 7; Stephen A. McNeary, "When Fire Came Down: Social and Economic Life of the Niska" (PhD diss., Bryn Mawr College, 1976), 382. See also Richard S. Mackie, *Trading beyond the Mountains: The British Fur Trade on the Pacific, 1793-1843* (Vancouver: UBC Press, 1997), 302.

93 Elmendorf, *Twana Narratives*, 61-63; Fort Victoria Journal, July 19, 1846, HBCA; Mackie, *Trading beyond the Mountains*, 301-6.

94 Suttles, *Economic Lives*, 305; according to Jones, each slave cost between six hundred and seven hundred blankets, though this seems high. See Charles Jones with Stephen Bosustow, *Queesto, Pacheenaht Chief by Birthright* (Nanaimo, BC: Theytus, 1981), 55.

95 Charles Wilson, "Report on the Indian Tribes Inhabiting the Country in the Vicinity of the 49th Parallel of North Latitude," *Transactions of the Ethnological Society of London* 14 (1866): 290; Captain John's descendants told Oliver Wells that the former rented slaves to the Boundary Commission. See K.C. Wells Collection, Chilliwack Archives, add mss 1, file 584.

96 Tolmie, "Utilization of the Indians," 7; Bolduc, *Mission of the Columbia*, 110; Donald, *Aboriginal Slavery*, 233, talks of slaves being rented out to the HBC to paddle canoes.

97 After 1876, "chief" acquires a legal meaning defined by the Indian Act.

98 Bolduc, *Mission of the Columbia*, 110; David Latasse, in Frank Pagett, "105 Years in Victoria"; Douglas to Lord Russell, 21 August, 1855, CO 305/6, 10048. For example, the Fort Rupert journals record that chiefs were paid at the same rate as were labourers to "supervise." Sealing schooners would negotiate with chiefs to bring a whole crew from a single village. See *Fort Rupert Post Journal*, 22 November, 1849, quoted in William Burrill, "Class Conflict and Colonialism: The Coal Miners of Vancouver Island during the Hudson's Bay Company Era, 1848-1862" (MA thesis, University of Victoria, 1987), 34. For sealing, see Cairn Crockford, "Changing Economic Activities of the Nuu-chah-nulth of Vancouver Island,

1840-1920" (BA honours thesis, University of Victoria, 1991), 58. One such arrangement with a chief went wrong in Puget Sound, when the chief was killed. See Drew W. Crooks, "Murder at Butler Cove: The Death of Tsus-sy-uch and Its Violent Consequences," *Occurrences* 14, 4 (1996/97): 3-12.

99　Douglas to Governor and Committee, April 16, 1851, in Bowsfield, *Fort Victoria Letters*, 17; Kane, *Wanderings of an Artist*, 145.

100　Dick, J.S. Helmcken's servant, who was paid two blankets and a shirt per month, probably hired himself out and owned his pay as personal property. Certainly, the diary of Arthur Clah, who came to Victoria from Port Simpson in the late 1850s, shows he hired himself out. See Robert Galois, "Colonial Encounters: The Worlds of Arthur Wellington Clah, 1855-1881," *BC Studies* 115/116 (1997-98): 104-47; Smith, *Reminiscences*, 131. Examinations of other west coast aboriginal groups have also suggested that the rise of wage labour coincided with the declining power of chiefs. See Doug Hudson, "Traplines and Timber: Social and Economic Change among the Carrier" (PhD diss., University of Alberta, 1983), 86; McNeary, "When Fire Came Down," 197.

101　Douglas to the Governor and Committee, November 6, 1847, and Douglas to Archibald Barclay, September 3, 1849 in Bowsfield, *Fort Victoria Letters*, 16, 39.

102　In fact, the formal text for these treaties was supplied some time after the agreement with the Lekwungen from a New Zealand treaty with the Maori. It was copied onto the page above the names of the Lekwungen men and their "Xs" were added, so the precise words in the treaty could not have been read to the Lekwungen. However, the written treaty closely follows the statements in Douglas's letter. See "Fort Victoria Correspondence Outward to the Hudson's Bay Company ... " May 16, 1850, BCA, A/C/Vi2; Duff, "Fort Victoria Treaties"; Paul Tennant, *Aboriginal People and Politics: The Indian Land Question in British Columbia, 1849-1989* (Vancouver, UBC Press, 1992), 17-25.

103　Pagett, "105 Years in Victoria."

104　Latasse in Pagett, "105 Years in Victoria"; an account by a Nanaimo elder, Quen-Es-Then (Joe Wyse), of the Nanaimo treaty making mirrors Latasse's very closely. See Beryl Cryer, BCA, F8.2/C88.1. vol. v3 11-14. As does Dave Elliot's story in *Saltwater People*, excerpted above.

105　Tennant, *Aboriginal Peoples and Politics*.

106　Douglas to Newcastle, October 24, 1853, CO 305/4 No, 9 89; Douglas to Captain Houston of HMS *Trincomali*, October 18, 1853, BCA, Report of the Provincial Archives Department ... for the Year Ended December 31st, 1913 (Victoria: King's Printer, 1914); Potlatch described in Martha Cheney Ella, "Diary," BCA, E/B/El 5A.

107　Quoted in Barnett, *Coast Salish*, 256.

108　The potlatch Kane was describing may be the same one mentioned by Frank Allen as having taken place ca. 1840-45, in Elmendorf, *Twana Narratives*, 39-41; Kane, *Wanderings of an Artist*, 145.

109　*Register* (Port Townsend), April 4, 1860; *British Colonist*, March 1, 1861, and April 26, 1863, 3; *British Colonist*, April 21 and 24, 1869; Wilson, *Mapping the Frontier*, 74; Royal British Columbia Museum, F. Dally, Album no. 5, 3; MacFie, *Vancouver Island*, 430-31; Edgar, "A Potlatch," 97. An 1872 potlatch on the Lekwungen reserve was photographed by Richard Maynard, photos at BCA, PN 6810.

110　The potlatch of 1869 is described by the Reverend H.B. Owen in "Reports of the Rev. H.B. Owen ... to the United Society for the Propagation of the Gospel," Rhodes House Library, Oxford, as cited in Keddie, *Songhees Pictorial*; *British Colonist*, April 23 and 28, 1874; *Victoria Daily Standard*, April 22, 1874; Dr. W.W. Walkem describes one day of yet another potlatch that occurred in 1875 on a Wsanec reserve, where he saw five hundred sacks of flour, two hundred HBC blankets, and eight goat's wool hand-made blankets distributed. See W.W. Walkem, *Stories of Early British Columbia* (Vancouver: News Advertiser, 1914), 114-15; I.W. Powell, DIAR, 1877, 32-34.

111　From 1870 to 1975, adjusted by F.H. Leacy, *Historical Statistics of Canada* (Ottawa: Statistics Canada, 1983), Index K44-46; and from 1975 to 2008, adjusted by the Consumer Price Index historical Summary from Statistics Canada, http//www.40.statcan.ca/cstolecon46.htm (site now discontinued; see new summary tables site at http://www40.statcan.ca/l01/cst01/econ46a.htm?sdi= consumer%20price%20index%20historical%20 summary).

112　On April 26 and 29, 1863, the *British Colonist* recorded a funerary potlatch; Mitchell, quoted in Barnett, *Coast Salish*, 257. Hosting potlatches spread from the upper class to commoners in other west coast societies around the same time: for Kwakwa̱ka̱'wakw see G.M. Dawson, "Notes and Observations on the Kwakiool People of Vancouver Island and Adjacent Coasts Made During the Summer of 1885," *Transactions of the Royal Society of Canada*, section 2 (1887) 17; for the Ts'msyen see Reverend William Henry Pierce, *From Potlatch to Pulpit*, ed. J.P. Hicks (Vancouver: Vancouver Bindery, 1933), 126.

113 Powell, DIAR, 1884, 107.

114 Edgar "A Potlatch" 99; Walkem, *Stories*, 119; Powell, DIAR, 1875, 34.

115 George M. Grant, *Ocean to Ocean: Sir Sanford Fleming's Expedition through Canada in 1872* (Toronto: James Campbell and son, 1873; reprinted Toronto: Coles, 1970), 319-20; Knight has a similar story from a different source that may describe a rival's response to Big George's potlatch. See Rolf Knight, *Indians at Work: An Informal History of Native Indian Labour in British Columbia, 1858-1930* (Vancouver: New Star, 1978), 114. See also Capt. C.E. Barrett-Lennard, *Travels in British Columbia: With the Narrative of A Yacht Voyage Round Vancouver's Island* (London: Hurst and Blackett, 1862), 60.

116 Brown, *Robert Brown*, 47, 66, 115; Douglas to Stuart, August 22, 1857, in Burrill, "Class Conflict," 127.

117 W.C. Grant in William Carew Hazlitt, *British Columbia and Vancouver Island* (London: G. Routledge, 1858), 179; M.B. Begbie in H.L. Langevin, *British Columbia: Report of the Honourable H.L. Langevin, Minister of Public Works* (Ottawa: I.B. Taylor, 1872), 23, put it another way: "Accordingly, after years of civilization [an Indian] constantly relapses, for a time at least into the painted savage, and goes hunting or fishing – or starving – as relaxation."

118 With the exception of the years immediately following the 1862 smallpox epidemic. See Douglas to Newcastle, October 24, 1853, CO 305/4 12345; Douglas to Russell, August 21, 1855, CO 305/6 10048. For more analyses of this migration, see John Lutz, "Work, Sex, and Death on the Great Thoroughfare: Annual Migrations of 'Canadian Indians' to the American Pacific Northwest," in *Parallel Destinies: Canadian-American Relations West of the Rockies*, ed. John M. Findlay and Ken Coates, 80-103 (Seattle: Center for the Study of the Pacific Northwest and University of Washington Press, 2002).

119 In July 1856, the American Indian Agent at Bellingham noted that most of the Aboriginal People from there had gone to Victoria. See Daniel Boxberger, *To Fish in Common: The Ethnohistory of Lummi Salmon Fishing* (Lincoln: University of Nebraska Press, 1989), 24. The Suquamish and the Stillaguaimish from Puget Sound also came to Victoria in the 1850s. See Ruby and Brown, *Guide to Indian Tribes*, 225, 228.

120 Dick and his wife preferred to live in their lodge in the Lekwungen village rather than in the Helmckens' house. Later, Dick became a sheep farmer. See Smith, *Reminiscences,* 131. For the preference for northern people over the Lekwungen for agricultural labour, see William Duncan to Rev. H. Venn, Secretary of the Committee of the CMS, July 27, 1857, LAC, Church Missionary Society, C.2./o, appendix C, reel A-105.

121 Rev. R.J. Staines to Thomas Boys, July 6, 1852, CO 305/3; Smith, *Reminiscences*, 134; Douglas to Earl Grey, October 31, 1851, CO/305/3. During the 1862 smallpox epidemic, special permits were granted to "Indian" servants so that they could not be compelled to leave with those Aboriginal People who were driven away. See *British Colonist*, May 28-30, 1862.

122 Latasse in Pagett, "105 Years in Victoria."

123 *San Francisco Times*, August 27, 1858, cited in Hazlitt, *British Columbia and Vancouver Island*, 208, 215. Cracroft passed through a street that "was chiefly the resort of the Indians." See Sophia Cracroft, *Lady Franklin Visits the Pacific Northwest: Being Extracts of the Letters of Miss Sophia Cracroft, Sir John Franklin's Niece, February to April 1861 and April to July 1870* (Victoria: Provincial Archives of British Columbia, 1974) 79; *Weekly Victoria Gazette* June 18, September 3, October 9, 1859; *British Colonist*, October 21, 1862, 3; Macfie, *Vancouver Island*, 484; Edgar Fawcett, *Some Reminiscences of Old Victoria* (Toronto: William Briggs, 1912), 284. James Bell to John Thomson, BCA MS659 E/8/B412, February 27, 1859.

124 *British Colonist,* 28 April 1862, 2.

125 Although tuberculosis has been found in precontact osteological remains elsewhere in the Americas, no evidence has yet been found on the Northwest Coast. See R.T. Boyd, "Demographic History, 1774-1874," in *Handbook of North American Indians*, ed. Wayne Suttles (Washington: Smithsonian, 1990), 7: 141-45. For an overview of the impact of colonization on the health of Aboriginal

Peoples in British Columbia, see Mary Ellen Kelm, *Colonizing Bodies: Aboriginal Health and Healing in British Columbia, 1900-50* (Vancouver: UBC Press, 2000).

126 Cole Harris, *The Resettlement of British Columbia: Essays on Colonialism and Geographical Change* (Vancouver: UBC Press, 1997), 19; Boyd, "Demographic History," 138; Deans, "Extract," 3.

127 Boyd, "Demographic History," 145; Bolduc, *Mission of the Columbia*, 108.

128 See Bolduc in Father P.J. De Smet, *Oregon Missions and Travels over the Rocky Mountains in 1845 and 1846* (New York: Edward Dunigan, 1847), 57-58.

129 James Douglas, Private Papers, 2nd series, BCA, B 20 1853; Fort Victoria Journal, February-July 1848. See also Duff, "Fort Victoria Treaties," 23. While Chief Factor Finlayson estimated a pre-1848 population of 1,300 for southeast Vancouver Island, comprising 700 Songhees (Lekwungen), 500 Wsanec, and 100 TSou-ke, Douglas's later census shows that his estimates are low. See Lt. Commander Wood to the Secretary of the Admiralty, November 19, 1848, BCA, O A P19. In 1847, the Lekwungen told Kane that they could muster five hundred warriors, but this may have been a strategic overestimate. See Kane, *Wanderings of an Artist*, 145; Robert Boyd, "The Pacific Northwest Measles Epidemic of 1847-1848," *Oregon Historical Quarterly* 95 (1994): 6-47.

130 James Mooney, "The Aboriginal Population North of Mexico," *Smithsonian Miscellaneous Collections* 80, 7 (1928): 15; Boyd, "Demographic History," 144. These estimates are based on the additive method of ethnohistorical population reconstruction, which enlarges a reliably dated anchor population through simple addition to compensate for known epidemics. Where specific mortalities are known, they are used; otherwise, average mortalities from epidemiological literature are applied.

131 This uses Douglas's count of 1,649 for the south Island in 1850 as the anchor and inflates it according to Boyd's formula, estimating a 10 percent mortality from the 1848 measles epidemic, a 5 percent mortality from the 1841 epidemic described by Bolduc, a 10 percent mortality in 1824, a 20 percent mortality in 1801, and a 30 percent mortality from the first smallpox epidemic in 1775. A slightly higher mortality would suggest a population of over five thousand. The difficulty in making these kinds of estimates is illustrated by John Belshaw, "Numbers from Brobdingnag: Confronting the Problem of Pre-Contact Population Figures in British Columbia," paper presented to the Canadian Historical Association Meeting, Quebec City, May 2001.

132 James Douglas, Letters to the Hudson's Bay Company, February 16, 1853, BCA A/C/20/Vi/2A.

133 Boyd argues that the Lekwungen suffered a 46 percent mortality in the 1862-63 epidemic; however, based on Garrett's report and newspaper reports, I am inclined to agree with Keddie that very few Lekwungen suffered from smallpox in 1862. See Boyd, "Demographic History," 144; Grant Keddie, "The Victoria Small Pox Crisis of 1862," *Discovery* 22 (1993): 4-5.

134 W.C. Grant, "Report on Vancouver Island," 1849, BCA, A/B/20/G76. Scrofula is apparently a reference to a cutaneous symptom of tuberculosis. See Boyd, "Demographic History," 137.

135 LAC, RG 10, vol. 11213, file 1. Consumption and cutaneous eruptions are likely references to tuberculosis.

136 James Douglas, Private Papers, 2nd series, BCA, B 20 1853; LAC, RG 88, vol. 499, 1876-77; *Census of Canada* (1891).

137 The membership of the Lekwungen was not rigidly defined in the 1870s and 1880s, despite the restrictions of the Indian Act. Consequently, whole families might relocate to take up residence with relatives on other reserves; however, it was equally true that others would move onto the Lekwungen reserve, which, from the point of view of work, was a desirable place to be.

138 *British Colonist*, November 11, 1864.

139 *Ibid.*, February 28, 1859; quote from *British Colonist*, May 14, 1872; Governor Kennedy to the Colonial Office, September 3, 1866, CO 305/29 10225.

140 *British Colonist*, November 11, 1864. Franz Boas, *The Ethnography of Franz Boas: Letters and Diaries Written on the Northwest Coast from 1886-1931*, ed. Richard Rohner, trans. Hedy Parker (Chicago: University of Chicago Press, 1969), 22, 45. Indian Agent Lomas added that the Aboriginal People acquired these "vices" from "degraded" whites. See DIAR, 1883, 53.

141 *British Colonist*, February 28, 1860; Edgar, "A Potlatch," 94; Bishop George Hills Diary, March 30 and September 22, 1862, Archives of the Ecclesiastical Province of British Columbia.

142 Blakey-Smith, *Reminiscences*, 329.

143 The negotiations leading up to the removal of the Lekwungen are described in Jeannie L. Kanakos, "Negotiations to Relocate the Lekwungen, 1843-1911," (MA thesis, Simon Fraser University, 1982). See also Keddie, *Songhees Pictorial*, 146-54.

144 *Victoria Gazette*, May 18, 1860; *Victoria Press*, May 8-19, 1862. "I do not hesitate to add, that two thirds if not more, of the Indian retail traders in Victoria depend for support upon the open prostitution carried on within the confines of the city. All the Indian liquor manufactured and sold in Victoria is purchased with means derived from the same source," I.W. Powell to George Walkem, November 6, 1873, in British Columbia, *Papers Connected with the Indian Land Question* (Victoria: R. Wolfenden, 1875; reprinted 1987), 122; *British Colonist*, September 6, 1861, 2; W.F. Tolmie to Sir Alexander Campbell, Federal Minister of Justice, August 21, 1883, BCA, A E Or3 C15; W.H. Lomas, "Annual Report for the Cowichan Agency," DIAR, 1887, noted that "several have regular employment in the city and these would have to rent or buy houses if their reserve was sold."

145 For more on the gendered impact of colonialism among the Lekwungen, see John Lutz, "Gender and Work in Lekwammen Families, 1843-1970," in *Gendered Pasts: Historical Essays on Femininity and Masculinity in Canada*, ed. Kathryn McPherson, Cecilia Morgan, and Nancy M. Forestell, 80-105 (Don Mills, ON: Oxford University Press, 1999).

146 Bishop George Hills Diary, November 9, 1862; Michael Cooper, who became chief, was conceived at the fishing site on San Juan in 1863. See *British Colonist*, January 11, 1936.

147 Bishop George Hills Diary, January 17, 1860; Herman Reinhart, *The Golden Frontier: The Recollections of Herman Francis Reinhart, 1851-1869*, ed. Doyce B. Nunis, Jr. (Austin: University of Texas Press, 1962) 143; Fawcett, *Some Reminiscences*, 283-84.

148 W.H. Lomas, DIAR, 1888, 105-7. In most years leading up to 1934, deaths exceeded births by two to three per year, with the exception of 1919, when the Spanish flu slightly increased the death toll.

149 See Chapter 3, this volume.

150 George Mitchell described the widening of the circle of those who could potlatch in Barnett, *Coast Salish*, 253.

151 "Registre de baptêmes" (Archives of the Catholic Diocese of Vancouver Island), records three baptisms and one marriage involving Lekwungen partners from 1861 to 1864. The difficulty faced by the Catholics and Anglicans is described in Bishop Hills Diary and William Duncan's letters to the Church Missionary Society. For an account of the Methodist missions, see Thomas Crosby, *Among the An-ko-me-nums or Flathead Tribes of Indians of the Pacific Coast* (Toronto: William Briggs, 1907), 27-30.

152 Crosby, *Among the An-ko-me-nums*, 97.

153 Sqwameyuks was sometimes written "Scomiach" or "Scomiax," and sometimes his English name "Jim" was used. Opposite the name of each adult male, Blenkinsop indicated the number of adult women as well as male and female youths and children in the immediate family. Other members of the "non-nuclear family" are listed under the adult male with whom they are associated and are identified as "orphan," "widow," "halfbreed," "sister," or often just "woman." Three Lekwungen families had unidentified, apparently unrelated, adult women (not widows or orphans) who may have been slaves living with them. The census does not allow us to be certain, but in counting the neighbouring Esquimalt band, adult sisters were clearly identified, and in both the Lekwungen and Esquimalt censuses, widows and orphans are indicated. See LAC, RG 88, vol. 494, 1876-77.

154 Canada, 1891, mss. census. Shoemaker raises the definite possibility that the census taker deliberately, or through misconception or deception on the part of Aboriginal People, failed to record multiple wives in 1891. But by this time the Indian Agent, if the census taker himself, would have had a personal acquaintance with the Lekwungen families and would have drawn attention to polygynous relationships. See Nancy Shoemaker, "The Census as Civilizer: American Indian Household Structure in the 1900 and 1910 US Censuses," *Historical Methods* 25, 1 (1992): 4-11; John Lutz, "'Relating to the Country': The Lekwammen and the Extension of European Settlement, 1843-1911" in *Beyond the City Limits: Rural History in British Columbia*, ed. Ruth Sandwell (Vancouver: UBC Press, 1999), 17-32.

155 Crosby, *Among the An-ko-me-nums*, 97.

156 Michael Harkin, *The Heiltsuks: Dialogues of Culture and History on the Northwest Coast* (Lincoln: University of

Nebraska Press, 1997); Jean Comaroff and John Comaroff, "Through the Looking-Glass: Colonial Encounters of the First Kind," *Journal of Historical Sociology* 1, 1 (1988): 6-32; Brett Christophers, *Positioning the Missionary* (Vancouver: UBC Press, 2000); Clarence Bolt, *Thomas Crosby and the Tsimshian: Small Shoes for Feet Too Large* (Vancouver: UBC Press, 1992).

157 Boas, *Ethnography of Franz Boas*, 21.

158 Sarah Albany worked in canneries before she married Chief Michael Cooper, and her children, including future Lekwungen chief John Albany, earned ten cents an hour washing cans. See Esquimalt Municipal Archives, "Interview with Joyce Albany" and Carmichael, "Account of a Season's Work." This has parallels in Tamara Harevan's description of the incorporation of preindustrial family production modes into factory life in New England. See Tamara Harevan, *Family Time, Industrial Time: The Relationship between Family and Work in a New England Industrial Community* (New York: Cambridge University Press, 1982.)

159 DIAR, 1883, 60. The industrial fishery apparently also eliminated the practice of the "first salmon" ceremony and aboriginal concerns about the ritual disposal of fish remains, which were recorded among the Lekwungen as late as 1859. See Wilson, *Mapping the Frontier*, 29.

160 McTeirnan, DIAR, 1882, 61, reports that 1,300 Indian men were employed at the fisheries and were paid an average of $1.75 per day for a season that lasted ninety days. During the same season, the canneries employed four hundred women, who earned one dollar per day.

161 Great West Packing Co. Ltd. to W.R. Robertson, Indian Agent, Cowichan, February 20, 1913, LAC, RG 10, vol. 1349, reel C-13917, item 412; British Columbia, Legislative Assembly, "BC Fishery Commission Report," testimony of F.L. Lord, 117, *BCSP* (Victoria: British Columbia, 1893); "Minutes of a Royal Commission at Victoria involving the fishing privileges of Indians of British Columbia," 1915, LAC, RG 10, vol. 3908, Black Series, file 107297-2, reel C-10160.

162 DIAR, 1887, 5, 92; DIAR, 1888, 13, 105; studies of other coastal groups suggest that the separation of the earnings of husbands and wives was common elsewhere as well. See Carol Cooper, "Native Women of the Northern Pacific Coast: An Historical Perspective 1830-1900," *Journal of Canadian Studies*, 27, 4 (1992-93): 56; Laura Klein,

"She's One of Us, You Know: The Public Life of Tlingit Women, Traditional, Historical, and Contemporary Perspectives," *Western Canadian Journal of Anthropology* 6, 3 (1976) 164-83. In 1913, Indian Agent Charles Cox reported that Nuu-chah-nulth men and women keep their incomes separate. See Royal Commission on Pelagic Sealing, Victoria, Indian Claims, December 1913, vol. 8, 135, in Crockford, "Changing Economic Activities," 43.

163 W.F. Tolmie to Sir Alexander Campbell, August 21, 1883, BCA, A E Or3 C15; W.H. Lomas, DIAR, 1882, 160-62; Lomas, DIAR, 1883, 53; J.A. Jacobsen, *Alaskan Voyage, 1881-83: An Expedition to the Northwest Coast of America*, trans. Erna Gunther (Chicago: University of Chicago Press, 1977), 5-6.

164 Edgar, "A Potlatch," 96; DIAR, 1876, 34.

165 I.W. Powell, in *Report of the Superintendent of Indian Affairs for British Columbia for 1872 & 1873* (Ottawa: I.B. Taylor, 1873), 8 (reprinted as CIHM No. 16227); Crosby, *Among the An-ko-me-nums*, 106. The best general description of the anti-potlatch legislation is in Douglas Cole and Ira Chaiken, *An Iron Hand upon the People: The Law against the Potlatch on the Northwest Coast* (Vancouver: Douglas and McIntyre, 1990). For a specific community's experience, see Daisy Sewid-Smith, *Prosecution or Persecution* (Cape Mudge, BC: Nu-Yum-Baleess Society, 1979).

166 Crosby, *Among the An-ko-me-nums*, 107.

167 Cole and Chaiken, *An Iron Hand upon the People*, 36-39.

168 Cowichan Agency, Departmental Circulars, 1892-1910, August 4, 1895, LAC, RG 10, vol. 1,350, reel C-13917.

169 Cole and Chaiken, *An Iron Hand upon the People*, 147-50.

170 Edward Sapir and Morris Swadesh, *Nootka Texts* (Philadelphia: Linguistic Society of America, University of Pennsylvania, 1939), 149.

171 DIAR, 1896, 185-87.

172 Fawcett, *Some Reminiscences*, 84. The Blue Books of the Colony of British Columbia for 1870 show 1,548 Chinese. Of these, 211 were in Victoria, where the non-aboriginal population at that time numbered 3,270. See *Census of Canada* (1870), 4: 376-77; *Census of Canada* (1881), 1: 290; 1891, 1: 332; McTiernan, in DIAR, 1884, 105; Loren P. Lewis to A.W. Vowell, January 29, 1887, LAC, RG 10, vol. 3772, file 35139.

173 An indication of the year-to-year fluctuation of the Lekwungen population is available after 1883, when the Indian Agent was supposed to conduct an annual census of each band. After 1917, a census was conducted every five years. See DIAR, 1891, 115; DIAR, 1892, 233. Agent Robertson, the Cowichan agent after 1900, reported in 1913 that he did not always visit each reserve each year, so sometimes he updated the census by deducting the deaths and adding the births reported by the band. See McKenna-McBride Commission, transcript of evidence, June 10, 1913, 263, BCA, GR 1995, file, reel B-1454; Powell, DIAR, 1876, 32-33; DIAR, 1877, 47-50; Letters received by the BC Indian Superintendent, 1873-76, no. 109, James Morrison to Lenihan, July 25, 1875, LAC, RG 10, vol. 1001; Lomas, in DIAR, 1888, 100-2; Cowichan Agency, Departmental Circulars, 1892-1910, A.W. Vowell, Visiting Indian Superintendent, July 9, 1892, August 22, 1898, and February 15, 1902, LAC, RG 10, vol. 1350, reel C-13917; Cowichan Agency, Miscellaneous Correspondence, 1893-1906, J.H. Todd and Sons to William Lomas, August 22, 1898, LAC, RG 10, vol. 1348, reel C-13917; W.R. Robertson, Diary, March 1903, LAC, RG 10, vol. 1351, reel C-13917; Cowichan Agency Miscellaneous Correspondence, 1906-1915, Letter 44, Indian Agent, New Westminster, to W.R. Robertson, Indian Agent, Cowichan, March 30, 1909, LAC, RG 10, vol. 1349, Reel C13917; J.H Todd and Sons to W.R. Robertson, Indian Agent, Cowichan, April 21, 1909.

174 DIAR, 1891, 115; DIAR, 1893, 116-18; W.H. Lomas and A.W. Vowell, DIAR, 1895, 153, 186.

175 Less than half the Lekwungen were enumerated in the census of 1881. And, of those who were enumerated, information on their work was either left blank or listed as "labourer." Although the enumerators did not ask about "race" or ethnicity, it is possible to locate the Lekwungen in this census by comparing names in the manuscript to those in DIA band censuses. These names can be further confirmed by tracking the enumerator until he arrived at the Lekwungen reserve in his circuit through the city and by checking the information that was collected concerning the birthplace of the respondent and her/his mother and father. Unlike the 1881 census, which missed over half the Lekwungen, the 1891 census includes virtually the whole band

176 DIAR, 1892, 223-24; DIAR, Annual Report of W.H. Lomas, 1894.

177 A.W. Vowell, Indian Superintendent for BC, in DIAR, 1901, 284-89. See also the *Colonist* editorial, December 20, 1898, stating "Chinese sawmill hands and the white longshoreman have taken [the Songhees'] places."

178 Vowell, in DIAR, 1901, 284-89; Lomas to Vowell, March 30, 1897, LAC, RG 10, vol. 3988, file 154,635; DIAR, 1891, 115-18; DIAR, 1903, 254-61; David J. Reid, "Company Mergers in the Fraser River Salmon Canning Industry, 1885-1902," *Canadian Historical Review* 56, 3 (1975): 285.

179 A.W. Vowell, in DIAR, 1901, 288-89; *Colonist*, December 20, 1898.

180 W.H. Lomas to A.W. Vowell, March 30, 1897, LAC, RG 10, vol. 3988, file 154,635.

181 Lomas, in DIAR, 1899, 222; 1900, 241; A.W. Vowell, in DIAR, 1902, 281-85.

182 *Colonist*, May 7, 1905, 1; Cowichan Agency, Miscellaneous Correspondence, 1906-15, J.H. Todd and Sons to W.R. Robertson, Indian Agent, Cowichan, August 23, 1909, LAC, RG 10, vol. 1349, reel C-13917; Michael Cooper, February 17, 1933, RG 10, vol. 4093, reel C-10,187, Indian Affairs Black Series 600,198, file; Lekwungen Indian Reserve Road Work, June 6, 1925, RG 10, vol. 9170 B-45.

183 The continuation of the organization of labour by "chiefs" in these two industries continued in other parts of British Columbia through at least to the 1950s, alongside the increasing tendency of Aboriginal People to sell their own labour as individuals or through Chinese or other labour contractors. Charley Nowell and Harry Assu both describe their experiences as labour contractors in their auto-ethnographies. See Ford, *Smoke from Their Fires*.

184 Mrs Edwards to Minister of the Interior, March 17, 1915, LAC, RG 10, vol. 11,050, file 33, part 7; *Colonist*, January 11, 1936. Fornsby also talks about the rivalry for the chieftainship between Cooper and the traditional chiefs, in Collins, "John Fornsby," 325. Cooper could claim connection to an important Lekwungen *siem*, his maternal grandfather. See Elmendorf, *Twana Narratives*, 39-41.

185 W.H. Lomas to A.W. Vowell, November 2, 1894, LAC, RG 10, vol. 3938, reel C-10,164, Black Series 121, 134,; A.H. Lomas, Indian Agent, to William Robert, August

8, 1922, RG 10, vol. 9,170, file B-45; *Victoria Times*, February 5, 1906, 5; *Colonist*, July 6, 1905, 3; *Colonist*, January 11, 1936.

186 J.H. Todd and Sons to W.R. Robertson, July 24 and 26, 1905, LAC, RG 10, vol. 1348, reel C-13,917, Cowichan Agency, Miscellaneous Correspondence, 1893-1906; *Colonist*, July 4, 1905, 7; *Colonist*, August 7, 1907, 7.

187 E.K. Nichols to A.B. Sutherland, June 19, 1909, United Church Archives, Toronto, 78.092c, file 97; *Colonist*, June 13, 1906, 9; *Colonist*, July 12, 1907, 5; *Vancouver Province*, September, 18, 1909, 1; Peter Baskerville, *Beyond the Island: An Illustrated History of Victoria* (Burlington, ON: Windsor, 1986), 68.

188 H. Dallas Helmcken to Richard McBride, October 26, 1910, LAC, RG 10, vol. 11,050, file 33/3, part 7.

189 The improvements taken together were valued at $20,172. *Colonist*, March 22, 1916, 3. The two negotiators for the province did even better, earning, $30,000 and $70,000, respectively; BCSP, 1912, C270; Canada, *Statutes of Canada* (Ottawa: Canada, 1911), 1-2: 225-27.

190 W.E. Ditchburn to Duncan C. Scott, December 11, 1913, LAC, RG 10, vol. 11,050, file 33/3, pt. 7.

191 McKenna-McBride Transcripts, June 14, 1913, BCA, GR 1995, reel B-1454, and Final Report Volume. In the final report the commissioners say that the Lekwungen are employed "in the mills, as stevedores, teamsters, fishermen, etc ... also two storekeepers, one baker, etc," but the evidence of Indian Agent Robertson explicitly states that no Lekwungen worked in the mills.

192 Sylvia Olsen, "'We Indians Were Sure Hard Workers': A History of Coast Salish Wool Working" (MA thesis, University of Victoria, 1998); Barbara Lane, "The Cowichan Knitting Industry," *Anthropology in British Columbia* 2 (1951): 18-19. A *Victoria Daily Times* article in 1949 claimed that Mrs. Ellen Roberts made the first "Cowichan Sweater" for her son Walter Joseph in 1906. "Songhees Made First Indian Sweater," *Victoria Daily Times,* October 20, 1949, 15.

193 DIAR, 1913, 283-84.

194 Department of Fisheries, General File, LAC, RG 23, reel 5, file 6, part 8. See also Dianne Newell, *Tangled Webs of History: Indians and the Law in Cananda's Pacific Coast Fisheries* (Toronto: University of Toronto Press, 1993), 77 and chap. 10.

195 DIAR, 1915, 102-3.

196 DIAR, 1912, 396; DIAR, 1911, 385.

197 Karl Marx, *Capital: A Critique of Political Economy* (New York: International, 1954), 644. Engels was not talking about Indian reserve labour, but he might as well have been, when he added that, when business is bad, the industrial reserve army "is paid below the value of its labour and is irregularly employed or is left to be cared for by public charity, but ... is indispensable to the capitalist class at times when business is especially lively." See Frederick Engels, *Karl Marx and Frederick Engels* (Moscow: Progress, 1962), 468.

198 DIAR, 1918, 38.

199 DIAR, 1919, 52-53.

200 Cowichan Agency, Agent's Diary, January 1898, May and June 1910, LAC, RG 10, vol. 1351, reels C-13917 and C-13918; *British Colonist*, 9 February, 1888 and January 20, 1901. See also Keddie, *Songhees Pictorial*, 136-44.

201 The best account of this transformation is in Wayne Suttles, "Spirit Dancing and the Persistence of Native Culture among the Coast Salish," in Suttles, *Coast Salish Essays*, 199-208. See also Michael Kew, "Central and Southern Coast Salish Ceremonies Since 1900," in Suttles, *Handbook of North American Indians*, 476-80.

202 LAC, RG 10, vol. 11,050, file 33/3, pt. 7; Suttles, *Economic Life*, 316. According to the McKenna-McBride Commission, there were "potlatch houses" on the Discovery Island reserve in use in 1911. See McKenna-McBride Commission, McKenna-McBride Transcripts, June 14, 1913, BCA, GR 1995, reel B-1454.

203 *Vancouver Sun*, August 21, 1916. Willie Jack was the son of King Freezy and a hereditary *siem* but was not the elected chief of the band. Keddie, *Songhees Pictorial*, 136.

204 For a fuller discussion of the laws and resistance, see Cole and Chaiken, *An Iron Hand upon the People*, 30-39.

205 LAC, RG 10, vol. 9174, file B-75; *Vancouver Sun*, August 21, 1916; *Colonist*, June 17, 1914.

206 *Colonist*, June 17, 1914.

207 *Vancouver Sun*, August 21, 1916.

208 Duncan Campbell Scott to all agents, October 21, 1918, LAC, RG 10, vol. 9,174, file B-75.

209 Indian Agent to Michael Cooper, January 24, 1921; W.E. Ditchburn to the Department of Indian Affairs, February 19, 1921, LAC, RG 10, vol. 9,174, file B-75.

210 Chief Michael Cooper to W.H. Lomas, Indian Agent, January 13, 1925, LAC, RG 10, vol. 9,170, file B-45. Cooper

asks about funds to do road work on the reserve: "I would like to get it done before some of the boys start working at the cannery next month." A.H. Lomas, Indian Agent, to Secretary, DIA, July 23, 1925 and November 8, 1924, See LAC, RG 10, vol. 9,170, file B-45. $1,000 was authorized to be spent on the Lekwungen road, and this employed thirteen Lekwungen men for a brief period. Similarly, repairs to the cemetery the previous year gave a week's wages ($17.60) to ten men.

211 Louie Kamia to Indian Agent, March 1, 1919, LAC, RG 10, vol. 11,050, file 33/3, pt. 6. Of the four who died in the 1920s, two still had a considerable amount of cash in their accounts, while one had no cash but owned property off-reserve. The fourth died with no assets. See LAC, RG 10, vol. 9,170, file B-4, Cowichan Agency, General, Rev. C.M. Tate to W.H. Lomas, Indian Agent, August 5, 1923; J.D. McLean, Assistant Deputy Superintendent, to A.H. Lomas, Indian Agent, April 4, 1924; Chief Michael Cooper to A.H. Lomas, January 13, 1925 and March 1, 1929; RG 10, series B3g, reel 2739-40, Songhees Estate Files.

212 Report of the Deputy Superintendent, DIAR, 1935, 10; J.L. Taylor, *Canadian Indian Policy during the Inter-War Years, 1918-1939* (Ottawa: Department of Indian Affairs and Northern Development, 1984), 93.

213 Lizzie Fisher to H. Graham, Cowichan Indian Agent, August 1932, and Charles to H. Graham, August 6, 1932, LAC, RG 10, vol. 9,170, file B-45.

214 Frank George to H. Graham, January 14, 1933.

215 Indian Affairs Black Series 600,198, Charles Perry, Assistant Indian Commissioner for BC, to H.W. McGill, Deputy Superintendent General, February 25, 1933, LAC, RG 10, vol. 4,093, reel C-10,187.

216 Sergeant C.C. Jacklin, British Columbia Police, to R.H. Moore, March 16, 1943, LAC, RG 10, vol. 9,172, file B-63. A spirit dance in 1939 on a Saanich Peninsula Reserve was also the subject of a police report. See RCMP Report, February 27, 1939, RG 10, vol. 11,297.

217 Mrs Percy Ross to H. Graham, January 8, 1935, LAC, RG 10, vol. 9,170, file B-45. This disparity is examined in more detail in Chapter 8.

218 Mrs Percy Ross to H. Graham, January 8, 1935, and H. Graham, to George Davidson, BC Superintendent of Welfare, January 17, 1935, LAC, RG 10, vol. 9,170, file B-45.

219 George Pragnell, Inspector of Indian Agencies, to Secretary DIA, December 14, 1934, LAC, RG 10, vol. 9,170, file B-44.

220 Susan Cooper to H. Graham, Indian Agent, March 15, 1933, and Elsie Kamia to H. Graham, December 6, 1933, LAC, RG 10, vol. 9,170, file B-48. The 1935 price is taken from a March 1993 interview with Priscilla on the Tsartlip Reserve. See Olsen, "We Indians Were Sure Hard Workers."

221 "Cecilia," interviewed by Sylvia Olsen in Olsen, "We Indians Were Sure Hard Workers."

222 Mrs. Percy Ross to H. Graham, January 8, 1935, and Robbie Davis to H. Graham, December 8, 1934, LAC, RG 10, vol. 9,170, file B-45.

223 George Pragnell to Secretary, DIA, June 15, 1933, LAC, RG 10, vol. 9,170, file B-44.

224 Pragnell to Secretary, DIA, July 30, 1932, LAC, RG 10, vol. 9,170, file B-44; see also file B-45, Frank George to H. Graham, April 4, 1933. "Please continue my relief as the Strawberries are getting on soon and then we won't be bothering you any more." Joe Thomas, Winslow to Mr. Moore, July 5, 1937, RG 10, vol. 9,172, file B-63. Thomas remarked that he paid eight hop pickers an advance of twenty dollars but they did not arrive, with the result that the employer wanted him to reimburse him in the amount of $160.

225 Memorial of the Songhees Band, March 15, 1935, LAC, RG 10, vol. 9,170, file B-45; Davey and Baker, Barristers and Solicitors, to R.H. Moore, October 6, 1939, LAC, RG 10, vol. 9,172, file B-63

226 Cowichan Agency, Miscellaneous Correspondence, 1906-15, Michael Cooper to W.R. Robertson, April 7, 1910, LAC, RG 10, vol. 1,349, reel C-13917.

227 Cooper was on salary from before 1910, when his wage was raised from twenty dollars to thirty dollars per month, until he resigned in 1916. His salary was reinstated in 1927 at forty dollars per month and cut off in 1933. See Cowichan Agency, Miscellaneous Correspondence, 1906-15, H. Dallas Helmcken to W.R. Robertson, March 17 and March 22, 1910, LAC, RG 10, vol. 1,349, reel C-13917; Indian File 600,198, A. Lomas to Secretary, DIA, August 13, 1928, and J.D. McLean to A. Lomas, October 3, 1928, RG 10, vol. 4,093, reel C-10,187.

228 A large part of the correspondence between the chief and the Indian Agent from 1910 through the 1950s

relates to the provision of welfare services to needy Lek-wungen. See, particularly, LAC, RG 10, vol. 4,093, reel C-10,187; vol. 1,349, reel C-13917; Black Series 600,198; RG 10, vols. 9170, 9172, 9173, and 9174. Jeremy Beckett described this new connection between the state and Aboriginal People, mediated by chiefs, as "welfare co-lonialism." See Jeremy Beckett, *Torres Strait Islanders: Custom and Colonialism* (Cambridge, NY: Cambridge University Press, 1987). See also Paine, "Brokers, Patrons and Clients." Cooper's death is reported in the *Colonist*, January 11, 1936.

229 Songhees Estate Files, LAC, RG 10, series B3g, reel 2739-40. This included nine of the heads of households who received the cash settlement.

230 DIAR, 1937, 112.

231 This included Percy Ross (who became a delegate to a convention of the Boilermaker's Union), Dave Fallard-eau, Jack Dick, George Thomas, and Louie Kamia. See Percy Ross to R.H. Moore, May 21, 1943, LAC, RG 10, vol. 9,172, file B-57 (see also file B-58).

232 R.H. Moore to D.M. McKay, Indian Commissioner, January 26, 1941, and McKay to Secretary Indian Affairs Branch, April 2, 1941, LAC, RG 10, vol. 11,050, file 33/3, pt. 6; Director, Indian Affairs Branch, to Moore, April 8, 1941. McKay argued against the leases because of protests against Asian farmers by the BC Minister of Lands, the BC Fruit Growers Association, the BC Marketing Board, and local farmers' organizations.

233 Information on employment at Empire Cannery comes from University of British Columbia Special Collections, J.H. Todd and Sons Business Records, boxes 2-6.

234 Lekwungen Hamlet Kamia worked casually for the cannery in 1941, earning only $31. In 1943, he earned $188, and in 1944, $200. He worked five and one-half months in 1948, grossing $960, and six months in 1949, grossing $1,474. C. Fletcher worked eight and one-half months in 1941 for $806, nine months in 1943 for $1,134, ten months in 1944 for $1,633, one month in 1944 for $171, and eleven and one-half months in 1945 for $1,799. Jack Dick worked two months in 1944 for $106.35, Harry Dick worked four months in 1944 for $271, and Edward Joseph worked four months in 1943 for $613 and nine and one-half months in 1944 for $1,447. J. James was a casual employee in 1943, earning $32, while George

Cooper earned $128 in 1944. The pay sheets for individual female employees have not survived.

235 DIAR, 1944, 46.

236 Those who were overseas included Frank and Walter George, George Patrick, Frank Albany, and one of the Dick brothers. See Minutes of Songhees Band Council Meeting, June 25, 1944; Percy Ross to R.H. Moore, July 20, 1944; Moore to W.A. Green, February 19, 1945, LAC, RG 10, vol. 9,172, file B-58. Lila Dick received a monthly allowance of $93.12 as her husband was in the armed forces. For a history of aboriginal soldiers see Fred Gaffen, *Forgotten Soldiers* (Penticton, BC: Theytus, 1985).

237 A.H. Brown, DND Dependents Allowance Board, to R.H. Moore, Indian Agent, April 14, 1941, LAC, RG 10, vol. 9,170, file B-49.

238 Susan Cooper, who could not find work during the Depression, was employed at a Steveston cannery in 1942 and at Empire Cannery in Esquimalt in 1943. See Susan Cooper to Moore, December 17, 1942, LAC, RG 10, vol. 9,172, file B-56B-57, and Cooper to R.H. Moore, October 16, 1943, LAC, RG 10, vol. 9,172, file B-56B-57; DIAR, 1946, 197. Norcross says that the annual sales of sweaters amounted to ten thousand dollars per year, or about four hundred sweaters in 1943. See E. Blanch Norcross, "The Cowichan Sweater," *The Beaver*, Outfit 276 (1945): 14-15.

239 This point is developed in Chapter 7.

240 Dennis Guest, *The Emergence of Social Security in Canada* (Vancouver: UBC Press, 1985), 132, 145.

241 Colonel Jones, Supervisor of Family Allowances Ottawa, Report delivered at Conference of Indian Agents and Executive Staff of Indian Affairs Branch, British Columbia, October 21, 1946, LAC, RG 10, vol. 8,571, file 901/1-2-2-5, pt. 1; W.R. Bone, Regional Director of Family Allowance, Victoria, to N.B. Curry, National Director of Family Allowance, February 2, 1946, LAC, RG 29, vol. 2,361, file 264-1-17, pt. 1; "Indian Migrant Workers," Report for the International Labour Organization, October 1953, LAC, RG 26, vol. 106, file 1/1-15, pt. 8.

242 In 1948-49, there was also an increase in the number of BC Aboriginal People doing seasonal logging work in Washington State. See DIAR, 1947, 1948, 1949, and 1950.

243 W.S. Arneil, Indian Commissioner for BC, to Indian Affairs Branch, May 27, 1957, LAC, RG 10, vol. 8,423 801/21-1, reel C-13835; J.V. Boys, Superintendent, Cowichan Agency, Report for the Quarter Ending June 30, 1956, July 18, 1956, Department of Indian and Northern Affairs, Central Registry Office (DIAND-CR), Ottawa, 974/21-1, vol. 1; Frances W. Thompson, "Employment Problems and the Economic Status of the British Columbia Indians" (MSW thesis, University of British Columbia, 1951).

244 H.B. Hawthorn, C. Belshaw, and S.M. Jamieson, *Indians of British Columbia: A Study of Contemporary Social Adjustment* (Toronto: University of Toronto Press, 1959), 115-16.

245 Other British Columbians had been receiving old age security since 1927. In 1948, the DIA started paying Indians over seventy eight dollars per month in lieu of old age security. In 1950, this was raised to twenty-five dollars per month. See "Indians Transferred from Aged Assistance to Old Age Security," December 31, 1951, LAC, RG 10, vol. 2375, file 275-3-4[1]; Department of National Health and Welfare, J.I. Clark to Joy Peacock, November 2, 1968, LAC, RG 29, vol. 1,889 R170/110.

246 J.V. Boys, February 1, 1956, DIAND-CR, 974/21-1, vol. 1.

247 K.R. Brown, Superintendent, Cowichan Agency, Semi-Annual Report for the Period Ending June 1954, June 23, 1954, DIAND-CR, 974/21-1, vol. 1, DIAR, 1958; K.R. Brown to W.S. Arneil, March 26, 1954, LAC, RG 10, vol. 6,933, file 901/29-1, pt. 1.

248 H.M. Jones, Director, Indian Affairs, to H.C. McQuillan, MP, August 5, 1960, LAC-Vancouver Regional Repository, RG 10, vol. 84-85 316 500351, file 29-12; LAC, RG 10, vol. 6933, file 901/29-1, pt. 2; *Colonist*, October, 16, 1960.

249 Kathleen A. Mooney, "Urban and Reserve Indian Economies and Domestic Organization" (PhD diss., University of Michigan, 1976), 89, 97. In 1970, on the Tsawout Reserve in Saanich, the main income earner in seven of the twelve households surveyed was employed only seasonally. The dentist was Roger Ross. See also Mooney's articles: "The Effects of Rank and Wealth on Exchange among the Coast Salish," *Ethnology* 17, 4 (1978): 391-406; "Social Distance and Exchange: The Coast Salish Case," *Ethnology* 15, 4 (1976): 323-46; "Suburban Coast Salish Inter-Household Co-operation, Economics and Religious Movements," *Culture* 7, 1 (1988): 49-58.

250 LAC-Vancouver Regional Repository, RG 10, V84-5, vol. 500351, file 41-12; DIAND-CR, 208/29-1.

251 "Excerpt from the Quarterly Report – Cowichan Agency for the period ending August 31 1962," DIAND-CR, 901/21-2, vol. 3.

252 Kathleen A. Mooney, "Urban and Reserve Coast Salish Employment: A Test of Two Approaches to the Indian's Niche in North America," *Anthropological Research* 32, 4 (1976): 402;

253 Occupational breakdown of Lekwungen men in the labour force in 1969: seven fishing and cannery workers, six forestry workers, six miscellaneous, and six unemployed for a total of twenty-five. See Mooney, "Urban and Reserve Coast Salish Employment," 402; Aziz, "Selected Aspects of Cultural Change," 34-35; Capital Region Planning Board of British Columbia, *Indian Communities and Land Use Planning* (Victoria: Capital Region Planning Board, 1968), appendix; D.B. Fields and W.T. Stanbury, *The Economic Impact of the Public Sector upon the Indians of British Columbia* (Vancouver: UBC Press, 1973), 48.

254 Mooney, "Urban and Reserve Coast Salish Employment," 399.

255 Mooney, "Urban and Reserve Indian Economies," 89, 259. Mitchell estimated that the sweaters brought in less than a dollar an hour in 1972 in exchange for "both physically hard work in washing the wool and monotony." See Marjorie Mitchell, "Social and Cultural Consequences for Native Indian Women on a British Columbia Reserve," *Atlantis* 4, 2 (1979): 183.

256 For the 1910 survey, see John Lutz, "Work, Wages and Welfare in Aboriginal-Non-Aboriginal Relations, British Columbia, 1849-1970," (PhD. diss., University of Ottawa, 1994), 222. No Lekwungen women were listed as having an occupation in the 1967 survey. This seems unlikely, even given other surveys that emphasized the very limited wage work available to Indian women, and it suggests that women may have been left out of the study altogether. Definitions of "employment" may vary over time, and the 1967 figures consider fifteen (not sixteen) to be "working age." Figures for 1891 are from

Census of Canada (1891), and figures for 1967 are from Capital Region, *Indian Communities and Land Use Planning*, appendix 1. Elliot is interviewed in Dorothy Haegert, *Children of the First People* (Vancouver: Tillacum Library, 1983), 19.

Chapter 5: The Tsilhqot'in

1 Robert Lane, "Cultural Relations of the Chilcotin Indians of West Central BC" (PhD diss., University of Washington, 1953), 267.

2 Alexander Mackenzie, *Journal of the Voyage to the Pacific*, ed. Walter Sheppe (New York: Dover, 1992), 185. He was apparently adapting aboriginal terminology. The Nazcot'in, whom he met along the river that the road followed, called the river "Tiyakoh," or the "Road River." See Elizabeth Furniss, *Changing Ways: Southern Carrier History, 1793-1940* (Quesnel, BC: Quesnel School District, 1993), 19.

3 Sage Birchwater, *Ulkatcho Stories of the Grease Trail: Anahim Lake, Bella Coola, Quesnel: Told by Ulkatcho and Nuxalk Elders,* ed. Leone Toney (Anahim Lake, BC: Ulkatcho Cultural Curriculum Development Committee, 1993), 11. Lane argues that Tsilhqot'in may have moved south since 1793 and that most of the people Mackenzie met west of the Fraser River may have been Tsilhqot'in. See Lane, "Cultural Relations," 271-83.

4 Mackenzie, *Journal of the Voyage to the Pacific*, 190.

5 Susan Vehik and Timothy Baugh, "Prehistoric Plains Trade," in *Prehistoric Exchange Systems in North America*, ed. Timothy Baugh and Jonathon Ericson (New York: Plenum, 1994), 249-74; Jerry Galm, "Prehistoric Trade and Exchange in the Interior Plateau of Northwestern America," 275-305; and Roy Carlson, "Trade and Exchange in Prehistoric British Columbia," in Baugh and Ericson, *Prehistoric Exchange Systems*, 249-361. The dates suggested by Besbut'a obsidian found at an archaeological site at Namu dated to 9500 BP. See Carlson, "Trade and Exchange," 312.

6 Birchwater, *'Ulkatchot'en: The People of Ulkatcho* (Anahim Lake, BC: Ulkatcho Cultural Curriculum Development Committee, 1991), 9; Mackenzie, *Journal of the Voyage to the Pacific*, 210; Al Elsey, *Grease: Ooligan Oil Production on the Bella Coola River* (videorecording, s.l., 1964) shows the Nuxalk harvesting and rendering of the oil in the late 1950s.

7 Phil Nuytten, "Money from the Sea," *National Geographic* 183 (1993): 109-17; Robert Galois and Richard Mackie, "A Curious Currency," *The Midden* 22, 4 and 5 (1990): 1-3, 6-9; James Teit, *The Shuswap*, Jesup North Pacific Expedition: Memoir of the American Museum of Natural History, vol. 2, ed. Franz Boas (New York: AMS Press, 1909), 451, 778.

8 Mackenzie, *Journal of the Voyage to the Pacific*, 310. Lane, "Cultural Relations," 111-12, also mentions dried berries as a commodity traded by the Tsilhqot'in.

9 J.J. Disa, J. Vossoughi, and N.H. Goldberg, "A Comparison of Obsidian and Surgical Steel Scalpel Wound-healing in Rats," *Plastic and Reconstructive Surgery* 92, 5 (1993): 884-87.

10 W. Karl Hutchings, "The Namu Obsidian Industry," in *Early Human Occupation in British Columbia*, ed. Roy Carlson and Luke Dalla Bona, 165-76 (Vancouver: UBC Press, 1996); Carlson, "Trade and Exchange," 313-21. Carlson states that dentalia from the coast is found in interior sites dating from 3000 BP to 3500 BP (Carlson, "Trade and Exchange," 37).

11 Carlson, "Trade and Exchange," 337; Galm, "Prehistoric Trade," 293. Not far away, at Lake Kamloops, there is a rare source of native copper.

12 British Columbia, Department of Lands, *Bulletin: Land Series* (Victoria: British Columbia, Department of Lands, 1939).

13 Mackenzie witnessed the hunting and preparation of ground hogs. See Mackenzie, *A Journal of the Voyage to the Pacific*, 45. A study of the archaeological remnants of hunting at the "Potlatch Site" on Anahim Lake showed that 83 percent of the bones recovered were mammalian, 13 percent were fish, and 3 percent were birds. See Frances Stewart, *Vertebrate Faunal Remains from the Potlatch Site (FcSi-2) in South Central British Columbia* (Ottawa: National Museum of Man, 1978), 45-52.

14 Lane, "Cultural Relations," 42-46; Teit, *The Shuswap*, 776, 779; Richard Hebda, Nancy Turner, Sage Birchwater, Michèle Kay, and the Ulkatcho Elders, *Ulkatcho Food and Medicine Plants* (Anahim Lake: Ulkatcho Indian Band, 1996). According to the Fort Chilcotin Journal the moult in the river valley was in late July. In October 1829, George McDougall wrote that the Indians were all on their "root grounds." See

"Correspondence etc relating to the Chilcotin District and Indians," BCA, A/E/Or3/C43. In the eastern part of their territory some families lived in pithouses (like their Secwepemc neighbours), but the Tsilhqot'in said that the many pithouse sites in their territory predated them. See Joseph McGillivray in Ross Cox, *Adventures on the Columbia River* (London: Henry, Colburn and Bentley, 1832), 321.

15 Cox, *Adventures on the Columbia River*, 321; William Connolly to the Governor and Council of the Northern Department," HBC, cited in "Fort Chilcotin," typewritten ms, PC Archives. Connolly says this happened three out of four years, but if this were true, then the Tsilhqot'in would have long since ceased to exist.

16 Lane, "Cultural Relations," 49.

17 Ibid., 198-99.

18 David Dinwoodie, "Reserve Memories: Historical Consciousness on the Nemiah Valley Indian Reserve" (PhD diss., University of Chicago, 1996), 74-77.

19 Lane, "Cultural Relations"; Irving Goldman, "The Alkatcho Carrier of British Columbia," in *Acculturation in Seven American Indian Tribes*, ed. R. Linton (Gloucester, MA: Peter Smith, 1963), 371.

20 The Toosey, the Nemiah, and the Stone; Alexandria, a mixed Tsilhqot'in-Carrier community, is located on the Fraser River.

21 Bernadette Rosetti tells the story on the videorecording "The Great Carrier Chief and the Chunlac Massacre," Yinka Déné Language Institute, 1989. See also A.G. Morice, *The History of the Northern Interior of British Columbia* (1904; reprinted Smithers, BC: Interior Stationary, 1978), 16-19.

22 Lane, "Cultural Relations," suggests that it may have been the trade that passed through Chinlac that was of interest to the Tsilhqot'in, but they did not seem to want to be major traders. For relations with the Homalco, see Lane, "Cultural Relations," 90-91. The Tsilhqot'in fought a major battle with the Homalco in the late 1850s, in which nineteen of the latter were killed. See "Mr. Waddington's Deposition," *British Colonist*, May 12, 1864.

23 The progress of this dispute in 1826-27 is recorded in Joseph McGillivray, "Report of Fort Alexandria ... 1827," in *Part of a Despatch from George Simpson*, ed. E.E. Rich (Toronto: Champlain Society, 1947), 213-14; Cox, *Ad-*

ventures on the Columbia River, 325; Fort Chilcotin Post Journal, 1839-40, HBCA, B37; Fort Alexandria Post Journal, 1824-1862, HBCA, B.5/a/11. See also Robert Lane, "Chilcotin," in *Handbook of the North American Indians: Plateau*, ed. William Sturtevant (Washington: Smithsonian, 1981), 6: 408.

24 For some of these stories, see H.S. Bostock, "Pack Horse Tracks: Recollections of a Geologist's Life in British Columbia and the Yukon, 1924-1954," Geological Survey of Canada, Open File Report no. 650 (Ottawa: Geological Survey of Canada, 1979), 19.

25 Stories from Felicity Walkus, Agnes Edgar, and Orden Mack, in Randy Bouchard and Dorothy Kennedy, British Columbia Indian Language Project, Fieldnotes, 1971-77; Sam Dunn, "Managing Multiple Narratives: Alexander Mackenzie at Nuxalk Territory, 1793," *BC Historical News* 32, 3 (1999): 16-23.

26 Teit, *The Shuswap*, 761-63; information on "midugh" ("nedo" in Carrier) from Bill Poser, personal communication.

27 McGillivray, "Report of Fort Alexandria ... 1827," 194.

28 Cox, *Adventures on the Columbia River*, 327.

29 McGillivray, "Report of Fort Alexandria ... 1827," 325; Department of Lands and Works, box 2, 431/72, Marcus Smith to George Walkem, November 29, 1872, BCA, GR 0983.

30 McGillivray, "Report of Fort Alexandria ... 1827," 216.

31 Fort Chilcotin Post Journal, 1839-40, July 1839, HBCA, B37/a/2.

32 Miscellaneous Information in Relation to Fort Chilcotin, BCA, MM/C43; Morice, *Northern Interior*, 268.

33 Beason's account of Dunlevy's actions comes via the diaries of Alex McInnes, who reportedly heard this from Dunlevy. See E. Beeson, *Dunlevy, From the Diaries of Alex P. McInnes* (St'at'imc, BC: St'at'imc Publishers, 1971), 118.

34 *British Colonist*, May 7, August 25, 1862.

35 Lt. H.S. Palmer, "Report of a Journey of Survey From Victoria to Fort Alexander, via North Bentinck Arm," (New Westminster: Royal Engineers, 1863), 4; Francis Poole, *A Narrative of Discovery and Adventure in the North Pacific* (1872; reprinted Vancouver, J.J. Douglas, 1980), 179-80.

36 Evidence of "Tennis" [Tenas] George, Homalco, at the trial of Klatsassin and others, in Begbie's Trial Notes:

"[I] knew the whole of the prisoners before, they had lived all last winter in my country." See also the evidence of Phillip Buckley, BCA, Colonial Correspondence, GR-1372, F142f/16, mflm B1308, Matthew Baillie Begbie, Begbie to the Governor of British Columbia, Including Notes Taken by the Court at the Trial of 6 Indians, September 30, 1864. These and other documents on the Chilcotin War are also available on John Lutz and the Mysteries Team, "We Do Not Know His Name: Klatsassin and the Chilcotin War," www.canadianmysteries.ca.

37   Notes taken by the court at the trial of six Indians, Telloot, Klatsassin, Chessus, Piell or Pierre, Tah-pit and Chedekki, Quesnelle Mouth, 28 September, 1864, an enclosure in Begbie's Trial Notes.

38   Begbie's Trial Notes.

39   British Columbia (Colony) Attorney General Inquisitions, 1859-1871, Bc 02 1864, Hom 21, Inquest May 1864 at murder camp, 23 May at Homathco, BCA, GR1328. See also Frederick Whymper, "Travel and Adventure in the Territory of Alaska" (Ann Arbor: University Microfilms, 1966), 19-20.

40   Ervin Charleyboy, interviewed by John Lutz, September 2, 1999, at Tsi Del Del (Redstone); Patrick Lulua, interviewed by John Lutz at Toosey, August 31, 1999.

41   Chartres Brew to Colonial Secretary from Waddington, May 23, 1864, BCA, Colonial Correspondence, F193/20.

42   Begbie's Trial Notes; Klatsassin statement to Cox, quoted in British Colonist, August 25, 1864.

43   A.W. Wallace, Customs Officer, Bentinck Arm, in British Colonist, June 28, 1864.

44   Great Britain Public Record Office, Colonial Office Records (CO) 60/19, 149, 10601, Frederick Seymour, Letter to Cardwell, no. 37, sent September 9, 1864, received November 17, 1864.

45   Ibid.

46   Ibid.

47   Frederick Seymour, Letter to Cardwell, no. 56, sent October 4, 1864, received November 29, 1864, CO 60/19, 298, 10955; Frederick Seymour, Letter to Cardwell, no. 37, sent September 9, 1864, received November 17, 1864, CO 60/19, 149, 10601.

48   Chedekki actually escaped on his way to New Westminster and was never recaptured. Two other Tsilhqot'in men were captured the following year, tried in New Westminster, and convicted; however, one – Lutas – was pardoned. See Matthew Baillie Begbie, Begbie to the Governor of British Columbia Including Notes Taken by the Court at the Trial of 6 Indians, September 30, 1864, BCA Colonial Correspondence, GR-1372, F142f/16, Mflm B1308; Special Assize, New Westminster, 3-4 July 1865 Before Henry P. Crease, in UBC Special Collections, R.L. Reid Papers, box 4, file 9.

49   British Colonist, September 7, 1864; Matthew Baillie Begbie, from Quesnelle Mouth to Colonial Secretary, September 30, 1864, BCA, Colonial Correspondence, microfilm reel B1308, file F142f.16.

50   Ibid. This sentence is part of a paragraph struck out in the original, but it echoes his trial notes.

51   British Colonist, February 29, 1872.

52   Ibid., July 10, 1872, 2; George M. Grant, Ocean to Ocean: Sir Sanford Fleming's Expedition through Canada in 1872 (Toronto: James Campbell and Son, 1873; reprinted Toronto: Coles, 1970), 328; Correspondence etc. relating to the Chilcotin District and Indians, L.W. Riske and D. McIntyre, June 6, 1872, BCA, A/E/O13/C43.

53   Draft Report of Peter O'Reilly to Provincial Secretary, August, 1872, BCA, A/E/O13/C43.

54   Charles S. Buckley Papers, LAC MG24 H43.

55   L.W. Riske and D. McIntyre, June 6, 1872, in BCA, MS-2894, O'Reilly family fonds A/E/O13.

56   Ibid. This account is confirmed by R.C. Lundin Brown in Klatsassin and Other Reminiscences of Missionary Life in British Columbia (London: Gilbert and Rivington, 1873).

57   Begbie in Begbie, O'Reilly, and Father McGuiggan in BCA, MS-2894, O'Reilly family fonds A/E/O13.

58   British Columbia, Legislative Assembly, "Return to an Address of the Legislative Assembly for ... all ... Correspondence ... Relative to Attempts Made for the Arrest of Emia, a Chilcotin Indian, 1885," BCSP (Victoria: British Columbia, 1885).

59   A.G. Morice to R.P. Tatin, March 1883, in "Missions de la Congregation des Missionaires Oblats de Marie Immaculée" (1883), BCA, GR 0429, Attorney General Files, box 1, file 12, 122, 141 and 356/83; translated in Dinwoodie, "Reserve Memories," 49-50,

60   William Laing-Meason, Indian Agent, Williams Lake Agency, Report for 1885, in Canada, Legislative Assembly, "Department of Indian Affairs Annual Report"

(DIAR), *Canada Sessional Papers* (Ottawa: Canada, 1885), 85-87; BCA, GR 0429, Attorney General Files, box 1, file 12, 18/83.

61 Indian Reserve Commission, 1876-78, McKinley and Sproat to Elliot, September 28, 1877, BCA, GR 0494, box 1, item 39, 366/77; GR0429 Attorney General Files, box 1, file 12, 141/83.

62 Centennial Committee, *History and Legends of the Chilcotin* (Williams Lake: Cariboo, 1957) 9; Witte Sisters, *Chilcotin: Preserving Pioneer Memories* (Surrey: Heritage House, 1995), 11.

63 Bostock, "Pack Horse Tracks"; Diana French, *The Road Runs West: A Century along the Bella Coola/Chilcotin Road* (Madeira Park, BC: Harbour, 1996); Terry Glavin and the People of Nemiah, *Nemiah: The Unconquered Country* (Vancouver: New Star, 1992); John L. Hall, "Ethnic Tensions and Economics: Indian White Interaction in a British Columbia Ranching Community," *Canadian Journal of Anthropology* 1/2 (1980): 179-90; Orrey Charleyboy, *Tsi Del Del: Redstone* (Williams Lake, BC: Chilcotin Language Committee, 1991), 11.

64 French, *Road Runs West*, 40, quoting the British Columbia Directory. The first reliable Indian Affairs Census, conducted in 1913, shows 489 Tsilhqot'in. Tsilhqot'in population taken from DIAR, 1913 and 1970.

65 See Charles Lillard and Terry Glavin, *A Voice Great within Us* (Vancouver: New Star, 1988) for a partial list of BC place names derived from Chinook.

66 Correspondence between I.W. Powell, Chief Commissioner of Lands and Works, and George Walkem, the Minister of the Interior, 1872-74, LAC, RG 10, vol. 3583, BCA Micro B2276 File 1102.

67 Indian Reserve Commission, 1876-78, McKinley and Sproat to Elliot, September 28, 1877, BCA, GR 0494, box 4, item 3, 146/88.

68 Shannon R.C. Pt. C., LAC, RG 10, vol. 11064.

69 DIAR, 1912; Teit, *The Shuswap*, 761-63.

70 Hall, "Ethnic Tensions," 179-90; Richmond Hobson, *Nothing Too Good for a Cowboy* (Philadelphia: Lippincott, ca. 1955).

71 George M. Dawson, *Journals of George M. Dawson,* 2 vols., ed. Douglas Cole and Bradley Lockner (Vancouver: UBC Press, 1989), 74, 232, notes that in 1875-76 there were only a few Tsilhqot'in at Anahim Lake and that most had moved to Anaham Flats near Alexis Creek.

He says the priest had ordered them to move east. See Teit, *The Shuswap*, 761-63.

72 "Report of the Indian Reserve Commission," 147-63, DIAR, 1887.

73 DIAR, 1892, 255.

74 Dinwoodie, "Reserve Memories," 14-15; Elizabeth Furniss, The *Burden of History: Colonialism and the Frontier Myth in a Rural Canadian Community* (Vancouver: UBC Press, 1999), 164-85; Goldman, "The Alkatcho Carrier," 371; Al Elsey, *Caribou Hunt in Tweedsmuir at Fenton, BC; Anahim Lake Stampede* (videorecording, s.l., ca. 1956). For more on the Indian-Cowboy phenomenon see John Lutz, "Interlude or Industry? Ranching in British Columbia, 1849-1885," *BC Historical News* 13, 4 (1980): 2-11; Morgan Baillargeon and Leslie Tepper, eds., *Legends of Our Times: Native Cowboy Life* (Vancouver: UBC Press, 1998); Peter Iverson, *When Indians Became Cowboys: Native Peoples and Cattle Ranching in the American West* (Norman: University of Oklahoma Press, 1994).

75 On October 6, 1842, Rev. Modeste Demers went where, in his words, "no minister of the gospel had yet penetrated" and stayed two weeks at Fort Chilcotin. See "Miscellaneous Information Relation to Fort Chilcoten," BCA, MM/C43; Dawson, *Journals*, 73, 8; DIAR, 1891; Birchwater, *'Ulkatchot'en*, 24.

76 "Report of the Indian Reserve Commission," DIAR, 1887, 147-63.

77 British Columbia Superintendency, Correspondence 1894-1905, Chris Carlson, Bella Coola, to A.W. Vowell, June 24, 1905, LAC, RG 10, vol. 1023, Mflm T-1459.

78 Quote from Williams Lake Indian Agent, in DIAR, 1897.

79 "Circular Letter from the Provincial Game Warden's Office, April 28, 1914, LAC, RG 10, 80-1/51, vol. 1, file 516,; Provincial Game Warden, BCA, GR 446, box 17, file 2, 100/1908.

80 Ibid.

81 McKenna-McBride Commission, July 22, 1914, BCA MS 1056, box 3.

82 Bostock, "Pack Horse Tracks," 19.

83 "Report of the Provincial Game Warden for 1918," BCSP, 1919, S16.

84 DIAR, 1906, 206-11; Cowichan Agency, Departmental Circulars, 1892-1910, A.W. Vowell to Indian Agents, June 20, 1905, LAC, RG 10, vol. 1350, reel C-13917; W.E.

Ditchburn testifying before the British Columbia Fisheries Commission, 1922, RG 23, vol. 1,233, file 726-34-4; Evelyn Pinkerton, "Indians in the Fishing Industry," in *Uncommon Property: The Fishing and Fish-Processing Industries in British Columbia*, ed. Patricia Marchak, Neil Guppy, and John McMullan (Toronto: Methuen, 1987), 251-54; McMullan, "State Capital and BC Salmon Fishing Industry," in Marchak, Guppy, and McMullan, *Uncommon Property*, 109-10.

85 Estimate of weight of average dried salmon taken from Daniel L. Boxberger, *To Fish in Common: The Ethnohistory of Lummi Salmon Fishing* (Lincoln: University of Nebraska Press, 1989), 15-16. For comparison, the Hudson's Bay Company allowed a ration of three pounds of dried salmon per man per day as a subsistence rate (two pounds for a woman and one pound for a child) in the 1820s, when it was the main food source, according to Archibald McDonald, HBCA, B.97/e/1 1827.

86 DIAR, 1916, 109; Henry Solomon, interviewed by John Lutz at his home in Nemiah, September 5, 1999.

87 E. McLeod, Indian Agent, Lytton, to M.B. Jackson, Chairman of the Game Conservation Board of BC, May 20, 1925, LAC, RG 10, vol. 10872, 901/20-10, pt. 2.

88 E. McLeod to M.B. Jackson, May 20, 1925, LAC, RG 10, vol. 10,872, file 901/20-10, pt. 2. In the winter of 1924-25, two Tsilhqot'in men, Henry Alexis and Billy Dagg, had made $960 from coyote skins alone. See Bostock, "Pack Horse Tracks."

89 Report of James Kew, Fisheries Inspector, Quesnel Subdistrict, 1938-48, LAC, RG 23, vol. 662, file 712-2-72, pt. 3.

90 DIAR, 1931, and 1934; Doug Hudson, "Traplines and Timber: Social and Economic Change among the Carrier" (PhD. Diss., University of Alberta, 1983), 140.

91 Bella Coola Agency, Agent's Report for the Month of December, 1941, LAC, RG 10, vol. 7332, file 989/20-7; RG 10, vol. 6736, file 4230-3-2; RG 10, vol. 6736, file 420-3-1-3. Information on ranch work taken from Glavin, *People of Nemiah*.

92 French, *The Road Runs West*, 230.

93 Report of James Kew, Fisheries Inspector Quesnel Subdistrict, LAC, RG 23, vol. 662, file 712-2-72, pt. 4; "Report on Williams Lake Agency for November 1941," RG 10, vol. 7332, file 989/20-7, pt. 1.

94 Report of James Kew, Fisheries Inspector, Quesnel Subdistrict, LAC, RG 23, vol. 662, file 712-2-72, pt. 4; "Report on Williams Lake Agency for November 1941" and "Report ... for 1943," RG 10, vol. 7332, file 989/20-7, pt. 1.

95 The source of information on the Puntzi base is French, *The Road Runs West*, 134-35.

96 The racism emerges clearly in Glavin's discussion of justice in the Chilcotin in "Last Day in Alexis Creek," in Terry Glavin, *This Ragged Place* (Vancouver: New Star, 1996), 123-69. See also Furniss, *Burden of History*.

97 Glavin records that the Setahs got their first cows in Nemiah in the 1950s. See Glavin, *People of Nemiah*. Quotes taken from DIAR 1951-52, 45; 1953-54 68; 1955-56, 60.

98 Ervin Charleyboy, chief of Redstone, interviewed by John Lutz at the Redstone Band Office, September 1, 1999; Cameron Beck, Economic Development Officer, Carrier Chilcotin Tribal Council, interviewed by John Lutz, August 30, 1999.

99 Quote from Hudson, "Traplines and Timber," 145; French, *The Road Runs West*, 230-31; W.J. Demerais, Superintendent's Quarterly Report Ending September 30, 1964, LAC, RG 10, vol. 5774, file 989/23-43. Demerais says that remoter communities are dependent on fur (he is likely referring to Ulkatcho and Nemiah and possibly Stone). Leslie Stump, chief at Anaham, interviewed by John Lutz at the Anaham Band Office, August 31, 2001. He agreed that trapping had dwindled in the early 1970s.

100 Cited in Andie Palmer, "Maps of Experience: Shuswap Narratives of Place" (PhD diss., University of Washington, 1994), 45. The dissertation has been revised and published as *Maps of Experience: The Anchoring of Land to Story in Secwepemc Discourse* (Toronto: University of Toronto Press, 2005). The importance of history being written onto the landscape has been stressed for a wide range of indigenous groups. See Fernando Santos-Granero, "Writing History into the Landscape: Space, Myth and Ritual in Contemporary Amazonia." *American Ethnologist* 25, 2 (1998): 128-48; Keith Basso, *Wisdom Sits in Places: Landscape and Language among the Western Apache* (Albuquerque: University of New Mexico Press, 1996).

101 Hall, "Ethnic Tensions," 179-90.

102 Quote from Palmer, "Maps of Experience," 170, describing the immediate Secwepemc neighbours of the Tsilhqot'in.

103 Hall, "Ethnic Tensions," 179-90.

104 Marilyn Bennett, *Indian Fishing and Its Cultural Importance in the Fraser River System* (Vancouver: BC Union of Indian Chiefs and Fisheries Canada, ca. 1974), 25.

105 McKenna-McBride Commission, in BC Union of Indian Chiefs, Transcripts of the Hearings, BCA, MS 1056, box 3; Henry Solomon, interviewed by John Lutz at his home in Nemiah, September 5, 1999.

106 Superintendent's Quarterly Report Ending September 30, 1964, LAC, RG 10, vol. 5774, file 989/23-43.

107 Compare DIAR, 1892, with Superintendent's Quarterly Report Ending August 31, 1963, in LAC, RG 10, vol. 5774, file 989/23-43.

108 If the agent thought the family was misspending the family allowance, then he would have dispensed it as food. This was known as distributing the allowance "in-kind." In a 1961 audit, twenty-eight of the 406 Williams Lake Agency Family Allowance recipients were getting their allowance in kind. See "Other British Columbians had been receiving old age security since 1927," LAC, RG 10, vol. 7906, file 40160-1, pt. 1. See also "Indians Transferred from Aged Assistance to Old Age Security," December 31, 1951, RG 10, vol. 2375, file 275-3-4[1], Department of National Health and Welfare, J.I. Clark to Joy Peacock, November 2, 1968, RG 29, vol. 1,889, R170/110. The family allowance rate in 1946 was $5.94 per child. See Dennis Guest, *The Emergence of Social Security in Canada* (Vancouver: UBC Press, 1985), 132, 145.

109 John Lutz, interviews with Charleyboy and Alphonse at the Tsilhqot'in National Government Office, August 2000.

110 John Lutz, inverviews with Patrick Lulua at the Tsilhqot'in National Government Offices and with Gilbert Solomon at the Nemiah Band Office, August 2000.

111 R.G. Cooper, Superintendent's Annual Report Ending March 31, 1967, LAC, RG 10, vol. 5774, file 989/23-43.

112 Don Wise, interviewed by John Lutz at the Tsilhqot'in National Government Office in September 1999; Henry Solomon, interviewed by John Lutz at Solomon's home in Nemiah, September 5, 1999.

113 Hall, "Ethnic Tensions" 183-84.

114 I.D. Desai and M. Lee, "Nutritional Status of British Columbia Indians: Biochemical Studies at Ahousat and Anaham Reserves," *Canadian Journal of Public Health* 62 (1971): 526-36. For a provincial discussion of this, see Mary-Ellen Kelm, *Colonizing Bodies: Aboriginal Health and Healing in British Columbia, 1900-1950* (Vancouver: UBC Press, 2000), 19-37.

115 Bennett, *Indian Fishing*, 13-20. Writing of the adjacent Carrier community of Nazko, Laura Boyd records the importance of country food in 1989 and the persistence of those few who continue to hunt and trap for their livelihood. See Laura Boyd, *My Home Forever* (Quesnel, BC: Developing Our Resources Curriculum Project, Quesnel School District, 1989).

116 M. Lee, R. Reyburn, and A. Carrow, "Nutritional Status of British Columbia Indians," *Canadian Journal of Public Health* 62 (1971): 289.

Chapter 6: Outside History

1 The full extent of the demographic catastrophe that struck Aboriginal Peoples in the eighteenth and nineteenth centuries will never be known: by the time the first censuses were taken, the worst was already over. Most scholars would agree, however, that it was not until 1950 that the total population of British Columbia reached the levels it had seen in 1750 (see Table 6.1). For a discussion of this, see Cole Harris, *The Resettlement of British Columbia: Essays on Colonialism and Geographical Change* (Vancouver: UBC Press, 1997), 3-30.

2 For an introduction to this diversity, see William C. Sturtevant, ed., *Handbook of North American Indians* (Washington, DC: Smithsonian) vols. 4, 6, 7.

3 Martin Robin, *The Rush for Spoils: The Company Province, 1871-1933* (Toronto: McClelland and Stewart, 1972), 30-31; Robin Fisher, *Contact and Conflict: Indian European Relations in British Columbia, 1774-1890* (Vancouver: UBC Press, 1977; reprinted 1992); Peter Carstens, *The Queen's People: A Study of Hegemony, Coercion and Accommodation among the Okanagan of Canada* (Toronto: University of Toronto Press, 1991).

4 See Arthur Ray, "The Hudson's Bay Company and Native People," in *History of Indian White Relations*, vol. 4, *Handbook of North American Indians*, ed. W.E. Washburn (Washington, DC: Smithsonian, 1988), 337.

5 Margaret Ormsby, *British Columbia: A History* (Toronto: Macmillan, 1958), 55.

6 E.E. Rich, ed., *Simpson's 1828 Journey to the Columbia* (London: Hudson's Bay Record Society, 1947), 10:26; see Richard S. Mackie, *Trading beyond the Mountains: The British Fur Trade on the Pacific, 1793-1843* (Vancouver: UBC Press, 1997), 283-310.

7 Eden Colvile to George Simpson, October 15, 1849, in *London Correspondence Inward from Eden Colvile 1849-1852*, ed. E.E. Rich (London: Hudson's Bay Record Society, 1956), 181.

8 Richard S. Mackie, *Trading beyond the Mountains*, 283-310; Richard S. Mackie, "Colonial Land, Indian Labour and Company Capital: The Economy of Vancouver Island, 1849-1858" (MA thesis, University of Victoria, 1984), 26-150.

9 HBCA, B.188/a/21., fol. 73, cited in Douglas Hudson, "Traplines and Timber: Social and Economic Change among the Carrier" (PhD diss., University of Alberta, 1983), 91.

10 James A. McDonald, "Trying to Make a Life: The Historical Political Economy of Kitsumkalum" (PhD diss., University of British Columbia, 1985), table 5. McDonald's figures are conservative since they do not include estimates for notations such as "several," "few," "some," or "gangs," and there may be instances where labour was not recorded at all. McDonald's work confirms the 1858 report of Missionary William Duncan, who noted "hundreds of Indians, in the course of the year, being employed about ... Fort [Simpson]." See Church Missionary Society Records, William Duncan, "First Report from Fort Simpson," February 1858, LAC, C2154.

11 BCA, Yale Family Papers, J.M. Yale to Simpson, October 22, 1850, in Mackie, "Colonial Land, Indian Labour," 89.

12 Douglas to Newcastle, October 24, 1853, CO 305/4, 12345. Chapter 3 examines the Songhees (Lekwungen) in detail and describes a potlatch.

13 Letters to the HBC from Vancouver Island Colony, James Douglas to Archibald Barclay, June 15, 1854, BCA, A/C/20/Vi2A.

14 Governor James Douglas to Russell, August 21, 1855, CO 305/6, 10048; Douglas to Colonial Office, August 8, 1860, CO 305/14, 9267; BCA, A/B/30/F49.1, in Roderick Finlayson, "History of Vancouver Island and the Northwest Coast," 57.

15 Indeed the "whites" became something of a tourist attraction for the local Songhees people. Skagit John Fornsby was given a tour of Victoria by Songhees Michael Cooper, who, in the late 1890s, took pains to show his visitors "the little log house where white people first stayed" and to explain the use of the plough and the stove. See June Collins, "John Fornsby: The Personal Document of a Coast Salish Indian," in *Indians of the Urban Northwest*, ed. Marian Smith (New York: Columbia University Press, 1949), 325; H.H. Bancroft, *History of British Columbia, 1792-1887* (San Francisco: The History Company, 1887), 130, 427.

16 Douglas to Barclay, July 13, 1853 in *Fort Victoria Letters: 1846-1851*, ed. Hartwell Bowsfield (Winnipeg: Hudson's Bay Record Society, 1979).

17 Douglas to Newcastle, July 28, 1853, CO 305/4, 9499.

18 See Fisher, *Contact and Conflict*, 71-72; Paul Tennant, *Aboriginal Peoples and Politics: The Indian Land Question in British Columbia, 1849-1989* (Vancouver: UBC Press, 1990), 35-39; John Adams, *Old Square Toes and His Lady: The Life of James and Amelia Douglas* (Victoria: Horsdal and Shubert, 2001).

19 The bills of the colony for 1852 included payments of goods and wages of £22.14.10 to Indians and other parties for improvements and repairs on the governor's premises, £6.15.5 to Indians for working on surveys, and £28.12.2 to "Indians and others" engaged in making public roads. See BCA, A/C/20/Vi/2A, Letters to the Hudson's Bay Company from Vancouver Island Colony, May 18, 1853. The Ts'msyen were from the Skeena River area around Fort Simpson. See William Duncan, "Journal," July 11, 1857, quoted in Jean Usher, *William Duncan of Metlakatla: A Victorian Missionary in British Columbia* (Ottawa: National Museums of Canada, 1974), 40; W.C. Grant in William Carew Hazlitt, *British Columbia and Vancouver Island* (London: G. Routledge, 1858), 179; Dorothy Blakey-Smith, ed., *The Reminiscences of Doctor John Sebastian Helmcken,* by J.S. Helmcken (Vancouver: UBC Press, 1975), 134. Mackie, "Colonial Land, Indian Labour," 140.

20 Douglas added: "Under proper restraints their labour would advance the Colony; but from their turbulent thievish disposition, it is impossible to prevent discord

arising between them and the white settlers and I would therefore rather dispense with their presence." Douglas to Barclay, June 15, 1854, BCA, A/C/20/Vi2A.

21 One account of these "pitched battles" on the outskirts of Victoria is given by Charles Wilson, *Mapping the Frontier: Charles Wilson's Diary of the Survey of the 49th Parallel, 1858-1862,* ed. G.F.G. Stanley (Toronto: Macmillan, 1970) 74. For a general discussion of these hostilities see John Lutz, "Work, Sex, and Death on the Great Thoroughfare: Annual Migrations of 'Canadian Indians' to the American Pacific Northwest," in *Parallel Destinies: Canadian-American Relations West of the Rockies,* ed. John M. Findlay and Ken Coates, 80-103 (Seattle: Center for the Study of the Pacific Northwest and University of Washington Press, 2002).

22 Homi Bhabha, "Frontlines/Borderposts," in *Displacements: Cultural Identities in Question,* ed. Angelika Bammer (Bloomington: Indiana University Press, 1994), 270. The idea of a moditional economy is developed in Chapter 1.

23 CO 305/6, 10048, Douglas to Lord Russell, August 21, 1855.

24 For the coining of the phrase, see United States, Report of the Commissioner of Indian Affairs, "Report of E.C. Fitzhugh, Special Indian Agent" November 11, 1857, 327; An examination of the Stó:lō pre-European and post-European seasonal cycle can be found in Colin Duffield and Albert McHalsie, "Contact Era Seasonal Rounds" and John Lutz, "Seasonal Rounds in an Industrial World," in *Stó:lō Coast Salish Historical Atlas,* ed. Keith Thor Carlson (Vancouver and Seattle: Douglas and McIntyre and the University of Washington Press, 2001), Plates 21 and 22.

25 William Duncan, First Report from Fort Simpson, February 1858, LAC, Church Missionary Society, C.2./o Appendix C. reel A-105.

26 June Collins, "John Fornsby: The Personal Document of a Coast Salish Indian," in *Indians of the Urban Northwest,* ed. Marian Smith (New York: Columbia University Press, 1949), 301; James Swan, "Northern Indians," *San Francisco Evening Bulletin,* October 4, 1860, reprinted in James Swan, *Almost out of the World: Scenes from Washington Territory: The Strait of Juan de Fuca* (Tacoma, WA: Washington State Historical Society, 1971), 99; CO 305/7, 3963, Douglas to Sir George Grey, March 1, 1856; and CO 305/7 5814, April 10, 1856; *Puget Sound Herald* (Seilacoom), April 23, 1858. This migration is described in more detail in Lutz, "Work, Sex and Death," and in John Lutz, "When Is an 'Indian War' Not a War? Canadian Indians and American Settlers in the Pacific Northwest, 1850s-1860s," *Journal of the West* 38, 3 (1998): 7-13.

27 References to the cheapness of provisions supplied by Aboriginal People and the dependence of the colonists on this food are ubiquitous. For the examples cited, see Rev. R.J. Staines to Thomas Boys, July 6, 1852, CO 305/3; Blakey-Smith, *Reminiscences,* 134; Douglas to Earl Grey, October 31, 1851, CO 305/3: "Deer and game of all kinds abound and could be bought for some trifle such as Tobacco Powder and shot; the price of a grouse in those days being two charges or twice as much as it cost to kill it." See Alfred Charles Bayley, "Early Life on Vancouver Island," BCA Mss. E/B/B34.2, 6; Letters to the Hudson's Bay Company from Vancouver Island Colony, James Douglas, February 2, 1853, BCA, A/C/20/Vi/2A; W.C. Grant in Hazlitt, *British Columbia and Vancouver Island,* 16.

28 James Douglas to the Governor and Committee of the Hudson's Bay Company, December 7, 1846, in Bowsfield, *Fort Victoria Letters,* 4.

29 E.E. Rich, ed., *The Letters of John McLoughlin from Fort Vancouver ... , 1825-1838* (Toronto: Champlain Society, 1941), 244, 334.

30 The reference is to a blanket of two and one-half points (the number of points specifies the quality of the blanket). See Douglas to the Governor and Committee, September 3, 1849, April 3, November 16, and December 22, 1850 in Bowsfield, *Fort Victoria Letters,* 46, 84, 132, 140; Eden Colvile to Sir J.H. Pelly, February 6, 1850, in Colvile, *London Correspondence,* 17. See also William Burrill, "Class Conflict and Colonialism: The Coal Miners of Vancouver Island during the Hudson's Bay Company Era, 1848-1862" (MA thesis, University of Victoria, 1987), 54. For the local population around the coalmines, see Robert Galois, *Kwakwa̱ka̱'wakw Settlements, 1775-1920: A Geographical Analysis and Gazetteer* (Vancouver: UBC Press, 1994).

31 Douglas to Pakington, August 28, 1852, CO 305/3, 10199; also November 11, 1852, CO 305/3, 933; James Douglas, Letters to the Hudson's Bay Company from Vancouver

Island Colony, September 3, 1853, BCA, A/C/20/Vi/A; "Nanaimo Correspondence," J.W. McKay to Douglas, September 9, 1852, BCA; James Douglas to Archibald Barclay, September 24, 1853, HBCA, B.226/b/12, and 2 November 1853 to Archibald Barclay, [not signed] B.226/b/14; Aboriginal People were also the first workers at the short-lived coal mine on the Skidegate River, Queen Charlotte Islands in 1867-69, see Mifflin W. Gibbs, *Shadows and Light: An Autobiography* (New York: Arno, 1968), 101-6; blanket values from Despatches about Vancouver Island, William Miller to H.A. Addington, October 23, 1848, quoting a letter of Capt. Courtenay dated September 12, BCA, GR-0328, Great Britain, Colonial Office.

32 Douglas to Stuart, August 22, 1857 quoted in Burrill, "Class Conflict," 127.

33 "Trip Up the Fraser," *Victoria Gazette*, 21 July 1858, 2.

34 Bayley, "Early Life," 6. Hazlitt, *British Columbia and Vancouver Island*, 166, also comments on the aboriginal men working in the mines and the women conveying coal to the ships in canoes.

35 In 1864, explorer Robert Brown tried to hire Indian packers at Nanaimo "but found it impossible ... every Indian being engaged at the coal mines." In 1882, the Indian Agent overseeing Nanaimo noted that the Aboriginal People there "[found] constant employment at the coal mines and wharves," and in 1883 George Dawson told the Immigration and Colonization Committee of the House of Commons "that a considerable number, not only of Chinese but of Indians are employed in the underground works and gain good wages," *The Resources of British Columbia* 1, 9 (1883): 10; DIAR, 1877, lx; DIAR, 1883, 54; Robert Brown, *Vancouver Island: Expedition, 1864* (Victoria: Colony of Vancouver Island, 1864). Albert Westly was among the Nanaimo people who worked in the mines at this time. Fifty years later, he was an informant for the anthropologist Homer Barnett. See Homer Barnett, *The Coast Salish of British Columbia* (Eugene: University of Oregon Press, 1955), 6.

36 The Department of Mines statistics do not include miner's assistants, which may account for part of this discrepancy as most conflicting reports do not specify what positions Aboriginal People held in the mines.

37 R.E. Gosnell, *Year Book of British Columbia and Manual of Provincial Information for 1897* (Victoria: R.E. Gosnell, 1898), 419.

38 DIAR, 1888, 100-2; DIAR, 1900, "Cowichan Report"; McKenna-McBride Commission Testimony, BCA, GR 1995, reel B-1454, 266, 276. The published report of the McKenna-McBride Commission gave the occupations of the Nanaimo band as: "Fishing, farming, and working for wages in the mines, as stevedores, trimming coal in ships, etc." See Appendix C.

39 Douglas to Earl Grey, January 29, 1852, CO 305/3, 3742; Staines to Boys, July 6, 1852, CO 305/3, 9263; Douglas to Earl Grey, October 31, 1851, CO 305/3; Captain A.L. Kuper to Admiralty, July 20, 1852, CO 305/3, 8866; Douglas to Labouchere, April 6, 1858, CO 305/9, 5180; Douglas to William Smith, July 20, 1857, HBCA, B226/b/15; and Douglas to Mssrs Allan Lowe and CO, April 24, 1858, HBCA, B/226/b/16.

40 James Douglas in T.A. Rickard, "Indian Participation in the Gold Discoveries," *British Columbia Historical Quarterly* 2 (1938): 13; and W. K. Lamb, "The Discovery of Hill's Bar in 1858," *British Columbia Historical Quarterly* 3, 22 (1939): 218. There are other estimates of between two hundred and five hundred Aboriginal People mining at Hill's Bar, compared to fifty to sixty white miners. See Hazlitt, *British Columbia and Vancouver Island*, 137; Robert M. Ballantyne, *Handbook to the Goldfields ...* (Edinburgh: A. Strahan, 1858), 18; Daniel Marshall, "Rickard Revisited: Native 'Participation' in the Gold Discoveries of British Columbia," *Native Studies Review* 11, 1 (1996): 91-99.

41 Mr. Walker at Fort Hope, May 1858, quoted in Bancroft, *History of British Columbia,* 392. For more on Indian mining and some estimates of returns, see Bancroft, 406-7, 454; Bishop George Hills, Diary, June 14 and 17, 1860, Anglican Church of Canada, Ecclesiastical Archives of British Columbia.

42 Bishop George Hills Diary, June 18, July 1, 1860; M.B. Begbie in H.L. Langevin, *British Columbia: Report of the Honourable H.L. Langevin, Minister of Public Works* (Ottawa: Parliament, I.B. Taylor, 1872), 27.

43 Mary Augusta Tappage, *The Days of Augusta*, ed. J.E. Speare (Vancouver: Douglas and McIntyre, 1992), 15; "The Story of the Conversion and Subsequent Experi-

ences of Captain John as Narrated by Himself" (1898), unpublished manuscript located in the Chilliwack Museum as told by Captain John in Chinook and transcribed by Reverend Barraclough.

44 Quoted in R.E. Gosnell, "Bygone Days of British Columbia," Vancouver *Daily Province*, November 14, 1908, 19. This reference is courtesy of Jeremy Mouat. Bishop Hills also commented in his diary on the importance and strength of aboriginal women packers.

45 *British Columbian*, October 1 and 15, 1862; George M. Grant, *Ocean to Ocean: Sir Sanford Fleming's Expedition through Canada in 1872* (Toronto: James Campbell and Son, 1873; reprinted Toronto: Coles, 1970) 313; interview with Annie York, BCA, Imbert Orchard Oral History Collection, tape 678: 1+2; K.C. Wells Collection, Chilliwack Archives, add mss 1, file 584.

46 James Cooper, "Report by the Harbor Master at Esquimalt to the Acting Colonial Secretary," BCA, Colonial Correspondence, F347/26a. Cooper also reports that a large number of the four hundred residents of "Laskick," a village on the Queen Charlotte Islands, were also in Victoria and that the Aboriginal People of Russian Alaska were familiar with the conditions there. See Usher, *William Duncan of Metlakatla*, 58. One of the Haida men from Skidegate was employed about this time as a domestic in the Victoria household of Mifflin Gibbs; see Gibbs, *Shadows and Light*, 102.

47 Douglas to Colonial Office, August 8, 1860, CO 305/14, 9267.

48 Douglas to Colonial Office, July 7, 1860, CO 305/14, 8319. One major shift that occurred during the gold rush involved aboriginal labour increasingly being paid in cash rather than in goods. Previously, the goods most sought after as pay were blankets, which were commonly used as potlatch gifts.

49 Stó:lō *Xe'ílhatel,* as well as Edmund Peter's grandfather worked on the boundary survey. See Oliver Wells, *The Chilliwacks and Their Neighbours* (Vancouver: Talonbooks, 1987), 137. See also Wilson, *Mapping the Frontier*; Edgar Fawcett, *Some Reminiscences of Old Victoria* (Toronto: William Briggs, 1912), 84; Robin Fisher, "Joseph Trutch and the Indian Land Policy," in *British Columbia: Historical Readings*, ed. W.P. Ward and R.A.J.

McDonald (Vancouver: Douglas and McIntyre, 1981), 155; Douglas to Barclay, October 8, 1851 in Bowsfield, *Fort Victoria Letters*, 222.

50 Fawcett, *Some Reminiscences*, 84.

51 Sophia Cracroft, *Lady Franklin Visits the Pacific Northwest: Being Extracts of the Letters of Miss Sophia Cracroft, Sir John Franklin's Niece, February to April 1861 and April to July 1870* (Victoria: Provincial Archives, 1974) 79; Fawcett, *Some Reminiscences*, 84; *British Colonist*, June 17, 1862, September 24, 1862. One of the thousands of coastal Aboriginal People who moved to Victoria for periods of up to several years, Arthur Wellington Clah worked in a variety of occupations in Victoria, including as a store clerk, builder, constable, and ship's crew. See Clah, Arthur Wellington, Wellcome MS American, LAC, MG 40, F11, microfilm A-1711, 140.

52 Bishop George Hills Diary, June 5, 1861, June 21, 1862; *British Columbian*, July 11, 1861; August 22, 1861; *British Colonist*, September 24, 1862.

53 It was not just neighbouring people who migrated to the gold rush town. In 1860, Chief Estercana of the Skidegate Haida on Haida Gwaii said that at least one of his people and perhaps more were at Yale or Hope. See James Cooper, "Report by the Harbor Master at Esquimalt to the Acting Colonial Secretary," BCA, Colonial Correspondence File F347 26a; M.B. Begbie to James Douglas, April 11, 1860, BCA B1307 F142c 6a.

54 Christine Quintasket, *Mourning Dove: A Salishan Autobiography,* ed. Jay Miller (Lincoln: University of Nebraska Press, 1990), 10, 166, 171; Cracroft estimates that there were one thousand Aboriginal People living at Yale in 1861, and she mentions that some of them were engaged as servants. See Cracroft, *Lady Franklin,* 53-54. At Lytton, the population of 250 was 80 percent Aboriginal and "the Indians ... very industrious and peaceable. Their chief employment is gold mining and packing supplies to and from the interior with their own horses of which they have in great numbers." See P.A. Crossby, *Lovell's Gazetteer of British North America* (Montreal: J. Lovell, 1873), 181; Fisher, *Contact and Conflict*, 111.

55 Alfred C. Selwyn, "Journal and Report of Preliminary Explorations in British Columbia," *Report of Progress for 1871-72* (Ottawa: Geological Survey of Canada, 1872), 56; *British Colonist,* November 26, 1872; Bishop George

Hills Diary, September 7, 1876, quotes the local missionary as estimating the annual yield at $20,000 and the local storekeeper as estimating it at $30,000. See J.W. McKay, in DIAR, 1887, 83.

56 Lena Hope "rocked gold" with her grandparents at Spuzzum early in the twentieth century: "They wash gold in them rockers, that was only the way that we got something to spend in stores." See Wells, *The Chilliwacks*, 193; DIAR, 1886, 4, 87-92; BCSP (1900), 724.

57 C.J. Grandidier to I.W. Powell, July 2, 1874 and Alexis to James Lenihan, September 5, 1875, LAC, RG 10, DIA, vol. 1001, items 82, 186.

58 George Walkem, "Report of the Government of British Columbia on the Subject of Indian Reserves," BCSP, 1875, 3. Walkem was trying to make the case that only a small fraction of BC Aboriginal People were agriculturalists. His point being that the remainder did not need reserves of 160 acres per family (which is what was being allotted on the Prairies).

59 In her study of Hawaiian women, Caroline Ralston argues that "the term 'prostitution,' with its undeniable sexist and moralistic connotations, is inapplicable as a description of the casual sexual encounters in which money or material favours are exchanged." See Caroline Ralston, "Ordinary Women in Early Post-Contact Hawaii," in *Family and Gender in the Pacific: Domestic Contradictions and the Colonial Impact*, ed. Margaret Jolly and Martha Macintyre (Sydney: Cambridge University Press, 1989), 57.

60 Matthew MacFie, *Vancouver Island and British Columbia: Their History, Resources, and Prospects* (London: Longman, Roberts, and Green, 1865), 471.

61 Captain J.C. Prevost to Secretariat of the Committee of the CMS, April 4, 1859, LAC, Church Missionary Society, C.2./0 appendix C, reel A-105. The Toquat tribe was reduced to "a few old men and women" by these raids. See Bishop George Hills Diary, February 6, 1860; Douglas Cole and David Darling, "History of the Early Period," in *Handbook of North American Indians*, ed. Wayne Suttles (Washington, DC: Smithsonian, 1990), 7: 130; Barnett, *Culture Element Distribution*, 267; Wayne Suttles, *Economic Life of the Coast Salish of Haro and Rosario Straits* (New York: Garland, 1974), 306.

62 William Banfield to Captain J.C. Prevost, November 21, 1859, Church Missionary Society, C.2./0, appendix C, reel A-105; Bishop George Hills Diary, February 6, 1860; Lutz, "Work, Sex and Death."

63 Bishop George Hills Diary, October 12, 1861, January 25, 1862; Sproat, in *Scenes and Studies*, 67, says that a young woman slave in Victoria would be worth fifty blankets or $150 (£30).

64 Franz Boas, *Contributions to the Ethnology of the Kwakiutl* (New York: Columbia University Press, 1925), 93-94; W.M. Halliday, *Potlatch and Totem: Recollections of an Indian Agent* (London and Toronto: J.M. Dent and Sons, 1935). See also Clelland S. Ford, *Smoke from Their Fires: The Life of a Kwakiutl Chief* (Hamden, CN: Archon, 1968); Carol Cooper, "Native Women of the Northern Pacific Coast: An Historical Perspective, 1830-1900," *Journal of Canadian Studies* 27, 4 (1992-93): 44-73. See also Jo-Anne Fiske, "Colonization and the Decline of Women's Status: The Tsimshian Case," *Feminist Studies* 17, 3 (1991): 509-35.

65 Albert P. Niblack, *The Coast Indians of Southern Alaska and Northern British Columbia* (1888; reprinted New York: Johnson Reprint Corporation, 1970) 338, 346-67; William Duncan, First Report Fort Simpson, February 1858, LAC, Church Missionary Society, C.2./0, appendix C, reel A-105; J.A. Jacobsen, *Alaskan Voyage, 1881-83: An Expedition to the Northwest Coast of America*, translated from the German text of Adrian Woldt by Erna Gunther (Chicago: University of Chicago Press, 1977), 8-9.

66 Daisy Sewid-Smith, interviewed by John Lutz, University of Victoria, October 19, 2000.

67 W.E. Banfield to the Colonial Secretary, September 6, 1860, from Lorne Hammond, unpublished manuscript on W.E. Banfield, BCA, Colonial Correspondence, file 107/5; James Morton, *The Enterprising Mr. Moody and the Bumptious Captain Stamp* (Vancouver: J.J. Douglas, 1977), 22-23; H.C. Langley, *Pacific Coast Directory for 1867* (San Francisco: H.G. Langley, 1867), 158.

68 For a discussion of the labour force and the disappearance of aboriginal labour, see Chapter 2. See also Frederick Whymper, *Travel and Adventure in Alaska* (London: J. Murray, 1868), 37, 62; G.M. Sproat, *The Nootka: Scenes and Studies of Savage Life* (London: Smith, Elder, 1868; reprinted Victoria: Sono Nis, 1989), 40. Taylor reports that, over its operation, the mill paid

out close to $300,000 in wages. He does not indicate his source, but the payroll of the Burrard Inlet Mills cited below suggests that this figure is credible. See G.W. Taylor, *Timber: History of the Forest Industry in BC* (Vancouver: J.J. Douglas, 1975), 23.

69 Morton, *Enterprising Mr. Moody*, 59; Taylor, *Timber*, 28.

70 R.H. Alexander, "Reminiscences of the Early Days of British Columbia, Address to the Canadian Club of Vancouver," in *Proceedings of the Canadian Club of Vancouver 1906-1911* (Vancouver: Canadian Club of Vancouver, 1911), 111; Visiting Burrard Inlet in November 1875, geologist George Dawson noted, disparagingly: "while Europeans or at least Whites fill the responsible posts, Indians (Squa'mich), Chinamen, Negroes, and Mulattoes, and Half breeds, and Mongrels of every pedigree abound." See George M. Dawson, *The Journals of George M. Dawson,* ed. Douglas Cole and Bradley Lockner (Vancouver: UBC Press, 1989), 115; Rev. C.M. Tate, "Thrilling Story of Missionary Adventure and Success: An Autobiographical Sketch of Nearly Sixty Years Labor among Indian Tribes of BC," *Western Recorder* 5 (1929): 3.

71 Walkem, "Report of the Government of British Columbia," 3; George Blenkinsop, "Report of the Proceedings of the Joint Commission," in DIAR, 1877, Special Appendix D, lii; Statistics Canada, *Census of Canada* (1881) (Ottawa: Canada, 1871-1971), 3: table 34, 380.

72 J.G. Swan, "The Haida Indians of Queen Charlotte's Island," in *Smithsonian Contributions to Knowledge* 21 (1876): 2, 8, 14.

73 Reverend William Henry Pierce, *From Potlatch to Pulpit*, ed. J.P. Hicks (Vancouver: Vancouver Bindery, 1933), 15.

74 Ford, *Smoke from Their Fires,* 134.

75 Morley Roberts, *The Western Avernus or, Toil and Travel in Further North America* (London: Smith, Elder, 1887), 181-82; J.S. Matthews, *Conversations with Khahtsahlano, 1932-1954* (Vancouver: Vancouver City Archives, 1955), 14; Boas recounts his meeting in Vancouver with an aboriginal man who had lost his arm in a sawmill accident and who was unemployed as a result. See Franz Boas, *The Ethnography of Franz Boas: Letters and Diaries of Franz Boas Written on the Northwest Coast from 1886-1931,* ed. Richard Rohner, trans. Hedy Parker (Chicago: University of Chicago Press, 1969), 87.

76 Matthews, *Conversations*, 14, 157; Rolf Knight, *Indians at Work: An Informal History of Native Indian Labour in British Columbia, 1858-1930* (Vancouver: New Star, 1978), 114; Nowell, in Ford, *Smoke from Their Fires*, 134; J.S. Matthews, *Early Vancouver: Narratives of Pioneers of Vancouver, BC* (Vancouver: Brock Webber, 1933), 44.

77 Khahtsahlano later worked in the W.L. Tait Mill and the Rat Portage Sawmill; see Matthews, *Conversations*, 56, 64; Wells, *The Chilliwacks*, 168. In 1876, the fifty-five men of the Sechelt band cut 1,300,000 cubic feet of saw logs for the mills, for which they received three dollars per thousand, the same rate paid to white loggers. See DIAR, 1878, 8, "Report of the Indian Reserve Commissioners," lix; Collins, "John Fornsby," 307. In May 1862, the *British Colonist* reported that the smallpox epidemic had caused the native longshoremen to leave the lumber yards, and the owners were obliged to hire white men and pay them $2.50 per day instead of the usual two dollars to unload lumber. See also Knight, *Indians at Work*, 123-30.

78 Duncan Stacey, *Sockeye and Tinplate: Technological Change in the Fraser Canning Industry, 1871-1912* (Victoria: British Columbia Provincial Museum, 1982); Keith Ralston, "James Symes," in *Dictionary of Canadian Biography* 11 (1982): 866.

79 Mackie, *Trading beyond the Mountains*, 221-30.

80 "Salmon Pack for 1883, Fraser River Canneries," *The Resources of British Columbia* 1, 4 (1883): 4; P. McTiernan, DIAR, 1882, 61. Visiting the Delta Cannery on the Fraser River in 1882, Newton Chittenden found that all the fishboats were worked by Indians and that the cannery labour force consisted of 160 Indians and 280 Chinese "under the supervision of experienced white foremen." See Newton Chittenden, *Travels in British Columbia* (Victoria: S.n., 1882; reprinted Vancouver: Gordon Soules, 1984), 29.

81 T. Revelly, Fisheries Agent to Nicholas Flood, August 22, 1884, printed in DIAR, 1885, 395.

82 DIAR, 1881, 130-60. Missionary Thomas Crosby remarked that, when the first cannery opened in Rivers Inlet in 1883, they immediately hired two hundred Aboriginal People. Quoted in Michael Harkin, "Dialogues of History: Transformation and Cultural Change in Heiltsuk Culture," (PhD. diss., University of Chicago, 1988), 289.

83 See Alfred Carmichael, "Account of a Season's Work at the Salmon Cannery, Windsor Cannery, Aberdeen, Skeena," BCA, Bp/C21.

84 Boas, *Ethnography of Franz Boas*, 6, 9.

85 *Census of Canada* (1881), 3: table 51, 474; *Census of Canada* (1891), 3: table 1, 149. In 1882, the Indian Agent for the Fraser River Area reported that 400 aboriginal women were employed inside the Fraser River canneries. In 1883, a journalist for *British Columbia Resources* estimated that the total cannery labour force on the Fraser River included 700 Chinese men. See "Salmon Pack for 1883, Fraser River Canneries," 4; McTeirnan, DIAR, 1882, 61.

86 He was surprised that many Indians consider a twenty-five-cent piece the smallest change. See J.A. Jacobsen, *Alaskan Voyage, 1881-83: An Expedition to the Northwest Coast of America*, trans. Erna Gunther (Chicago: University of Chicago Press, 1977), 6.

87 Unless otherwise cited, the following data relating to 1881 is taken from the Canada, Legislative Assembly, "Department of Indian Affairs Annual Report" (DIAR), *Canada Sessional Papers* (Ottawa: Canada, 1881), 130-60.

88 The Ts'msyen also conducted a freighting industry along the Skeena, which began in 1865 and, by 1895, was employing two hundred people and forty canoes. A fuller account of the Ts'msyen economy can be found in J.A. McDonald, "Images of the Nineteenth-Century Economy of the Tsimshian," in *The Tsimshian: Images of the Past; Views for the Present*, ed. M. Seguin (Vancouver: UBC Press, 1984), 45. For a Ts'msyen perspective, see the Diary of Arthur Wellington Clah, LAC, MG 40, F11, microfilm A-1711, MS American 140 (1).

89 Powell, in DIAR, 1881, 139-40, 148. For the Fort Rupert people, see Charles Nowell cited in Philip Drucker and R.F. Heizer, *To Make My Name Good: A Re-examination of the Southern Kwakiutl Potlatch* (Berkeley: University of California Press, 1976), 215.

90 Harry Guillod, in DIAR, 1882, 57; Cairn Crockford, "Changing Economic Activities of the Nuu-chah-nulth of Vancouver Island, 1840-1920" (BA honours thesis, University of Victoria, 1991), nicely charts the expansion of paid work among the Nuu-chah-nulth as an extension of their subsistence economies.

91 In the 1870s, a missionary complained that "in less than two months they are able to make money enough to buy food and clothing for a whole year and without much labour. They understand that in farming they must work very hard all year to make *less* than they do now by two months sealing and fishing." Quoted in Crockford, "Changing Economic Activities," 38; DIAR, 1915, in Crockford, 47. For the sealing industry, see Peter Murray, *The Vagabond Fleet: A Chronicle of the North Pacific Sealing Schooner Trade* (Victoria: Sono Nis, 1988); and Briton Cooper Busch, *The War against the Seals: A History of the North American Seal Fishery* (Montreal and Kingston: McGill-Queen's University Press, 1985).

92 W.H. Lomas, in DIAR, 1882, 160-62; and McTiernan, in DIAR, 1882, 166. The first cannery opened on Rivers Inlet in 1883, and by 1891 virtually the entire Heiltsuk population of Bella Bella moved to the Rivers Inlet canneries in the summer. See Michael Harkin, *The Heiltsuks: Dialogues of Culture and History on the Northwest Coast* (Lincoln: University of Nebraska Press, 1997), 141.

93 "Salmon Pack for 1883, Fraser River Canneries," 4; Chittenden, *Travels in British Columbia*, 29; McTiernan, in DIAR, 1882, 61; McTiernan, in DIAR, 1885, 84.

94 DIAR, 1882, 130-60; Fisher, *Contact and Conflict*, 111. Since coastal people put such great emphasis on wealth, he argued that this "stultified" their culture. There are numerous indications that the peak of prosperity for many aboriginal groups came after settlement.

95 DIAR, 1886, 81, 84.

96 DIAR, 1885, 81-84; Collins, "John Fornsby," 324-30; Edward Sapir and Morris Swadesh, *Nootka Texts* (Philadelphia: Linguistic Society of America, 1939), 149-50; Matthews, *Conversations*, 82; Ford, *Smoke from Their Fires*, 133-34.

97 Powell, in DIAR, 1884, 107; McTiernan, in DIAR, 1882, 166; "George Swanaset: Narrative of a Personal Document," University of Washington, Special Collections, Melville Jacobs Collection, mss. 1693-71-13, box 112; Wells, *The Chilliwacks*, 164.

98 DIAR, 1882, 61; Tsimshian from Port Simpson and the Nass also came to work on the E&N railroad construction on Vancouver Island in the mid-1980s. See DIAR, 1885, 80.

99 *British Colonist*, March 8, 1860; Clah Diary; Charles Jones with Stephen Bosustow, *Queesto, Pacheenaht Chief by Birthright* (Nanaimo, BC: Theytus, 1981), 47; Sapir and

Swadesh, *Nootka Texts*, 141-47 and passim. Edenshaw is now one of the best known Haida argillite carvers. See Margaret Blackman, *During My Time: Florence Edenshaw Davidson, a Haida Woman* (Vancouver: Douglas and McIntyre, 1982), 72; Knight, *Indians at Work*, 60-62.

100 Knight, *Indians at Work*, 114, 123-24; Pierce, *From Potlatch to Pulpit*, 69-70; Charley Nowell worked in the Alert Bay mill in 1897-98. See Ford, *Smoke from Their Fires*, 167.

101 Canada, Department of Agriculture, *Census of Canada, Bulletin Nos. 8 and 10* (Ottawa: Department of Agriculture, 1892). By 1891, largely on the basis of the rapid, proportional expansion of the canneries, more people were employed in manufacturing in British Columbia than in any other province. Aboriginal cannery employees accounted for a large part of this figure.

102 This estimate subtracts from the total aboriginal population the population figures of the Indian Affairs census for those bands listed as living primarily or exclusively on trapping, hunting, and fishing. The bands subtracted are: 239 people in the Chilcotin, 600 on the coast, 300 in the Kootenays, and 2,000 from tribes not visited. See Wilson Duff, *The Indian History of British Columbia: The Impact of the White Man* (Victoria: British Columbia Provincial Museum, 1964), 35-40, for estimates of tribes not visited.

103 "The majority of the Indians on the Lower Fraser River prefer working for the whites to cultivating their lands ... During the fishing season these Indians earn from $1 to 2½ dollars per diem which gives them a sufficiency of cash to supply all themselves with all the necessaries of life without resorting to the cultivation of the soil for a livelihood." See George Blenkinsop, Census Taker for the Indian Reserve Commission, Notebook, 1879, LAC, RG 10, 10,012A.

104 Powell, in DIAR, 1884, 107; McTiernan, in DIAR, 1882, 166; "George Swanaset: Narrative."

105 James Lenihan, DIAR, 1876, 56. See also a similar statement by Indian Superintendent Powell, DIAR, 1877, 33-34.

106 An account of the circumstances surrounding the creation of the manuscripts is given in Appendix 1.

107 Cowichan Agency, Departmental Circulars, 1892-1910, A.W. Vowell, March 9, 1896, LAC, RG 10, vol. 1350, reel C-13917; Bill Russell, "The White Man's Paper Burden:

Aspects of Record Keeping in the Department of Indian Affairs, 1860-1914," *Archivaria* 19 (1984-85): 50-72.

108 In particular, the different forms of racialization of Aboriginal Peoples by different agencies affects the comparability of statistical data.

109 Phillip John, interviewed by Ulli Steltzer and Catherine Kerr for their book, *Coast of Many Faces* (Vancouver: Douglas and McIntyre, 1979), 134.

110 Pierce, *From Potlatch to Pulpit*, 56; Dave Elliot, *Saltwater People* (Saanich, BC: School District 63, 1983), 67-68; Collins, "John Fornsby," 309; Harry Assu with Joy Inglis, *Assu of Cape Mudge: Recollections of a Coastal Indian Chief* (Vancouver: UBC Press, 1989), 23-24; Bridget Moran, *Stoney Creek Woman: The Story of Mary John* (Vancouver: Tillacum Library, 1988), 19-24; Blackman, *During My Time*, 63-4, 113. See also Mary-Ellen Kelm, "British Columbia First Nations and the Influenza Pandemic of 1918-19," *BC Studies* 122 (1999): 23-47.

111 *Census of Canada* (1881, 1901, 1961).

112 Swanaset, "Personal Narrative." Some Lillooet also found work for the railway. See Joanne Drake Terry, *The Same as Yesterday: The Lillooet Chronicle the Theft of Their Land and Resources* (Lillooet, BC: Lillooet Tribal Council, 1989), 317n2.

113 DIAR, 1885, 87-88, 118. This would average $50,000 a year for six years and so roughly agrees with the estimate that Onderdonck paid $40,000 to aboriginal labourers in 1882 alone. See DIAR, 1882, 61.

114 Chittenden, *Travels in British Columbia*, 43.

115 Although immigration records show that 15,701 Chinese arrived in British Columbia between January 1881 and July 1884, in 1884 a Royal Commission found 10,492 Chinese in the province, an increase of 6,142 over the census of 1881. These figures roughly coincide with the estimate of the contractors, which indicates that 6,500 Chinese were employed in 1882. The use of these Chinese labourers peaked in late 1883, after which they increasingly looked for other work. See Peter S. Li, "Immigration Laws and Family Patterns: Some Demographic Changes among Chinese Families in Canada, 1885-1971," *Canadian Ethnic Studies* 12, 1: (1980): 61; Canada, *Report of the Royal Commission on Chinese Immigration* (Ottawa: Printed by Order of the Commission, 1885), 363-65; David Chuenyan Lai, *Chinatowns* (Vancouver: UBC Press, 1988), 32.

116 McTiernan, DIAR, 1884, 106.

117 A.W. Vowell in DIAR, 1892, 223-24.

118 For number of aboriginal sealers, see Figure 6.2. For population, see "West Coast Agency, Annual Report," DIAR, 1896; Canada, Department of Fisheries, *Annual Reports*, 1895-1905; Cairn Crockford, "Nuu-Chah-Nulth Labour Relations in the Pelagic Sealing Industry, 1868-1911" (MA thesis, University of Victoria, 1996), 51, 84.

119 Ford, *Smoke from Their Fires*; Jones, *Queesto*, 35; Peter Webster's father was also a sealer, and he was at sea for as long as six months at a time in the early 1900s. See Peter Webster, *As Far as I Know: Reminiscences of an Ahousat Elder* (Campbell River, BC: Campbell River Museum and Archives, 1983), 22. The pelagic seal hunters were all men, but several took their wives or daughters along as boat steerers, and at least one aboriginal woman, Mary, the wife of Chief Joseph of Opitsaht, worked as a cook on these vessels. See George Nicholson, *Vancouver Island's West Coast, 1762-1962* (Vancouver: G. Nicholson, 1965), 254-55; Crockford, "Nuu-Chah-Nulth Labour Relations," 55.

120 DIAR, 1915, cited in Crockford, "Changing Economic Activities," 38, 47; Jones *Queesto*, 8, 35. Jones also says that his father could make between $9,000 and $14,000 a year principally from sealing, but this seems high. See Dorothy Haegert, *Children of the First People* (Vancouver: Tillacum Library, 1983), 68.

121 *British Colonist*, April 22, 1885; Crockford, "Nuu-Chah-Nulth Labour Relations," 55-65, 77-79, 91-104.

122 Crockford, "Nuu-Chah-Nulth Labour Relations," 104; Haegert, *Children of the First People*, 68.

123 For Nuu-Chah-nulth involvement in the industry, see Crockford, "Nuu-Chah-Nulth Labour Relations." For a history of the sealing industry, see Peter Murray, *The Vagabond Fleet: A Chronicle of the North Pacific Sealing Schooner Trade* (Victoria: Sono Nis, 1988); and Busch, *The War against the Seals*.

124 James Spradley, ed., *Guests Never Leave Hungry: The Autobiography of James Sewid, a Kwakiutl Indian* (Montreal and Kingston: McGill-Queen's University Press, 1989), 27; Moran, *Stoney Creek Woman*, 29, 78, 81; Beth White in Yukon Archives, Yukon Women's History Project Sound Recording (Transcripts) file 13-5; Blackman, *During My Time*, 109; Assu, *Assu*, 62; Ruth Cook in Haegert, *Children of the First People*, 23; Leona Marie

Sparrow, "Work Histories of a Coast Salish Couple" (MA thesis, University of British Columbia, 1976), 263.

125 George Pragnell to the Provincial Game Board, August 21, 1954, LAC, RG 10, vol. 10872, file 901/20. Emphasis in original.

126 Mary John describes the family trapping enterprise in her biography. See Moran, *Stoney Creek Woman*. For statistics, see LAC, RG 10, vol. 6736, file 420-3-1-1; Department of Indian and Northern Development, Treaty and Historical Research Office, file U-24, F.R. Butler at Indian Affairs Branch, Department of Citizenship and Immigration, Indian Superintendent's Conference, British Columbia and Yukon Region, January 16-20, 1956, 9; Arthur Ray, *The Canadian Fur Trade in the Industrial Age* (Toronto: University of Toronto Press, 1990), 202-3, argues that this pattern of displacement also occurred on the Prairies and in the North. See H.B. Hawthorn, C. Belshaw, and S.M. Jamieson, *Indians of British Columbia: A Study of Contemporary Social Adjustment* (Toronto: University of Toronto Press, 1960), 101.

127 McDonald, "Trying to Make a Life," figs. 9 and 10. The declining trapping economy of the Carrier in south central British Columbia is documented in Hudson, "Traplines and Timber." The declining trapping economy of the Nisga'a along the Nass River in northwest BC is documented in Stephen A. McNeary, "When Fire Came Down: Social and Economic Life of the Niska" (PhD diss., Bryn Mawr College, 1976), 197.

128 Ray, *The Canadian Fur Trade*, 200. The total aboriginal population in 1954 was approximately 31,000. See Hawthorn, Belshaw, and Jamieson, *Indians of British Columbia*, 23, 101.

129 Maureen Cassidy, *From Mountain to Mountain: A History of the Gitksan Village of Ans'payaxw* (Kispiox: Ans'payaxw School Society, 1984), 39; DIAR, 1901, 285; Joan Skogan, *Skeena: A River Remembered* (Vancouver: British Columbia Packers, 1983), 77.

130 Canada, Legislative Assembly, "Department of Fisheries Annual Report," *Canada Sessional Papers* (Ottawa: Canada, 1929-30), 105; M.C. Urquhart and K.A.H. Buckley, *Historical Statistics of Canada* (Toronto: Macmillan, 1965), 396; M.S. Todd to J.A. Motherwell, July 23, 1936, "Fishing 1914-41," LAC, RG 10, vol. 11,147. In 1925, Aboriginal People held 3,352 of the 11,750 fishing

licences issued in the BC House of Commons. See Canada, House of Commons, Special Committees of the Senate and House of Commons to Inquire into the Claims of the Allied Indian Tribes of British Columbia ... Session 1926-27, *Proceedings, Reports and Evidence* (Ottawa: F.A. Ackland, 1927).

131 Sayach'apis, John Fornsby, August Khatsahlano, George Swanaset, John Wallace, and James Spradley fished but do not mention owning their own boats. Other aboriginal fishers are highlighted in Skogan, *Skeena: A River Remembered.*

132 Sparrow, "Work Histories," 30; Spradley, *Guests Never Leave Hungry,* 58; Blackman, *During My Time,* 82; Collen Bostwick, "Oral Histories: Theresa Jeffries," *Labour History* 2, 3 (1980): 8-15; Clayton Mack, with H. Thommasen, *Grizzlies and White Guys: The Stories of Clayton Mack* (Madeira Park, BC: Harbour, 1993), 19.

133 John McMullan, "State Capital and the BC Salmon Fishing Industry," in *Uncommon Property: The Fishing and Fish-Processing Industries in British Columbia,* ed. Patricia Marchak, Neil Guppy, and John McMullan (Toronto: Methuen, 1987), 107-52; and Keith Warriner, "Regionalism, Dependence, and the BC Fisheries: Historical Development and Recent Trends," in Marchak, Guppy, and McMullan, *Uncommon Property,* 326-50; Dianne Newell, *Tangled Webs of History: Indians and the Law in Canada's Pacific Coast Fisheries* (Toronto: University of Toronto Press, 1993).

134 BCSP, 1893, "Report of the British Columbia Fishery Commission," estimated that each of twenty canneries employed an average of forty to fifty aboriginal women. The 1953 figure is taken from Hawthorn, Belshaw, and Jamieson, *Indians of British Columbia,* 113.

135 *Colonist,* December 12, 1948, 13. The 1960s witnessed another round of cannery closures and layoffs. See Evelyn Pinkerton, "Indians in the Fishing Industry," in Marchak, Guppy, and McMullan, *Uncommon Property,* 260-61; Alicja Muszynski, "The Creation and Organization of Cheap Wage Labour in the British Columbia Fishing Industry," (PhD diss., University of British Columbia, 1986), 140-41.

136 Prince Rupert, *Daily News,* June 10, 1914, cited in Karla Greer, "Race, Riot, and Rail: The Process of Racialisation in Prince Rupert, BC, 1906-1919" (MA thesis, University of Victoria, 1999).

137 McKenna-McBride Commission, BCA, MS 1056, box 1.

138 British Columbia Fisheries Commission, 1922, transcripts, LAC, RG 23, vol. 238, file 726-34-4 C3.

139 Steltzer and Kerr, *Coast of Many Faces,* 46, 49.

140 Hawthorn, Belshaw, and Jamieson, *Indians of British Columbia,* 115; M.J. Friedlaender, *Economic Status of Native Indians in British Columbia Fisheries,* Technical Report Series PAC/T-75-25 (Vancouver: Environment Canada, Fisheries Operations Branch, 1975).

141 *The Resources of British Columbia* 1, 4 (1883): 4; DIAR, 1885, 84; Hawthorn, Belshaw, and Jamieson, *Indians of British Columbia,* 114.

142 Art Dick, interviewed by Byron Plant and Chris Cook III on Dick's seine boat in Alert Bay, July 6, 2003. Billy Wasden, interviewed by John Lutz, Byron Plant, and Chris Cook III in Alert Bay, May 19, 2003.

143 See Chapter 7 for a discussion of the buy-back plans.

144 John Pritchard, "Economic Development and the Disintegration of Traditional Culture among the Haisla" (PhD diss., University of British Columbia, 1977), 108-9.

145 The reliability of these estimates is discussed in Appendix 2.

146 Quintasket, *Mourning Dove,* xxi-xii, 10, 157, 166, 171, 185. Quintasket worked as a seasonal agricultural labourer for much of her life, but she also took vocational courses and worked as a teacher at the Inkameep Indian Reserve near Penticton, British Columbia, around 1917-18.

147 Hawthorne, Belshaw, and Jamieson, *Indians of British Columbia,* 140-41. There is also a brief sketch of Okanagan Harry Robinson's ranching career in Harry Robinson, *Write It on Your Heart: The Epic World of an Okanagan Storyteller,* ed. and comp. Wendy Wickwire (Vancouver: Talonbooks/Theytus, 1989), 13.

148 Ranching and agriculture among Aboriginal People in BC is discussed in Duane Thomson, "History of the Okanagan: Indians and Whites in the Settlement Era, 1860-1920" (PhD diss., University of British Columbia, 1985), 245-334; Michael Ames, "Fountain in a Modern Economy: A Study of Social Structure, Land Use and Business Enterprise in a British Columbia Indian Community" (BA essay, University of British Columbia, 1956). See a brief discussion of Harry Edward's Fraser Valley dairy farm, which operated from 1917 to 1950, in Wells, *The Chilliwacks,* 97-98.

149 Ford, *Smoke from Their Fires*, 133-4; Collins, "John Fornsby," 329; Wells, *The Chilliwacks*, 197. Harry Robinson was also born when his mother was working as a seasonal agricultural worker. See Robinson, *Write It on Your Heart*, 11.

150 Henry Pennier, with Herbert L. McDonald, *Chiefly Indian: The Warm and Witty Story of a British Columbia Half Breed Logger* (Vancouver: Graydonald Graphics, 1972).

151 Vancouver, *News Advertiser*, September 28 and 29, 1912, in LAC, RG 10, vol. 11197.

152 Ibid.; McKenna-McBride Royal Commission Transcripts, January 27, 1916, BCA, add mss 1056, box 2, file 5-6, 431; *Chilliwack Progress*, August 16, 1934, 1; Frances Densmore, *Music of the Indians of British Columbia* (New York: Da Capo Press, 1972), 13.

153 James Burrows found that, in 1910, agricultural employment opportunities for Aboriginal People in the southern Interior Plateau were decreasing from a peak that he thought occurred before the turn of the century. See James Burrows, "'A Much Needed Class of Labour': The Economy and Income of the Southern Interior Plateau Indians, 1897-1910," *BC Studies* 71 (1986): 27-46. In 1885, the DIA estimated that one-quarter of British Columbia's aboriginal population migrated to the hop fields of Washington State. See DIAR, 1885, 81, 84.

154 Chief Peter D. Peters, interviewed by Larry Commodore, July 21, 1985, Stó:lō Nation Archives, Chilliwack, BC, tape 85-84.

155 "Indian Migrant Workers," Report for the International Labour Organization, October 1953, LAC, Department of Citizenship and Immigration, RG 26, vol. 106, file 1/1-15, pt. 8; W.S. Arneil, Indian Commissioner for British Columbia to Indian Affairs Branch, May 27, 1957, LAC, RG 10, vol. 8423, file 801/21-1, reel C-13835. The published annual reports of the DIA mention the declining participation in the seasonal migration in 1951-53, 1957, and 1959.

156 Today in Canada Aboriginal People are slightly over half as likely to be in agriculture and related fields as are other Canadians. See Ames, "Fountain," 54. The fisheries officers often noted when Aboriginal People in this area stopped fishing to go to the hop fields. In 1948, the local official noted: "On August 20th almost the entire fishing population moved from this area to the hop-yards on the lower Fraser Valley," from which they returned on September 21. See K.C. Messer, Fisheries Inspector, Yale-Lytton Subdistrict, 1948, LAC, RG 23, vol. 662, file 712-2-72, pt. 4; Chief Peter D. Peters, Interview, tape 85-84; Stewart Clatworthy, Jeremy Hull, and Neil Loughran, "Employment of the Aboriginal Labour Force: Patterns of Employment, Unemployment and Poverty," in *Economy: Project Area 3* (Ottawa: Four Directions Consulting Group for the Royal Commission on Aboriginal Peoples, 1995), 80-81.

157 R.E. Gosnell, *Year Book of British Columbia and Manual of Provincial Information for 1897* (Victoria: R.E. Gosnell, 1898), 420-21, adds that Chinese received from six to eight dollars per week and that Japanese received from seven to nine dollars per week. See McKenna-McBride Royal Commission Hearing Transcripts, January 27, 1916.

158 Frances W. Thompson, "Employment Problems and the Economic Status of the British Columbia Indians" (MSW thesis, University of British Columbia, 1951), 34.

159 Jones, *Queesto*, 91. Jones also worked as a brakeman on a logging railway, in a machine shop, as a farm labourer, as a telegraph repairman. In the forest industry, he was, at one time or another, a boom man, a chokerman, a rigging slinger, a faller, a hook tender, and a woods foreman.

160 Frank Fuller, "Gilbert Joe," *Labour History* 2, 3 (1980): 16-19; Blackman, *During My Time*, 109; Jones, *Queesto*, 90-91.

161 Helen Codere, *Fighting with Property: A Study of Kwakiutl Potlatching and Warfare, 1792-1930* (Seattle: University of Washington Press, 1972) 43-48; Blackman, *During My Time*, 109; Assu, *Assu*, 66; Spradley, *Guests Never Leave Hungry*, 75. Pritchard reports extensive hand-logging among the Haisla of Kitimat and also discusses its decline. See Pritchard, "Economic Development and Disintegration," 122-27; Jones, *Queesto*, 94, writes about how forest unions excluded Aboriginal People. See McKenna-McBride Commission Transcripts, October 17, 1915, BCA MS 1056.

162 In Canada, Aboriginal People are 2.8 times more likely to be in the forest industry than are other Canadians. Interviews with Dave Dawson at Kingcome and Charlie Johnson at Owikeno, in Steltzer and Kerr, *Coast of Many Faces*, 68, 82, 135; Amy O'Neill, "Identity, Culture and the Forest: The Stó:lō" (MA thesis, University of British

163 Pennier, *Chiefly Indian*.

164 Hudson, "Traplines and Timber," 145; George "Porgie" Jolliffe, interviewed by Chris Cook III, at Alert Bay, July 6, 2003; Billie Wasden, interviewed by John Lutz, Byron Plant, and Chris Cook III, May 19, 2003.

165 For descriptions of the early gypo operator hiring process, see A. Grainger, *Woodsmen of the West* (London: Edward Arnold, 1908 [Toronto: McLelland and Stewart, 1996]); Gordon Hak, *Turning Trees into Dollars: The British Columbia Coastal Lumber Industry, 1858-1913* (Toronto: University of Toronto Press, 2000). And, for the 1930s, see Roderick Langmere Haig-Brown, *Timber* (London: Collins, 1946). For the "company era," see Richard S. Mackie, *Island Timber: A Social History of the Comox Logging Company, Vancouver Island* (Victoria, BC: Sono Nis, 2000); Richard A. Rajala, *Clearcutting the Pacific Rainforest: Production, Science, and Regulation* (Vancouver: UBC Press, 1998). Some aboriginal men did find work in the modern corporate industry. See "Doug White Labours Long Hours for Nanaimo Indians," *Crown Zellerbach News* 7:9 (February 1964), 2 (thanks to Richard Mackie); see also John Williams, interviewed by Imbert Orchard, BCA Acc2428 Tape 1, Track 1.

166 Moran, *Stoney Creek Woman*, 99, 103.

167 Pierce, *Potlatch to Pulpit*; A.P. Morley, *Roar of the Breakers: A Biography of Peter Kelly* (Toronto: Ryerson, 1967); Quintasket, *Mourning Dove*, xii.

168 Clatworthy, Hull, and Loughran, *Economy*, 80-81.

169 Thompson, "Employment Problems," 36. Interview with John Barrie, Regional Director of the International Longshoremen and Warehouseman's Union, May 23, 1951.

170 Interview with Mr. Y, Squamish Band Councillor, May 24, 1951, in Frances W. Thompson, "Employment Problems and the Economic Status of the British Columbia Indians" (MSW thesis, University of British Columbia, 1951), 44.

171 Mack, *White Guys*, 46-49.

172 Transcripts, "Claims of Sheshaht to the Royal Commission on Pelagic Sealing, December 1913," cited in Crockford, "Changing Economic Activity," 66. This is an excellent study of Nuu-chah-nulth cultural adaptations to wage work opportunities and their moditional economy.

173 DIAR, 1894, 204; DIAR, 1902, 281-85; Harkin, *The Heiltsuks*, 143.

174 Mary John remembers asking: "Would you like to trade a pair of moccasins (or a trout or a whitefish or a pail of berries) for some of your old clothing for my children?" See Moran, *Stoney Creek Woman*, 70, 78, 100.

175 Blackman, *During My Time*, 72, 86, 112, 122, 128; Tappage, *The Days of Augusta*, 52; White, "Yukon Women's History Project"; Sparrow, "Work Histories." Assu, *Assu*, 63, records that, after the Cape Mudge cannery burned down, the Cowichan women still accompanied their husbands to Cape Mudge, where the latter fished. Instead of engaging in their former cannery work, the women spun wool and knitted. See Barbara Lane, "The Cowichan Knitting Industry," *Anthropology in British Columbia* 2 (1951): 14-27. See also Hawthorn, Belshaw, and Jamieson, *Indians of British Columbia*, 257-67; Sylvia Olsen, "'We Indians Were Sure Hard Workers': A History of Coast Salish Wool Working" (MA thesis, University of Victoria, 1998).

176 "Indian Migrant Workers," Report for the International Labour Organization, October, 1953, LAC, RG 26, vol. 106, file 1/1-15, pt. 8.

177 Assu, *Assu*, 88; Incoming Correspondence, 1895-96: A.W. Powell to R.H. Pidcock, May 15 and 27, 1895; R.J. Walker to R.H. Pidcock, May 28, 1896, LAC, RG 10, vol. 11,137; Incoming Correspondence, 1900-3: Jim Chackidl, Chief at Cape Mudge, to G.W. Debeck, Indian Agent, December 28, 1903, LAC, RG 10, vol. 11,138. See also LAC, RG 10, vol. 10,888-93/011, file 979/8-3/03, 1942.

178 Blackman, *During My Time*, 111-14; Moran, *Stoney Creek Woman*, 27, 70.

179 Jones, *Queesto*, 38; Webster, *As Far as I Know*, 42-44; Andrew Paul speaking at a conference on the Indian Act, July 20-21, 1955, LAC, RG 10, vol. 8570, file 901/1-2-2-2; aboriginal testimony before the McKenna-McBride Commission, quoted in Thomson, "History of the Okanagan," 203, 209.

180 Quintasket, *Mourning Dove*, 174.

181 Eight percent attributed the decline to dropping fish populations and government regulation.

182 Marilyn Bennett, *Indian Fishing and Its Cultural Importance in the Fraser River System* (Vancouver: BC Union of Indian Chiefs and Fisheries Canada, ca. 1974). The

Columbia, 1999); Clatworthy, Hull, and Loughrun, *Economy*, table 8.

key respondents were elected band council members or elders.

183 Jo-Anne Fiske, "Fishing Is Women's Business: Changing Economic Roles of Carrier Women and Men," in *Native People, Native Lands: Canadian Indians, Inuit and Metis*, ed. Bruce Alden Cox (Ottawa: Carleton University Press, 1988), 186-97.

184 Vowell, in DIAR, 1902, 284-89; Vowell, in DIAR, 1904, 314-20.

185 Shannon, "Fishing 1914-41," M.S. Todd to J.A. Motherwell, July 23, 1936, LAC, RG 10, vol. 11,147.

186 Codere's study of the Kwakwaka'wakw shows that their real incomes peaked before 1914. See Codere, *Fighting with Property*, 43-48.

187 See the reports by A.W. Vowell, Indian Superintendent for British Columbia, in DIAR, 1892 to 1903. Quote from DIAR, 1903, 314-20. Burrows suggests that the income of the interior people in the Kamloops-Okanagan probably peaked prior to 1900 and that it has declined in the twentieth century. See Burrows, "A Much Needed Class," 45.

188 Moran, *Stoney Creek Woman*, 77-81. See also Pennier, *Chiefly Indian*, 58; Assu, *Assu*, 66; Spradley, *Guests Never Leave Hungry*, 95.

189 Blackman, *During My Time*, 120.

190 Report of the Department of Labour, BCSP, 1943, K28.

191 R.W. McLeod, Supervisor of Fisheries, "Report," 1943, LAC, RG 23, vol. 662, file 712-2-72, pt. 4, The provincial situation is described in Chapter 4.

192 DIAR, 1945, 161.

193 Helen Clifton, interviewed in Hartley Bay by John Lutz, June 9, 2004.

194 Spradley, *Guests Never Leave Hungry*; Blackman, *During My Time*; Ford, *Smoke from Their Fires*; Sparrow, "Work Histories"; Assu, *Assu*; Collins, "John Fornsby," 287-341; Bostwick, "Oral Histories," 8-15; Fuller, "Gilbert Joe," 16-19; Sapir and Swadesh, *Nootka Texts*; see also McDonald, "Trying to Make a Life"; McNeary, "When Fire Came Down."

195 Moran, *Stoney Creek Woman*; Tappage, *The Days of Augusta*; Pennier, *Chiefly Indian*. Burrows has explored this economy for the turn of the century in "A Much Needed Class of Labour"; Robinson, *Write It on Your Heart*, 12-3. See also Hawthorn, Belshaw, and Jamieson, *Indians of British Columbia*, 141-58; Bennett, *Indian*

Fishing, 43 (80 percent of the survey respondents were men).

196 White, Yukon Women's History Project; Moran, *Stoney Creek Woman*; Hudson, "Traplines and Timber."

197 The exceptions are William Pierce, who became a minister in his early twenties, and Joyce Albany, who became a secretary and had a white-collar career.

198 Bennett's 1972 survey of one band councillor or elder from each of eighty-five interior bands shows that 69 percent desired full-year work but that only 40 percent were able to find it, and many of those were presumably in full-time employment with their bands. See Bennett, *Indian Fishing*, 43. See also Chapters 3 and 4.

199 W.T. Stanbury, "Indians in British Columbia: Level of Income, Welfare Dependency and Poverty Rate," *BC Studies* 20 (1973-74): 78.

Chapter 7: The White Problem

1 Only the Squamish and the Musqueam, whose reserves are now surrounded by Greater Vancouver, had equivalent access, but because of the later development of Vancouver, the Lekwungen had a forty-year head start.

2 James A. McDonald, "Trying to Make a Life: The Historical Political Economy of Kitsumkalum" (PhD diss., University of British Columbia, 1985); Michael Harkin, *The Heiltsuks: Dialogues of Culture and History on the Northwest Coast* (Lincoln: University of Nebraska Press, 1997); Duane Thomson, "The History of the Okanagan: Indians and Whites in the Settlement Era, 1860-1920" (PhD diss., University of British Columbia, 1985); Peter Carstens, *The Queen's People: A Study of Hegemony, Coercion and Accommodation among the Okanagan of Canada* (Toronto: University of Toronto Press, 1991); Douglas Hudson, "Traplines and Timber: Social and Economic Change among the Carrier" (PhD diss., University of Alberta, 1983); Stephen A. McNeary, "When Fire Came Down: Social and Economic Life of the Niska" (PhD diss., Bryn Mawr College, 1976); Helen Codere, *Fighting with Property: A Study of Kwakiutl Potlatching and Warfare, 1792-1930* (Seattle: University of Washington Press, 1972); John Pritchard, "Economic Development and the Disintegration of Traditional Culture among the Haisla" (PhD diss., University of British Columbia, 1977); Hugh Brody, *Maps and Dreams: Indians and the British Columbia Frontier* (London: Jill

Norman and Hobhouse, 1982); Keith Thor Carlson and John Lutz, "Stó:lō People and the Development of the BC Wage Labour Economy," in *You Are Asked to Witness: The Stó:lō in Canada's Pacific Coast History*, ed. Keith Thor Carlson, 109-24 (Chilliwack, BC: Stó:lō Heritage Trust, 1997).

3 W.E. Ditchburn to Bryan Williams, July 4, 1929, LAC, RG 10, vol. 10872, file 901/20-10, pt. 1.

4 Robert Galois, *Kwakwaka'wakw Settlements, 1775-1920: A Geographical Analysis and Gazetteer* (Vancouver: UBC Press, 1994); Daniel Clayton, "Geographies of the Lower Skeena," *BC Studies* 94 (1992): 31.

5 Douglas to Colonial Secretary, October 24, 1853, CO 305/4, 12345; Douglas to Governor and Committee, February 24, 1851 in Bowsfield, *Fort Victoria Letters*, 156; DIAR, 1881, no. 5, 143; W.H. Collinson to the Reserve Commissioner, October 10, 1887, LAC, RG 10, vol. 11007.

6 "The Kwakiutl had a potential demand for European goods in excess of any practical utility the goods might have possessed. This can be seen both as a stimulus to the Kwakiutl integration in their new economy and as a direct stimulus to the potlatch." Codere, *Fighting with Property*, 126.

7 Codere, *Fighting with Property*, 126.

8 Ibid., 124; Assu, *Assu*, 39. Contemporary value calculated using Consumer Price Index for Canada, 1911-71, in F.H. Leacy, ed., *Historical Statistics of Canada,* 2nd ed. (Ottawa: Statistics Canada, 1983); and Statistics Canada, Consumer Price Index Historical Summary 1914-2004, at http://www40.statcan.ca/l01/cst01/econ46a.htm (site now discontinued; see new summary tables site at http://www40.statcan.ca/l01/cst01/econ46a.htm?sdi=consumer%20price%20index%20historical%20summary).

9 DIAR, 1882, 160, 170; DIAR, 1885, 101; J.H. Van Den Brink, *The Haida Indians: Cultural Change Mainly between 1876-1970* (Leiden, The Netherlands: E.J. Brill, 1974) 42.

10 These quotes taken from Bishop Hill's Diary, June 5 and August 8, 1861, Archives of the Ecclesiastical Province of British Columbia. See also June 21, 1862; I.W. Powell and P. McTiernan, in DIAR, 1882, 155, 166.

11 *British Colonist*, February 19, 1861, 2.

12 Ibid., September 24, 1862, 2.

13 Victoria *Gazette*, May 18, 1860, 2.

14 This is explored more fully in Chapter 2.

15 See Chapter 2 and Kay Anderson, *Vancouver's Chinatown: Racial Discourse in Canada, 1875-1980* (Vancouver: UBC Press, 1991), 47.

16 Heather Lee Wilke, "One Too Many: Imbibing and Resistance in the Cowichan Indian Agency, 1888-1899" (MA thesis, University of Victoria, 2006).

17 Patrick Everett to I.W. Powell, September 22, 1875, LAC, RG 10 vol. 3623, file 5119.

18 Frederick H. Fullerton, Manager, Pharmaceutical Association of the Province of British Columbia, to the Indian Advisory Committee of British Columbia, November 29, 1950, BCA, GR 1071, box 1, file 9; see also BCA, Gr 1071, box 2, file 8. It is unclear from this correspondence whether or not this prohibition was enforced and, if so, whether it disadvantaged aboriginal store owners.

19 A fuller discussion may be found in Paul Tennant, *Aboriginal Peoples and Politics: The Indian Land Question in British Columbia, 1849-1989* (Vancouver: UBC Press, 1992), 39-52; George Edgar Shankel, "The Development of Indian Policy in British Columbia" (PhD diss., University of Washington, 1945), 89-144; Robert E. Cail, *Land, Man and the Law: The Disposal of Crown Lands in British Columbia, 1871-1913* (Vancouver: UBC Press, 1974); Duane Thomson, "A History of the Okanagan: Indians and Whites in the Settlement Era, 1860-1920" (PhD diss., University of British Columbia, 1985); Cole Harris, *Making Native Space* (Vancouver: UBC Press, 2002).

20 Crown Colony of Vancouver Island, *Laws of Vancouver Island* (Victoria: Crown Colony of Vancouver Island, 1864); Crown Colony of British Columbia, "An Ordinance to further define the law regulating the acquisition of Land in British Columbia," *The Laws of British Columbia* (Victoria: Crown Colony of British Columbia, 1865-70), March 31, 1866; "An Ordinance to amend and consolidate the Laws Affecting Crown Lands in British Columbia," June 1, 1870; British Columbia, "Lands Act," *Statutes of British Columbia* (Victoria: British Columbia, 1888), section 5, prohibits Indians from occupying Crown land except by special permission of the lieutenant-governor in council.

21 A.W. Vowell in DIAR, 1903, 314-20; E. McLeod, Indian Agent, Lytton, to M.B. Jackson, Chairman of the

Game Conservation Board of British Columbia, May 20, 1925, and H.E. Taylor, Indian Agent, Williams Lake, to C.C. Perry, Assistant Indian Commissioner for British Columbia, January 24, 1936, LAC, RG 10, vol. 10,872, file 901/20-10, pt. 2; DIAR, 1880s. An eloquent condemnation of the province's policy towards grazing and water rights for Aboriginal People is provided by Chief Johnny Chillitza's testimony to the House of Commons, in Canada, House of Commons, Special Committees of the Senate and House of Commons to Inquire into the Claims of the Allied Indian Tribes of British Columbia ... Session 1926-27, *Proceedings, Reports and Evidence* (Ottawa: F.A. Ackland, 1927), 141-45. For other instances of discriminatory allocation of water and grazing rights, see Thomson, "History of the Okanagan," 273-75, 330-32; Cole Harris, *The Resettlement of British Columbia: Essays on Colonialism and Geographical Change* (Vancouver: UBC Press, 1997), chap. 3.

22 McKenna-McBride Commission Testimony, June 10, 1913, BCA, GR 1995, reel B-1454, 279.

23 The fishing rights of the Lekwungen had been interrupted by the colonial government. See Chapter 3.

24 Dianne Newell, *Tangled Webs of History: Indians and the Law in Canada's Pacific Coast Fisheries* (Toronto: University of Toronto Press, 1993), 10.

25 See Chapter 6.

26 Newell, *Tangled Webs*, 64-70.

27 Pritchard, "Economic Development and Disintegration," 72.

28 William Henry Barker, BC Packers, to the Hon. J.D. Hazen, Minister of Fisheries, August 19, 1913, LAC, RG 23, Department of Fisheries, General File, reel 5, file 6, pt. 8.

29 Indians of Northern British Columbia to the Minister of Fisheries, August 11, 1913, LAC, RG 23, reel 5, file 6, pt. 8.

30 W.M. Halliday to Duncan Scott, July 28, 1916, LAC, "Fishing 1914-41," RG 10, vol. 11,147.

31 Fisheries Commission Evidence, 1917, 274, quoted in Pritchard, "Economic Development and Disintegration," 79.

32 Shannon, "Fishing 1914-41," W.M. Halliday to W.E. Ditchburn, June 16, 1919, and E.G. Taylor, Inspector of Fisheries, Nanaimo, to W.M. Halliday, May 14, 1919, LAC, RG 10, vol. 11,147.

33 BCA, GR 2043, vol. 1655, 219, 248; Shannon, "Fishing 1914-41," W.A. Found, Department of Fisheries and Marine, to J.D. McLean, Acting Deputy Superintendent of Indian Affairs, September 9, 1920, and "W.M. Halliday to Johnny Scow, May 20, 1922, LAC, RG 10, vol. 11,147.

34 DIAR, 1908, xxx.

35 Quoted in Geoff Meggs, *Salmon: The Decline of the British Columbia Salmon Fishery* (Vancouver: Douglas and McIntyre, 1991), 79. For the prohibition of the food fishery, see Meggs, *Salmon*, 74-79; Newell, *Tangled Webs*; Douglas C. Harris, *Fish, Law and Colonialism: The Legal Capture of Salmon in British Columbia* (Toronto: University of Toronto Press, 2001).

36 Canada, Legislative Assembly, "Department of Fisheries Annual Report," *Canada Sessional Papers* (Ottawa: Canada, 1906), 206-11; Cowichan Agency, Departmental Circulars, 1892-1910, A.W. Vowell to Indian Agents, June 20, 1905, LAC, RG 10, vol. 1350, reel C-13917; W.E. Ditchburn testifying before the British Columbia Fisheries Commission, 1922, LAC, RG 23, vol. 1,233, file 726-34-4; Evelyn Pinkerton, "Indians in the Fishing Industry," in *Uncommon Property: The Fishing and Fish-Processing Industries in British Columbia*, ed. Patricia Marchak, Neil Guppy, and John McMullan (Toronto: Methuen, 1987), 251-54; John McMullan, "State Capital and the BC Salmon Fishing Industry," in Marchak, Guppy, and McMullan, *Uncommon Property*, 109-10.

37 Peter Webster, *As Far as I Know: Reminiscences of an Ahousat Elder* (Campbell River, BC: Campbell River Museum and Archives, 1983), 37, 43.

38 Helen Clifton, interviewed by John Lutz and Liam Haggerty in Hartley Bay, June 9, 2004.

39 Newell, *Tangled Webs*, 150-52.

40 These events accelerated an ongoing process involving the merging of the major cannery companies and the closure of canneries. See Newell, *Tangled Webs*, 152-53.

41 Helen Clifton, interviewed by John Lutz in Hartley Bay, June 9, 2004; Pete Cook, interviewed by Byron Plant and Chris Cook in Alert Bay, 8 July 2003.

42 Ulli Steltzer and Catherine Kerr, *Coast of Many Faces* (Vancouver: Douglas and McIntyre, 1979), 82.

43 M.J. Friedlaender, *Economic Status of Native Indians in British Columbia Fisheries,* Technical Report Series PAC/

T-75-25 (Vancouver: Environment Canada, Fisheries Operations Branch, 1975); Assu, *Assu*, 74.

44 August Jack Khahtsahlano was one of these loggers, as were George Swanaset and Peter Kelly. See J.S. Matthews, *Conversations with Khatsahlano* (Vancouver: Vancouver City Archives, 1955); "George Swanaset: Narrative of a Personal Document," University of Washington, Special Collections, Melville Jacobs Collection, mss. 1693-71-13, box 112. I wish to thank Sasha Harmon for suggesting the Swanaset narrative to me. See Allan Morely, *The Roar of the Breakers: A Biography of the Reverend Peter Kelly* (Toronto: Ryerson, 1967). For work histories of twentieth-century aboriginal loggers, see the account of John Wallace in Oliver Wells, *The Chilliwacks and Their Neighbours* (Vancouver: Talonbooks, 1987), 199-94; Henry Pennier, with Herbert L. McDonald, *Chiefly Indian: The Warm and Witty Story of a British Columbia Half Breed Logger.* (Vancouver: Graydonald Graphics, 1972); James Spradley, ed., *Guests Never Leave Hungry: The Autobiography of James Sewid* (Montreal and Kingston: McGill-Queen's University Press, 1989); Leona Sparrow, "Work Histories of a Coast Salish Couple" (MA thesis, University of British Columbia, 1976).

45 A hand-logger paid an annual fee of ten dollars and could cut timber on unalienated lands providing he did not use power equipment. Hand-loggers cut timber on steep slopes close to the shore, limbed the trees, took the bark off one side, and used the weight of the tree and the natural lubrication of the sap to propel the tree into the water. The system required little equipment other than axes, saws, and a jack to lift the trees over obstacles. See R.E. Gosnell, *Year Book of British Columbia and Manual of Provincial Information for 1897* (Victoria: R.E. Gosnell, 1898), 249; British Columbia, Task Force on Crown Timber, *Crown Charges for Early Timber Rights: Royalties and Other Levies for Harvesting Rights on Timber Leases, Licenses and Berths in British Columbia* (Victoria: Information Division of the British Columbia Forest Division, 1974), 10; British Columbia, "Lands Act," 1888.

46 Indian Reserve Commissioners, in DIAR, 1877, li; P. O'Reilly, Indian Reserve Commissioner, in DIAR, 1888, 147; P. O'Reilly, Indian Reserve Commissioner, in DIAR, 1889, 195ff; Inspectorate of Indian Agencies, Cor-

respondence Out, W.E. Ditchburn to Secretary, DIA, November 7, 1910, LAC, RG 10, vol. 1312, reel C-13,908; Codere, *Fighting with Property*; McDonald, "Trying to Make a Life; Pritchard, "Economic Development and Disintegration."

47 British Columbia, *Crown Charges for Early Timber Rights*, 10; DIAR, 1902, 292 (the Kwawkewlth agent says that hand-loggers cannot get timber there). By 1916, it was even difficult for the Haida in the remote Queen Charlotte Islands to find unalienated land. See DIAR, 1916, 96.

48 W.M. Halliday, in DIAR, 1909, 245.

49 McKenna-McBride Royal Commission, BCA; Codere, *Fighting with Property*, 30-39.

50 Pritchard, "Economic Development and Disintegration."

51 Timber Sale Records, 6710, 1924, BCA, quoted in Pritchard, "Economic Development and Disintegration," 147.

52 Timber Sale 31736, 1942, quoted in Pritchard, "Economic Development and Disintegration," 148.

53 McKenna-McBride Commission, Transcripts, William Robertson Examined, June 10, 1913, BCA, GR 1995, reel B-1454. See also Cowichan Agency, Miscellaneous Correspondence, 1893-1906, item 273, John Coburn to W.R. Robertson, Indian Agent, Cowichan, May 22, 1903, LAC, RG 10, vol. 1348, reel C-13917. Codere, *Fighting with Property*, 37, documents other instances in which DIA policies put obstacles in front of aboriginal loggers.

54 Charles Jones, with Stephen Bosustow, *Queesto: Pacheenaht Chief by Birthright* (Nanaimo, BC: Theytus, 1981), 38. In 1951, Indian Agent Earl Anfield told the Indian Committee for British Columbia that "another problem is growing more prevalent these days with the advent of large logging concerns under management licenses, such as Columbia Cellulose Company Ltd., whose timber operations are wiping out a great many traplines which have been hereditary areas for Indians for generations. These people feel that they are entitled to compensation for loss of livelihood as trappers." See LAC, RG 10, vol. 11080, file 168/20-10, pt. 1, letter, April 11, 1951.

55 *Vancouver Island Acts*, "An Act for the Preservation of Game," April 20, 1859; "An Act to Amend an Act for the Preservation of Game," September 5, 1862.

56 Crown Colony of British Columbia, "An Ordinance to Prohibit the Unseasonable Destruction of Game," *Laws of British Columbia*, April 1, 1865 and March 4, 1867; "An Ordinance Entitled the Game Ordinance, 1869," *Laws of British Columbia*, March 12, 1869, further reduced the hunting season, as did "An Ordinance Entitled the Game Ordinance, 1870," *Laws of British Columbia*, April 20, 1870. For an example of Aboriginal People charged under these acts, see: "Jim and Mary Sauwek [?], Saanich Indians charged with possessing 4 deer skins contrary to statute. Fined $10 each to be levied by distress in default of such distress, one weeks imprisonment and the skins forfeited, 28 June 1878," Victoria Police Archives, Charge Book, 1877-08-08 to 1878-11-12, and Gaol Charge Books, October 1876 to April 1878.

57 British Columbia, *Statutes of British Columbia*, 1888, 52, 3,1, Game Protection Act, 1895, and Game Protection Amendment Act, 1896; *Statutes of British Columbia*, 1897, C88; *Statutes of British Columbia*, 1927, 98, 9; Gosnell, *Year Book of British Columbia*, 318; Thomson, "History of the Okanagan," 201-2.

58 Circular Letter from the Provincial Game Warden's Office, April 28, 1914, LAC, RG 10, 80-1/51, vol. 1, file 516; Williams to Lemmens, January 15, 1914, quoted in Thomson, "History of the Okanagan," 202.

59 Quoted in Thomson, "History of the Okanagan," 202, LAC, RG 10, 80-1/51, vol. 1, file 516.

60 According to many aboriginal trappers, the trapping season did not coincide with the season of prime furs but, rather, started and ended a month late. See Geo. S. Pragnell, "Special Report re: Trapping," September 12, 1923, LAC, RG 10, vol. 10872, file 901/20, pt. 1.

61 George Pragnell to Chairman and members, Provincial Game Board, August 21, 1924, LAC, RG 10, vol. 10,872, file 901/20, pt. 1 (emphasis in original).

62 Grace E. Bloomfield, Field Matron, Fort St. James, to J.H. Pragnell, January 28, 1929, LAC, RG 10, vol. 10872, file 901/20-10, pt. 2. For accounts from the Finlay River-Peace River area in northeastern British Columbia, see George Pragnell to the Chairman and Members of the Provincial Game Board, October 1, 1924, LAC, RG 10, vol. 10872, file 901/20-10, pt. 2. For Vancouver Island, see Trapping, M.S. Todd, Indian Agent, Alert Bay, to B. Harvey, Game Warden, Courtenay, November 30, 1938, RG 10, vol. 11,153.

63 LAC, RG 10, vol. 10872, 901/20-10, pt. 2.

64 Harper Reed, Indian Agent, Telegraph Creek, to W.E. Ditchburn, April 2, 1929, LAC, RG 10, vol. 10,872, file 901/20-10, pt. 1.

65 Frank Calbreath, Merchant, Telegraph Creek, to J.H. McMullan, Provincial Game Warden, December 31, 1928, and Harper Reed, Indian Agent, Telegraph Creek, to W.E. Ditchburn, Chief Inspector of Indian Agencies, December 31, 1928, LAC, RG 10, vol. 10872, file 901/20-10, pt. 1.

66 W.E. Ditchburn to Bryan Williams, July 4, 1929, LAC, RG 10, vol. 10872, file 901/20-10, pt. 1.

67 British Columbia, Legislative Assembly, "Game Warden's Report," *BCSP* (Victoria: British Columbia, 1894-1927), 1917, O16.

68 Report of District Officers Conference, October 21, 1946, LAC, RG 10, vol. 8,571, file 901/1-2-2-5, pt. 1.

69 "Game Warden's Report," 1907, F11. The game department also harassed "Asiatics" and recommended that they be "prohibited from shooting altogether."

70 Louis B. Prince to J.H. Pragnell, Indian Inspector, Kamloops, January 1, 1929, LAC, RG 10 vol. 10872901/20-10, pt. 1; DIAR, "Special Report on Trapping," September 12, 1923, and other correspondence in LAC, RG 10, vol. 10872, file 901/20-10, pt. 2.

71 Alfred Adams and H.D. Bailey, Native Brotherhood of British Columbia, to Indian Commissioner for British Columbia, January 27, 1941, LAC, RG 10, vol. 10872, file 901/20-10, pt. 2; Report of District Officers Conference, October 21, 1946, RG 10, vol. 8571, file 901/1-2-2-5, pt. 1; Trapping, T.R.L. MacInnes to the Secretary, DIA, February 27, 1939, RG 10, vol. 11,153, contains a petition signed by 153 Aboriginal People from the north coast region protesting the reallocation of traplines.

72 Department of Indian and Northern Affairs, Treaty and Historical Research Office, file U-24, F.R. Butler at Indian Affairs Branch, Department of Citizenship and Immigration, Indian Superintendent's Conference, British Columbia and Yukon Region, January 16-20, 1956, 9. The shrinkage of Kitsumkalum trapping areas between the 1920s and the 1980s is pictorially illustrated in McDonald, "Trying to Make a Life," figs. 9 and 10.

73 Cowichan Agency, Miscellaneous Correspondence, 1893-1906, letter 350, John Baird to W.R Robertson, July

24, 1904, LAC, RG 10, vol. 1348, reel C-13917; British Columbia Superintendency, Correspondence, 1894-1905, Ralph Smith, MP, to A.W. Vowell, August 31, 1905, LAC, RG 10, vol. 1023, reel T-1459; "Report of a Meeting," May 4, 1894, LAC, RG 10, vol. 3688, file 13,886-1.

74 Stó:lō Harry Joe of Squatisse and Katzie band chief Joe Isaacs made this complaint to the McKenna-McBride Royal Commission. See 1916, BCA, add mss 1056, 379. The same complaint is made by George Archie, secretary of the Canim Lake band, to W.E. Ditchburn, on December 1, 1927. See LAC, RG 10, vol. 10872, file 901/20-10, pt. 2. See also Francis W. Thompson "Employment Problems and the Economic Status of the British Columbia Indians" (MSW thesis, University of British Columbia, 1951," 41, for an interview with an unidentified aboriginal man who was fired from his public works job in Vancouver in the 1930s due to complaints that the city was employing someone who was not a taxpayer.

75 H.E. Taylor, Indian Agent, Williams Lake, to C.C. Perry, Assistant Indian Commissioner for British Columbia, January 24, 1936, and the response on February 6, 1936, LAC, RG 10, vol. 10872, file 901/20-10, pt. 2.

76 Report of the Deputy Superintendent, DIAR, 1935, 10; "Report of a Meeting," May 4, 1894, LAC, RG 10, vol. 3688, file 13,886-1; Thompson, "Employment Problems," 41.

77 "Game Warden's Report," BCSP, 1907, F11. During the Second World War, when once more there was a labour shortage and Aboriginal People were hired in large numbers in the commercial fishery, the abundance of wage work was used as an argument to deprive them of their subsistence fishery. See William Henry Barker, BC Packers, to the Hon. J.D. Hazen, Minister of Fisheries, August 19, 1913, LAC, RG 23, General File, reel 5, file 6, pt. 8; Shannon, "Fishing 1914-41," J.A. Motherwell, Chief Supervisor of Fisheries, to M.S. Todd, Indian Agent, May 20, 1940, LAC RG 10, vol. 11,147.

78 E. McLeod, Indian Agent, Lytton, to M.B. Jackson, Chairman of the Game Conservation Board of British Columbia, May 20, 1925, LAC, RG 10, vol. 10872, 901/20-10, pt. 2.

79 Ross Modeste and Chief Richard Thevarge, November 21, 1963, LAC, RG 10, vol. 8423, 801/21-1, reel C-13835; Salim Aziz, "Selected Aspects of Cultural Change among American Indians: A Case Study of Southeast Vancou-

ver Island" (MA thesis, University of Victoria, 1970), 46, 80. This survey was confined to southeast Vancouver Island, but there is similar evidence from around the province.

80 Helen Clifton, interviewed by John Lutz in Hartley Bay, June 9, 2004; Mary John, in Bridget Moran, *Stoney Creek Woman: The Story of Mary John* (Vancouver: Tillacum Library, 1988), 131; Terry Glavin, "Last Day in Alexis Creek," in Glavin, *This Ragged Place* (Vancouver: New Star, 1996), 123-69; Hugh Brody, *Indians on Skid Row* (Ottawa: DIAND, 1971); Elizabeth Furniss, *The Burden of History: Colonialism and the Frontier Myth in a Rural Canadian Community* (Vancouver: UBC Press, 1999).

81 Jones, *Queesto*, 94; McKenna-McBride Royal Commission, BCA, add mss 1056. See also Thompson, "Employment Problems," 9.

82 *Colonist*, 30 January 1973.

Chapter 8: Prestige to Welfare

1 H.M. Moffat to the Superintendent of Indian Affairs, December 21, 1888, LAC, RG 10, vol. 3803, reel C-10,141. By law, the revenue from leased Songhees reserve land belonged to the band, but it was held by the DIA.

2 *Weekly Victoria Gazette*, June 18, September 3, October 9, 1859; *British Colonist*, October 21, 1862, 3; Matthew MacFie, *Vancouver Island and British Columbia: Their History, Resources, and Prospects* (London: Longman, Roberts, and Green, 1865), 471; Edgar Fawcett, *Some Reminiscences of Old Victoria* (Toronto: William Briggs, 1912), 284.

3 This is discussed more fully in Chapter 7.

4 G.M. Sproat, *The Nootka: Scenes and Studies of Savage Life* (London: Smith, Elder, 1868; reprinted Victoria: Sono Nis, 1989), 42. Sproat was appointed as the Indian reserve commissioner, but the provincial government considered his land, water, and timber right allocations to Aboriginal People to be too generous. See Robin Fisher, "An Exercise in Futility: The Joint Commission on Indian Land in British Columbia, 1875-1880," *Historical Papers* 10 (1975): 81.

5 DIAR, 1887, 105. For the different effects of colonialism by age and gender, see John Lutz, "Gender and Work in Lekwammen Families, 1843-1970," in *Gendered Pasts: Historical Essays on Femininity and Masculinity in*

Canada, ed. Kathryn McPherson, Cecilia Morgan, and Nancy M. Forestell (Don Mills, ON: Oxford University Press, 1999).

6 W.H. Lomas, DIAR, 1887, 105-7; DIAR, 1888, 100-2. In 1915 another Indian Agent, H. Graham, made the same statement with regard to elderly Aboriginal People at Yale. See Royal Commission on Indian Affairs for the Province of British Columbia, BCA, add mss 1056.

7 W.H. Lomas, DIAR, 1887, 105-7; DIAR, 1888, 100-2. This is reinforced by the reminiscences of Charles Jones, a Nuu-chah-nulth neighbour of the Lekwungen, in Charles Jones with Stephen Bosustow, *Queesto: Pacheenaht Chief by Birthright* (Nanaimo, BC: Theytus, 1981), 54.

8 There were, however, variations in access to these resources by family and community as well as seasonal variation and annual fluctuations in supply, which made scarcity a possibility. See Wayne Suttles, "Coping with Abundance: Subsistence on the Northwest Coast," in *Coast Salish Essays*, ed. Wayne Suttles (Vancouver/Seattle: Talonbooks/University of Washington Press, 1987), 45-67; and Wayne Suttles, "Variation in Habitat and Culture on the Northwest Coast," in Suttles, *Coast Salish Essays*, 26-44. Unlike other coastal groups, the Lekwungen do not tell stories that dwell on starvation or scarcity.

9 DIAR, 1893, 116-18.

10 Cowichan Agency, Departmental Circulars, 1892-1910, A.W. Vowell, Indian Superintendent for British Columbia, November 30, 1893, LAC, RG 10, vol. 1350, reel C-13917.

11 Cowichan Agency, Departmental Circulars, 1892-1910, A.W. Vowell to all Indian Agents, August 20, 1894, LAC, RG 10, vol. 1350, reel C-13917.

12 Dave Elliot, *Saltwater People*, ed. Janet Poth (Saanich, BC: School District 63, 1983), 60; John McMullan, "State, Capital, and the BC Salmon-Fishing Industry," in *Uncommon Property: The Fishing and Fish Processing Industries in British Columbia*, ed. Patricia Marchak, Neil Guppy, and John McMullan (Toronto: Methuen, 1987), 110.

13 Jeannie L. Kanakos, "The Negotiations to Relocate the Songhees Indians, 1843-1911" (MA thesis, Simon Fraser University, 1983), 57; Canada, *Statutes*, 1890, LXII-LXIII; 1878, LII; 1889, XLI-XLII.

14 Cowichan Agency, General, B-48, Simon Johns to A.H. Lomas, Indian Agent, November 10, 1911, LAC, RG 10, vol. 9, 170; Johns, who was himself from the Sooke band, was subsequently declared persona non grata by the agent and ordered to leave the Songhees reserve. See W.E. Ditchburn, testifying before the British Columbia Fisheries Commission, 1922, in RG 23, vol. 1,233, file 726-34-4.

15 "Fishing 1914-41," G.S. Pragnell, Inspector of Indian Agencies, October 5, 1928, LAC, RG 10, vol. 11,147; McKenna-McBride Royal Commission Transcripts, January 27, 1916, BCA, add mss 1056, box 2, file 5-6, 431.

16 E. McLeod to M.B. Jackson, May 20, 1925, and McLeod to All Chiefs in His District, June 30, 1926, LAC, RG 10, vol. 10872, file 901/20-10, pt. 2.

17 Emphasis mine. See "Extract from Kwakewlth Agency Monthly Report for February 1934," LAC, RG 10, vol. 11,153; "Fishing 1914-41," M.S. Todd, Indian Agent, to Secretary, DIA, November 11, 1940, LAC, RG 10, vol. 11,147.

18 Inspectorate of Indian Agencies, Correspondence Out, 1910-11, W.E. Ditchburn, Indian Inspector, to Secretary, DIA, November 10, 1910, LAC, RG 10, vol. 1312, reel C-13,908. In this letter Ditchburn authorizes fifty pounds of flour to one recipient, perhaps because the relief was intended for his wife as well, but twenty-five was the standard rate for Aboriginal People. The ration list for Indians changed little between 1888 and 1945. Rates for non-Indians from BCARS, GR 150, cited in Bonnie Thompson, "Voices from a Not Too Distant Past: Pre-1930s Indigent Fund," paper presented to the Qualicum Conference, Parksville, British Columbia, January 1994. For policy on sugar and tea only for the sick, see Cowichan Agency, Departmental Circulars, 1892-1910, A.W. Vowell to All Agents, May 11, 1900, RG 10, vol. 1350, reel C-13917.

19 There also seems to be an undercurrent in the DIA records indicating that "Indians were content with less," but this is seldom stated explicitly.

20 Allan Irving, "The Development of a Provincial Welfare State: British Columbia, 1900-1939," in *The "Benevolent" State: The Growth of Welfare in Canada*, ed. Allan Moscovitch and Jim Albert (Toronto: Garamond, 1987), 159, 162; Thompson, "Voices from a Not Too Distant Past."

21 At the beginning of the Depression, men working in relief camps were paid two dollars per day, though this was soon reduced to $7.50 per month. See Irving, "Development of a Provincial Welfare State," 163; Cowichan Agency, General, B-45, Mrs. Percy Ross to H. Graham, January 8, 1935, LAC, RG 10, vol. 9,170; Cowichan Agency, file B-48, E.M. George to H. Graham, Indian Agent, February 9, 1932, LAC, RG 10, vol. 9,170. George writes: "I wrote to you at the begging [sic] of last month about getting some relief but I haven't heard anything of it yet. The white people here are getting five dollars per week; so I don't expect to get that much." The agent wrote back on February 9, telling him he could get relief worth four dollars per month.

22 H. Graham to Henry John, Indian, April 20, 1931, LAC, RG 10, vol. 9172, file B-63; Cowichan Agency, General B-45, Mrs. Elizabeth Joseph to H. Graham, Cowichan Indian Agent, April 1, 1930, LAC, RG 10 vol. 9,170.

23 Bridget Moran, *Stoney Creek Woman: The Story of Mary John* (Vancouver: Tillacum Library, 1988), 8, 101.

24 A.F. MacKenzie, Secretary, DIA, to C.C. Perry, Assistant Indian Commissioner, British Columbia, 1931, LAC, RG 10, vol. 11,155, file CR 37, pt. A; Cowichan Agency, General, B-44, George S. Pragnell, Inspector of Indian Agencies to Secretary, DIA, July 30, 1932, LAC, RG 10, vol. 9, 170.

25 Cowichan Agency, General, B-45, Dora Ross to Mrs. Murie, BC Department of Social Welfare, January 4, 1935, LAC, RG 10, vol. 9,170.

26 Ibid., Mrs. Percy Ross to H. Graham, January 8, 1935.

27 Irving, "Development of Provincial Welfare State," 163.

28 Cowichan Agency, General, B-45, H. Graham to George F. Davidson, BC Superintendent of Welfare, January 17, 1935, LAC, RG 10, vol. 9,170.

29 A.F. MacKenzie, Secretary, DIA, to E.G. Newnham, April 20, 1933, LAC, RG 10, vol. 11,155, file CR 37, pt. A.

30 Cowichan Agency, General, B-44, George S. Pragnell, Inspector of Indian Agencies to Secretary, DIA, December 21, 1936, "Cowichan Indian Agency Report No. 7," LAC, RG 10, vol. 9,170.

31 Hugh Shewell, *Enough to Keep Them Alive: Indian Welfare in Canada, 1873-1965* (Toronto: University of Toronto Press, 2004), 123, Table 43, 330.

32 Thomas Lightly, Fisheries Inspector, "Report 1942," LAC, RG 23, vol. 662, file 712-2-72, pt. 4; F.J. Winlow,

Fisheries Inspector, Squamish Subdistrict, "Report 1943," LAC, RG 23, vol. 662, file 712-2-72, pt. 4; Percy Ross to R.H. Moore, May 21, 1943, LAC, RG 10, vol. 9172, file B-57; Cowichan Agency, General, B-44, LAC, RG 10, vol. 9,170.

33 Shannon, "Fishing 1914-41," J.A. Motherwell, Chief Supervisor of Fisheries, to M.S. Todd, Indian Agent, Alert Bay, May 20, 1940, LAC, RG 10, vol. 11,147. This repeated the pattern established during the First World War, when, during the period of peak wartime labour demand, the fisheries officer decided not to give licences to people who had other jobs. See Shannon, "Fishing 1914-41," W.M. Halliday to W.E. Ditchburn, June 16, 1919, LAC, RG 10, vol. 11,147.

34 *Vancouver Sun*, Letters, August 23, 1940.

35 Moran, *Stoney Creek Woman*; James Redford, "Attendance at Indian Residential Schools in BC, 1890-1920," *BC Studies* 44 (1979-80): 41-56.

36 The monthly ration for a family of three in 1946 consisted of 49 pounds of flour, 24 ounces of baking powder, 10 pounds of rolled oats, 10 pounds of sugar, 1 pound of tea, 4 pounds of lard, 6 pounds of beans, 2 pounds of butter, 6 tins of milk, 10 cakes of soap, 3 tins of tomatoes, 5 pounds of fresh meat, 1 small bag of salt, and 1 jar of peanut butter. See R.H. Moore to Cowichan Merchants, January 9, 1946, LAC, RG 10, vol. 9174, file B72; Moore to Indian Commissioner, April 3, 1945, LAC, RG 10, vol. 9174, file B72.

37 Andy Paull, speaking at a conference on the Indian Act, July 20-21, 1955, LAC, RG 10, vol. 8570, file 901/1-2-2-2.

38 *Colonist*, October 18, 1960, 1; Cowichan Agency, General, B-45, Lizzie Fisher to H. Graham, Cowichan Indian Agent, August, 1932, LAC, RG 10, vol. 9,170; Cowichan Agency, General, B-45, Charles to H. Graham, August 6, 1932, LAC, RG 10, vol. 9,170; Cowichan Agency, General, B-45, Robbie Davis to H. Graham, December 8, 1934, LAC, RG 10, vol. 9,170.

39 Kathleen Mooney, "Urban and Reserve Indian Economies and Domestic Organization" (PhD diss., University of Michigan, 1976), 227, 236; Michael Kew describes the same pattern among the Musqueam in "Coast Salish Ceremonial Life: Status and Identity in a Modern Village" (PhD diss., University of Washington, 1970).

40 Mooney, "Urban and Reserve Indian Economies," 235-36. There have been long-term adverse health implications for many Aboriginal People as a result of the shift away from a diet based on hunted, fished, and gathered foods. See Mary Ellen Kelm, *Colonizing Bodies* (Vancouver: UBC Press, 1999); Hugh Brody, *Maps and Dreams* (London: Jill Norman and Hobhouse, 1982), 203.

41 Mooney, "Urban and Reserve Indian Economies."

42 Ibid., 231.

43 W.H. Lomas, DIAR, 1887, 105-7.

44 Wayne Suttles, "Spirit Dancing and the Persistence of Native Culture among the Coast Salish," in *Coast Salish Essays*.

45 Suttles, "Spirit Dancing"; See also Pamela Amoss, *Coast Salish Spirit Dancing: The Survival of an Ancestral Religion* (Seattle: University of Washington Press, 1978); and Kew, "Coast Salish Ceremonial Life."

46 Dennis Leon, interviewed by Liam Haggarty and Heather Watson at Sardis, May 25, 2005. Keith Carlson, personal communication, May 18, 2005.

47 Brody, *Maps and Dreams*, 212. According to Brody, in 1978 the average per capita annual income (including from the bush economy) in the three communities was $1,875, compared to the Canadian average of $6,600. Douglas Hudson, "Traplines and Timber: Social and Economic Change among the Carrier" (PhD diss., University of Alberta, 1983), iv-v, 136; Brody, *Maps and Dreams*, 178-213; Kenneth Coates, *Best Left as Indians: Native-White Relations in the Yukon Territory, 1840-1973* (Montreal and Kingston: McGill-Queen's University Press, 1991), 65, 69.

48 I.W. Powell, *Report of the Superintendent of Indian Affairs for British Columbia for 1872 and 1873* (Ottawa: I.B. Taylor, 1873), 10 (reprinted as CIHM No. 16227). Colonial officials confirm Powell's observations, with the exception of the colony distributing "gifts" (rather like at a potlatch) to mark the Queen's birthday celebrations. See James Hendrickson, ed., *Journals of the Colonial Legislatures of the Colonies of Vancouver Island and British Columbia, 1866-1871* (Victoria: Provincial Archives of British Columbia, 1980) 5:568.

49 Statistics Canada, *Social Security: National Programs, A Review for the Period 1946-1975* (Ottawa: Statistics Canada, 1976), December 1976, 4-2003-501 p 690-1. D.B. Fields and W.T. Stanbury, *The Economic Impact of the Public Sector upon the Indians of British Columbia* (Vancouver: UBC Press, 1973), 46; Andrew Siggner and Chantal Locatelli, *An Overview of the Demographic, Social and Economic Conditions among British Columbia's Registered Indian Population* (Ottawa: Research Branch, Corporate Policy, Department of Indian Affairs and Northern Development, 1981), 39.

50 Inspectorate of Indian Agencies, Correspondence Out, 1910-11, W.E. Ditchburn, Indian Inspector, to Secretary, DIA, November 10, 1911, LAC, RG 10, vol. 1312, reel C-13,908; James Smith to W.E. Ditchburn, September 14, 1931, LAC, RG 10, vol. 11,155, C.R. 37, pt. A; Johnny Galakawmei to E.G. Newnham, August 1, 1933, LAC, RG 10, vol. 11,155, C.R. 37, pt. A; Marjorie Mitchell, "A Dictionary of Songish: A Dialect of Coast Salish" (MA thesis, University of Victoria, 1968), 143.

51 Rena Peters and Joanne Jefferson, interviewed by Liam Haggarty and Heather Watson, Chilliwack, BC, May 24, 2005. Copy at Stó:lō Nation Archives.

52 Herb Joe, interviewed at Sardis, BC, by Liam Haggarty and Heather Watson, May 20, 2005.

53 Chief Pat Sterritt, interviewed by Nancy Turner, Anne Marshall, and John Lutz in her office at Hartley Bay, December 8, 2003; Helen Clifton, interviewed by John Lutz in Hartley Bay, June 9, 2004.

54 Verna Ambers, interviewed by Byron Plant at the Community Development Office, Namgis First Nation, Alert Bay, July 7, 2003.

55 Edwin Newman, interviewed by Byron Plant and Chris Cook III at Alert Bay, July 6, 2003.

56 Doug Kelly, interviewed by Liam Haggarty and Heather Watson at the Soowahlie Band Office, May 27, 2005.

Chapter 9: Conclusion

1 So states the Supreme Court of Canada in *Delgamuukw v. The Queen*, 1997.

2 Allan McEachern, *Reasons for Judgement: Delgamuukw v. BC* (Smithers, BC: Supreme Court of British Columbia, 1991), 17, 52. For a discussion of the importance of this case to historians and other social scientists see *BC Studies* (special issue) 95 (1992); and Dara Culhane, *The Pleasure of the Crown: Anthropology, Law, and First Nations* (Vancouver: Talonbooks, 1998).

3 McEachern, *Reasons for Judgement*, 129. On rereading fur trader documents with an eye to their partiality, see

Mary Black Rogers, "Varieties of 'Starving': Semantics and Survival in the Subarctic Fur Trade, 1750-1850," *Ethnohistory* 33, 4 (1986): 353-83; and Elizabeth Vibert, *Traders Tales: Narratives of Cultural Encounters in the Columbia Plateau, 1807-1846* (Norman: University of Oklahoma Press, 1997).

4 Douglas to Newcastle, July 28, 1853, CO 305/4, 9499; Matthew Baillie Begbie, in H.L. Langevin, *British Columbia: Report of the Honourable H.L. Langevin, Minister of Public Works* (Ottawa: Parliament, 1872), 27; George Walkem, in British Columbia, Legislative Assembly, "Report of the Government of British Columbia on the Subject of Indian Reserves," *BCSP* (Victoria: British Columbia, 1875), 3.

5 Linda Tuhiwai Smith, *Decolonizing Methodologies Research and Indigenous Peoples* (London: Zed Books, 1999), 35.

6 Hudson uses "bush economy," which has the advantage of being more intuitive, but it suggests a heavier reliance on subsistence than is often the case. See Douglas Hudson, "Traplines and Timber: Social and Economic Change among the Carrier" (PhD diss., University of Alberta, 1983). See also N.G. Canclini, *Hybrid Cultures: Strategies for Entering and Leaving Modernity* (Minneapolis: University of Minnesota Press, 1995); Hugh Brody, *Maps and Dreams: Indians and the British Columbia Frontier* (London: Jill Norman and Hobhouse, 1982); and "Postscript: Subordination without Subjugation."

7 A.W. Vowell in DIAR, 1903, 281-85; Sifton in Canada, *Debates*, 1897, col. 4076, June 14, 1897.

8 This supports the observations by Alicja Muszynski, *Cheap Wage Labour: Race and Gender in the Fisheries of British Columbia* (Montreal and Kingston: McGill-Queen's University Press, 1996); Evelyn Pinkerton, "Competition among BC Fish-Processing Firms," in *Uncommon Property: The Fishing and Fish Processing Industries in British Columbia*, ed. Pat Marchak, Neil Guppy, and John McMullan (Toronto: Metheun, 1987), 107-52; and Kenneth Coates, *Best Left as Indians: Native-White Relations in the Yukon Territory, 1840-1973* (Montreal: McGill Queen's University Press, 1991).

9 W.T. Stanbury, "BC Indians Living Off Reserve: Some Economic Aspects," speech delivered to the Union of BC Indian Chiefs (November 8, 1972), table 7, Simon Fraser University Archives; H.L. MacMillan, A.B.

MacMillan, D.R. Offord, and J.L. Dingle, "Aboriginal Health," *Canadian Medical Association Journal* 155, 11 (1996): 1569-78, reported that, in 1965, the high school graduation rate was only 2 percent.

10 The term is from Robert Paine, *The White Arctic: Anthropological Essays on Tutelage and Ethnicity* (St. John's, NF: Memorial University, 1977), 3, 46. See also Jeremy Beckett, *Torres Strait Islanders: Custom and Colonialism* (Cambridge: Cambridge University Press, 1987), 16-17, 172-77.

11 W.T. Stanbury, "Indians in British Columbia: Level of Income, Welfare Dependence and Poverty Rate," *BC Studies* 20 (1973-74): 66-78. According to this data, 25.1 percent of all Canadian families lived below the poverty line in 1970 (i.e., they earned less than two thousand dollars per year). See Simon Fraser Archives, W.T. Stanbury, "The Social and Economic Conditions of Indian Families in British Columbia," paper prepared for the British Columbia Family and Children's Law Commission, Simon Fraser University, November 1974, 18, 37, 40.

12 Hugh Brody, *Indians on Skid Row* (Ottawa: DIAND, 1971), R72-6470; Edgar Dosman, *Indians: The Urban Dilemma* (Toronto: McClelland and Stewart, 1972); Heather Robertson, *Reservations Are for Indians* (Toronto: James Lorimer, 1970, 1991); Geoffrey York, *The Dispossessed Life and Death in Native Canada* (London: Vintage, 1990). The identification with cowboys comes from a discussion with an aboriginal friend.

13 See, for example, Bridget Moran, *Stoney Creek Woman: The Story of Mary John* (Vancouver: Tillacum Library, 1988); Terry Glavin, "Last Day in Alexis Creek," in Glavin, *This Ragged Place* (Vancouver: New Star, 1996), 123-69; John L. Hall, "Ethnic Tensions and Economics: Indian White Interaction in a British Columbia Ranching Community," *Canadian Journal of Anthropology* 1, 2 (1980): 179-90.

14 In 1993, all visible minorities had an unemployment rate of 16 percent, compared to 18 percent for off-reserve Indians. The on-reserve rate is not given for this date. See Ruth Dibbs and Tracey Leesti, *Survey of Labour and Income Dynamics: Visible Minorities and Aboriginal Peoples* (Ottawa: Statistics Canada, Interdepartmental Working Group on Employment Equity Data, Catalogue no. 95-08, 1995); Rachel Bernier, *The Dimensions of Wage*

Inequality among Aboriginal Peoples (Ottawa: Statistics Canada, 1997), 11F0019MPE no. 109, pp. 8, 12.

15 Stewart Clatworthy, Jeremy Hull, and Neil Loughran, "Employment of the Aboriginal Labour Force: Patterns of Employment, Unemployment and Poverty," in *Economy: Project Area 3* (Ottawa: Four Directions Consulting Group for the Royal Commission on Aboriginal Peoples, 1995), 6.

16 Chris Cook, personal communication, September 20, 2002; Wayne Suttles, "Spirit Dancing and the Persistence of Native Culture among the Coast Salish," in *Coast Salish Essays*, ed. Wayne Suttles, 199-208 (Vancouver/Seattle: Talonbooks/University of Washington Press, 1987).

17 Robin P. Armstrong, *Geographical Patterns of Socio-Economic Well-Being of First Nations Communities in Canada*, Working Paper no. 46 (Ottawa: Statistics Canada Agriculture Division, 2001), 13.

18 In 1996, the on-reserve unemployment rate was 29 percent, while the off-reserve rate was 26 percent. See Armstrong, *Geographical Patterns*, 13-16; W.R. Avison, "Summary of Health Consequences of Unemployment," paper prepared for the National Forum on Health, Ottawa, Health Canada, 1999; DIA study quoted by the *Globe and Mail*, October 12, 1998.

19 Don Kerr, Andrew Signer, and Jean Pierre Bourdeau, *Canada's Aboriginal Population, 1981-1991: Summary Report* (Ottawa: Royal Commission on Aboriginal Peoples and Statistics Canada, 1996), 29; Armstrong, *Geographical Patterns*, 13-16, 23; Michael Mendelson and Ken Battle, *Aboriginal People in Canada's Labour Market* (Ottawa: Caledon Institute of Social Policy, 1999), 2-3.

20 Bernier, *Dimensions of Wage Inequality*, 12; Kevin Lee, "Measuring Poverty among Canada's Aboriginal People," *Insight* 23, 2 (1999): 11; Armstrong, *Geographical Patterns*, 6, 22; DIA study quoted by Erin Anderson, "Canada's Squalid Secret," *Globe and Mail*, October 12, 1998, A1.

21 In Vancouver, half of all Aboriginal People (49 percent) lived below the poverty line compared to 23 percent of non-Aboriginal People. In Victoria, the respective rates were 41 percent and 15 percent. See Mendelson and Battle, *Aboriginal People in Canada's Labour Market*, 2-3; Lee, "Measuring Poverty," 11; Chief Pootlas interviewed on CBC Radio, *Vancouver Morning Edition*, September 23, 1999.

22 Rob Shaw, "Legislature Land Dispute Settled at Last," *Victoria Times Colonist*, November 19, 2006.

23 Sage Birchwater, *Chiwid* (Vancouver: New Star, 1995); Sage Birchwater, interviewed by John Lutz at his home at Tatlayoko Lake, September 2, 2000.

24 Overwaitea is the main grocery store in Williams Lake. Gilbert Solomon, interviewed by John Lutz at the Nemiah Band Office, August 23, 2000; Joe Alphonse, interviewed by John Lutz at the Tsilhqot'in National Government Offices, August 24, 2000.

25 Chief Charleyboy, interviewed by John Lutz at his home at Redstone; Gilbert Solomon, interviewed by John Lutz at the Nemiah Band Office, April 23, 2000; Commission on Resources and Environment, *Cariboo-Chilcotin Land Use Plan* (Victoria, British Columbia, 1994), 44.

26 Nemiah Declaration and chronology available at http://xenigwetin.com.

27 Chief Cassidy Sill of the Ulkatcho Band, interviewed by John Lutz, August 31, 1999 at Toosey.

28 Sage Birchwater, "Land Deal Signed at Redstone," *Williams Lake Tribune*, April 14, 2005.

29 Patrick Lulua, interviewed by John Lutz at Toosey, August 31, 1999. For an elaboration of this observation with regard to the neighbouring Carrier people, see Jo-Anne Fiske, "Fishing Is Women's Business: Changing Economic Roles of Carrier Women and Men," in *Native People, Native Lands: Canadian Indians, Inuit and Metis*, ed. Bruce Alden Cox (Ottawa: Carleton University Press, 1988), 186-97.

30 Robin Ward, *Echoes of Empire: Victoria and Its Remarkable Buildings* (Madeira Park, BC: Harbour Publishing, 1996); Avery Gordon, *Ghostly Matters: Haunting and the Sociological Imagination* (Minneapolis: University of Minnesota Press, 1997), 17-18; Renée Bergland, *The National Uncanny: Indian Ghosts and American Subjects* (Hanover, NH: University of New England Press, 2000), 22. Thanks to Christina Nilson for introducing me to these books.

31 A prominent recent example is John Stackhouse, "Canada's Apartheid," a fourteen-part series in the *Globe and Mail*, November-December 2001.

32 Kyle Campbell, *American Indian Languages: The Historical Linguistics of Native America* (New York: Oxford University Press, 1997), 19; R.J. Gregg, "Local

Lexical Items in the Sociodialectical Survey of Vancouver English," *Canadian Journal of Linguistics/La Revue Canadienne de Linguistique* 28, 1 (1983): 17-23. There is a gazetteer of British Columbia place-names derived from Chinook in Lillard and Glavin, *A Voice Great within Us*. For Oregon, see Lewis L. McArthur, "Anglicized Native American Place Names in Oregon: Their Number and Distribution," *Names* 44, 4 (1996): 322-32. The fluidity of Chinook jargon has particularly attracted the poets. See Charles Lillard, *Cultus Coulee* (Surrey, BC: Sono Nis, 1971); Gary Geddes, *Skookum Wawa: Writings of the Canadian Northwest* (Toronto: Oxford University Press, 1975); Terry Glavin, "Rain Language," in *A Voice Great within Us*, ed. Charles Lillard and Terry Glavin (Vancouver: New Star, 1998), 17-34.

33 Clatworthy, Hull, and Loughran, *Economy*, 8. For example, in 2002 British Columbia eliminated its Human Rights Branch.

34 The Province of British Columbia appealed a 2002 Supreme Court decision requiring the Crown to consult with Aboriginal People before transferring a timber licence, arguing that the province had "no duty of consultation until aboriginal title had been proven in court." See Court of Appeal for British Columbia, *Haida Nation* v. *BC and Weyerhaeuser*, 2002, BCCA 462, August 19, 2002. Full transcript available at http://www.courts.gov.bc.ca/jdb%2Dtxt/ca/02/04/2002bcca0462.htm.

35 *Haida Nation* v. *BC and Weyerhaeuser*, 2002, BCCA 462, August 19, 2002. The court declared that the government and the interested companies "have legally enforceable duties to [Aboriginal People] to consult with them in good faith and to endeavor to seek workable accommodations between the aboriginal interests ... on the one hand, and the short-term and the long-term objectives of the Crown ... in accordance with the public interest, both aboriginal and non-aboriginal, on the other hand.

Postscript

1 Douglas Cole and Ira Chaikin, *An Iron Hand upon the People: The Law against the Potlatch on the Northwest Coast* (Vancouver: Douglas and McIntyre, 1990), 35-36.

2 Mikhail Bakhtin, *The Dialogic Imagination: Four Essays,* ed. Michael Holquist, trans. Caryl Emerson and Michael Holquist (Austin: University of Texas Press, 1996), 427.

3 David Dinwoodie, *Reserve Memories: The Power of the Past in a Chilcotin Community* (Lincoln: University of Nebraska Press, 2002) 104.

4 Néstor García Canclini, *Hybrid Cultures: Strategies for Entering and Leaving Modernity* (Minneapolis: University of Minnesota Press, 1995), 47, 54.

5 Michel de Certeau, *The Practice of Everyday Life*, trans. Stephen Randall (Berkeley: University of California, 1988).

6 "Moral economy" is sometimes used, but it implies that "morals" are not part of the neoliberal economy; "bush economy" captures part of the concept. Gérard Bouchard has carefully theorized this economy among settler society in Saguenay Quebec and calls it "co-integration." His 'co-integration model' comprises a distinct version of the moditional economy, with family farming and inputs from wage work forming the main components. See Bouchard, *Quelques arpents d'Amérique: Population, économie, famille au Saguenay, 1838-1971* (Montreal: Boréal, 1996); and his "Marginality, Co-Integration and Change: Social History as Critical Exercise," *Journal of the Canadian Historical Association* New Series 8 (1997): 19-38.

7 As surely as Euro-Canadians who entered aboriginal communities, missionaries, especially, were transformed by their encounters.

8 Bouchard, *Quelques arpents d'Amérique*; Ruth W. Sandwell, *Contesting Rural Space: Land Policy and the Practices of Resettlement on Saltspring Island, 1859-1891* (Montreal and Kingston: McGill-Queen's University Press, 2005).

9 Sarah Deutsch also adds Protestantism and Anglo-Saxonism to the values embedded in capitalism. See Deutsch, "Landscape of Enclaves: Race Relations in the American West," in *Under an Open Sky: Rethinking America's Western Past*, ed. W. Cronon, Jay Gitlin, and George Miles (New York: Norton, 1992), 113.

10 Renée Bergland, *The National Uncanny: Indian Ghosts and American Subjects* (Hanover, NH: University of New England Press, 2000), 10-12.

Appendix 1: Auto-Ethnographic Sources and Interviews

1 Following Mary Louise Pratt, *Imperial Eyes: Travel Writing and Transculturation* (London: Routledge, 1992).

2 H. David Brumble III, *An Annotated Bibliography of American Indian and Eskimo Autobiographies* (Lincoln: University of Nebraska Press, 1981).

3 Clah learned English from the missionary William Duncan, to whom he taught the Ts'mshyen language sm'algyax. The original manuscript is in the library of Wellcome Institute London, with a copy at Library and Archives Canada, Arthur Wellington Clah, MG 40, F11, microfilm A-1711. For more description, see Robert Galois, "Colonial Encounters: The Worlds of Arthur Wellington Clah, 1855-1881," *BC Studies* 115/16 (1997-98): 104-47.

4 Much of the editorial work was by Morris Swadesh. The Aboriginal text is printed alongside an English translation in Edward Sapir and Morris Swadesh, *Nootka Texts* (Philadelphia: Linguistic Society of America, 1939) and in their *Native Accounts of Nootka Ethnography* (Bloomington: Indian University, 1955). Sayach'apis' biography has been published in different forms, including Sapir, "The Life of a Nootka Indian," *Queen's Quarterly* 28, 3-4 (1921): 232-43, and 351-67; and Sapir, "Sayach'apis, a Nootka Trader," in *American Indian Life*, ed. E.C. Parsons, 297-323 (New York: B.W. Huebsh, 1922; reprinted Lincoln: University of Nebraska Press, 1922).

5 Charles Jones, with Stephen Bosustow, *Queesto: Pacheenaht Chief by Birthright* (Nanaimo, BC: Theytus, 1981).

6 Captain John, "The Story of the Conversion and Subsequent Experiences of Captain John as Narrated by Himself," 30 March 1898, translated from Chinook by Rev. W.H. Barraclough, Chilliwack Archives, add mss 1, file 253 and file 584.

7 June Collins, "John Fornsby: The Personal Document of a Coast Salish Indian," in *Indians of the Urban Northwest*, ed. Marian Smith (New York: Columbia University Press, 1949), 287-341.

8 Rev. William Henry Pierce, *From Potlatch to Pulpit*, ed. J.P. Hicks (Vancouver: Vancouver Bindery, 1933).

9 J.S. Matthews, *Conversations with Khahtsahlano, 1932-1954* (Vancouver: Vancouver City Archives, 1955); and Oliver N. Wells, *The Chilliwacks and Their Neighbours* (Vancouver: Talonbooks, 1987).

10 "George Swanaset: Narrative of a Personal Document," University of Washington, Special Collections, Melville Jacobs Collection, mss. 1693-71-13, box 112.

11 Clelland S. Ford, ed., *Smoke from Their Fires: The Life of a Kwakiutl Chief* (New Haven: Yale University Press, 1941).

12 Ronald Olson, "The Life Story of a Bella Bella Woman," in "Notes on the Bella Bella Kwakiutl," *Anthropological Records* 14, 5 (1955): 341-43.

13 Christine Quintasket, *Mourning Dove: A Salishan Autobiography*, ed. Jay Miller (Lincoln: University of Nebraska Press, 1990), xxxiii.

14 A more detailed look at the role of women and men in paid and unpaid labour is available in John Lutz, "Gender and Work in Lekwammen Families, 1843-1970," in *Gendered Pasts: Historical Essays on Femininity and Masculinity in Canada*, ed. Kathryn McPherson, Cecilia Morgan, and Nancy M. Forestell (Don Mills, ON: Oxford University Press, 1999), 80-105.

15 Leona Marie Sparrow, "Work Histories of a Coast Salish Couple" (MA thesis, University of British Columbia, 1976).

16 Mary Augusta Tappage, *The Days of Augusta*, ed. J.E. Speare (Vancouver: Douglas and McIntyre, 1992).

17 Henry Pennier, with Herbert L. McDonald, *Chiefly Indian: The Warm and Witty Story of a British Columbia Half Breed Logger* (Vancouver: Graydonald Graphics, 1972), reintroduced and edited by Keith Carlson and Kristina Fagan as *"Call Me Hank": A Stó:lo Man's Reflections on Logging, Living and Growing Old* (Toronto: University of Toronto Press, 2006).

18 Harry Assu, with Joy Inglis, *Assu of Cape Mudge: Recollections of a Coastal Indian Chief* (Vancouver: UBC Press, 1989), xviii.

19 Wells, *The Chilliwacks,* 197-204.

20 Yukon Women's Project Sound Recording, 1974, 13-5, Yukon Archives.

21 Clayton Mack, with H. Thommasen, *Grizzlies and White Guys: The Stories of Clayton Mack* (Madeira Park, BC: Harbour Publishing, 1993).

22 Simon Baker, *Khot-La-Cha: The Autobiography of Simon Baker,* Verna J. Kirkness, comp. and ed. (Vancouver: Douglas and McIntyre, 1994).

23 See James Spradley, ed., *Guests Never Leave Hungry: The Autobiography of James Sewid, a Kwakiutl Indian*

(Montreal and Kingston: McGill-Queen's University Press, 1989).

24 Joyce Albany interview, 17 August 1990, Oral History Project, Esquimalt Municipal Archives, file 990.16.1.

25 Earl Maquinna George, *Living on the Edge: Nuu-Chah-Nulth History from an Ahousat Chief's Perspective* (Victoria: Sono Nis, 2003).

26 Colleen Bostwick, "Oral Histories: Theresa Jeffries," *Labour History* 2, 3 (1980) 8-15; and Frank Fuller, "Gilbert Joe," *Labour History* 2, 3 (1980): 16-19.

27 Beth White, Yukon Women's Project Sound Recording (Transcripts), Yukon Archives, file 13-5.

28 Bridget Moran, *Stoney Creek Woman: The Story of Mary John* (Vancouver: Tillacum Library, 1988), 29, 78, 81.

Appendix 2: Reliability of Department of Indian Affairs Estimates

1 She notes that income from fishing and wages may not be clearly distinguished. Cannery income appears under a separate category in some years and under fishing in others, which Codere attributes to a change in agents. See Helen Codere, *Fighting with Property: A Study of Kwakiutl Potlatching and Warfare, 1792-1930* (Seattle: University of Washington Press, 1972), 34-35, 41.

2 James K. Burrows, "'A Much Needed Class of Labour': The Economy and Income of the Southern Interior Plateau Indians, 1897-1910," *BC Studies* 71 (1986): 27-46.

3 J.H. MacKay to W.H. Lomas, August 4, 1898, LAC, RG 10, vol. 1350, 252-53.

Bibliography

The conventional distinction between primary and secondary sources breaks down in this book for several reasons. First, since I examine both the material and rhetorical construction of aboriginal lives, what might be considered a secondary source for describing aboriginal lives will be a primary source when it comes to considering the rhetorical construction of those lives. Second, the traditional reasons for distinguishing primary and secondary sources, the prima facie reliability of the former compared to the latter, dissolve under close scrutiny, as David Murray and Ian MacLaren show in their works cited below. Finally, in this book, which spans 140 years, there are many works, like Hawthorn, Belshaw, and Jamieson, dated 1958, that are both a primary source, according to the traditional division, for the period in which they were written, and a secondary source for later periods.

Archival Sources

Anglican Church of Canada. Ecclesiastical Province of British Columbia and the Yukon Archives. Vancouver.
Bishop George Hills, Diary.

British Columbia Archives (BCA). Victoria.
Anderson, James Robert. "Notes and Comments on Early Days and Events in British Columbia, Washington, and Oregon." Add. Mss. 1912, box 8/18.
Aural History Program. Acc No 2428 Tape 1 Tract 1.
Aural History Program Collection. John Williams. Interviewed by Imbert Orchard, 1969.
Bayley, Charles A. "Early Life on Vancouver Island." E/B/B34.2.
Bell, James, to John Thomson. February 27, 1859, MS 659 E/8/B412.
Boas, Franz. *Indianische Sagen von der Nord-Pacifischen Küste Amerikas*. Berlin, 1895, translated in an unpublished manuscript by Dietrich Bertz.

British Columbia, Colony of. Blue Books of the Colony of British Columbia.
British Columbia, Colony of. Attorney General Inquisitions, GR 1328.
British Columbia. Attorney General Files. GR 0429.
British Columbia. Indian Advisory Committee of British Columbia. GR 1071.
BC Union of Indian Chiefs. MS 1056.
Campbell, Alexander. "Report on the Indians of British Columbia to the Superintendent General of Indian Affairs." October, 19 1883. A/E/Or3/C15.
Canada. Manuscript Census. 1881, 1891, 1901.
Carmichael, Alfred. "Account of a Season's Work at a Salmon Cannery, Windsor Cannery, Aberdeen, Skeena," ca. 1885. Add. Mss. 2305.
Colonial Correspondence. GR 1372.
Correspondence, etc. relating to the Chilcotin District and Indians. A/E/Or3/C43.
Commission on the Salmon Fishing Industry in British Columbia, 1902. GR 213.
Cooper, James. "Report by the Harbor Master at Esquimalt to the Acting Colonial Secretary." F347/26a.
Deans, James. "Settlement of Vancouver Island," 1878. E/B/D342.
Department of Lands and Works. GR 0983.
Douglas, James. Diary of a Trip to Victoria March 1-21, 1843. A/B/40/D75.4A.
Douglas, James. Private Papers, 2nd Series. B/20 1853.
Douglas, James, to W.F. Tolmie. Country letter book, August 13, 1857.
Ella, Martha Cheney. "Diary," 1853-1911. E/B/El 5A.
Finlayson, Roderick. "Biography." A/B/30/F49A.
Finlayson, Roderick. "History of Vancouver Island the Northwest Coast." A/B/30/F49B.

"Fort Chilcotin." MM/C43.

Grant, W.C. "Report on Vancouver Island, 1849." A/B/20/G76.

Great Britain. Colonial Office, Vancouver Island Acts. Micro B-63. CO 305/4.

Great Britain. Colonial Office. Despatches about Vancouver Island. GR 0328, CO 305 vols. 1-2, 1847-51.

Hanna, James. "Bring Sea Otter from Macao." A/A/20.5

Hudson's Bay Company. Letters to the Hudson's Bay Company from Vancouver Island. A/C/20/Vi/2A.

Hudson's Bay Company. "Fort Victoria Correspondence Outward to the Hudson's Bay Company." A/C/Vi2.

Imbert Orchard Oral History Collection. Interview with Annie York. Tape 678:1-2.

Indian Reserve Commission. GR 0494. Micro B-1391.

Jenness, Diamond. "The Saanich Indians of Vancouver Island." Unpublished manuscript.

McKenna-McBride Royal Commission. Transcript of Evidence. GR 1995. Micro B1454.

Maynard, Richard. Photographic Collection. PN 6810.

O'Reilly Family Papers. MS 412.

Premier's Papers. GR 441.

Provincial Game Warden. GR 446.

Union of British Columbia Indian Chiefs. Transcripts of evidence taken at hearings of the Royal Commission on Indian Affairs in British Columbia, 1913-1916. Typescript, 1914-1915. MS 1056.

Vancouver Island, Colony of. Blue Books of the Colony of Vancouver Island.

Vancouver Island, Colony of. Letters to the Hudson's Bay Company. A/C/20/Vi2A.

Yale Family Fonds. MS 0182.

British Columbia Indian Language Project, Fieldnotes, 1971-77. Victoria.

Interviews with Felicity Walkus, Agnes Edgar, and Orden Mack by Randy Bouchard and Dorothy Kennedy.

Copy of Letter to the Secretary of the United Society for the Propagation of the Gospel, from Victoria, June 6, 1862, original in Rhodes House Library, Oxford, vol. E 10, p. 2208.

Catholic Diocese of Vancouver Island Archives. Victoria. "Registre de baptîmes."

Chilliwack Archives. Chilliwack, BC.

K.C. Wells Collection. Add Mss. 1. File 584.

"The Story of the Conversion and Subsequent Experiences of Captain John as Narrated by Himself," and transcribed by Rev. Barraclough.

Coqualeetza Resource Centre. Sardis, BC.

Interview with Ernest Pearson, 1976, tape 1, 971.hop/1/1.

Department of Indian and Northern Affairs, Treaty and Historical Research Office. Ottawa.

Indian Affairs Branch, Department of Citizenship and Immigration. Indian Superintendent's Conference, British Columbia and Yukon Region, January 16-20, 1956. File U-24.

Department of Indian and Northern Affairs, Central Registry. Ottawa.

File 901/21-2, vol. 3.

Esquimalt Municipal Archives. Esquimalt, BC.

Oral History Project. Joyce Albany Interview, August 17, 1990. File 990.16.1.

Hudson's Bay Company Archives. Winnipeg.

Fort Chilcotin Post Journal. B.37/a/2.

Fort Alexandria Post Journal. B.5/a/11.

Fort Victoria Post Records. B.226.

Library and Archives Canada. Ottawa.

Clah, Arthur Wellington. Papers. MG 40 F11, Micro A1711.

Buckley, Charles S. Papers. LAC MG24 H43.

Church Missionary Society Records. Micro C2154.

Department of Citizenship and Immigration. RG 26.

Department of Fisheries and Oceans. RG 23.

Department of Indian Affairs. British Columbia Superintendency, Correspondence, 1894-1905. RG 10.

Department of the Interior. RG 88.

Department of National Health and Welfare. RG 29.

Library and Archives Canada. Vancouver Regional Repository.

Department of Indian Affairs. RG 10.

Lutz, John.

Field Notes in possession of the author.

Alphonse, Joe. Director of Government Services for the Tsilhqot'in National Government. Interviewed at the Tsilhqot'in National Government Office, August 24, 2000.

Beck, Cameron. Economic Development Officer, Carrier Chilcotin Tribal Council. Interviewed August 30, 1999.

Birchwater, Sage. Interviewed at his home at Tatlayoko Lake, BC, September 2, 2000.

Charleyboy, Ervin. Interviewed at Tsi Del Del (Redstone) Band Office, September 1, 1999.

Charleyboy, Orrey. Interviewed at Tshilqot'in National Government Office, September 1999.

Sill, Chief Cassidy of the Ulkatcho Band. Interviewed by John Lutz, at Toosey, August 31, 1999.

Lulua, Patrick. Interviewed at Toosey, August 31, 1999.

Sam, Robert. Interviewed at Songhees Band Office, 2000.

Sam, Sammy. Interviewed at Songhees Bighouse, 2000.

Solomon, Gilbert. Interviewed at the Nemiah Band Office, August 2000.

Solomon, Henry. Interviewed at his home in Nemiah, September 5, 1999.

Stump, Leslie, chief at Tl'etinqox-t'in (Anaham). Interviewed at the Anaham Band Office, August 31, 2001.

Wise, Don. Interviewed at the Tsilhqot'in National Government Office, September 1999.

Public Record Office. London, UK.

Colonial Office. Original Correspondence, Vancouver Island, 1846-67, 305.

Royal British Columbia Museum. Victoria.

Photographic Archives. PN 8927.

Simon Fraser University Archives. Burnaby, B.C.

Stanbury, W.T. "BC Indians Living Off Reserve: Some Economic Aspects." Speech to the Union of BC Indian Chiefs, November 8, 1972.

Stanbury, W.T. "The Social and Economic Conditions of Indian Families in British Columbia." Paper prepared for the British Columbia Family and Children's Law Commission, Simon Fraser University, November 1974.

Stó:lō Nation Archives. Sardis, B.C.

Chisholm, Brian, and Toshio Nakamura. "Prehistoric Diet at DgRl 5 (Esilao Village) and DjRi 46." Paper prepared for Stó:lō Nation. August 9, 1994.

Ware, Reuben, and Albert Phillip. "Stalo History Field Notes." Interviews with Richard Malloway, Susan Peters, Andy Commodor, Burns Mussell, and Amelia Douglas, n.d.

Oral History Collection.

Campo, Pat. Interviewed by Sarah Eustace, November 20, 1997; December 15, 1997; February 2, 1998.

Charlie, Jimmie, and Dean Louie. Interviewed by Sarah Eustace and Keith Carlson, December 8, 1997.

George, Rosaline. Interviewed by Sarah Eustace, November 18, 1997.

Malloway, Sweetie. Interviewed by Sarah Eustace, November 14, 1997.

Nelson, Ed. Interviewed by Sarah Eustace, November 12, 1997.

Peters, Chief Peter D. Interviewed by Larry Commodore, July 21, 1985.

Victor, Aggie. Interviewed by Sarah Eustace, November 13, 1997.

Ethnohistory Field School Interviews

Gutierrez, Tilly, and Al Gutierrez. Interviewed by Liam Haggarty and Heather Watson, May 26, 2005.

Joe, Herb. Interviewed by Liam Haggarty and Heather Watson, May 20, 2005.

Kelly, Doug. Interviewed by Liam Haggarty and Heather Watson at the Soowahlie Band Office, May 27, 2005.

Leon, Dennis. Interviewed by Liam Haggarty and Heather Watson, May 25, 2005.

Peters, Rena, and Joanne Jefferson. Interviewed by Liam Haggarty and Heather Watson, May 24, 2005.

United Church of Canada Archives. Toronto.

A.B. Sutherland Papers. Incoming Correspondence of the General Secretary, Foreign Department, Missionary Society, Methodist Church. 78.092c.

University of British Columbia, Special Collections. Vancouver.

J.H. Todd and Sons Business Records, boxes 2-6.

R.L. Reid Papers, box 4, file 9.

University of Victoria, Special Collections (Coast under Stress Fond). Victoria.

Clifton, Helen. Interviewed by John Lutz, June 9, 2004. Copy at the Gitga'at Band Office, Hartley Bay.

Dick, Adam, and Kim Recalma Clutesi. Interviewed by John Lutz, October 23, 2001.

Dick, Adam, and Daisy Sewid-Smith. Interviewed by John Lutz, October 18, 2003.

Dick, Art. Interviewed by Byron Plant and Chris Cook III, July 6, 2003. Copy at the Namgis Band Office, Alert Bay.

Jolliffe, George "Porgie." Interviewed by Chris Cook III at Alert Bay, July 6, 2003. Copy at the Namgis Band Office, Alert Bay.

Newman, Edwin. Interviewed by Byron Plant and Chris Cook III at the Namgis Band Office, Alert Bay, July 6, 2003.

Wasden, Billy. Interviewed by John Lutz, Byron Plant, and Chris Cook III, May 19, 2003. Copy at Namgis Band Office, Alert Bay.

University of Washington, Special Collections. Seattle.
   Melville Jacobs Collection.
Vancouver City Archives. Vancouver.
   Bell-Irving Papers. Mss 485.
Victoria Police Archives. Victoria.
   Charge Book, 1877-08-08 to 1878-11-12
   Gaol Charge Books, October 1876-April 1878.
Wellcome Institute, London.
   Arthur Wellington Clah Papers. MS American 140.
Washington State Library, Olympia.
   Mary Bourque, MS 283.
Yukon Archives. Whitehorse.
   Transcript of Yukon Women's Project Sound Recording,
      1974. File 13-5.

Court Documents

Court of Appeal for British Columbia. *Haida Nation* v. *BC
   and Weyerhaeuser,* 2002 BCCA 462, August 19, 2002.
   Full transcript at http://www.courts.gov.bc.ca/jdb-txt/
   ca/02/04/2002bcca0462.htm.
Supreme Court of Canada. D*elgamuukw* v. *The Queen,* 1997.
Supreme Court of British Columbia. Songhees and Esquimalt
   bands, "Statement of Claim," August 23, 2001.

Newspapers/Periodicals

Columbian (Olympia, Washington Territory)
Indian Missionary Record
Daily News (New Westminster)
Columbian (New Westminster)
Register (Port Townsend)
Daily Province (Vancouver)
Vancouver News Advertiser
Vancouver Sun
British Colonist (also *Daily British Colonist* and *Colonist*)
   (Victoria).
Victoria Daily Standard
Victoria Times Colonist
Gazette (also *Weekly Victoria Gazette* and *Daily Gazette*).
Victoria Times
Williams Lake Tribune

Published Sources

Abel, Kerry M., and Jean Friesen. *Aboriginal Resource Use in
   Canada: Historical and Legal Aspects.* Winnipeg: University of Manitoba Press, 1991.

Adams, John. *Old Square Toes and His Lady: The Life of James
   and Amelia Douglas.* Victoria: Horsdal and Shubert, 2001.
Albers, Patricia C. "From Legend to Land to Labor: Changing Perspectives on Native American Work." In *Native
   Americans and Wage Labor,* ed. Alice Littlefield and
   Martha C. Knack, 245-73. Norman: University of Okla-
   homa Press, 1996.
Alexander R.H., "Reminiscences of the Early Days of British
   Columbia, Address to the Canadian Club of Vancou-
   ver," *Proceedings of the Canadian Club of Vancouver 1906-
   1911.* Vancouver: Canadian Club of Vancouver, 1911.
Ames, Michael M. *Cannibal Tours and Glass Boxes: The An-
   thropology of Museums.* Vancouver: UBC Press, 1992.
–. "Fountain in a Modern Economy." BA thesis, University
   of British Columbia, 1956.
Anderson, Alexander C. *Hand Book and Map to the Gold
   Region of Fraser's and Thompson Rivers.* San Francisco:
   J.J. Le Court, 1858.
–. "Notes on the Indian Tribes of British North America and
   the Northwest Coast." *Historical Magazine* 7 (1863):
   73-81.
Anderson, Karen. *Chain Her by One Foot: The Subjugation of
   Native Women in Seventeenth-Century New France.* New
   York: Routledge, 1993.
Anderson, Kay. *Vancouver's Chinatown: Racial Discourse in
   Canada, 1875-1980.* Montreal and Kingston: McGill-
   Queen's University Press, 1991.
Anderson, Srin. "Canada's Squalid Secret." *Globe and Mail,*
   October 12, 1998, A1.
Anonymous. "Founding of Fort Victoria." *The Beaver.* March
   1943, 3-9.
–. "A New Vancouver Journal." *Washington Historical Quar-
   terly* 6 (1915): 129-37, 215-24, 301-8, 51-68.
Appadurai, Arjun. *The Social Life of Things: Commodities in
   Cultural Perspective.* Cambridge: Cambridge University
   Press, 1986.
Armstrong, Robin P. *Geographical Patterns of Socio-Economic
   Well-Being of First Nations Communities in Canada.*
   Agriculture and Rural Working Paper Series no. 46.
   Ottawa: Statistics Canada Agriculture Division, 2001.
Assu, Harry, with Joy Inglis. *Assu of Cape Mudge: Recollections
   of a Coastal Indian Chief.* Vancouver: UBC Press, 1989.
Avison, W.R. "Summary of Health Consequences of Unem-
   ployment." Paper prepared for the National Forum on
   Health. Ottawa: Health Canada, 1999.

Aziz, Salim Akhtar. "Selected Aspects of Cultural Change among Amerindians: A Case Study of Southeast Vancouver Island." MA thesis, University of Victoria, 1970.

Babcock, Barbara. "Arrange Me into Disorder." In *Rite, Drama, Festival, Spectacle: Rehearsals toward a Theory of Cultural Performance*, ed. Ron MacAloon: 102-28. Philadelphia: Institute for the Study of Human Issues, 1984.

Baillargeon, Morgan, and Leslie Tepper, eds. *Legends of Our Times: Native Cowboy Life*. Vancouver: UBC Press, 1998.

Baker, Simon. *Khot-La-Cha: The Autobiography of Simon Baker*. Comp. and ed. Verna J. Kirkness. Vancouver: Douglas and McIntyre, 1994.

Bakhtin, Mikhail. *The Dialogic Imagination: Four Essays*. Ed. Michael Holquist. Trans. Caryl Emmerson and Michael Holquist. Austin: University of Texas Press, 1981.

Bancroft, H.H. *History of British Columbia, 1792-1887*. San Francisco: The History Company, 1887.

Barman, Jean. *The West beyond the West: A History of British Columbia*. Toronto: University of Toronto Press, 1991.

Barnett, Homer. *The Coast Salish of British Columbia*. Eugene: University of Oregon Press, 1955.

–. "Culture Element Distributions: Gulf of Georgia Salish." *Anthropological Records* 1, 5 (1939): 221-95.

–. "The Nature of the Potlatch." In *Indians of the North Pacific Coast*, ed. Tom McFeat, 81-91. Toronto: McClelland and Stewart, 1966.

Barrett-Lennard, Capt. C.E. *Travels in British Columbia: With the Narrative of a Yacht Voyage Round Vancouver's Island*. London: Hurst and Blackett, 1862.

Barry, J. Neilson. "Broughton's Reconnaissance of the San Juan Islands in 1792." *Washington Historical Quarterly* 21 (1930): 55-60.

Baskerville, Peter A. *Beyond the Island: An Illustrated History of Victoria*. Burlington, ON: Windsor Publications, 1986.

Baskerville, Peter, and Eric Sager. *The 1881 Canadian Census: Vancouver Island*. Victoria: Public History Group, 1990.

Basso, Keith. *Wisdom Sits in Places: Landscape and Language among the Western Apache*. Albuquerque: University of New Mexico Press, 1996.

Baugh, Timothy, and Jonathon Ericson, eds. *Prehistoric Exchange Systems in North America*. New York: Plenum, 1994.

Beckett, Jeremy. *Torres Strait Islanders: Custom and Colonialism*. Cambridge: Cambridge University Press, 1987.

Beckwith, Brenda. "'The Queen Root of This Clime': Ethnoecological Investigations of Blue Camas (Camassia leichtlinii, C. quamash; Liliaceae) and Its Landscapes on Southern Vancouver Island, British Columbia." PhD diss., Department of Biology, University of Victoria, 2004.

Beeson, E. *Dunlevy, from the Diaries of Alex P. McInnes*. St'at'imc, BC: St'at'imc Publishers, 1971.

Begbie, Matthew Baillie. "Journey into the Interior of British Columbia." *Journal of the Royal Geographical Society* 31 (1861): 237-48.

Belshaw, John. "Numbers from Brobdingnag: Confronting the Problem of Pre-Contact Population Figures in British Columbia." Paper presented to the Canadian Historical Association Meeting, Quebec City, May 2001.

Bennett, Marilyn. *Indian Fishing and Its Cultural Importance in the Fraser River System*. Vancouver: BC Union of Indian Chiefs and Fisheries Canada, ca. 1974.

Bergen, Myrtle. *Tough Timber: The Loggers of British Columbia – Their Story*. Toronto: Progress, 1966; reprinted Vancouver: Elgin, 1979.

Bergland, Renée. *The National Uncanny: Indian Ghosts and American Subjects*. Hanover, NH: University of New England Press, 2000.

Berkhofer, Robert Jr. *The White Man's Indian: Images of the North American Indian from Columbus to the Present*. New York: Vintage, 1978.

Bernier, Rachel. *The Dimensions of Wage Inequality among Aboriginal Peoples*. Ottawa: Statistics Canada, December 1997. Cat. 11F0019MPE, no. 109.

Bhabha, Homi. "Frontlines/Borderposts." In *Displacements: Cultural Identities in Question*, ed. Angelika Bammer, 269-73. Bloomington: Indiana University Press, 1994.

–. *The Location of Culture*. London, New York: Routledge, 1994.

–. "Signs Taken for Wonders: Questions of Ambivalence and Authority under a Tree outside Delhi, May 1817." In *Europe and Its Others: Proceedings of the Essex Conference of the Sociology of Literature*, ed. Francis Barker, Peter Hulme, Margaret Iverson, and Diana Loxley, 89-106. Colchester: University of Essex, 1985.

Birchwater, Sage. *Chiwid*. Vancouver: New Star, 1995.

–. "Land Deal Signed at Redstone." *Williams Lake Tribune*, April 14, 2005.

–. *Ulkatcho Stories of the Grease Trail: Anahim Lake, Bella Coola, Quesnel –Told by Ulkatcho and Nuxalk Elders,* ed. Leona Toney. Anahim Lake, BC: Ulkatcho Cultural Curriculum Development Committee, 1993.

—. *'Ulkatchot'en: The People of Ulkatcho*. Anahim Lake, BC: Ulkatcho Cultural Curriculum Development Committee, 1991.

Blackman, Margaret B. *During My Time: Florence Edenshaw Davidson, A Haida Woman*. Vancouver: Douglas and McIntyre, 1982.

Blakey-Smith, Dorothy. *Texts, Facts and Femininity: Exploring the Relations of Ruling*. London: Routledge and Kegan Paul, 1990.

—, ed. *The Reminiscences of Doctor John Sebastian Helmcken*. By J.S. Helmcken. Vancouver: UBC Press, 1975.

Boas, Franz. "Chinook Songs." *Journal of American Folk-Lore* 6 (1888): 220-26.

—. *Contributions to the Ethnology of the Kwakiutl*. New York: Columbia University Press, 1925.

—. *The Ethnography of Franz Boas: Letters and Diaries of Franz Boas Written on the Northwest Coast from 1886-1931*. Ed. Ronald Rohner. Trans. Hedy Parker. Chicago: University of Chicago Press, 1969.

—. *Indian Myths & Legends from the North Pacific Coast of America: A Translation of Franz Boas' 1895 Edition of Indianische Sagen von der Nord-Pacifischen Kuste Amerika*. Ed. Randy Bouchard and Dorothy Kennedy. Trans. Dietrich Bertz. Vancouver: Talonbooks, 2002.

—. "The Lku'ñgen." *Report of the British Association for the Advancement of Science* 59 (1890): 563-82.

Bolduc, Jean B.Z. *Mission of the Columbia*. Ed. and trans. Edward J. Kowrich. Fairfield, WA: Ye Galleon Press, 1979 (reprint of 1843 edition).

Bolt, Clarence. *Thomas Crosby and the Tsimshian: Small Shoes for Feet Too Large*. Vancouver: UBC Press, 1992.

Bostock, H.S. "Pack Horse Tracks – Recollections of a Geologist's Life in British Columbia and the Yukon, 1924-1954," *Geological Survey of Canada Open File Report 650*. Ottawa: Geological Survey of Canada, 13-27.

Bostwick, Colleen. "Oral Histories: Theresa Jeffries." *Labour History* 2, 3 (1980): 8-15.

Bouchard, Gérard. "Marginality, Co-Integration and Change: Social History as Critical Exercise." *Journal of the Canadian Historical Association* New Series 8 (1997): 19-38.

—. *Quelques arpents d'Amérique: Population, économie, famille au Saguenay, 1838-1971*. Montreal: Boréal, 1996.

Bowen, Lynne. *Boss Whistle: The Coal Miners of Vancouver Island Remember*. Lantzville, BC: Oolichan, 1982.

Bowsfield, Hartwell, ed. *Fort Victoria Letters: 1846-1851*. Winnipeg, Hudson's Bay Record Society, 1979.

Boxberger, Daniel L. *To Fish in Common: the Ethnohistory of Lummi Salmon Fishing*. Lincoln: University of Nebraska Press, 1989.

—. *San Juan Island National Historical Park: Cultural Affiliation Study*. Seattle: National Park Service, n.d.

Boyd, Laura. *My Home Forever*. Quesnel, BC: Developing Our Resources Curriculum Project, Quesnel School District, 1989.

Boyd, Robert T. "Demographic History, 1774-1874." In *Handbook of North American Indians*, vol. 7, ed. Wayne Suttles, 135-48. Washington: Smithsonian, 1990.

—. *Indians, Fire, and the Land in the Pacific Northwest*. Corvalis: Oregon State University, 1999.

—. "The Pacific Northwest Measles Epidemic of 1847-1848." *Oregon Historical Quarterly* 95 (1994): 6-47.

Bracken, Christopher. *The Potlatch Papers: A Colonial Case History*. Chicago: University of Chicago Press, 1997.

Brink, J.H. Van Den. *The Haida Indians: Cultural Change Mainly between 1876-1970*. Leiden, the Netherlands: E.J. Brill, 1974.

British Columbia. Commission on Resources and Environment. *Cariboo-Chilcotin Land Use Plan*. Victoria: British Columbia, 1994.

—. Department of Lands. *Bulletin, Land Series*. Victoria: British Columbia, Department of Lands, 1939.

—. Legislative Assembly. "Annual Report of the Minister of Labour." *BCSP*. Victoria: British Columbia, 1940-45.

—. Legislative Assembly. "Annual Report of the Minister of Mines." *BCSP*. Victoria: British Columbia, 1875-1924.

—. Legislative Assembly. "BC Fishery Commission Report." Testimony of F.L. Lord. *British Columbia Sessional Papers*. *BSCP*. Victoria: British Columbia, 1893.

—. Legislative Assembly. "Game Warden's Report." *BCSP*. Victoria: British Columbia, 1894-1927.

—. *Papers Connected with the Indian Land Question*. Victoria: R. Wolfenden, 1875. Reprinted 1987.

—. Legislative Assembly. "Report of the Government of British Columbia on the Subject of Indian Reserves." *BCSP*. Victoria: British Columbia, 1875.

—. Legislative Assembly. "Return to an address of the Legislative Assembly for ... all ... correspondence ... relative to attempts made for the arrest of Emia, a Chilcotin Indian." *BCSP.* Victoria: British Columbia, 1885.

–. *Statutes of British Columbia.* Victoria: British Columbia, 1888-1927.

–. Task Force on Crown Timber Disposal. *Crown Charges for Early Timber Rights: Royalties and Other Levies for Harvesting Rights on Timber Leases, Licenses and Berths in British Columbia.* Victoria: Information Division of the British Columbia Forest Service, 1974.

British Columbia, Crown Colony of. *The Laws of British Columbia.* Victoria: Crown Colony of British Columbia, 1865-88.

Brody, Hugh. *Indians on Skid Row.* Ottawa: Department of Indian Affairs and Northern Development, 1971.

–. *Maps and Dreams: Indians and the British Columbia Frontier.* London: Jill Norman and Hobhouse, 1982.

Brown, Robert. *Robert Brown and the Vancouver Island Exploring Expedition,* ed. John Hayman. Vancouver: UBC Press, 1989.

–. *The Races of Mankind: Being a Popular Description of the Characteristics, Manners and Customs of the Principal Varieties of the Human Family,* vol. 3. London: Cassell, Petter and Galpin, Belle Savage Works, 1873.

–. *Vancouver Island: Expedition, 1864.* Victoria: Colony of Vancouver Island, 1864.

–. "On the Vegetable Products Used by the North-West American Indians." *Transactions of the Botanical Society of Edinburgh* 27 (1868): 378-96.

Brumble, H. David III. *An Annotated Bibliography of American Indian and Eskimo Autobiographies.* Lincoln: University of Nebraska Press, 1981.

Buckley, Helen. *From Wooden Ploughs to Welfare: Why Indian Policy Failed in the Prairie Provinces.* Kingston and Montreal: McGill-Queen's University Press, 1992.

Burrows, James. "'A Much Needed Class of Labour': The Economy and Income of the Southern Interior Plateau Indians, 1897-1910." *BC Studies* 71 (1986): 27-46.

Busch, Briton Cooper. *The War against the Seals: A History of the North American Seal Fishery.* Montreal and Kingston: McGill-Queen's University Press, 1985.

Caglar, A.S. "Hyphenated Identities and the Limits of Culture." In *The Politics of Multiculturalism in the New Europe: Racism, Identity and Community,* ed. T. Modood and P. Werbner, 169-85. London: Zed, 1997.

Cail, Robert E. *Land, Man and the Law: The Disposal of Crown Lands in British Columbia, 1871-1913.* Vancouver: UBC Press, 1974.

Campbell, Kenneth. *Persistence and Change: A History of the Tsimsyen Nation.* Prince Rupert, BC: First Nations Education Council, 2005.

Campbell, Kyle. *American Indian Languages: The Historical Linguistics of Native America.* New York: Oxford University Press, 1997.

Canada. Department of Agriculture. *Census of Canada, Bulletins Nos. 5, 8, and 10.* Ottawa: Canada, 1892.

–. Department of Indian Affairs. *Census of Indians in Canada.* Ottawa: 1924-59.

–. Department of Indian Affairs and Northern Development. Corporate Services. Information Quality and Research Directorate. *Socio-Economic Indicators in Indian Reserves and Comparable Communities 1971-1991, Departmental Statistics.* Ottawa: Department of Indian Affairs and Northern Development, 1997. Catalogue no. R32-181/1991E.

–. Dominion Bureau of Statistics. Fur Production. Ottawa: Canada, 1919-61.

–. House of Commons. *Debates.* Ottawa: Canada, 1897.

–. House of Commons. Special Committees of the Senate and House of Commons to Inquire into the Claims of the Allied Indian Tribes of British Columbia ... Session 1926-27. *Proceedings, Reports and Evidence.* Ottawa: F.A. Ackland, 1927.

–. Legislative Assembly. "Annual Reports of the Department of Fisheries." *Canada Sessional Papers.* Ottawa: Canada, 1895-1945.

–. Legislative Assembly. "Department of Indian Affairs Annual Reports" (DIAR). *Canada Sessional Papers.* Ottawa: Canada, 1873-1972.

–. "Report of the Royal Commission on Chinese Immigration in 1885." Ottawa: Printed by Order of the Commission, 1885.

–. Statistics Canada. *Census of Canada.* Ottawa: Canada, 1871, 1881, 1891, 1901, 1911, 1921, 1931, 1941, 1951, 1961, 1971.

–. Statistics Canada. *Social Security: National Programs, a Review for the Period 1946-1975,* December 1976. 4-2003-501 pp. 690-91. Ottawa: Canada, 1976.

–. *Statutes of Canada, vols. 1-2.* Ottawa: Canada, 1911.

Canadian Broadcasting Corporation. *The Way of the Indian*. Radio Series, 1961. Toronto: CBC, 1969.

Canclini, N.G. *Hybrid Cultures: Strategies for Entering and Leaving Modernity*. Minneapolis: University of Minnesota Press, 1995.

Capital Region Planning Board of British Columbia. *Indian Communities and Land Use Planning*. Victoria: Capital Region Planning Board, 1968.

Carlson, Keith Thor. "The Power of Place, the Problem of Time: A Study of History and Aboriginal Collective Identity." PhD diss., University of British Columbia, 2003.

–. "Stó:lō People and the Development of the BC Wage Labour Economy." In *You Are Asked to Witness: The Stó:lō in Canada's Pacific Coast History*, ed. Keith Thor Carlson, 109-24. Chilliwack, BC: Stó:lō Heritage Trust, 1997.

–, ed. *A Stó:lō-Coast Salish Historical Atlas*. Vancouver: Douglas and McIntyre/University of Washington Press/Stó:lō Heritage Trust, 2001.

–. "Stó:lō Exchange Dynamics." *Native Studies Review* 11, 1 (1996): 5-47.

–. *You Are Asked to Witness: The Stó:lō in Canada's Pacific Coast History*. Chilliwack, BC: Stó:lō Heritage Trust, 1997.

Carlson, Roy. "Trade and Exchange in Prehistoric British Columbia." In *Prehistoric Exchange Systems in North America*, ed. Timothy Baugh and Jonathon Ericson, 249-361. New York: Plenum, 1994.

Carstens, Peter. *The Queen's People: A Study of Hegemony, Coercion and Accommodation among the Okanagan of Canada*. Toronto: University of Toronto Press, 1991.

Carter, Sarah. *Lost Harvests: Prairie Indian Reserve Farmers and Government Policy*. Montreal and Kingston: McGill-Queen's University Press, 1990.

Cassidy, Maureen. *From Mountain to Mountain: A History of the Gitksan Village of Ans'payaxw*. Kispiox: Ans'payaxw School Society, 1984.

Centennial Committee. *History and Legends of the Chilcotin*. Williams Lake: Cariboo Press, 1957.

Certeau, Michel de. *The Practice of Everyday Life*. Trans. Stephen Randall. Berkeley: University of California Press, 1988.

Charleyboy, Orrey. *Tsi Del Del: Redstone*. Williams Lake, BC: Chilcotin Language Committee, 1991.

Chiaro Productions Inc. *A Forgotten Legacy: Spirit of Reclamation*. Produced and directed by Martin de Valk. Victoria: Chiaro Productions, 2002.

Chittenden, Newton H. *Travels in British Columbia*. Victoria: S.n., 1882. Reprinted Vancouver: Gordon Soules, 1984.

Chow, R. "Where Have All the Natives Gone?" In *Displacements: Cultural Identities in Question*, ed. A Bammer, 125-51. Bloomington and Indianapolis: Indiana University Press, 1994.

Christophers, Brett. *Positioning the Missionary*. Vancouver: UBC Press, 2000.

Clark, Ella E. "George Gibbs' Account of Indian Mythology in Oregon and Washington Territory." *Oregon Historical Quarterly* 56, 4 (1955): 293-325.

Clark, Jerry L. "Thus Spoke Chief Seattle: The Story of an Undocumented Speech." *Prologue* 17, 1 (1985): 58-63.

Clatworthy, Stewart, Jeremy Hull, and Neil Loughran. "Employment of the Aboriginal Labour Force." *In Economy: Project Area 3*. Ottawa: Four Directions Consulting Group for the Royal Commission on Aboriginal Peoples, 1995.

Clayton, Daniel. "Geographies of the Lower Skeena." *BC Studies* 94 (1992): 29-59.

Claxton, Earl Jr., and John Elliot Sr. *Reef Net Technology of the Saltwater People*. Saanich, BC: Saanich Indian School Board, 1994.

Clifford, James. *The Predicament of Culture*. Cambridge, MA: Harvard University Press, 1988.

Clifford, James, and George E. Marcus. *Writing Culture: The Poetics and Politics of Ethnography*. Berkeley: University of California Press, 1986.

Coates, Kenneth. *Best Left as Indians: Native-White Relations in the Yukon Territory, 1840-1973*. Montreal and Kingston: McGill-Queen's University Press, 1991.

Codere, Helen. *Fighting with Property: A Study of Kwakiutl Potlatching and Warfare, 1792-1930*. Seattle: University of Washington Press, 1972.

Cole, Douglas, and Ira Chaikin. *An Iron Hand upon the People: The Law against the Potlatch on the Northwest Coast*. Vancouver: Douglas and McIntyre, 1990.

Cole, Douglas, and David Darling. "History of the Early Period." In *Handbook of North American Indians*, vol. 7, ed. Wayne Suttles, 119-34. Washington: Smithsonian, 1990.

Collins, June. "John Fornsby: The Personal Document of a Coast Salish Indian." In *Indians of the Urban Northwest*, ed. Marian Smith, 287-341. New York: Columbia University Press, 1949.

Collison, W.H. *In the Wake of the War Canoe*. London: Seeley, Service and Co., 1915.

Comaroff, Jean, and John Comaroff. *Of Revolution and Revelation: Christianity, Colonialism, and Consciousness in South Africa*. Chicago: University of Chicago Press, 1991.

–. "Through the Looking-Glass: Colonial Encounters of the First Kind." *Journal of Historical Sociology* 1, 1 (1988): 6-32.

Cook, James. *The Voyage of the Resolution and Discovery, 1776-1780*, vol. 1, ed. J.C. Beaglehole. Cambridge: Hakluyt Society, 1967.

Cook, Warren L. *Flood Tide of Empire*. New Haven: Yale University Press, 1973.

Cooke, Katie. *Images of Indians Held by Non-Indians: A Review of Current Canadian Research*. Ottawa: Research Branch, Department of Indian Affairs and Northern Development, 1984.

Coull, Cheryl. *A Traveller's Guide to Aboriginal British Columbia*. Vancouver: Whitecap, 1996.

Cox, Ross. *Adventures on the Columbia River*. London: Henry Colburn and Bentley, 1832.

Cox, Thomas. *Mills and Markets: A History of the Pacific Coast Lumber Industry to 1900*. Seattle: University of Washington Press, 1974.

Cracroft, Sophia. *Lady Franklin Visits the Pacific Northwest: February to April 1861 and April to July 1870*. Victoria: Provincial Archives of British Columbia, 1974.

Crockford, Cairn. "Changing Economic Activities of the Nuu-chah-nulth of Vancouver Island, 1840-1920." BA honours thesis, University of Victoria, 1991.

–. "Fort Victoria Journals." Paper presented to Columbia Department Fur Trade Conference, Victoria, British Columbia, October 1-3, 1993.

–. "Nuu-Chah-Nulth Labour Relations in the Pelagic Sealing Industry, 1868-1911." MA thesis, University of Victoria, 1996.

Crooks, Drew W. "Murder at Butler Cove: The Death of Tsus-sy-uch and Its Violent Consequences." *Occurrences* 14, 4 (1996/97): 3-12.

Crosby, Alfred. *The Columbian Exchange: Biological and Cultural Consequences of 1492*. Westport, CT: Greenwood Press, 1972.

–. *Ecological Imperialism: The Biological Expansion of Europe, 900-1900*. Cambridge: Cambridge University Press, 1986.

Crosby, Thomas. *Among the An-ko-me-nums or Flathead Tribes of Indians of the Pacific Coast*. Toronto: William Briggs, 1907.

Crossby, P.A. *Lovell's Gazetteer of British North America*. Montreal: J. Lovell, 1873.

Cruikshank, Julie, with Angela Sidney, Kitty Smith, and Annie Ned. *Life Lived Like a Story*. Vancouver: UBC Press, 1990.

Culhane, Dara. *The Pleasure of the Crown: Anthropology, Law, and First Nations*. Vancouver: Talonbooks, 1998.

Cwynar, C. "Fire and the Forest History of the North Cascade Range." *Ecology* 68, 4 (1987): 791-802.

Dawkins, H. "Paul Kane and the Eye of Power: Racism in Canadian Art History." *Vanguard* 15, 4: (1986): S.p.

Dawson, George M. *Journals of George M. Dawson*. 2 vols., ed. Douglas Cole and Bradley Lockner. Vancouver: UBC Press, 1989.

–. "Notes and Observations on the Kwakiool People of Vancouver Island and Adjacent Coasts Made during the Summer of 1885." *Transactions of the Royal Society of Canada*. Sec. 2 (1887).

Deans, James. "Extract from the Traditional History of Vancouver Island." *Victoria Daily Times*, December 22, 1900, 3.

Dening, Greg. *Performances*. Chicago: University of Chicago Press, 1996.

De Laguna, Frederica. *Under Mount Saint Elias: The History and Culture of the Yakutat Tlingit*. Washington: Smithsonian, 1972.

Desai I.D., and M. Lee. "Nutritional Status of British Columbia Indians: Biochemical Studies at Ahousat and Anaham Reserves." *Canadian Journal of Public Health* 62 (1971): 526-36.

De Smet, Father P.J. *Oregon Missions and Travels over the Rocky Mountains in 1845-46*. New York: Edward Dunigan, 1847.

Densmore, Frances. *Music of the Indians of British Columbia*. New York: Da Capo Press, 1972.

Deutsch, Sarah. "Landscape of Enclaves: Race Relations in the American West." In *Under an Open Sky: Rethinking America's Western Past*, ed. W. Cronon, Jay Gitlin, and George Miles, 110-31. New York: Norton, 1992.

Dibbs, Ruth, and Tracey Leesti. *Survey of Labour and Income Dynamics: Visible Minorities and Aboriginal Peoples*. Ottawa: Statistics Canada Interdepartmental Working

Group on Employment Equity Data. Catalogue no. 95-08, March 1995.

Dinwoodie, David. "Reserve Memories: Historical Consciousness on the Nemiah Valley Indian Reserve." PhD diss., University of Chicago, 1996.

–. *Reserve Memories: The Power of the Past in a Chilcotin Community.* Lincoln: University of Nebraska Press, 2002.

Dippie, Brian. *The Vanishing American: White Attitudes and US Indian Policy.* Middletown, CT: Wesleyan University Press, 1982.

Disa, J.J., J. Vossoughi, and N.H. Goldberg. "A Comparison of Obsidian and Surgical Steel Scalpel Wound-Healing in Rats." *Plastic and Reconstructive Surgery* 92, 5 (1993): 884-87.

Donald, Leland. *Aboriginal Slavery on the Northwest Coast of North America.* Berkeley: University of California Press, 1997.

Downey-Bartlett, Laura B. *Chinook-English Songs.* Portland, OR: Kubli Miller, 1914.

Duff, Wilson. "The Fort Victoria Treaties." *BC Studies* 3 (1969): 3-57.

–. *The Indian History of British Columbia: The Impact of the White Man.* Victoria: Provincial Museum, 1964.

Dunn, John. *History of the Oregon Territory and British North American Fur Trade ...* London: Edwards and Hughes, 1844.

Dunn, Sam. "Managing Multiple Narratives: Alexander Mackenzie at Nuxalk Territory, 1793." *BC Historical News* 32, 3 (1999): 16-23.

Dyck, Noel. *What Is the Indian "Problem": Tutelage and Resistance in Canadian Indian Administration.* St. John's: Institute of Social and Economic Research, 1991.

Easton, N. Alexander. "The Archaeology of Straits Salish Reef Netting: Past and Future Research Strategies." *Northwest Anthropological Research Notes* 24, 2 (1990): 161-77.

Edgar, J.D. "A Potlatch among Our West Coast Indians." *Canadian Monthly and National Review* 6, 2 (1874): 93-99.

Eells, Myron. *The Indians of Puget Sound: The Notebooks of Myron Eells*, ed. George Pierre Castile. Seattle: University of Washington Press, 1985.

Elliot, Dave. *Saltwater People*, ed. Janet Poth. Saanich, BC: School District 63, 1983.

Elmendorf, William W. *Twana Narratives: Native Historical Accounts of a Coast Salish Culture.* Seattle: University of Washington Press, 1993.

Elsey, Al. *Caribou Hunt in Tweedsmuir at Fenton, BC; Anahim Lake Stampede ...* Videorecording. S.l., ca. 1956.

–. *Grease: Ooligan Oil Production on the Bella Coola River.* Videorecording. S.l. 1964.

Engels, Frederick. *Karl Marx and Frederick Engels.* Moscow: Progress, 1962.

Farrand, Livingstone. *Traditions of the Chilcotin Indians.* New York: S.n., 1900.

Fawcett, Edgar. *Some Reminiscences of Old Victoria.* Toronto: William Briggs, 1912.

Fields, D.B., and W.T. Stanbury. *The Economic Impact of the Public Sector upon the Indians of British Columbia.* Vancouver: UBC Press, 1973.

Fisher, Robin. *Contact and Conflict: Indian-European Relations in British Columbia, 1774-1890.* Vancouver: UBC Press, 1977. Reprinted 1992.

–. "An Exercise in Futility: The Joint Commission on Indian Land in British Columbia, 1875-1880." *Historical Papers* 10 (1975): 79-94.

–. "Joseph Trutch and the Indian Land Policy." In *British Columbia: Historical Readings*, ed. W.P. Ward and R.A.J. McDonald, 154-83. Vancouver: Douglas and McIntyre, 1981.

Fisher, Robin, and Hugh Johnstone, eds. *From Maps to Metaphors: The Pacific World of George Vancouver.* Vancouver: UBC Press, 1993.

Fiske, Jo-Anne. "Colonization and the Decline of Women's Status: The Tsimshian Case." *Feminist Studies* 17, 3 (1991): 509-35.

–. "Fishing Is Women's Business: Changing Economic Roles of Carrier Women and Men." In *Native People, Native Lands: Canadian Indians, Inuit and Métis*, ed. Bruce Alden Cox, 186-97. Ottawa: Carleton University Press, 1988.

Forbes, Charles. *Vancouver Island: Its Resources and Capabilities as a Colony.* Victoria: Colony of Vancouver Island, 1862.

Ford, Clellan S., ed. *Smoke from Their Fires: The Life of a Kwakiutl Chief.* Hamden, CN: Archon, 1968.

Foucault, Michel. *Discipline and Punish: The Birth of the Prison.* New York: Vintage, 1979.

Franchère, Gabriel. *Narrative of a Voyage to the Northwest Coast of America, in the Years 1811, 1812, 1813, and 1814, or, The First American Settlement on the Pacific*. Trans. and ed. by J.V. Huntington. New York: Redfield, 1854.

Francis, Daniel. *The Imaginary Indian: The Image of the Indian in Canadian Culture*. Vancouver: Arsenal Pulp Press, 1992.

French, Diana. *The Road Runs West: A Century along the Bella Coola/Chilcotin Road*. Madeira Park, BC: Harbour, 1996.

Friedlaender, M.J. *Economic Status of Native Indians in British Columbia Fisheries*. Technical Report Series PAC/T-75-25. Vancouver: Environment Canada, Fisheries Operations Branch, 1975.

Fuller, Frank. "Gilbert Joe." *Labour History* 2, 3 (1980): 16-19.

Furniss, Elizabeth. *The Burden of History: Colonialism and the Frontier Myth in a Rural Canadian Community*. Vancouver: UBC Press, 1999.

–. *Changing Ways: Southern Carrier History, 1793-1940*. Quesnel, BC: Quesnel School District, 1993.

–. "Pioneers, Progress and Myth of the Pioneer: The Landscape of Public History in British Columbia." *BC Studies* 115/16 (1997/98): 7-44.

Gaffen, Fred. *Forgotten Soldiers*. Penticton, BC: Theytus, 1985.

Galm, Jerry. "Prehistoric Trade and Exchange in the Interior Plateau of Northwestern America." In *Prehistoric Exchange Systems in North America*, ed. Timothy Baugh and Jonathon Ericson, 275-305. New York: Plenum, 1994.

Galois, Robert. "Colonial Encounters: The Worlds of Arthur Wellington Clah, 1855-1881." *BC Studies* 115/16 (1997-98): 104-47.

–. *Kwakwaka'wakw Settlements, 1775-1920: A Geographical Analysis and Gazetteer*. Vancouver: UBC Press, 1994.

Galois, Robert, and Cole Harris. "Recalibrating Society: The Population Geography of British Columbia in 1881." *Canadian Geographer* 38, 1 (1994): 37-53.

Galois, Robert, and Richard Mackie, "A Curious Currency." *The Midden* 22, 4-5 (1990): 1-3, 6-9.

Geddes, Gary. *Skookum Wawa: Writings of the Canadian Northwest*. Toronto: Oxford University Press, 1975.

Geertz, Clifford. "Thick Descriptions: Towards an Interpretive Theory of Culture." In *The Interpretation of Cultures: Selected Essays*. New York: Basic Books, 1973.

George, Earl Maquinna. *Living on the Edge: Nuu-Chah-Nulth History from an Ahousaht Chief's Perspective*. Victoria: Sono Nis, 2003.

Gibbs, Mifflin W. *Shadows and Light: An Autobiography*. New York: Arno Press, 1968.

Gill, John Kaye. *Gill's Dictionary of the Chinook Jargon, with Examples of Use in Conversation and Notes upon Tribes and Tongues*. 15th ed. Portland, OR: J.K. Gill, 1909.

Ginzburg, Carlo. "Microhistory: Two or Three Things That I Know about It." *Critical Inquiry* 20 (1993): 10-35.

Gladstone, Percy. "Native Indians and the Fishing Industry of British Columbia." *Canadian Journal of Economics and Political Science* 19 (1953): 20-34.

Glavin, Terry. *This Ragged Place*. Vancouver: New Star, 1996.

Glavin, Terry, and the People of Nemiah Valley. *Nemiah: The Unconquered Country*. Vancouver: New Star, 1992.

Glazebrook, G.P.T., ed. *The Hargrave Correspondence*. Toronto: Champlain Society, 1938.

Goldman, Irving. "The Alkatcho Carrier of British Columbia." In *Acculturation in Seven American Indian Tribes*, ed. R. Linton, 333-89. Gloucester, MA: Peter Smith, 1963.

Gonzalez, Ellice B. *Changing Economic Roles for Micmac Men and Women: An Ethnohistorical Analysis*. Ottawa: National Museums of Canada, 1981.

Gordon, Avery. *Ghostly Matters: Haunting and the Sociological Imagination*. Minneapolis: University of Minnesota Press, 1997.

Gordon, Daniel. *Mountain and Prairie: A Journey from Victoria to Winnipeg via Peace River*. Montreal: Dawson Bros., 1880.

Gosnell, R.E. "Bygone Days of British Columbia." *Daily Province* (Vancouver), November 14, 1908-19.

–. *Year Book of British Columbia and Manual of Provincial Information for 1887*. Victoria: R.E. Gosnell, 1911.

Gould, Ed. *Logging: British Columbia's Logging History*. North Vancouver: Hancock, 1975.

Grant, G.M. *Ocean to Ocean: Sir Sanford Fleming's Expedition through Canada in 1872*. Toronto: James Campbell and Son, 1873. Reprinted Toronto: Coles, 1970.

Gregg, R.J. "Local Lexical Items in the Sociodialectical Survey of Vancouver English." *Canadian Journal of Linguistics/La Revue Canadienne de Linguistique* 28, 1 (1983): 17-23.

Gregory, C.A. *Gifts and Commodities*. London: Academic Press, 1982.

Guest, Dennis. *The Emergence of Social Security in Canada*. Vancouver: UBC Press, 1985.

Guha, Ranajit. *Dominance without Hegemony: History and Power in Colonial India*. Cambridge, MA: Harvard University Press, 1997.

Gunther, Erna. "A Further Analysis of the First Salmon Ceremony." *University of Washington Publications in Anthropology* 2, 5 (1928): 129-73.

–. *Indian Life on the Northwest Coast of North America*. Chicago: University of Chicago Press, 1972.

–. *Klallam Ethnography*. Seattle: University of Washington Press, 1927.

Haegert, Dorothy. *Children of the First People*. Vancouver: Tillacum Library, 1983.

Haig-Brown, Roderick Langmere. *Timber*. London: Collins, 1946.

Hale, Horatio. "The 'Jargon' or Trade Language of Oregon." In *Ethnology and Philology*, ed. H. Hale, 635-50. 1846. Reprinted Ridgewood, NJ: Gregg Press, 1968.

Hall, John L. "Ethnic Tensions and Economics: Indian White Interaction in a British Columbia Ranching Community." *Canadian Journal of Anthropology* 1/2 (1980): 179-90.

Hall, Lizette. *The Carrier, My People*. S.l.: Lizette Hall, 1992.

Hall, Stuart. "Gramsci's Relevance for the Study of Race and Ethnicity." *Journal of Communication Inquiry* 10, 2 (1996): 123-27.

Halliday, W.M. *Potlatch and Totem: Recollections of an Indian Agent*. London and Toronto: J.M. Dent and Sons, 1935.

Hammond, Lorne. "Adulterers, Murderers, Orphans and Transvestites: A Look at the Periphery of Fur Trade Masculinity." Paper presented to the Columbia Department Fur Trade Conference, Victoria, 1993.

Harevan, Tamara. *Family Time, Industrial Time: The Relationship between Family and Work in a New England Industrial Community*. New York: Cambridge University Press, 1982.

Harkin, Michael. "Dialogues of History: Transformation and Change in Heiltsuk Culture." PhD diss., University of Chicago, 1988.

–. *The Heiltsuks: Dialogues of Culture and History on the Northwest Coast*. Lincoln: University of Nebraska Press, 1997.

Harmon, Alexandra. *Indians in the Making: Ethnic Relations and Indian Identities around Puget Sound*. Berkeley: University of California Press, 1998.

Harris, Barbara. "Klohowiam Mr. Smis: Context of Culture as a Factor in the Interpretation of a Chinook Jargon Text." *Anthropological Linguistics* 27, 3 (1985): 303-17.

Harris, Douglas C. *Fish, Law and Colonialism: The Legal Capture of Salmon in British Columbia*. Toronto: University of Toronto Press, 2001.

Harris, R. Cole. *Making Native Space: Colonialism, Resistance, and Reserves in British Columbia*. Vancouver: UBC Press, 2002.

–. *The Resettlement of British Columbia: Essays on Colonialism and Geographical Change*. Vancouver: UBC Press, 1997.

Harvey, A.A. *A Statistical Account of British Columbia*. Ottawa: G.E. Desbarats, 1867.

Hawthorn H.B., C.S. Belshaw, and S.M. Jamieson. *The Indians of British Columbia: A Study of Contemporary Social Adjustment*. Berkeley and Vancouver: University of California Press, and the University of British Columbia, 1958.

Hazlitt, William Carew. *British Columbia and Vancouver Island*. London: G. Routledge, 1858.

Hebda, Richard, Nancy J. Turner, Sage Birchwater, Michèle Kay, and the Ulkatcho Elders. *Ulkatcho Food and Medicine Plants*. Anahim Lake: Ulkatcho Indian Band, 1996.

Heckewelder, John. "Indian Tradition of the First Arrival of the Dutch at Manhattan Island, Now New York." In *Collections of the New York Historical Society*. 2nd set, 4 vols., 1:71-74. New York: I. Riley, 1841.

Hendrickson, James E., ed. *Journals of the Colonial Legislatures of the Colonies of Vancouver Island and British Columbia, 1851-1871*, vol. 5: *Journals of the Legislative Council of British Columbia, 1866-1871*. Victoria: Provincial Archives of British Columbia, 1980.

–. "Two Letters from Walter Colquhoun Grant." *BC Studies* 26 (1975): 3-15.

–. "Vancouver Island: Colonial Correspondence Despatches." Unpublished Manuscript.

Hesse-Wartegg, Ernst von. "A Visit to the Anglo Saxon Antipodes." Chapter 18 of *Curiosa aus der Neuen Welt, 1893*. Trans. John Maass. *BC Studies* 50 (1981): 29-38.

Hibben, T.N. *Guide to the Province of British Columbia for 1877-78*. Victoria: T.N. Hibben, 1877.

Hill-Tout, Charles. *The Salish People*, vol. 4, ed. Ralph Maud. Vancouver: Talonbooks, 1977.

Hobson, Richmond. *Nothing Too Good for a Cowboy*. Philadelphia: Lippincott, ca. 1955.

Honour, Hugh. *The European Vision of America*. Cleveland: Cleveland Museum of Art, 1975.

Howay, F.W. "The Dog's Hair Blankets of the Coast Salish." *Washington Historical Quarterly* 9, 2 (1918): 83-91.

Howay, F.W., and E.O.S. Scholefield. "Authorship of the Traits of Indian Life." *Oregon Historical Quarterly* 35 (1934): 42-49.

–. *British Columbia from the Earliest Times to the Present*. Vancouver: S.J. Clarke, 1913.

Hudson, Douglas. "Traplines and Timber: Social and Economic Change among the Carrier." PhD. diss., University of Alberta, 1983.

Hunt, M. "Racism, Imperialism, and the Traveler's Gaze in Eighteenth Century England." *Journal of British Studies* 32 (1993): 333-57.

Hutchings, W. Karl. "The Namu Obsidian Industry." In *Early Human Occupation in British Columbia*, ed. Roy Carlson and Luke Dalla Bona, 165-76. Vancouver: UBC Press, 1996.

Hyde, Lewis. *Trickster Makes This World, Mischief, Myth, and Art*. New York: Farrar, Straus and Giroux, 1998.

Igartua, José E. *Arvida au Saguenay: Naissance d'une ville industrielle*. Montreal and Kingston: McGill-Queen's University Press, 1996.

Iggers, Georg G. "From Macro- to Microhistory: The History of Everyday Life." In *Historiography in the 20th Century: From Scientific Objectivity to the Postmodern Challenge*. Hanover, NH: University Press of New England, 1997.

Inglis, Richard. "The Spanish on the North Pacific Coast: An Alternative View from Nootka Sound." In *Spain and the North Pacific Coast*, ed. Robin Inglis, 133-36. Vancouver: Vancouver Maritime Museum, 1992.

Irving, Allan. "The Development of a Provincial Welfare State: British Columbia 1900-1939." In *The "Benevolent" State: The Growth of Welfare in Canada*, ed. Allan Moscovitch and Jim Albert, 155-74. Toronto: Garamond, 1987.

Iverson, Peter. *When Indians Became Cowboys: Native Peoples and Cattle Ranching in the American West*. Norman: University of Oklahoma Press, 1994.

J. A. Jacobsen. *Alaskan Voyage, 1881-83: An Expedition to the Northwest Coast of America*. Translated from the German text of Adrian Woldt by Erna Gunther. Chicago: University of Chicago Press, 1977.

Jacobson, Cardell. "Internal Colonialism and Native American Indian Labor in the United States from 1871 to World War II." *Social Science Quarterly* 65 (1984): 158-71.

Jane, Cecil. *A Spanish Voyage to Vancouver and the North-West Coast of America*. London: Argonaut, 1930.

Jenness, Diamond. *The Faith of a Coast Salish Indian*. Victoria: BC Provincial Museum, 1955.

–. "The Saanich Indians of Vancouver Island." National Museum of Canada, Mss no. VIIOG-8M p114ff.

Jolly, Margaret. "The Forgotten Women: A History of Migrant Labour and Gender Relations in Vanuatu." *Oceania* 58, 2 (1987): 119-37.

Jolly, Margaret, and M. Macintyre. *Family and Gender in the Pacific: Domestic Contradictions and Colonial Impact*. Sydney: Cambridge University Press, 1988.

Jonaitis, Aldona, and Richard Inglis. "Power, History and Authenticity: The Mowachaht Whaler's Washing Shrine." *South Atlantic Quarterly* 91, 1 (1992): 193-213.

Jones, Charles, with Stephen Bosustow. *Queesto: Pacheenaht Chief by Birthright*. Nanaimo, BC: Theytus, 1981.

Kan, Sergei. "Shamanism and Christianity: Modern-Day Tlingit Elders Look at the Past." *Ethnohistory* 38, 4 (1991): 363-87.

Kanakos, Jeannie. "The Negotiations to Relocate the Songhees Indians, 1843-1911." MA thesis, Simon Fraser University, 1983.

Kane, Paul. *Wanderings of an Artist: Among the Indians of North America: From Canada to Vancouver's Island to Oregon, through Hudson's Bay Company's Territory and Back Again*. 1859. Edmonton: Hurtig, 1968.

Keddie, Grant. "Legend of Camosun." *Discovery* 19 (1991): 3.

–. "The Question of Asiatic Objects on the North Pacific Coast of America: Historic or Prehistoric?" *Contributions to Human History* 3 (1990): 1-26.

–. *Songhees Pictorial: A History of the Songhees People as Seen by Outsiders, 1790-1912*. Victoria: Royal BC Museum, 2003.

–. "The Victoria Small Pox Crisis of 1862." *Discovery* 22 (1993): 4-5.

Kelm, Mary-Ellen. "British Columbia First Nations and the Influenza Pandemic of 1918-19." *BC Studies* 122 (1999): 23-47.

–. *Colonizing Bodies: Aboriginal Health and Healing in British Columbia, 1900-50*. Vancouver: UBC Press, 2000.

Kendrick, John. "The End of the Northern Mystery: The Spanish in Juan de Fuca and Beyond, 1790-1792." In *Spain and the North Pacific Coast*, ed. Robin Inglis, 100-10. Vancouver: Vancouver Maritime Museum, 1992.

–. *The Men with Wooden Feet*. Toronto: NC Press, 1986.

–. *The Voyages of the Sutil and Mexicana 1792*. Spokane: Arthur H. Clark, 1991.

Kerr, Don, Andrew Signer, and Jean Pierre Bourdeau. *Canada's Aboriginal Population 1981-1991 Summary Report*. Ottawa: Royal Commission on Aboriginal Peoples and Statistics Canada, 1996.

Kew, J.E. Michael, "Central and Southern Coast Salish Ceremonies since 1900." In *Handbook of North American Indians*, vol. 7, ed. Wayne Suttles, 467-80. Washington: Smithsonian, 1990.

–. "Coast Salish Ceremonial Life: Status and Identity in a Modern Village." PhD. diss., University of Washington, 1970.

Klein, Laura. "'She's One of Us, You Know': The Public Life of Tlingit Women, Traditional, Historical and Contemporary Perspectives." *Western Canadian Journal of Anthropology* 6, 3 (1976): 164-83.

Knack, Martha, and Alice Littlefield. "Native American Labor: Retrieving History, Rethinking Theory. In *Native Americans and Wage Labor: Ethnohistorical Perspectives*, ed. Alice Littlefield and M. Knack, 3-44. Norman: University of Oklahoma Press, 1996.

Knight, Rolf. *Indians at Work: An Informal History of Native Indian Labour in British Columbia, 1858-1930*. Vancouver: New Star, 1978.

Lai, David Chuenyan. *Chinatowns*. Vancouver: UBC Press, 1988.

Lamb, W. Kaye. "The Discovery of Hill's Bar in 1858." *British Columbia Historical Quarterly* 3, 22 (1939): 215-20.

–. "Early Lumbering on Vancouver Island, I and II." *British Columbia Historical Quarterly* 2 (1938): 31-53, 95-144.

–. "The Founding of Fort Victoria." *British Columbia Historical Quarterly* 7 (1940): 71-92.

Lane, Barbara. "The Cowichan Knitting Industry." *Anthropology in British Columbia* 2 (1951): 14-27.

Lane, Robert. "Chilcotin." In *Handbook of North American Indians: Plateau*, vol. 6, ed. William Sturtevant, 402-12. Washington: Smithsonian, 1981.

–. "Cultural Relations of the Chilcotin Indians of West Central BC." PhD diss., University of Washington, 1953.

Langevin, H.L. *British Columbia: Report of the Hon. H.L. Langevin, Minister of Public Works*. Ottawa: I.B. Taylor, 1872.

Langley, H.C. *Pacific Coast Directory for 1867*. San Francisco: H.C. Langley, 1867.

Latour, Bruno, and Steven Woolgar. *Laboratory Life: The Social Construction of Scientific Facts*. Beverly Hills: Sage, 1979.

Leacy, F.H. *Historical Statistics of Canada*. Ottawa: Statistics Canada, 1983.

Lee, Kevin. "Measuring Poverty among Canada's Aboriginal People." *Insight* 23, 2 (1999): 11-12.

Lee, M., R. Reyburn, and A. Carrow. "Nutritional Status of British Columbia Indians." *Canadian Journal of Public Health* 62 (1971): 285-96.

Levi, Giovanni. "On Microhistory." In *New Perspectives on Historical Writing*, ed. Peter Burke, 93-113. University Park: Penn State Press, 1991.

Li, Peter S. "Immigration Laws and Family Patterns: Some Demographic Changes among Chinese Families in Canada, 1885-1971." *Canadian Ethnic Studies* 12, 1 (1980): 58-73.

Lillard, Charles. *Cultus Coulee*. Surrey, BC: Sono Nis, 1971.

Lillard, Charles, and Terry Glavin. *A Voice Great within Us*. Vancouver: New Star, 1998.

Locke, John. *Second Treatise of Government*. Ebook no. 7370. http://www.gutenburg.org/dirs/extext05/trgov10.txt (accessed January 2005).

Lugrin, N. De Bertrand. "Aged Indian Princess Recalls Childhood." *Victoria Sunday Times Magazine*, May 3, 1952, 5.

–. "Chief David's Saga." *Daily Colonist*, May 17, 1936, 6.

Lutz, John. "Gender and Work in Lekwammen Families, 1843-1970." In *Gendered Pasts: Historical Essays on Femininity and Masculinity in Canada*, ed. Kathryn McPherson, Cecilia Morgan, and Nancy M. Forestell, 80-105. Don Mills, ON: Oxford University Press, 1999.

–. "Interlude or Industry? Ranching in British Columbia, 1849-1885." *BC Historical News* 13, 4 (1980): 2-11.

–. "Making 'Indians' in British Columbia: Power, Race and the Importance of Place." In *Power and Place in the North American West*, ed. John Finlay and Richard White, 61-86. Seattle: University of Washington Press, 1999.

–. "Myth Understandings." In *Myth and Memory: Stories of Indigenous-European Contact*, ed. John Sutton Lutz, 1-14. Vancouver: UBC Press, 2007.

–. "Preparing Eden: Aboriginal Land Use and European Settlement." Paper presented to the Canadian Historical Association Annual Meeting, Montreal, August 25-27, 1995.

–. "'Relating to the Country': The Lekwammen and the Extension of European Settlement, 1843-1911." In *Beyond the City Limits: Rural History in British Columbia*, ed. Ruth Sandwell, 17-32. Vancouver: UBC Press, 1999.

–. "Seasonal Rounds in an Industrial World." In *A Stó:lō Coast Salish Historical Atlas*, ed. Keith Carlson, 64-67. Vancouver/Seattle: Douglas and McIntyre/University of Washington Press, 2001.

–. "When Is an 'Indian War' Not an Indian War? Canadian Indians and American Settlers in the Pacific Northwest, 1850s to 1860s." *Journal of the West* 38, 3 (1998): 7-13.

–. "Work, Sex, and Death on the Great Thoroughfare: Annual Migrations of 'Canadian Indians' to the American Pacific Northwest." In *Parallel Destinies: Canadian-American Relations West of the Rockies*, ed. John M. Findlay and Ken Coates, 80-103. Seattle: Center for the Study of the Pacific Northwest and University of Washington Press, 2002.

–. "Work Wages and Welfare in Aboriginal-Non-Aboriginal Relations, British Columbia, 1949-1970." PhD diss., University of Ottawa, 1994.

Lynch, Michael, and Steven Woolgar, eds. *Representation in Scientific Practice*. London: MIT Press, 1990.

Lyons, Cicely. *Salmon Our Heritage*. S.l.: S.n., 1969.

Lyotard, Jean François. *The Differend: Phrases in Dispute*. Trans. Georges Van Den Abbeele. Minneapolis: University of Minnesota Press, 1988.

Macdonald, Joanne. "From Ceremonial Object to Curio: Object Transformation at Port Simpson and Metlakatla, British Columbia, in the Nineteenth Century." *Canadian Journal of Native Studies* 10, 2 (1990): 193-217.

MacFie, Matthew. *Vancouver Island and British Columbia*. London: Longman, Roberts, and Green, 1865.

Mack, Clayton, with H. Thommasen. *Grizzlies and White Guys: The Stories of Clayton Mack*. Madeira Park, BC: Harbour, 1993.

Mackenzie, Alexander. *Journal of the Voyage to the Pacific*, ed. Walter Sheppe. New York: Dover, 1992.

Mackie, Richard S. "Colonial Land, Indian Labour and Company Capital: The Economy of Vancouver Island, 1849-1858." MA thesis, University of Victoria, 1984.

–. *Island Timber: A Social History of the Comox Logging Company, Vancouver Island*. Victoria: Sono Nis, 2000.

–. *Trading beyond the Mountains: The British Fur Trade on the Pacific, 1793-1843*. Vancouver: UBC Press, 1997.

MacLaren, Ian S. "Exploration/Travel Literature and the Evolution of the Author." *International Journal of Canadian Studies* 5 (1992): 39-67.

–. "The Metamorphosis of Travellers into Authors: The Case of Paul Kane." In *Critical Issues in Editing Exploration Texts: Papers Given at the Twenty-eighth Annual Conference on Editorial Problems, University of Toronto, 6-7 November 1992*, ed. G. Warkentin, 67-108. Toronto: University of Toronto Press, 1992.

MacMillan, H.L., A.B. MacMillan, D.R Offord, and J.L. Dingle. "Aboriginal Health." *Canadian Medical Association Journal* 155, 11 (1996): 1569-78.

Maranda, Lynn. *Coast Salish Gambling Games*. Mercury Series, vol. 93. Ottawa: National Museums of Canada, 1984.

Marshall, Daniel. "Claiming the Land: Indians, Goldseekers, and the Rush to British Columbia." PhD diss., University of British Columbia, 2000.

–. "Rickard Revisited: Native 'Participation' in the Gold Discoveries of British Columbia." *Native Studies Review* 11, 1 (1996): 91-99.

–. *Those Who Fell from the Sky*. Duncan, BC: Cowichan Tribes, 1999.

Martin, Robert Montgomery. *The Hudson's Bay Territories and Vancouver's Island*. London: T. and W. Boone, 1848.

Marx, Karl. *Capital: A Critique of Political Economy*. New York: International, 1954.

–. *Grundrisse*. Hammondsworth, UK and Boston: Penguin, 1973.

Matthews, J.S. *Conversations with Khahtsahlano, 1934-1954*. Vancouver: Vancouver City Archives, 1933.

–. *Early Vancouver: Narratives of Pioneers of Vancouver, BC*. Vancouver: Brock Webber, 1933.

Mayne, R.C. *Four Years in British Columbia and Vancouver Island*. London: John Murray, 1862.

McArthur, A.A., ed. *The Resources of British Columbia*. Victoria: A.A. McArthur, 1882-1886.

McArthur, Lewis L. "Anglicized Native American Place Names in Oregon: Their Number and Distribution," *Names* 44, 4 (1996): 322-32.

McCracken, Grant. *Culture and Consumption: New Approaches to the Symbolic Character of Consumer Goods and Activities*. Bloomington: Indiana University Press, 1988.

McDonald, James A. "Trying to Make a Life: The Historical Political Economy of Kitsumkalum." PhD diss., University of British Columbia, 1985.

McEachern, Chief Justice Allan. *Reasons for Judgement: Delgamuukw vs. British Columbia*. Supreme Court of British Columbia, 1991.

McMullan, John. "State Capital and the BC Salmon Fishing Industry." In *Uncommon Property: The Fishing and Fish-Processing Industries in British Columbia*, ed. Patricia Marchak, Neil Guppy, and John McMullan, 107-52. Toronto: Methuen, 1987.

McNally, David. "Political Economy without a Working Class." *Labour/Le Travail* 25 (1990): 17-226.

McNeary, Stephen A. "When Fire Came Down: Social and Economic Life of the Niska." PhD diss., Bryn Mawr College, 1976.

Meggs, Geoff. *Salmon: The Decline of the British Columbia Salmon Fishery*. Vancouver: Douglas and McIntyre, 1991.

Mendelson, Michael, and Ken Battle. *Aboriginal People in Canada's Labour Market*. Ottawa: Caledon Institute of Social Policy, 1999.

Merk, Frederick, ed. *Fur Trade and Empire; George Simpson's Journal Entitled Remarks Connected with the Fur Trade in the Course of a Voyage from York Factory to Fort George and back to York Factory 1824-25*. Cambridge, MA: Belknap Press of Harvard University Press, 1968.

Miki, Roy. "Unclassified Subjects: Question Marking 'Japanese Canadian' Identity." Paper presented at the Making History: Constructing Race conference, University of Victoria, 1998.

Miller, Bruce. "Centrality and Measures of Regional Structure in Aboriginal Western Washington." *Ethnology* 28, 3 (1989): 265-76.

Miller, Christopher, and George R. Hammell. "A New Perspective on Indian-White Contact: Cultural Symbols and Colonial Trade." *Journal of American History* 73, 2 (1986): 311-28.

Miller, J.R. *Skyscrapers Hide the Heavens: A History of Indian-White Relations in Canada*. Toronto: University of Toronto Press, 1989.

Miner, H. Craig. *The Corporation and the Indian: Tribal Sovereignty and Industrial Civilization in Indian Territory, 1865-1907*. 2nd ed. Norman: University of Oklahoma Press, 1989.

Mitchell, Donald H. "Predatory Warfare, Social Status and the North Pacific Slave Trade." *Ethnology* 23, 1 (1984): 39-48.

Mitchell, Donald H., and Leland Donald. "Some Economic Aspects of Tlingit, Haida, and Ts'msyen Slavery." *Research in Economic Anthropology* 7 (1985): 19-35.

Mitchell, Marjorie. "A Dictionary of Songish: A Dialect of Coast Salish." MA thesis, University of Victoria, 1968.

–. "Social and Cultural Consequences for Native Indian Women on a British Columbia Reserve." *Atlantis* 4, 2 (1979): 179-88.

Mitchell, Timothy. *Colonizing Egypt*. Cambridge: Cambridge University Press, 1988.

Monet, Don, and Ardythe Wilson. *Colonialism on Trial*. Gabriola, BC: New Society Publishers, 1992.

Mooney, James. "The Aboriginal Population North of Mexico." *Smithsonian Miscellaneous Collections* 80, 7 (1928): 1-40.

Mooney, Kathleen A. "The Effects of Rank and Wealth on Exchange among the Coast Salish." *Ethnology* 17, 4 (1978): 391-406.

–. "Urban and Reserve Coast Salish Employment: A Test of Two Approaches to the Indian's Niche in North America." *Journal of Anthropological Research* 32, 4 (1976): 390-409.

–. "Urban and Reserve Indian Economies and Domestic Organization." PhD. diss., University of Michigan, 1976.

Moran, Bridget. *Stoney Creek Woman: The Story of Mary John*. Vancouver: Tillacum Library, 1988.

Morice, A.G. *The History of the Northern Interior of British Columbia*. 1904. Smithers, BC: Interior Stationery, 1978.

Morley, A.P. *Roar of the Breakers: A Biography of Peter Kelly*. Toronto: Ryerson, 1967.

Morris, Gary J. *Straits Salish Prehistory*. Lopez Island: Morris, 1993.

Morton, James. *The Enterprising Mr. Moody and the Bumptious Captain Stamp: The Lives and Times of Vancouver's Lumber Pioneers*. Vancouver: J.J. Douglas, 1977.

–. *In the Sea of Sterile Mountains: The Chinese in British Columbia*. Vancouver: J.J. Douglas, 1974.

Murray, David. *Forked Tongue: Speech, Writing and Representation in North American Indian Texts*. London: Pinter, 1991.

Murray, Peter. *The Vagabond Fleet: A Chronicle of the North Pacific Sealing Schooner Trade.* Victoria: Sono Nis, 1988.

Muszynski, Alicja. *Cheap Wage Labour: Race and Gender in the Fisheries of British Columbia.* Montreal and Kingston: McGill-Queen's University Press, 1996.

–. "Class Formation and Class Consciousness: The Making of Shoreworkers in the BC Fishing Industry." *Studies in Political Economy* 20 (1986): 85-116.

–. "The Creation and Organization of Cheap Wage Labour in the British Columbia Fishing Industry." PhD diss., University of British Columbia, 1986.

–. "Major Processors to 1940 and the Early Labour Force: Historical Notes." In *Uncommon Property: The Fishing and Fish Processing Industries in British Columbia,* ed. Patricia Marchak, Neil Guppy, and John McMullan, 46-65. Agincourt, ON: Methuen, 1987.

–. "Race and Gender: Structural Determinants in the Formation of BC's Salmon Canning Labour Forces." *Canadian Journal of Sociology* 13, 1-2 (1988): 103-20.

Nadasdy, Paul. *Hunters and Bureaucrats: Power, Knowledge, and Aboriginal-State Relations in the Southwest Yukon.* Vancouver: UBC Press, 2003.

Nater, H.F. *A Concise Nuxalk-English Dictionary.* Mercury Series no. 115. Ottawa: Canadian Museum of Civilization, Canadian Ethnology Service, 1990.

Newell, Dianne. *Tangled Webs of History: Indians and the Law in Canada's Pacific Coast Fisheries.* Toronto: University of Toronto Press, 1993.

Newsome, Eric. *The Coal Coast: History of Coal Mining in British Columbia.* Victoria: Orca, 1989.

Niblack, Albert P. *The Coast Indians of Southern Alaska and Northern British Columbia.* 1888. New York: Johnson Reprint Corporation, 1970.

Nichols, Roger L. *Indians in the United States and Canada: A Comparative History.* Lincoln: University of Nebraska Press, 1998.

Nicholson, George. *Vancouver Island's West Coast, 1762-1962.* Victoria: G. Nicholson, 1965.

Norcross, E. Blanch. "The Cowichan Sweater." *The Beaver,* Outfit 276 (1945): 14-15

Olsen, Sylvia. "'We Indians Were Sure Hard Workers': A History of Coast Salish Wool Working." MA thesis, University of Victoria, 1998.

Olson, Ronald. "The Life Story of a Bella Bella Woman." In "Notes on the Bella Bella Kwakiutl." *Anthropological Records* 14, 5 (1955): 341-43.

O'Neill, Amy. "Identity, Culture and the Forest: The Stó:lō." MA thesis, University of British Columbia, 1999.

Ormsby, Margaret. *British Columbia: A History.* Toronto: Macmillan, 1958.

Pagett, Frank. "105 Years in Victoria and Saanich! Chief David Recalls White Man's Coming; 80 Years Rent Unpaid," *Victoria Daily Times,* July 14, 1934, Features 1.

Paine, Robert. *The White Arctic: Anthropological Essays on Tutelage and Ethnicity.* St. John's, NF: Memorial University Press, 1977.

Palmer, Andie. *Maps of Experience: The Anchoring of Land to Story in Secwepemc Discourse.* Toronto: University of Toronto Press, 2005.

–. "Maps of Experience: Shuswap Narratives of Place." PhD diss., University of Washington, 1994.

Palmer, H.S. *Report of a Journey of Survey from Victoria to Fort Alexander, via North Bentinck Arm.* New Westminster: Royal Engineers Press, 1863.

Parry, Benita. "Problems in Current Theories of Colonial Discourse." *Oxford Literary Review* 9, 1-2 (1987): 27-58.

Peacock, Catherine Kirby. "Salmon Canning in British Columbia." *Good Words* 35 (1894): 605-9.

Pennier, Henry, with Herbert L. McDonald. *Chiefly Indian: The Warm and Witty Story of a British Columbia Half-Breed Logger.* Vancouver: Graydonald Graphics, 1972.

Peterson, Jan. *The Albernis.* Lantzville, BC: Oolichan, 1992.

Phillips, Paul. "Confederation and the Economy of British Columbia." In *British Columbia and Confederation,* ed. W. George Shelton, 43-66. Victoria: University of Victoria, 1967.

Phillips, W.S. *The Chinook Book.* Seattle: W.S. Phillips, 1913.

Pierce, William Henry. *From Potlatch to Pulpit,* ed. J.P. Hicks. Vancouver: Vancouver Bindery, 1933.

Pinkerton, Evelyn. "Competition among BC Fish-Processing Firms." In *Uncommon Property: The Fishing and Fish Processing Industries in British Columbia,* ed. Patricia Marchak, Neil Guppy, and John McMullan, 66-96. Toronto: Methuen, 1987.

–. "Indians in the Fishing Industry." In *Uncommon Property: The Fishing and Fish Processing Industries in British Columbia,* ed. Patricia Marchak, Neil Guppy, and John McMullan, 66-96. Toronto: Methuen, 1987.

Poole, Francis. *A Narrative of Discovery and Adventure in the North Pacific.* 1872. Vancouver: J.J. Douglas, 1980.

Povinelli, Elizabeth. *Labor's Lot: The Power, History and Culture of Aboriginal Action.* Chicago: University of Chicago Press, 1993.

Powell, I.W. *Report of the Superintendent of Indian Affairs for British Columbia for 1872 and 1873.* Ottawa: I.B. Taylor, 1873. Reprinted CIHM no. 16227.

Pratt, Mary Louise. *Imperial Eyes: Travel Writing and Transculturation.* London: Routledge, 1992.

Pritchard, John. "Economic Development and the Disintegration of Traditional Culture among the Haisla." PhD. diss., University of British Columbia, 1977.

Quintasket, Christine. *Mourning Dove: A Salishan Autobiography*, ed. Jay Miller. Lincoln: University of Nebraska Press, 1990.

Rabinow, Paul, ed. *The Foucault Reader.* New York: Pantheon, 1984.

Rahala, Richard A. *Clearcutting the Pacific Rainforest: Production, Science, and Regulation.* Vancouver: UBC Press, 1998.

Ralston, Caroline. "Ordinary Women in Early Post-Contact Hawaii." In *Family and Gender in the Pacific: Domestic Contradictions and the Colonial Impact*, ed. Margaret Jolly and Martha Macintyre, 45-64. Cambridge: Cambridge University Press, 1989.

Rathbun, Richard. "A Review of the Fisheries in the Contiguous Waters of the State of Washington and British Columbia." *Report of the US Commissioner of Fisheries for 1899.* Washington: United States Government Printing Office, 1900.

Ray, Arthur. *The Canadian Fur Trade in the Industrial Age.* Toronto: University of Toronto Press, 1990.

–. "The Hudson's Bay Company and Native People." In *History of Indian-White Relations: Handbook of North American Indians*, vol. 4, ed. W.E. Washburn, 335-50. Washington: Smithsonian, 1988.

Redclift, N., and E. Mingione. *Beyond Employment: Household, Gender, and Subsistence.* Oxford: Blackwell, 1985.

Reid, David J. "Company Mergers in the Fraser River Salmon Canning Industry, 1885-1902." *Canadian Historical Review* 56, 3 (1975): 277-306.

Reinhart, Herman. *The Golden Frontier: The Recollections of Herman Francis Reinhart, 1851-1869*, ed. Doyce B. Nunis, Jr. Austin: University of Texas Press, 1962.

Reksten, Terry. *Illustrated History of British Columbia.* Vancouver: Douglas and McIntyre, 2001.

Rich, E.E., ed. *The Letters of John McLoughlin from Fort Vancouver ... 1825-1838.* Toronto: Champlain Society, 1941.

–. *London Correspondence Inward from Eden Colville, 1849-1852.* London: Hudson's Bay Record Society, 1952.

–. *Part of a Despatch from George Simpson.* Toronto: Champlain Society, 1947.

–. *Simpson's 1828 Journey to the Columbia.* London: Hudson's Bay Record Society, 1947.

Rickard, T.A. "Indian Participation in the Gold Discoveries." *British Columbia Historical Quarterly* 2 (1938): 3-18.

Ridington, Robin. "Fieldwork in Courtroom 53." *BC Studies* 95 (1992): 12-24.

Roberts, Morley. *The Western Avernus or, Toil and Travel in Further North America.* London: Smith, Elder, 1887.

Robin, Martin. *The Rush for Spoils: The Company Province 1871-1933.* Toronto: McClelland and Stewart, 1972.

Robinson, Harry. *Write It on Your Heart: The Epic World of an Okanagan Storyteller.* Ed. and comp. Wendy Wickwire. Vancouver: Talonbooks/Theytus, 1989.

Rogers, Mary Black. "Varieties of 'Starving': Semantics and Survival in the Subarctic Fur Trade, 1750-1850." *Ethnohistory* 33, 4 (1986): 353-83.

Rosetti, Bernadette. *The Great Carrier Chief and the Chunlac Massacre.* Videorecording, Yinka Déné Language Institute, 1989.

Roy, Patricia. *A White Man's Province: British Columbia Politicians and Chinese and Japanese Immigrants, 1858-1914.* Vancouver: UBC Press, 1989.

Ruby, Robert H., and John A. Brown. *A Guide to Indian Tribes of the Pacific Northwest.* Norman: University of Oklahoma Press, 1986.

–. *Indian Slavery in the Pacific Northwest.* Spokane, WA: A.H. Clark, 1993.

Russell, Bill. "The White Man's Paper Burden: Aspects of Record Keeping in the Department of Indian Affairs, 1860-1914." *Archivaria* 19 (1984-85): 50-72.

Said, Edward W. "Representing the Colonized: Anthropology's Interlocutors." *Critical Inquiry* 15 (1989): 205-25.

Samson, Daniel, ed. *Contested Countryside: Rural Workers and Modern Society in Atlantic Canada.* Fredericton: Acadensis, 1994.

Sandwell, Ruth W. *Contesting Rural Space: Land Policy and the Practices of Resettlement on Saltspring Island, 1859-1891.*

Montreal and Kingston: McGill-Queen's University Press, 2005.

–. "The Limits of Liberalism: The Liberal Reconnaissance and the History of the Family in Canada." *Canadian Historical Review* 84, 3 (2003): 423-50.

–. "Negotiating Rural: Policy and Practice in the Settlement of Saltspring Island, 1859-91." In *Beyond the City Limits: Rural History in British Columbia*, ed. R. Sandwell, 83-101. Vancouver: UBC Press, 1999.

Santos-Granero, Fernando. "Writing History into the Landscape: Space, Myth, and Ritual in Contemporary Amazonia." *American Ethnologist* 25, 2 (1998): 128-48.

Sapir, Edward. "The Life of a Nootka Indian." *Queen's Quarterly* 28, 3-4 (1921): 232-43, 351-67.

–. "Sayachi'apis, a Nootka Trader." In *American Indian Life*, ed. E.C. Parsons, 297-323. New York: B.W. Huebsh, 1922. Reprinted Lincoln: University of Nebraska Press, 1978.

Sapir, Edward, and Morris Swadesh. *Native Accounts of Nootka Ethnography.* Bloomington: Indiana University Press, 1955.

–. *Nootka Texts.* Philadelphia: Linguistic Society of America, University of Pennsylvania, 1939.

Scott, J.C. *Seeing Like a State: How Certain Schemes to Improve the Human Condition Have Failed.* New Haven: Yale University Press, 1998.

Seed, Patricia. *Ceremonies of Possession in Europe's Conquest of the New World, 1492-1690.* Cambridge: Cambridge University Press, 1995.

Seemann, Berthold. *Narrative of the Voyage of HMS* Herald *during the Years 1845-51.* London: Reeve and Co., 1853.

Selwyn, Alfred C. "Journal and Report of Preliminary Explorations in British Columbia." *Report of Progress for 1871-72.* Ottawa: Geological Survey of Canada, 1872.

Sewid-Smith, Daisy. *Prosecution or Persecution.* [Cape Mudge, BC]: Nu-Yum-Baleess Society, 1979.

Shankel, George Edgar. "The Development of Indian Policy In British Columbia." PhD diss., University of Washington, 1945.

Shewell, Hugh. "*Enough to Keep Them Alive*": *Indian Welfare in Canada, 1873-1965.* Toronto: University of Toronto Press, 2004.

Shoemaker, Nancy. "The Census as Civilizer: American Indian Household Structure in the 1900 and 1910 US Censuses." *Historical Methods* 25, 1 (1992): 4-11.

Siggner, Andrew, and Chantal Locatelli. *An Overview of the Demographic, Social and Economic Conditions among*

British Columbia's Registered Indian Population. Ottawa: Research Branch, Corporate Policy, Department of Indian Affairs and Northern Development, 1981.

Skogan, Joan. *Skeena: A River Remembered.* Vancouver: British Columbia Packers, 1983.

Slotkin, Richard. *Regeneration through Violence: The Mythology of the American Frontier, 1600-1860.* Middleton, CT: Wesleyan University Press, 1973.

Smedley, Audrey. *Race in North America: Origin and Evolution of a Worldview.* Boulder, CO: Westview Press, 1993.

Smith, Linda Tuhiwai. *Decolonizing Methodologies: Research and Indigenous Peoples.* London: Zed Books, 1999.

Smith, Marian W. *The Puyallup-Nisqually.* New York: Columbia University Press, 1940.

Smith, Merrit Roe. *Harpers Ferry Armory and the New Technology.* Ithaca: Cornell University Press, 1977.

Sparrow, Leona Marie. "Work Histories of a Coast Salish Couple." MA thesis, University of British Columbia, 1976.

Sperlin, O.B. "Two Kootenay Women Masquerading as Me? Or Were They One?" *Washington Historical Quarterly* 21 (1930): 120-30.

Spivak, Gayatri Chakravorty. "Can the Subaltern Speak?" In *Post-colonial Studies Reader*, ed. Bill Ashcroft, Gareth Griffiths, and Helen Tiffer, 24-28. New York: Routledge, 1995.

–. "The New Historicism: Political Commitment and the Post Modern Critic." In *Post-Colonial Critic: Interviews, Strategies, Dialogues*, ed. Sarah Harasym, 152-68. London: Routledge, 1990.

Spradley, James, ed. *Guests Never Leave Hungry: The Autobiography of James Sewid, a Kwakiutl Indian.* Montreal and Kingston: McGill-Queen's University Press, 1989.

Sproat, G.M. *The Nootka: Scenes and Studies of Savage Life.* London: Smith, Elder, 1868. Reprinted. Victoria: Sono Nis, 1989.

Stackhouse, John. "Canada's Apartheid." Fourteen-part series in the *Globe and Mail*, November-December, 2001.

Stanbury, W.T. "Indians in British Columbia: Level of Income, Welfare Dependency and Poverty Rate." *BC Studies* 20 (1973-74): 66-78.

Steltzer, Ulli, and Catherine Kerr. *Coast of Many Faces.* Vancouver: Douglas and McIntyre, 1979.

Stepan, Nancy. *The Idea of Race in Science: Great Britain, 1800-1960.* London: MacMillan, 1982.

Stern, Bernhard. *The Lummi Indians of Northwest Washington*. New York: Columbia University Press, 1934.

Stewart, Frances. *Vertebrate Faunal Remains from the Potlatch Site (FcSi-2) in South Central British Columbia*. Ottawa: National Museum of Man, 1978.

Sturtevant, William C., ed. *Handbook of North American Indians*, vols. 4, 6, 7. Washington, DC: Smithsonian, 1978-96.

Suttles, Wayne. *Coast Salish Essays*. Vancouver/Seattle: Talonbooks/University of Washington Press, 1987.

–. *Economic Life of the Coast Salish of Haro and Rosario Straits*. New York: Garland, 1974.

–. "Post-Contact Culture Change among the Lummi Indians," *British Columbia Historical Quarterly* 18 (1954): 29-102.

Swan, Brian, and Arnold Krupat. *Recovering the Word*. Berkeley, University of California Press, 1987.

Swan, James. *Almost Out of the World: Scenes from Washington Territory – The Strait of Juan de Fuca, 1859-61*. Tacoma: Washington State Historical Society, 1971.

–. "The Haida Indians of Queen Charlotte's Island." In *Smithsonian Contributions to Knowledge* 21 (1876): 2,8,14.

–. *The Northwest Coast: Or, Three Years' Residence in Washington Territory*. New York: Harpers, 1857. Reprinted Seattle and London: University of Washington Press, 1972.

Tappage, Mary Augusta. *The Days of Augusta*, ed. J.E. Speare. Vancouver: Douglas and McIntyre, 1992.

Taussig, M. *Shamanism, Colonialism and the Wild Man: A Study in Terror and Healing*. Chicago: University of Chicago Press, 1987.

Taylor, G.W. *Timber: History of the Forest Industry in British Columbia*. Vancouver: J.J. Douglas, 1975.

Taylor, J.L. *Canadian Indian Policy during the Inter-War Years, 1918-1939*. Ottawa: Department of Indian Affairs and Northern Development, 1984.

Teit, James. *The Shuswap*. Jesup North Pacific Expedition: Memoir of the American Museum of Natural History, vol. 2, ed. Franz Boas. New York: AMS Press, 1909.

Tennant, Paul. *Aboriginal Peoples and Politics: The Indian Land Question in British Columbia, 1849-1989*. Vancouver: UBC Press, 1992.

Terry, Joanne Drake. *The Same as Yesterday: The Lillooet Chronicle the Theft of Their Land and Resources*. Lillooet, BC: Lillooet Tribal Council, 1989.

Thomas, Edwin Harper. *Chinook: A History and Dictionary of the Northwest Coast Trade Jargon*. Portland, OR: Metropolitan, 1935. Reprinted Portland, OR: Binford and Mort, 1970.

Thomas, Nicholas. *Entangled Objects: Exchange, Material Culture and Colonialism in the Pacific*. Cambridge, MA: Harvard University Press, 1991.

–. "Partial Texts: Representation, Colonialism and Agency in Pacific History." *Journal of Pacific History* 25, 2 (1990): 139-58.

–. "Sanitation and Seeing: The Creation of State Power in Early Colonial Fiji." *Comparative Studies in Society and History* 32 (1990): 149-70.

Thompson, Bonnie. "Voices from a Not Too Distant Past: Pre-1930s Indigent Fund." Paper presented to the Qualicum Conference, Parksville, British Columbia, January 1994.

Thompson, E.P. *The Making of the English Working Class*. Hammondsworth, UK: Penguin, 1968.

Thompson, Frances W. "Employment Problems and the Economic Status of the British Columbia Indians." MSW thesis, University of British Columbia, 1951.

Thomson, Duane. "A History of the Okanagan: Indians and Whites in the Settlement Era, 1860-1920." PhD diss., University of British Columbia, 1985.

Todorov, T. *Mikhail Bakhtin: The Dialogical Principle*. Minneapolis, University of Minnesota Press, 1984.

Tolmie, William Fraser. *The Journals of William Fraser Tolmie: Physician and Fur Trader*. Vancouver: Mitchell Press, 1963.

–. "Utilization of the Indians." *The Resources of British Columbia* 1, 12 (1884): 7.

Tough, Frank. *As Their Natural Resources Fail: Native People and the Economic History of Northern Manitoba, 1870-1930*. Vancouver: UBC Press, 1996.

Tuan, Y.F. *Topophilia*. Englewood Cliffs, NJ: Prentice-Hall, 1974.

Tully, James. *A Discourse on Property: John Locke and His Adversaries*. Cambridge: Cambridge University Press, 1980.

Turner, Nancy J., John Thomas, Barry F. Carlson, and Robert Ogilvie. *Ethnobotany of the Nitinaht Indians of Vancouver Island*. Occasional Papers no. 24. Victoria: Royal BC Museum, 1983.

United States. Governor Stevens. Report of the Commissioner of Indian Affairs. November 25, 1854. Senate Exec. Doc. 33rd Congress, 2nd sess., no. 746.

University of British Columbia Museum of Anthropology and First Nations House of Learning. *Symposium on the Tsilhqot'in War of 1864 and 1993 Cariboo Chilcotin Justice Inquiry.* Vancouver: University of British Columbia, November 19, 1994.

Urquhart, M.C., and K.A.H. Buckley. *Historical Statistics of Canada.* Toronto: Macmillan, 1965.

Usher, Jean. *William Duncan of Metlakatla: A Victorian Missionary in British Columbia.* Ottawa: National Museums of Canada, 1974.

Vancouver, George. *A Voyage of Discovery to the North Pacific Ocean and Round the World.* London: G.G. and J. Robinson, 1798. Reprint Ed. W. Kaye Lamb. London: Hakluyt Society, 1984.

Vancouver Island, Crown Colony of. *Laws of Vancouver Island.* Victoria: Crown Colony of Vancouver Island, 1864.

Vattel, Emmerich de. *The Law of Nations: Or, Principles of the Law of Nature: Applied to the Conduct and Affairs of Nations and Sovereigns.* 1758. Philadelphia: T. and J.W. Johnson, 1861.

Vehik, Susan, and Timothy Baugh. "Prehistoric Plains Trade." In *Prehistoric Exchange Systems in North America,* ed. Timothy Baugh and Jonathon Ericson, 249-74. New York: Plenum, 1994.

Verne, Ray F. *Lower Chinook Ethnographic Notes.* Seattle: University of Washington, 1938.

Vibert, Elizabeth. *Traders' Tales: Narratives of Cultural Encounters in the Columbia Plateau, 1801-1846.* Norman: University of Oklahoma Press, 1997.

Wagner, Henry R. *Spanish Explorations in the Strait of Juan de Fuca.* New York: AMS, 1933.

Waisberg, Leo, and Tim Holzkamm. "'A Tendency to Discourage Them from Cultivating': Ojibwa Agriculture and Indian Affairs Administration in Northwest Ontario." *Ethnohistory* 40, 2 (1993): 175-211.

Walkem, W.W. *Stories of Early British Columbia.* Vancouver: News Advertiser, 1914.

Walker, Alexander. *An Account of a Voyage to the Northwest Coast of America in 1785 and 1786,* ed. Robin Fisher and J.M. Bumsted. Toronto: Douglas and McIntyre, 1982.

Wallace, Anthony. *Rockdale: The Growth of an American Village in the Early Industrial Revolution.* New York: W.W. Norton, 1978.

Warburton, Rennie, and Stephen Scott. "The Fur Trade and Early Capitalist Development in British Colum-

bia." *Canadian Journal of Native Studies* 5, 1 (1985): 27-46.

Ward, Robin. *Echoes of Empire: Victoria and Its Remarkable Buildings.* Madeira Park: Harbour, 1996.

Ward, W.P. "Regionalism, Dependence, and the BC Fisheries: Historical Development and Recent Trends." In *Uncommon Property: The Fishing and Fish-Processing Industries in British Columbia,* ed. Patricia Marchak, Neil Guppy, and John McMullan, 326-50. Toronto: Methuen, 1987.

Weber, Max. *The Protestant Ethic and the Spirit of Capitalism.* New York: Scribner, 1958.

Webster, Peter. *As Far as I Know: Reminiscences of an Ahousat Elder.* Campbell River, BC: Campbell River Museum and Archives, 1983.

Wells, Oliver N. *The Chilliwacks and Their Neighbours.* Vancouver: Talonbooks, 1987.

Whipple, Fred L. *The Mystery of Comets.* Washington, DC: Smithsonian, 1985.

White, Richard. *Land Use, Environment, and Social Change: The Shaping of Island County, Washington.* Seattle: University of Washington Press, 1980.

–. *The Middle Ground: Indians, Empires and Republics in the Great Lakes Region, 1650-1815.* Cambridge: Cambridge University Press, 1991.

Whymper, Frederick. *Travel and Adventure in Alaska.* London: J. Murray, 1868.

Wickwire, Wendy. "To See Ourselves as the Other's Other: Nlaka'pamux Contact Narratives." *Canadian Historical Review* 75, 1 (1994): 1-20.

–. "Women in Ethnography: The Research of James A. Teit." *Ethnohistory* 40, 4 (1993): 539-62.

Wike, Joyce. "Problems in Fur Trade Analyses: The Northwest Coast." *American Anthropologist* 60, 1 (1958): 1086-101.

Wilkes, Charles. *Life in Oregon Country before the Emigration,* ed. Richard Moore. Ashland: Oregon Book Society, 1974.

Williams, David. *The Man for a New Country.* Victoria: Sono Nis, 1972.

Williams, Judith. *Clam Gardens: Aboriginal Mariculture on Canada's West Coast.* Vancouver: New Star, 2006.

Wilson, Charles. *Mapping the Frontier: Charles Wilson's Diary of the Survey of the 49th Parallel, 1858-1862,* ed. G.F.G. Stanley. Toronto: Macmillan, 1970.

–. "Report on the Indian Tribes Inhabiting the Country in the Vicinity of the 49th Parallel of North Latitude." *Transactions of the Ethnological Society of London.* New series 14 (1866): 275-332.

Witte Sisters. *Chilcotin: Preserving Pioneer Memories.* Surrey: Heritage House, 1995.

Wood, Phillip. "Barriers to Capitalist Development in Maritime Canada, 1870-1930: A Comparative Perspective." In *Canadian Papers in Business History*, ed. P. Baskerville, 33-57. Victoria: Public History Group, 1989.

Yeomans, Donald K. *Comets.* New York: John Wiley and Sons, 1991.

Young-Ing, Greg. "Talking Terminology: What's in a Word and What's Not." *Prairie Fire* 22, 3 (2001): 130-40.

Zenk, Henry B. "A Chinook Jargon and Native Cultural Persistence in the Grand Ronde Indian Community, 1856-1970: A Special Case of Creolization." PhD diss., University of Oregon, 1984.

Zenk, Henry B., and Tony A. Johnson. "Uncovering the Chinookan Roots of Chinuk Wawa: A New Look at the Linguistic and Historical Record." *University of British Columbia Working Papers in Linguistics (Papers for International Conference on Salish and Neighbouring Languages 31)* 14 (2004): 419-51.

Websites

Canada. Statistics Canada. Consumer Price Index historical Summary. http://www.statcan.ca/english/Pgdb/Economy/Economic/econ46.htm (site now discontinued; see new summary tables site at http://www40.statcan.ca/l01/cst01/econ46a.htm?sdi=consumer%20price%20index%20historical%20summary).

International Association for Obsidian Studies, http://www.peak.org/obsidian/index.html.

Lutz, John, and the Mysteries Team. "We Do Not Know His Name: Klatsassin and the Chilcotin War." http://www.canadianmysteries.ca.

Xeni Gwet'in. *Nemiah Declaration.* http://xenigwetin.com.

Acknowledgments

This book is both about, and the result of, *makúk*: meaningful and often unequal exchanges. I have benefited disproportionately from the intellectual generosity of many people and the financial generosity of several organizations. It is a pleasure to acknowledge these debts.

Much *wawa* has gone under the bridge during the fifteen years this book has been in the making. It will not be a surprise that a book about dialogue is the product of innumerable dialogues with aboriginal and non-aboriginal friends, colleagues, interviewees, research assistants, and students. If there is any knowledge or new insights to be found in *Makúk: A New History of Aboriginal-White Relations*, it is the result of a "collaborative wisdom" that comes from dozens of people.

The exchanges start and end in Victoria, British Columbia. The questions worked out in this book were sparked during my MA research at the University of Victoria, and the book was completed here, where I am privileged to teach. I could not ask for a more stimulating and congenial department in which to have launched a scholarly career or of which to be a member. Peter Baskerville is responsible for bringing me to a position where I could consider a doctorate, and he and Eric Sager continue to challenge, assist, and inspire me. At UVic I have the benefit of a remarkable community of scholars who may recognize some of their thoughts in this work. These include Martin Bunton, Patrick Dunae, Hamar Foster, Jo-Anne Lee, John MacLaren, Richard Mackie, Patricia Roy, Ian MacPherson, Lynne Marks, Rosemary Ommer, Nancy Turner, Elizabeth Vibert, Bill White, Wendy Wickwire, and others too numerous to name. Andrew Rippin, Dean of Humanities, has perpetuated a culture of interdisciplinary collegiality, consistently supported all of us, and given financial support to allow this book to have an expanded format.

The origins of the idea and much of the archival research derive from a PhD dissertation begun at the University of Ottawa in 1991 and finished in 1996. My foremost debt there is to Chad Gaffield, who revealed to me the insights of social history and taught me how to critically evaluate evidence when I thought I had already learned these things. I am one of many who has been inspired to pursue a scholarly career by the work, example, and encouragement of Chad, Peter, and Eric. I feel privileged to have them as mentors.

Michael Piva and Beatrice Craig made excellent suggestions, which propelled me towards writing this book. Ken Coates, the external examiner, has assisted me in this and in a thousand other ways. My friends at the University of Ottawa made that campus a stimulating and pleasant place to work. Liz Coombs, Barry Cottam, Michel Girard, Lorne Hammond, Marcel Martel, Lorna McLean, Wayne Melvin, and Bill Shannon all deserve special mention.

The manuscript got launched into the world of postcolonial and postmodern thought during a postdoctoral sojourn at the geography department at the University of British Columbia. There Dan Clayton, Derek Gregory, and Cole Harris significantly muddied my thinking and made this book the multilayered text that it is. A year-long doctoral Fulbright and a later a postdoctoral fellowship with Richard White at the University of Washington introduced me to the literature on the American West and environment. I hope a small part of Richard's wisdom and ability to write clearly about the complex rubbed off, and I can only hope his generosity to me is reflected in my relationships with my students. Richard, John Findlay, Sasha Harmon, and Laura McKinley befriended and inspired me while I was homeless in Seattle.

Other scholars who have been particularly generous with their support and ideas, include Jacques Barbier, Donald Davis, Jim Hendrickson, Cornelius Jaenen, Dan Marshall, and Barbara Neis. Many, including Peter Baskerville, Randy Bouchard, Cairn Crockford, Dorothy Kennedy, Lorne Hammond, Jim Hendrickson, Tony Johnson, Grant Keddie, Sylvia Olsen, Bonnie Thompson, and Henry Zenk, have given me access to their research-in-progress. These same people, along with Jean Barman, Ken Campbell, Ira Chaikin, Ken Coates, Douglas Cole, Bob Galois, Dorothy Kennedy, Richard Mackie, Jeremy Mouat, Bill Poser, David Robertson, and Pat Roy, suggested or lent source material and/or made valuable suggestions. No one has provided this book with as many key details as Brad Morrison.

I want to acknowledge all the rich resources to which I have had access to at archives in Canada, England, and the United States. Scholarship such as this depends on public support for archives and the availability of resources in which archivists may do their work. Ron Denman at the Chilliwack Archives and David Smith and Tia Halstead at the Stó:lō Nation Archives deserve special thanks, as do staff at the Barkerville Historic Town Archives, British National Archives in Kew, the Hudson's Bay Company Archives in Winnipeg, Stark Museum of Art, the Wellcome Institute in London, the Williams Lake Library and Archives, the Secwepemc Museum and Heritage Park, the Yukon Archives in Whitehorse, and Special Collections at the University of Victoria, the University of British Columbia, and the University of Washington. Many staff at the Archives of Canada and British Columbia Archives have earned my thanks and appreciation, but none more than Brian Young in Victoria. In a cooperative and timely fashion, Ernie Fraser at Archives of Canada patiently reviewed tens, perhaps hundreds, of metres of Department of Indian Affairs documents ordered under the Freedom of Information Act.

Several artists, including Briony Penn, Don Monet, and Brian Seymour, have agreed to let me use their work, and the Stó:lō Nation has permitted the use of Stan Greene's artwork. For the front cover image, my thanks goes to the Catriona Jeffries Gallery and, in particular, Brian Jungen, a BC artist with Swiss and Dunne-za roots, whose art embodies *makúk*.

Stuart Daniels provided the maps. Different photographers have allowed me to use their images including: Veera Bonner, Dorothy Haegert, Liam Haggarty, Bruce Johnson, Diana Nethercott, Uli Steltzer, Nancy Turner, and Robert Turner. Leslie Kopas has generously allowed me to use his father Cliff Kopas' amazing images. Thanks too to Helen Clifton, Adam Dick, Greg Dening, Terry Glavin, Tilly Guteriez, Giovanni Levi, Sonny McHalsie, Kim Recalma Clutesi, Ruth Sandwell, Daisy Sewid-Smith, and Nicholas Thomas for permission to print images of them in this book.

For sharing their enthusiasm, stimulating ideas, research, and kind spirits, Keith Carlson, Colin Coates, Megan Davies, Patrick Dunae, Peter Gossage, Larry Hannant, Craig Heron, Sylvia Olsen, and Ruth Sandwell have been model scholars and friends who have provided me examples to which to aspire. Their help and humour have added so much joy to this journey.

Several people have read all or part of drafts of this book, suggesting important avenues of analyses and correcting errors. These people include Cheryl Coull, José Igartua, Mary Ellen Kelm, Richard Mackie, and Wayne Suttles. Keith Carlson's detailed comments prevented many errors. Cheryl Bryce of the Songhees Nation and Don Wise of the Tsilhqot'in National Government agreed to look over the book and offer their input.

In my current role as a teacher I have the unbelievable good fortune of being able to learn from students whenever I am able to keep up with them. The History of Racialization Reading Group taught me what I know about race, and numerous others have helped seed this book, particularly Ben Bradley, Dennis Flewelling, Karl Preuss, and Adam Rudder. Also among these are the student researchers, including Emmy Campbell, Jon Clapperton, Chris Cook III, Jamie Disbrow, Jennifer Gamble, Liam Haggarty, Allan Heineman, Peg Kelly, Emma Lowman, John Lund, Jason Miller, and Byron Plant, without whom this book would be much impoverished.

Many people have participated in interviews, have guided me, and have answered my questions, and I mention them by name in Appendix 1. It has been impossible to include all their voices. And, with regard to those voices that have been included, I could only present embarrassingly small fragments of complex discussions. I will continue to pass on what you have taught in other works, and the tapes or transcripts of our discussions will be available for others, so that they may learn from them. I hope this will be a small compensation to all of you.

I owe a special debt to the staff and people of the Stó:lō Nation and Stó:lō Tribal Council, who have welcomed me and other students to work with them in a biennial field school since 1998. Sonny McHalsie has shared his knowledge, time, and home. It is impossible to thank him enough. My co-instructor, Keith Carlson, has shared his vast knowledge with me, and, over the years, the field school students have taught me much and have made teaching so much fun. Tia Halstead, Tracey Joe, Nikki Larock, Kat Pennier, Dave Smith, and Dave Schaepe have helped out in innumerable ways. The people we have interviewed and those whose interviews we have been granted access to, are named in Appendix 1. I extend a giant, collective "thank you" to all of you: *Haishka Siem.*

In the Chilcotin, many people have extended themselves to help me: Joe Alphonse, Don Wise, Orrey Charleyboy, and Patrick Lulua (Tsilhqot'in National Government); Cameron Beck (Cariboo-Chilcotin Tribal Council); Henry and Gilbert Solomon and Chief Roger Williams (Nemiah); Chief Leslie Stump (Ulkatcho) and Chief Cassidy Sill (Anaham); Chief Ervin Charleyboy (Redstone); and Chief Ivor Myers (Stone). Chilcotin historian Sage Birchwater shared his hospitality, photos, and knowledge very generously. *Sechanalyagh!*

I would like to thank Chief Pat Sterritt and her council in Hartley Bay and Dan Cardinal for inviting the "Coast under Stress" project to work there. We were generously received by the whole community. Helen Clifton and the Hill family (Ernie, Lynne, Cameron, and Eva) hosted us and generously offered their knowledge. Thanks to all the elders and community members who shared their histories with us and to my colleagues in the project who have taught me so much. *T'oyaks'ŝm!*

Thanks, too, to the Namgis Tribal Council, who invited us to work in Alert Bay, and to the many people we interviewed there. Chris Cook III, particularly, helped us gain the trust of his community and, with Byron Plant, conducted many of the interviews there. Outside of Alert Bay, Kwakwaka'wakw elders and historians Chief Adam Dick (Kwaxsistala) and Daisy Sewid-Smith (Mayanilth) have been very generous with their time and ideas, as has Chief Kim Recalma Clutesi (Ogwilogwa). *Gílla kas la*!

In Victoria, I particularly thank Chief Robert Sam and Cheryl Bryce of the Songhees Nation.

The happy fact that most of the debts I have racked up have been intellectual and personal rather than financial is the result of the faith of all those people who have refereed innumerable grant applications and a number of funding agencies. Over the past fifteen years, the British Columbia Heritage Trust, the University of Ottawa, the University of Victoria, the Social Sciences and Humanities Research Council of Canada, the Association of Canadian Universities for Northern Studies, the Canada-United States Fulbright Program, and the Secretary of State for Multiculturalism have funded different parts of my research. I thank them all. From 2003 to 2006, the Multi Council Research Initiative "Coasts under Stress Project" has funded students and me to conduct research in the aboriginal communities of Alert Bay and Hartley Bay. Without this funding this research could not have happened.

At UBC Press, an amazing team put this book together. Jean Wilson has been a bedrock of support and a font of encouragement over the many years it took to get this book to press. Holly Keller shepherded all the complex pieces of this book into its final shape; Joanne Richardson's careful copy editing has made it so much more readable; Irma Rodriguez typeset the book and created the amazing book design; and George Kirkpatrick crafted the arresting cover.

For encouragement, faith, love, and sharing of insight, my ultimate debt for the most meaningful of exchanges is to

Cheryl Coull. I promised her that this book would be done before our child was born. Sylvan, now eight years old, is a loving reminder that this book is an unkept promise.

This book belongs to all of you. Thank you.

Haiyu Mahsie.

Credits

NOTE: Illustrations are indicated by an open bullet (○) and quotations by a closed bullet (●).

ABBREVIATIONS: BCA (British Columbia Archives), CMC (Canadian Museum of Civilization), CVA (City of Vancouver Archives), DIAR (Department of Indian Affairs Annual Reports), LAC (Library and Archives Canada), RBCM (Royal British Columbia Museum), VPL (Vancouver Public Library).

A reasonable attempt has been made to secure permission to reproduce all illustrative materials used. If there are errors or omissions, they are wholly unintentional and the publisher would be grateful to learn of them.

PAGE IX
● James Cook, *The Voyage of the Resolution and Discovery, 1776-1780*, ed. J.C. Beaglehole (Cambridge: Hakluyt Society, 1967), 1: 307. See also James King's account of hearing the word before they ventured ashore in the same volume, p. 1394.
○ Captain James Cook. From James Cook, *A voyage to the Pacific Ocean. Undertaken by the command of His Majesty, for making discoveries in the Northern hemisphere, to determine the position and extent of the west side of North America ...* (Dublin: Printed for H. Chamberlaine, et al., 1784), in University of Victoria, Special Collections.
○ Maquinna, Chief of the Mowachaht. From John Meares, *Voyages de la Chine à la côte nord-ouest d'Amérique, faits dans les années 1788 et 1789; précédés de la relation d'un autre voyage exécuté en 1786 sur le vaisseau le Nootka ...* (Paris: F. Buisson, An 3ᵉ de la République [1794 or 5]), in University of Victoria, Special Collections.

PAGE X
● William Fraser Tolmie, *The Journals of William Fraser Tolmie: Physician and Fur Trader* (Vancouver: Mitchell, 1963), 210.
● Harry Guillod, *Chinook Dictionary*, BCA, microfilm 225A(3), n.d. [1862-88].
○ Harry Guillod, ca. 1880. BCA, A-02187.

PAGE XI
● W.S. Phillips, *The Chinook Book* (Seattle: W.S. Phillips, 1913), 9.
● James Swan, *The Northwest Coast: Or, Three Years' Residence in Washington Territory* (New York: Harpers, 1857; reprinted Seattle: University of Washington Press, 1972), 319.
○ James Swan and Johnny Kit Elswa, 1883. University of Washington Libraries Special Collections, NA1412.

PAGE XII
○ James Cook's crew and Mowachaht at Friendly Cove, 1778. Engraving after a painting by John Webber. Reproduced from James Cook, *A voyage to the Pacific Ocean. Undertaken by the command of His Majesty, for making discoveries in the Northern hemisphere, to determine the position and extent of the west side of North America ...* (Dublin: Printed for H. Chamberlaine, et al., 1784), in University of Victoria, Special Collections.
● Ernst von Hesse-Wartegg, "A Visit to the Anglo-Saxon Antipodes (Chapter 18 of *Curiosa aus der Neuen Welt*, 1893)," trans. John Maass, *BC Studies* 50 (1981): 36.

PAGE 3
○ John Morton. Painting by G.H. Southwell, CVA, AO4872.

PAGE 6

○ Exchange of fish for blankets. Painting by Stó:lō Stan Greene, courtesy of Stó:lō Nation.

PAGE 7

● Emmerich de Vattel, *The Law of Nations: Or, Principles of the Law of Nature: Applied to the Conduct and Affairs of Nations and Sovereigns* (1758; reprinted Philadelphia: T. & J.W. Johnson, 1861).

PAGE 9

● Rev. W.H. Collison, *In the Wake of the War Canoe* (London: Seeley, Service, 1915), 57-58.

○ Rev. Collison with Kincolith Chief Paul Klaydach and Councillor James Robinson, Kincolith, 1915. BCA, H-07284.

● Chief Justice Allan McEachern, *Reasons for Judgement: Delgamuukw v. British Columbia* (Supreme Court of British Columbia, 1991), 129.

PAGE 10

○ Captain George Vancouver. Portrait by William Bright Morris. http://www.west-norfolk.gov.uk/images/Captain%20George%20Vancouver.jpg

○ August Jack Khahtsahlano. CVAS, Port N632P920

PAGE 11

○ The Chief of Langara Point who met with Vancouver in 1792. Ink and wash drawing by José Cardero, 1792, Museo Naval MS 1725-5-2.

PAGE 13

● Giovanni Levi, "On Microhistory," in Peter Burke, ed., *New Perspectives on Historical Writing* (University Park: Penn State Press, 1991), 110.

○ Giovanni Levi. Photo by Pere Duran, *El Pais,* courtesy of Giovanni Levi.

PAGE 15

● Nancy Farriss, Foreword, in Arjun Appadurai, *The Social Life of Things: Commodities in Cultural Perspective* (Cambridge: Cambridge University Press, 1986), x.

PAGE 16

● Ruth W. Sandwell, *Contesting Rural Space: Land Policy and the Practices of Resettlement on Saltspring Island, 1859-*

1891 (Montreal and Kingston: McGill-Queen's University Press, 2005), 229.

○ Ruth Sandwell. Photo by Steven Baxter, with permission.

PAGE 17

○ Ts'msyen diarist Arthur Wellington Clah. BCA, AA-00678.

PAGE 19

○ Aboriginal spinning group, ca. 1881. BCA, B-03573.

PAGE 20

○ Wet'suwet'en fishing at Moricetown. BCA, AA-00673.

PAGE 22

● Mikhail Bakhtin in T. Todorov, *Mikhail Bakhtin: The Dialogical Principle (*Minneapolis: University of Minnesota Press, 1984), 30.

● Nicholas Thomas, *Entangled Objects: Exchange, Material Culture, and Colonialism in the Pacific* (Cambridge: Harvard University Press, 1991), 123.

○ Nicholas Thomas. Photo by Annie Coombes, courtesy of Nicholas Thomas.

PAGE 23

● Michel Foucault, in Paul Rabinow, ed., *The Foucault Reader* (New York: Pantheon, 1984), 211.

○ Michel Foucault. Photo by Bruce Jackson, with permission.

● Letter from Mr. E.W. Gordon to Mr. Dewdney, 1891, BCA, Cornelius Bryant Fonds, add mss 2819, box 1.

PAGE 25

● The Honourable Leonard Marchand, Okanagan, in the film *A Forgotten Legacy: Spirit of Reclamation*, produced and directed by Martin de Valk (Victoria: Chiaro Productions, 2002).

PAGE 26

● Edward W. Said, "Representing the Colonized: Anthropology's Interlocutors," *Critical Inquiry* 15 (1989): 212.

○ Edward W. Said. Photographer unknown.

PAGE 27

● Greg Dening, *Performances* (Chicago: University of Chicago, 1996), 124.

○ Greg Dening. Photo courtesy of Greg Dening.

PAGE 28

○ B.J. Spalding, *A Dictionary of the Chinook Jargon* [Sidney (BC): B.J. Spalding, 1947], courtesy of the University of Victoria Special Collections.

PAGE 31

● Burton Kewayosh, in Canadian Broadcasting Corporation, transcript of *The Way of the Indian* radio series, 1961 (Toronto: CBC, 1969), Part 5.

● Homer Barnett, *The Coast Salish of British Columbia* (Eugene: University of Oregon Press, 1955), 5.

○ Tommy Paul, early 1930s. RBCM, PN-11743.

PAGE 32

○ *America* (ca. 1600). Engraving by Théodore and Phillipe Galle of Jan Van der Straet's late-16th-century painting *America* showing Amerigo Vespucci discovering America. Reproduced from Rachel Doggett, ed., *New World of Wonders: European Images of the Americas, 1492-1700* (Washington, DC: Folger Shakespeare Library, 1992) 37.

PAGE 35

● William Spragge, Deputy Superintendent of Indian Affairs, in DIAR, 1865, 5.

● Homer Barnett, *Coast Salish of British Columbia* (Eugene: University of Oregon Press, 1955), 248.

PAGE 37

○ Sketch of Chief Kakalatza. Drawn by Frederick Whymper, 1864, in Beinecke Rare Book and Manuscript Library, WA MSS 525.

PAGE 40

● R.E. Gosnell, *Year Book of British Columbia and Manual of Provincial Information for 1897* (Victoria: R.E. Gosnell, 1898), 420-21.

PAGE 41

● Fred Greer, enumerator, in Canada, Department of Agriculture, *Census of Canada, Bulletin no. 5* (Ottawa: Department of Agriculture, 1892), 6-7.

PAGE 42

● James Douglas and Peter S. Ogden to J.A. Duntze, quoted in Robert Montgomery Martin, *The Hudson's Bay Territories and Vancouver's Island* (London: T. and W. Boone, 1849), 39.

○ James Douglas, Chief Factor of Fort Victoria, 1849-58. CVA Port N626P32.

PAGE 43

● Henry David Thoreau, cited in *The Journal of Henry David Thoreau*, ed. Bradford Torrey and Francis H. Allen (Boston: Houghton, Mifflin, 1906), 11: 437-38.

PAGE 45

● Rolf Knight, *Indians at Work: An Informal History of Native Indian Labour in British Columbia, 1858-1930* (Vancouver: New Star, 1978), 22.

○ Aboriginal sawyers captured in Haida argillite carving. RBCM, Cat No. 15679,

PAGE 51

● Wayne Suttles, *Economic Life of the Coast Salish of Haro and Rosario Straits* (New York: Garland, 1974), 486.

PAGE 52

○ Spanish ships *Sutil* and *Mexicana*. Pen and ink wash drawing by José Cardero, 1792, courtesy of Museo Naval, Madrid, MS 1723(3), 2942.

PAGE 54

○ Makah Chief Tetacus (Tatoosh). Ink and wash drawing by José Cardero, 1792, Muséo de America 2-276.

● Dionisio Alcalá Galiano, cited in Cecil Jane, *A Spanish Voyage to Vancouver and the North-West Coast of America* (London: Argonaut, 1930), 40. Compare to the translation in John Kendrick, *The Voyage of the Sutil and Mexicana 1792* (Spokane: Arthur Clark, 1991), 106.

PAGE 56

○ Lekwungen house posts, sketched by Franz Boas, 1885. Reproduced from Franz Boas, "The Lku'ñgen," *Report of the British Association for the Advancement of Science* 59 (1890), 563-82.

PAGE 58

● Patrick George, quoted in Suttles, *Economic Life of the Coast Salish of Haro and Rosario Straits* (New York: Garland, 1974), 384.

- Harry Assu, Kwakwa̱ka̱'wakw, *Assu of Cape Mudge: Recollections of a Coastal Indian Chief,* with Joy Inglis (Vancouver: UBC Press, 1989), 10.
○ Lekwungen Chief Sqwameyuk's potlatch, April 1874. RBCM, PN6810.

PAGE 62

○ Lekwungen house profile, sketched by Franz Boas, 1885. Reproduced from Franz Boas, "The Lku'ñgen," *Report of the British Association for the Advancement of Science* 59 (1890), 563-82.
- James Robert Anderson, "Notes and Comments on Early Days and Events in British Columbia, Washington, and Oregon," BCA, add mss 1912, box 8/18.

PAGE 63

○ Lekwungen weaver and loom. Paul Kane, *A Woman Weaving a Blanket* (oil on board). Royal Ontario Museum, 912.1.93.

PAGE 64

- Louie Pilkey, Wsanec, quoted in Suttles, *Economic Life of the Coast Salish of Haro and Rosario Straits* (New York: Garland, 1974), 163.
○ Reef net with crew. Original artwork by Briony Penn.

PAGE 65

- Reef net songs, by Julius Charles. Recorded by Henry Smith, December 13, 1942, Melville Jacobs Collection, University of Washington Special Collections, box 112, file 3 (recording 42A2).
○ Julius Charles, ca. 1949. Center for Pacific Northwest Studies, Bellingham, WA, Buswell Collection, 22.
○ Boas sketch of a reef-net camp site. Reproduced from Franz Boas, "The Lku'ñgen," *Report of the British Association for the Advancement of Science* 59 (1890), 563-82.

PAGE 66

○ Flower and bulb of the camas plant. Original artwork by Briony Penn.

PAGE 68

○ The Lekwungen burning forest cover. Reproduced from Frederick Whymper, *Travel and Adventure in the Territory of Alaska* (London: J. Murray, 1868).

PAGE 69

○ *The Great Comet of 1843.* Painted by astronomer Charles Piazzi Smyth and courtesy of the eThekwini Municipal Library Services (Durban): Don Africana Library.
- James Douglas, March 17, 1843, "Diary of a Trip to Victoria, March 1-21," 1843, BCA, A/B/40/D75.4A.
- Lekwungen story, in *Robert Brown and the Vancouver Island Exploring Expedition,* ed. John Hayman (Vancouver: UBC Press, 1989), 179-80; Franz Boas also recorded this story; see Randy Bouchard and Dorothy Kennedy, eds., *Indian Myths and Legends from the North Pacific Coast of America: A Translation of Franz Boas' 1895 Edition of* Indianische Sagen von der Nord-Pacifischen Küste Amerikas (Vancouver: Talonbooks, 2002).
- John Herschel, *Outlines of Astronomy* (London: Longman, Brown, Green, and Longmans, 1849), 200.

PAGE 70

○ Lekwungen Chief Chee-ah-thluc. Painting by Paul Kane, titled *Clea-clach, Head Chief of the Clallam* [sic], 1847 (oil on paper), Stark Museum of Art, Orange Texas, 31.78/200, WOP 3.
- John Gill, *Gill's Dictionary of the Chinook Jargon, with Examples of Use in Conversation and Notes upon Tribes and Tongues,* 15th ed. (1881; reprinted Portland, OR: J.K. Gill Company, 1909), 77.

PAGE 71

- Harry Guillod, *Chinook Dictionary,* BCA, microfilm 225A(3) n.d. [1862-88].
○ Lekwungen canoe, sketched by Franz Boas. Reproduced from Franz Boas, "The Lku'ñgen," *Report of the British Association for the Advancement of Science* 59 (1890), 563-82.

PAGE 74

○ Chee-ah-thluc, 1864. Photographed by Charles Gentile, February 1, 1864, BCA, F-08917.

PAGE 75

- James Swan, *The Northwest Coast: Or, Three Years' Residence in Washington Territory* (New York: Harper, 1857; reprinted Seattle and London: University of Washington Press), 316.
- W.S. Phillips, *The Chinook Book* (Seattle: W.S. Phillips, 1913), 117.

PAGE 76

o Sister of James Sqwameyuks with basket of fish. Photographed by Frederick Dally, BCA, F-08291.

● *Columbian*, January 15, 1853. This Olympia, Puget Sound, paper was the main newspaper in the Pacific Northwest. It circulated in Victoria, which did not have a local paper until 1858.

● John Dunn, *History of the Oregon Territory and British North American Fur Trade ...* (London: Edwards and Hughes, 1844), 287.

PAGE 77

● *Robert Brown and the Vancouver Island Exploring Expedition,* ed. John Hayman (Vancouver: UBC Press, 1989), 158.

o Robert Brown. BCA, G-03439.

PAGE 79

o Chief David Latasse, early 1930s. RBCM, PN-11743.

PAGE 80

● Dave Elliot, *Saltwater People (Saanich, BC: School District 63, 1983)*, 71-72.

PAGE 81

● Martha Cheney Ella, "Diary" (1853-1911), BCA, E/B/El 5A, 1853.

PAGE 84

o Aboriginal washerwoman. Photograph by Hannah Maynard, BCA, F-09011.

PAGE 85

● Edgar Fawcett, *Some Reminiscences of Old Victoria* (Toronto: William Briggs, 1912), 284.

● Traditional story of the Lekwungen, recorded by James Deans, in "Extract from the Traditional History of Vancouver Island," *Victoria Daily Times*, December 22, 1900, 3.

o Stan Greene's interpretation of smallpox. Painting by Stó:lō Stan Greene, courtesy of Stó:lō Nation.

PAGE 86

● Rev. A.C. Garrett, Letter to the Secretary of the United Society for the Propagation of the Gospel, from Victoria, June 6, 1862, Rhodes House Library, Oxford, vol. E10, p. 2208 (thanks to R. Bouchard and D. Kennedy).

PAGE 87

● "Whiskey Kills My Friends," recorded by Mary Bourque at Neah Bay, 1908, to the tune of "The Bear Went over the Mountain," Washington State Library, MS 283.

o Detail of a photo of Henry Rocky with a whiskey bottle. Barkerville Historic Archives, P-1651.

PAGE 88

● Horatio Hale, "The 'Jargon' or Trade-Language of Oregon," in *Ethnography and Philology* (1846; reprinted Ridgewood, NJ: Gregg, 1968), 645.

PAGE 91

o Thomas Crosby preaching to an unidentified man. Photo by Hannah Maynard, in Beinecke Rare Book and Manuscript Library, WA Photos 199.

PAGE 92

o Husband and wife rowing, 1913. BCA, E-05024.

PAGE 93

● George Chictlan, Lekwungen, "Report of a Meeting," May 4, 1894, LAC, RG 10, vol. 3688, file 13,886-1.

● A.W. Vowell, Indian Superintendent, in Canada, Legislative Assembly, DIAR, *Canada Sessional Papers* (Ottawa: Canada, 1903), 320.

PAGE 94

● Sayach'apis, Nuu-chah-nulth, ca. 1888, in Edward Sapir and Morris Swadesh, *Nootka Texts* (Philadelphia: Linguistic Society of America, 1939), 149.

o Sayach'apis (Tom). Photo by Edward Sapir, 1914, CMC, 26543.

PAGE 95

o Field boss captain and Soowahlie hop pickers. Chilliwack Museum and Archives, P5759

PAGE 96

● Edgar Fawcett, *Some Reminiscences of Old Victoria* (Toronto: William Briggs, 1912), 84.

PAGE 99

● A.W. Vowell, Indian Superintendent, DIAR, 1902, 281-85.

PAGE 101
○ Songhees Chief Michael Cooper and Premier Richard McBride. BCA, AA-00677.

PAGE 103
● W.E. Ditchburn to the Secretary of the Department of Indian Affairs, February 16, 1911, Inspectorate of Indian Agencies Correspondence Out, 1910-11, LAC, RG 10, vol. 1312, Mflm C-13, 908.

PAGE 105
● Cowichan Chiefs, to Superintendent of Indian Affairs, LAC, RG 10, vol. 9, 174, file B-75, December 22, 1914.
○ Cowichan chiefs at a potlatch in Duncan, 1899. BCA, AA-00400.

PAGE 108
○ The Charlie family (Cowichan) knitting sweaters. BCA, I-27571.

PAGE 109
● Memorial of the Songhees Band, March 15, 1935, LAC, RG 10, vol. 9,170, file B-45.

PAGE 111
○ Aboriginal worker, Inverness Cannery, 1947. BCA, I-28895.

PAGE 113
○ Empire (Todd) Cannery. Drawn by Lindley Crease, ca. 1904, BCA, PDP-06571.

PAGE 114
● Cowichan Agency, Quarterly Report for the period ending August 31, 1962, Central Registry Office, DIAR, file 901/21-2, vol. 3.

PAGE 117
● Dave Elliot, Wsanec elder, quoted in Dorothy Haegert, *Children of the First People* (Vancouver: Tillacum Library, 1983), 19.
○ Dave Elliot, ca. 1981. Photo by Dorothy Haegert, from her collection.

PAGE 119
● Ray Hance, Tsilhqot'in National Government, quoted at the University of British Columbia Museum of Anthro-
pology and First Nations House of Learning symposium on "The Tsilhqot'in War of 1864 & 1993 Cariboo Chilcotin Justice Inquiry," Vancouver, UBC, November 19, 1994.
● James Teit, *The Shuswap*, Jesup North Pacific Expedition, Memoir of the American Museum of Natural History, vol. 2 (New York: AMS Press, 1909), 763.
○ James Teit and his Nlaka'pamux wife Lucy Antko, ca. 1910. Photographed by V.V. Vinson, Sigurd Teit Collection (courtesy Wendy Wickwire).

PAGE 120
● Joe Alphonse, Director of Government Services, Tsilhqot'in National Government, interviewed by John S. Lutz at the Tsilhqot'in National Government Offices, August 24, 2000.

PAGE 122
○ Nuxalk Pat Schooner on the Bella Coola River, 1935. Photographed by Cliff Kopas, from the collection of Leslie Kopas.

PAGE 125
○ Homathco River. Engraving by Frederick Whymper for the *Illustrated London News,* September 5, 1868.

PAGE 126
○ Tsilhqot'in fish trap, sketched by James Teit, 1900. Reproduced from James Teit, *The Shuswap*, Jesup North Pacific Expedition: Memoir of the American Museum of Natural History, vol. 2, ed. Franz Boas (New York: AMS Press, 1909), 528.

PAGE 127
○ Spirit carvings on trees near Anahim Lake, 1900. Reproduced from James Teit, *The Shuswap*, Jesup North Pacific Expedition: Memoir of the American Museum of Natural History, vol. 2, ed. Franz Boas (New York: AMS Press, 1909), 528.
● Livingstone Farrand, *Traditions of the Chilcotin Indians* (New York: S.n., 1900), 3.
● Chief Leslie Stump, Tl'etinqox, interviewed by John S. Lutz at Anaham Reserve, September 1999.

PAGE 128
○ Tsilhqot'in cradle, sketched by James Teit in 1900. Reproduced from James Teit, *The Shuswap*, Jesup North

Pacific Expedition: Memoir of the American Museum of Natural History, vol. 2, ed. Franz Boas (New York: AMS Press, 1909), 727.

PAGE 129
- Fort Chilcotin Journal, December 25, 1838, HBCA B37/a/2 Chilcotin Post Journals.
○ Alexnder Mackenzie. Engraving of a painting by Thomas Lawrence, ca. 1800, in *Voyages from Montreal on the River St. Lawrence through the Continent of North America, to the Frozen Pacific Oceans in the Years 1789 and 1793 ...* (London: Printed for T. Cadell and W. Davies [etc.] by R. Noble, 1801).

PAGE 131
○ The Chilcotin River cutting through the Chilcotin Plateau. Photograph by John S. Lutz, 2000.

PAGE 132
- Letter from Lieut. H.S. Palmer, R.E., July 16, 1862, BCA, Colonial Correspondence, file 1302A.

PAGE 135
○ Attack on McDonald's pack train. Detail of painting by Brian Seymour, from his collection.

PAGE 136
- Chartres Brew to the Colonial Secretary, May 23, 1864, BCA, Colonial Correspondence, 193/20.

PAGE 137
- R.C. Lundin Brown, *Klatsassin and Other Reminiscences of Missionary Life in British Columbia* (London: Gilbert and Rivington, 1873), 100.
- Correspondence from Matthew Baillie Begbie to the Governor of British Columbia, April 8, 1869, BCA, Colonial Correspondence, F142-8.

PAGE 138
○ Klatsassin. From R.C. Lundin Brown, *Klatsassin and Other Reminiscences of Missionary Life in British Columbia* (London: Gilbert and Rivington, 1873), frontispiece.
- Testimony of Ach-pie-er-mous, Special Assize, New Westminster, July 3-4, 1865, before Henry P. Crease, UBC Special Collections, R.L. Reid Papers, box 4, file 9.

PAGE 139
○ CPR survey map (1875-76). CPR Survey Division X, BC Surveyor General's Office Vault.

PAGE 140
- George M. Dawson, *Journals of George M. Dawson*, ed. Douglas Cole and Bradley Lockner (Vancouver: UBC Press, 1989), 1: 80.
○ George Mercer Dawson. Reproduced with the permission of the Minister of Public Works and Government Services Canada, 2007, and Courtesy of Natural Resources Canada, Geological Survey of Canada, KGS-2375.

PAGE 141
- Leonard Johnson, Tsilhqot'in, in David Dinwoodie, "Reserve Memories: Historical Consciousness on the Nemiah Valley Indian Reserve" (PhD diss., University of Chicago, 1996), 122.
- William L. Fernie, quoted in Witte Sisters, *Chilcotin: Preserving Pioneer Memories* (Surrey: Heritage House, 1995), 415.

PAGE 142
- Indian Agent William Laing-Meason, DIAR, 1892, 255.
- Xeni Gwet'in elder, Henry Solomon, 1999, interviewed by John S. Lutz at his home in Nemiah, September 5, 1999.
○ A young Henry Solomon and friends. Courtesy Sage Birchwater.

PAGE 145
○ Haying on a swamp grass meadow near Anahim Lake, 1934. Photograph by Cliff Kopas from the collection of Leslie Kopas.

PAGE 147
- Ewan Bell, Williams Lake Indian Agent, DIAR, 1906, 260.

PAGE 148
○ Tsilhqot'in Tsulin and party with pack horses, 1924. Photographed by Harlan Smith, CMC 49074.

PAGE 149
- H.S. Bostock, "Pack Horse Tracks: Recollections of a Geologist's Life in British Columbia and the Yukon, 1924-

1954," Geological Survey of Canada, Open File Report no. 650 (Ottawa: Geological Survey of Canada, 1979), 19.

○ Eagle Lake Henry (Henry Alexis) and his wife Alietta. Courtesy Sage Birchwater.

PAGE 150

● Correspondence from BC Game Commissioner M.B. Jackson to Indian Agent E. McLeod, June 10, 1925, LAC, RG 10, vol. 10,872, file 901/20-10, pt. 2.

PAGE 151

● Correspondence from Indian Agent E. McLeod to M.B. Jackson, Chairman of the Game Conservation Board of BC, May 20, 1925, LAC, RG 10, vol. 10872, file 901/20-10, pt. 2.

○ Nuxalk boys bringing salmon home, 1920. Photographed by Harlan Smith, CMC 49074.

PAGE 153

● James Kew, Fisheries Inspector, Quesnel Subdistrict, RG 23, vol. 662, file 712-2-72, pt. 4, "Report on Williams Lake Agency for November 1941."

PAGE 154

○ Trading coyote pelts, 1938. Photographed by Cliff Kopas from the collection of Leslie Kopas.

PAGE 156

○ Chief William Charleyboy and his wife Elaine, 1910s. Photographed by C.D. Hoy, Barkerville Historic Town Archives, P1583.

PAGE 157

● Dave Stockland, "Ageless Cheewhit Spurns a House, Prefers Nomadic life in Chilcotin," *Vancouver Sun*, June 26, 1973 (thanks to Keith Carlson).

○ Tsilhqot'in Cheewhit. Photographed by Verra Bonner from her collection.

PAGE 158

● Henry Solomon, Xeni Gwet'in, interviewed by John S. Lutz at his home in Nemiah, September 5, 1999.

PAGE 159

● Henry Solomon, Xeni Gwet'in, interviewed by John S. Lutz at his home in Nemiah, September 5, 1999.

PAGE 160

○ Ulkatcho woman scraping moose skin, 1922. Photographed by Harlan Smith, CMC, 56862.

PAGE 162

○ Aboriginal railway labourers between Yale and Spuzzum. Yale Museum and Archives, ca. 1914.

PAGE 166

● Arthur Wellington Clah, Ts'msyen, February 26, 1868, Wellcome MS American, 140, LAC, MG 40, F11, microfilm A-1711.

● Horatio Hale, "The 'Jargon' or Trade-Language of Oregon," in *Ethnography and Philology* (1846; reprinted Ridgewood, NJ: Gregg, 1968), 644.

PAGE 167

● John Gill, *Gill's Dictionary of the Chinook Jargon, with Examples of Use and Notes upon Tribes and Tongues*, 15th ed. (1881; reprinted Portland, OR: J.K. Gill, 1909), 79.

○ Aboriginal family packed for long-distance travel. From the *Illustrated London News,* March 1, 1862.

PAGE 169

● James Douglas, Douglas to Barclay, June 15, 1854, BCA, A/C/20/Vi2A.

PAGE 170

● Arthur Wellington Clah, Ts'msyen from Fort Simpson, Wellcome MS American, 140, LAC, MG 40, F11, microfilm A-1711.

PAGE 171

● Dick Whoakum, Snuneymuxw of the Nanaimo band, May 28, 1913, to the Royal Commission on Indian Affairs for BC meeting at the Nanaimo (No. 1) Town Reserve.

○ Coal Tyee. CVA, A22904.

PAGE 172

● Told by Quen-Es-Then and interpreted by Tstass-Aya to Beryl Cryer in the 1930s, BCA, F8.2/C88.1, vol. 3, 11-14.

PAGE 174

○ Nlaka'pumx gold miners. RBCM, 8770.

- A.C. Anderson, *Hand Book and Map to the Gold Region of Frazer's and Thompson Rivers* (San Francisco: J.J. Le Count, 1858), 30.

PAGE 175

- Chief Spintlam, Nklakapmux, July 1, 1860, Bishop George Hills Diary, Anglican Church of Canada, Ecclesiastical Archives of British Columbia.
- ○ Wet'suwet'en packers at Moricetown, 1910s. BCA, G-04121.

PAGE 176

- A.C. Anderson, *Hand Book and Map to the Gold Region of Frazer's and Thompson Rivers* (San Francisco: J.J. Le Count, 1858), 30.
- Arthur Wellington Clah, Ts'msyen, Wellcome MS American, 140, LAC, MG 40, F11, microfilm A-1711.

PAGE 177

- Arthur Wellington Clah Diary, Tuesday, March 6, 1860, Wellcome Institute MSS 5501 AMS 140(1).

PAGE 178

- Mary Augusta Tappage, Secwepemc (Shuswap), in *The Days of Augusta,* ed. Jean Speare (Vancouver: Douglas and McIntyre, 1973), 15.
- ○ Group of Interior Salish on their way to diggings, ca. 1899. LAC, C56761.

PAGE 179

- Daisy Sewid-Smith, Kwakwaka'wakw, interviewed by John S. Lutz, University of Victoria, October 19, 2000.

PAGE 182

- Charley Nowell, Kwakwaka'wakw, in Ford, *Smoke from Their Fires: The Life of a Kwakiutl Chief* (Hamden, CN: Archon, 1968), 134.

PAGE 184

- Dialogue between foreman and aboriginal man, 1865, Pope and Talbot Papers, University of Washington Special Collections, acc. 1744; file VF 715.
- ○ Puget Mill Co. sawmill and log pond, Port Gamble, WA, ca. 1882. Photographed by Carleton Watkins, University of Washington Libraries Special Collections, NA 3059 PH Coll 286.17.

PAGE 186

- Albert (Sonny) McHalsie, interviewed in the film, *A Forgotten Legacy: Spirit of Reclamation*, prod. and dir. Martin de Valk (Victoria: Chiaro Productions, 2002).
- ○ Stó:lō Sonny McHalsie, 2006. Photographed by John S. Lutz.

PAGE 187

- Alfred Carmichael, "Account of a Season's Work at the Salmon Cannery, Windsor, Cannery, Aberdeen, Skeena," BCA, Bp/C21.
- ○ Carmichael sketch of aboriginal women at work at Windsor Cannery, Skeena River Cannery. Alfred Carmichael, "Account of a Season's Work at a Salmon Cannery, Windsor Cannery, Aberdeen, Skeena," ca. 1885, BCA, Add. Mss. 2305.

PAGE 189

- Letter from Jack to Mr. Smith, dated February 7, 1881, quoted in Barbara Harris, "Klohowiam Mr. Smis: Context of Culture as a Factor in the Interpretation of a Chinook Jargon Text," *Anthropological Linguistics* 27, 3 (1985): 307.
- ○ Fort Rupert Kwakwaka'wakw people en route to Steveston canneries, ca. 1898. CVA, A26353.

PAGE 191

- ○ Ts'msyen Chief A.S. Dudoward's house in Port Simpson. DIAR, 1905.

PAGE 192

- Franz Boas, June 1889, *The Ethnography of Franz Boas: Letters and Diaries Written on the Northwest Coast from 1886-1931,* ed. Richard Rohner, trans. Hedy Parker (Chicago: University of Chicago Press, 1969), 6, 9.
- Franz Boas, September 1886, *The Ethnography of Franz Boas,* 28.
- ○ Aboriginal cook on west coast trading schooner, ca. 1880s. From Joseph Van Der Heyden, *Life and Letters of Father Brabant* (Louvain: J. Wouters-ickx, 1920), 144.

PAGE 193

- Deputy Superintendent of Indian Affairs in DIAR, 1895, xxviii.
- Story told to to Marius Barbeau, recorded in BCA, Barbeau, Field Notes, micro-reel A1413, 91011.

PAGE 194

- A.W. Vowell, Indian Superintendent, DIAR, 1894, 202.
- Murphy Stanley, Nisga'a, quoted in Ulli Steltzer and Catherine Kerr, *Coast of Many Faces* (Vancouver: Douglas and McIntyre, 1979), 8.

PAGE 195

- *Census of Canada* (1951), 4: xiv.
- Mary Augusta Tappage, *The Days of Augusta,* ed. J.E. Speare (Vancouver: J.J. Douglas, 1973), 30-31.

PAGE 196

- Dave Elliot, *Saltwater People* (Saanich, BC: School District 63, 1983), 67-68.

PAGE 197

- Andrea Laforet and Annie York, *Spuzzum: Fraser Canyon Histories, 1808-1939* (Vancouver: UBC Press, 1998), 85.
- Detail of unnamed photo of aboriginal railway labourers between Yale and Spuzzum. Yale Museum and Archives, ca. 1914.

PAGE 198

- Aboriginal sealers and their equipment, ca. 1894. University of Washington Libraries Special Collections, NA3062.

PAGE 199

- Bruce McKelvie, "Saga of Sealing," written by B.A. McKelvie from the recollections of Captain Ernst Jordan, BCA, add mss 115, box 3, file 2.

PAGE 201

- Franz Boas, "Chinook Songs," *Journal of American Folklore* (1888): 220-26. This song was sung by an aboriginal man left behind by a sealing schooner in Alaska.
- Aboriginal sealers on Victoria-based sealing schooner, *Favorite,* ca. 1894. University of Washington Libraries Special Collections, NA3059.

PAGE 203

- Furs being unloaded in Prince Rupert, ca. 1910. BCA, C-08954.

PAGE 204

- Correspondence from E. McLeod, Indian Agent, to M.B. Jackson, Chairman of the Game Conservation Board of

BC, May 20, 1925, Lytton, LAC, RG 10, vol. 10872, file 901/20-10, pt. 2.

PAGE 205

- "Song of a Traveller." Recorded by Francis Densmore, in *Music of the Indians of BC* (New York: Da Capo, 1943), 91.
- Sophie Wilson. Photograph by Francis Densmore in her *Music of Indians of British Columbia,* Bureau of American Ethnography Bulletin 136 (Washington: Government Printing Office, 1943), 91 and Plate 9.

PAGE 206

- Mary Hopkins, Klemtu, quoted in Ulli Steltzer and Catherine Kerr for their book, *Coast of Many Faces* (Vancouver: Douglas and McIntyre, 1979), 134.
- Mary Hopkins, ca. 1977. Photo by Ulli Steltzer and reproduced with permission.

PAGE 208

- Harry Assu, Kwakwa̲ka̲'wakw, *Assu of Cape Mudge: Recollections of a Coastal Indian Chief,* with Joy Inglis (Vancouver: UBC Press, 1989), 8.
- James Sewid and crew of his seiner *Twin Sisters,* 1963. Reproduced from William Dunstan, "Canadian Indians Today," reprinted from the *Canadian Geographical Journal,* December 1963, p. 7.

PAGE 209

- Verna Ambers, Namgis, interviewed by Byron Plant, Alert Bay, July 7, 2003.

PAGE 210

- Daniel Gordon*, Mountain and Prairie: A Journey from Victoria to Winnipeg, Via Peace River* (Montreal: Dawson Bros., 1880), 13-14.

PAGE 212

- Aboriginal hop pickers at Hulbert's hop fields, Agassiz, BC, ca. 1896. Photo by J.O. Boen, Chilliwack Museum and Archives 1622.
- Ernest Pearson, storekeeper, Columbia Hop Yards Sardis, interviewed by Mr. Charlie, June 29, 1976, Coqualeetza Resource Centre, tape 1 971.hop/1/1.

PAGE 214
- Chil-lah-minst [Jim Frank] Squamish, to Major Matthews, November 20, 1932, quoted in Matthews, *Early Vancouver: Narratives of Pioneers of Vancouver, B.C.* (Vancouver: Brock Webber, 1933), 44.

PAGE 216
○ Stó:lō logger Hank Pennier. Chilliwack Museum and Archives, 2003.39.7.
- Leonard Point interview, cited in Frances W. Thompson, "Employment Problems and the Economic Status of the British Columbia Indians" (MSW thesis, University of British Columbia, 1951), 34.

PAGE 217
- Mary Augusta Tappage, *The Days of Augusta*, ed. J.E. Speare (Vancouver: Douglas and McIntyre, 1992), 52.

PAGE 218
○ Aboriginal girl servants, Yale, DIAR, 1902.

PAGE 219
- Clayton Mack, Nuxalk, with H.T. Thommasen, *Grizzlies and White Guys: The Stories of Clayton Mack* (Madeira Park, BC: Harbour Publishing, 1993), 19-20.
○ Mrs. Willie Mack, Nuxalk, 1923. Photographed by Harlan Smith, CMC 58531.
- Art Dick, Namgis, interviewed by Byron Plant and Chris Cook III, in Alert Bay, July 6, 2003.

PAGE 221
○ Jessie Wilson, Nuu-chah-nulth, selling her baskets, 1930s. Photographer: Associated Screen News Ltd., Vancouver Public Library, 13440, cd no. 120.
- Chief Jim Chackidl, We Wai Kai (Cape Mudge), to Indian Agent G.W. Debeck, December 28, 1903, LAC, RG 10, vol. 11,318.

PAGE 222
- Billy Wasden, Namgis, interviewed by John S. Lutz, Chris Cook II, and Byron Plant, May 19, 2003, Alert Bay.

PAGE 224
- Thomas McIlwraith, quoted in John Barker and Douglas Cole, eds., *At Home with the Bella Coola Indians: T.F. McIlwraith's Field Letters, 1922-24* (Vancouver: UBC Press, 2003), 68.
○ Thomas McIlwraith with Willie Mack and sons, Bella Coola, 1922. Photographed by Harlan Smith, CMC 56872.

PAGE 225
○ Tlingit woman applying labels to salmon cans, Alaska. Alaska State Library, Winter and Pond Collection, PCA 87-190.

PAGE 226
- John Williams, Haida, interviewed by Imbert Orchard 1969, BCA Acc No 2428, Tape 1, Track 1.

PAGE 227
○ Okanagan men wearing World War I uniforms. O'Keefe Historic Ranch, F30-6.

PAGE 228
- Helen Clifton, Gitga'at, interviewed by John S. Lutz in Hartley Bay, June 9, 2004.

PAGE 229
○ Aboriginal railway crew, 1909. Photographed by Joseph W. Heckman, VPL 352.

PAGE 230
- Adam Dick, Kwakwaka'wakw, interviewed by John S. Lutz at the University of Victoria, October 23, 2001.
○ Hereditary Chief Adam Dick. Photo by Nancy Turner.

PAGE 233
- DIAR, 1912, 396.
- Charles Jones, with Stephen Bosustow, *Queesto, Pacheenaht Chief by Birthright* (Nanaimo, BC: Theytus, 1981), 55.

PAGE 234
- Harry Assu, with Joy Inglis, *Assu of Cape Mudge: Recollections of a Coastal Indian Chief* (Vancouver: UBC Press, 1989), 10.

PAGE 235
○ Potlatch at Alert Bay, 1910-12. Photographed by A.M. Wastell, Vancouver City Archives, A26475.

Page 237

- Doreen Jensen, Gitksan, interviewed in the film, *A Forgotten Legacy: Spirit of Reclamation*, produced and directed by Martin de Valk (Victoria: Chiaro Productions, 2002).

Page 238

- James Bell to John Thomson, February 27, 1859, BCA, MS659 E/B/B412.
- ○ Threshing machine. DIAR, 1901.

Page 239

- William Henry Barker, BC Packers, to the Hon. J.D. Hazen, Minister of Fisheries, August 19, 1913, LAC, RG 23, Department of Fisheries, General File, reel 5, file 6, pt. 8.

Page 240

- ○ David Moody rowing gill-netter, 1934. Photo by Cliff Kopas from the collection of Leslie Kopas.

Page 241

- Indian Agent Graham, Lytton Agency, to McKenna-McBride Commission, October 27, 1915, BCA, Royal Commission on Indian Affairs for the Province of B.C., add mss 1056.

Page 242

- "Fishing 1914-41," Agent W.M. Halliday to Johnny Scow, May 20, 1922, LAC, RG 10, vol. 11,147.

Page 243

- Dave Dawson, Kingcome, ca. 1978, quoted in Ulli Steltzer and Catherine Kerr, *Coast of Many Faces* (Vancouver: Douglas and McIntyre, 1979), 82.
- ○ Hartley Bay wharf with band-owned seine boats, 2004. Photo by John S. Lutz.

Page 244

- Dave Elliot, Wsanac, *Saltwater People* (Saanich, BC: School District 63, 1990), 71-72.

Page 245

- Chief Jim Chackidl of Cape Mudge to G.W. Debeck, Indian Agent, December 28, 1903, LAC, RG 10, vol. 11,138.
- Wilson from Kimsquit, to the McKenna-McBride Royal Commission, BCA, MS 1056, box 1.
- ○ Log drivers, ca. 1930. Enderby and District Museum, No. 286.

Page 246

- Peter Webster, *As Far as I Know: Reminiscences of an Ahousat Elder* (Campbell River, BC: Campbell River Museum and Archives, 1983), 43.
- ○ Nuu-chah-nulth Peter Webster with wife Jessie and grandchild, ca. 1980. Photo by Dorothy Haegert from her collection.

Page 247

- W.H. Lomas, Cowichan Indian Agent, DIAR, 1888, 100-1.
- ○ Mathilda Joe of Alexandria. Photographed by C.D. Hoy, Barkerville Historic Town Archives, P1631.

Page 248

- Chief Louis Prince and Councillors, Secwepemc (Shuswap) Kamloops, to J.H. Pragnell, Indian Inspector, January 1, 1929, LAC, RG 10, vol. 10872, file 901/20-10, pt. 2.
- ○ Secwepemc Chief Louis Prince of Kamloops, ca 1920. Secwepemc Cultural Society.

Page 249

- George Archie, Secwepmec, Secretary Canim Lake Band, to W.E. Ditchburn, December 1, 1927, LAC, RG 10, vol. 10872, file 901/20-10, pt. 2.
- ○ Daniel Wigaix with winter's catch of furs, 1923. Photographed by Marius Barbeau, CMC 59501.

Page 250

- John Gill, *Gill's Dictionary of the Chinook Jargon, with Examples of Use and Notes upon Tribes and Tongues,* 15th ed. (1881; reprinted Portland, OR: J.K. Gill, 1909), 80.
- ○ Secwepemc people waiting to meet the game warden, 1891. Photographed by C.W. Holliday, Enderby and District Museum, 0281.

Page 251

- Premier Richard McBride, July 6, 1909, BCA, GR 441, section 30, box 35, item 340.

PAGE 252

○ Tsilhqot'in entrepreneurs, Quesnel, 1910s. Photographed by C.D. Hoy, Barkerville Historic Town Archives.

● George Archie, Secretary of the Canim Lake band, to W.E. Ditchburn, Indian Superintendent for British Columbia, December 1, 1927, LAC, RG 10, vol. 10872, file 901/20-10, pt. 2.

PAGE 253

● M.B. Jackson, Provincial Game Warden, "Game Warden's Report," 1917, 6.

PAGE 254

● Chief John Albany, Songhees (Lekwungen), in Canadian Broadcasting Corporation transcript of *The Way of the Indian* radio series, 1961 (Toronto: CBC, 1969), 53.

PAGE 257

● Leslie John, Sne ney mux, 1948, BCA, GR1070, box 1, file 2, Indian Advisory Committee.

● Edwin Newman, Heiltsuk, July 6, 2003, interviewed by Byron Plant and Chris Cook III, at Alert Bay.

PAGE 258

● Bishop George Hills Diary, February 6, 1860, Archives of the Ecclesiastical Province of British Columbia.

○ Anglican Bishop George Hills. BCA A-09771.

● Indian Agent E. McLeod, Lytton, to M.B. Jackson, Chairman of the Game Conservation Board, May 20, 1925, LAC, RG 10, vol. 10872, file 901/20-10, pt. 2.

PAGE 259

○ Discovery Island woman. BCA, AA-00675.

PAGE 260

● Correspondence Indian Agent F.G. Newnham from James Smith for Louisa McKenzie, September 14, 1931, LAC, RG 10, vol. 11,155, file C.R. 37, pt. A.

● Indian Agent O'Byrne to McKenna-McBride Royal Commission, January 27, 1916, BCA, add mss 1056, box 2, file 5-6, 431.

PAGE 261

○ Frank Kibbie, game warden at Bowron Lake, ca. 1890. BCA, A-02259.

PAGE 262

● Indian Agent E. McLeod, Lytton, to M.B. Jackson, Chairman of Game Conservation Board, May 20, 1925, LAC, RG 10, vol. 10872, file 901/20-10, pt. 2.

PAGE 264

● Daisy Sewid-Smith, Kwakwa̱ka̱'wakw, interviewed by John S. Lutz at the University of Victoria, October 19, 2000.

○ Daisy Sewid-Smith and Kim Recalma-Clutesi. Photo by Nancy Turner, from her collection.

PAGE 265

● Interview with Tully Gutierrez, by Liam Haggarty and Heather Watson, May 26, 2005.

○ Tilly Gutierrez, Stó:lō elder, 2005. Photographed by Liam Haggarty.

● Daisy Sewid-Smith, Kwakwa̱ka̱'wakw, interviewed by John S. Lutz at the University of Victoria, October 19, 2000.

PAGE 267

○ Clam label. Photo by Robert Turner, from his collection.

● Dave Elliott, Wsanec, quoted in Dorothy Haegert, *Children of the First People* (Vancouver: Tillacum Library, 1983), 19.

PAGE 270

● Letter from Johnny Galakawmei, August 1, 1933, LAC, RG 10, vol. 11,155, file C.R. 37, pt. A.

PAGE 271

● Helen Clifton, Gitga'at, former social worker, interviewed by John S. Lutz and Liam Haggerty, Hartley Bay, June 9, 2004.

○ Helen Clifton, 2004. Photographed by John S. Lutz.

PAGE 272

● Doug Kelly, Stó:lō, interviewed at Soowahlie Band Office by Liam Haggarty and Heather Watson, May 27, 2005.

PAGE 274

○ John Webber painting depicting Cook's ship, *Resolution*, in Nootka Sound. British Museum, Add Ms 15514 F10 c7546-04.

PAGE 275
- James Hanna, August 9, 1785, "Bring Sea Otter from Macao," BCA A/A/20.5.

PAGE 276
- Transcript, *Delgamuukw* v. *The Queen*, cited in Don Monet and Ardythe Wilson, *Colonialism on Trial* (Gabriola, BC: New Society Publishers, 1992), 42.
- Mary Johnson sings her history into the court record at the *Delgamuukw* trial, 1987. Artist Don Monet reproduced with permission from Don Monet and Ardythe Wilson, *Colonialism on Trial* (Gabriola, BC: New Society Publishers, 1992), 41.

PAGE 278
- Aboriginal longshoremen at Moodyville, 1889. CVA, A32533.

PAGE 279
- Tatoosh to the Royal Commission on Indians Affairs, 1914, West Coast Agency, 46, BCA, add mss 1056.

PAGE 280
- Suggesting resistance. CVA, A26351.

PAGE 282
- Theodore Winthrop, *The Canoe and the Saddle* (Tacoma: John H. Williams, 1913), 11.

PAGE 283
- Chief David Bailey of the Coquitlam Band and Commissioner Shaw, McKenna-McBride Commission Transcripts, January 8, 1915, BCA GR 1995.

PAGE 284
- Clifford Sifton, Superintendent of Indian Affairs, in Canada, House of Commons, *Debates* (Ottawa: Canada, 1897), col. 4076, June 14, 1897.
- Clifford Sifton, Superintendent of Indian Affairs. LAC, PA-27942.

PAGE 285
- Laura B. Downey-Bartlett, *Chinook-English Songs* (Portland, OR: Kubli Miller, 1914), 34-35.

- Aboriginal boys learning trades. DIAR, 1905.

PAGE 288
- Wilson, a Nuxalk from Kimsquit, to the McKenna-McBride Royal Commission, August 22, 1913, BCA, MS 1056, box 1.
- Weeping Woman Totem. Photographed by John S. Lutz.

PAGE 289
- Transcript of *The Way of the Indian* radio series, 1961 (Toronto: CBC, 1969), 53.

PAGE 291
- The Honourable Len Marchand, Okanagan, in the film *A Forgotten Legacy: Spirit of Reclamation*, produced and directed by Martin de Valk (Victoria: Chiaro Productions, 2002).

PAGE 295
- David Dinwoodie, "Reserve Memories: Historical Consciousness on the Nemiah Valley Indian Reserve" (PhD diss., University of Chicago, 1996), 104.

PAGE 296
- Gilbert Solomon, Nemiah [Tsilhqot'in] councillor, interviewed by John S. Lutz at Nemiah Band Office, August 23, 2000.

PAGE 297
- Chinook poem, cited in in Charles Lillard and Terry Glavin, *A Voice Great within Us* (Vancouver: New Star, 1998), 30, 31.
- Terry Glavin. Photo courtesy of Terry Glavin.

PAGE 298
- Richard Rorty, *Philosophy and the Mirror of Nature* (Princeton: Princeton University Press, 1979), 378.

PAGE 300
- Painting of a railway labourer by Stó:lō Stan Greene. Courtesy of Stó:lō Nation.

PAGE 302
- Throwing blankets to crowd at potlatch, 1895. BCA, AA-00679.

PAGE 304

○ Charley Nowell at World's Fair in St. Louis, 1904. BCA, D-1503.

PAGE 305

● Daniel Gordon, *Mountain and Prairie: A Journey from Victoria to Winnipeg Via Peace River* (Montreal: Dawson Bros., 1880), 85.

PAGE 306

● George Clutesi, "The Viewpoint of the Native Indian," in *Western Goals in Social Work,* cited in Frances W. Thompson, "Employment Problems and the Economic Status of the British Columbia Indians" (MSW thesis, University of British Columbia, 1951), 57.

● Ruby Dunstan, former chief of the Lytton Band, quoted in James Clifford and George E. Marcus, *Writing Culture: The Poetics and Politics of Ethnography* (Berkeley: University of California Press, 1986), 2.

Index

Printed and bound in Canada by Friesens

Set in Garamond and News Gothic by Artegraphica Design Co. Ltd.

Text design: Irma Rodriguez

Copy editor: Joanne Richardson

Proofreader: Dianne Tiefensee

Indexer: Dianne Tiefensee